OVER AN ANGEL'S SHOULDER

ONE SOUL'S JOURNEY
THROUGH TIME

✳

BONNIE ANN GILCHRIST

D1603444

RAINBOW BOOKS, INC.

Library of Congress Cataloging-in Publication Data

Gilchrist, Bonnie Ann, 1925-
　　Over an angel's shoulder : one soul's journey through time /
Bonnie Ann Gilchrist.
　　　　p.　cm.
　　ISBN 1-56825-23-1
　　1. Gilchrist, Bonnie Ann, 1925-　. 2. Spiritual biography.
I. Title.
BL73.G45A3　1995
291.4'092–dc20　　　　　　　　　　　　　　　　　　95-4330
[B]　　　　　　　　　　　　　　　　　　　　　　　　CIP

OVER AN ANGEL'S SHOULDER
One Soul's Journey Through Time
by Bonnie Ann Gilchrist
Design by Marilyn Ratzlaff
Cover Design by Betsy Lampé
$16.95

Printed in the United States of America

DEDICATION

I wish to dedicate this book to my mother,
Marlena Marjorie L. Beckington,
who graduated to the Higher Realms of life in 1976,
and whose loving support with wise and early
guidance showed me the more expansive view of
life in which a sense of humor should always play
a part.

ACKNOWLEDGEMENTS

I wish to acknowledge with much appreciation the time and loving efforts of my son, Garth Allen Gilchrist, whose editing of this book was invaluable.

And my loving thanks to an intuitive and beautiful young lady named Heather, who at age seventeen brought forth the title of this book *out of the blue*, so-to-speak, two years after I had been told by Spirit, "You will change the title of your book. It will be given to you."

And last, but most certainly not least, my heartfelt gratitude ever extends to the Loving Presence and encouragement of my Angel Guides, Friends, Teachers, including the wisdom of the Ascended Masters, whose support is never-failing.

I also wish to extend thanks to Marilyn Ratzlaff, editor and Betty Wright, publisher of Rainbow Books, Inc., for faith in my work that led to the publication of my book, and to Allen Wiseman and Betsy Lampé for smoothing the way.

The Author

CONTENTS

POEM — THE DAYS OF MY YEARS —
JOURNEY THROUGH TIME — 11

PROLOGUE — 13

CHAPTER ONE:
THE EARLY DAYS — ON THE FARM — 19
    Help From Heaven — 30
    School Days — Those Golden Rule Days — 36
    Threshing Time — 48
    My Fall From the Haymow — 53
    The Wonder of Music — 54
    Some Gory Details — 57
    Our Funny Hired Men — 58
    Night Time Visitors — 66
    Papa and the Blizzard — 76
    Christmas — and the Clan at Grandma's — 80
    Summertime Joys — 84
    My First Love — and We Leave "The 80" — 87
    My Specially Gifted Great Aunts — 91
    Life On Our Other Farm — 96

CHAPTER TWO:
DEATH, LIFE AND A WONDERFUL REVELATION — 102
    Electric Storms and Barn Dances — 106
    Roger Returns — 111
    Death of Princess and A Nocturnal Visitor — 115
    World War II Strikes Our Community — 120

CHAPTER THREE:
DISCOVERY OF THE INNER WORLD — 128
 The Miracle of Cousin Will — 132

CHAPTER FOUR:
GO WEST YOUNG LADY — GO WEST — 143
 Touched by the Hand of Destiny — 150
 An Affair With Los Angeles County — 155
 I Flirt With Hollywood — 159
 Papa Has a Stroke — And I Go Home — 162
 Discovery of An Indian Master — 169
 Finding the Past in the Present —
  At the Agashan Temple — 173
 Poem — ENERGY — 181

CHAPTER FIVE:
A NEW WOMAN, A NEW MAN AND A NEW LIFE — 194
 Papa Leaves This Earth — 201
 Out of the Blue — A Proposal — 207
 A Shadow Appears — 215
 My Soldier Comes Home — 223
 Evelyn Comes to Visit — 236
 Holy Presence Answers A Call For Help — 237
 A Yogi In the House — Maharishi Arrives — 242

CHAPTER SIX:
ANOTHER WORLD — THE OLDE WORLD — 251
 Our New Baby Boy — 263
 Mama Sails The Atlantic — 264
 Dachou — A Very Dark Shadow — 266
 A Lost Soul Is Found — 270
 Poem — THROUGH VISION'S DOOR — 277
 A Step Into the Past — in Italy — 278
 A Gift From Angel Guides — 287
 Pompeii — A Picture of the Past — 290
 Poem — ODE TO POMEII — 293
 A Glimpse of North Africa —
  And the Middle East — 294

CHAPTER SEVEN:
HOME TO THE U.S. — 300
    Experiences with Miracles of Healing — 305
    A Return to California — 311
    Illness — and an Answer — 316
    Heart Attack — 322
    C.F.O. — And a Dramatic Flashback — 325
    A Near-Death Experience — 329
    Poem — "LIFE EVERLASTING" — 341
    We Find an Answer — 341
    A Warning — Cancer — 346
    Death — A Graduation — 350

CHAPTER EIGHT:
PRISON — 357
    Dreams and Visions — 386
    Mama Receives Her Diploma — 389
    Poem — THE BUTTERFLY — 392
    Release from Prison — and Earth — 393
    Poem — THE FENCE — OR THE AMBULANCE? — 408

CHAPTER NINE:
SLAYING THE DRAGON — A CANCER CURE — 410
    Poem — LOVE — 427
    The Joy of Music — 428
    Poem — THE ORCHESTRA! — 429
    Visions of Adrian — 431
    A Vision of Hawaii Past — 436

CHAPTER TEN:
THE WONDER OF CREATIVE HEALING — 440
    Poem —IMMORTALITY — 454
    The Healing Power of Wellsprings Therapy — 455

CHAPTER ELEVEN:
GUESS WHO CAME TO MY HOUSE —
    AND SURPRISING ADVENTURES — 468
    Off To India — 482
    Psychic Healing Experiences — 493

CHAPTER TWELVE:
A STRANGE VISION —
    AND A HEAVENLY VISITOR APPEARS — 501
        A Heavenly Visitor Appears — 505
        I Receive Vision Confirmation — 534

CHAPTER THIRTEEN:
THE MIND MIRACULOUS — 544
        Poem — THE PEARL — 552
        Poem — THE ILLUSION — 556

EPILOGUE — 571

POEM — THE DAYS OF MY YEARS — 574

REFERENCES — 577

PREFACE

It is an early Fall evening, warm and gentle; I feel the whisper of Spirit in my heart urging me to write a book, for myriad memories clamor behind the door of my mind, begging to be heard. My concern is for the many people who have hopeless days and sleepless nights, when dreams are shattered and there appears no light in the tunnel, when life seems a trap with no escape. And so I begin. I ask that my pen be guided that I shall write of the hidden realities of Life — the yearnings of the soul and the "answerings" from the Universe that I have found, that those who hunger for knowledge and Truth may find in these pages some words of comfort and help to guide them through the maze we call earth-living.

Perhaps my story will lend courage to those who feel a kinship, for I have found the spirit within us all, that spirit that is connected to and part of the Great Universal Spirit, to be stronger than circumstances on this earth plane, and that spirit has the power to make dreams a reality and life a joy.

THE DAYS OF MY YEARS —
A JOURNEY THROUGH TIME

The days of my years are many
   and few
For this journey through life is old
   and yet new.

Each day brings new wonders,
   new tests of our strength,
But how can one measure
   the breadth and the length?

For many a man
   in the search for his goal,
Has made a wrong turn
   and near sold his soul.

May I tell you my story?
Strange tales — real and true.
One may wonder, dear reader,
Might they have happened to you?

But faith in God's Love
   and guidance each day,
Brought me through - safe and sound,
For you too, 'tis the way.

The search for answers to life
   is as the search for pure gold.
May the reader find light
   on their path — in my story
As told

               The Author

PROLOGUE

The heavy steel prison gate slammed shut behind me with a deafening crash of finality and I stood alone outside in the hot summer sun. As I walked away I stopped to look back at the huge grey stone fortress with gun towers positioned menacingly above, and my eyes followed the high wall circling around it. Strangely, the Great Wall of China drifted through my mind and I thought of walls in general, that kept unfortunate people in, and others out. It would be a brave desperate man who attempted to escape those walls.

I felt as if I were standing in a dream. How could this be real? My son, my beautiful son, was inside those grey walls, locked in like an animal, for God knows how long. I had long since ceased to cry . . . and my heart was leaden in my chest. A certain numbness had taken hold, cushioning the grief I had carried for years. I had almost lost track of how many. It seemed that the agony would never end, despite my best efforts. I had searched for help for his problems through every available avenue since he was eight years old, and now it had come to this. The son whom I loved and who loved me was now in the dreaded *Lifer's Prison*, Folsom, at the age of eighteen.

This was a nightmare from which I could not awaken. It was dangerous inside; I knew that at any time I could have word that he had been killed, knifed at the hands of other inmates or even shot by the guards. Yes, that formidable rock fortress was a symbol of the last frontiers of violence in this, our beautiful America.

My mind again envisioned the sweet, smiling blue-eyed little boy. He had always laughed so happily as a child, was eager to please, delighted in reading to his baby sister, worshiped his older brother and followed him everywhere. He had much preferred a hand-me-down shirt from his brother to a new one, saying proudly, "This is 'Jeremy's' shirt!" 'Jason's' sense of humor never failed to entertain us; he always saw the lighter side of things and never once complained or was angry if he was last in games or when goodies were handed out. Even as a baby of fourteen months his desire to share what he had appeared early, as he sat in his highchair feeding himself a bite, then offering me a bite. My other two babies had never been that generous. He very early showed musical ability and had a rich and sweet singing voice, perfectly on pitch. During those early years he never said "No" to any request, but was always eager to help and please in all the little ways. I often thought, "I would have a dozen children were they all like Jason." (Little did I know those would be the ultimate famous last words.)

When Jason was three, the wonderful friend who had been my employer before I married and whom I called the Greek god, only saw him once, but stated in rapt sincerity, "That is the most beautiful child I have ever seen, bar none."

Yes, he was physically beautiful. His large, wide-set expressive eyes of misty blue had a unique darker ring around the iris and were framed in long curling lashes under perfectly formed brows. His white, even teeth often flashed an eager smile through full curving lips. Jason's thick brown hair refused conformity and whorled into a mischievous cowlick above his forehead. But mostly it was those eyes that captured one's attention. They had an innocent, trusting straight forward gaze, yet were deep and magnetic as though they knew age-old secrets.

Perhaps he had been too trusting; his spirit had come to earth and become entangled. Strange, I mused, the tricks that Fate appears to play upon us, though I knew in my heart-of-hearts there are no tricks, but only answers hidden like the hidden pictures in puzzle games. Somehow, some way, I would find them.

I walked woodenly away, leaving my son whom I loved as life itself in the only hands I could; the God who watches over us all and knows our destiny. I was totally helpless to do anything at all now except pray and accept Jason's destiny, whatever came. Had it not been for my knowledge of the power of prayer, and faith in the positive Divine Destiny that guides each of us, I would not, I believe, have been able to survive emotionally the ten years past, or the years of travail still ahead. For this son, as a little boy, had been special, sweeter than most, loving and gentle and always caring of others. If he was hurt by his older brother in play, if I tried to reprimand, he would stop me with, "No-No, Mama! Jeremy didn't mean it. Don't scold him!" He was sensitive in the extreme, never able to withstand stress, and therein, I later found, lay part of the crux of the problem.

Rivulets of heat waves reflected like running water in the azure blue California sky and I thought of the 103° heat in the top tiers behind those walls where my boy said men sweltered and sweat and swore as tempers rose with the temperature, where there was nothing to do and nowhere to go to escape for relief, and they sometimes turned on one another like rats in a cage just to relieve the tension. I gazed into the brilliant sky and asked the God of the Universe, as I had so many times before, what we had done to deserve this heartbreak, this soul-searing trauma that seemingly had no end. And I knew that I asked for many other mothers who suffered as I, with sons or daughters, the fruit of their womb and their dreams, locked away as outcasts of life.

Over the years the Universe has answered me, not in a moment of vivid enlightenment, but bit by bit like the pieces of a puzzle coming together, sometimes after much study and research, but often in strange and subtle ways in response to meditation and intense prayer. I was like one continually knocking and seeking. One who wants to know, "Why?" For there is never a question without an answer or a result without a cause.

I reflected on the unique circumstances and events that had brought me to this point in time, and wondered at the apparent quirks of fate that can change the entire course of a person's life, forcing one to face the mysteries of the often frightening unknown. I have come to know beyond a shadow-of-a-doubt that these so-called tricks of fate of earth-living are the perfect Plan our Higher Consciousness has built into our lives that we may better understand the Universal Law of Cause and Effect, or more plainly, the results of the causes that we ourselves have set in motion at some point in everlasting time.

The immortality of life is not a theory — it is a fact. The sooner we face the understanding that we ourselves are the Captain of our Ship and the Master of our Soul, the better off we will be. One must set their compass to the high road and not to the low road of personal gain at the expense of others. Unfortunately, often it is only through pain and suffering that we grow into a true understanding and compassion for all of our brothers on this planet. This too seems necessary even in nature, for it is only in what must be pain for the bulb while in the dark of the earth, to split open its body that the beautiful flower that is its true Self may burst forth into the light!

Many volumes of philosophy are available, filled with uplifting words or formulas for living. I have read many fine ones and it is most gratifying to see that, especially in recent years, bookshelves everywhere are flooded with self-help guides and spiritual teachings of every conceivable kind. Many of these ideas were a rarity, even unheard of by the majority, only fifteen years ago.

The words of this book are written more simply, in everyday language, for folks who laugh and cry and love together, folks who may enjoy the story of another who grew up the hard way, but became strong in spirit and plain grit because of it, one who has tales to tell that encompass an eventful life, tales that stretch over several continents and half a dozen decades, of a life that began before the depression years in mid-America with the historic happenings of those times — and more, much more.

And so I ask that my pen be guided, that these pages be not only a history of days gone by, but a chronicle of visions and healings, and a source of guidance for those who seek and wonder "Why?"

In most instances I have changed names to insure the

privacy of the living and the dead, though certain names are true as given for authenticity, with permission of those involved. All the tales as told herein are true in every respect exactly as they happened. This needs to be remembered, for in truth there is courage, as the Spirit in Man is strong — and that Spirit has the power to overcome all of this world's troubles and illusions and to find joy instead!

As I stood in the hot summer California sun gazing at the rivulets of heat against the endless sky, my mind drifted back to another hot summer's day. The year is 1930. I am on a farm in Illinois — back in Corn Country.

※

CHAPTER ONE

THE EARLY DAYS —
ON THE FARM

Standing under the hot summer sun in the corn field, dwarfed by the tall stalks of corn that marched row upon row for what seemed like miles, I squished the soft warm mud from a sudden rainstorm between my toes and wondered what to do. I was breathless, for I had run up and down between the rows for an hour, panting with anxiety and worry, hunting for the only pair of shoes I owned. I had taken them off in the corn field earlier in the day when my feet became hot and now I could not find them, for all the corn rows looked alike. I was five years old. My parents said we were leaving shortly to attend the funeral of my baby cousin who had died at only ten days of age. We would drive the fourteen miles in our old 1918 Mitchell auto with the isinglass windows that were hard to see out of. I was afraid they might leave without me, but then I reasoned that they couldn't, as I was an only child and we lived way out in the country. There was no one at home to stay with me. But I couldn't find my shoes! One simply could not attend a funeral barefooted, but it appeared 'one' would have to. I did not know exactly what a funeral was, but it must be very important if both my parents were going, for my father never left his daily work.

In great distress I returned to the house, washed my

feet and face, and slipped into my only good dress. My mother, understanding, did not chastise me, but my humiliation upon arriving barefoot at the home of my aunt and uncle on this solemn occasion was chastisement enough. (I never again left my shoes in the cornfield.) Most of our relatives were already there, talking in low tones to one another and attempting to comfort Auntie Grace.

I tucked my bare feet as far under my chair as I could and tried to listen to the minister. I gazed in awe at the tiny grey casket laden with flowers. Somehow I could not feel sad for the baby boy, for I knew from my mother's teachings that he was pure and good and would return to the Heaven-world from whence he had come. I felt sorry though for my aunt and uncle, who I could see were very sad. I heard Mama tell Papa the baby had a heart problem at birth. Uncle had a nice big farm with a brick house and a big red barn that sat on a hill. It was the 'family farm' on which my mother, who was his sister, had also been raised. Folks needed lots of boys in those days to help them run the farms, but my poor Papa had only me, a skinny little girl. Papa said I was so thin he could almost look through me, like the angels Mama talked about.

There had been nine children in Mama's family and she was the eldest. So even though I was an only child, I had what seemed like dozens of cousins. I normally saw them only at Easter or Christmas or on other rare and special occasions, which were very exciting times for me, since we lived quite a few miles away on the South 80, and folks did not socialize much over what was a fairly long distance in those days. The work days were long. My father was tired when he finally came in from chores and milking the herd every evening after a full day that had begun at 4:30 a.m. Even on Sundays and holidays the dairy cattle needed to be fed and milked mornings and evenings. Papa did it all by hand as he didn't believe in those new-fangled milking machines. Besides, we didn't even have electricity, so there wasn't any use thinking about it. Papa was too tired to go visiting and Mama never did learn to drive. She was "too nervous," she said. She tried once and promptly backed into a tree. Papa yelled at her so she refused to even try again.

So attending a funeral where one had an opportunity to see relatives was a very special happening, though this time even the children felt the overtones of solemnity. There was always something good to eat afterward. My aunts, like my mother, were excellent cooks, and food then was all homegrown. Even the meats folks raised on their own green pastures had a richer flavor than generally found nowadays. But this day I was ashamed of my bare feet and although no one spoke of it to me, I went to hide in our auto, so I missed playing with my cousins. It is strange in retrospect to think how the trauma of embarrassment left such an indelible mark on my memory through the years.

You may wonder why I had only one pair of shoes, and no other for Sunday best. It wasn't that we were poor. Oh no! Papa owned two farms, a herd of dairy cattle, big strong work horses and several race horses. We also had pigs, turkeys, ducks and geese and chickens, as well as fruit orchards with cherry, apple, and walnut trees, and a large vegetable garden, all of which Mama and I had to tend. As for my shoes, the trouble was that Papa always told Mama and me that he "didn't have money for women's foolishness," as he had to buy machinery and such for the fields or more cattle. And "one pair of shoes is all any child needs." He carefully counted out the necessary money for staples we bought from the country store once a month, such as sugar, rice, and other food items we did not raise ourselves, and for coal to stoke the heavy metal stoves in the winter time. Hard coal would hold overnight, some embers burning red 'til morning, so the fire would not be so difficult to start on those icy cold winter mornings. Our old farm house was not insulated so Mama piled straw around the foundation in the late Fall to help keep out the terribly cold drafts.

These were the Depression Years of 1929 and the early 1930's, and we were lucky to have food from our garden and milk from our cows. People were going bust all over the country, Papa said, so he had to be careful with every nickel in order to pay taxes and keep the farm. Papa would count out the money exactly down to the penny, so there was never any left over for a candy sucker for a little girl who yearned for a treat. I sometimes got to ride with Papa to the old country store at Herbert, a tiny village eight miles away. It was the only store for miles around. Usually he would hitch up the team of horses and go by wagon, but in the winter we hitched to the sleigh, and that was great fun as Papa always had jingle bells on the harnesses then! He was proud of his horses and kept them in good condition. Sometimes the snow would be so deep that the roads and five foot high fences completely disappeared. The snow could hold the horses weight, having frozen solid between repeated snowfalls. On those days we could take off as the crow flies, across the fields, not paying attention to where the roadways were. The day would be clear and Mama would bundle me up against the sting of the crisp, cold air. Papa had a heavy black robe of buffalo skin to cover our laps and knees. We used that same robe for many cold winters. Snow crackled under the horses hooves and the sleigh bells jingled merrily giving our ride a holiday air.

I shall never forget those trips to the store when I was a very small girl. The lady who ran the little grocery knew my father and me and I suspect she could read my eager eyes and his careful counting of the money. If I sometimes dared ask for a treat from Papa outloud, his answer was always the same, "No child, there's no need." The store-keeper was a very wise and kind lady whose name was Mrs. Tucker. Sometimes just as we were leaving, when my father was halfway out the door, and I reluctantly and disappoint-edly lagging behind, Mrs. Tucker would slip quietly out from behind the counter and press a very small paper bag into my hands. It was too late for me to give her anything but a wide and grateful smile from a small joyous heart. Clutching my precious bag, I scrambled up onto the high seat beside Papa. He gave a sharp "k-k-k-" of his tongue to the horses, and we sailed off across the clean snow. It was not until we were part way home that I dared peek in my bag to see what surprises Mrs. Tucker had given me. There would be an assortment of four or five small candies and maybe a gum. Oh, what a happy day that was! It may be difficult for anyone now to imagine how important such a small gift could be, but to a child who hardly ever received a treat of any kind, it was heaven itself. The trip home was a happy daze. I allowed myself one candy, saving the rest to show Mama and to portion out to last as long as possible.

Through the ensuing years since those days of the Great Depression I have often thought of and silently blessed Mrs. Tucker, and wondered if she really knew the far-reaching effect of her small acts of kindness. For it was in those very days that an appreciation was born in me for the importance of the gentle touch, of being sensitive to the quiet unspoken needs of others we meet, when we can be helpful without fanfare and without the need for acknowledgement.

Papa didn't mind my having the candy, just so he didn't have to buy it. He likewise never spent money on himself or Mama. He did not drink or smoke or go to taverns at night with other men. In that way he was a good husband and father as he was always home nights. But Mama in later years told me that in her forty years of marriage to him, the one and only time he ever took her to dinner out in a restaurant was the weekend marriage honeymoon they spent in a Chicago hotel in 1913. After the ceremony they rode the seventy miles into the city on the little Interurban railway that ran through their farm and the small village nearby.

I came to realize in later years that my father was truly the personification of the old-fashioned miser. It cost my mother her health, for she had no help but me with the many farm chores, nor enough warm clothing during those cold winter months in an old farm house that was drafty and difficult to keep warm. Mama was delicate in many ways, and contracted tuberculosis while I was very young. She said I had colic as a baby and cried every two hours with a need to be fed day and night for two years, so she lost much sleep.

My father would not allow Mama to go to a sanitarium as it would cost money and, she told me, he was deathly afraid of and hated doctors. When he was twelve years old his mother had died on the kitchen operating table at home under the hands of a doctor, from a bowel stoppage. (Mama said it may have been a burst appendix — they were never sure.) This would have been in 1881, as Papa was born in

1869. So Mama and I went to live at Grandma's house where Mama stayed in bed for a year. I was six years old. Mama had the TB for four years, but she was strong in spirit and courage and recovered all by herself through periods of rest and a deep faith in God and prayer — and lots of sunbaths! She later said to me, "I had to get well to take care of you! I didn't want to leave my little angel." X-rays taken years later showed her lungs to be full of healed scar tissue which she carried to her dying day.

Mama was a wonderful and lovely woman, and wise in many ways. She was my first teacher, as she began to explain life to me at a very early age. And so, although it seemed there were few privileges, or the usual comforts of other families available to us, I had something far more valuable: her words of wisdom, telling me of God's love for us all. She told me we each have a special Guardian Angel to take care of us no matter where we are, and that life is happy if we keep joy in our hearts and treat everyone we meet with kindness, just as we would wish to be treated. She told me of Jesus and the Holy family, and we talked a lot together. We were alone out in the country without the amenities of radio, television, or even near neighbors or the rest of her family.

Mama was always very honest with me and there were no secrets about the facts of life. I grew in wisdom and also in the ways of the world rather quickly, for I detected early that my parents were not suitably mated. My father was earthy and strong, very healthy in body and handsome in a rugged way but he cared nothing for the aesthetics of life or for philosophy as my mother did. Mama enjoyed good literature, music and flowers, the things that beautify a home and please the eye. She made time to read used books she found on philosophy and to study the spiritual side of life. When she tried to share these ideas with Papa he would scoff and say this was a waste of time. "Poppycock! When you're dead, you're dead. And that's the end of it."

Mother made our home attractive and pleasant with only pennies eeked from the sale of eggs in town. She built with her own hands seven lovely flower beds and rock gardens in the big yard on the South 80, and later on our larger farm on the highway where I spent my teens, she built a graceful grape and gourd arbor with walkway and climbing roses, with a bench to sit and view the beauty in summer. She often was given or swapped seeds such as hollyhocks and jack-o-lanterns with neighbors.

Colorful and uniquely shaped rocks were spotted along the roadway on our infrequent and bumpy auto trips to town. At that time in the 1930's some elegant and unusually colorful large rocks were turned up in the fields by farmers' plows and deposited along the fence rows. Keeping her eye peeled, Mama would suddenly shout, "Stop! I see a rock!" Papa would grudgingly bring our old auto to a screeching halt several yards past the spot, then sit and wait while she hopped out to retrieve her prize, lugging it back to the auto, exclaiming, "Isn't it a beauty?" And usually it was. I do not recall Papa ever getting out of the car, even once, to carry the rocks for Mama although many were fairly large with strange shapes. Mama told me that Papa had suffered and recovered from spinal meningitis when he was only ten years old and as a result still had a stiff neck which bothered him, and so he did not like to turn to look at things, especially a rock! Such an illness usually was sure death in those days so it was amazing he lived at all. I often wondered in later years what ever happened to my mother's beautiful and unique rock gardens after the farm was sold. I know her hobbies gave her pleasure during those years that must have been very lonely and desolate for a woman of finer tastes.

There were many verbal disagreements between my parents, usually involving money for some necessity Mama needed for the house. She was not built to be the workhorse and farmhand that many farm women were in those days and I know Papa was disappointed not to have such a helpmate, so she lacked the love from my father that brings joy and lightness of heart that contributes to a woman's good health. My father just did not understand love. Nevertheless, Mama carried out her duties and daily chores. She also usually had a hired man or two to feed. All of this broke her health. Mama contracted tuberculosis, and also a fibrous tumor that caused heavy monthly hemorrhaging. Usually such a tumor is removed, but since Papa would never consent to a doctor or surgery for her, she had no choice but to treat herself with home remedies, with as much rest as possible, and with prayer. Papa would angrily shout, "Your sickness is all in your head!"

In a sense there is truth in that, for unhappiness can, I have since found, bring on many maladies. Sexual incomparability over time can result in uterine and related illnesses, but at the time Papa's accusations did not help Mama nor alleviate the heavy bleeding she suffered. By then they no longer shared the same bedroom, so he did not see that she was often at such times too weak to lift her head off the pillow, having hemorrhaged all night, soaking the bed with blood. At a very early age I nursed her at such times and changed the blood soaked muslin rags, washed and hung them on the line to dry. Papa literally did not want anything to do with *women's problems.* He simply did not understand and sometimes called Mama, "Lazy." I think now it is a miracle that she did not bleed to death at some point. Mama carried that tumor the size of a muskmelon to her grave at the age of eighty nine. The tumor had gone dormant finally in her menopause years. She never did have surgery and lived remarkably long due to strength of spirit.

Mama explained to me that Papa did not understand women because he had not had a mother since he was twelve years old and no other woman had been around to teach him since. In the 1800's little boys did not learn about girls, as they do now. Such things were never spoken of. Papa was the eldest of four boys and two girls. My grandfather was left by his wife's death to raise five children alone on their family farm, which happened to be next door to my mother's family. There had been six children, Papa was the eldest, but one of the little girls, sister Kate, passed away while yet tiny and the other, named Jennie, left home very early in life to live with a relative and then became a teacher. And so, my grandfather and his four sons batched it together for many years so my father was raised never having a woman's touch or teaching.

My Mother, Marlena Lampert Beckington, age 26, the year of her marriage.

Mama said Papa jokingly told her after marriage, with a twinkle in his eye, that "I was so surprised to find you had legs!" He always thought women's feet were attached to their petticoats. At that time of course all dresses were to the floor with layers of petticoats that touched high button shoes. This was even more amusing in that Papa was forty-seven years old when he married Mama. He had lived all those years as a bachelor with his father and brothers, and to our knowledge, had not courted any other woman. So perhaps, Mama said to me, he could not be blamed then for knowing so little about women. It occurred to me in later years, perhaps he really didn't want to learn either.

In those days neighbors lived far apart and only a precious few had eligible daughters. If a chap knew of a girl 'round about he had to hitch up a horse to the buggy of an evening, after all the milking and chores were done and supper eaten, then at 8:00 p.m. ride for an hour to go a'courtin'. Upon arrival he was escorted into the parlor to sit with the girl on a horsehair stuffed sofa. Mama told me the horsehairs were like wire and sometimes poked up through the upholstery, often sticking one in the bottom, so staying any longer than an hour became an itchy ordeal. (One suspects the 'love seats' were stuffed with horsehairs purposely to discourage too ardent a romance.) After the hour, the beau would take leave and arrive back home by midnight in his open buggy (having to rise again by 4:00 or 5:00 a.m.), sometimes in the cold and icy wintertime. "So courting was a major task, not to be taken lightly," Mama said, "often of short duration, and was seldom indulged in without marriage in mind. Under these conditions there was not much opportunity to get to know your prospective mate. This was not considered too important; people were expected to adjust."

Mama told me a tale one time about her sister, Millicent, that was at once comical and very sweet. When Millicent was sixteen years old it seems a young neighbor boy in his late teens saw her and fell in love at first sight. His home was not near, but actually on a road behind, perhaps a mile away. Apparently it was possible to get a view of my Mama's and Millicent's house from the haymow of the young man's family barn.

Mama said that one day the lad's father came to see Grandma, begging her to allow her youngest daughter, only age sixteen, to marry his son, for, as he lamented, "Steven isn't worth a tiddly to me! All he does is sit up in the haymow all day with his spy glass trained on your yard hoping to catch a glimpse of her, while all his chores go untended! He moons around and doesn't hear a word I say! I am at wits end about him." I could understand it, for Millicent was slender and blonde with a beautiful smile. Grandma decided to give assent, and they were married. He was Mama's youngest sister's first and only beau and it was a very loving happy marriage, for I noticed even years later, after four children, that Uncle Steven still couldn't walk past Aunt Millicent without gently patting her 'behind.' Later however there was tragedy. After twenty or so years of happy marriage a cow kicked him in the breastbone and that began cancer of the bone from which he did not recover. So sweet Millicent was widowed early in life.

My father, on the other hand, was not a romantic type, nor one to give his time or money to such frivolous matters. Mama always said he chose her because she was "handy-by," one of six girls who lived next door (next door being the farm one-half mile down the road). Most of the other sisters had beaus through those years, but even so, Papa found my Mama the most pleasing to his eye. Her name was Marlena. She was tall and willowy with a shock of dark hair piled high on her head above her straight neck, creamy smooth face and hazel eyes. Especially appealing was her mischievous sense of humor. Papa too liked to kid around, so they hit it off that way.

As a handsome bachelor, the man who later would become my papa was, in his prime, considered to be the catch of the county, Mama said. Clyde was well-built, with strong broad shoulders, sun-bronzed complexion, dark auburn wavy hair, his cobalt blue eyes set in chiseled symmetrical features. Also he was the eldest son of a respected landowner. Two of his brothers became attorneys and the third brother went to Michigan to farm. They all sold their shares in the farm to Papa upon grandfather's death. Clyde also had the most handsome high-stepping horses and shiny well-kept rig of any man around, Mama said. He prided himself on being a good horseman, and every year competed with his trotting horses in the sulky races at the County Fairs. A sulky is a light-weight, two-wheeled cart drawn behind a single horse, with driver perched upon the cart's seat, his legs spread apart and braced against the whippletree. Young Clyde would pace the horse exactly, for the entire race must be run only at a fast trot. If the horse broke his pace and went into a cantor it was disqualified. My father always made a good showing in these races and kept a number of handsome shiny-coated racing horses in his pasture during those years, in addition to the heavier work horses. He was well-known for many miles around not only for his fine race horses, but also as an accomplished auctioneer, much sought after for farm sales, as he was knowledgeable about the value of farm equipment. My parents were married for twelve years before they finally got me. Mama being so poorly that way, she lost four babies during pregnancy. Papa never forgave her. He always thought such things were the woman's fault. Mama was sad that she never received sympathy even from her own mother, as she said she knew Grandma favored Papa, maybe even loved him, for he was a hard worker like her and closer to Grandma's age than to Mama's!

✳

HELP FROM HEAVEN

One of the first miracles in my life happened when I was still a toddler of two years old, and involved one of the race horses that Papa had retired. I was always fascinated to hear my father tell the story of the day Mama allowed me to be in the barn with him while she rested, but while he was busy working he failed to notice that I had wandered off out into the barnyard. Suddenly he heard a commotion and through the open door he saw that two horses were having

Mama, age 37 — the year before I was born.

a terrible fight, their backsides reared in the air kicking at each other, with tremendous bucking and flying hooves. To his horror, he saw his baby girl standing watching in fascination — not four feet from those sharp and deadly hooves! Papa said he felt rooted to the ground, frozen with fear. He knew if he shouted to me I might run into the hooves rather than back to him. And besides, he added, his throat was closed with shock and he could not utter a word. As Papa stood petrified for a long moment, as in a time warp, he saw a third horse come from across the barn lot and place herself between the two horses and me, taking some vicious kicks as she did so. With lowered head she gently nudged me over to the barnyard gate.

By then Papa was able to move and rushed to rescue me. But the real heroine was the horse Princess, who later Papa gave to me for my very own, my riding horse upon whom I spent hundreds of happy hours, both at work and in play.

Horses are very smart animals and are seldom given the credit they deserve. That horse had a special kind of intelligence, as you have already seen. She intuitively knew I was very small and even though I rode her almost daily by age five, to my intense disgust no amount of urging would ever get her to go beyond a light trot, though she would gallop at any time with any adult. Not until I was six years old, a full year later when she decided I could handle it, did she finally gallop. It was a day I shall never forget. We sailed like the wind across the field and after that, any time I chose. Sometimes Bowzer came with us. Bowzer was a mutt of unknown breed, but a good and faithful friend and always game to go anywhere and hopefully to chase a rabbit along the way. There was a limit as to what he could do. Often he gamely ran along behind my horse, Princess and me, but finally — panting — he gave up and limped home.

There was earlier trauma involved with riding however. At age four Papa decided I should learn to ride. He placed me up with him on the western style saddle, squeezing me between himself and the saddle horn. He was a sturdy man, as I've indicated, and did not understand deli-

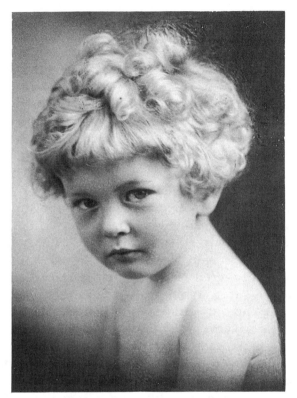

The author — age three years.

cate females. I cried loudly, Mama told me later, but Papa thought I was only frightened and would have no sissy for a daughter, so he kept on with the riding lesson. About two weeks later Mama discovered two lumps the size of chicken eggs hanging out on either side of my belly. A double rupture of the intestinal lining was the verdict. Immediate surgery was required and this time Papa did not object to a doctor.

The anesthesia of ether and hospital experience are still vivid in my memory. I dreamed when I was under the mask that I was flying in the air with a flock of ducks, when suddenly I began falling . . . and falling . . . and falling . . . into oblivion.

The very first night I had a terrible reaction to the ether that had been used, and reared up in a nightmare, screaming, which tore my new stitches wide open. I carry the scars to this day — wider than normal near my groin. It is good that ether is no longer used as an anesthetic. The worst misery in my memory was the terrible thirst. I was not allowed water of any kind for two days. That was the medical practice then. There was nothing to allay the intense fever. I shall never forget it, though I was only five years old. Nowadays a patient is immediately allowed, in most cases, to suck on precious ice in the mouth — a cooling godsend. Strange how medical ideas change through the years, fortunately in many ways for the better, but even yet there is a long way to go to really understand the complex and wonderful mechanism we call the body.

I soon recovered from my hernia operation and returned home. After my chores were finished I would play with my one and only girl friend who lived on a farm about two miles away across the fields. Her name was Angeline. I called her "Angie," and I loved her dearly. We romped with the dog, climbed trees in true tomboy fashion, tumbled in the haymow and swung on our makeshift swing, an old rubber tire attached to a rope on a tree limb. We were outdoor girls, seldom playing house or with dolls, mainly because we didn't even own a doll in those early years.

One warm summer's day Angie and I were down in the pasture, a quarter mile from the house, swinging merrily back and forth on the unlatched huge steel cattle gate. It had two rows of barbed wire strung across the top. Papa said this was to discourage cattle from leaping over out of the pasture. The entire gate swung free of the ground, hung by two bolts on one side. This day apparently one bolt had slipped free and the other broke under the extra weight; it suddenly came crashing down with Angie and me clinging to it. I was quick and jumped clear, but Angie was pinned beneath. To my horror I saw blood gushing from her head where the barbed wire had ripped through. Instinctively I called out, "Oh God! Please help me!" Mama had often taught me to remember that my Guardian Angel and Jesus were *always* with me. I knew I had to help her as we were alone and a long way from the house. I bent down and with one heave and all my strength of will lifted the steel gate off Angie so she could crawl out and then helped her to the house. We were by then both covered with blood and my horrified Mama bound her wound and went to pull the rope to ring the big heavy farm bell calling Papa to quickly drive her to the hospital fourteen miles away. I ran panting across the fields to tell her family what had happened.

Later my father had a hard time believing my story, even though Angie insisted it was true, that I had actually lifted the gate. "Child," he exclaimed, "that steel gate weighs 1,000 pounds and you are only five years old!" Whether he ever believed me or not, I know what happened. I know God answered my call because I do not recall the gate to even seem heavy, and it lifted on my very first try. I wasn't surprised, for I still had childlike faith. I knew Jesus was with me and would help me because Mama had told me so.

Years later I read of a similar case, even more dramatic, in *Guideposts Magazine*,* of a woman who held a two-thousand pound tractor up off her husband's chest for over an hour by bracing her shoulder against the hot radiator so he would not be crushed until help came. The tractor had tipped over on him in the field pinning him beneath. She saw what happened from her kitchen window and ran out to him. It took over an hour for a passing motorist to see the situation from the highway some distance away and bring help. The woman's upper arm was burned clear through to the bone, but she felt no pain — as she said she called on God for help. Her name and her husband's and the area they lived were clearly stated in the article. It was an authentic story and happened about twenty years ago when I read it. There have been many such miraculous happenings through the years. I have been privileged to know the truth of the reality of spiritual guidance and help and that we need not feel alone on this earth plane, no matter how desperate the problem. If we cannot feel it or receive the answer, the blockage is within us.

* *Guideposts*, 39 Seminary Hill Road, Carmel, N.Y. 10512-9954

*
SCHOOL DAYS — THOSE GOLDEN RULE DAYS

I was heartbroken when Angie, who was six years old, got to start school. I was only five and there was no kindergarten in those days, so I was not old enough to begin first grade. I raised such a ruckus at losing my playmate and being left behind that my mother sought and received special dispensation for me to begin also, so I entered first grade at age five and loved school from day one, for I truly enjoyed learning. Due to Papa's reluctance to spend money, I did not own a single new dress, but I was blessed with my cousins' hand-me-downs. Those dresses never fit me very well and I recall sometimes being ashamed, but then, in our little schoolhouse all the children came from farm families and no one dressed fancy, for goodness sake. Sometimes Mama was able to buy a swatch of gingham with the egg money and stitch a new dress for me at the start of a new school year.

In the late spring and then in early fall, on Indian Summer days when the air was balmy and seemed often tinted with a soft yellow haze, when spider webs sometimes floated in the air tangling across one's face, we all went to school barefoot. There was a wonderful sense of freedom in running barefoot in soft clean grass and down warm dusty roads, then to stop at the little creek that ran across our path halfway to school to wash one's feet in the cool gurgling water and usually to dawdle awhile under the bridge, stepping from one slippery stone to another to see how far we could get without falling in the knee deep water.

This first year of school was memorable. Not only was school new and wonderful, but I had the opportunity to see and play with someone besides Angie and my dog Bowzer. But the most memorable part of that first year was the fear of coming home. Even if I had played along the way and was late, it wasn't Mama or Papa I was frightened of; It was the gander! All went well as I trudged along the three miles carrying my empty lunch bucket until I reached the bottom of our long lane down by the road. We had a flock of geese that Mama tended, partly for the wonderful goosedown featherticks and pillows that they provided, and partly so we could have goose for dinner on special occasions like Christmas. Also Mama sold the eggs, as one big egg would almost make a whole breakfast. The geese ran loose to catch bugs and eat green grass in our big front pasture that was a long down-hill slope between the house and the road. The patriarch master of the flock was an old mean gander — and I mean, MEAN! He strutted about like a king of all he surveyed, hissing at dogs and cats alike who all made a point of staying out of his way. He seemed huge to a little five year old girl (actually he was nearly my size), and that wiley fellow knew I was afraid of him. He soon caught on that I came home every afternoon about the same time and he was ready and waiting down at the end of the lane. He stood there, hissing loudly with open beak and wide outstretched wings, daring me to pass. If I ran he chased me, nipping at my legs, while I screamed for Mama. His beak was sharp and could pinch hard and was not to be reckoned with. Sometimes I didn't even try to run past him, but stood screaming and crying until Mama, a quarter mile up the hill, finally heard and looking down, saw my plight. She came running, carrying a big stick, giving him a few good whacks, chasing him off so I could get to the house.

One day I shall never forget. Mama finally got tired of that old gander's brassiness and of having to come down the hill to rescue me. As I stood in awed admiration, Mama walked right up to that mean gander with hissing beak above his long arched neck, and wide menacing wings, grabbed him around the neck with both hands, lifted that huge heavy goose right off his feet into the air, and began swinging him around and around in a circle — until Mama finally let him go with a fling, and he fell with a hefty flop onto the grass. That old gander tottered around as he tried to get up, then staggered off as dizzy as a whirligig. I'll bet he had a sore neck for awhile and do you know, he never bothered me again. He was, in fact, quite subdued for days, hiding out alone in corners of the pasture. The love and admiration I already felt for Mama swelled a hundred-fold that day.

Our schoolhouse, in my memory, was a wonderful little schoolhouse of only one room, plus coat closets. It was called Pinegar School because the land for the school had been purchased from the Pinegar farm. Our teacher taught all eight grades in one room. Thinking back, I believe she was a magician, for everyone studied all the necessary subjects at his own level. Her name was Miss Gracie Hollembeck and she was a charmer of twenty three, with curly dark hair and bright dancing blue eyes, pretty as a picture, and she was vivacious with a merry laugh and a way of making studying fun. She had to be smart, too, to juggle teaching eight separate grades each day while keeping everyone busy. (There was no Junior High in those days. One went right from eighth grade into High School.) The number of students in the room varied, as I recall, from the least of twelve in one year, to the most of twenty-three some other years.

"Teacher" (as we called her), always came out of doors at recess time and played games with us too, like King of the Hill, or Fox and Geese, and even baseball. She was full of ideas and truly made the school years of my youth an enjoyable experience. In fact, she made some of the school days, for now and then, in the darkest winter months when the snow was far too deep for little feet and short legs to manage, she actually came around with her high-wheeled Model-A Ford to pick us up, careening along, charging through the snowbanks at top speed so she wouldn't get stuck, with powdery snow flying out from under the running boards like the roostertail on a speedboat. Her cheery horn was a welcome sound, just when we'd given up to being snow-bound at home for a boring day. Those days school was our excitement, where we got to see our friends, unlike modern times when children have so many alternative pleasures they often welcome skipping school. Never a day was missed if I could possibly help it, as I truly loved school, even though it usually meant a long daily walk of nearly three miles through snow and ice in the wintertime. Being an only child, I had to go it alone most of the way.

The winters out on Midwest prairie lands were often bitter cold. Central heating in homes, and heaters in autos were nonexistent. No one had the time or machinery to clear the backroads and the howling winds would repeatedly fill the roads with drifting snow. We children got to school as best we could. We were made of sturdy stuff and you didn't question what you had to do. You just did it. Of course, if it were really storming one was not allowed out, unless there was a ride, for safety's sake. Sometimes in the worst days I would rise an hour earlier to catch a ride with the milkman in his sleigh, as he came to pick up our cans of fresh milk to take to the dairy for processing. But then one had to sit through all the stops at other farms to pick up their milk and the ride was a long cold one in the open sleigh. I did have high boots and warm scarves and a stocking cap. But, after all these years, I still have an aversion to cold because of those bitter days.

One of my most vivid memories is of the dreaded chilblains. Sometimes arriving at school by 9:00 a.m., after having left home at 7:30, my feet would be numb with cold. On such days Teacher held classes around the old fat pot-bellied stove in the corner, so we could all take off our wet coats and shoes and stockings and put our cold feet near the stove to thaw out. Often they would be bright red and swollen, and itch like thunder, so badly I could hardly study for scratching my feet. Dratted chilblains! I recall scratching until blood came. I have found that after once being affected in this manner, the feet are always more sensitive to cold forever after. But even chilblains did not stop us from going out in the snow at recess to stomp out a Fox and Geese circle for games.

One morning Mama and Papa and I arose to find an ice storm had come in the night. An ice storm is rain that freezes and sticks as it falls, covering everything with several layers of ice. I gasped as I peered out the windows in little clear spaces I made by blowing on the glass with my breath and wiping it clean. *Jack Frost* had come in the night too, creating lovely patterns all over the window panes. These were delicate creations of Nature. One could find hidden pictures; beautiful scenes of trees and birds and flowers in the frosty patterns if one looked hard enough and used a little imagination.

But this particular morning the glory was out-of-doors. Oh, how it all sparkled in the clear, cold morning sunlight! A fairyland! The familiar sights around the yard had been transfigured into odd caricatures; exotic creatures of strange grace and beauty. The scene is still vivid in my memory, lo, these many years. Tree branches had broken under the weight of the ice, creating strange shapes as though people with snow top-hats were leaning against the trunk; telephone wires were thick as a man's thumb and hanging low like ropes to be swung on; fence posts resembled sentinels marching down the lane with fluffy white fur caps. One step outside — your feet flew out from under you — and you were flat on the ground in a twinkle. This was extra slippery glass-ice!

It was a wondrous sight, but rubbing my sore bottom, I wondered how was I to get to school? There had to be a way. Picking myself up I inched back into the house to fashion a sling to tie my lunch bucket on my back so I would have both hands to catch myself when I fell (for I knew I would fall many times) and the bucket would not then go flying every time with its precious contents. After finishing the few chores I could (I never did know how Mama fed the chickens and ducks that day), and bundling up extra warm, off I went, sliding on my bottom most of the way down our long lane to the road below. Our farmhouse stood on a high hill with a grand view in all directions. It was quite easy to get down the hill and slither along the road beyond, but after turning the corner onto the main gravel road, now also covered with ice, I met some of the other kids as we came to the hill leading to the schoolhouse. It wasn't a hill really, more like a rise, but it might as well have been Mt. Everest on that icy morn. After attempts and failures, red faced and out of breath, with sore bottoms and knees from slipping back down, we took another tack. "Lets form a chain," somebody said, "and hold onto the fence over there and pull ourselves along!" It was a great idea. We crunched and slid our way over to the fence, then hand over hand we pulled along like a pulley rope, giving each other shouts of encouragement. Ice covered the otherwise sharp barbs on the wire, which now were almost like knots in a rope to hold onto. Needless to say, the four of us were very late for school, but proud to be only the few who had not missed that day.

Not missing school was a kind of badge of honor we wore with pride in those days, as it was so often a struggle. Buses were unheard of and didn't come into existence until a number of years later when those small one-room school houses were closed, the district was consolidated, and a new large elementary school was built in the village.

The era of the one-room schoolhouse was picturesque and carried a special kind of charm and memory that will never be replaced by the large and crowded classrooms of today. From the friendly pot-bellied stove in the corner (Teacher had to always arrive early in order to lay the fire and warm the room in the wintertime), to the large and colorful schoolyard filled with special trees to climb and swing from, or to build playhouses in, our one-room school-house, and all one-room schoolhouses, should have a place in history alongside covered bridges, for they personify an era long gone, that molded three generations of midwest and western farm families.

On balmy early spring days when students had spring fever, when birds arrived back from the south caroling their joyous songs outside our windows, and we sometimes heard the nostalgic far-off honking of Canadian geese and we rushed outside to see their sky-high V-for-victory sign in the heavens as they migrated north for the summer, our won-derful kind-hearted, understanding teacher would hold classes outside under the elm tree with its wide spreading branches. We delighted to sit in the soft, cool grass while taking turns reading aloud portions of the Tales of King Arthur, Longfellow's poems, the stories of Louisa May Alcott, Jean Stratton-Porter and other wonderful tales.

One special tree stood in a corner of the schoolyard near the road. It was a very large weeping willow and it was

our friend. This huge tree had graceful trailing branches
that reached to the ground all the way around, like a lady's
full golden-green skirt. We girls soon discovered that inside
those branches was a perfect little house. We were totally
hidden, with just enough light filtering through the branches
to create a soft green, cool, quiet atmosphere. How delightful! We spent many happy noon hours playing house inside
the branches of our magnificent tree. And, best of all, it was
off limits to rowdy boys who preferred more rough-and-
tumble games.

One Fall we returned to school to find a devastating
sight. A road crew had come by and, being clip-happy, had
trespassed onto our hallowed school grounds and had given
our tree a hair-cut, cutting the branches high off the ground
all the way around, ruining forever our playhouse. Our grief
was deep and long-lasting. We thought black thoughts of
grown-ups who had no feeling for the needs of children and
the simple gifts of nature that make them happy.

The boys, and girls too, liked to play Leap Frog. In
those years girls always wore dresses to school, for trousers
were only in the form of coveralls for performing chores at
home. Under our dresses we wore petticoats, long stockings and bloomers. Bloomers were underpants that were
quite loose and blousey, with elastic to hold them just
above the knee, so we were really very well covered, and
we could play leap frog with the best of the boys. One day,
however, remains seared in my mind.

While we were all leap-frogging at recess, the boys
began to snicker and whisper to one another and seemed
eager to get in line quickly again. They ended up rolling on
the ground laughing and finally the truth came out. I had a
split in the crotch of my bloomers that I was unaware of,
and this was the highlight of their day. For me — a mortal
embarrassment. I never again put on a pair of bloomers without searching it several times for unsuspected holes.

One of our male playmates named Pete had older brothers at home, and I gathered later on that he picked up some
interesting conversation and ideas from them, for one year
when I was about seven years old, he suddenly became my

plague. It didn't matter what game the group was playing, he would find an excuse to knock me down, none too gently, falling flat on top of me and holding me there for a time until I struggled free. I was becoming furious with his harassment, but it took awhile for me to catch on to his intentions. This was my first introduction to the sexual approach of the male animal, and I was put-off, to say the least. I think it influenced me to be wary of most males from then on.

My wariness held me in good stead, for on my way home I often used a shortcut through the farmyard of three bachelors. They were brothers and the youngest was about twenty three. I found later he was *simple*, as we used to call it then, that is, somewhat slow mentally. Everyone accepted such folks as being a natural part of nature, and treated them with kindness. The brothers were neighbors, therefore considered friends and trustworthy. So when this young chap, whom I shall call Clem, called to me from his porch one day as I was passing through, I stopped to see what he wanted. He held out a book he said he had for me. I was a lover of books so was curious. As I walked up to him he reached for me and pulled me onto his lap and said he wished to read it to me. I thought this rather sudden and strange, but I didn't want to be rude, as Mama had taught me to be polite to my elders. It was only a few moments, however, before his hands reached under my dress. It took me only a split second to bolt off his lap and run like sixty before he knew what had happened. One of my attributes was being quick in my movements, and in this instance it held me in good stead. I didn't need to think twice about things! I told Mama what had happened, because now I could never again take the shortcut and it would take me longer to get home. She understood and praised me for having "good horse sense," as she called it.

Mama was very strict with me. Even though she was the gentle one, a lover of beauty and books, she was also the disciplinarian, and she could come down hard when I didn't obey. Papa was busy in the fields and the barn and didn't pay that much attention to my training. This was left to

Mama to accomplish, and accomplish it she did! She was also my friend and confidante and gave me much love. I was not only high-spirited but strong-willed, and as Mama put it, she only had one chick, and she wasn't going to be ashamed of her. She was not averse to using a good springy willow switch when occasion called for it, and memory tells me that was more than seldom, for I can still feel the sting of her ire when I conveniently forgot or tried to weasel out of my chores.

I was held tightly to my two or more hours of daily chores after school. It seemed that work was never-ending on those old family farms, and men usually expected their wives to deliver strong strapping sons who would grow up to help. This carryover from old European customs, that sons were a necessity, held even to the generations of the American family in this century. My father never forgave my mother for giving him only one stringy little girl. So my role in the plan seemed inescapable and I was expected to produce. "One who doesn't work, doesn't eat," was the familiar chant. Mama had not been strong in her organs of reproduction, as mentioned, and (I later found) had had several miscarriages. Finally, after many years, when my father was about fifty-seven years of age and Mama thirty-eight, she carried one baby to delivery. She, of course, prayed for a boy to please my father. When the doctor told her she had a lovely little red-headed girl, she told me she very nearly fell out of bed! I now know that I came to her to be a help and comfort, as she needed it even more than Papa did. Perhaps I came to have the experience that only that kind of life could bring me. There is always a Divine Plan working in our lives, although sometimes it remains hidden under strange and even harsh appearance until many years later. When one can then look at the chain of events, a light goes on in the mind and one will exclaim, "Ah-ha! So that explains it all."

So Mama and I had to be buddies to each other. We were way out there in the country with no others with whom to talk personal girl talk. Mama told me tales of her girlhood, of our unique and interesting extended family and their gifts or idiosyncracies, while Papa fell asleep and snored on the sofa after supper till Mama woke him up to make him go to bed. At such times Mama shared many things that she had learned relating to who we really are in God's Kingdom. Mama told me we are not just the bodies we see, but rather spiritual beings of wonderful creation, come to earth for special purposes to learn and help and love one another for a time, before returning again to heavenly realms. These realms were many and unique, as Jesus taught, (". . . in my Father's house are many mansions . . .") and where we went after we died depended on how we had lived and conducted ourselves here, and how kind we were to one another and to the animals.

But that didn't mean we could be soft. Oh No! We had to learn to work hard and do every chore placed before us to the best of our ability. For to be lazy and shiftless was shameful; not to do our share would be to put a burden on others to carry. But most of all we were to love God, the source of our life and to be grateful for what we did have, for when one has no gratitude for what he has been given, he may lose it.

Even so, Mama encouraged reading and day-dreaming at proper times. We often shared fairy tales on dark winter evenings before bedtime, and the moral of the story would be pointed out if there was one. Mama had a sense of humor and often wove funny stories and jokes around events that had happened to me or to others that day, so that I looked at my experiences in a lighter vein — objectively, we would say now, rather than being caught up in personal trauma and taking myself and my importance in the event too seriously. Then we would laugh together and sometimes poke gentle fun at others who huffed and puffed and blew themselves all out of shape in an effort to impress their listeners, like our turkey gobbler out in the chicken yard. Mama told me that folks who really impressed others were those who didn't talk and blow their own horn about what they were going to do. They just quietly did it, and surprised everyone. And if these works were helpful to others, as well as themselves, God — who saw everything we did — took note of it and rewards would come in due time.

Naturally, I know now there is far more to the Law of Cause and Effect, and that can be discussed later, but this was the way Mama put it all in a nutshell in story fashion for a little girl who was eager to listen. In later years Mama gave me one choice bit of wisdom that has always held me in good stead, "If someone says something mean or accuses you of something that you know very well you did not do, think of it as a bag of garbage they are trying to hand you to ease their own mind. If you do not reach out to take it, it will never be yours, and they are left holding the bag."

I was required to carry a large share of the chores, both inside and out, not for any rewards, but simply because the work had to be done and my parents needed the help. Mama's health was frail and Papa had many acres and long tiring days. I carried in all the water for cooking from a deep, cold well where, in the heat of the summer, we hung the butter and cream down in a bucket at the end of a long sturdy rope. This was our refrigeration. At harvest time we had to pick and carry in the apples, and from the garden, turnips and potatoes, to be stored in the root cellar in a special corner of the cool underground basement. I carried wood to replenish the woodboxes even in summer, for Mama cooked on a large old-fashioned black iron cookstove with warming ovens above where bread and other baked goods could rise, permeating the whole house with good smells. If the wood box got low, believe me I heard about it!

Sometimes on nice fall days I went with Papa up to our big eight acres of woods to help him chop up trees that had fallen and bring it down in the wagon. One day I chopped into my foot with the big ax (I was ten years old), and bled like a stuck pig. Papa dropped everything and whipped the horses into a run for home, but Mama said it "wasn't too bad," and just put black salve on my foot and bound it up. I hobbled about awhile and still have the scar. That ax was sharp. I used to watch Papa as he sat on the seat of his whetstone, pedaling hard so the big stone wheel went round and round while he held the ax against the stone to sharpen it — fine as a knife blade.

There were chickens and ducks and turkeys, as well as

the geese, to throw grain and corn to, though they ran free around the yard and fed on grasshoppers and June bugs and such, keeping the flowerbeds and orchards free of insect nuisances. Our food was not poisoned by insecticides in those days. This was unheard of. The barnyard fowl did their work well. Also Mama always said that fowl that fed naturally outdoors were healthier and had a better color to their skin. However, we kept a tight chicken wire fence around the vegetable garden which was planted with all manner of good things, even horseradish, which Papa grew, ground up and bottled for the winter months, as meat without horseradish relish was not a proper meal in his mind. Boy! It could blow the top of your head off if you forgot and took a big bite.

One of my jobs in summer was to walk up and down the garden rows carrying a small can of kerosene, searching for big brown potato bugs and fat green tomato worms clinging to the vines, and when I found them I would pick them off and drop them into the can. A farm girl couldn't afford to be squimish.

Vegetables were fresh and the soil was fertilized only with barnyard manure, rich in nitrogen, and our garden produced big healthy plants with wonderful flavor; different kinds of squash, big red radishes and juicy tomatoes, lettuce and celery, peas and carrots and cucumbers for pickles, fat pumpkins for Mama's wonderful pies, and even that horseradish. Papa would never have dreamed of spending money to buy commercial fertilizers. Every Fall he carefully spread all of the barnyard manure that had been sitting to one side composting all winter and summer on the fields that would later produce abundant crops of corn, wheat, oats and barley. The big, wide spreader was pulled by two large workhorses with broad flanks and heavy legs. A few farmers then, who could afford it were buying tractors, but Papa didn't believe in motorized machinery that broke down, rusted and gave problems. Horses were more dependable, he said, and he was a horse man. So all the field work, including plowing, planting, cultivating, raking and harvesting, was done in this manner and later Papa taught me to drive the big work horses, sometimes a team of four, to help when I was not in school.

*
THRESHING TIME

Haying season and threshing season were especially busy times, for the hay had to be cut and carried in at a precise time before the rains came that would cause it to mildew. Papa always hired help then if we didn't have a steady man, but good help was always hard to find. The big wagon piled high with enormous loads would trundle up to the barn and the hay was lifted by a large forklift and carried on a pulley-rope up into the haymow above. The pulley-rope went across the mow high in the rafters of the barn and down the other side outdoors, where it attached to the whippletrees hitched to a team of strong horses. It was my job to drive these horses on signal by a shout from the other side of the barn, indicating the fork was set into a large forkful of hay ready to be hoisted. It was very tricky, because the rope had to be kept taut and the pull steady, up and across into the high open mow, but not too fast. If the horses should stop and then start again with a jerk at any point during the pull, the fork would release and dump the whole load off in the wrong place, even on the ground, or bury the chap on the wagon who was setting the fork. Papa taught me to keep close rapport with my horses to start and stop them at precise moments. "I'm counting on you, my girl. Drive them in a steady strong pull straight forward, until you hear a loud shout 'WHOA!' from the man in the mow who is directing the fall." This went on for several days until all the hay was in the barn. This was a responsible job for a girl of ten years, but I became very proficient at it during the next several seasons. The horses knew me. Horses are very intelligent and try hard to obey, and they too seem to understand their job, for actually the success of it depended far more on them than on me.

One fall there was a serious accident. Papa had hired a man whom he knew from town to help with the haying. I do not know if he was too old and not agile enough, we never knew just what happened. But while he was in the mow directing the fork lift, suddenly there came a strange and strangulated shout that did not resemble "WHOA!" and it was wrong timing. I stopped the horses and called out, but an ominous silence came from the barn. Then shouts went up from the other side where the wagon stood. My father found that the poor man had fallen to the main floor below and was badly hurt. He was rushed to the hospital, but later died. We all, especially Papa, felt very badly about this tragedy and our little family was somber for days.

Threshing time in the fall when grain was ripe was a really big event, as one huge expensive old threshing machine was used co-operatively by all the farmers together and trundled around to all the farms in perhaps a twenty mile radius, since no one could afford to own such a machine alone. A schedule was arranged and the men all worked together (some had sons to bring), threshing the grain of each farm successively, staying from one to three days each, depending on how large the farm and how much grain there was to be threshed, mainly oats, wheat and barley. My father, after his morning milking and other barn chores, would hitch up his team to the wagon and be gone daily for three or four weeks during this season, working at other farms.

What excitement when our turn came! Men and their teams would begin to arrive from miles around very early in the morning. There would be anywhere from eighteen to twenty very hungry men to feed a noon meal, perhaps for two or three days running if the harvest was large. Any one of those men could eat as much as three men normally might, it seemed. Forever after, if anyone made a pig of himself, it was said that he "ate like a thresher." My Mama sometimes enlisted the help of her closest neighbor lady and began baking luscious pies days ahead; cherry, berry, apple, walnut and pumpkin. The aroma of many loaves of fresh bread permeated the house. She prepared all that she could, and I helped, for when the men from all over the county came to eat, a lady's reputation as a cook was on the line. We served huge beef, pork loin and chicken dishes and of course many vegetables. The men had a golden opportunity to compare the culinary skills of all the local women for miles around and were not loath to report home to their wives who it was that served up the tastiest dishes, and who the worst. When Mama slyly asked Papa his opinion on this delicate subject a few days later, he would pretend to give it deep thought and then with a twinkle in his eye, would magnanimously concede that Mama could "hold her own with the best of them." I will say, Papa was never prone to gossip about anyone, for good or ill, but by the same token he never gave any undue praise, either. We knew my Mama was a very good cook, having German heritage, as the Germans were well-known for flavorful, hearty and filling food. I'll say, those men would lick up every scrap, a compliment in itself. If I desired a sample of something special I'd jolly well better put some on a plate and hide it before those men descended from the fields like the seven-year locusts, for we women never got to eat until the men were finished, and usually there wasn't much of anything left.

It was my job also to set up the washstands. These consisted of several sawhorses placed apart, with long planks on them. On these planks we set perhaps eight or ten metal wash basins with big bars of soap and towels, with several pails of fresh water nearby. For hungry men, hot and perspiring from their labors, did not wish to take time for turns at only a couple of basins. They wanted to eat! They joked and laughed over dinner, tossing around local gossip, which I had to strain to hear because Mama kept me busy running back and forth replenishing the fast-emptied serving dishes. I'll never forget one fellow loudly telling his impressions of Mrs. So-and-So's house the day before. He said he had seen her that morning chasing the big unlucky rooster around the chickenyard, and not much later, at noon, the poor bird was served up, tough and still quivering and jumping on the platter! This tale brought a hoot of laughter and agreement from his listeners, and I felt sorry for poor Mrs. So-and-So, who must not have known that one must always leave a slaughtered chicken sit at least twelve hours or overnight before cooking, or it does not taste right. That repulsive but comical picture lodged in my imagination and has remained all through the years.

It was always a big relief to my parents to have the

autumnal threshing season finished with the precious grain safely in the bins before fall rains came, and off to one side huge fresh golden straw piles to be used for bedding for the animals all winter. We loaded freshly threshed bags of choice hard wheat and rye into the wagon, hitched up the horses and trundled it to the local mill in our village for grinding, as we used all our own grain for flour in home baking, and also ground corn for cornmeal as well. Very little of our food was store-bought in the early years, only black molasses, sugar, coffee, tea, a little cocoa and spice, sometimes dried codfish for delicious codfish gravy in the wintertime. And, oh yes, Vermont natural maple syrup. For a while we had our own bees for honey, but they kept stinging neighbors and other now-and-then visitors, and Papa said, "Enough of that!" and sold them. It is amazing that even bees come to know their keeper and invariably only sting strangers.

Our eggs were stored to winter-over by stacking them in big enamel crocks in the cool basement. Mama would stand the eggs on their pointy ends in a layer of salt so they did not touch, then lay down another layer of salt and a layer of eggs on that, and so on, until the crock was full, with salt the last layer over the top. She packed duck and goose eggs as well. This way the eggs kept fine and were used mainly for baking through the winter. Mama tried to raise turkeys and we had them awhile, but she said, they were too delicate, catching croup, keeling over and dying at the slightest change in temperature. They were stupid, too, and didn't even know enough to come in out of the rain to their turkey house. Mama and I were always out there chasing turkeys around during every storm, and the silly things would run backwards between your legs before they would go where you wanted them. They weren't only stupid, they were stubborn as well. So we finally gave up on the turkeys. Nowadays, of course, turkeys are raised by the thousands on big farms. It is interesting the changes that can take place in fifty years.

My father favored my mad passion for cats, as they were inexpensive insurance against mice and gophers, which otherwise would over-run our corncrib and granaries. During my first year at school, when I was five, I was given and carried home a wild and unruly grey and white female kitten that struggled and scratched all the long two miles home from the farmer who gave her to me. I remember that day as clear as a bell for my arms were a mass of scratches. But I held tight for I desperately wanted that kitten! That one cat proved to be very fertile and prolific, producing two litters a year for the next ten years. Of course, those litters had litters as well, and it turned out that I supplied cats to the farmers for miles around for those ensuing years, and one year we still had twenty-three cats left over! Most were barn cats, wild and hard to catch, but three or four became house pets with special privileges. Not having brothers and sisters, cats and dogs were my friends and playmates, along with my fine horse.

That old Mama Cat never did get over being mean and unruly right to the end, but she was a wonderful mother, taking every single litter for training at the right age out into the fields to teach them to hunt. At such times she would sneak home without them to teach them to find their own way home. They'd come dragging in, one at a time, almost at dark, bedraggled and wet, yowling their heads off about it all. But they had found their way, and after that they were on their own. Papa set large pans of warm fresh milk out at milking time for those barn cats and some he even trained, for fun, to catch warm squirts of milk from the cows' teats straight into their open mouths, as he playfully aimed in their direction while milking. Otherwise, they had to comb the fields and granaries for their food, or starve. No one ever heard of buying cat food, and Papa would not have spent one dime for such foolishness anyway. The dog was luckier. He always had table scraps and juicy steak or stew-meat bones.

The summer that I was seven years old the accident happened that has affected my entire life.

✳

MY FALL FROM THE HAYMOW

I screamed — the pain shot up my spine like a hot poker! Then I felt nothing; I lay in a daze. The kids were shouting and scrambling down the barn-loft ladder to where I lay on the cement floor below. We had all been playing in the hayloft above. I had gotten too close to the edge while jumping into the hay and a boy visiting with neighbors had given me a playful shove at the wrong moment. The others helped me to walk up to the house. I felt numb, not feeling my legs.

For some reason not much was made of it. Children around farm yards fell down a lot in play and parents didn't coddle them or stop their work to run to the hospital unless there was blood. So I was told to lie down and rest awhile. Besides, you know Papa distrusted the entire medical profession, and didn't care for their charges either. I had pain in my lower back for a long time, but recovered after a time and continued work and schooling.

But as the years advanced, my backaches became worse and I experienced an increasing loss of energy. By the time I was twelve years old Mama finally took me to a doctor for ex-rays, despite Papa. The doctor found I had sustained a broken coccyx in that fall, which had developed into a calcification of the tailbone and curvature of the lower spine with abnormalities in the lower lumbar vertebras. Doctors told Mama if the body had not adjusted itself with the curvature, my spine would have ended up at my right shoulder. They said they could rebreak and reset the bones and put me in a cast for nine months, but they would then give only a 50/50 chance that I would walk again. Mama said, "Leave it alone."

This condition has been a challenge intermittently through life causing backache in my teen years and early twenty's. Later I found answers and conquered pain. I managed to continue a normal life in those early years with the help of back rubs from Mama and a wonderful lady Osteopath in town Mama knew who gave therapeutic massages, and who gave us a reduced rate for she knew we hadn't much money. I remember she massaged an hour for only $2.00. She was a big heavy set lady, very strong but very gentle, and I'll always remember the touch of her healing hands that felt so good on my aching back. This was my first real experience with the wonder of the healing touch in alleviating pain in the body and it left a lasting impression that influenced my later years.

I have always had determination, so did not stop participating in life, and even set a county record in High Jump at the competition one year. In later years I found while practicing natural childbirth exercises that gentle consistent exercise of the lower spine was my greatest self help, and since those long ago days, the medical profession has finally come to this same conclusion.

*

THE WONDER OF MUSIC

Music was one of our greatest joys and entered into my life very early as Mama had an old-fashioned victrola that one had to wind up with a crank on the side. It played wonderful records she had brought from her girlhood home or collected at farm auctions. This pastime livened up the long winter evenings, for we had no other entertainment, not even radio, until a few years later when we got an old-timer that ran on a battery. The battery, I recall, was forever running down and needing to be taken to town for a charge. I got hooked on those exciting classical episodes of *The Lone Ranger, Little Orphan Annie*, and *The Shadow*, but many times right at the crucial part, to my intense frustration, the battery would run down and I'd be left hanging for a couple weeks until it could be taken to town and charged again. Papa put up with this luxury because he liked to listen to the prize fights now and then, when Joe Louis was world champion.

So mostly we listened to Mama's victrola and she would dance me around the sitting room, as Papa didn't care for that foolishness, never having learned to dance a single step. Besides, he always fell asleep on the sofa after supper and snored loudly, sometimes in time with the music. It was really very funny. One of Mama's favorite records, and the lullaby she sang to me when I was little, was :

'Til We Meet Again

Smile the while you kiss me sad adieu,
When the clouds roll by I'll come to you.
Then the skies will seem more blue,
Down in lover's lane, my darling —
Wedding bells will ring for you and me,
All our friends will sing so merrily.
So wait and pray each night for me —
'Till we meet again.

I loved those old time records. It brings back sweet sad memories to hear those songs now and then, for I know this is how Mama kept her spirits up during those difficult, work-worn years.

Mama wanted a piano for me, as she had taught herself to play in her teen years, but her piano had burned with the house fire of her family home in 1911, along with all of her early pictures and personal belongings. She always looked sad when speaking to me about that, for it had been a traumatic happening in the dead of winter on a very cold and snowy night. Her brother, Leslie, who was six years old and who's leg was broken from a cow kicking him, was quickly carried out and laid in the snow. The water the family poured onto the roof in attempts to quell the blaze quickly froze into ice and made their efforts slippery and impossible. There were no telephones or fire engines in those days, but the little interurban train that happened to be going past across the road stopped, and the people all jumped out and tried to help, to no avail. My grandpa and grandma's house burned to the ground. Mama lost everything since she was not at home at the time to rescue her own things from her room, and the piano, too, was lost.

Mama was, however, determined I should have piano

lessons by hook or by crook. So she carefully saved enough over the years to pay twenty dollars and acquire an old but tuneful upright in good condition at a farm sale. I began lessons at age eight from Evelyn Pinegar who lived near our little school house. If twenty dollars seems like not much to pay for a decent piano, I remember that ten dollars was an entire month's salary Papa paid our hired men during those depression years when he could find the help. Twenty dollars was two months' salary. Mama told me in later years that although Papa seemed stingy with money, it had helped him save his farmland during the depression when many others lost theirs and ended up as tenants to others on their own land, or became displaced and had to work at the CCC Camps begun by President Franklin D. Roosevelt.

When I was five, Papa gave me a gift and he didn't even know it. He inspired me to whistle. He used to whistle around the barnyard and I followed him around, begging him to teach me how to do that. He would only say, "Well . . . All you have to do is pucker and blow." Well, I "puckered and blowed" till I was red in the face. I finally got it right, and it was fun! Whistling turned out to be something special for me that changed the course of my life.

I found that I could listen to the birds and get new ideas for trills, and then later I whistled with the tunes I learned on the piano, and this was an unusual combination that surprised and fascinated folks who came to call on Mama now and then. For me it was a wonderful way to express the joy of music, because I never thought I had much of a singing voice like others.

Mama also decided I should have elocution lessons, and somehow she managed enough egg money to afford several years of these. So I also learned to speak properly, to overcome stage fright, and acquire a modicum of poise on stage. Amazingly, there was a young neighbor woman who had been to the big city (probably Chicago) and had returned home to teach. She was within riding distance for me and my horse, and I rode to her home between the ages of eight to eleven, while we were yet living on The 80, as my folks called our south farm. In a few years word of my playing, whistling, and recitation talents spread and I found myself in school programs, performing at local harvest festivals and Grange entertainments. Since I came free of charge, I was in demand. The experience was rewarding for me, as I recall those days with fondness and gratitude for the grassroots experience. Folks would clap and make a bit of a fuss over me, and soon I was well known over most of the countryside.

*
SOME GORY DETAILS

All this attention might lead you to think I became spoiled. Well, I wasn't. Far from it. I was required to daily help Papa bring in the cows for milking, throw down hay for the horses, and swill the pigs. I especially remember swilling the pigs. We mixed a special swill mix with water and carried it in big heavy buckets to their troughs. They were a mess. The pen was always a huge mudhole, which they loved, and they sloshed around and squealed and oinked shrilly at feeding time. Papa kept the sows with litters of piglets separated from the rest, as the piglets might otherwise be trampled to death underfoot. Some of those old sows were huge and very heavy and didn't care where they laid or stepped.

Butchering time once a year in the fall was not a pleasant affair. Papa brought in professional help. A big sow or two would be chosen, and the ritual began. I usually ran off to hide, for I could not stand it. One day especially stands out in horror in my memory. After one of the chosen ones throat had been cut, she somehow got loose from the men and her moorings, got on her feet and began careening all over the yard, with blood splashing out on everything, all the while squealing bloody murder, for that's exactly what it was!

I knew of course that meat was needed not only for family, but to feed hungry hired men for the long winter months. The larder had to hold over 'til spring. Papa raised hogs for this express purpose and some to sell for income. Finally this day, the old sow weakened, fell over, and died, and the men hoisted her up by the heels and cleaned the carcass by pouring boiling water over the rough skin, which loosened the hair and bristles, which all had to be scraped off by hand. The meat was cut in portions, some smoked in our smokehouse down by the barn, and the rest taken to town for refrigeration, to be used later. It was a grisly affair and I hated it. I have in later life become mostly vegetarian, but I don't recall at that time having any reservations about sharing in the delicious dishes Mama served up as a result of that red-letter day. Papa and a hired man would often come in at 8:00 a.m. for a big porkchop and fried potato breakfast, having been up working since 4:30 a.m.

Saturday mornings were the times for my music and elocution lessons. My mode of transportation was my horse, Princess, but for a long time when I was small I had to climb up on a fence post in order to jump on her. Sometimes though, when Duke was home, I could count on him to stop work to lift me up on my horse. Which reminds me, I really must tell you about Duke and the wild thing that happened.

✳

OUR FUNNY HIRED MEN

Papa didn't have very good luck with hired men. In those days our hired men were a crazy bunch. Those were hard years and we were so far out in the country it was difficult to find dependable young men who would stay on, as they preferred being closer to town so they could carouse around on Saturday night. The hired man who was with us most often was Duke. Duke was slender and good looking in a debonair way, I thought, with dark hair, soft brown eyes and a small dark moustache that really made him look the part of the gambling man Mama said he was. Duke was definitely not a work-hand type, for he had a certain kind of class. He was the nephew of some longtime neighbors, but he took a shine to our family and semi-adopted us as his own. Trouble was, we never knew how long Duke would stay, for he gambled periodically on the horse races and would come and go after working awhile to make a little money. But when he returned it was always unexpected and he would usually bring some candy for Mama and me to help smooth over his last sudden departure. He also brought news and gossip of the city; Chicago or Milwaukee and roundabout. I know Mama was happier when Duke came, for he represented the world outside, and she could talk with him evenings of the latest happenings and hear his stories of the people he had seen and places he'd been. It was clear to me Mama didn't approve of Duke's lifestyle, but that didn't keep her from cooking extra good things when he was around or probing for stories of his adventures. His presence lifted us for a short while out of the dreary existence of winter farm life.

Duke always seemed to show up when Papa needed help, so he was kind of a godsend. I also suspect that he and Mama had an intellectual understanding, and that he felt sorry for Mama, an imprisoned bird, so to speak, in a cage of hard work and he recognized she wasn't physically built to be a farmer's wife who received little appreciation from Papa for her inner beauty and spiritual knowledge. Papa had no belief to speak of in the saving of his soul, and for that matter I doubt he even believed he had one.

Duke was more like a grownup wayward son than a hired man, and Papa liked him just fine, but there was this problem. He had itchy feet and couldn't stay put for long. As soon as he earned enough so his pockets jingled, as Mama put it, he would announce he was leaving and disappear for a couple months, leaving Papa with the work, and that didn't set very well.

Duke liked to hear about the books Mama had read, as Papa was a loss in that department and couldn't be bothered. One particular out-of-print book Mama was especially thrilled to find and which was discussed at length was called *The Strange Story of Ahrinziman*.* This book was very finely leather bound, and related the amazing karmic tale, over many lifetimes, of a Persian prince who had been

*A.F.S., Anita Silvani, Office of Light, 110 St. Martins Lane, London 1906

exceedingly cruel to his followers. When the prince died he was taken into the depths of Hell. He described in detail the many strange levels he found there, and of his struggles through the centuries to rise to higher heavenly realms. The story was conveyed from Spirit, through a medium who took the dictation, and it was professed to be totally true. It was an astonishing revelation and confirmed much to Mama, who already had a great deal of inner knowing. She loaned the book and, unfortunately, never got it back. Mama complained long about that to me, even years later, as it was an amazing book, and she could not find another. The man she loaned it to insisted he had given it back, when she knew he had not, but she could do nothing about it.

I relate this detail to you because of the unusual follow-up incident. Forty years later after Papa had died and while Mama was retired and living in Los Angeles, she received an excellent psychic reading through a medium there. That very man, who had long since passed over, came in spirit. The medium, who would have no way on earth to know of this, described him, even to his name, which was Mr. Fitzer, and the medium said, "He wants desperately to tell you how sorry he is that he lied about your book. He tells me he also had loaned it on and not received it back, and he was too embarrassed to tell you. He says this lie has held him back in consciousness on the inner planes and he is asking your forgiveness." Well, you see, that book was so good no one wanted to turn loose of it.

Not only was that medium's unique message, forty years later in a different state, absolute proof of the continuity of life and consciousness after so-called *death*, but also it shows even small untruths can be very damaging to the spirit and its forward progress on the other side of life we know as the Astral.

In these intervening years, I have often wondered what will be the karmic repercussions on the many corporate white collar thieves we are seeing in society today, not to speak of the out-and-out murder of thousands taking place all over the world at the orders of evil and greedy rulers. How very strange it is that humankind as a whole seems never to learn from the past, but continues in each age to make money and power its god, completely overlooking the fact that none of it can be taken with one, but actually is often the greatest detriment to growth into beauty and knowledge and splendor on the next level of life. In addition, the soul has to face the consequences of those actions in succeeding lifetimes, here or elsewhere, and that will not be pleasant.

I have come to know that no one escapes the Law of Cause and Effect. The Judge is one's own *Higher Self* that knows all. One cannot escape. The Christ said, "Even the Spirit of truth; . . . the world seeth him not, neither knoweth him, but ye know him for he dwelleth with you, and shall be in you," (John: 14:17).

So few pay attention or take seriously the warnings of Christ Jesus — that ". . . Every jot and tittle shall be accounted for." The Universe always seeks balance, and so, "as ye give, so shall ye receive."

It is unfortunate for the Christian Religion that the doctrine of reincarnation, with the reality, wonder, and grace of an exact pattern for the spiritual growth of souls, and which had been accepted by the early Church for the first 500 years, was removed from the teachings in the 2nd Ecumenical Council of Constantinople in 553 A.D. during the reign of the Roman Emperor Constantine. The Church decided this teaching was contrary to the interests of its ecclesiastics who preferred the populace to be governed by fear and to seek forgiveness only from their priests.* The grace and forgiveness of a loving Father/Mother God, on the other hand, allows freedom of choice and broad stretches of time to Its children, offering them second, third and endless chances to make good.

So, back to my story. Duke was a kind of errant member of the family who came and went on his own timing. Well, one day Duke received an inheritance, (Mama said it

* *The Christian Agnostic,* 1965, Abingdon Press, is a writing in great depth on this subject by Leslie Weatherhead, who for more than 20 years was pastor of the City Temple of London.

was a tidy sum of about $1,000, which was a lot in those days), and of all things, he bought a small airplane, as somewhere in his past he had learned how to fly. Jiminy Crickets! That was exciting! He kept the plane in our cow pasture, and when Duke was home with us on a Sunday he would take off with a roar, flying several times in a big circle overhead and then coming in very low, would buzz our farm, scaring the chickens and barnyard animals to death and worrying us a little too. Those were the barnstorming days of the 1930's when Charles Lindberg was so popular and many young men were inspired to fly, especially right there in the midwest where Lindberg himself flew. Rides were a big attraction at County Fairs, offered by some of those chaps with biplanes, who would take folks up for a ride for fifty cents.

Duke always wanted to take Mama and me up for a ride, but Papa wouldn't hear of it. I guess it was a good thing, too, for one day while buzzing around over our yard doing tricks, he took a nosedive in that plane square into our grove of cottonwood trees! By heaven's grace, the trees helped break the fall, so amazingly, Duke survived, though the plane was demolished. Duke only had a broken nose and his front teeth knocked out. That took the wind out of his sails for awhile.

I recall Duke stayed around helping Papa long enough to get enough money to go to town to have some false teeth made and then he disappeared again.

Mama took this opportunity to lecture me on the evils of gambling, for no matter how much money Duke made, he was never able to save a dime, and he always arrived broke and willing to work awhile. Papa always needed help, and I was tickled for the uplift that his presence and town news brought Mama, as he was good humored and joking, and we had more fun then. He was always nice to me and helped me climb up on my horse, so I liked Duke a lot.

One day when Duke was gone, along came two brothers named Fred and Elmer. I do not recall where Papa found them to hire, as I was about nine years old then, but they were young and lively and Papa said they were hard workers. The brothers were not at all alike, reminding me of a Mutt-and-Jeff team. Fred was tall and lanky, dark and big-boned and his overalls hung loose on his lean frame. He had a long solemn funereal face. One would assume Fred thought the world a gloomy place, for he never, ever smiled, but then he would suddenly surprise us with an off-beat dry or caustic wit that he came up with at unexpected times. Mama sometimes called him "that big holliker," which did seem descriptive. Fred's brother Elmer didn't look like he even belonged in Fred's family. Short and stocky, with blonde, curly hair and a wide lovely smile, he laughed a lot and talked a lot, being the spokesman for them both. He liked to kid Fred and to tease me, and reminded me at times of a kind of pesky elf, because he never took anything seriously. Despite their distinct differences they never argued, but made fun of everything. Elmer with his uninhibited laughter and Fred with his dry quiet wit, always seemed to enjoy one another's company. They lived for Saturday nights when they could go to town to dance and look for girls. The presence of those two brothers kept our home from being dull that year as I could always watch the crazy antics of Fred and Elmer.

The brothers sometimes griped to my mother about Papa, saying that he gave them too much work, and they called him the Old Man. It is hard to now realize that their wage was ten dollars a month (for which they rose at 5:00 a.m. and did not finish their day until sometimes 7:00 p.m.) plus room and good board, of course. That was the going wage then. Mama's cooking was not to be sniffed at, and this I think kept them staying during those hard times, as it was a long trek to town.

The memory that stands out in my mind about Fred and Elmer is rather off-beat. One day, as usual, Mama sent me upstairs to change the bed linens. I finished Papa's room and then went to Fred and Elmer's room. In the process of tucking the sheet under the mattress, something struck my hand. I lifted the edge of the mattress and was intrigued to find comic books. I pulled them out and sat down to look them over. Jumpin' Jehosaphat! If eyes could pop out, mine nearly did! I was stunned for a moment and felt a shameful flush creep up my neck. This was my first introduction to anything pornographic. Even at the age of nine, in days that were much more puritan, I was no dummy and knew the natural course of life, having worked around farm animals, and Mama had of necessity in her illness talked to me a lot, but I had no idea there could be picture books like this. Heavens! What would Mama think if she knew this?

I quickly tucked the books back where I had found them and hurried downstairs as I had been gone too long and didn't want her to question me. I never told Mama or Papa or *anyone* about the books, for I guessed rightly that it would only cause a great deal of trouble, and for me as well. Papa needed the help, but if he chastised and embarrassed the boys they might leave, and then I would have a great deal more work to do to help Papa. Not that I could or would be asked to help replace the work of two men. No way. But I would have many, many more chores. So I kept my mouth shut, but I could not look the boys in the eye after that, because I knew their shameful secret.

Little girls were raised pristinely in those days, even on a farm, and my parents were well-bred in such matters and off-color remarks were never heard around our house. There was always humor, but it was clean humor. Even on the radio our favorite evening programs were Fibber McGee and Molly and Amos 'n Andy, and later Edgar Bergen and Charlie McCarthy, just as they were the favorites in thousands of homes that had radios at that time. Those programs became classics in later years and can now be purchased on tape. After awhile Fred and Elmer moved on and I never heard what became of those two unusual brothers.

There were intervals during those depression years when Papa had to hire "bums off the road," as Mama called them, men who had no home and no destination.She didn't enjoy feeding such motley members of the human race and having them sleep in our house because they were not other farmers or hired hands out of work, which one could feel good about helping, but generally bums in the real sense of the word, even in good times. However, she swallowed her pride as she knew Papa needed the help. Fred and Elmer were right though — Papa wasn't the easiest man in the world to work for as he demanded a lot of work from them, and these men often did not stay long as they were usually looking for a soft spot to spend their time.

One bum even brought bedbugs to our house. This naturally gave Mama fits, and she and I waged a mighty battle, even to burning his mattress in the yard after pouring kerosine all over it, and then we had to scrub the metal springs with kerosine as well. She exclaimed in a voice of great indignation as the smoke rose skyward, "It is not a disgrace to catch bedbugs, but it is a disgrace to keep them."

Then there came a very hard winter when temperatures plummeted to 35 and 40 to 50 degrees below zero. That winter Duke disappeared again, so Papa hired a drifter, who, it turned out, only cared about his bed and meals. For a week Papa complained the man was slow and didn't get any work done. He was given the hired hand's room upstairs, of course. Our two story frame house, built sometime in the 1860's was poorly insulated, if at all, with cold wintry drafts blowing in cracks around the wooden window frames and under the ill-fitting doors. Mama piled more straw against the outside door of the back storeroom to help keep out the cold.

This particular winter Old Jake, the lazy bum hired only the week before, did not come down one morning early enough to help Papa with the milking. Nor did he come to breakfast. Papa went up to see if he overslept, and he told Papa he was ill with a cold and could not get up. "Well, okay, stay there a day or so," Papa said. Well! The upshot of it was Old Jake never did get up that whole winter! He lay in bed a full three months, pretending to be sick. He didn't have a fever that Papa could determine and never used up any handkerchiefs. "He's just a loafer pretending to be sick," said Papa, who was by then madder'n hornets! The snows came and the wind howled and one could not throw a man out in such weather miles from town, even if he was a scoundrel and a sponger. My father was irate to think that he and Mama had to house and feed that bum and he wasn't giving us one lick of work in return.

So Papa and I had all the chores to do alone. It was not an easy winter, I'll tell you. It also fell my lot to carry up Old Jake's trays of food at mealtime, as my folks didn't want to lay eyes on him. If they went up and tried to talk to him, he would not answer but instead pretend to be asleep. However, the food I took up was always eaten. Mama was humane and wouldn't let him starve, but the meals were very simple fare. Besides, she commented, maybe he really was ill with something we couldn't tell. But Papa wouldn't think of calling a doctor out from town to come fifteen miles in all that snow, especially when he was sure that Jake was a fake. The cold increased, and one morning I shall never forget, a Saturday when I was home from school, I took the breakfast tray up the narrow, steep old-fashioned stairs to Jake. After knocking to announce my coming, I exchanged the trays and saw he was still just a hump of covers in the bed. Then I carried the tray with dishes from last night's supper back down- stairs. When we opened the pot, we found that the leftover tea had frozen solid overnight! That's how cold it was inside our house upstairs where there was no heat. The big round stove in the living- room, and the kitchen range, heated only the downstairs. I might also add that the contents of Jake's slopjar was frozen solid as well, and was my unpleasant task to tend. I don't recall when he left, but it was a happy day for me.

*

NIGHT TIME VISITORS

We always took a hot soapstone wrapped in towels to bed on those cold winter nights, or sometimes a warmed and wrapped flat- iron. Even though it was as hard as a rock in bed, it held heat for many hours and helped make our beds, with their deep goosedown feather ticks from Mama's geese, toasty warm and snug. Mama and I slept together downstairs in a room off the living room that had a wide arched ceiling between, which was built open to take advantage of the warmth from the stove in the living room. If we stoked it well, it might hold some glowing coals till early morning. Papa slept upstairs in another bedroom alone as he was healthy and strong and didn't mind the cold; also he rose at 4:30 A.M. to begin barn chores. As I said, Mama and he did not share the same bedroom those years while she wasn't well. Papa didn't seem to mind. He worked hard and fell asleep early, snoring loudly. Mama would usually lie down with me to tell a story and give me a bedtime hug and stay until I fell asleep. Then she would rise and finish her evening work, preparing for the next day's baking.

One evening, just shortly after eight o'clock when she was lying beside me, but still wide awake, watching the red glow from the hot coals as it shone through the isinglass window of the living room stove, she suddenly saw a young soldier of maybe eighteen years of age, wearing a World War I uniform, sitting in our rocking chair and looking into the fire. He looked very young, rather sad, sitting quietly as though in contemplation, Mama said later. After about ten minutes he arose and just disappeared into thin air! He was no one she recognized. When she told Papa and me about this in the morning, she asked Papa, as she described him, if he knew who it could be. Papa said, "No, I have no idea. Maybe you dreamed it."

A few months later Papa happened to meet the man from whom he had bought this 80-acre farm a few years back, and felt compelled to tell him the story, and to describe the boy.

The man turned pale, staring at Papa and then he said, "Clyde, you have described my son. He was killed in France in 1918. He was only eighteen years old and he was raised in that house."

Mama was relieved to hear that it really was an authentic visitation from a young lad in spirit, drawn back with nostalgia to his old homestead for a few moment's contemplation.

You see, Mama sometimes had what we called *second sight*. She often seemed to know things about people before they knew it themselves. She was not only interested, but fascinated, with the deeper knowledge of what happens to us after we leave this earth-plane in the transition we call death, and in what we can learn now to help us understand our time here and the reasons for our many unique, often harsh and seemingly unfair experiences and relationships with each other. Her desire wasn't so much just to communicate with those passed on, but rather to find answers that would help solve some of the above mentioned mysteries, and to understand our lot in life.

My Mama, like so many others in this world, felt totally out of place in the role she was compelled to play as a farmer's wife with a heavy work load. Poor health kept her trapped in an era when even healthy women did not generally work for a living out in the world, other than as servants in well-to-do homes or as school teachers. Mama had not been given training for anything other than marriage, for that was what was expected then of daughters, and life was a struggle. Everyone had to help at home just to keep their land intact. Both families, my mother's parents and my father, managed that miraculous feat during those depression years when most people lost everything. Some of Mama's brothers-in-law and neighbors and friends had terrible struggles and lost their properties. Papa's frugal ways that caused Mama and me such hardship those years did save our land, and the family farm is intact to this day, producing good corn, wheat, and soybeans.

One night during those years on The 80 when Mama was studying the unique books she had found, a strange thing happened. In the middle of the night we awakened to hear my father's muffled strangled shouts, "NO! NO! HELP! HELP!" coming from upstairs.

Mama jumped out of bed and rushed up the stairwell. I lay petrified, wondering if this was a dream, and crouched under the covers. Papa was a sound sleeper and never awoke in the night, so I knew something awful must have happened. When Mama came down she was very quiet and said, "Wait 'til morning. He's alright. It was a . . . a kind of dream. Go back to sleep."

The next day everything seemed as usual, but remembering, I asked again, "Did Papa really have a bad dream?" She then told me a very strange story (for we had always talked over everything). She said in reading her book of spiritual studies that very day before, she had found a passage on the Dark Forces in spirit, and it said that they actually can, in certain circumstances, physically harm humans on this earth-plane. She said she strongly questioned that in her mind, always believing that all spirit was ethereal and could not affect flesh bodies for harm. So she asked God in her mind, "How could this be?" and then dismissed it, in continuing with the evening's activities. And then,that very night my father shouted out for help. Mama said that as she approached him upstairs he appeared to be battling an unseen assailant while lying on his bed. As she grabbed his arms and shook him, thinking it a nightmare, he immediately spoke to her, showing her he was not asleep at all, and croaked in that strangled voice, "A black cloud with evil eyes is trying to smother me." Then he praised her for coming and saying IT left the moment she touched him. The whole thing was astonishing to us as my father never had nightmares, and never had such an occurrence again. It only happened the very night after Mama had questioned the validity of such a preposterous idea, "And," she added, "It came only as if to show me that such can happen."

Papa was not harmed, nor would he have been, I'm sure. She was very quiet and thoughtful for several days after that scary nighttime spook event.

Mama sought answers, and found several books, books that were classics in their time. How she unearthed those books or how they reached her hands I do not know, but "when the student is ready . . . the teacher appears." This is an apt saying. A book then cost only one or two dollars new. In addition, her family was not your run of the mill family. Having a form of sixth sense seemed to be natural with several family members, beginning with Mama's father, who passed away before I was born.

Mama was born in 1887 and she told me that when she and her brothers and sisters were young, there was no entertainment of an evening other than family games and songs, and so sometimes they did *table tilting* with my grandfather acting as the power center. Everyone sat quietly around the table while he began with devotional prayer. Then they lightly placed their hands upon the top of the heavy oak table. Soon one side would gently rise up a few inches off the floor and they could ask questions. The table would tilt to tap the legs to the floor once for No and twice for Yes. The family was able in this way to gather a certain amount of information about those members who had passed on, or other information considered important. In her family it was not questioned in the least that there was life after death, or that loved ones existed on the *other side of life*, who were able to converse in this primitive way. Besides, a few family members had the psychic sight to see discarnate beings. I will tell of this later.

My grandfather, Christopher, who had this power in table tilting (psychokinesis), was a perfectly normal hard-working farm gentleman, well-liked and respected by all his neighbors. Mama loved her father dearly and told me he was a scholar with a great love for good literature, which love she shared with him. They would read together evenings when day's work was done and the younger children were in bed.

My Mama was the eldest child of the nine, so it was one of her jobs in her youth at home to care for her younger brothers and sisters. The youngest was the pretty blonde baby girl, Millicent, born when Mama was eighteen years old. Mama said some of the younger ones were three years old before they discovered she was not their mother. For, you see, Grandmother Augusta had a tremendous responsibility, cooking and baking for at least thirteen people three meals a day. There were the nine children, at least one hired man, and Great Grandmother, who lived with them too.

Great Grandmother was Grandfather's mother. She had become mentally incompetent, and in those days folks cared for their own at home; there were no nursing homes. Mama told me that she and all the other children avoided Great Grandma because she couldn't stand children's noise and would whack your legs with her cane if you came near her. Most times she carried on a running conversation with herself and the empty air, and would sometimes laugh in a high-pitched cackle that frightened visitors who might hap-

pen to be downstairs in the parlor if they didn't know of
her presence. Those years, Mama said, her mother never went to bed
before 1:00 or 2:00 a.m., and then she got up at 5:00 a.m. to
begin baking the morning coffeecakes and hot breads. It
was a good thing Grandmother had a strong constitution
and never had any health problems. Mama said Grandma
would catch catnaps only as she sat ten minutes now and
then nursing a baby. Grandma often was cross with my
Mama, however, as she would now and then find her sitting
down on the job when she had been sent to do a chore.
Mama's explanation that she was "tired and out of breath"
fell on deaf ears, however, and met with Grandma's harsh
chastisement and a scolding for laziness. Grandma had much
work to do and couldn't tolerate or understand such inad-
equacies in her eldest daughter.

Mama was very unhappy at home because of this and, as
a result, did not have a love relationship with her mother, so
really married my father, I believe, to escape. It was almost a
case of jumping from the frying pan into the fire, for as a
farmer's wife she still had more work to do in our home than
her health warranted, but at least she was her own boss and
could lie down to rest now and then without punishment,
except sometimes for Papa's angry remarks.

Miraculously, and to her great relief and absolvement,
the doctors found a number of years later, when she finally
had ex-rays for her tuberculosis condition, that she had
been born and lived her entire life with what is called a
blue-baby heart. In recent years this condition commands
immediate surgery on newborns, for they may die if it is not
corrected. The problem is a faulty aorta valve in the heart
that blocks proper blood flow, causing lack of oxygen throughout the body, with ensuing weakness. So Mama's unhappy
condition was very real, and it was a miracle that she not
only lived her life with this burden, but accomplished as
much as she did.

It is sad, often tragic, how many people have been
misunderstood and condemned through the ages because of
a lack of knowledge, which the accusers replaced with a

judgmental sense of self-righteousness. We have come a long way in medicine and science, and researchers are to be truly commended for their efforts. But I am going on record to say we still have a long way to go. There are thousands and thousands in mental hospitals and prisons today suffering the same misunderstood condemnation by society, and I now know my second son was one of these. It is shocking to see how difficult it is to get changes made for enlightened treatment in our institutions. Those in charge say, "We've always done it this way," or "it costs too much," and refuse to bend.

Only in very recent years have brave men and women stepped forth with new research documenting the detrimental effects of environmental poisonings on the blood and brain chemistry. The chemical imbalances cause, in many people, physical and even emotional problems which result in social deviancy. The American taxpayer is paying dearly for this ignorance. We are housing and caring for thousands who we could otherwise help to become harmonious, productive members of our society. This I will discuss more fully later in my story.

My Grandfather Chris was a sweet and understanding man, with a sense of the spirit in things and in people.He knew my mother needed more quiet time to dream, read poetry, and to play music on the piano, so he helped buffer Grandmother's ire and tried to make life more bearable for Mama. Unfortunately, my own Papa was again more like Grandmother; both found life's joy in their work alone. So my mother often wondered about her lot in life and what it all meant to be ill at times to the point of exhaustion and despair and yet to be surrounded only by those whom it seemed had not a drop of the milk of human kindness in their veins to attempt to understand.

Mama used to say whimsically that she "seldom received any sympathy because she always looked so well."

Papa, on the other hand, was never harsh with me. He enjoyed my Geminian bounce and love for activity. I recall musingly the quiet evenings when I was small, around three years of age, when Papa would sit me up on his knee and ask me with a twinkle in his bright blue eyes, "Well, Wee

One, has the honeywagon come today and brought something for your old Papa?" I would giggle and say, "Yes it did
Papa." Knowing just what he expected, I'd give him a whole
bunch of kisses on his whiskery cheek. His disappointment
in not having the four sons he hoped for to help on the
farm, but only one skinny little girl, was never evidenced in
his treatment of me, which was always gentle and kind
when he had the time. Papa loved me in his own way,
though he had to work hard on his land all of his life.

One vivid and chilling memory of those cold winter
days was of our "3-holer" out back of the house. Plumbing
was unheard of in those old farm houses in the 1930's. The
three-holer sat behind a big full lilac bush that blossomed
fragrantly in summer with deep purple, heavy hanging clus-
ters of blooms, wafting a natural deodorant through the air.
In winter, however, that bush might reach out with icy twig
fingers to slap you in the face as you hurried past. The door
often blew open, allowing swirling snow to create mounds
around my ankles, but the worst of all was having to sit my
bare bottom down on the ice-edged hole in the middle of a
winter storm! Often I waded through knee-deep snow at
6:00 a.m.to make the journey and carry the night-time emergency pail along for emptying. One really had to be brave
those times. Absolute necessity knows no fear, but it wasn't
condusive to relaxation. And the old Sears catalog wasn't
placed there for reading. Papa wouldn't dream of spending
hard-earned money on toilet paper when another means
was available. So one tended one's business quickly and left.

A funny story was brought back from Texas in those
days about some of our shirt-tail relatives that lived down
there. Great Uncle Oscar was my Grandpa's brother and
considered to be the family black sheep, more or less. He
never did anything really wrong — he just didn't ever stay
home to do anything right, and he was always making a
mess of things. Uncle Oscar finally ran away and the family
later heard he had settled in Texas with a new wife and had
children.

Many years later one of Mama's sisters and her hubby
went down to look them up and found them in rather poor

circumstances, but happy. What I remember most about the tales of their journey was Uncle Marvie telling how he feared for his life when he had to use Uncle Oscar's ramshackle outhouse, which sat precariously on the edge of a cliff. It really looked, he said, like it might let go at any moment and tumble backward, giving up its ghost together with that of anyone in it at the time! The reality of gravity, the sheer face of the cliff, and the thin tentacles by which it clung to its moorings gave one real cause for alarm. Luckily there was an elderberry bush growing out in front of it Uncle said, so he reached out, grabbed hold of the branches and held on for dear life all the while he was in there, just in case. Uncle Marvie came home to tell the tale so I guess he didn't fall in. But that incongruous mental picture has clung with fingers of laughter in my mind through the years. For all I know that old Toonerville Outhouse is still hanging in there, doing its duty.

Indoor plumbing was a luxury we never had until much later when Papa quit farming at age 73 years and retired to a house in town — the little village nearby. I was sixteen. Meanwhile, on the farm with a soft water cistern that caught rainwater and, an old-fashioned pump on our backporch, we raised washwater which we heated in a built-in tank on one end of our big black kitchen range. This warmed water served for baths on Saturday nights in the summer before going to town.

Stores stayed open on Saturday nights and the main street of the next larger town in northern Illinois was the social gathering place for everyone from miles around. If you wanted to see someone, all you need do was plan to go to town come Saturday night. Town seemed an amazing gossip-fountain to a young girl with big ears, as the ladies had a golden opportunity to share the news: Who had a new baby, who was expecting another, whose man got drunk last Saturday night and had to be taken home, or perhaps the latest engagement announcement. Our world was much smaller in those days and folks paid a great deal of attention to what happened to their neighbors, also by way of helping out if needed. Women took eggs to town to sell at the old-fashioned grocery and did their shopping. Men sat along the walled curbing on the side street near the store that sold wagon parts and horse harnesses, exchanged the latest word on crop and land prices, griping about the current administration, and arguing politics, while others spent their time in the taverns. My father was not one to do much gossiping. He purchased what he needed — the least possible — very quickly, and went back to the car. There he sat impatiently honking the horn at my mother, who raced up and down the street, hurrying to finish her shopping, all the while pulling me along by one hand. Mama knew that the quicker she finished, the less chance there was of raising Papa's ire and hearing a tirade all the way home. It was on these shopping trips to town I learned to walk fast, a lifelong habit that later caused friends to call me a race horse when we were only out for a stroll.

I think it was partially the problem of Papa's impatience with any and all shopping that caused my parents to agree to my learning to drive at the tender age of eleven. I was tall for my age, and bright enough it seems, and I pestered them to distraction to let me drive. Well, Mama couldn't, or wouldn't, drive, always contending that she was too nervous and would probably hit another tree, and Papa resented the time driving to town took from his work. So they propped me up on a pillow, my feet just barely touching the pedals, and away we went. It was all country backroads to town with farm residences far and few between so not much danger of meeting other cars. Mama and I solved the legality of it by parking the old square-topped 1918 Mitchell out on the edge of town, walking in to shop, then walking back to the auto with our purchases and driving home. I was in Seventh Frog Heaven and had that fun all one summer before Papa decided we would move to the other farm on the highway, closer to town. Meanwhile we lived through some terribly stormy winters while on the South 80.

✳
PAPA AND THE BLIZZARD

It is a challenge to describe the severity of Prairie winters and the snowstorms we experienced during those years far out in the country. The Midwest and East nowadays frequently receive the same freezing temperatures and depths of snowfall we did then, but there are snowplows to deal with it, homes are heated, and neighbors live close by. In those days we sometimes had to battle the elements for survival, with families isolated from one another and many miles to travel to buy coal for the furnace.

One such winter when I was only about eight years of age, I recall the snow had come early and heavy. One morning we awakened to find everything totally covered over. The bushes, the pump at the well, the chicken house, and even the pig pen were simply huge mounds of snow, with the animals and chickens buried beneath. Papa shoveled his way to the barn to feed the animals and to milk the cows. Later in the morning Mama decided she should try to feed the chickens and see if they were alive under there. So out she went, and she didn't come back.

I waited quite awhile, then becoming worried, I bundled up and plunged out, following her footprints in the deep snow. I shouted to her as I went, and suddenly heard her muffled calls in answer. Then, I saw the footprints disappear into a mound of snow. Frantically I began digging and found she had fallen through a huge clump of bushes, hidden by the mounds that all looked alike. She had been unable to scramble out because the heavy wet snow had fallen in on top of her and she was buried. I shouted, "I'll save you Mama! Wait! I'll go get a shovel." And so I did. Then I shoveled as fast as I could to uncover my brave mother. She was a bit shaken and cold and wet, but fine otherwise. Laughing and hugging me, Mama said, "Now I know you are My Angel." I do not recall somehow if we ever did find and feed those chickens in their house under the snow, but I'm sure we did, as Mama wasn't one to give up.

That winter the snow was so deep that no one could

get to town except with horses and sleigh. So four families arranged to take turns going on Saturdays to buy the necessary food staples and some coal for all four families. The Saturday it was Papa's turn, he hitched up our team of strong, sturdy horses with their jingle bells on the harnesses to our big bobsled which was like a wagon, except that it had runners instead of wheels, and after chores, he set out early for town across the fields as the crow flies, because roads and fences were completely covered from view. About 11:00 a.m., to our dismay, the wind rose and snow again began to fall thick and fast. By 2:00 p.m. the storm had grown into a full-blown, howling Midwest blizzard with snow swirling in such masses a person could not see beyond two feet.

By 4:00 p.m. Papa should have been home. We began to worry. The hours ticked by. Suppertime came and no Papa. We ate our hot soup and bread silently without him. Mama looked strained, but reminded me that we just must know in our hearts that Papa was alright, that God would take care of him and he would be safe. And we prayed for him. The phone lines were down, and had been for days, so that communication was lost. By 8:00 p.m. the unmilked cattle were bawling in the barn. Mama never had milked and wouldn't dare go out in that storm. We could hear the cattle once in awhile in breaks when the wind died down. Then it would begin to howl again, starting low and increasing to a scream like a wild banshee clawing at the rattling window panes. It seemed to me it wanted to get at us even in the house.

I had become somewhat accustomed to winter blizzards, but this one seemed different, more intent on tearing us loose from our moorings in the snug house on the hill with coal fire radiating warmth and the kerosene lamp throwing its golden glow across the table. We could not help but think continually of Papa, out in that icy cold and wind, and I shoved visions of him and the horses buried in a snowbank out of my mind with insistent deliberateness, clinging to Mama's words that God would take care and he would be safe. Mama reminded me again of our Guardian Angels always present, and of Jesus' promise to be with us always, and led us again in a prayer to guide Papa home.

I did not want to go to bed this night and Mama did not ask me to, knowing I needed to keep the vigil with her. We tried to rest but could not, and so she read stories to me and talked of God's love for all of us, how we were never alone in our troubles even when it seemed so, and I was always to remember that and not be frightened. I believed this, for hadn't God and the Angels helped me lift the heavy steel gate off of bleeding Angie?

The hours ticked by. At 11:00 p.m. I had dozed off from sheer exhaustion. I came to with a start, as Mama shook me awake. "Listen!" she said. "The jingle bells!! We raced to the door, shoving it open against the wind and heavy snow. There in the swirling snow and vicious, icy wind stood our beautiful horses with little icicles of frost hanging from their steaming nostrils and their wet coats. And there on the seat of the sleigh was their precious cargo. But Papa did not speak, or turn, or make a single move to come down from the sled.

"Papa!" I screamed into the wind . . . but it threw the shout back in my face. Mama rushed out into the storm, and climbing onto the sleigh, grabbed hold of him. He appeared to be asleep, but then she discovered he was frozen to the seat! Mama ran back into the house, and grabbing a tea-kettle of hot water from the stove, dashed back out and poured the hot water over Papa's coat and the seat to dislodge him. His gloves were frozen to the reins, his eye-lids were frozen shut and his scarf and face were covered with ice particles. Mama told me calmly but urgently, to bring more hot water from the register. Mama shook Papa partially out of unconsciousness and together we joggled him off the seat and half-carried, half-dragged his heavy body into the kitchen. Working fast, Mama took off his icy-stiff outer clothing, wrapped Papa in warmed blankets, and put his feet in a pail of warm water. She began then to rub his face and upper body vigorously, shaking him a little, making him talk to her. When he came to and realized he was home and in our warm kitchen, tears began to roll down his face and he choked as he said, "The horses brought me home." It was the only time in my whole life I'd ever seen my father cry.

Then Mama told me to stay close and keep talking to Papa and give him sips of warm broth. She bundled up and bravely went out in the storm to put the heroic horses in the barn and give them some feed. We later spoke of the unique intelligence of those wonderful animals that caused them to pull the sled up to the house — and to us — where they never, ever came, rather than to the barn down below where they were familiar and normally would go. If the horses had gone to the barn, Papa would certainly have died in that storm, for we never would have heard the jingle bells in the shrieking wind.

Answers to prayer ofttimes seem like miracles. And God uses animals as well as people to answer our prayers. Through this experience and others like it, my faith in prayer and the love of God were firmly cemented early in my life.

Soon Papa was back to normal, happily eating hot soup and pouring out his adventure to our eager ears. He said the storm was bad before he ever left town at noon with the sleigh loaded with purchases for all the families. But he felt that if he waited the storm could only get worse and so he started home. By 2:30 p.m., because of the blackness of the storm, it was completely dark. At 4:00 p.m., and halfway home, by sheer accident he drove through the yard of some folks we knew named Gustafson. To come upon their home now and recognize the house was a godsend, as he was nearly lost. He went in to get warm and had a little hot food. Someone fed the horses, which had not eaten or drank since morning, and then Papa started out again. Four hours later at about 8:00 p.m., he said he came upon a landmark that, to his horror, he recognized as one he had passed a couple hours before. He realized he had guided the horses in a complete circle. Papa said he now knew he was totally lost in the swirling snow. He could barely make out the horses tails in front of him. In complete despair he let the reins loose in his hands, shouted to the horses, "Go home!" and gave them their heads. All he could do now was sit in a daze, and try not to fall into sleep from the cold and fall off the sleigh.

The faithful horses, counting the extra driving in a circle, had trudged some forty miles through deep snow and bitter cold winds that day and night, and then had instinctively found their way home when no man could manage such a feat. Horses have always been and always will be my favorite animals.

Do you wonder that those bitter winters are indelibly engraved in my mind?

*

CHRISTMAS — AND THE CLAN AT GRANDMA'S

The most special social event of the entire year for me and, I believe for many of my cousins, was Christmas at Grandma's. As the days approached and time grew short, I became more and more eager. Present-giving was not emphasized in our little family as Papa never gave a gift of any kind to anyone, not to Mama nor to me. I knew better than to expect anything from him, so I was not disappointed. Mama read the Christmas story to me and we talked of the true meaning of Christmas. We did have a small tree. That was a wonder and a joy, because Mama, in the German fashion, waited to put it up and decorate it secretly on Christmas Eve after I was sound asleep. And so, wonder of wonders, Christmas morning its glittering and shining beauty reflected the morning sunlight off ornaments Mama had somehow saved and treasured, bringing Christmas right into our living room. Oh Joy! It never ceased to be a surprise. That was truly my first and best present, the Christmas tree.

But look! Santa *had* come! There was a present for me after all. Mama had said she wasn't sure if Santa could make it way out in the country, as he had so many places to stop, and I wasn't to be too expectant. But yes, he had left a small dolly, my first and what was to be my only doll. I named her Rosalie, after a favorite song of the day, and my dolly was with me many years. There was fruit, and cookies too. The doll, I later realized, represented many weeks of saving dimes and nickels from household money on Mama's part, so that I would not be disappointed on Christmas.

The following year she saw to it that Santa brought a small wicker buggy for the dolly, and some hand-stitched doll clothes. The year after that the glittering branches stretched over a precious set of small doll dishes and a child-size wooden table painted green to put them on, which in later years she confessed she had asked a neighbor man to build. Each Christmas brought just one gift. Sometimes it was a new gingham jumper for school that Mama had stitched. One of the most exciting presents one year was a small hand-dialed typewriter, on which one could turn the dial, punch a key and write letters. I can still see that treasure in my mind's eye. There were no presents as such during the twelve months intervening, but I do not recall feeling deprived, as I did not expect them.

The advantage, I have seen clearly as the years passed, to being raised in an atmosphere of austerity where creature comforts are concerned, is that one's value system does not become centered around the worth of an individual being judged by what he/she owns in the way of possessions. More important was one's character, his or her honor and integrity, and concern for others. Also important was being able to stand on one's own feet in the world and not to expect handouts as a God-given right — they were to be earned.

Another advantage in not receiving very many material things as a child has been an ever-increasing appreciation of life and all that it has offered through the ensuing years. When others around me seemed bored and have taken for granted the wonderful conveniences used every day, while finding very little new to be excited about, I have, rather, felt a never-ending gratitude for the simple gifts that daily living has brought in our modern world. The convenience of electricity is in itself a miracle, for until we left the farm when I was sixteen, we cleaned the chimneys of the kerosene lamps with wadded up newspaper, and I was careful to trim the wicks lest the flame smoke and smudge up the newly cleaned glass.

I always helped Mama get ready for Christmas as much as a little girl can, and we made special breads and pies, and other dishes to take to Grandmother's for the family gathering. Although I was an only child, there was always a sense of belonging, for our extended family clan was large indeed. Grandfather had died before I was born, as mentioned, but I felt I knew and loved him from what Mama had told me of his gentle nature and sensitive gift. Grandma, too, was a wonderful hospitable woman whose home was always open to everyone. In all the years I knew her she never locked a door, front or back; her house was open to shelter anyone, day or night.

In later years when the main highway that carried through traffic from Chicago to Dubuque, Iowa passed by her front door and became a speeding thoroughfare, with drivers traveling so fast they were through the little village before they knew they had entered it, there would sometimes be accidents at a trouble spot on the road where there was a curve and huge tree, very near her home. The victims were usually carried into Grandma's house, especially in the cold of winter, as everyone in town knew her doors were not locked, even at 3:00 a.m., and she never once experienced a robbery.

Grandmother was slender and sprightly, like a small grey roadrunner. Her hair was wound into an austere business-like and efficient bun at the nape of her neck. She could accomplish a lot of work, for she was stronger than she looked, with an amazing amount of endurance. After Grandpa passed on (from a heart condition), Mama told me Grandmother carried on alone, as some of her nine children were still at home.

Grandmother was born in June. Mama used to say that people born in June were generally pretty strong, and strong-minded, too, with a lot of mental tenacity as well as physical endurance. I think it always bothered Mama that her own Mother was so strong and healthy and she herself was not. Mama may have inherited her father's faulty heart, as well as his love for books and the aesthetics of life. Daily living can be a real struggle when you haven't good health, but Mama made up for it with a fine sense of humor. Later in life she often said, "I could not have made it if I couldn't laugh at life's crazy happenings." I think God has a sense of humor too, for He placed it in us. Some things in life are so ridiculous, it has to be a joke.

Grandma liked company. She was happiest if she could bustle around and feed somebody. Mama said in the early years before she married and was still at home with all the younger children, the family never got to eat somewhere else on a Sunday because Grandma always invited one or another family from town, out to the farm for Sunday dinners. So she and Mama spent every weekend cooking. Grandpa complained it kept him in the poorhouse feeding town relatives.

Anyway, come Christmas, there was always a huge crowd at Grandma's. It was the event of the year. One Christmas Day I counted forty-five relatives for dinner at noon, and an additional twenty or so showed up later for the cold buffet supper. Those Johnny-come-latelies had been to various in-laws earlier in the day.

Christmas Day was a real highlight for me as I got to see all my cousins at once, and to eat all kinds of good food, as my aunts were marvelous cooks and everyone had brought two or three of her most favorite dishes. Great Aunts and Uncles arrived even from Chicago (a far distance in those days), and second cousins and in-laws of all sorts, some shirt-tail relatives even from other states, as it was the place to see everyone from far and near, and to share in a scrumptious meal.

As I grew older I liked to sit inconspicuously in a corner of the kitchen just to listen to my aunts (there were eight of them) and Mama all talking at once, for it seemed they could talk and listen at the same time, and they never missed a beat.They had to talk fast to catch up on all the news that had piled up for months. There was much laughter and their happy spirits shone, just to be together once again. The gossip was fascinating to Little Big Ears from the Backwoods. I think I learned a lot about life very early just by listening.

One special memory of the afternoon was the Fish Pond. Someone had taken time to find a humorous gift for each of the main family members, something that related to a quirk or habit that each might have. Then those folks took turns fishing with a pole, the hook and line of which was hung over the top of a sheet stretched across the open door to an adjoining room. One chosen person stationed behind the sheet in that second room would hook a comical gift that had been picked ahead of time with forethought, just for that particular fisherman onto his line. The catch always brought shrieks of hilarity as it poked fun, but in a good natured way, as only loved ones can do. Trouble was, Papa never allowed us to stay very late because it was winter with snowy roads, and we had a long way to go home. Sometimes if the weather turned bad we had to leave before supper, and that was the pits. The animals always needed to be fed and milked daily, even on Christmas, of course, and often we had no hired hand. This was very upsetting to me as the others were still there having fun, and it would be many long winter months before I saw them again.

I never shall forget the closeness of our family clan, for it gave me a sense of stability, of belonging, and roots that in later years stayed with me no matter where I found myself around the globe. This special sense of family was brought over from the Old Country by Grandma and Grandpa as they immigrated from Europe. Most Europeans carry that trait even today. I believe it is valuable for children to have this sense of heritage, and regrettable that in America this has slipped away for too many. The lack of this family bonding has contributed to the social unrest we are experiencing, which is very evident, and it is very sad.

*
SUMMERTIME JOYS

The summers, however, were another story, sometimes hot in the opposite extreme, but usually a wonderful time for children. Angie and I would romp barefoot in the grass and play with the dog, swing on tree branches and play house in cool vine-covered nooks or wade in the gurgling creek that ran through a neighbor's pasture. All these carried an open invitation to pleasure. The cold water felt so good on hot dusty feet (but not so good in the winter when we would sometimes break through the ice when we went sliding, as we had no skates, get wet feet and stockings, and run home cold, then maybe get a spanking too). I liked our old house and yard on The 80 in summer. The house was dignified and picturesque, standing high on a hill, painted a soft cream with contrasting brown gingerbread trim around the roof- line, with a portico front entrance held up by two stately pillars. Later a screened-in sunporch was added. This turned long summer evenings into cool delightful hours to anticipate, when we would gently rock back and forth on the big wide porch swing, listening to the crickets chorusing their mating song, and watch the fireflies blink their magic lanterns in the evening twilight on the lawn. We had zillions of fireflies in our yard. Their lights were so bright some nights one could almost see his way to the barn without a lantern. Sometimes, for fun, I would catch a whole lot of them and put them in a jar to make my own lantern, soon letting them go free as they seemed like magical insects of special favor. For really, how many creatures on this earth have a fluorescent light in their tail? So many of Nature's wonders are beautiful to behold, like the fabulous butterfly that comes in a radiance of multicolored iridescence. I often wonder why . . . it is not called a Flutter By?

Those warm summer nights were so peaceful. After the crickets quieted, the silence was almost intense. Mama put an old but clean mattress out on the big woodpile and it was my delight to sleep out-of-doors, gazing at the brilliant stars sprinkled across the clear, dark blue heaven and to wonder about the universe and whether anyone lived on those stars as we did here on earth. (Clear skies covered with an immense canopy of bright stars is a very special memory and a rarity now.) Sometimes a star would fall and I'd catch my breath and make a wish, a wish that I might travel and see the world someday.

Those clear nights under the stars carry very precious personal memories for me, as it was there I first began to commune with God and talked to Him in the simplicity of a child. Sometimes I included my Guardian Angel, and Jesus too. We did not attend church in my early years. We lived miles from town as mentioned, besides Papa did not believe any of that stuff, and would not go for love-nor- money, and

Mama did not drive. In a way, it was a blessing as it turned out, for I did not experience the hell-fire and damnation sermons that I later heard some preachers gave, frightening children and warping minds. I had, rather, a closer communion with the Unseen through faith in the wonderful stories Mama told and read to me, and the way she explained God's love for us and the protection of His Angels. Mama taught that prayers would always be heard and answered in God's right time, but then, I'd already had proof of that.

Those nights out under the stars I could feel a Presence with me, and in the years since, have often had a sense of knowing and of receiving a clear thought in my mind; usually it was very different from my own thoughts. So I never have been afraid of the dark, or of hidden evils in the dark as some children have suffered, for that early darkness to me was soft and sweet, smelling of newly mown hay, filled with night sounds of crickets and cooing barn doves, and those beautiful twinkling stars that seemed to wink just to me.

I believe it is a real crime for parents to place fears in their small child's mind of boogey men or other fearsome things that are "gonna getcha" so that their lives may forever after be shadowed with vague fears, and they know not why. Of course, the proper training of caution with strangers and such on city streets is in order, and unfortunately becoming much more-so in recent years. I speak, rather, of those hidden unrevealed fears that one cannot face because they remain unidentified, the source not remembered, hidden in the closeted recesses of the mind, placed there by unthinking, uncaring adults who themselves have lived with fear, and pass it on to the innocent children. Such an individual may then look upon the world and all in it as vaguely unfriendly, while he carries unwarranted suspicions, and is ready to do battle at the drop of a hat, or of an off-beat remark from someone.

One such summer morning very early, around 4:30 a.m., as I awakened with the early sunrise warm on my face, refreshed in the clear brisk air after sleeping out-of-doors on my mattress on the woodpile, a unique and entrancing sight met my eyes. There was a small gravel pit on the side of our front pasture just a short way down the hill. From the base of the pit emerged a mother skunk, proudly taking her six new baby skunks for a morning stroll. They obediently marched behind her in a perfectly straight line, the cutest sight one might ever see. Each little one sported the distinctive fluffy black tail with the wide white stripe, curled proudly like a plume straight up in the air behind. They resembled uniquely marked baby kittens, as they marched past my quiet outdoor bedroom, paying no attention to me whatsoever. The mother led them across the yard and they disappeared, still in single file, into the cornfield beyond.

In all those years the distinct and obnoxious odor of skunk was never a problem, unless we had an innocent dog who unknowingly tangled with one. But once burned — twice shy. It never happened to that dog again.

People are so unique. In later years a friend in San Francisco once told me that "The smell of skunk was his favorite aroma above all others in all the world." And he was serious!

*

MY FIRST LOVE — AND WE LEAVE "THE 80"

At the tender age of ten I fell in love. He was a gorgeous boy with black wavy hair, twinkling brown eyes, and was about thirteen years old. The occasion for our meeting was the Ladies Aid Society. My mother by then had begun to feel better through treating herself with sunbaths, rest whenever possible, and happy faith-filled thoughts, and so she socialized once a month by attending Ladies Aid Society. The children, at home on Saturdays, usually went along and played in the yard while the ladies met indoors over their quilting bees, bake sale plans, and what-not.

This was the first time I'd ever seen Roger, and my heart did instant flip-flops. Most girls in those days were very shy to let on that they liked a boy, and I was no exception. However, while playing tag as a group, I always made sure he caught me. His name was Roger Morgan and he was nice to everyone. I knew I had never before seen

such a handsome well-mannered boy, who at the same time
was not a sissy. He organized the games in a helpful way and
laughed a lot, and was not one bit like the boys I'd known at
school. I thought Roger was a dreamboat, and my daydreams
were about him a great deal after that for several years.
Unfortunately, I saw him only a few times during the next
two years, since he was too old to tag along to Ladies Aid
Society meetings by then, and they lived many miles from
us. (I wish to tell you about Roger for a very special reason.)
    The following year we moved away from my childhood
home on The 80 and over to my father's larger farm on the
highway. This farm was closer to town and to the village
consolidated school. Papa's renters had left this farm, buying one of their own, so Papa decided we would move onto
it ourselves and rent The 80 out instead.
    Oh! I just remembered something funny about those
renters. Their name was Bee and Mama was, of course,
neighborly with "Miz Bee." They had four big strapping
grown sons. One time I heard her talking with Mama when
they had come calling on business. She was complaining
loudly because her boys never did get married and leave
home. It seems they were then ages 38, 40, 42, and 44, so
she still was feeding and washing heavy overalls for five
grown men, including her husband, all those years. She was
a sturdy lady and used to hard work, but "It isn't fair, there
ought to be end to it!" Miz Bee exclaimed to Mama. Old Mr.
Bee would not kick the boys out as he liked having their
help around the place. There wasn't anything wrong with
them, as I recall, they just were too shy to go courtin' and
they were comfortable with their Mama's cooking. They
knew a good thing when they had it! I always felt sorry for
poor Miz Bee having to cook and clean for five grown men
for forty years.
    Where was I? Oh yes, Papa announced we would move
now, as Bee's had bought their own place. I was eleven
years old and felt the wrench of leaving my familiar one-
room schoolhouse, beloved Teacher and the only few friends
I'd known. I surely wouldn't miss Pete though, that rowdy
that always knocked me down and fell on me, but oh, I'd be

closer to Roger's home!

Moving day arrived. I climbed up one last time to the tip-top of the windmill that sat on the very top of our hill for a look around at the far-flung countryside, as I knew in my heart I would never see that familiar view in the same way again. There stood the long row of tall, stately and symmetrical poplar trees Mama had planted for a windbreak seven or eight years ago. Now they were mature and marched up our long lane from the road far below, making a kind of rustling harp in the wind as they whispered their secret song. I watched a flock of wild ducks settle on the pond in McKeown's pasture next door, where an icy cold spring gushed up from under the ground to feed the pond, that it might water the cattle that grazed in the pasture. Often in the summer, Mama and I had braved that shallow icy cold water with bare feet to wade out to pick fresh crisp green watercress as it grew wild in the cold mineral water. We hurried to fill our buckets before our feet turned blue, as we squealed with laughter just short of pain! In the wintertime that pond never froze completely over because of the bubbling spring, so when I went sliding on the edges I had to be very careful not to break through.

Mama was a fun companion on those few outings we had time for, as she had a sense of adventure and would point out Nature's wonders to me. She showed me where the wily woodduck carefully hid her nest of eggs in the tall grasses and bullrushes, safe from the keen eye of the chicken hawk who always seemed to be floating very casually overhead, but who really had evil intent. We had to watch out for him even in our chicken yard, as he was known to raid the chicken pen. Sometimes weasels did too, at night, and we'd hear a terrible squawking and ruckus from the chickenhouse. Mama or Papa would quickly light the lantern and rush out in their night clothes into the dark, but usually too late to save a hen or two. The chicken house would be in shambles, full of loose flying feathers, blood and hysterical chickens. Papa fixed the hole where the weasel had dug under and repaired the fence right then and there, even in the middle of the night, if he should come back. The kill was useless to the weasel as he couldn't drag the fat chicken back through the hole, or stay to devour it. We always hated weasels. The many sides of Nature were a fact of life that one learned to live with.

The sharp March wind whipped my dress about my legs and the blades of the windmill whirled crazily overhead as I clung to the ladder at the very top. I was never frightened of heights, rather it was a marvelous vantage point from which to view the earth. I strained my eyes to see as far, as far as I could across the countryside, for this felt to me as close to flying like the birds as one could get. Remember, this was not only the top of a windmill, but the windmill also sat on the top of our hill, so the view was extraordinary.

On rare occasions Mama invited one of her sisters and family to come for Sunday dinner. As it neared time for their arrival, I would climb to the top of my windmill and watch for them, spotting the auto while it was still six or eight miles away. There were very few cars on our backroads in those days, so a moving black spot, raising a cloud of dust from their direction, was a dead giveaway. I would hastily climb down and run back to the kitchen shouting, "They're coming, Mama! They're coming!" So Mama could pretty well tell the timing of her cooking to our guests actual arrival that way. Telephones were not always working or dependable.

Sometimes, when in climbing the windmill I disturbed the small, but feisty, big-eyed barn owl that always made her nest up there on the platform in the spring, she would bravely swoop at my head, attempting in flight to knock me off my perch. Then, the very last second, she would swerve in a sharp arch to avoid actually hitting me with her wings. The first time this happened I very nearly did let go and fall off in surprise. I hastily retreated down the ladder. She had won her stand. In later years I learned to first check to see if she was nesting in the springtime and then, respecting her privacy, did not intrude.

In the heat of summer, during haying season, in mid-afternoons Mama would ask me to take a big jug of ginger ale out to the men working in the back fields. It was home-made, with cold, hard water from our deep well at the windmill, rich in minerals, clear and fine tasting, that truly quenched the thirst. Then we'd add sugar and ginger, just the right amount, and m-m-m, it was delicious! My mission of mercy was always greeted with hearty cheers by those helpers whose bare backs and tan muscles glistened with sweat in the hot sun from long hours of hoisting hay onto the big wagons.

As these thoughts rambled through my mind and I said my sad goodbyes to my friend, The Windmill, I heard my mother's shouts below and saw her flapping her arms around beckoning me down. It was time to leave my childhood home.

✳

MY SPECIALLY GIFTED GREAT AUNTS

We heard the crash, and our hearts jumped into our throats. Who would it be this time? The two-lane highway with its heavy flow of traffic west out of Chicago, at what seemed then like break-neck speed, ran right past our new home and a few rods down the road was a very dangerous curve. Since we moved into our house on Papa's other farm, there had already been two accidents at that curve. And now — Oh No! Not another! We rushed out, with Mama grabbing blankets to cover the injured, just in case, and sure enough, a young couple on a motorcycle had been hit and, we soon found, killed instantly. It was a very traumatic sight for a child, not easily forgotten. The paper carried the story of the young married couple, who in death had left three small children, now orphans. This experience alone caused me to be very wary of motorcycles after that. In recent years they are, of course, very popular but demand more driving examination and skill than was required then. Mama took the opportunity to point out that it was not wise for a couple with small dependent children to both be riding the same cycle. That dangerous curve claimed a few more lives before it was finally straightened by the county road department some years later.

So living on the farm on the highway brought a different outlook on life, as I saw that some people lived a much faster pace, but also often came to an end much sooner too! I talked to Mama about what happens when people die so suddenly. Does God have another home ready for them, and did He know they were coming when it is an accident? Mama did not always have ready answers. She said there are different circumstances surrounding each individual, depending upon his (or her) Divine Plan of life and death, but that God would know. Later in life I pursued the studies that would bring answers, answers authentic because they came from master teachers on the Higher Planes of life, and also from my own inner enlightenment.

Mama often spoke of my two great aunts who had special gifts of the spirit. They lived in towns quite a distance away. Mama's Aunt Kate was known as a healer, one who was able to heal the sick of all kinds of ailments without medicines. This was during the late 1800's and early 1900's when surgery was not only dangerous, but often sure death. Folks would bring their ill family members, ofttimes lying on a pallet in a buckboard wagon, traveling many miles to be seen by Aunt Kate. Her gifts of healing first were discovered when her young son, age seven, was badly burned in a gasoline explosion. It wasn't thought he could live. Frantic as a mother would be, she turned to prayer, then heard a voice in her head telling her to apply such-and-such. Aunt Kate followed those instructions and the boy not only recovered, but lived to be a fine-looking man. After that, spirit voices directed her healing work, and she became known for many miles around.

Great Aunt Kate turned her home into a sanitarium in order to accommodate the many who came. She was the sister of my grandfather, the one with table-tilting power. Kate could lay hands upon a person and simply know what the illness was and heal by her touch, or she would hear an inner voice tell her a natural remedy or solution.

I recall one remedy Mama told me Aunt Kate used, and some folks were cured of gallstone attacks without medicines. One of those cured was my Uncle Marvie, in fact it was at Aunt Kate's sanitarium where he first met my Mama's sister, Etta, who later became his wife! The remedy given was simple, but must be followed carefully, and was perfectly harmless as it involved food. The patient was required to not eat for twenty four hours. Then, beginning at 8:00 a.m. the first day, rotating every two hours, they must take the juice of a lemon, two hours later the juice of an orange, the next two hours the juice of a grapefruit, for twelve hours around. No water was allowed. This schedule was to continue for three days, twelve hours each day, and still no water or other food. On the evening of the third day the patient was to drink a full cup of olive oil and keep it down, with the help of a lemon. If he urped it up, he had to take another until he kept one cup of olive oil down. The following morning, which was the fourth day, Aunt Kate gave the patient a dose of a certain salts (a form of laxative). Then, amazingly, within six or so more hours the stones would come pouring out. One patient eliminated forty-two stones of all sizes, Mama said. It seems that the three days of strong undiluted citric acid softened the stones, the olive oil provided a lubricant, and the salts shot them out.

Many people avoided surgery in those years through Aunt Kate's help and the guidance she received from Spirit. Folks were more than grateful, as surgery in those days was so dangerous. (Sometimes that is true even today.) This was just one example, as it seems she dealt with all kinds of ailments.

The Medical Association got wind of her work and gave her trouble, charging her for practicing medicine without a license, even though she gave no medicine. So while tending a family of six children, she had to go to school for a number of years. Kate obtained a professional degree in nursing, I believe, and a cursory knowledge of the medical practice of the day, only to return to her original methods, which were more successful and safe as well.

In the past one hundred years the medical community has not advanced as a whole in its outlook on prevention and natural cures, in fact, often try to block such practice at every turn. In very recent years there are now some young doctors who recognize the body as a total finely-tuned electromagnetic mechanism. These open-minded professionals are beginning to really look at the influence of diet and stress on the body, which affects the glandular system, and in turn major organs. Thus, it is gratifying that the need to remember and practice that old saying; "an ounce of prevention is worth a pound of cure," regarding our health and general well-being, is finally being more widely emphasized.

In my opinion, there will come a day when some of the medical practices of the twentieth century, even into the 1990's will be considered medieval, when man discovers the body truly is a finely tuned electromagnetic mechanism and needs to be viewed in that light, with appropriate understanding and enlightened treatment. But I have wandered from my story.

My other Great Aunt, named Minnie, who lived in Elgin, Illinois, was someone we revered, for she had the wonderful ability to see those on the Other Side of the Veil as easily as she could see you or me. Even so, it also seemed quite natural because of what we already knew, and because Aunt Minnie was so natural herself. She was a sprightly, slender, kind-hearted lady, small of stature, with grey hair and keen sparkling eyes that peered through round glasses with gold rims, making her eyes seem even more penetrating. She was warm and caring and liked to have company, but always asked that we let her know when we were coming, as she was sensitive and didn't like surprises. Well, I think that's true of everybody. I wouldn't want someone to come halfway across the state and just blow in without letting me know! What if I were taking a bath?

Anyway, Aunt Minnie always had a stream of clients for readings, mostly folks who had had a death in the family and were grieving, and they wanted to know if their loved one was still alive somewhere. Back then folks had lost sons or husbands in World War I. Most who came were strangers to her, having heard of her work through others. Mama told me that many times before the person who came for a reading even sat down or could ask a question, Aunt Minnie would surprise her client by describing their passed on loved one, and even calling the name, saying he or she "just walked in the door with you!" That usually set them back a bit. Aunt Minnie was truly remarkable, and through her beautifully developed clairvoyance and clairaudience she brought much comfort to many bereaved folks.

Many times the one in Spirit would request the client, through Aunt Minnie, "Please do not grieve so much for me as you are tying me to the earth-plane with your emotions and I cannot go on as I should. I am more alive now than I ever was, and I love you very much. We will meet again one day when you come over here, but now I need to go on, and you must release me from your sorrow. Please know that I am just fine." There were other times when the one in spirit would be exceedingly grateful for the opportunity to give very pertinent messages to the family that only that one could possibly know, or to clean up some important business left undone, if their death had been sudden. So then, such a soul was very happy for this unique opportunity to communicate with those left behind on earth. In this way the naturalness of communication with loved ones who had passed over became quite common knowledge in my Mama's family.

I wish to emphasize that if a sitting with a recognized and authentic medium (or channel, as it is now called) is always begun with prayer and devotion, asking the Holy Spirit's guidance and protection, and that all present be surrounded with the Light of the Christ, communication between the two worlds is quite safe and usually very beneficial to all involved. The consciousness of the medium, or channel, and that of the client also makes a difference. For example, if a client came in who was overly skeptical and suspicious, who came simply to disprove her work, Aunt Minnie told Mama that sometimes created a negative block, and she then could not receive as well. Thus, the person did himself or herself a disfavor with disbelief, and usually went away without as much comfort or information as they might have otherwise received.

The word 'medium' was used as the clairvoyant actually was the medium through which a message could find a pathway between the two dimensions of life, just as a radio is the medium to bring air waves into our living rooms. Can you envision that the human being, when finely-tuned, was originally created to become the finest medium in existence? On all levels?

Great Aunt Minnie first discovered her gift, when after losing her husband in death, she saw him in her bedroom one evening and he even spoke to her. In speaking of this to her clergyman she was told, "Have nothing to do with that! It is the Devil!"

Well, Aunt Minnie had not seen anything devilish, only her husband. So she followed her own inner guidance. She was devoted to God and felt she was doing His work in her calling, as after that she saw plainly for everyone. She was an honest and kind woman, using the gifts He had given her for the alleviation of suffering, and to bring an added dimension of knowledge and enlightenment to those who needed it. She accepted only love offerings for her time, but from those who were in financial difficulty she would accept nothing.

As a child of ten, I remember seeing Great Aunt Minnie, a widow with one grown son, but Mama used to tell me all these things through the years. Unlike parents today who are often too busy to communicate on deeper levels with their children, Mama always talked with me about almost everything. She always had time to answer all my questions. In later years, while apart, we continued sharing via letters and news clippings. When, as a young mother and wife of an Army Officer traveling about the world, I became too busy to read as much, Mama kept me informed with her avid interest in many different fields and subjects of life, sending me pertinent news clippings and entertaining letters.

However, in my teen years while I was still at home, our Aunt Minnie played the key role in a most startling scenario, clinching my belief in the reality of the hereafter and of life after death for all time. I do not just believe this to be true, I *know* it is true! But I will tell you of that amazing happening later.

✳

LIFE ON OUR OTHER FARM

Excitedly I jerked hard on the reins turning her head too quickly and we fell, my horse and I, in the slick black mud of the wet cornfield, she on her side and I clinging to her and the saddlehorn for dear life. Fortunately, I had instinctively and quickly yanked my foot out of the stirrup, lifting my leg away from under her body as she went down hard (she was a big horse), or I would surely have suffered a broken leg. As it was, I was still astride her belly with my free right foot on the muddy ground. I gave her her head, and she struggled to rise while I clung on. Up we went, both of us more than a little shaken and covered with mud. Princess and I found ourselves in this ungainly position because I had goofed my job and let some of the cows sneak into the maturing field corn. Feverish and muddy, there was no time for self-pity. Quickly we finished chasing those wandering and munching out-of-bounds members of the dairy herd out of the cornfield.

Watching cows was one of my main summertime jobs. You see, we had quite a lot of pasture land, but not all of it was fenced, as fencing was costly and time-consuming to erect. So Papa merely stationed me on my horse, Princess, in the pasture. My only duty was to keep the cows from wandering out of the pasture into the growing corn. These were some of the happiest days of my youth, ages eleven through fourteen, out in the warm summer sun. I later realized that it was during those long quiet days that I learned to enjoy my own company, to deeply appreciate nature and the value of my daydreams.

So many hours were spent astride that gentle horse that I am surprised I did not acquire a cowboy's bowlegs. The sweet aroma of alfalfa and clover blossoms from Papa's hayfields attracted honeybees and many brilliant butterflies of every size and color. Our eight-acre woods contained precious red and white oak trees, where a variety of birds sang and built nests, and there were secret dark places to investigate, filled with ferns growing from fallen logs and many small animals. Wild flowers lined the fence-rows: buttercups, black-eyed susans, johnny jump-ups, jack-in-the-box, and wild violets. (In recent years I am told these woods also now harbor deer.) I was supposed to keep a sharp eye on those cows though, for it was a disaster if they got into the new crop of young corn!

On those warm days Princess contentedly munched grass, with the reins tied loosely on the saddlehorn, while I pursued my favorite hobby — reading. We were privileged to have a mobile library, a truck-van that came around once a month. I recall, one long hot summer, reading ninety-eight books while seated on my horse, with each current exciting book braced against the saddlehorn. These stories transported me in my imagination to many places around the world. There were the wonderful classical series of Jean Stratton Porter, a favorite was "The Beekeeper," and all of Louisa May Alcott's books, the most famous of course being *Little Women*, that was later made into a movie starring the actress, Katherine Hepburn as a young woman. Sherlock Holmes Stories and other neck-tingling mysteries were favorites. Is it any wonder that the cows strayed into the corn that misty summer day? I was lucky with the outcome of it.

I washed down my muddy horse and me with pails of water from the well so that Papa never knew, but believe-you-me, I didn't let that happen again.

We had fencing to separate our land from neighbors, of course, and all along the road on both sides, for our land stretched also on the other side of the highway, clear to the next road, or section. Our farm included a portion of the meandering Kishwaukee River with its oasis of many thick trees along the banks. The Kishwaukee, an Algonkian Indian name, flowed into the Rock River which later joined the Mississippi. This land was roamed by the Iroquois Indians in the old days before my grandfather farmed it, and my Papa plowed up great numbers of fine Indian arrowheads while working the fields as a boy of twelve and fourteen. That would have been 1881 to 1884, over one hundred years ago, as Papa was born in 1869. Many of those arrowheads were perfect, without chips. In later years my husband placed them in frames under glass, beautifully patterned on velour.

I helped Papa put up some fences in my teen years, holding the heavy posts in place in the holes he had dug, while he tamped them in. Then while I used all my strength to brace the barbed wire stretcher after he had pulled it taut, Papa wound and secured the wire with heavy staples. Papa always watched The Farmers Almanac to decide when was the best time to put in fence posts, as I do not recall wood preservative being used then. Posts put in the ground during the dark of the moon would not rot as quickly. Potatoes and other root vegetable seeds, on the other hand, should be planted in the light of the moon to assure good growth. That may sound superstitious to some folks, but Papa, of all people, was most practical, and he knew what worked.

One might think I was a big strong tomboy. Quite the opposite. I was a slight-built, skinny, small-boned, sunny-faced blonde. Strong muscles, however, are developed through necessity and outdoor work and play, in sun and snow alike. So also are strong will and character built, honed on the so-called hardships of life that chisel away the weaknesses, in doing what has to be done.

Once or twice a week in summer I was allowed to walk two miles down the railroad track to the old swimming hole where the Kishwaukee River made a sharp bend, creating a deep spot for swimming. The summers were very hot and humid, and this was a much anticipated treat. There was one problem, if you stepped off into the muddy places along the bank, you usually came up with blood suckers stuck to your feet and legs. And it was tricky pulling them off, for the heads, strangely enough, would break off and remain under your skin, creating a mean, red infected area. So one had to squeeze the flesh around it and pull the sucker out gently at the same time to remove it. Yuk! We endured anything for the pleasure of swimming in the cool river on those sizzling hot days.

School now was in a larger county cooperative building in the village a mile away. Those years were busy with studies, and woven through with the usual emotional growing pains of boy/girl traumas, such as love notes that sometimes were intercepted by others who jeered and taunted and made life humiliating for a few days for the unfortunate writer. It seems I was ahead in my studies, so was given seventh and eighth grades together in one year, graduating

early and ready for high school at age thirteen. There was
no junior high then.

Entering high school is a turning point in every child's
life. In addition to the usual adjustments, for me it meant
finding a way to travel six miles from home to the next
larger town every day. There were no school buses. Fortunately, some of the other young people drove autos and I
sometimes caught a ride. We each paid the driver ten cents
toward his gas cost. I had worked all summer in the fields
detasseling the hybrid corn, and selling our fresh-picked
sweetcorn and other vegetables at a roadside stand to make
the money for my rides and clothes, and school books which
we had to buy then. I knew I could not ask Papa. Would you
believe the sweetest sweet corn in all the world was raised
there, and I sold it for ten cents *a dozen*? Often we dried
the sweetcorn ears in the hot sun, shucked and ground the
kernels, and that fresh cornmeal made cornbread that was
out-of-this-world delicious! The year was 1938.

High School was great, as learning continued to be fascinating, and I did well. Socially though, I was a dud. The
town kids had a very tight clique and I was, of course a farm
kid. (Many people can relate to that.) It didn't matter too
much. I somehow had my dream, and the secret in my heart
that there was more to me than what met the eye, and
somehow, someway, I'd make Mama and God proud of me.
Because of that special communion I felt with the Unseen, I
had faith in myself, although I could not put the why of it
into words if I'd been asked. So it didn't really matter what
those snooty peers thought of this gangly teenager from the
farm, too tall and too thin, with flat breasts and pimples on
her face. I made the Honor Roll every month, a satisfaction
to me and, I think, to Mama, if to no one else. Besides, glory
be!, I saw Roger in the halls once in awhile now, but only in
passing or just a nod in greeting, as he was always nice,
never aloof or high-hat like many others. Even so, he was a
beautiful senior and I just a plebeian freshman, and as everyone knows, seniors never have time to talk to freshmen. I
understood that, so I adored him from a distance.

Roger was an only son and had a car, so he drove to

school and picked up a carload of young people from his area, which to my dismay was too far away to include my road. Everyone liked Roger, young and old alike. He had that certain charm that was natural and unaffected and always pleasant, but I knew that I cared for him most of all, and just the secret of it warmed my heart. I tell you all this for a very special reason that will shortly be revealed.

Soon I heard through the school grapevine that he had a girl friend now, a pretty redhead from Cherry Valley.

And then, something happened in the spring in a unique way, shocking and sudden, that shaped my life, confirming forever my inner knowing of the continuity of life and communication between worlds, and this is the reason I am relating all of this to you.

※

C H A P T E R   T W O

DEATH, LIFE AND A WONDERFUL REVELATION

The news spread like wildfire through the community. By Monday morning it was all over — Roger Morgan was dead! It seems he had taken ill on Friday. By Friday night paralysis began in his legs. The next day, Saturday, the doctors pronounced it polio and said they could do nothing. The paralysis crept up to his chest. He begged to see his girl friend, but only his parents were allowed into the room. Being Saturday the State offices were closed and since poliomyelitis was considered very contagious, a special permission from the State was required for anyone but parents. Permission finally came through on Sunday noon, but by the time his girlfriend was allowed in to see him the paralysis had passed his throat, and he could only look at her with tears in his eyes. Very late Sunday night he left his body, and everyone who knew was in shock. He was ill only three days.

I walked as though in a daze — a kind of disbelief. Why him? Why the nicest boy in the community, the only one I cared for? His poor parents were devastated. I could only believe that God thought him worthy to be taken up to Heaven, and my solace was in prayer, alone in my room at night.

Upon moving to this farm on the highway, Mama and I had been attending the church in our small village, but somehow the sermons weren't very satisfying. The minister was a rather stuffy looking fellow with a round bald head and a tummy out in front. His name was Reverend Dobbs. He wore glasses and peered at us very accusingly, I thought, probably because we had not come before. I had been expecting to hear wonderful things in the sermons to answer my unspoken questions, but instead I felt let down and disappointed, as he usually spoke of events that did not seem to relate to our daily lives and were therefore soon forgotten, at least by me. Rev. Dobbs often admonished that we must ask forgiveness for our sins. I didn't feel like a sinner. What had I done that was so terrible? I had tried to be a good girl and help Mama and Papa every day, working long hours to finish outdoor chores and my studies as well. There were berries, cherries, and apples to pick in season, as we had a large raspberry patch (with swarms of mosquitoes), and our walnut tree dropped big green balls that while shucking to get out the nut, stained one's hands black as coal from the juice, which did not wash off for weeks.

Sometimes the minister raised questions about the inequities in life, but he seldom had answers for his own questions. We were left hanging and wondering, and told to "just have faith" when we saw some born sick and crippled, while others were healthy and strong, some born so very rich, and others poor as church-mice. "Well," he said, "that's just the way the cookie crumbles." He actually said that!

It seemed to me from the things Mama had told me of God's love for us, that God would be more fair than that. There surely had to be reasons for such important things, for even parents demanded reasons for everyday happenings, saying, "Now, why did you do that?" and one had to search one's mind for a tolerable explanation. Surely the wondrous God must have reasons for the treatment of His children.

Through all my wondering I felt surely God really loved me, for hadn't He already helped me at important times? He also must love Roger enough to take him to a better world, even though it was terribly sad for his parents, as well as friends, especially as Roger was not only their only son, but their only child.

The day of the funeral came on the following Thursday

afternoon. I had never skipped school for any reason at all, but this day I skipped the whole afternoon, for I wanted to attend the service for Roger. I walked fast, all the way across town from the High School to the funeral home. When I arrived the large room was already full. There was only a chair or two way in the back. This was fine, for I hoped that no neighbors would see me and report to Mama. The room was literally piled to the ceiling with flower wreaths and bouquets of every color and kind, all across the front and down the sides. I have never seen so many flowers at any funeral since, through all the years of my life. It was just breathtaking. Roger had been very popular even with the grown-ups for miles around, for he was often involved in community happenings and helping whenever he could. Everyone knew and admired his parents, as well.

The service began. I soon was overcome with a great wave of intense emotion, not exactly grief, for I had never had him to lose, but in realizing this lovely young man would no longer be in our world. And perhaps I may have secretly carried a hope in my heart, though never consciously admitted. Tears streamed down my face in what seemed like torrents. I shall never forget. I begged God to comfort his poor parents, who had lost their only child, and to bring them peace from their sorrow. Over and over I blessed Roger and asked the Angels to care for him in his new home.

Suddenly the service was over; I rose and hurried out, among the first to leave, and ran back to school to catch my ride. I never did tell Mama or anyone else I had gone to the funeral, or how I felt about Roger; somehow my feelings were for my secret heart alone. And so, life went on . . . but also, sometimes holds surprises.

Subsequent days seemed bleak for awhile, with no more chance to catch a glimpse of him at school. But finally the hurt faded as it always does. Time can be kind, and Life again caught me in its rush of youthful occupations. Music continued to be my happiest diversion. I had a new piano teacher in our village, a very pleasant and pretty lady named Rose Davies. She was a fine teacher too and more and more

I was asked to whistle, play, and speak on local programs for Grange meetings, harvest festivals and the like. That was most enjoyable; it was a wonderful exhilaration to be able to express music, for I felt I did not have a good singing voice. The whistling was different, and folks really liked it, clapping and calling for more.

The year passed rather quickly and life remained full of work and studies. One wonderful pet I had was a blind lamb. It had been given to me by my uncle, who lived nearby. Because it was blind, it could not feed itself nor get its share of the food among Uncle's flock, often being pushed aside in the scramble, so was losing out and getting thin. He asked if I would take it and care for it.

'Lambie' soon discovered I was his benefactor and recognized my voice and footsteps. When allowed to run free around the yard, Lambie would follow me around like a dog. He was such a cute sight, now fat and cuddly, all curly and white, with four black feet and a black nose and face. In the mornings he would bleat with expectant happiness in hearing the bang of the screen door and my footsteps on the porch. I was always amazed at that little lamb's sensitivity. When he grew older and it came sheering time, Mama kept the wool and made a warm throw comforter of it. She kept some out to wear in a scarf for sore throats, and do you know, it worked? For many years after, whenever I caught a cold that included a sore, scratchy throat, Mama gave me that little sheep's wool in the scarf to wrap around my neck upon going to bed, and the next morning my sore throat would be gone. Nowadays they are again discovering the healing benefits of wool, advertising a Woolrest underlay sheepskin to put beneath one's sheet to sleep upon nights, for relief of pain due to arthritis and related problems. No one seems to know exactly why wool has healing qualities. But my Mama knew of this help years ago. Finally Papa had to sell Lambie when we later left the farm. He was a sweet friend.

*

ELECTRIC STORMS AND BARN DANCES

Then there were the barn dances. Oh! Those were a highlight in our lives! A few times through the many years of my youth, someone would erect a brand new barn, either to improve their farm or because the old one had caught fire in a lightning storm and burned down. The lightning could be horrendous in those summer electric storms. I've never seen such lightning anywhere as we used to have in the midwest. Huge jagged slashes would shoot across the night sky, creating a weird Halloween-like landscape, artificially bright as day for a few split seconds, then repeated in successive flashes, often with dagger-like tips stabbing the ground, followed by monstrous rolls of drumming thunder that literally shook the earth. Those summertime electric storms on the prairie plains were the biggest show on earth. All living there became accustomed to them, and we seldom felt truly frightened, but it could become a little scary, as we watched in awed fascination when the lightening came really close. Now and then the bright sizzling gashes would split a huge tree right in half in someone's front yard with a crack that really was frightening, or we would hear the next day that the storm had set someone's barn on fire.

One night we saw the fire and my father raced out into the night to help fight it. Owners had to act fast to get the animals out in time. Most everyone had lightning rods attached to their buildings to forestall such a happening by grounding the dangerous currents. If the farmer had just filled his mow with this season's hay crop, it was all the more tragic.

Soon after such a disaster there would be a barn raising. All the able-bodied men who could, would leave their own work to gather on a given day to help the unfortunate family, and a magnificent new barn would go up before one's very eyes, sometimes in one day, or three at the most. There was always a huge haymow with brand new floor boards, and this called for a barn dance to celebrate the raising. A few fiddlers would be rounded up, word was spread for miles around, and folks came that Saturday night wearing their best bib-and-tucker country dance clothes.

Oh! It was a roaring good time, I'll tell you. There were always barrels of beer on the main floor below for the men, with lemonade and other goodies for women and children. Children ages ten and up were usually allowed to go. My first dance was a most memorable event. I was ten years old. A neighbor lady named Minnie took me with her, as my Papa never had danced a step in his life, much to Mama's disappointment, so she seldom went either. So Minnie took me this first time and taught me a simple two-step. What a joy! I had discovered a whole new world, and went to as many dances as I could ever after. The fiddle players were tops and played long and valiantly, far into the night, at those old time barn dances. They really made those fiddles sing, and would-be songsters and callers were encouraged to get up in front and show their stuff. Everybody, bar none, had a good time. Even if a few shy wallflowers didn't dance, just listening and watching was fun, as some folks knew how to do an old-fashioned jig, and they made those new floor boards ring.

Sometimes it seems the memories of such events as those great barn dances made all the hardships seem worthwhile. For from that very music grew the Grand Ole Opry in Nashville and the Country Western music craze that has swept the nation and the movie industry in these years since. And it all started right around back home.

One thing about those days though, it seemed like everyone knew everyone else's business. There wasn't as much entertainment then, very little of the world-wide information that is available now. So there was more time to have an avid interest in what all the neighbors were doing. It wasn't considered nosey, you see, because folks for a number of miles around were thought of as the community, a kind of extended family. It had its good points, for if anyone had real trouble, all the others rallied around with whatever help was needed. The telephones were party lines, so it was pretty difficult to keep anything a secret. We had the old crank phone that hung on the wall, and we called one another without an operator by winding one long ring and two short, — or a long, then a short, and another long — or two shorts then a long, etc., depending on who you were ringing. Everyone had a ring code. One could hear all the receivers go up along the wire soon after, as everyone listened in.

The other side of the coin was that no one could stray over the lines of decent behavior without the whole county knowing it. Maybe that was good in a way, as it deterred those who might otherwise be mischief makers. Youngsters who got into minor trouble were often chastised and reprimanded by any adult on the spot at the time, and it was considered a favor by the parents. But it seemed not to stop those few who became locally notorious for their actions. There were a few husbands who spent their free evenings in the local tavern, squandering their money so that their wives and children were objects of pity, and folks took home-canned goods to them with cover-up remarks such as, "I made more canned fruit (beans, corn) this year than we can possibly eat and we want to get rid of some," so the recipients wouldn't feel embarrassed. They were good upstanding folks, you see. It just happened the husband had a drinking problem.

One incident though was downright scandalous. I've often thought in later years that I was not shocked when I arrived in the big city of Los Angeles and ran into the usual bold sexual advances that a woman receives, because of the amazing cross-cut of human nature with all of its varigated colors that we had right there at home in our little midwestern community.

One teenage neighbor girl was especially memorable. She was an only child of parents who thought themselves to be prime stock in the whole area as to pioneer ancestry, and therefore a cut above the rest of us. This couple had a way of letting this be known to others in subtle condescending remarks made in casual conversation, and also of always being out front running the show in any community event. They became known far and wide and were accepted as they were, usually huffing and puffing indignantly over someone or something whenever we'd meet either him or her. They each stuck out their chests, she resembling a portly grey pigeon and he a turkey gobbler in full strut, offering their opinions on everything, whether asked or not. It can be said they were sincere, for they did believe themselves to be the moral backbone of our small community, and they did do good works.

Trouble was, they always bragged on their only child as though she were unique just by being their progeny. However, this girl was something else.

At age eighteen Georgia was a large girl, stocky in build, with brooding dark heavy-lidded eyes, thick sensuous, curling lips and short, dark curly hair. She might have been pretty except for a very sullen stormy expression. Her body reminded one of a young bull, for she was exceedingly strong and worked like a man on her father's farm, always wearing men's coveralls. One never saw her in a dress. This seemed to be her life, for she had no friends among other young women that anyone was ever aware of, nor did she attend any local social gathering in a normal way. Rumors began to spread that when men came to their farm to do business with her father, she would find excuses to take the man out back, alone, to the barnyard to see her bull, and would talk openly about his prowess, for it was she who acquired a prize bull and tended to breeding him with other farmers' heifers. (Not very lady-like, all the women observed, but that was her business, even so.)

This went on for a few years with more basis for local eyebrows to be raised as the months went by. For now she spent many nights in the tavern with the menfolks and always wore men's work clothes, day or night. In the 1980's and 1990's this may not seem strange, and is even acceptable, but do remember, in the late 1930's very early '40's such behavior was very irregular and unheard of; that is, for a young woman to be so openly crude.

One evening I overheard my father (who ordinarily never gossiped or gave an opinion on the actions of others, because generally he didn't really care) tell my mother a scandalous tale that was spreading among the men who weren't at the tavern the night before. (Those who were, were being close-mouthed, except for one long-time neighbor friend of Papa's, who had stopped in at the tavern only a few minutes for a beer that night.) Now salt-of-the-earth type farmers did not ever make up tales, as they had no time for idle gossip. They were very down-to-earth factual folk who had enough hard-luck tales of their own and hard times to deal with. But this happening was so outlandish, it created a stir. It seems the men who were at the tavern were clamming up, so no one knew later who actually was involved. But Papa was telling Mama that it was said Georgia had taken on every man who came in the place, one after the other all through the night in an upstairs loft over the tavern. An electric silence fell over the kitchen. (I was supposed to be asleep and lay still as a mouse stunned at this news, waiting to hear Mama's response). Finally, in a quiet voice she spoke.

"Well, I'm not surprised. And no doubt Carl and Clarissa will never know and will continue to brag about their Georgia as though she were better than any other ever born."

I could hardly picture such a degrading affair, and tried to put it out of my mind. (But as you see, I was not successful, for in those days such actions were truly unheard of. At least in small local farm communities.) A few years later Georgia married a man who drifted through who was not known in the community. A good thing, it was said, as none of the local boys would have considered her, and she surely needed a man. Everyone was relieved and we heard no more rumors.

Another strange case was a local woman who was so desperate to leave her vulgar husband that she ran off leaving six children. With a sly smile the eldest daughter confided to me in high school, "I am my Daddy's new wife!" and she meant it in every sense of the word. So one could understand why his wife left him. Incest happened even then in our small community, which was a cross-cut of America. This is why I say nothing surprised me later while in the big city. I had been exposed to the many sides of human nature.

However, many fine young people grew up in our

community, as in most communities across our country.
Some became merchants, others founded lumber companies or began their own businesses in farm equipment.
Some bought acreage and became large landowners, later
farming one thousand acres. My girl friends married up-and -
coming young men. Later, at sixteen and seventeen, I had
proposals of marriage from not only three young farmers,
but from two very handsome soldiers whom I met at U.S.O.
dances held in Rockford during the war years of the 1940's.
One tall and dark, very elegant chap was from Washington,
D.C., and the other sweet one from La Crosse, Wisconsin.
They were wonderful, and I was deeply infatuated, but I
had dreams that were not of marriage. Not yet. The world
was big and my soul longed to fly.

*

ROGER RETURNS

An amazing thing happened! I lay in bed that night
thinking back over the events of the day, and I could not fall
asleep. It was all just too wonderful. I hugged my pillow in
joy and said my prayers over and over, thanking God for the
blessing of Great Aunt Minnie, who had come to visit us
from her home many miles away, and for the message she
had brought. The message had been such a surprise — and
such a personal thing that I knew without a single doubt
that it was true-as-true could be. And that is the wonderful
part. I know now that what Mama had told me about our life
here on earth being just a short while in our over-all existence, only a preparation for our life in other heavenly realms,
is really so. I know now we need not fear the change called
death because it is just another birth into a new life, like
taking a trip to another country. And I know now that God
hears prayers and that He does love me. I hugged myself
again and nearly laughed out loud for joy. How do I know?
Because He let Roger come back to tell me so!
    You see, it was like a miracle, because Great Aunt
Minnie made a trip to see our big family, my Mama and her
sisters and brothers, one last time, for she is now about

eighty-two years old and seldom travels very far. You recall it was she who was the fine medium I spoke of earlier, who had second sight? Well, she came to our house today to visit with Mama. My Aunt Blanche drove her here from her home where she had spent yesterday.

Mama and Great Aunt Minnie really had a fine visit and talked up a storm. It is so lucky that she came in summertime when I am home from school, and so we were all together in the kitchen dining nook having tea time, with berry pie Mama had made. They were just talking about family news, and I sitting quietly listening, enjoying my sweets, when suddenly Aunt Minnie stopped in mid-conversation.

Closing her eyes, Aunt Minnie motioned for silence. She appeared to be listening with her head slightly cocked. Then with eyes still closed, she reached her hand out to take mine, and said, "There is someone here for Bonnie Ann. Yes . . . he is standing here beside you, and he is a most shining Being. He has soft brown eyes . . . and appears to have dark wavy hair. He is smiling very sweetly. He is a young man and comes in a beautiful clear light, a very fine Soul because he passed over young and pure. He has not been gone long."

She paused again as though listening.

"Yes . . . he tells me his name is Roger, and he wants to tell you that . . . he is so sorry . . . he did not know." (That I cared for him?) "And he is saying that . . . he wants you to know how valuable your prayers were in helping him to make the transition . . . and he says to tell you . . . that because you blessed him, God will bless you."

I was just taken aback, with this happening so sudden like that. I had not told anyone about my crush on Roger, or about my prayers at the funeral nor since; not Mama, not even a girl friend, and certainly Great Aunt Minnie would have no way on earth to know or his name. I wasn't even thinking of Roger that afternoon, as it had been two years since he died. I finally found my voice and said I wished to thank him so much for coming to me, and I asked if he really felt the same as when he was alive here, and was he happy?

Aunt listened a moment and then said, "He smiles broadly

and says, 'Oh Yes! Much more alive.' And it's beautiful where he is, and he is very happy."

I then asked, "What is he doing with his time there in Heaven?"

"With another big smile, he is saying you will understand when he tells you he is still picking up people."

Well! That was a clincher too, for remember I told you that Roger drove to school and picked up kids all along the way till his car was full? I could only guess he meant he was picking up those who had passed on, here on earth, and was helping them find their way to their proper place in the Heaven Realms.

In the years since, I have found this to be true. (Recall the words to the spiritual song: "Swing low, sweet chariot . . . coming for to carry me home . . .") This refers to those many angelic entities like Roger whose work it is to help the newly deceased, who leave the earth plane and their body, adjust to their new level of existence in the plane above, in whatever level the developed consciousness dictates. This is a very valuable work and requires many thousands of sensitive caring angelic souls who have already come that route through "The valley of the shadow of death." For these entities understand the fear and confusion of the many thousands dying daily on this earth, who are not prepared for true reality there, nor how to function on that level of existence, having neither given it much thought or preparation. There are also the many who have been misled by uninformed ministers to expect wings and harps and a vengeful God on a throne. For it is not like that at all. Much dedication and patience is required of these angelic souls, having been themselves human, to help and guide the newly deceased to understand and function in their new surroundings. For although it resembles the earth plane (at first levels), it is also very different, being a higher dimension which does not know time nor space as it is known here.

Roger, in his very personal and intimate message, had given me a priceless gift — the gift of not only believing — but of knowing the truth that I had perceived within myself was real, that all life continues after the death of the body, and it can be a wonderful and beautiful existence if one has lived kindly and well. But also that it is possible to communicate with loved ones; they are not gone.

He went on to say through Aunt Minnie that anytime I had a need for assistance, I was to think of him strongly in my mind, and he would be there. Again, he expressed a blessing, and vanished.

Aunt Minnie concluded this amazing impromptu reading by saying she had a further message for me from Holy Spirit. Her words are recalled clearly, as that afternoon was a red-letter day for me.

Aunt Minnie held my hands in hers, and said, "You will survive a life-threatening illness in mid-life, but you will recover and continue to grow, and grow, in God's love and in Truth, slowly but surely, without the blowing of bugles or beating of drums, so when you arrive at your pinnacle in this life it will not be a flash-in-the-pan, but rather as one who will have built the necessary foundation to keep the laurels you will have rightfully earned. And I want to say when that time comes, *be sure to tell your right age.* This will be very important!"

Not understanding all this, I recall thinking in my sixteen-year old mind that I would be in the entertainment world (as I yearned to whistle with the U.S.O. troupes like those that went with Bob Hope overseas). Perhaps I would attempt to give an age older than I really was in order to qualify for certain shows.

How naive can we be? I could not know that there would, instead, be fifty or more chronological years before I would begin to see those prophecies fulfilled, and in a totally different way than I could then ever have imagined.

Then it was night. I lay in my bed in my room reliving the unexpected joy and amazement of that message, and I resolved to learn more about the mysteries of that Heaven realm where Roger was, for the whole idea fascinated me totally and in fact confirmed the feelings I'd had all along that conflicted so harshly with what Reverend Dobbs preached in our little church. But if this earth was only a drab reflection of that beautiful reality, why were we here? I fell asleep pondering.

Now, many years later I think back on Aunt Minnie's message and realize the great solace it has given me. Much water has passed under the bridge and much more over the dam. There have been many lessons learned and challenges overcome. Now I have the courage to write this book. If we can help one soul along the way with faith and insight, we have served God. Some may disbelieve what I write. No matter, for that shall not concern me. It is gratifying that in recent years there are many, many more who have since received proof for themselves and do believe. So I write for those who have ears to hear, who may find inspiration herein and help for the needs in their own lives.

*

DEATH OF PRINCESS
AND A NOCTURNAL VISITOR

I raced to get Papa. Princess lay on her side in the barn emitting deep guttural moans. I knew what was wrong and I knew it was terrible. She had gotten into the green oats in the field that bordered our yard that very morning and Papa had often said the animals must never be allowed to eat green oats as they would get a bellyache and could even die. The gate to the barnyard had somehow been left open, and I found her out in the field munching away when I went out to the barn. I quickly grabbed a halter to put on her, pulling her back into the barn, but fearing the worst. And now, here she was, her belly all bloated up and moaning in agony. I was just heartsick.

Papa called Mr. Chisam, the old gentleman who tended sick horses, and he came right out. He was the closest thing our area had to a veterinarian. I tried to comfort Princess, stroking her muzzle and talking to her to hang on, help was coming. However, after his examination, he gave us the dire news that there was nothing he could do. She was terribly bloated with gas that continued to expand as the green oats fermented, and it seems her age was against her. She was pushing thirty years now, and most likely would not survive surgery, he told Papa. His advice: Put her out of her misery.

I stood in abject despair. What had I done? I had not come out that morning to her as early as usual; if I had this might not have happened. I sat down again in the straw beside her and stroked her soft muzzle one last time as my hot tears began to flow. I thanked her for the many years of joy she had given me. Then I ran back to the house, and curled up in a corner. It wasn't long before I heard the single shot that spelled the end of our youthful wild rides together across the open fields, in free exhilaration and our love for life — Princess and me — sharing the wind in our face and the sun on our thighs, enjoying the moment in wild abandon, not once contemplating then that there would be an end to that special companionship that exists between an animal and her mistress.

My only solace was that she had lived a good life and actually achieved an age of thirty years, which was old for a horse. She never showed those years. I think she did live so long because she had received much love. My prayer was that she would be happy in Horse Heaven if there was such a place, and would have rewards for her many years of faithful service. She had carried me to music lessons, elocution lessons and sometimes to school in the spring, not to speak of those many hours watching the cows or chasing them home from the river pasture for milking time. I mourned my companion's passing for many weeks.

As it turned out, the timing was right for her demise, if it had to be, for later that very year Papa announced he was retiring from farming and had bought a house in the village for us. There would have been no place to keep her there. Meanwhile, I labored in the fields all summer, working for a large hybrid seed-corn company to make the necessary funds for school books and other expenses that Fall, preparing to be a Senior in high school. The year was 1941.

Winter came early that year and for a reason I do not recall there was not an auto ride with other students available. If I had the money I could catch a Greyhound Bus. Otherwise, I had to hitchhike. It was safer then, as passing motorists recognized local students carrying books. Today's problems were generally unheard of. There were some deep snows, and I vividly recall one late afternoon in the beginning of a blizzard, standing for two hours in the cold at the edge of town. Drivers were reluctant to stop their autos on the slippery shoulder. One kind motorist picked me up just after dark.

Exposure may have been a contributing factor, for soon after, at mid-term, I developed a very high fever, nausea, and my skin became red as a beet. Mama put me to bed, and this time immediately called a doctor. The verdict: Scarlet Fever. And as though that wasn't enough, shortly after on that sensitive red flesh, blisters began to appear that itched and burned like thunder. I asked Mama for a mirror the second morning, and recoiled in horror. For the creature looking out at me was ugly beyond description, with eyes almost swollen shut, the flesh puffed twice its size, literally covered with huge purplish-blue, and dark red discolorations. I counted ninety-six of those ugly splotches on my face alone, while my neck, chest and upper body was a mass of them as well. Sinking back in abject despair, I wondered would I ever regain a shred of my own appearance, or was my life ruined? At sixteen, this was no less than the end of the world.

The upshot of it was that I had contracted both Scarlet Fever and Chicken Pox at the same time and became dangerously ill. These illnesses are much worse when a person is past childhood, and the double dose was an added factor. As a small child, far from town in that one room schoolhouse, we had not been given vaccinations.

The doctor came those days, Mama said, but I was not aware of it. The fever caused deliriums, as the splotches progressed to horrid pustules. Sometimes I was aware of Mama dabbing soda paste on my face and chest to relieve the terrible itching and burning

No medicine was given; it had to run its course. The nights through the next four weeks were a kind of nightmare, alone in the dark, unable to sleep except to doze in spasmodic periods. I was always reluctant to disturb Mama who needed her rest.

I tell this event for a particular reason that I wish to

share with you, for I know many children are ill many times in many worse ways, but I was again given evidence of God's love and caring for us.

One very special night, near the end of four weeks time, is engraved in my memory. I often prayed to God to help me get well and relieve this misery. It was a comfort to know He must hear and I had only to trust, but the illness seemed at the time to have no end. Physically, I was in total misery with my entire body burning and itching all over and my eyes swollen shut. Daytime, too, the room remained darkened, there was no TV then, I could not read, and I spent many long hours alone as Mama had her work. The blisters would break and every spot the infected fluid touched, as it oozed out, another horrid blister would form, until it seemed I was one solid mass of inflamed flesh. Mama taped my fingers to keep me from scratching and making open wounds which can cause deep scars.

One memorable night I lay half awake, half in fitful dozing, when I became aware of a Light in the darkness beside my bed. My first thought, "It's Mama, come to check on me." But no, this was not Mama, for there stood a shining female Being dressed in gleaming white with a golden glow around her. An angel! Oh, she was so beautiful. She stood beside me for a long moment. There was a light touch on my forehead, and then I felt, rather than heard her say, "You will be well now." That's all. Nothing more. Soon she faded and disappeared, leaving a soft and peaceful feeling in the room that seemed to be filled with love and caring. To be frightened never occurred to me.

Immediately I fell into the first sound sleep since the beginning of my illness, and in the morning I was delighted, but not surprised, to find those miserable blisters, hundreds of them all over my body, had begun to dry and form scabs. The fever was gone, the itching and burning had ceased. I also knew too that my face would soon clear.

This again confirmed my knowing that God hears our prayers and sends angels to bless and heal. I was so very happy, thinking of my beautiful nocturnal visitor and the love and peace she had brought.

It was six weeks all told before I returned to school and was allowed to take late mid-year exams, which I had missed, in a special test. I finished High School, graduating with highest honors at the age of sixteen.

That summer I took a job working in an insurance office in a nearby town. One day after work before going home, I decided to see a card reader I had heard of. I thought it would be interesting to see what she would say, as my future seemed to be in a mist. Strangely, I do not recall anything she told me, except one very vivid statement which stands out in my memory as clear as a bell.

"Your four brothers in Spirit want to send greetings to you." Well! I thought she was full of beans, and upon arriving home jauntily told Mama, "That crazy lady said I had four brothers in the spirit world. Why would she say something like that?"

Mama, seemed rather startled and sat down. After a moment she took my hands, and said quietly, "How very interesting. I had never told you that I had four early miscarriages before you were born and they were all boys."

(I have mentioned this earlier in my narration, in telling about Mama, but this was the moment I first learned of it.)

She continued. "I had trouble carrying babies, you were the only one who hung in there. Your father never forgave me for the losses, even though I could not help it." She went on to muse that she had not before realized that an unborn child, once conceived, even though lost, retains its tie to the family and continues to remain in the family circle even while growing up on the other side of the veil. (As a postscript: Many years later another psychic reader in Honolulu gave me the message to "Please pray for your two sons [lost in miscarriages in early months of pregnancy in my marriage], as they are not maturing normally, never having known earth-living.") Neither medium had any way whatsoever to know of these occurrences. So it was proven again that the tie that binds the family — even the unborn — remains.

The summer I was sixteen Papa allowed me to travel for the first time to visit my cousins on his Beckington side of the family near Yipsilanti and Ann Arbor, Michigan. There were eight, all older then me in their early twenties. The boys and one girl were a handsome lot — all the Beckingtons were — my father being no exception. With their well-built bodies, twinkling eyes and flashing teeth I was quite taken. Later that year my other Beckington uncle from Washington D.C. came to visit and brought along his youngest son, my cousin, aged twenty-one. He and I promptly fell in love in the exciting way that happens to the very young. Bruce and I corresponded for years, particularly since he then went into service in World War II, and was one of the chief concerns on my prayer list of the fifteen fine young men for whom I prayed daily. I am glad to say he came back un-scathed. But with this experience I understood how it is that cousins would sometimes marry, as did Franklin Delano Roosevelt and Eleanor Roosevelt, even though we are told it is not wise.

That summer we left the farm and my life changed. The Japanese bombed Pearl Harbor, and the shock was touching our community in very personal ways.

✳

WORLD WAR II STRIKES OUR COMMUNITY

December,1941. The Japanese bomb Pearl Harbor, and the convulsive waves of this tragic event wash across America in an ever-increasing tide. Coupled with the escalating war in Europe that was already stripping our homeland of its finest young men, this was a dark and tragic reality. Our community, like all others, was struck hard.

The year prior to the war, I had been allowed to attend dances at our large and congenial country dance hall, lo-cated only two miles down the highway from our farm. It was called Rainbow Gardens, a picturesque name that the conviviality lived up to, if not the outer physical appear-ance. One didn't have to have dates to attend, for almost everyone came as a single or in groups, and was therefore free to dance with whomever they wished. It was great!

Mama was sympathetic to my longing for music and dancing, since she had been denied the opportunity for so many years. Papa didn't pay much attention to my social life. He was seventy-two years old by then, and left it all up to Mama because I was a girl, and "women raised girls." The exercise seemed to help my often recurring backache from that old injury. So my girlfriend, Agnes, and I went almost every week. Agnes was very pretty with a beautiful smile, vivacious, and loaded with energy. Everyone liked her and we laughed, danced, and always had fun.

Rainbow Gardens was fortunate in being a kind of off-Broadway testing grounds for new bands out of Chicago, and we quite often were favored with the big bands that played Chicago's famous ballrooms, the Trianon and the Aragon. We had those great Big Bands of the '40's right there in our own backyard. In those early days the music of Eddie Howard, Tex Benneke, Mitch Miller, Ray Ebberle, and lesser bands imitating Wayne King or Guy Lombardo were our usual fare. Tuesday and Saturday nights attracted dance fans from miles around, farm and cityfolks alike, and we had to arrive early or risk not being allowed in due to the crowd.

We girls met quite a wide array of interesting young men, and had many months of genuine good times, just dancing and drinking deeply of the draft of youth. Mama's strict discipline generally held me in good stead, for I knew without a doubt that if I dared to smoke or drink alcohol I might as well leave home. In later years I blessed Mama in her ever-present wisdom for saving me from habits that others have since suffered mightily from. Although drinks were served at the bar at the end of the large hall, drunkenness was not tolerated anywhere on the premises. Most all of the patrons were there to dance, as the music was the very best. There were mixer-dances and ladies' choice, so one could easily meet new people. Those evenings at Rainbow Gardens remain wonderful memories, and I had no fear of strangers in those long-ago days, as Midwest folks were generally honorable and decent. But there was one incident that stands out in my memory as a wild struggle to retain my virginity!

One night a nice-looking chap from another town had spent most of the evening dancing with me, even the last Sweetheart Waltz. He then asked if he could escort me home.

He had been a wonderful dancer and a perfect gentleman all evening, so I agreed. Getting into his small coupe outside, I was a little surprised to find a friend of his at the wheel. I was introduced, then asked to sit in the middle. I thought little of it until halfway home, when suddenly the friend pulled over and stopped the car on a quiet side road. I was sixteen that year, and quickly realized this meant trouble.

Without any warning whatsoever I found myself battling two men who definitely were not gentlemen. No fair! What a dirty trick! I was so furious at this sneakiness I didn't take time to be afraid. Being a farm girl who had lifted heavy milk cans and driven four horses, I was no wimp and stronger than they suspected. Plus, I believe, my anger gave me additional strength. My arms and legs flailed around like a windmill in a windstorm. My shoes came off; I managed to grab them and toss them out the window with my bag. I gouged one man in the eye with my thumb and kicked the other in the groin at the same time. As they momentarily let go, grabbing themselves in pain, I dove out the open car window headfirst into the ditch, my legs and feet flailing in their faces. I think they were surprised at the wild creature they had tangled with, and in great haste, they drove off. It wasn't far for me to walk home, contemplating my narrow escape. I didn't dare tell Mama, as she would not have allowed me to go dancing anymore. But I was more careful of my choice of company after that, I'll tell you.

Sometimes a band would invite local talent to do a number with them, as that was an audience-pleaser. One such time my friends urged me to go up on stage and whistle with the band. As it turned out it was quite a hit, and the orchestra, called Charles Wolfe and The Sweet Sounds, asked me to be a regular with them as singer and whistler! That began a nostalgic era for me and the beginning of my dream, for the following year on weekends we played the Lake Resorts in southern Wisconsin and a few clubs on Chicago's northside, as well as our own Rainbow Gardens at home.

Listeners and friends began to urge me to try out for radio in Chicago. Major Bowes Amateur Hour was popular on radio then, (he was the early forerunner of the Ed Sullivan

Show), but by then I had taken a position as a stenographer, attempting to earn the sum necessary to attend business school, and thus had no time to arrange an audition.

The social climate was quickly changing, as our neighbor boys, friends I had grown up with, cousins and boy friends began to disappear into the draft. Some were already in Europe, and now others were being sent to the South Pacific. We girls still went to the dances, but more and more we were reduced to dancing with each other, practicing the Jive and Swing routines. This was acceptable as their were fewer and fewer men, until finally those few left scattered around the sidelines were 4-F's — Army rejects — and they were too shy to dance, as some were crippled. We attended the dances.less and less.

The big bands had stopped coming to Rainbow Gardens, so we stayed home nights writing long letters to our boys overseas, and looking up the strange sounding names of places we heard on the news, like Okinawa and Iwo Jima. I was writing to fifteen correspondents. They were neighbor boys, my cousins, brothers of girl friends, and my own casual boyfriends, who all wanted letters from home. The beautiful part was that of all those fifteen young men to whom I wrote faithfully during their absence, only one did not return home. He was lost on Iwo Jima. His name was Red Burns. An unusual name, so I always remembered it, though it was natural as he had red hair. He was Duke's nephew. (You recall, Duke had been our special hired man.) This was far below the average losses reported. To this day I give credit to Jesus and the Holy Spirit to whom I prayed for the lives of those fifteen, individually, every night through all the years they were away. I still own bracelets made of coral and unusual shells sent to me from Okinawa, in those years from one young man. We girls got together also in prayer groups to pray for not only the boys we knew, but the many across the land, now far from home, who were giving their courage and strength that our homeland might remain safe and free. World War II was a very long and terrible war, with many casualties, quite unlike the recent Desert Storm. Over 6,490 lives were lost on Iwo Jima alone.

I went to church regularly and played the organ for part of the service. Still my heart longed to know more of God's love and of the inner mysteries of our relationship to Him — why He would allow wars that killed fine innocent young boys. For now the news regularly reported losses of the sons of townspeople and farm folks alike. Everyone was leveled to mourning together. Old Reverend Dobbs never threw any light on those subjects to satisfy me.

As mentioned, I joined the U.S.O. (the United Services Organization), formed early in the war to help entertain soldiers on leave or passes from their camp. A branch of this organization opened in Rockford and held dances in a large hall there, as Camp Grant at Rockford was a large induction center for men from many states. It was important for the soldiers to have a place to go off-Post that was sanctioned by the Army. A girl had to be interviewed and pass strict requirements (age, character, etc), before being allowed to join. There I met many young fellows who hailed from all over the U.S. We danced and talked, but there was no feeling of the freedom and joy I'd known at Rainbow Gardens. Now the ever-present specter of war hung like a grey veil. Young men headed overseas knew the carefree nights of their youth were numbered. Their demeanor was serious. They needed desperately to cling to anyone that represented home and gentle love. Many of these boys were so young, and I'm sure, inside, more than a little scared. Most had never been out of their hometown, and now they were headed for France or the South Pacific. Their future was a question mark.

My future, too, was a question mark. I had dreams of leaving this small town, but it remained a mystery. How would I ever leave if not with a U.S.O. Troupe? Some troupes were already traveling about the country and even overseas to entertain the boys. That was still a longed-for possibility. I knew Papa would never pay my way anywhere, and I had now, of necessity, recently found this daytime position as stenographer for the (then) grand sum of $50.00 a month, half of which went to Mama for my room and board. I was adept at all things secretarial and studying business courses nights as well, knowing in that way I could always support myself, but music was my first love. Somehow, something would have to happen to lift me out of this small town environment − perhaps into radio in Chicago. It wasn't improbable, for I had already whistled there on Radio Station WLS, on talent shows and other spots, receiving several enthusiastic letters from listeners, but so far nothing further had come of it. I could not go to college and study music or broadcasting. Papa would not hear of it or pay for it either. I also worried my health would never endure full-time schooling and a job for support, as my back, at times, still troubled me.

And then, at one of these dances I met Don. He was a dreamboat. His warm gentle eyes, that crinkled when he smiled, looked long and deeply into mine and I was lost. He was twenty-two years old, a sharp guy who had been studying dentistry at home in Wisconsin when he was called up. His smile was inviting; 'cupid's bow' curving lips revealed perfect teeth and his voice disarming, like liquid honey. We danced. He held me close, and gave me his rapt attention, never leaving my side from the moment we met that first evening. He seemed as entranced as I was.

Soon he was coming to my home for dinner on weekends and to meet my parents. We walked and talked. It was thrilling to be together. "As Time Goes By" became our song, for those were the years of Humphrey Bogart and the movie, Casablanca. Soon our love was a brilliant blossom floating through all my days, but, he was headed for France, didn't know if he'd ever come back.

"If I do, will you be waiting?" His eyes pleaded with me. "There is one thing," he paused hesitating. "There is a girl at home; I've grown up with her and known her all my life. Its been kind of understood by both families for a long time that we would marry upon my return. And really, I thought it was okay, until I met you. Honey, I've known her so long she is like a sister. But now I know it is you I want to marry. Will you wait?" He was so sweet and tender, pleading with me, melting my heart with his beautiful eyes.

Don's proposal threw me into a quandary. I recalled the local boys I had dated in casual ways. I had found no trouble in refusing their proposals of marriage, as I'd known them for a long time and would not — could not — remain in this small farming community as a farmer's wife, for that would be forfeiting all my dreams. Besides, I'd really had all the hard farm-life I could take for one lifetime.

I knew there was a greater plan for my life. I felt different somehow from my girlfriends, whose only dream was to marry early and raise a family, as had their mothers before them.

And now, Don was offering an avenue of escape that could change everything for me. I cared deeply for him, but was gripped with a chill of disappointment, for *life as his wife would never include my nebulous dream,* the dream I knew was there, though I could not quite see it, the dream that always lay just beyond my vision. My heart knew too that I could never be happy or at peace taking a man who had been promised to another, even though he said he loved me. Putting it all together, I knew it could not be, I had to be true to myself — that part of me that had not yet truly lived.

And so I explained to my dear young man all these feelings as best I could, but also that I did love him dearly and would write all the months he was away, until he came home to marry the girl who waited in Wisconsin. "If you had loved her once, you will love her again."

Every girl was writing to someone, and love letters carried secret signs because all letters overseas were censored, that is, read by federal agents. Anyone who wrote letters in those days would tell you that a latter carrying "SWAK" on the back stood for "sealed with a kiss," and an upside down stamp meant, "I love you." This seemed to be a national code understood by all.

Don left for France, still hoping I would change my mind, but I could not. I somehow knew God had another plan for me. Music and the hope of expressing its beauty in entertaining lay deep within, and like an inner call, superseded all else. I had to follow my Star. Years later I quietly made an inquiry while passing through his hometown and found he had married his lady and fathered five children. I was not surprised, as he was a most romantic lover, and she, I mused, a lucky girl.

Anthony, another very tall and very handsome young soldier from the military camp attending the U.S.O. dances also proposed to me two years later, when I was nineteen. His home was Washington D.C. and his family were wealthy furriers. Standing 6 ft. 4" tall, with black wavy hair, and sparkling dark eyes, Anthony was a really bewitching guy. He too was sent to France, from where he wrote steamy love letters to me for eighteen months. Even so, again I refused, for by then something unusual and exciting had happened. The Hand of Destiny had opened the door to my new life, the life my Inner Self had dreamed about and prayed for.

*

CHAPTER THREE

DISCOVERY OF
THE INNER WORLD

I am alone in my room — but I'm not *in my room, and I don't feel alone at all. I am suspended in space with a clear perception of being part of everything that is. It is beautiful, so peaceful — a wondrous bliss permeates my entire being. It's almost unbelievable. How can I relate what is happening to me? It defies description. One would have to experience this to understand. I am* wide *awake, more awake in fact than I have* ever *been. My 'awakeness,' an awareness and sensitivity to everything around and about is vivid. All that I view is amazingly* alive, *and I am a part of it. Oh, it is so exhilarating! And yet deeply peaceful.*

This experience was the culmination of over two years of daily meditation. I had spent an hour or more alone in my room every night (and many mornings) practicing meditation, special breathing exercises and affirmations which I spoke consistently and firmly, until they became a part of my subconscious self. This meditation routine had become a satisfying habit.

Great good fortune had smiled on me two years before when, still yearning for a more satisfying relationship with God (whom I talked to as a friend), and wanting to know more of His Plan for me which caused this restless hungry desire inside, I had, incredibly, been led to see a small ad in a newspaper from the *Rockford Morning Star*, to which I normally never had access. Papa did not subscribe, and I seldom read the paper anyway. But this day, in the home of an aunt, I had picked up the paper while waiting for her. That ad might as well have been written in red ink, for it jumped right out at me!

> *Learn to meditate and know the One God.*
> *The Institute of Mentalphysics*
> *Church of the Holy Trinity,*
> *Hobart Avenue in Los Angeles, Calif.*

I was astounded. To this day I can only wonder how that kind of ad happened to be in a Midwest farming community newspaper in 1940. No one I knew then had ever used the word meditation, or even knew what it really meant. And they certainly wouldn't have ever responded to such an advertisement. *Instantly I knew — this was where I would write.*

I was fascinated from the first lesson. I learned of the I AM within each of us. I was introduced to internal breath control, to concentration, to the silence within, with its immense depth and quiet peace.

The lessons were prepared by an American man said to be over 100 years old, but who looked only fifty. His picture was enclosed but only his oriental name was given. Ding Li Mi had returned from thirty years study with Tibetan monks in the Himalayas. He was offering the benefit of his studies through the basic discipline of deep meditation which leads to man's inner world and the peace of the God-Self within.

And so in this way, my friend, my prayer was answered. God heard a little girl of fifteen, different from others, living in a small farm community with few advantages. He gave her the gift of meditation thirty years before it was to become generally known, or even heard of, in an obscure midwestern community.

I looked forward eagerly to my nightly appointment with God, and I studied the lessons that came regularly by mail teaching me the practices and disciplines which after a time brought a wonderful peace that held me as though on a velvet pillow in the blissful silence of the soul. The days seemed brighter and I was happier. Many days and nights passed — sixteen, eighteen, twenty months.

Then one soft balmy evening came that was different, oh, so different. After intoning my affirmations and then quieting my breath as usual to a mere whisper, the inner silence that came seemed deeper, more intense. Then it seemed I had no boundaries, I could not feel flesh and bones. I could not have described where my hands and feet were. I was not in the least aware of a body, or even of being in a body. This night I seemed to be only Mind, with an intense, alive awareness. Then, gradually around me formed a radiant ball of golden light. My awareness was in the center of this warm glowing sun, yet it was not glaring as an outward sun would be. I saw no Being, yet there was something different about this Light, and it was oh, so wonderful!

How can one describe Love? The Love that permeates your whole being like water swelling a sponge, or air filling a balloon — this Light that was Love filled my whole being. It filled me and lifted me, but the feeling was at the same time emotionally thrilling, like being held close by a sweetheart, only so-much more. There is an indescribable joy that tells you when you are truly loved. Reveling in this Light that was Love for a time — who knows how long, for time seemed not a factor — filled me with deep awe and reverence. I held no thoughts, only joy and gratitude. And then, something more.

I began to feel an expansion of my being, my room disappeared and suddenly my consciousness was above the earth. I could see clearly, as though in broad daylight, for many miles in a complete 360 degree visionary range, though there was no use of eyes. I had experienced no feeling of leaving my body, for I had not been aware of my body, as mentioned, and I had not looked back to see a body, nor did I sense a body now. It was only pure Mind. This was an expansion of consciousness that included all. There was no need to turn to see in different directions, for I was aware of all — all at once, and it was beautiful!

It was around 11:00 p.m. It would be dark in our village, but in my soul's sight, the earth shone with pure Light and sparkling Life! The trees, plants, the sleeping animals, people in homes, even the houses, had a kind of brightness, but some more than others. That brightness included lines of Light that passed from one object to others, connecting everything in a vast gossamer shimmering web — overlaying the earth and everything in it. The world was truly wondrous; the glowing web connected all living things with a kind of electricity that I knew was life-force. This seemed not startling or unnatural or new; I realized, as if I had always known it, that this was Life in its Reality.

All of this lasted perhaps moments; one cannot tell time for there seemed none. It does not matter, for I saw and felt all this in a kind of totality that is timeless. I was a part of the indescribable completeness, of inner peace that words as we use them can only vaguely hint at.

After a time there began a kind of receding, or shrinking back into myself, and in seconds I was back inside my room. The warm glowing light was still around me. I felt it permeating my entire being with quiet, yet intense, joy. I gave fervent thanks to God for His goodness and mercy in giving me such a gift of Love and Peace, the knowledge of the rightness and order of things. My prayer had been answered, for now I knew beyond-the-shadow-of-a-doubt that we are not just a body with thoughts and feelings contained therein. We are beings, with the potential to become vast, tremendous! We are a consciousness that is one with the Greater Mind and all else that is.

I lay in my bed, meditating on the wonder of this night. Why, I thought, if our true nature is oneness with the Light and all of creation, are we not aware of this at all times? In the years since I have come to understand — we could not handle it. We are not ready; it would blow our minds, so to speak. Most of us live in the tiny world of our own self-chosen limitations, identifying ourselves with our bodies, our personalities, our surroundings and our personal desires, refusing to believe in anything beyond what is the most obvious. We are as children in the kindergarten of life, who grab for themselves, cry over broken toys and skinned knees, and who rage over a piece of candy another child takes away. This totality space, this Oneness with all living things could be likened to the college level consciousness or beyond. A glimpse is all we are sometimes given, in answer to fervent desire and prayer, that we may have the courage to push on, to follow the teachings of those teachers gone before us; the teaching that we must cease to harm our brothers, for in so doing we harm ourselves. There is a need to forgive one another and ourselves for past errors in our lack of love, wisdom and judgment, to love the Seen — knowing it contains the Beautiful Unseen.

Never through the years since has such an expanded consciousness experience come to me again in that way, but it has not been necessary. One experience placed it indelibly in my mind and heart. Later, spiritual visions of another kind came in response to intense emotional needs for personal answers. I'll share them as my story unfolds.

As my consciousness returned that night to the world of my quiet room, I went to sleep thinking of the Light and aglow with the wonder of what I had been shown.

Very soon after that memorable happening, circumstances in my outer world took a sudden new turn as well. I secretly believed these events to be a follow-up to the spiritual experience I had been given. Miraculously I was transported out of my Midwestern hometown village into an exciting adventure. What's more, it entailed no effort on my part.

*

THE MIRACLE OF COUSIN WILL

As the Greyhound Bus pulled up to our little village store, I climbed aboard and was dismayed to see that the bus was full with all seats taken. But No. There was one vacant seat. I had a long distance to go and I didn't relish standing.

Every single Greyhound Bus that passed through our village was loaded-to-the-gills with people these days, even though the buses passed through every hour, on the hour, twenty-four hours a day. I sometimes wondered where eve-

ryone was going. But then, these were the last months of
World War II. Some soldiers had served their time and were
coming home, and folks were traveling in all directions,
moving and taking new jobs. Many were going West.

Gratefully I sat down and thought of my happy jaunt. I
was taking the day off work. My seventeenth birthday was
approaching and I had made an appointment in the next
city to have my picture taken as a present for Mama. Dressing especially nice in a pretty green and blue flowered
jersey dress that she liked, I chose to take along a big black
lacy picture hat, for I did look well in hats, if I do say so
myself. But I was carrying it while on the bus as I didn't
wish to look conspicuous. I had barely sat down in the seat
which seemed to have been saved just for me, when the
man in the next seat spoke to me.

"Pardon me, is this 'Prairie Valley?'"

Surprised, I turned and looked at him for the first time.
I saw a very elderly gentleman, quite bald and rather shrunken
with age. He was squinting at me intently.

"Why yes," I replied. "This is Prairie Valley. Did you
wish to get off here? The driver will stop if we pull the
cord." I made a move towards the trip cord.

He spoke again with a gentle courtesy, touching my
hand to detain me from having the driver stop the bus.

"No, no. I'm only passing through to get a glimpse of the
countryside 'round about. Do you live here? As I see you just
got on."

"Yes, I do live here," I answered.

"Do you then happen to know anyone here named Fitz-
Randolph?" he pursued.

I was thunderstruck, and stared at him in astonishment.

"Why, that was my grandmother's maiden name! My
father's mother was Anne Fitz-Randolph. But how in the
world would you know that name? She has been dead many
years, even before I was born." Now it was *his* turn to be
astonished.

"Your grandmother, you say? Well, fancy that! For Anne
Fitz-Randolph was my aunt, my mother's sister. My mother
was Kathryn Fitz-Randolph. I knew my family had their

roots in these parts of Illinois. I am on my way home from a last trip to New York. My train was stopping over in Chicago so I just thought I would take a bus ride out and view this countryside that fostered my family."

Well, for Heaven's Sake! ("Fancy that" seemed altogether inadequate.) Would you believe, here I was sitting next to a long-lost second cousin? The little old gentleman became very excited, and of course I was having a bit of wonderment over it myself. How could this be coincidence? These buses went through our village on this main highway every hour, on the hour, twenty-four hours a day, seven days a week, as I mentioned. I had taken this one day off, a Thursday, not a Wednesday or a Friday; boarded this particular bus at 1:00 p.m. not the 12:00 or the 2:00; was forced to sit in this only available seat, not in behind or in front of, but *next to* a member of my father's family!

Papa later told me this gentleman's mother, my father's aunt, Kathryn Fitz-Randolph, had married a man named Matson, and had migrated with him to Tacoma, Washington many years before. This branch of the family later moved to Los Angeles, unbeknownst to Papa's branch and, as a result, were lost track of. My grandmother, Anne Fitz-Randolph, had married a Beckington and stayed here in Illinois.

It came out in conversation as we conversed that this gentleman cousin was eighty-three years old and had taken this one last trip across the U.S. to see his New York publisher about a book he had written. He was tickled all shades of pink to have found me, as he'd never dreamed of really looking up anyone after all those long years, thinking only to see the countryside where our pioneer family had first settled. His name was William Matson, and he naturally struck up an enthusiastic correspondence with my parents in the wake of our meeting, which continued for one and a half years. As it turned out, this correspondence was the spring-board that changed my life. For it was two years after meeting Cousin Will that the real importance of the event became clear.

However, while I am speaking of heritage, I wish to tell you of an interesting fact discovered by my father's brother,

On the day I met Will – picture taken for my 17th birthday.

who was a retired attorney living in Washington, D.C. Uncle Boyd took up genealogy as a hobby, even traveling to England to trace old records in church rectories, since he knew our family, only one generation before, had come from the British Isles. (I have since been told also that the 'Fitz' preceding an English name denotes that the first ancestor with that name had been sired by the King, but since the mother was not the Queen, the King publicly recognized his offspring in this manner, although he/she could not become an heir to the crown.)

Through traveling to England and intensive research there, my uncle found that the family name of "Beckington" (my maiden name, as Anne Fitz-Randolph had married a Beckington), was still quite preserved in Somersetshire, England, as the family had been sheep barons. Beckington Castle in Beckington, England still stands, eleven miles south of Bath in King Arthur Country, near Stonehenge. The castle had been built in 1049 and when the last Beckington to live there died without an heir, the castle, which was really a very large natural stone Manor House built in Norman style, was taken over by the Crown in World War II and used as a hospital. It was later converted into a boys' Prep or boarding school called Ravenscroft. In recent years this ancient structure was purchased privately. The new owner intended to turn the lower floor into an antique shop.

It rather fascinated me when my Uncle Boyd found, in tracing the family tree, that I am a cousin, twenty-two times removed, to the present Queen Elizabeth II of England! Our ancestor, in early times was named Beaconton, in the service of King Henry II, and knighted by the Crown. The family crest still exists. Well, I didn't get too puffed up over it, being twenty-two times removed.

I have a picture of Beckington Castle, taken when I visited Beckington Village in 1978. The castle was built entirely of fieldstone taken from the pastures round-about in 1049, and placed together to fit perfectly without the use of mortar. The garden behind was filled with elegant climbing roses, run wild along the walls, for it had been long neglected. I was pleasantly surprised to find myself treated as visiting royalty by the local populace, for there had not been a Beckington there for a few hundred years! Beckington Village School was recessed so the children could talk with me. It is fascinating and enlightening to trace one's ancestral roots.

During the ensuing two years after meeting Cousin Will in 1943, I worked at my steno-secretarial position day-time, saving my small salary and attending Business College some evenings, while continuing to pursue my love for music by whistling and singing with the Charles Wolfe Orchestra, as well as a few local functions such as the Fall Festival.

Fall Festivals were big events with apple dunkin', jack-o-lantern cutting, sack races and pie and watermelon eating contests. Barbecue feasts and entertainment drew large crowds, celebrating the bounty that Nature had provided, with the storing once more of the grain and corn in the granaries. The crowds were so large that this event usually had to be held down at the old cemetery grounds, one-half mile out of the village. It was a picturesque cemetery with a lovely garden appearance, well cared-for and spacious, not scary at all. Speaking of the cemetery reminds me — I must tell you a wild and very true story.

Across the street from our home lived a retired couple that our family had known for many, many years. They were a pretty ordinary couple as small towns go, except that they argued and quarreled a lot, never seeming to agree on anything at all. The husband's hollering carried clear across the street to our house. Maude was a thin, pleasant little woman, very down-to-earth and practical. She liked to chat with Mama now and then, and every Sunday she walked to church a block away. But Fred wouldn't go with her. No siree! He, like my Papa, always said in a loud sure-of-himself voice, "That's a lot of hog-wash! When you're dead, you're dead." He was a strong-minded retired farmer and tavern owner, very set in his ways, determined about his opinions, and that was one of them. Fred truly believed this life was all there was, and the rest of that 'hog-wash' was just people's pipedreams. His only recreation was to walk up to the tavern every evening, chew the fat with other retired farm-ers, and have a few beers. (His pot-belly showed it). Otherwise he stuck pretty close to home.

All of a sudden Fred up and died. Well, for awhile Maude was inconsolable. Mama was surprised and remarked to me, "I should think she would be glad for the peace and quiet! But I suppose she misses the fighting." After a month or so Maude calmed down with Mama's help and the consolation of her grown children's frequent visits.

Suddenly, one morning six months later, Maude came pounding on our door at 6:00 a.m. Mama opened the door, and there stood Maude, looking distraught and disheveled, as if she hadn't slept all night, and she hadn't.

"I couldn't go to bed! I was too frightened!" cried Maude. Mama bade her sit down and calm herself, and served her some hot coffee. She said she had sat up all night, waiting for morning so she could come tell Mama her horrifying experience.

"I stayed up late, till eleven p.m. sewing on a dress for my granddaughter's twelfth birthday, you see. The lights were all on and I was wide awake. Suddenly I heard a kind of soft scratching at the screen door of the kitchen, as though a dog were nosing around. It was warm last night so I'd left the door open for fresh evening air with only the screen latched. I laid down my sewing and walked out to the kitchen to see.

"When I peered through the screen, there to my horror stood Fred, right on the steps! He was wild-eyed and white as a sheet!

"He yelled, 'For God's sake, let me in, woman!' I was so stunned I just unlatched the screen door and he came into the kitchen and said in a most agitated voice, 'Those damn fools buried me alive! I just now managed to get home from the cemetery!'

"I was thunderstruck and just stood there staring. Fred sat down at the kitchen table and seemed to relax a little. I just stood dumbfounded. 'Quit gawking woman! What have you got to eat?'

"In a kind of daze I turned to the pantry to bring out some bread and jam and when I turned back to the table, he was gone! Completely vanished into thin air!"

Now that her story was out, Maude seemed to wilt like a flower, and began to whimper, "What does it mean? What happened to Fred?," she pleaded to Mama. "Where is he?"

Mama was a little shocked too, but she tried her best to explain.

"The words of Jesus are more true than people realize, she said. 'Whatsoever ye believe in your heart,' Christ said, 'so shall it be done unto you . . .' You know, Maude, that Fred always believed and said, 'When you're dead, you're dead!' so for him, there was no rising to the glory of heaven. He didn't believe in heaven. All he believed in was the body, so his soul stayed within his dead body in that grave at the cemetery for six months, possibly asleep. When he came to and found himself in the casket, he thought he'd been buried alive because his consciousness, the soul was 'alive.' Of course he was hopping mad. All he wanted was to get out and come home. And he did." Maude seemed to accept this idea, but it took her awhile to calm down, even so.

It has been shown that intense emotion can sometimes cause physical materialization for a short while because of the power of the emotions. Emotional desire has more power than we give it credit for. Fred was intensely angry as he thought of having been buried alive; thus he became dense enough in material essence to be seen by Maude. But when he relaxed, feeling he was at last in his own home, the anger — and power — diminished so he disappeared from her sight. Fred definitely was not buried alive since this was 1945, and bodies were always embalmed. A funeral service had been held several days after his passing, which we attended.

This erie story shows the tragedy of ignorance of the soul, and the result of refusing to open one's mind to the possibility of Life beyond the body and beyond earth-life. This same problem in varying degrees is the cause of ghostly hauntings at certain places, houses, castles and such, where people who have died refuse to believe it, and so remain at the site of their earthly interest. Usually, in such cases, there is a strong emotional tie to the site, generally a negative one such as a suicide or murder, in which they are the victim — or the murderer. This strong emotion causes them to be dense enough to be seen at times by some who have clear sight. It is one of the laws of the Universe that we are bound by our emotions whether dead, or alive. We are bound to people and places about whom we have *very strong* emotional ties.

Thus it is that we must conquer our own emotions, become masters of ourselves so to speak. This is actually the first order of business here in this earth-life. For if you think emotional ties are strong here, wait and see what they can do to you when you pass over! You may find yourself totally earthbound to your money, your house, to someone you despise, or to sensual pleasures. Anything to which you have given intense emotional power through a lifetime does not let you go so easily just because you drop your body. A person may find an unhappy state of affairs for their soul. One may have to work long years (as earth time goes) to disentangle themselves, or with a need to be born again and again before the lessons are learned and they are able to rise in Light to the glories of the Heaven worlds.

This does not mean we are wrong to feel strongly about good causes, or to work to aid and assist in areas of need. Quite the contrary. Generous, positive feelings put us in tune with the Light, and expand our sense of connection to life larger than our own ego.

It is strong negative emotions in the form of hate, anger, envy, jealousy, unforgiveness, revenge, and sensual lusts which become albatrosses around our necks, weighing us down so the soul cannot rise to its true place. We are given free choice in what we will worship, and our choices have powerful consequences. Fred's worship of his earth life as the only reality, and his total identification with his body kept him in the grave with that body even after it was dead. But as the soul begins to understand its true nature as greater than the body, as eternal, it is free to move to higher realms after death.

It takes time, many lifetimes perhaps, for a soul to learn to relax its grasp on its own self-interest, its identification with the ego. As we begin to sense our connectedness, we start to feel concern for others' needs, to love and be as concerned for others as we are for ourselves. We learn to forgive others' faults or offenses even against ourselves, as we are all connected, all parts of the wholeness of life, as I was shown in my vision. Glimpses of the Transcendent may come to us to give us strength and courage to deal with the inevitable challenges and pains of life which constitute our training and which are the vehicle of our growth. As we learn to love in the midst of every difficulty, our love capacity grows, allowing us to advance slowly in grace and wisdom, that we might one day become that which we were created to be — Beautiful Beings of the Creation, inheritors of Heaven and Earth, who can, with the Creator, "look upon the world and call it good," (Gen.1:31).

As I was saying before I got sidetracked at the cemetery, my parents were having a lively correspondence with Cousin Will Matson. That is, Mama was. Papa never wrote a letter in his life unless it concerned money someone owed him. It seems when Cousin Will had moved to the Los Angeles area with his parents, he married and raised a family there. He was a grandfather by now, so there was quite a clan, but his wife had passed on some years before. One day after one of Cousin Will's letters arrived, my parents announced, "Bonnie Ann, Cousin Will is inviting you to come to California to visit them. Would you like that?"

Would I like it? I whooped with joy! An opportunity to go to sunny, warm southern California legitimately — with my folks' blessing — it was a dream come true! I had never had good health with the Midwest winters bringing colds and sore throats and even anemia; the thought of balmy winter sunshine was glorious. Here was my passport out of the colloquial world of small-town interests, a passport to a place where my spiritual studies could flourish, and where I might follow my dreams of becoming an entertainer. Papa would never have allowed me to leave home to go so far, even to college, except as in this sort of arrangement, to relatives he could trust.

I thanked the Holy Spirit that had put both Cousin Will and me on that certain bus, that certain day and certain hour, on his trip through Illinois. To me that was not coincidence, but rather the answer to the deep prayers of my soul. In great wonderment, I thought again of my vision of that great all-encompassing Light and Love, and I now felt my life was being guided in a wondrous way, that something new and wonderful was about to happen.

✳

C H A P T E R   F O U R

GO WEST YOUNG LADY — GO WEST

*I'm having a ball! The train to Los Angeles is loaded
with dozens of young men in uniform. They're all soldiers
and sailors going home after the war and we talk far into
the nights. They tell me harrowing war stories and we play
cards. Days, we gawk at the mountain scenery which is all
new and amazing to me.*

It was difficult leaving Mama, but she knew I needed to
leave. She had reconciled herself to it a long time ago,
sensing with her special intuition that my destiny would
lead me far from home. Mama gave me a lovely wristwatch,
my very first, as a going-away present. She hugged me goodbye
at the station, not knowing what temptations I might be
facing, but harboring no fear for my future; she had faith in
what she had taught me.

I was then twenty years old. But I was not as sophisticated as twenty-year-old's are today, never having had television, and seldom even going to Chicago, seventy miles
away, so rolling down the tracks surrounded by scores of
celebrating young men, all dashing in their uniforms, was
an overwhelming experience.

It was November of 1945, and I spent Thanksgiving
Day on the train. Early snows made the mountains a fairyland of shining peaks and snow-filled pines. It was sheer

delight to one who had seen only the prairie plains all of her life. I watched sunrises and sunsets that were always new, freshly painted on Mother Nature's canvas, and I gloried at the sheer grandeur of our vast country. There was more open space then, big cities were fewer, and far between, and the air was crystal clear.

Having been raised in the Midwest in the small-town atmosphere of community spirit, I was open hearted, and a friendly person by nature. I had enjoyed the camaraderie of my male cousins for years, so I was taken aback to have my friendliness received as an invitation to intimacy by more than one young war hero on that train. I'd been thrown to the wolves and I hadn't yet arrived in the big city.

I had plenty of opportunity during those five days and four nights to hone my skills at fending off advances and out-and-out propositions. One night I was awakened by a rustling sound. Quick as a flash, I braced my feet against the curtains of my upper berth and gave a mighty shove in an effort to discourage one young amorous sailor who seemed determined to visit me in the middle of the night. Tumbling backward off the ladder, he decided to give up.

What a thrill to see Cousin Will and his family waiting for me at the station. And that magnificent California sunshine, brilliant even in November! Truly I believe I have arrived in heaven at a very early age. Los Angeles has clean wide streets lined with tall palm trees, with strange, luxuriant tropical plants in the yards of residences. The air is so clean and clear it literally sparkles. This indeed is the highlight of my young life, and I am on Cloud Nine.

My new cousins greeted me enthusiastically and Cousin Will took me around sightseeing. The La Brea Tar Pits, which now has cement walks and a big museum, was all open ground with only a small wire fence around the actual pits that day in 1945. We stood within feet of the hot tar bubbling out of the ground. Skeletons and picture signs described prehistoric animals the tar had entrapped in ages past.

Cousin Will took me to all the well-known places. At Forest Lawn, I was thrilled to see the memorials of Rudolph

Valentino, Jean Harlow, and other famous people of the day. We went to Griffith Park with its fabulous Planetarium, and I discovered for the first time the taste of fresh figs, ripe papayas, and plump red persimmons, fruits that had never found their way to the Midwest in those long ago days. It was all new to me. Manna from Heaven!

Will took me to his church every Sunday, a small Presbyterian chapel in Southgate. My Cousin Will was very devout. His published book, which had been the cause of his trip to New York three years previously, was of a religious nature. Being the wonderful age of eighty-five, he no longer drove an automobile, so we rode the streetcars and buses and I soon learned my way around.

A younger cousin introduced me to the beach at Santa Monica, where I soon acquired my first sunburn. Being thrilled with the warmth, I overdid it. But I was amazed. "Just think," I raved, "A sunburn in December! Back home they are freezing." I decided right then and there that this was where I belonged. I had no intention of returning to the frozen midwest. I wrote Mama and Papa, describing the wonders of the sunshine, the lush, tropical foliage, the fabulous fruits, and told them how good I felt. I was thrilled when they agreed I should stay the winter and then decide.

It seemed appropriate after six weeks that I find my own place to live, as I had no wish to wear out my welcome by overstaying at Cousin Will's. By then, Will appreciated my need to be on my own a little and it was a pleasant transition, as he took a room for me in the private home of a most gracious and kind lady friend whose daughter was away at college. Will and I still made dates for little excursions around and about, and to visit his sons and families who were wonderful to me, and with whom I have kept in touch through these many years since.

Now there was time of my own and I soon found my way across the city to Hollywood. Oh, it was delightful. Clean wide streets lined with tall palms led up into the foothills of the San Gabriel mountains, showcasing to perfection the homes built with artistic ingenuity. Many were of Spanish design, each more stately than the last, with the most elegant perched in reigning majesty high on the crests of the layered distant hills.

There was a quiet dignity and elegance to the residential sections of town in Hollywood. Since there were no high-rises to dim the view, sunlight cast a golden brilliance over the entire landscape. Even the best apartment houses were only three-stories at that time. Tropical foliage, flowers and blooming trees, abundant in the landscaping, were all unfamiliar, exotic and fascinating to me.

Sunset Boulevard! It lived up to its legendary name, the ultimate in class, with shops containing jewels, furs, elegant clothing and furnishings, with riches of every kind and description, and restaurants that offered exotic foods from Thailand, Java, Scandinavia and other faraway lands. A smorgasbord of wonder to me.

Wilshire Boulevard was similar to Sunset; both were wide, clean thoroughfares leading to the mighty Pacific. The beaches at Malibu were open and peaceful on weekdays. Very few people marred the long stretches of cream-colored sand. It was like another world to this farm girl from the prairie land.

All would have been perfect except for one thing. I lacked money. My small savings was fast running out. So I had no choice but to set out job hunting. Since I played the piano, I was able to secure a position in a music store on Santa Monica Boulevard selling pianos by demonstration, and on commission. I did very well, too well it seemed, for the owner's wife soon became jealous of me. I was young, blonde and sold too many pianos. She dropped in often and sat, just watching me with hawk eyes. Her husband, the owner, was an older European gentleman of quiet demeanor, who was apologetic and nervous when he told me, "It might be better if you look elsewhere for a position." Needless to say, I was disappointed. I had worked just three weeks.

But I now knew that I wanted to work and live on the west side of Los Angeles, in the Hollywood-Wilshire Districts. The lady with whom I had taken a room told me her daughter was returning from college and would need my bedroom, so necessity backed up my inclination. However, there was no greater housing shortage anywhere in the United States that Spring of 1946 than in Los Angeles. Half of the servicemen who had passed through California on their way to the South Pacific had decided, as I had, that this was the place for them. Many who lived to return, moved there now with their families, so in these years immediately following the war, Los Angeles grew like Topsy.

I could fill a book just with my string of weird experiences renting rooms that year. One had to be up and out by 6:00 a.m. on a Sunday morning as only one or two "Room to Rent-Females Only" ads appeared in the early edition paper, and there would be as many as twelve or fourteen girls waiting on the advertised doorstep at that hour. The girl the landlady fell over first when she opened the door got the space. I use the word "space" deliberately, for often what was being rented wasn't even a room. One of my lucky finds (desperate as I was) was a walk-in clothes closet. It contained shelving on the wall, a very narrow army-type cot, and a bare light bulb hanging from the ceiling with a pull-chain. The charge for this luxury was $15.00 a week, which in 1946 was a grand sum of money. I had been making only $12.50 a week at my full-time insurance job in Illinois.

I moved several times during those months, constantly seeking to upgrade my situation, and hoping and praying to find a home that might have a piano I would be allowed to play. I was always on the lookout for opportunities to perform musically. Charitable events often needed performers, and I did some of these to keep in practice and be useful.

When I took a parttime job as a sales clerk at Macy's, a girl at work, feeling sorry for me in my closet, took me home to share her little apartment. Well! If ever I'd jumped from the frying pan into the fire, this was it, for there was only one bed for the both of us. I didn't mind that too much — until her boyfriend showed up around 11:00 p.m., and darned if he didn't crawl in with us, too. I couldn't believe it. It turned out this was normal for her, but something she had failed to mention.

I was exhausted from my day's work and I faced another work day in the morning, so I closed my ears and tried to sleep, clinging precariously to my edge of the bed. After a time I felt the boyfriend press against my backside. When he said, "Now, how about you?" I jumped out of bed like a shot and finished the night on the floor, curled up in one thin blanket. This may sound humorous in the 1990's, but in the 1940's it was shocking, especially to a girl from the country, who was quite unaccustomed to such shenanigans.

I rose early and packed my things, having slept very little. Lugging my suitcase along, I got on the first bus that came past. I didn't have the faintest idea where I would sleep that night after work, so I sat with my eyes closed, praying as I had done so many times before to the Beloved Presence who I knew was always near me for help and guidance. I couldn't look for a room and keep my job commitment both. Besides, I had only $10.00 to my name until payday.

I felt a tug at my sleeve. Opening my eyes, I saw a small Mexican lady whose dark eyes were peering at me with concern. "Are you alright, Dear?" she asked gently. "Is anything wrong?" Her genuine sincerity disarmed me and I found myself blurting out my dilemma. She was instantly sympathetic.

"You must come home with me. I live very near. Come, we'll take your suitcase and you can see where I live. Then you can catch a later bus to work."

Good fortune — or Divine Intervention? I knew it was the latter, but I didn't then realize the full extent of the grace and protection God was extending to me through this kind little Mexican lady.

Three days after I had gratefully accepted a lovely room in Rosita Rodriguez' home, I had lunch at a fast-food beanery near my workplace. Suddenly that afternoon I developed horribly painful stomach cramps and barely made it home before becoming deathly ill. I lay in bed retching every ten minutes into a basin. This went on for hours, all night, and several more days, until I thought I would turn inside out. Rosita hardly left my side for many days, ministering to my poor body as I lay semi-conscious, as she offered cleansing potions to my poisoned stomach. My rib cage ached so from the convulsions that I could scarcely endure the slight movement of each breath. Later I realized

I had suffered ptomaine poisoning. I now believe I could have died had it not been for Rosita's kindness and expert ministrations. She, the angel who had taken me in when she knew me not at all. I fervently thanked the Holy Spirit who watches over us for answering a need that was greater than either of us knew when on that bus Rosita kindly asked, "Are you alright dear?"

Recovering I set out looking for new work. Perhaps because of weakness from having been ill, overwhelming homesickness hit me without warning. To my surprise, I found it indeed to be a sickness. I couldn't eat or sleep well and my heart hung heavy like lead in my chest. This was more than mere nostalgia, and I knew then what others had suffered when they speak of real homesickness.

Soon I also knew I could not impose on my gracious Rosita any longer, as she had intended only a kindness, and hadn't counted on a permanent resident. I thought to turn to Cousin Will and the relatives, but no, I couldn't return to them again, for they had already hosted me nearly two months, and also, I was too proud to admit need. Besides, Will might write my parents, who would demand my return home. I knew better than to ask Papa for financial help for the same reason. I had not come this far only to give up and turn back. I was determined — I would make it on my own.

In my weekly letters to Mama, I had related the beauty of what I had seen, the tropical climate in the dead of winter with its fragrant blossoms, the masses of flowers smiling brilliantly under a golden sun, and of the roaring ocean with water warm as a summer bath. But mainly I wrote of the feeling of new beginnings in a land that seemed bursting and eager as my own spirit. And I fervently prayed that Mama could one day come here to enjoy it as well, for she deserved some happiness and loveliness in her life after all the difficult years. I thought of her inner beauty and expansive thinking that had been stifled for too long. I knew in my heart that some way, I had to stay, if only so Mama could come and join me.

*
TOUCHED BY THE HAND OF DESTINY

Once again I set out at dawn one Sunday morning, to answer one of those rare "Room to Rent" ads this time in the Wilshire District. By the time I arrived, the room was already taken, but I refused to lose hope. I knew I would be alright, for my Inner Guide had brought me this far. Surely there was a Plan. Assessing my surroundings, I saw that I stood on a street corner in a wholly unfamiliar residential area. The streets and houses slept peacefully as they do only on very early Sunday mornings. Not a soul was to be seen in any direction. It was about 8:00 a.m. The grey mists of morning were melting softly under the thin rays of winter sunlight. I felt a sudden urge to attend church — but where? There was no phone booth anywhere in sight in this residential area, and I couldn't knock on a door at that early hour. Once again I turned inwardly to the Beloved Presence and said, "Father, if you wish me to attend church, direct my feet in the direction I should walk." Then I stood quietly awaiting guidance.

Now, you may not believe this, but suddenly I felt someone touch my sleeve. I turned and saw a well-dressed prim little lady. *Moments before there had been no one on the street in any direction,* and I had not even heard footsteps. Before I could open my mouth in surprise, she quietly spoke:

"Dear, if you are looking for Unity Church, it is one block over and one block down." Motioning the direction and without another word or even waiting for my reply, she turned and walked away. I stood there in utter amazement.

And that is how I found Christ Church Unity* of Los Angeles, pastored by Dr. Ernest Wilson, one of the finest men that ever walked this earth. Dr. Wilson ministered to a congregation of over 5,000, so many in fact, that in the spring of 1946 he was giving three services every Sunday morning at this attractive brick church on Manhattan Blvd. In ensuing months I had to arrive at least forty minutes early

*Christ Church Unity, Unity Village Hdqtrs, Lee's Summit, Mo. 64065

to be seated in the main sanctuary, as latecomers were relegated to upstairs chapels with piped in sound. I liked to watch Dr. Wilson, a tall handsome older man, with a shock of white hair and a warm smile. He was given to lively humor in his sermons which kept his audience rollicking and raptly attentive.

I cannot fully describe the inner elation I felt during my first visit, for here finally was a minister speaking to my heart and saying the things I knew within myself all these years. He talked of our inner divinity, that each of us is a child of God, created in His likeness, with the potential to manifest perfection and beauty as Christ did. He said that we are to know ourselves to be "inheritors of the Kingdom of God," joint heirs with Christ. His words assured us that each of us carries the spark of Divinity within, pure and untouched, which assures our immortality, and that it is only up to us to align ourselves with that Perfect Being in order to achieve the Oneness that is All Knowledge and Wisdom, all Love and Beauty.

My mind flashed back — This was what had happened to me in those marvelous lighted, expanded moments in my room at home three years before, when there was no time, nor space. In that eternal moment I had felt myself to be a part of, One with, that Divine Essence that is within each of us, and which has no boundaries on this earth.

Dr. Wilson's talk sparkled with gentle delightful humor, like bright stars across a velvet sky and the peace of it was as balm to my soul. At the same time his words made sense, and appealed to my down-home, close-to-the-earth upbringing.

And so began my thirty-year association with Unity's Truth principals, which emphasized the importance of connecting spiritual understanding to our daily living. These teachings gave new force and application to the language of love and wisdom that Mama had instilled in me. I had found a church home that spoke the language of the heart, the guileless love I had innately shown, and for which I had often been misunderstood. I felt like the ugly duckling who had finally found the swans and her place in the pond.

As so often happens when events are guided by the

Unseen Presence, there was an added blessing. New friendships through church led to a lovely permanent home with two wonderful people who also attended. Their names were June and Hal Court, a couple in their mid-fifties who, I found to my delight, were singers and dancers, duo-performers on some of the programs at which I hoped to entertain. June was as pretty as an angel, blonde, with sparkling brown eyes and a smile to match. Her gorgeous creamy complexion, reminiscent of European beauties, made her look like a Renaissance portrait come to life. June weighed over 200 pounds, but her weight was invisible as she moved with floating grace on tiny feet, dancing and singing with Hal by her side. In my mind's eye I see them even now: June in her pink satin gown, Hal in a tall silk black hat, white tie and tails, a thick shock of styled white hair and crisp moustache giving him the air of a debonair man-about-town. They are singing "Side By Side" and they could have stepped off the cover of a Broadway Review magazine.

Hal was very sharp and always witty. In conversation, he had a quick comeback to every remark, usually with a humorous twist that cut to the core of things. He used his wit to cover up a heart of gold which, like most men, he did not wish to expose. June, always sweet and gentle, laughed at his cleverness.

June and Hal took a shine to me when we first met, and so invited me to take a room in their comfortable home. I had the run of the house and was treated like their own daughter. And, to my joy, they had a piano!

Fascinated by my whistling, they gave me huge encouragement at a time when I needed it, proudly taking me to perform with them on shows of various kinds all over Hollywood. They were well-known and loved in the entertinment world, so I met some wonderful vaudeville performers during those days.

My prayer had been answered — I felt safe and sound at last. I now could cease to worry about a place to call home and set my mind to finding permanent work daytime and entertainment spots evenings. I was not overly starry-eyed, for I knew I was only one of hundreds of young hopefuls, all

Bonnie Ann in Hollywood studio picture — age 22.

full of dreams, most of which would be dashed by disappointment. But I was unique! How often, I asked myself, does one run across a whistling girl who can accompany herself at the piano, speak poetry, and who can even ride a horse? I wanted to shoot for the stars, for that had been my dream.

A number of single shows filled those next months. A highlight was when I was voted "Queen for a Day" on the popular radio show by that name. Ralph Edwards was host and moderator of the show at the old Orpheum Theatre in downtown Los Angeles. Out of an audience of hundreds, a few women who had unusual abilities were chosen to be contestants, based on cards we had submitted beforehand describing our talents. My heart leaped when I heard by name called.

Ralph called us up on stage and interviewed each of us in turn looking for stage presence, personality and personal goals. Then we performed. There were several singers, a dancer, and a comedienne. The crowd's response to each performer was gauged on an Audience Applause Meter.

My turn came. Ralph Edwards engaged me in conversation for a time and then I whistled a merry tune, accompanying myself at the piano. Lo-and-behold, the needle went clear off the applause-meter! Feet stamped and many whistled back. The audience loved it! I had won, over all the other contestants — hands down. It was so exciting I hardly heard all my prizes being listed off, a great variety. Money was not given in those days, but I had won new clothing, a beautiful cedar chest, a set of records, dinner at the famous Brown Derby, a day's limousine tour of the large movie studios with introductions, and finally a full make-up session with the famous make-up artist, Wally Westmore, to be followed by a photographic session at one of Hollywood's best photography studios. I was floating on air!

Nothing special career-wise came out of it, but t'was fun and a real boost to know the audiences in California liked my whistling, too.

Then Cousin Will, with whom I had kept close touch, (but spared him my worst trials), came up with a suggestion, and it brought a brand new chapter into my life.

*
AN AFFAIR WITH LOS ANGLES COUNTY

"Look, my dear. I cut this out of the paper for you. It's an ad saying the County of Los Angeles is offering exams for secretaries and stenographers. I think you should look into it."

Cousin Will was quite excited as he waved a news clipping under my nose, for he knew that I badly needed a steady income. I took Will's advice and went for an interview and test by Civil Service. I passed with flying colors and was given an immediate position in the Budget Division of the Chief Administrative Office. I was elated!

How amazing, I thought later, that for the second time this little man was instrumental in changing the course of my life, for as it turned out, I was to work as an administrative secretary for Los Angeles County, both in the Chief Administrative Office and later for the Board of Supervisors as secretary to Supervisor Hahn, for the next eight years. It was one of the most interesting, informative and educational periods of my life. Our office was located in the old Hall of Records Building in downtown Los Angeles. This department was the heart and pulse beat of Los Angeles County, as nothing could be done without money, and all budget planning and approval took place here.

Los Angeles County was growing so rapidly during those years, that the equivalent of the entire population of Salt Lake City was moving into Los Angeles County *every month!* All one hundred and six County departments were bursting with projects, and all of them cleared their budgeting needs through our administrative channel, from the Assessor to the Department of Weights and Measures, so we were a most important and responsible entity in the guiding of County business.

At that time the Chief Administrative officer was General Wayne Allen, a retired Army officer from W.W.II who continued to run his administrative ship as though he, and we, were still in the military. General Allen was a charged bolt of energy that sent electric shock waves through the staff from one end of the office to the other the moment he

stepped through the door. Somehow he managed to draw a
subtle feeling of fear from even his top male administrative
assistants, graduate business degrees not withstanding. Very
seldom did anyone express what they thought about a situation at hand; rather they listened and then turned and marched
out to carry out his explicit orders. He was fair, however.
He thoroughly read the written reports of his department
heads and incorporated those ideas into the decision at
hand. Wayne Allen surrounded himself with brilliant and
capable men. I was privileged indeed those years to work
with and for some of the finest minds in the business world,
as this office also encompassed the Personnel Division, Maintenance and Operations, Capital Outlay, etc., as well as
Budgeting, of all Los Angeles County operations.

On my third day of work, my immediate boss appeared
for the first time and introduced himself saying, "Hello. I'm
Smith Griswold. Glad to have you aboard. If there is anything you need, let me know."

I caught my breath — a Greek god! A striking man —
tall, blonde wavy hair, piercing cobalt blue eyes that looked
directly into mine, and broad shoulders tapering to a narrow waist, a build his trim suit showed to perfect advantage. His hand shake was firm, but easy, his demeanor in
command without being commanding, his smile friendly
and genuine. He had perfect teeth and a square-cut firm jaw.
In short, here stood the handsomest man I had ever seen.

Having been on stage, poise and an easy response came
naturally to me, but at this moment I was at a loss for words.
My tongue stuck in my mouth and I mumbled something
incoherent and idiotic. He was too gracious to take notice,
but left me with another quick smile and reassurance about
my work. I stood there, startled to realize that this position
would be no mere job as long as this man were anywhere
around. All my previous images of the man of my dreams (a
dark and dashing Robin Hood?) flew out the window, replaced with six-foot two, eyes of blue and a flashing smile
that lit a spark in my heart. Love at first sight can happen. It
did that day for me.

As the days progressed, I discovered that this man

(who in my mind resembled the pictures I had seen of the Greek gods Adonis or Appolo), had been a full Commander in the Navy during World War II, holding the position of Supply Officer for the entire South Pacific, and had recently returned to the States from that tour of duty. No wonder he had such regal bearing and seemed so obviously in command. Smith was accustomed to a position of authority, but he had no need to demand respect. His very demeanor and charisma elicited an eagerness to please from those around him, including me. As the weeks passed, I learned something else that I had felt all along . . . he was married. The disappointment was hard to accept. The one man I totally respected, and felt I could truly care for, was already married.

Strangely, the words of that old minister in my home-town in Illinois came back to me, "Well, that's the way the cookie crumbles," as if life's complexities were all chance. But I knew better. I'd seen that even the disheartening, disappointing happenings in our lives are undergirded by order and hidden purpose. My life had been guided thus far by an Intelligence greater than my conscious mind, and I trusted that there must be good in store for me in this instance too, beyond the disappointment.

I decided to enjoy each day for the good that it brought, and not dream dreams that were out of reach. So in just being myself, in throwing my energies into doing the best work I was capable of doing, I found happiness in having the privilege to be in the same office with Smith, to enjoy the person of this man whom I admired so much.

With each passing day my admiration grew. Smith was never condescending and was genuine in his dealings with everyone. He even took the blame for mistakes of his subor-dinates, he never passed the buck. All the men who were heads of departments were wonderful to work with. The atmosphere was cordial — we secretaries were treated with respect and courtesy, and sometimes teased with jovial good humor. There was not the slightest hint of sexual harass-ment that seems to plague many work places nowadays. These men were real gentlemen. Everyone liked my boss, and that deference extended to me.

After a few years, my capability and devotion to my work was rewarded. I was made Smith's personal Administrative Secretary, but only after I had made Number One among all applicants on the extensive oral and written Civil Service exams required for that position. I had won it fair and square, not just because he liked me.

For Smith did like me — very much. We had a kind of simpatico. I knew when he was happy or when he had problems. I became a kind of sounding board for thoughts he could not voice to anyone else. He knew his thoughts were safe with me, and he trusted me. In short, we became close friends. With God's grace, this soon extended to a lifelong friendship with his lovely wife and their two beautiful little daughters, all striking nordic blondes.

I came to love and care for not only Smith, but his family too, and I spent many happy times in their home. The resulting days of working together were with joy that made the years seem as months.

It's an often sung rag, the so-called affair between the boss and the secretary. But our rich friendship did not fit into that usual category, and I say this for two reasons. One, because we were able to guide our love and admiration into a channel for good for both of us, which did not bring danger or trauma to his family nor to me, and for this I am eternally grateful. The opposite opportunity was there, daily: for an extremely exciting romance. I was young and blonde, shapely, and attractive, and Smith admired my country-fresh personality. A farm girl of twenty-three, I was honest and guileless, with no hidden motives. He also appreciated that I was sharp as a secretary and often told me so. We shared compatibility and common interests. In short, our respect for one another forged a deep and lasting bond.

This is not the end of this episode. Another intriguing reason I tell this tale will have to wait to be shared in a later chapter.

*
I FLIRT WITH HOLLYWOOD

During those early months the entertainment field continued to draw me like a moth to the flame, and I took every one night stand that I was offered, as well as everything else that came along. I found my whistling ability taking me across thresholds and through doors I might never have otherwise entered, to meetings with Hollywood celebrities and quite a few sleazy agents and producers as well.

Some of my most memorable times were fill-in spots with Sammy Kaye's Orchestra, which was one of the big bands of the '40's, advertised as the "Sweetest Sound This Side of Heaven," and also a show with "Kaye Kyser's College of Musical Knowledge." That was a real kick.

A palm reader Kaye Kyser had interviewed on his show just before I came on told him he was going to marry again. When I appeared he exclaimed excitedly, "Why, here she is now!" and pretended to fall head over heels for me. He talked about running off with me, and prodded, "When can I pick you up for our elopement?"

It was really humorous because he appeared to put his whole heart into it. He said he was impressed with my speaking ability, and asked, "Why, with that voice, aren't you in radio?" When he found that I held down a position in the County of Los Angeles Chief Administrative Office, he raved, "She's intelligent too!" Kay didn't try to hide his admiration. He was a big-name band leader and I blushed pink under his glowing praise. I knew it was just a bit of horseplay, but one of the band members later whispered to me aside, "This is the first time I've seen The Prof flip out like that on stage! I think he really likes you."

When the show was released over the air, that bit of titillating conversation had been deleted, and I wasn't surprised.

A girlfriend of mine named Marsha was the personal hairdresser for Ann Sheridan at MGM, so I had access to visit the movie sets where Marsha worked, as guests were allowed in by invitation in those early days. The stars I met were genuinely nice people who chatted with the crew between takes, and I often was included in this exchange. One day Dean Martin discovered me standing on the edge of the set of a Martin-and-Lewis picture. Pulling up a chair for me, he then sat down to visit. He described the *visuals* of the set, in particular a strange cobweb-making machine with a blower that turned the cardboard interior of this particular scene into a very realistic looking and scary castle dungeon. The illusion was fascinating. I found it heartwarming that Dean took time to describe this to me.

Ginger Rogers and Joseph Cotton were always warm and friendly to everyone. I recall the evening they sat next to me in a theater and we conversed naturally about the play we were attending. It seems to me folks talked more to one another in those days. I spent time with Ann Blythe, and had my picture taken with her when we were on the same stage show together. Sometimes I went to different sets to watch a movie being made with Maureen O'Sullivan or Burt Lancaster. One could do that then if one had connections.

It was an exciting time. I was a bit star-struck, but I think these years of the 1940's were generally a memorable time for the stars as well. It was the day of the big extravaganza, a wonderful era of movie-making that will probably never come again. Even now, in the 1990's those stars still living and in their gentle years speak with nostalgia of the glitter and excitement of the '40's. The war was over, the country rebuilding, people loved entertainment and were going to the movies in droves. Things were generally looking up.

Television was just coming in and there were spots for my whistling. I had invitations to after-theater gatherings — people began to notice me. I did a show with Terry Moore, and I was taking advanced piano lessons from Eleanor Powell's accompanist. It seemed my career was opening up.

One day an agent called from a Hollywood suite with an offer.

"How would you like to be Barbara Stanwyck's stand-in? You resemble her in many ways, especially profile and build. One of the executives has asked for you. Your hair is blonde, but we could fix that. You're a natural."

The salary was attractive, but the job wasn't. I knew very well that a stand-in took the prat-falls into mud puddles, fell off horses, got slapped around by the leading man and generally did the dirty scenes, then the star stepped in on the close-ups. I didn't need to think twice. That would do nothing toward getting my talents exposed or further my career, even though I might be seen more. "Thanks, but no thanks," was the answer I shot back.

I continued to entertain some evenings with Hal and June, and performed a few spots on weekends which opened some doors for me. Suddenly an agent asked me to audition for Disney Studios who were producing bird whistling tapes for their pictures. It was a wonderful experience in later years to hear the birds in Cinderella and other full-length films and wonder which trills were mine. A few other whistlers' work was also used, the tapes interlocked and overlayed, so one never could really tell. It is nice to know one's efforts are preserved in such a beautiful way.

About that time, Horace Heidt, a famous band leader of the day, was touring the country with his troupe, and holding auditions to discover new talent around the U.S. which he would later present in debut on his weekly radio show. When I heard Horace Heidt would arrive in Los Angeles, I made sure I was at the try-outs. Arriving at the studio I was chagrined to see at least five hundred hopefuls waiting their turns! Each of us was interviewed and given try-out times for future days. Most were singers, many with fabulous voices. I wondered how it would ever be possible to choose only a few for the finals.

Amazingly, among the five-hundred or so, I was called back with the ten finalists! We would be narrowed down to five who would perform on the nation-wide show. I was elated! As it happened, there was also a male whistler among the ten chosen. Although he had more lung power, I did not feel emotionally moved by his artistry. (Secretly, I thought my tone was sweeter and more melodic.) Well, he beat me out and I had to accept it. Later, listening to his act on the broadcast show, the spot I felt I should have had, I shed tears of disappointment. This was the only time in my years in and about Hollywood that I cried over the breaks. I knew that if I'd tried out in any of the dozens of small towns across America where Horace Heidt traveled, against only a handful of contestants instead of against that crowd in Los Angeles, I would have been a shoo-in. I consoled myself with the thought that to be chosen one of ten out of five hundred was in itself an accomplishment. I dried my tears, and went on with life.

Quite a number of Horace Heidt's young artist discoveries later rose to varying levels of fame and fortune.

*

PAPA HAS A STROKE – AND I GO HOME

The year was 1947. Suddenly word came that my father had suffered a stroke. Not much could be done for him, and after spending a few months in a convalescent center which depleted my parents' small savings, Papa was sent back home and put under Mama's care. (Health insurance was something Papa never considered nor would have dreamed of paying for, as he had always been very healthy.) He was by then seventy-eight years old and I was twenty two. Caring for Papa was a big strain on Mama, so I hastily made arrangements for a leave from work, bought an airline ticket with my small savings, and flew home on an old United four-propeller driven plane to help. It was sad indeed, for Papa was bedridden, incontinent, heavy to lift, and at times delirious for eighteen hours at a time. At night he would pound the wall with his one good fist (his other side was paralyzed), and shout incoherently, disrupting the little rest Mama tried to get. My presence was a welcome relief; she was filled with joy to see me.

Papa became more quiet as I sat with him, praying silently, and talking gently of many things. He gave no sign of understanding, but grasped my hand. Sometimes at night in his delirium he would roll out of bed. Mama and I struggled together to lift him back in, for he was a sturdy man and heavy.

I want to tell you an interesting phenomenon that developed. Papa's body refused all food. He continually clenched his teeth against our attempts to feed him. This appeared to be involuntary, for he was not mentally with us or able to speak or communicate in any way, except for this one stubborn action. "Out of his mind," it was called then. He did accept water and orange juice through a straw, and that is all he would take in the way of nourishment. This went on for six to eight weeks, with the body continuing to excrete solid material four to five weeks of that time. In those days, intravenous feeding was not generally given except in extreme emergencies in hospitals. Doctors had actually sent my father home to die, plainly stated. They had given up on his case.

Over the period of those weeks, as he continually clenched his teeth against food, something unusual happened. After receiving no solid food whatsoever for six to eight weeks Papa began to recover. His body became slender and youthful appearing, without the wrinkles one might expect from weight loss. His mind cleared and he began talking to us a little. At night he slept like a baby, and those awful deliriums we had all suffered through vanished. Papa seemed so gentle and now called me "Dear," a term he had not used since I was a very small girl. Soon he was up and walking again. In a few more weeks the paralysis actually disappeared and his body resembled the flesh of a young boy, smooth and clear. Amazingly, he regained some of his strength and his mind, and Papa looked even better than before he became ill. It was wonderful and quite a revelation.

My father totally recovered — to his doctor's amazement — and went on to live fairly healthily another four years. In those days we had never heard of fasting to cleanse the body and regain health, but I had here seen its beneficial effects with my own eyes. It appears that Papa's inner body intelligence knew what to do, even if his conscious mind was totally out of it. Many years later I was to recall this valuable lesson in body cleansing when I faced a major health challenge of my own. I came to fully appreciate the amazing ability of the body to mastermind its own healing, provided it is given the opportunity.

Although I was loath to leave my Mother, my three-month leave of absence was up. I returned to my job in Los Angeles (it was wonderful they'd held it for me as it was my bread and butter), and to continuing my search for the elusive show that needed a first-class whistler.

A new agent who seemed to believe in me arranged a meeting with one of the King Brothers, producers who had discovered and launched the careers of Burt Lancaster, Kirk Douglas, and Ann Sheridan, among others. As I entered Maurie King's office I saw a sparsely furnished room with a desk, a chair, and a leather couch. There was not even a secretary to clear my way.

"Can you ride a horse?" Mr. King shot at me as I approached. "I grew up astride a horse," I smiled back, eyeing this short stocky dark man with tousled hair and a cigar stuck in his mouth at a jaunty angle He didn't really look as important as I had been led to believe.

"Good! We have a western coming up. If you can ride a horse, we can write in the whistling and give it an interesting twist." He asked various pertinent questions about me in an animated way, talked of the movie plot, said I would fit in, but we would need to run a screen test, etc. Then, to my surprise, he asked me to go to a movie.

"Well, that would be nice," I answered, as I thought I should be agreeable, but in the next instant he had come out from behind his desk and I found I was being steered toward the couch. A heated disagreement followed, and soon it became clear I had lost the part in the new movie.

Finding morally decent agents and producers was really tricky in those days. Everything you ever heard about the shady side of Hollywood was true, and then some. The 'casting couch' was a reality and a girl was accepted or rejected to a large degree on her physical performance – or lack of it. For the most part, talent seemed secondary. Of course, there were exceptions. Those with tremendous singing voices, like the young Judy Garland and Deanna Durbin, or those discovered and taken as proteges by established stars might avoid this usual prerequisite. Janet Leigh was discovered and helped by Norma Shearer, I was told. Those of moderate talent, or unpolished like myself, those who were fresh from the country, or who had not a hawk-eyed mother, were fair prey.

Another attractive-at-first-sight offer came from Johnny Green, who was then head of MGM's Music Department, and in that capacity was a very important man indeed. He attended an audition I had appeared for, singled me out, and asked me to do another number for him. He seemed surprised by and genuinely interested in my whistling. "It's unique," he said, and then, chin in hand, he asked me to walk around the room and pose against the window. I felt hopeful.

"Mmmm . . .Yes, I think we could find a place for you. I have a few people to talk to about it. You're different. Perhaps with a little polishing up . . . one of the acting workshops, and I'll arrange a screen test . . . leave your number out front . . ." His voice was warm and his manner genuinely sincere.

I felt ecstatic! Maybe this was it — the break I'd been waiting for. I sailed home hardly touching the ground. "The head of MGM Music really likes my whistling!" I bubbled out the news to June and Hal, who had been my main support all along. I took the screen test, as he arranged, and passed with flying colors.

A few evenings later, the phone rang. June called to me, "It's Johnny Green, dear."

"Hello?"

"Bonnie Ann? This is Johnny Green. May I pick you up? I want to talk things over with you." His voice was warm, friendly, cordial. "We can talk while we drive. I'd like to show you around."

I was a bit surprised, yet I'd heard many decisions were made outside office hours at the studio. I wasn't in a position to refuse and was eager for a part in a musical, even a very small part.

Johnny pulled up half an hour later in a beautiful silver grey Cadillac. He held the door for me and then we drove through many lovely hillside sections of Hollywood and Beverly Hills that I had not before seen. Johnny talked animatedly about the new movie he was planning. He emphasized again that parts would be written especially for me around my talents.

Pulling up before an elegant apartment house, he turned to me and said significantly, "I own this apartment house. One apartment is reserved for you. I've brought you here especially to show it to you, and I know you will like it. There is a new red convertible roadster in the garage below. It's for you too, of course."

Realizing his intentions, I sat in stunned silence, which he must have interpreted as assent, or gratitude, for he prattled on.

"I know you'll be very happy here. It's a lovely apartment, and I'll be coming by to keep in touch, and to work with you, as there is every indication we'll have a good part for you soon."

I couldn't find my voice and sat in a mute void, hearing him as though from a distance. Here was the same old wolf, only clothed in classier lamb's wool. I knew now he wasn't truly interested in *me*, or my unique ability that he had raved about. At least that wasn't his main interest. He was using my talent so he could use me. Disappointment and anger seared like a hot stone in my chest. The futility of it all! The insincerity and opportunism of these power-mongers whose real interest was only to serve themselves.

Coming up from my thoughts, I saw he had now driven to and stopped on a quiet canyon road above the city. The view below lay like a fairyland of twinkling lights, but the beauty was lost on me. Suddenly, without speaking, Johnny put his hand on my knee and then his head ducked down to go under my skirt as he grabbed me in a sudden clutching hold. This was nothing like the hesitant approach of the boys back home! I struggled, shouting my outrage, and finally managed to throw open the car door. Battling my way out, I fell backwards onto the street, losing my shoes in the process. I fled into the night, running in stocking feet. After some hours, I found my way home to June and Hal. I was disgusted and felt ill, as disappointment in people I once admired had reached the saturation point. Indiscriminate sex was not the norm in the 1940's where I came from.

But it seemed to be a fixation in Hollywood.

I had earlier decided to improve my piano chording skills, so took lessons each week from a man who was the accompanist for Eleanor Powell, the famous tap dancer and wife of Glenn Ford. Maurie was a short stocky man in his early forty's, a marvelous pianist, but with an overbearing manner that masqueraded as very friendly interest. After the first few excellent lessons, instead of paying attention to my musical progress, he enthusiastically regaled me with vivid gossip of the infidelities of the stars to which he was privy. I wanted to tell him to just shut up about that stuff and get on with our lesson, which I was paying him for. But I was too young, too shy of the luminous circles in which he moved. I had also been taught to not be rude to my elders.

The straw that broke the camel's back came the day my teacher could barely contain his excitement until we sat down so he could relate the latest lurid tale: the tryst a famous actress had just discovered when she climbed a ladder and looked over the transom of a dressing room on the movie lot. With her own eyes she saw her equally famous husband (whom we all know) going hot and heavy with an up-and-coming nineteen-year-old starlet.

"She has instantly filed for divorce," he added, with a smirking smile that seemed to say he was relishing the whole picture.

I decided I could not listen to any more of this rubbish and canceled my future appointments. It was the end of my otherwise beneficial piano lessons and it was sad, for he was a fine pianist, and other good teachers were very expensive.

Looking back over my life, I realize it was a kind of protection that the doors to this part of the world were closed to me, or that I chose to close them. Perhaps the Angels or my Higher Self knew I had a life to live that would lead to much greater meaning and inner growth this time around. But I was given the freedom to take a stab at it, to have a glimpse into that inner sanctum that I might see for myself what it would have been like, and to decide that I would not be missing much.

My up-bringing was on a farm, but I was not a babe in

the woods as far as sex was concerned. There was in me a strong sense of morality and innate personal dignity. This, coupled with the knowledge of our truly wonderful — if hidden — Beingness of who we really are, the beauty of our Spirit and its body temple that cannot be desecrated without paying a price, was my saving grace. These kept me from compromising myself and my ideals just to attain a sought-after goal. I thought sadly of those who believed such compromise was worth it, to attain stardom. History has since shown the tragic fate of more than a few famous ones whose movie careers have ended in suicide, or early demise due to indulgences into drugs or alcohol, or the fast pace those roles seemed to demand.

I saw this life wasn't for me. Letting go meant abandoning my girlhood dream of looking toward a career in Hollywood. I was disillusioned by the scenario repeating itself over and over again, for there were other incidents, from which I spare the reader further detail. I decided to entertain in simpler and safer ways for hospitals, fund-raisers for charities, some daytime television, etc. This proved uplifting for me and for others, and I now felt free to turn my attention to higher pursuits.

Even so, there were good times too, and now I am grateful for having had the opportunity to be a part of the Hollywood scene during those glamourous years that began in the 1930's, into the 1940's and early '50's, when stars were really STARS, pampered and petted by the studios into icons of beauty and stature. Many stars are still revered, many worldwide, years after their passing, some of whom I had spoken to and mingled with personally. Nothing like those years had been known before, nor has it been so since.

The air in Southern California was clear, weather warm and temperate, very few autos on the streets, and folks were laid back enjoying life. Those days will never come again, an era stamped in time, like the many photos taken then that one takes out in memory and gazes upon with fond bitter-sweet nostalgia, The Golden Age of Hollywood.

Later in life I came to realize that my destiny could not have included the entertainment world, for there was a work for me to accomplish on a level many would call mundane. It was challenging, even harsh at times. I was to be an Army wife to a man who needed me, and the mother of three very special souls, but I am getting ahead of my story.

*

DISCOVERY OF AN INDIAN MASTER

When one needs balm for the soul, God often answers in dramatic yet subtle ways. Very soon after those disappointing happenings, I heard of a Master Yogi who had come from India to California and who spoke at a small church on Sunset Boulevard. His organization was called Self-Realization Fellowship, and his name was Paramhansa Yogananda. I decided to visit this church and see for myself what a real yogi from India was like. That special Sunday morning when I made the plan to go to Hollywood to attend, the sun was warm and bright and my heart was filled with a glow of anticipation, though I had heard very little about him.

The church was quite new and small, set back from the sidewalk along Sunset Boulevard, gently nestled behind magnolia bushes and other rich greenery. There was an air of dignity at the entrance, quiet humility, not at all pretentious. I was warmly but quietly greeted at the door by a white-robed disciple and offered a seat. There were only a few in attendance, but the peace inside this simple room lay gentle like a down coverlet upon us as we waited for the renowned Yogi Master to appear. There was no conversation, as one finds before service in many churches; the scattered few sat with closed eyes, in prayer and meditation. This was quite natural for me also, and I was pleased to prepare silently for his coming.

There was a rustle of robes — noiselessly a figure floated into our vision. A slender young chap appeared and rather quickly introduced Master Yogananda to us, and as quickly left the stage. I was unprepared for the one who stepped forth from behind the curtains. Yogananda bowed most graciously to us, clasping small brown folded hands before his face. I am not sure what I expected a Yogi Master to look like. Tall of stature perhaps, with a commanding manner. Not so Yogananda. The one who greeted us with such gentle humility was quite small, almost insignificant at first glance. His face was smooth and soft, one might even say expressionless, as he stood there with eyes closed. He wore a robe of white cotton with one side draped across his shoulder. His hair was a soft brown, parted in the middle and flowing to shoulder-length, thick and luxuriant. In this he resembled those of Jesus' time, and one could picture him on a road in Galilee. There was an even deeper quiet than before, a kind of expectant hush in the room. Moments passed as he appeared to be in prayer, still as an alabaster statue.

Suddenly Yogananda raised his eyes and looked at us, and it was as though a light came on in that small church, although he made no attempt to project a personality, as one comes to expect from those on stage. The Master's dark eyes were large and luminous and filled with tenderness as he quietly gazed a moment upon each one in turn. As his penetrating look met mine, a kind of ethereal peace settled over my mind which before had been active with curiosity. With this peace came a clear feeling that I had received my reward for coming, whether or not I ever heard him speak. It was into this well of bliss that my ears relayed the ideas that he had begun to offer us. His voice seemed far away and on a higher plane somewhere. It was of a tone difficult to describe, that did not seem to fit his diminutive figure. But no matter; the words, somehow, were not what was important. I do not even recall precisely anything he said other than his proclaiming the wonders of God's Love and its blessing to the spirit of all men. It was the peaceful bliss that surrounded me, which I was intensely aware of, that was the master's real message. I seemed to be wrapped in a cocoon and his voice came only from afar as he led us into meditation.

Time was nonexistent. I do not know if he stayed twenty minutes or an hour, but when I looked up he was gone, as silently as he had come. No one moved; we sat as if one for some time longer, absorbing the light that the Master's presence had brought to the sanctuary. It had been an unusual service, with no extra appurtenances, no singing or prayers spoken aloud, no other attendants on the platform, and yet it had moved me deeply, as it obviously had the others in attendance as well. It was quite some time before everyone came back to earth enough to rise and quietly leave.

The bright light of the sun and the flashing traffic outside was in sharp contrast to the soft light and other world atmosphere of the small chapel, and I wondered at this profoundly different culture that the man from India had brought to America, and what it would mean to people here who, especially in Hollywood, were so materially oriented and flashy in the extreme. How many would really be interested in his message? How many were concerned enough about their souls and to want to feed their inner selves with the wonderful manna that this gentle little man was offering. How brave to bring this message to this city, right into the midst of those who obviously were in hot pursuit of only worldly goods and sensual pleasures. Only a Messenger of God would be so confident – or so naive – to think he would be heard.

In my heart I knew there were not too many who understood as I did the reality of the Spirit and the awareness of God's love that could be tapped, which the Master was entreating us to search for. He was so gentle, so humble, how many would be impressed, would be sensitive enough to recognize this peace that he offered, the importance of his message?

I was able to return a few more Sundays. Sometimes he was not there and one of the disciples would speak. But when Yogananda was there, we could bask in his love and peace. Often he only led us in meditation. Once his gaze fell upon me and I had the clear feeling he could read my soul. I never approached him – I dared not be so bold.

Paramhansa Yogananda, who had come to the U.S. originally in 1920 as India's delegate to an International Congress on Religion, was to become a tremendous influence in America where, over time, he attracted a large following. His book, *Autobiography of a Yogi,** which would

Autobiography of a Yogi, 1969 - Self-Realization Fellowship, 3880 San Rafael Ave., L.A. CA

be published in 1949, has become a spiritual classic world wide. In those years he and his disciples also built a beautiful monastery, retreat and temple at Encinitas, California for his teaching. He was to become a major influence in my future family but I had no way to know that then, as the future has a way of casting a veil over our eyes.

Why didn't I feel a compelling urge to join Yogananda's Self-Realization Fellowship, even though I was in complete agreement with its purpose and was so moved by his presence? Something within me answered, "It is not necessary. You have made the contact . . . that is enough. You will be shown your way."

Yes, I had made the contact. The mills of the gods grind slowly, but they grind exceedingly fine. The year was 1947. In the years since then I clearly saw that had I followed the Master then, as a part of me desired to do, into the life of a celibate disciple, my soul's plan in this life would never have been accomplished. Even so, his influence stretched far into my future, as you shall see.

It is only in looking back, along the path we have already trod, looking back and seeing the miracles that were often disguised as challenges, disappointments or apparent tragedies, that we can gather the faith to know that the path ahead, too, though hidden in the mists of the future, carries the perfect design for each one of us.

One day, not long after, just as I had finished a spot on a weekend daytime television show, something quite out of the ordinary occurred. After the show went off the air, a gentleman from the live audience approached me and out-of-the-blue handed me a calling card.

"I feel you should go here," he said. Before I could recover to ask his name, he turned on his heel and walked away. He had singled me out, not introducing himself, nor speaking to anyone else, or even waiting for my answer. Startled, I watched as he disappeared into the crowd before I thought to look at the card. It read:

Reverend Richard Zenor
The Agasha Temple of Wisdom

The address was in Los Angeles. How very curious! Why would he choose to hand this card to me? I did not at that moment suspect that a new chapter in my life was about to begin. Destiny once again was pointing the way.

*

FINDING THE PAST IN THE PRESENT
AT THE AGASHAN TEMPLE

The Agashan Temple of Wisdom proved to be just that, for in the days to come I was to hear wonderful truths, wisdom of the ages, that furnished answers to questions I had pondered for years and others I had never thought to ask. My curiosity led me to follow the directions on the card I had received from the mysterious stranger in the television studio, who had appeared — then disappeared — without any explanation.

The Agashan Temple was a small white building, beautiful in its simplicity. I was graciously welcomed as a new student searching for . . . well, more specific answers to the mysteries of life. It is wonderful to be childlike and trusting, as somehow there is protection in that. If you ask for and expect protection, you will receive it. I knew there truly was a reason the door had opened for me to come to California. If it was not for a career, as I had originally thought (even a small one in a musical), then the adventure must lie elsewhere. How could it be coincidence that a perfect stranger in that big crowd should reach out only to me, with an introduction to this Temple of Wisdom? Was he guided? And if so, by whom?

I mulled this over in my mind that day in the studio, as I looked at the card handed to me. These questions interested me immensely as my background knowledge of spiritual possibilities made of me a believer, filled with faith in the unseen world around us, rather than a skeptic who believes that the physical holds all the answers. I knew a person shouldn't be gullible — oh no! But I also know it is sad indeed if, in ignorance and skepticism, a person automatically slams the door on an opportunity to higher learning when it is made available, simply because it is the unknown. Even though that channel of availability may be unique and not heretofore accepted, I believe we should indeed walk through that door, look around and check it out. We have been given free will in the Kingdom. We can always walk out again if we find that what is taught does not harmonize with our own inner gut-level feelings.

If we prejudge a teaching before even investigating it, turn our back and call it of the Devil, or some-such, we may miss an opportunity to grow in spiritual awareness and stature that could have been priceless. One who does this, as Mama used to say, "has a mind set in cement and is in danger of becoming a blockhead."

Thus I began classes, attending every Friday night. It was most amazing, for I found the Reverend Richard Zenor to be a gifted trance medium. He had discovered this ability while he was still a very young boy. As he grew to young manhood in the ministry, a Teacher from a high Inner Plane had made contact with him and asked his permission to teach through the instrumentality of his body and spiritually attuned mind. It is necessary to have the express permission of the human, whose chemical make-up and spiritual awareness are such that he or she is a medium between the two worlds, physical and non-physical.

This Master Teacher had been a prophet of wisdom in Egypt during the Third and the Seventh Dynasties. His name was Agasha,* and he desired, we were told, to bring together his students presently incarnated on this earth plane, who had lived and studied with him in those times. (Yes, he definitely taught the Law of Reincarnation.) He wished to continue teaching those disciples whose souls he felt responsible for, who were still lingering on earth. It appeared it was he who had helped clear the way for many of these students to come to him in Los Angeles to this Temple pastored by Reverend Zenor. Students had come from all parts of the United States, from New York and other points in the east,

---

Agasha: Master of Wisdom and *Agashan Discourses*, by William Eisen, 1977, DeVorss & Co., P.O.Box 550, Marina del Rey, CA 90291

from Texas and the South, many from the Midwest like myself, and many who were already on the west coast.

Our previous soul-connection seemed to be true because immediately on arriving, in making the acquaintance there of other students of all ages, I felt a special rapport with many of them, feelings of old friend and where have we met before? Often the affection was instantaneous and overwhelming. Indeed, for some it was almost a reunion, and for me it opened a new heart's joy in a city where I was as yet fairly new. Whatever our previous connections, a number of these fellow disciples have remained lifelong friends for over forty years. These reunions, in addition to the fascinating teachings, made attending the Agashan Temple meetings a most eagerly anticipated weekly experience.

As Reverend Zenor relaxed, entering into a state of upright *sleep*, Agasha descended in a shaft of Light, described by those among us who had clairvoyant sight, and took control of the body in order to speak to us. No one ever saw the Master in form, as the Light was so brilliant. There was a Protector there in spirit also, who was The Gatekeeper, a guardian to Reverend Zenor, to assure that nothing amiss could happen such as an unwelcome or negative entity stepping in during the short interim before the Master Agasha entered. It took several minutes to make the transition and connection. I later learned that a change in vibration is required of the one descending to this plane from the mental plane where he resides. It is a willing sacrifice for a Master to do this, as this plane is very heavy by comparison; an analogy would be the pressure a deep sea diver might feel descending hundreds of feet under water. A suit of light is required as protection.

After Agasha made contact and was fully in alignment with the body, he sat up with an entirely new demeanor, tall and erect. The voice spoke perfect English, and took on a masterly command, yet was very gentle.

"Greetings, my beloved disciples." Then he would launch into the text of the evening's lesson.

But I barely heard three or four sentences of his opening remarks before I dropped into a sound sleep. I went out like a light, and stayed out until it was over and time to leave. I could remember nothing at all. I was bewildered and ashamed, and disgusted too, as I wanted to hear the message. I even took a nap at home before going to class in an attempt to alleviate the problem. To no avail. I continued to be gone (in consciousness) through every class for three weeks. I finally complained to my new friends, and they had a hearty laugh at my obvious consternation.

"We wondered when you would say something. This also happened to each of us when we first began. Don't worry, it seems the power of Agasha's presence is so strong that your consciousness goes out at first, but the subconscious is receiving the message, so don't be too concerned. During this period your body is being chemicalized, (it seems there is a subtle change in cell structure when the human enters the presence of a Higher Light), and your vibration is raised from the spiritual side to withstand the power. Soon you will remain awake." And soon I did.

After about three or four weeks I had no more inclination to drop into unconsciousness (or sleep), and the message was exciting to my now finely tuned awareness. Agasha told tales of our lives as his students in Ancient Egypt, with references also to Atlantis, its history of technology and later destruction, which rang bells of memory for many students, but the teaching that was to be applied to current spiritual growth was most pertinent and memorable. It is impossible to relate, due to space or ability, the content of Agasha's messages in this narrative. I will pass along some of the wonderful truths he taught, which in *1947-48* were quite electrifying in context, but which have since been proven out, even very recently through the 1970's and 1980's by scientists and other researchers. It was necessary to hear the message over and over again, each week couched in different terminology and stories, as Agasha tried to penetrate our minds that had been conditioned by the stultified laws of the earth-plane, and to refresh our inner memory. It occurred to me that Jesus had this same problem with His disciples, who could not comprehend even a small part of what he really was saying. Many times through the New

Testament, Jesus' frustrations with His disciples is evident. Fortunately for me, the expanded consciousness experience I had in the sanctity of my room five years previous gave foundation to all the Master's words, which explained much to my conscious mind.

Agasha spoke to us of the *Law of Vibration* that truly governs all that is, and includes the *Law of Attraction* which works in tandem with the *Law of Cause and Effect,* creating necessarily the reincarnation of souls. These truths can be voiced in many ways, from scholarly dissertations to simple statements, as Jesus made. I choose the latter method, because I do not write for verbal glorification, but rather to reach those who are seeking answers, as I was. Thus the message must be as clear as possible.

What the Master Agasha taught is the same essential Truth that all great Masters teach, in different tongues, using the language of different parts of the world. But always it is the one Truth: that Man is created one with God, and one with all others. All the masters, in accord with Jesus, teach "Seek and ye shall find . . . Ask and it shall be given . . . Knock and it shall be opened unto you . . . " (Notice the first letters of 'Ask' 'Seek' and 'Knock' again spell *Ask*.)

Many people have in the past actually been afraid to 'Ask' or to 'Seek' or to 'Knock' on the door of any religion, or teaching, that was not the one they were raised in. *Afraid* is the key word here. Fear has been used by many religious leaders through ages past to hold the masses under their power. Fear of retribution from a supposed angry or jealous God that would deal harshly with sinners who did not obey the Word, as interpreted by those self-appointed leaders, who in reality were often the blind, taught by the blind, and who continued down a path — blindly. And the masses followed, afraid to question in any way, until recent years.

The time has come when humankind must take a giant step in understanding. We must come to know who we truly are and were intended to be by the Creator — gods in the making. God created Man in His own image, "in the image of God created he him," (Gen.1:27). The inner levels of our spiritual being must be awakened to balance outer technological growth. Knowledge without Wisdom, and Power without Love, are so dangerous that they will turn and destroy, as they already are, humankind's best laid plans.

Wide-scale destruction has happened before on this planet and it is dangerously close to happening again. We are hearing and seeing the warning signals. Even the simplest peasant understands this. In fact, he knew it all along, but has been led by those in power to believe that war can bring peace, that violence can bring justice. Have we not truly been brainwashed to actually believe such a philosophy? Were not the wars — each one — to be the war to end all wars? Are we finally awakening to the reality of this falsehood? The simplest soul knows that weed seeds do not bear roses. How many generations must die until the planet itself is dead through the destruction caused by the horror of war? Every civilization that depended upon military aggression for its greatness has fallen.

Witness the Roman Empire for one. The lust for power over other men and nations has only one eventual outcome: its own eventual annihilation. The alarm has been sounded. It rings loudly throughout the lands. "For he who has ears . . . let him hear," (St.Luke:8:8) and take heed.

Master Agasha and other great masters have told us there is One God, One Power in the Universe and that power is translated as Love Energy. This energy is in constant motion throughout the entire Universe, subject to the Law and Order of Universal Mind which we call God. This energy is Life Force and it vibrates at various rates of speed according to its form and purpose. From the highest to the lowest, from the largest to the smallest, all things are vibrating energy, their atomic particles held together in a particular form by the rate of vibration, according to the Law of Attraction.

The Law of Attraction could also be called the Law of Love. It is literally the glue of the universe, that which holds all forms together. Each form has its own rate of vibration, for the energy to create its cells and molecules was drawn out of universal life force, and all the cells in each form are vibrating in harmony under this Law of Attraction that brought that form into being. This vibrating rate is slowest in the

mineral world and progresses up through the plant kingdom, animal kingdom, and in the human, at varying higher
rates (or speed) of vibration.

It is this attraction of the sparks of Life Energy for one
another that creates and then holds all forms together. This
is the reason we can say "God is Love" and "All is God," for
this Force is the life energy that manifests all things. And
Love — as attraction — is the glue that holds all forms of life
on all levels together in a particular unit. We then call this
energy a rock, or a tree, or a horse, or a human, or a planet.

Love also brings relationships and even circumstances
to us, which we then call good or bad. All come through the
Law of Attraction, for like attracts like through this magnetic life-force that cannot be denied. Thus Master Agasha
taught us in many analogies.

The great teachers whom we call Masters have taught the
Truth that all is Life Energy, or all is God, for many centuries.
But only in recent decades have scientists observed proof of
this reality. Technical advances have allowed matter to be
photographed on a subatomic level. These photographs have
shown modern physicists something very surprising: There is
no such thing as solid matter. In simple words, there is nothing at the heart of anything. What physicists find are whirling points of *light*, or energy, that make up the heart of the
atom. When atoms were bombarded in scientific experiments
with other atoms, they exploded into sparkling points of light
in geometric patterns of beautiful design. Still pictures were
taken of these energy patterns at different moments. Remember, these views are supposedly of solid objects. However,
they appear solid only to our physical eyes, which really do
not see reality at all.

One of the foremost pioneers in this exciting work is
Dr. Fritjof Capra, a distinguished physicist from the University of California, Berkeley, Dept. of Physics. His first book,
*The Tao of Physics,** explored his and his colleagues findings. Capra boldly states that the scientific community has

* *The Tao of Physics*, 1983 Random House, Distr.400 Hahn Rd., Westminster,
MD 21157

come to a meeting of minds with the esoteric religious traditions, particularly the Eastern teachings, that describe the real substance of all things as being energetic in nature; that is, that there is no solid reality or material substance to matter as we have thought. Rather, all life is a manifested projection of an unseen world of energy that is electrical in nature, vibrating at varying speeds according to the unseen intelligence of that form. The slower the vibration, the more solid the form we see physically. One could liken this to fan blades that are seen at a slow speed, but the faster they whirl, they appear to disappear, making it possible to see through them. Thus it is with all objects, seen and unseen. The higher the rate of vibration, the less seen by the physical eye.

The atom is actually a miniature universe and under the microscope of the subatomic camera, vast spaces are revealed between the central sun of an atom's nucleus and the electrons whirling in orbit around it, just as the planets whirl around a central sun in our larger universe with millions of miles between. This is common knowledge now, available to the interested reader, and has been for some years, but it was news of great import to we students of the Master Agasha in the 1940's.

To hear the Truths of the science of religion was exciting to me beyond all telling! How fascinating it was to listen to Agasha's clear authoritative voice explaining to us the precise and wonderful Order of the Universe, with Divine Laws that extend throughout all Creation. "As above, so below." A number of years later, while in meditation on this most enlightening concept, the following poem flowed through my mind:

ENERGY

Energy! — Can there be
    Anything but energy?
Can't you see — all you see
Are only forms of ENERGY!

Singing wires — whining tires
Trains that steam — eagles scream
Planes that stream — across
    the landscape so serene,
And yet that landscape too it seems
    Is ENERGY!

Eyes that shine,
Machines that whine,
Bullets zing and live wires sting,
Voices sing — and bells that ring
All proclaiming —
    ENERGY!

Voices hum — guitars strum,
Feet that stomp,
Hands beat the drum.
Violin sings — light and clear
Notes of ENERGY upon our ear.

This — the Symphony of Joy!
The planet sings —
    Oneness Rings
A Universal Melody —
    ENERGY! ENERGY!

Bonnie Ann Gilchrist

Agasha described to us the Hierarchy of spiritual masters who work to guide our planet earth and the life upon it, not interfering with humankind's free will, but attempting to influence and help leaders of nations in the crucial decisions they must make. Many leaders, of course, do not listen to inner guidance, but instead allow greed and power hunger to run rampant in themselves as well as in their countries. Free Will was a God-given right for all, and none are allowed to interfere, unless asked to, in prayer.

Agasha also told us there are spiritual teachers assigned to each of us, who have been with us for long ages, waiting patiently for us to become aware. All these work together to assist all to evolve out of the difficulties that have been created on earth so that we may move forward into the Golden Age of Light and Peace that is the plan for earth in the coming new age. A finer, brighter dimension will then unfold.

However, as time advances toward that day, hope becomes increasingly slim that the transition into a new era will be safe — or easy. In fact, tremendous, even cataclysmic difficulties seem inevitable. Whether we realize it or not, we humans are creators. The Law of Cause and Effect is fundamental to the Universal Order. Any action creates a re-action. The Creator has given everyone the freedom to mentally guide their own actions. Thus, we are creators through our actions, which create re-actions. The Law of Cause and Effect is inescapable, and functions throughout the evolution of the soul. In no other way can we truly understand the effects of our actions unless we suffer those effects ourselves. Slowly then, through this process, discrimination and wisdom grow in the soul of the human (we learn not to do that again). No person stands alone. Such an idea is the root of all selfish action, and is purely delusion. Humankind is a Body. Most of us have not yet grasped that *all of humankind is intrinsically connected by lifelines of a subtle, unseen, but very real form of electrical life force,* through the connecting grids of Light Energy that encircles the planet, as I was clearly shown years ago in my consciousness expansion experience (Chapter Three). Because of this connectedness, *the effect of individual and collec-*

tive actions are eventually suffered in some fashion by one and all. Would that these actions were all for man's highest good. Through modern communication we see more clearly every day that what happens on the other side of the world affects the rest of the earth's nations and their people. I will mention that it is also on this subtle level of unseen electrical life-force that prayer for others achieves results, and on this level that thought transference, or mental telepathy, takes place.

The spiritual teachers who have been with us for long ages, wait patiently for us to become aware. In this way the Holy Comforter is always with us as promised. The Christ essence, the High-Self superconscious that is the innate immortal part of our very own being, also serves as our guide. It is this level of our beingness, our High-Self, which we attempt to align ourselves to in meditation. In that Oversoul we find peace, guidance, and harmony.

On the spiritual level, all is order and Divine Plan. It is we who, with free will and ego, slow down our own progress by emotions and actions that often are not in harmony with that order, and then we must face the consequences. Humankind has not generally understood the tremendous power that was bequeathed us by the Creator in giving us Mind. Notice, I do not say "a mind," because Mind has separate parts, but for purposes of this moment we will speak only of two pertinent parts: conscious and subconscious. These are, of course, known by everyone. These aspects of mind can be likened to the parts of an iceberg above and below the water. The visible part, the conscious mind, is only one-seventh, if that, of the total. The remaining six-sevenths lies, as in the iceberg, hidden from view. The hidden parts of the iceberg play a major role in its course. So it is with the hidden parts of the mind. The part we call the subconscious, though not seen, determines to a large extent the daily course of our lives, feelings, thoughts, and actions, more than is realized. The subconscious mind, with the personality pattern it brings with it to earth-living, directs the building of the body while it is yet in the womb. Yes, the genes of the parents and the lifeblood of the mother are of course used to build the new cells, but *the subconscious carried over from past lives, exerts tremendous influence in the formation of the fetus (its strengths, weaknesses, and talents), and to a certain extent the emotional pattern, which is carried over through the subconscious of the new babe, for it is clear that our emotions are closely tied into our subconscious memory bank.*

As we well know, it is the intelligence of the hidden parts of our mind that continues operating all the complex body systems through the span of our life, never sleeping, the wonder of which astounds the conscious mind. The more we learn of the Intelligence at work in the body, its ability to constantly create new cells, fight disease with its immune system, and to generally heal the physical of all manner of damage, provided it is given a chance, the more awe-struck we become at its magnificence.

Just think of the gift that has been given humankind to which we rarely pay heed. For how much thought do you consciously give to the flow of your blood, the beat of your heart, or the creation of digestive juices?

However, from the very beginning of the new life of the human, the subconscious mind takes new instructions from the conscious mind, or from the environment it sees and is taught through the conscious mind, much as a computer takes instructions from a programmer. Once those instructions are entered and believed as fact, the subconscious mind takes them and runs with it, that is, proceeds to carry them out. These instructions then become manifest in the physical body or the outer circumstances in a short time, or over years, depending upon a variety of factors. *The subconscious mind is not a reasoning mind as is the conscious mind. The subconscious does not discriminate between right and wrong, but goes by what it has been given as true, and proceeds to act on it.* If the messages a child hears are of a positive nature, the outcome or manifestation in its life will be beneficial. If they are negative or in some way disruptive to Universal Order, the outcome will undoubtedly be detrimental. This latter is common knowledge. But, as important as this new input is to the new soul, what that one brings in with him or her, buried in the subconscious soul's memory, also greatly influences its life.

Therefore, it is of the utmost importance to our lives, our goals, our health, and the circumstances which we wish to experience, that we watch what thoughts, self-definitions, and attitudes with which we program our subconscious minds. And it is of utmost importance to our children's present and future well-being that we use words and actions that help them to build a healthy, positive self-image.

Now you may be saying, "This is elementary. Everyone understands the control the subconscious mind has, for look at hypnosis and the amazing things the hypnotist can make a person do." True. But how many of us apply this known principle seriously to our everyday lives? How many of us become the Watcher and observe what we think and feel strongly? With what are we programming our subconscious? For the subconscious is literally our servant, our Genie in the Magic Lamp. It will carry out (manifest), and truly believe whatever instructions we give it. Therefore if, in ignorance, we fail to consciously entertain thoughts and feelings of a positive — happy, joyful, confident — nature, we may allow, by default, strong negative emotions or thoughts to have powerful influence over us. The effects of these negative emotions and thoughts will, sooner or later, become evident in our lives.

It has perhaps taken many of us a good many years, even lifetimes, to reach the conclusion that something is wrong with the effects we are experiencing. If some of us become miserable enough, and have an intelligent mind that seeks to know why, we may finally be led to look at causes — at our own thoughts and actions. Most people prefer to abdicate all responsibility for what they experience in life and instead will blame it on bad luck or even on God for the state in which they find themselves. It has always been said that to blame someone else, even God, for one's problems is a childish attitude, has it not?

The first step toward maturity and conscious spiritual evolvement then is to take responsibility for one's life. We must choose to act and think positively, in partnership with the Creative Life Force.

Thus the Master Agasha spoke to us, and was teaching us, as all Masters have through the ages, that we are Divine Beings with the innate ability and Mind to create whatever we choose for ourselves. However, this knowing must be strong enough to be woven into the belief system of the subconscious, as it is the womb of creation. Thus the saying, "Whatsoever the mind can believe — the mind can achieve."

. The emotions play a major role in this process, as they are closely connected through the glandular system to the subconscious mind. Feelings tend to program the subconscious mind quite easily, much more easily than simple thoughts. Thus the emotions and the subconscious play back and forth upon one another, often creating situations, looking back on which, one may say, "I don't know what made me do that," or "I couldn't help myself." Something someone near and dear said, or did, punched a subconscious button, and like a jukebox, we dropped in one of our old records to play its theme.

Usually we aren't even aware of this connection, we only feel the instant emotional reaction and tend to blow a situation up out of all proportion to its present reality, often to the astonishment and puzzlement of others involved.

This recurring problem can be 90% of the trouble with relationships that become rocky. One of the partners, or even both, may have old sore spots from childhood, or even past lives, that their conscious mind has forgotten. It is these sore spots which flare up out of all proportion when certain buttons are punched by a phrase, expression, attitude, on the part of the partner or friend. The hurt has not been forgotten by the subconscious. Oh, no. Not only does it never sleep, it also never forgets until deliberately cleared. Thus the subconscious mind, the seat of the emotions, raises its defenses instantly, in order not to be hurt again.

We often don't know why we became so angry, or perhaps offended, or experience a guilty feeling. We seldom look within ourselves, but tend instead to place the blame outside on the loved one, saying such phrases as, "It's your fault!" or "You always do that to me!" Thus we have a vicious cycle that continues to repeat.

The situation can resolve in two ways. Either the parties become mature enough to look at themselves objectively and become The Watcher, seeing if reactions are appropriate to circumstances, or, as more often happens, they finally split, having achieved no growth in the relationship. If this happens, they may have to go around again in life's arena at some future time.

In reality, sincere and consistent work is needed to reprogram the subconscious mind through prayer and desire, to get to the root of these negative feelings and change them, with the help of Love, to a positive wholesome reaction. Then there can be understanding and freedom at last, and a peaceful relationship.

For if we cannot be at peace with ourselves, how can we be at peace with the world? And as we know only too well, the need for peace in the world has become the one most important priority in these times. There is not much time left — the sand is fast flowing through the hour glass of this Age. Humankind will soon be called to deal with the effects of our causes. And the picture is not a pretty one.

For Master Agasha also told us of the challenge that lay ahead due to man's aggression against man, the trials that would test the mettle of America's people and other countries around the world: mass hunger, economic difficulties, and wars. Since those days of Master Agasha's teachings have come the Korean War, the Viet Nam War, Desert Storm, to name only conflicts of U.S. involvement, not to speak of continued fighting in the Middle East, Ireland, Yugoslavia, Africa, Central and South America and other regions of the globe.

Agasha spoke of coming geographical upheavals, the intensity of which would be increased in part due to dense clouds of negative mass consciousness surrounding our home in space. These upheavals, he said, would cause the death of many, but were part of the inevitable cleansing. Our planet would be moving into a new vibrational dimension, and those elements of greed and selfishness could not survive the new, higher vibrations. These changes, Agasha told us in 1948, would come subtly through the next forty years, becoming more clearly apparent beginning in the late 1980's and early 1990's.

The Hierarchy and all in the Brotherhood of Light are working to bring us through safely, but they need our awakened consciousness, the power of humankinds' prayers for peace and the active cooperation of everyone, to pray and meditate daily in the Light of God's Love.

Since those far off days in the 1940's, when the 1990's seemed a lifetime away to me then, I am happy to say that many groups in America and around the world have heard the call to join forces with the Brotherhood of Light Workers, and the community spirit has spread like wildfire in the past ten to twenty years. It is very encouraging and truly could be the saving grace. The Masters are credited with bringing many of these age-old, long-hidden, teachings back to light once again through guiding the founding of the Masonic Lodge, The Theosophical Society, The Philosophical Research Society, the I AM Foundation, the original Rosicrucians, the Society for Research and Enlightenment (followers of Edgar Cayce teachings), Self-Realization Fellowship, and Astara, to name a very few. All have helped bring illumination to the planet.

In recent years also, new and legitimate spiritual communities have been founded, dedicated to the highest ideals of the Christ Spirit, that have risen not only in North America but around the world. Two of the earliest, largest and most successful communities that have acted as way-showers are the Findhorn Community in Scotland* and the Ananda Community** in Northern California. There are many, many more, too numerous to mention here, led by dedicated inspired souls.

Each of these organizations reaches hundreds and even thousands of students and disciples, helping to bring Light and a higher mental vibration to our planet, that the mass of negativity may be alleviated and dispelled. In this way, help is being given to move more peacefully into the approaching New Dimension.

It would not have been possible to bring these large

The Magic of Findhorn, by Paul Hawken, Harper & Row, N.Y.18022
**Ananda Brotherhood, 14618 Tyler Foote Rd, Nevada City, CA 95959

spiritual organizations into being (and they are still growing), had it not been for the strong guidance of these blessed
masters, working through the founding leaders on this physical
plane. Astara Foundation* in Upland, California has had the
faithful leadership on the physical plane of Drs. Robert and
Earlyne Chaney, spiritually guided from the beginning in
1951 by Master Kuthumi, Master Rama, and the Healer
Pharoah, Zoser. Astara's healing ministry has helped many
hundreds through the years in often miraculous ways, and
continues to be a source of comfort and spiritual fellowship
for me as well as continuing to reach thousands of seekers
around the globe, lo – these forty-plus years.

The Astarian Teachings are available by correspondence
course, comprehensively guiding the student who seeks to
know his/her true relationship to God. Eight Degrees of twenty-
two lessons each address in-depth questions which most fundamental religious teachings do not cover. In addition, both
Dr. Earlyne and Dr. Robert Chaney have written many marvelous and enlightening books dealing with these subjects, and
were among the first teachers of Truth in this century, with
their founding of Astara – a Church of All Religions.

Ananda Community, since its inceptions in 1967, has
had the guidance and blessing of the great Master Paramhansa
Yogananda (1896-1952). Yogananda came from India to
America in 1925 with the mission to help unite East and
West through encouraging mutual appreciation of the best
that both countries had to offer and to awaken in westerners,
through the ancient soul science of Yoga, the desire for
God-Realization, or illumination. In addition to founding
Self-Realization Fellowship, mentioned earlier, Yogananda
envisioned successful self-supporting communities (which
he liked to refer to as World Brotherhood Colonies), with
How-to-Live Schools for children. His dream, though not
realized in his lifetime, has been achieved through his early
disciple, Donald Walters, a.k.a. Swami Kriyananda, founder
of Ananda Community, together with the dedication of many
others who gathered round through the thirty years since in

*Astara, 800 West Arrow Hwy., P. O. Box 5003, Upland, CA 91785-5003.

this great work.

May I interject here a glance into the future and say that as the Divine Plan would have it, many years later, in 1972, our eldest son, at the age of sixteen heard the call of Spirit and joined the Ananda Community. 'Jeremy' graduated from Ananda's High School and, after attaining a college degree in literature, returned there to teach. More recently his sister, 'Jeannine,' in 1990 also answered the inner call and has become a disciple and student. Thus the gentle Master from India, whom I had had the privilege of seeing in person in the early 1940's, has touched my life in a very personal way.

Yogananda's teachings have been a Lighted Torch of Truth igniting flames that are spreading across America and the world. There are Ananda Centers now in many cities, plus a thriving Retreat Center at Assisi, Italy, bringing these life-changing teachings of Yoga Philosophy and Self-Realization to the thousands who yearn for the truth of God's love.

Yogananda recommended daily meditation, always at the same hour if possible, that we may become more sensitive to receiving the uplifting vibrations that the Teacher seeks to bring. Meditation finely attunes us to our own inner center, as well as to divine guidance.

It has been said that an atheist is one who has no invisible means of support. It is sad to think that love and guidance, as well as the truest friendship ever attainable is only a thought away, but few among the multitudes avail themselves of it. I am urged to write, to share these wonderful truths, but I pray that those who read may have ears to hear.

The Blessed Lord Jesus is our Master among masters in the Christian world, and yet He walks with the masters of all religions, for they are all members of the Great White Brotherhood of Light, who work in devoted unison for the peace and glory of planet earth and all the children upon it.

During those early years, while attending the classes, I was introduced to Emil Spaulding's books, *The Life and*

---

* *The Life and Teachings of the Masters of the Far East*, by Baird T. Spalding 1927, California Press, San Francisco, CA

*Teachings of the Masters of the Far East.** The novels of
Marie Corelli also fascinated me — stories that were far more
than novels, with mystical truths providing the warp and
woof of the engaging themes. They held me spellbound. So
began my serious study of the writings of the wise ones who
had traveled ahead on the path to becoming, and my journey became one of greater enchantment with each passing
year. Attending Agasha's Master Lectures had opened a new
horizon to life that offered conscious understanding, and
confirmation, of what I had instinctively felt within, plus
much, much more.

The vista, glimpsed through the eyes of spirit, is beautiful and unending, for at each plateau of awakening one
discovers another mountain to climb, another opportunity
for growth. It is exciting to find that you can evolve as far as
you can dream and aspire. It was clearly shown, however,
that the lessons learned must be applied to daily living —
and carry the responsibilities thereof, for if one knows the
truth and the Law, but fails to live it, he /she may suffer more
remorse for time lost than one who never learned it at all.

Truly, I had been led by God's grace and love to these
wonderful studies, led from my roots in a small midwest
village, where in my meditations I had faithfully followed
guidance to 'ask', 'seek' and 'knock.'

God is always centered in us — it is our need to be
centered in Him.

All the while I continued my work as secretary to the
County Administrator and later in the Office of the Board of
Supervisors of Los Angeles County as it provided the steady
income I needed to survive. The Universe always seeks
balance, and it is well to tend the areas of life that may not
be so glamorous, but that build a practical foundation, and
in the process, one's character.

A highlight of those years was the honor of being named
Miss Los Angeles County of 1947. A nice picture of me
appeared in the Los Angeles Times, along with a story on
the phenomenal growth of that glamorous city and county
on America's west coast. I was pleased that my ability and
hard work was respected in the office and I especially appreci-

ated the fine calibre of all the men I had the privilege to work with, not only my Greek-god boss, who made the days a joy by his good humor and appreciation of everyone, but all the men who had a kind word or a joke to lighten the load for us hard working secretaries when some days were extra burdensome. These gentlemen were very much higher on the ladder of male esteem than the men I had encountered in the movie industry.

One day the big boss, General Wayne Allen, who was the Chief Administrative Officer for the County, called me into his office to show me a letter from a judge from Dade County, Florida, interestingly also named Wayne Allen. The Judge Wayne Allen was writing to compliment our General Allen on "not only having the distinguished name of Wayne Allen, but of having in your employ one Miss Beckington, whose sultry tones and intriguing whistling ability I was privileged to hear over the airwaves on my car radio the other evening, when she performed on the Kay Kaiser Show. Please give that charming young lady my compliments!" General Allen actually seemed a bit surprised and even proud, as he offered the letter to me with a grand flourishing sweep of his arm. I was, of course, secretly pleased to receive acclaim for other accomplishments than my secretarial skills from a quite unexpected source.

But even as I basked in the sunshine of approval from various quarters, I was becoming more aware that I could not continue to pursue two careers. My health was not sturdy enough to carry both and do justice to either. The old back injury, sustained in my youth, left a sometimes recurring pain, and at times I battled anemia. A serious musical career would entail training which cost both money and time I did not have, while the business world, in which I was doing well, was paying for rent and food plus making possible the small savings needed to fly home once again to see my parents.

And so it was that Destiny led me away from the stage. In later years I understood why. We all have a Soul Plan when we come to this earth, whether we are aware of it or not, that carries us on a wave of experiences that close some doors and open others, all necessary for the soul's growth and learning at various points in time. Our lives may not unfold according to the plan we thought we had at all. In fact, challenges can appear which we never dreamed of.

Many may be surprised to know that they had already chosen a lifeplan before coming into this body, a plan they are not consciously aware of. This spiritual blueprint can be a very powerful force in life, a magnet that sweeps one down often uncharted and unexpected pathways to astonishing experiences. It has been jokingly said that, "Life is what happens to you while you are busy making other plans."

There is always free will, however, our gift from the Creator, which allows us to choose if we will intuitively go with inner guidance or choose to go against divine flow, allowing ego to demand its own way. The latter choice can create a tangled tale that may take years, sometimes centuries, to unravel. And so, if we can accept what comes to us in life with grace and good cheer, always holding our highest goal in the mind's eye, while making the best of those experiences we cannot change, then it will be shown to us one day that each experience of our life has been exactly what we needed at that particular time, each event an essential link in the chain of events, all moving in the proper direction — in our journey to becoming that beautiful Being we were created to be.

194

✳

C H A P T E R   F I V E

A NEW WOMAN, A NEW MAN
AND A NEW LIFE

The flight home to Illinois had been a most marvelous experience: my first plane trip. To look down upon the majestic Rocky Mountains and on the plains of midwest farmland, cut into colorful, many shaded squares of green, gold and brown, had been a thrill, especially since the plane flew so low over the land. Now, three months later, I was returning to Los Angeles. After nine hours of flight, wrapped in the drone of the 1940's propeller-driven plane, I woke drowsily to see a glow in the sky. I pressed my nose hard against the glass of the window beside me and could hardly believe the sight that met my eyes. Far below, against the dark blue velvet of an early evening sky, a glorious fairyland of sparkling jewels spread as far as the eye could see. I gasped in amazement. The early evening twinkling lights of the city lay far ahead and stretched out on all sides like a sequinned fan, its bright jewels spread to the very horizon.

There is no city in America that covers an area comparable to Greater Los Angeles. I could see from the edge of San Bernardino in the east, to the Pacific shores in the west. The metropolis spread below me like a science-fiction city of another planet — over 150 miles of solid lights cut into geometric patterns by the here-and-there red, orange and green strings of major boulevards. It was a sight I shall never forget. In 1947 the night air was clear as crystal and the beauty was almost unearthly. One could understand why it was named the City of Angels. My heart leaped, as I had come to love my new home, and seeing it spread out like this below me, it seemed all the more wonderful.

Upon arriving, I found that June and Hal were planning to move to a smaller house. It was the right time, in any case, to look for larger living quarters of my own — an apartment I decided, now that my job was secure. Well! Easier said than done. It was like looking for a needle in a haystack. In my recent security I had forgotten the shortage of living space due to the immense population influx.

After a number of weeks I got a lucky break. A contractor chap I had met and dated a few times was remodeling the home of Lloyd Mangrum, the nationally known golfer, converting some rooms of their home into a small furnished apartment which they planned to rent out. Lloyd Mangrum and his wife traveled on the national golf circuit ten months out of every year and they wanted their home to have a lived-in look during their absences. Bob went to bat for me, giving them a consideration on the cost of the remodeling if they agreed to rent it to him when finished. Bob then subleased it to me.

I was elated! It was just the right size, with a nice bright and airy studio room plus kitchen and bath, all on the main floor. It's private entrance faced a secluded fenced backyard for sunbathing. I finally had my own little nest to add touches to as I pleased, and all brand-new. Oh Joy!

The year was 1948. Lloyd Mangrum won the National Open Golf Tournament. What excitement! He became famous overnight, as had his friend, Ben Hogan, who held the title for several years running in that decade. I felt my home was special — not just your run-of-the-mill apartment. It was in a lovely quiet neighborhood near Highland Boulevard, boasting wide sunny streets with lush tropical plantings, and with easy bus access to my job in the Civic Center downtown.

Immediately I rented a piano, moved it in and played and whistled to my heart's content without having to worry about disturbing others. It was real quiet for my meditation time. It wasn't long, however, before I began to think of finding a compatible apartment-mate to share costs and companionship, as expenses ran higher than expected, even then.

I advertised for female only, and no less than eighteen girls answered the first week. What an interesting array. There were short girls, tall girls, sophisticated beauties who smoked, and plain girls who didn't. To interview with an eye toward a roomy who would be as close as breathing for most of my at-home time, and who would share interests similar to mine as well, was quite a challenge. I decided to ask my intuition to tell me who would be the right one in this all important choice. One evening a girl came who really stood out above the rest. After her visit I continued to receive others who had called and applied, but somehow I could *see* no one else, for her distinctive face kept floating before me, even while I spoke with new applicants. She was the one, hands down. I phoned her.

Evelyn was a smaller edition of Sophia Loren, and seemed even more beautiful. Her wide-set eyes were large and golden hazel; her hair, a deep red-brown copper color, was cut classically in a straight and shining soft page-boy bob. As she strolled about, examining the quarters, her every move exuded class. I noted that her smooth, tawny tan body was like one of the jet-set who spend their days on their yachts in the sun. From her manner and astute questions, it was also apparent Evelyn was very intelligent, a quality I appreciated. For me it was love at first sight, and we began then a joyous and rewarding friendship that included not only four years as perfect apartment mates, but has extended to a lifelong friendship of over forty-five years.

My intuition fully answered my call to help me make the right choice. We have long since adopted one another as family. Such friendships, for anyone, are indeed a blessing and come only too rarely in life. Since I had been an only child, to have a friend who was truly a soul-sister, and with whom I could share secrets of my heart, was indeed a great happiness, and a blessing I would wish for everyone.

Evelyn hailed from Montana, so we had our mid-America roots in common, as well. She appreciated music and literature; we hit it off like two peas in a pod. I can honestly say that in four years of being under the same roof we never had even one disagreement over anything. We were totally different in many basic ways: I was tall, slender and blonde, open and enthusiastic, knowing no strangers, while she seemed more quietly mysterious and sultry with a kind of sexy magnetism behind those almond eyes that always attracted men. We each admired qualities in the other that we ourselves did not have, so together we were harmonious. Sometimes we double-dated, always asking upon meeting a new chap, whether or not he had a friend for the other.

We enjoyed the theater and Hollywood Bowl Concerts especially, as in all the West the Bowl was unique with its outdoor setting, magical music floating crystal clear under a canopy of velvet blue sky laced with stars. But mostly we took great joy in simple pleasures, like taking walks down the quiet residential streets in the warm summer evenings when the scent of night-blooming jasmine hung heavy in the air and one became heady with the rich perfume. Orange blossom, too, mixed with the jasmine, for in those early years, smog was a word seldom heard, perhaps only read in a rare report. Generally the air was clear and sweet, the perfume of many flowers wafting on the evening breezes which blew off the ocean to the west. We took pleasure in attempting to identify the various tropical scents, many of which were foreign to our inland upbringing. Truly, it was a heavenly, happy time when life held a minimum of responsibilities.

It was during this carefree period that we first discovered my psychic ability, quite by accident. In the evenings after our walks, Evelyn and I would sometimes relax before bedtime, sharing tea and cookies. We used loose herbal tea, which leaves leaf-grounds scattered in the bottom of the cup.

One evening in a relaxed mood, I picked up and gazed idly into Evelyn's empty cup, thinking of nothing in particular. Pictures seemed to form among the leaves and unusual thoughts popped into my mind with the pictures. That evening I recall exclaiming, "There's a large bouquet of flowers in your cup tonight — all colors. Isn't that interesting?" Then, guess what — the very next evening her boyfriend (of the moment) showed up on our steps carrying a huge spring bouquet to present to her, of all colors and varieties! He had never brought any before, nor had Evelyn even mentioned that she liked flowers. We looked at each other, astonished at the coincidence. And he, poor fellow, stood there puzzled at our delighted laughter over his love offering. I don't recall that we ever did explain to him.

There were other times when scenes from Evelyn's childhood years appeared to me, certain pets and events of note in Montana, even the physical appearance and characteristics of her mother, whom I had never seen and who was deceased. It became a kind of entertainment for us, nothing serious, and I thought little of it.

One night, however, I gazed into her cup and surprised, I found myself asking, "What in the world are you doing riding in a gondola on a canal in Venice, dabbling your hands in the water alongside?"

We chuckled with amusement, thinking this time my vivid imagination had gone too far. We forgot all about this incident, but, three years later, in 1951 my interesting friend, Evelyn, suddenly chose to sign up with the U.S State Department. Being a natural linguist, she was flown to Washington, D.C., trained for six weeks, then sent to Florence, Italy to work in the American Consulate there. Soon after Evelyn arrived in Italy and settled into her work, she began exploring other cities and hill towns. One day I received in the mail a really mammoth postcard. The colorful picture was of a large and lovely black and gold gondola, floating gracefully down the Royal Canal of Venice, with a gondolier in distinctive costume artfully guiding its glide. On the back of the card Evelyn had written one ecstatic sentence, " Here I am! And just for the record, I believe in your tea leaves!" I have kept that card to this day.

Evelyn's frequent long letters soon were filled with the fascinating wonders and beauty of her new surroundings: the romantic River Arno flowing lazily through the center of Florence, the palaces of dukes and princes, containing famous statues and the wondrous art of the Renaissance, the Ponte Vechio — that most famous bridge over the Arno, housing shops filled with precious gold, silver, and leather goods. Evelyn wrote of elegant shops on narrow winding streets that displayed the handiwork of hundreds of artisans. I read her letters over and over, almost memorizing every word. To a young girl in her early twenty's, back in 1951, who felt lucky just to have come to California, Evelyn's tales from the other side of the world were like an astounding dream.

Years later upon finally visiting Italy, I had the unreal feeling of having already been there, as I gazed upon sights she had so carefully described that they had become vividly etched in my mind's eye. And yet, I also had the weird and unreal feeling that I had come home once again, but that I will explain later.

My lovely friend had a full and interesting career with the U.S. State Department, which took her to posts in Yugoslavia, Brazil and Canada. She also worked in the U.S. Consulate under Claire Booth Luce in Rome, while Mrs. Luce was American Ambassadress to Italy. The variety of Evelyn's work included hostessing foreign diplomats at evening receptions, so Evelyn's language expertise was very necessary.

While in Florence Evelyn met and was courted by a handsome and brilliant young Italian medical student. They later married. He has since become a Doctor/Professor, Director of the Neurology Department of Johns Hopkins University Hospital in Bologna, Italy. Later, upon retiring from the U.S.State Department, Evelyn served as Registrar of Johns Hopkins University in Bologna for several years. As of this writing, Evelyn and Giancarlo have lived happily in Bologna for forty years.

I must tell you one other rather important thing I saw in Evelyn's teacup those evenings. The pictures plainly showed me that she would never have children, but I did not tell her that. It seemed harsh and unkind, for most women desire children, and then too, I hoped I might be wrong. But now, after forty years of marriage, Evelyn and Giancarlo never have had children. Interesting — those tea leaves.

Those years in the apartment on Highland Avenue remain a joyful, bright ray among the colorful memories of my life. Evelyn and I experienced a communion of souls, feeling contentment in natural gentle friendship without the need even to converse, and yet finding uplifting energy, humor and joy in sharing everyday happenings. Truly a good friend is a gift from God and not to be taken lightly, but to be appreciated, for many people never know that grace.

And so, the months slipped past. I continued working, playing music some evenings, and on other evenings I attended the philosophy and metaphysical classes at the Agashan Temple. These were a great source of inspiration, and I appreciated the unique friendships I made there.

One bronzed, curly-haired young man in his twenties was of special interest. Eddie was vivacious, artistic, open and disarmingly charming. He had skated for a number of years with the world-famous Sonja Heinie Ice Follies until he fell and broke his knee, which brought an abrupt end to that career. Eddie since became a well-known artist, creating beautiful original bowls of colorful enamel on copperware that are shown in some of the finest gift shops in the world, and were purchased by such world figures as Queen Elizabeth II of England. Verna was another special friend, a unique soul whom I met at the Agashan classes. Verna was a woman of depth who possessed rare spiritual insight and wisdom. I mention this as both she and Eddie figured significantly in a rather startling psychic event the three of us had several years later.

Meanwhile, back at the apartment, before our lives separated so dramatically, while Evelyn and I dated a few nice fellows, there seemed to be no man of the calibre that seriously interested me, for I had subconsciously set pretty high standards in my desires. The only chap I'd seen who fit them was the handsome, and oh-so-intelligent Greek god with the winning smile and warm personality I was privileged to call my boss — and that man was married. In my heart I somehow knew that destiny had already chosen the man that was to be my husband, and when the time was right he would appear. So I was not unduly concerned or out hunting, as were many young women of the day.

*
PAPA LEAVES THIS EARTH

In the spring of 1951, I awakened with a start. The dream-vision was still so real I felt I could step right back into it. My body tingled and every hair on my head prickled. I lay in wonder at the intensity of it. It had been vivid, brightly colorful, leaving me with a strange other-world sensation. Unlike most dreams, wispy, fading seconds after awakening, the clarity of this dream carried through that day, the week, and has endured for more than forty years.

That morning I lay very still in bed, retracing the scenes of the dream in my mind. The setting had been the Illinois farm home of my Aunt Millicent, my mother's youngest sister who was then a matron with grown children. In my dream-vision it was a bright spring day. I was alone, swinging in a swing we had enjoyed as children in her yard. Suddenly I felt an urge to go into the house. The rooms were all empty until I reached the living room. It, too, was empty except for a desk. To my surprise, seated at the desk was my father.

"Child," he said, "go bring pen and paper. I wish to make out my will."

Leaving the room, I fetched the desired items and returned. But as I approached the threshold of the living room, I saw to my horror it was no longer my father seated at the desk, but Death, The Grim Reaper, with ashen white skull, and black holes for eyes and nose, above grisly teeth. This skull peered out at me from under the black hood, heavy black drapery falling around it to the floor, as it sat there at the desk. The arms stretched toward me and long bone-white skeletal fingers groped for the pen and paper. Aghast, I could go no closer. I bent down and slid the paper and pen across the floor toward the desk. Then I turned and fled outside.

The scene suddenly changed. I stood behind the house in the morning sunlight, looking across the field. The grassy hillside was intensely green, on it brown and white Guernsey and Jersey cows grazed contentedly under trees which arched against the sky. Then, into this lovely scene strode my father, appearing again in his normal mature physical form. He quickly hiked up and over the hilltop, waving to me as he disappeared from my sight, and then all was stillness. At this point I awakened, my scalp tingling, and feeling a strange immediacy.

Could this dream mean what it seemed to mean, I wondered? It was an ominous feeling. Mama had written that caring for Papa had become more strenuous with each passing day.

Yes. Exactly three weeks to the night of my dream Papa passed from this earth-life and made his transition to higher realms. The all-knowing spirit had quite obviously warned me, with a picture-prophecy.

Something about the dream puzzled me. Why had the setting been my Aunt Millicent's farm home, but she nowhere in sight? Why not our own village home where my parents now lived, or our farm recently left? Strangely, the answer came only a few years later, as my Aunt Millicent was unfortunately the next member of our family to pass. She had contracted cancer. It was unexpected and shocking, as she was the youngest of all nine in Mama's family, as I have said.

So, my vision had, in its symbolic way, given me the prophecy of two deaths, my father's and my Aunt Millicent's, for it had been in her empty house I had seen the Grim Reaper. Millicent was still young and her death was sad indeed. She was the first of many poignant losses of beloved family and friends to the horror of cancer. In the years immediately after, I was to see no less than fourteen family members and friends contract cancer, and every last one passed away slowly and painfully under the current medical treatments of surgery and/or chemotherapy. There had to be a better answer. It was at that time I began a personal search for an answer to cancer, for I knew it was not a loving God's will that so many should suffer such a painful and demeaning death.

I prepared to fly home to my father's funeral service. His death was a shock, but I was relieved that my mother was, at long last, free of the care that had become a heavy drain on her health. I worried about Mama, and now I again had to take leave from work to return to Illinois. It was at this same time that Evelyn announced her State Department plans and told me she had been called to report to Washington, D.C., and she, too, was soon to fly away. "Breaking up is hard to do . . ." as the song goes, even for platonic friends, but life is there to be faced, and we do what we must, as our destiny unfolds.

Mama was worn and tired, showing the effects of her long and faithful vigil. She stood up well to Papa's passing, for our knowledge of the continuity of life caused our family to never grieve unduly when someone graduated to the Higher Life if they had lived long and full, and the time was not premature. In reality, this time of graduation should be a time for rejoicing, and it is a shame that so many unenlightened folks still go into deep and prolonged grief, thinking it to be the end.

In her inimitable way and much to my delight, Evelyn made time to come through Illinois to visit all of us for a few days and say a last goodbye to me on her way to Washington, D.C. During the years of our acquaintance I had described to Evelyn the individual characteristics of my various relatives, their idiosyncracies and eccentricities. Now, we laughed at how well the *real people* she was meeting fit her mental images. I thought to myself, a little sadly, oh, how I will miss Evie's wonderful humor. She always had an active interest in people, and had adopted my family in her imagination as though they were her own. She would, for instance, cook up a dish and then ask, "Is this the way Aunt Henrietta would have made it?" For my Aunt H. was a superb cook and the head chef of a fine country golf club.

Destiny has a way of quietly changing our lives.

Shortly after Papa's funeral service, I was seated on the sofa, resting and reading in my Aunt Elsie's house when a tall, good-looking man walked through the front door unannounced, as though it were his home.

"Hello," he said in a gentle, softly modulated tone. "You must be Bonnie Ann. I had expected to meet you. I'm Allen."

Lifting my eyes from my book, I was momentarily puzzled, but then I recalled that Aunt Elsie had spoken of a man to whom she had given room and board for over a year, but who traveled in his work. In the rush of events surrounding my father's passing, I had forgotten this. He was, he said, just returning from a trip to Wisconsin.

"I had hoped to return before you left, as I've heard so much about you."

This left me slightly at a disadvantage as I didn't wish to admit I had heard virtually nothing about him. Quickly scanning the figure before me, I was surprised to find I was impressed with what I saw — his face was handsome, but also his physique. He was broad-shouldered and there was a natural dignity in his bearing. He was blonde, but tan, his facial features were perfect in symmetry, with a rather high forehead and hairline, and a perfect mouth that curved upward in the corners in a kind of cupid's-bow, even when he wasn't smiling. His gaze was direct and clear. I felt instantly that I could trust this man, but otherwise, I felt nothing dynamic in our meeting. He was handsome, thirtyish, and a gentleman.

"Don't let me disturb you," he continued. "I'm sure we'll meet again later."

Little did I know then what events that seemingly insignificant encounter would trigger. The amazing thing about life is that every day is a surprise package. Sometimes what's under the wrapper seems plain, but it is never wise to judge any day as unimportant, for it could prove a most precious link in our unseen chain of destiny.

The following week was filled with helping Mama to plan and adjust to her new situation, entertaining and talking delightedly with Evelyn who had arrived, and being dined in the homes of various relatives. I saw hardly anything at all of Allen, and, frankly, thought no more about him. He had been present at one of the evening gatherings, but did not enter conversation, sitting quietly and courteously in one corner of the room, respecting the family occasion of my father's passing.

Evelyn and I had arranged for our planes to depart the

same day, within an hour of each other, one flying east, the other west. Uncle Harold planned to drive us the two-hour trip to the Chicago Airport seventy miles away. Again, Destiny stepped in. That very day Uncle's car broke down and there was no time to repair it. What were we to do? Most folks were away working and Mama still did not drive, but suddenly she brightened.

"I've got it! We'll ask Allen to drive you girls in!"

"Oh No, Mama! I hardly know the gentleman," I protested. "I cannot ask him!"

"Then I shall ask him," she flatly stated. And so she did. (Mama never was a shrinking violet.) Allen was instantly and courteously agreeable. "Certainly, I have the time," he told her. "It would be an honor." Good heavens! I felt reluctant to impose on an almost stranger.

My cousin Don came along for company and the drive was pleasant and uneventful. Allen said very little, but made enormous sense when he did offer an opinion, and I found a subtle admiration growing in me for this quiet-spoken, dignified man who was every inch a gentleman. We talked mainly of the exciting adventure looming in Evelyn's life as she entered the State Department, and of what mysteries that might entail.

I found, upon questioning him, that Allen had recently re-enlisted in the Army. The year was 1951 and the U.S. had by then decided to fight militarily against communism and gone to the aid of South Korea. Allen said he felt it was his duty as a single man to help protect the freedom of our country for the future of his nieces and nephews and all other young people. Drafted in 1940 when he was twenty two, Allen had fought through World War II, having seen duty in Italy battling the Nazi's, and had come out a Captain, and alive. (I found later he had had some harrowing near misses with death, but he did not speak of that this day, for he was reticent to speak of himself.) He had now been a civilian only a few years.

At the airport while we awaited our departure, a family with a little three-year old girl sat near us. I was interested to see that Allen talked with her, keeping her happy while her mother wrestled with baggage and tickets, etc. I thought he looked rather sad, yearning, as he gazed at the little girl. He told me he missed seeing his own nieces and nephews, who were six in number.

At my gate Evelyn and I exchanged a nostalgic farewell. It was our inevitable parting of the ways. As my plane took to the air, and I left my old midwest home behind, I found myself overwhelmed by a sudden and inexplicable wave of grief. It took me completely by surprise. The tears flowed in a steady stream and sobs shook my body. I was relieved that the seat next to me was empty. I didn't understand this deep trauma that was rising in my breast.

Was it because of my father's passing? No. I had not been aware of grief through the past week, for in fact, I was grateful for his release from a worn-out body, freeing my poor mother from her heavy bondage of nursing him. Was it because of parting from Evelyn? No. I had long since become reconciled to this and I was happy for the new life opening for her. Granted, I did not relish returning to an empty apartment, but that prospect certainly didn't warrant this flood of tears and inner grief.

Searching my feelings, I was amazed to realize that it was Allen I wept for. I hardly knew this gentle man. He had made no personal advance of any kind to me, and on my part I was not even aware of an attraction to him. I was not reluctant to leave him. Rather, I simply felt a huge sadness sweeping over me as I connected with his life. I was amazed to find myself longing to give him a little girl to bring him joy, for I knew intuitively this man had suffered a great deal in his life and deserved some happiness. I believe I had tapped into the sadness he carried within. Now, because of his patriotism, he was returning again to war, this time to Korea. I wondered why I had such a spontaneous and intense emotional compassion for this man? There had been no noticeable physical spark that I was aware of. My feelings came from some deep inner level over which my *mind* had little control.

Life and Time have a way of bringing answers, often surprises we least expect. I didn't dream of it then, but in a short nine months I would become Allen's wife.

*
OUT OF THE BLUE — A PROPOSAL

It seemed like it came about almost by accident — for it happened so fast! I must write Allen, I thought, now that I was safely back to Los Angeles, to thank him for his kindness in driving Evelyn and me to the airport. My letter was simple and courteous. His re-enlistment had activated and he'd been sent to Ft. Sill, Oklahoma, an Artillery Training Base, as Allen had been an artilleryman in W.W.II. He responded immediately to my note with a beautiful letter that was impressive in both its style and content. I read it over several times. He wanted to hear from me again and his plea was very touching. How could I not respond?

Military correspondence was not new to me. (You will recall that in my younger years I had written to fifteen young men during World War II to help cheer them with letters from home.) But Allen's letters were entirely different than any I had received over those years. They were exceptional. Every line revealed a mind that was well-educated, but not egotistical, a person who was well-read, observant of nature and people around him, and possessed of a unique ability to communicate his observations in colorful and brilliant phrases. He drew word-pictures so clearly, that in reading them I could see what he saw. He wrote of places he had been, the people and sights he had seen in Europe, and described his impressions of where he was now stationed. I was surprised, even amazed, and continued to write to him.

Through the following four months of correspondence I found a man whose mind fascinated me. His gentle reflections portrayed a spirit of idealism similar to my own, tempered with faith that one seldom meets in today's materialistic world. His letters contained humor, everyday happenings dressed up with pen and ink to intrigue and amuse me. No run of the mill person — this man.

Soon the letters contained words of tenderness and beauty, as he was able to express his feelings in ways that I sensed he never could have spoken aloud, for he had a certain innate shyness that kept him verbally reticent. On paper, with pen and ink, he felt free — and his true spirit became visible.

We had met in March. Already in July a letter came with a sweet entreaty, a proposal of marriage! "Before I leave for Korea in early January, I will come to Los Angeles, to you."

I could hardly believe what I was reading. He was asking me to be his wife! And this year! But how could I? I had met him only four months before. It was true, I admired his mind and his character — this was a real man, husband material if there ever was. But a woman has to feel more than admiration — she has to feel love. I hardly had time with him, just one short ride to the airport. How could I be a wife when we hadn't had a single date? This was amazing. I had not so much as looked at him sideways at home in Illinois, much less said or done anything that he could have construed as encouragement. He told me later that while he lived in the home of my aunt, he had heard about me for eighteen months, and thus came to know me and admire me. But I hadn't had the same advantage.

"Well!" I exclaimed to myself, "Of course I cannot marry this man. I do not know him! He'd shown me an inkling of his mind and his spirit, but I didn't *know* him." It frightened me even to think of it.

So I sat down to struggle over a letter to him that would not be harsh or hurtful, suggesting postponing the decision, until he returned from Korea.

But my frightened girlish ideas were inconsequential to the Divine Plan. Soon after mailing that letter, I had another startling dream. It was simple, yet very clear. I saw nothing, but a voice which seemed to be The Beloved Presence, strong, clear, and not to be questioned, instructed me.

"You are to marry this man for he needs you, as he will die." I awoke with a start. My every cell was alert and tingling, as I scanned my moonlit flooded bedroom to see if someone was standing there — but there was no one. The commanding, yet gentle voice still rang in my ears. Everything was the same as it had always been. There was my writing desk with the vase of flowers, and my dresser and bookcase. And there were my clothes, laid out for work in the morning. Yet suddenly, everything was different. I felt that I must obey that command spoken so clearly in my mind, and I knew that it would change my life. Was this the way Joseph had heard the voice from God? The voice who told him to arise and flee with the Child into Egypt? Surely it must be, for this voice was just as commanding and just as real.

It then occurred to me with a shock that if the voice was right, Allen would not return from the war in Korea. I realized now the sadness, Allen's sadness, I had felt so deeply as I flew home from Illinois. Maybe I was to give this man a little of the happiness he deserved before leaving this earth plane. His life had been hard. He had written that in the recent years since returning from Europe and World War II, he had lived at home in Columbia, Missouri with his elderly parents. He had cared for them, nursing his father who suffered cancer, until his death, while also finishing his schooling at the University of Missouri where he attained a degree in Agriculture and was awarded Phi Beta Kappa.

After his father's passing he came to Illinois to work in agricultural sales, settling there in my hometown. He'd had little time for socializing or the joyful side of youth. Allen's life had been one of struggle and hardship. There were six children, his father was often ill and Allen carried much of the load of supplying the family. Then came the war and he was sent off to fight at a very tender age. He'd had some narrow brushes with death in Italy. His jeep was blown up, along with his driver, before his horrified eyes, barely moments after he had gotten out to walk on ahead because of an uneasy feeling, to check for mines.

So, obeying the voice in my dream, (although I did not tell him of it), and following my own resolve as well, I wrote to Allen again, courageously accepting his proposal of marriage.

This fine man came to Los Angeles in December of 1951 to claim me as his bride. He had obtained a leave in order to be married before shipping out to Korea. He was visibly and tremulously shaking as he kissed me for the very first time. I felt myself moving as in a dream scenario. Could this be real? And, in the midst of this dream another dream was coming true.

Wonderfully, my dear Mama arrived from Illinois, just a month before Allen, in answer to my prayer that she come to live here. It was the fulfillment of my yearning for six long years — to have her see the sunshine and beauty and wonder of California. Now that Papa was gone she was free to rent her home and escape the cold midwest winters.

Mama was delighted with it all, just as I had been, and would you believe, she went on living in California for twenty-five years? When she arrived she was sixty-four years old. When I joyously met her at the train, her appearance was of an elderly lady, tired, careworn from the many years' burden of nursing Papa and holding things together. I felt so sad to see her *lost* expression. But she soon perked up, for like me, she felt she had arrived in heaven.

Would you believe, within a year's time, with sunshine and rest and some fun, Mama was looking at least twenty years younger. I was overjoyed. She could pass for forty-five any time, with a bubbling personality that others enjoyed. Mama was so happy during those years. She joined an Authors' Club, and later published a book of her own. She attended musicals and lectures, hearing nationally known speakers, but above all Mama loved people. She easily made many interesting friends, delighting in the new horizons and experiences. Not once did she ever express a desire to go back to live in Illinois.

Mama had enough experiences of her own to fill several books. In addition to her published work, two of her manuscripts have remained unpublished. She always was quite a gal, as I've already indicated, being my first teacher of philosophy and the mystical. Southern California had always been avant garde in this area, so naturally she was in Seventh Frog Heaven, reading new books and attending new churches and lectures at every opportunity. You might as well turn a little kid loose in a candy store as to introduce Mama to Southern California in the early 1950's. She lived it to the fullest.

It was God's grace that brought her out to me just a month before Allen arrived; so, to my joy, Mama was there to attend my small and intimate wedding.

It was, I thought, a unique marriage in anyone's book. Allen arrived at my door wearing his military uniform on a Tuesday evening and kissed me for the first time. Wednesday we got our marriage license and on Thursday, December 13th, we were married in Christ Church Unity. We had never even had the pleasure of a date. This had to be some kind of record! It seemed wonderful and yet strange after waiting so many years for the right one. I was twenty-six years old and Allen was thirty-four, so ostensibly, we were responsible adults by now, but our courtship had been entirely on paper and thus was a real gamble. But apparently, in God's Book it was not. In a way, I mused, I had an edge on other girls, for I could keep for years all the sweet things my lover had written to me in his letters, and take them out to read again when there came a time (and I knew there would be) when I was left alone. The spoken word is gone with the breeze and often remains only vaguely in one's memory, but Allen's words of love had come to me in a form that would last.

Our wedding, performed by white-haired and majestic Dr. Ernest Wilson, a legend among ministers, was a quiet one. As though by divine arrangement, a favorite cousin from Illinois and her husband happened to be passing through Southern California on their vacation, so conveniently they stood up with us as best man and brides' matron. Through the ceremony the feeling that I was in a dream grew stronger.

Anyone who has not been a bride cannot understand the waves of feeling that washed over me. There was trepidation bordering on fright. *What am I doing!* There was excitement and joy. I'm marrying a wonderful man. But lurking behind the veil of the unknown is the question, "What lies ahead with this man I barely know?" The instructions from Spirit had been explicit. So whatever it was, I knew it would be for the good of all. I must obey. I truly was going on faith, as I always had done.

I looked at my new husband. He was the essence of

caring and consideration, and *so* handsome in his Army
Captain's uniform. At six-feet, two-inches he towered over
me and I must admit to feeling somewhat proud. I thought,
if only the girls back home who had long since married
hometown or farm boys could see me now. Isn't that just
like a young girl?

Allen had six weeks leave before having to report to
the Port of Seattle where he would embark for Korea by
ship. The plan was to take our honeymoon driving back to
Missouri to meet his mother and two of his four sisters and
their families who lived nearby. It seemed strange somehow
that I should be marrying a man whose family I had never
met, but I knew many others had done this through history
and especially in war-time. To my surprise, Allen told me
that his mother was the oldest living member of Unity Church
in Kansas City, and had known the founders, Myrtle and
Charles Filmore personally. I thought that to be a remarkable coincidence, and it helped my inner quakings a great
deal with regard to meeting my new mother-in-law.

A lovely wedding supper party was hosted in Pasadena
by a few of my friends. I was in a daze and do not in any way
recall what was served. Mama kissed me goodbye with a
tear in her eye and we were off on our honeymoon.

As we drove down the coast to Laguna Beach where I
had made arrangements for a cottage on the ocean, I saw
through the window the most huge and brilliant harvest
moon I have ever seen before or since lying right on the
horizon directly ahead. It was astonishing, almost like another world hanging in our earth's orbit, so close and a
brilliant orange. Guiding our way all along the coast highway, it seemed a celestial wedding gift to me. I relaxed
against Allen's side in a warm glow of tenderness. It was a
new feeling and I silently prayed that I would be given a
deep love to help me to be a good wife. There had been
growing in me for some time a sincere respect for this
gentle, yet strong man with high ideals. (I now know respect to be the real seed of true love, the kind of love that
lasts and grows ever deeper through the years.) Respect and
admiration are not built upon a passion that flares hot as a

grass fire on the prairie, but then as quickly dies. Respect, rather, is the enduring flame that remains in the heart to warm a marriage through the cold blasts of any and all circumstances.

We continued on through the twilight, bathed by the golden red glow of our huge harvest moon, each savoring in reflective silence, the reality of this moment in time that was changing both our lives. There was an unearthly dream-like quality about that drive. Was this really me? Was this really happening? To whom, and what, had I committed the rest of my life? I felt like I was silently floating in a boat, headed for the falls.

Suddenly we arrived at our destination. As Allen went to the office to check in, I gazed out across the moonlit beach at the string of shadowed cottages overlooking an ocean that sparkled with diamond points of reflected moonlight, here and there swathed white with the foam of incoming waves. The dark ocean seemed to reflect an endless unfathomed universe that held secrets, yet veiled to mortal eyes.

Allen walked back toward the car and leaned in the window. "The attendant who's just arrived for the night-shift says he's forgotten his keys to the office, so he can't get in, and the keys to the cottages are locked inside! The day shift chap has gone home and took his keys with him. This fellow doesn't think he can reach him. There's no way he can let us into our cottage until he gets the keys."

I walked back to the office with Allen. The attendant was most apologetic. "There is just no way to let you folks into your cottage until I find a way to get into the office. Usually by midnight most folks are already checked in. Wait here. I'll be right back."

And so, our wedding night was spent in the front seat of our car . . . talking and waiting. By 3:00 a.m., the Southern California night was getting quite chilly, and the new growth of Allen's whiskers began to scratch my face in our few attempts at romance. This had overtones of comedy, but certainly fell short of our dreams! Another hour . . . I dozed a bit on Allen's shoulder, on the edge of consciousness when the sharp crackling sound of shattered glass

Charles Allen Gilchrist — age 34, taken at the time of our marriage.

brought me wide-eyed awake. "What was that?"

"The attendant brought the police and they've broken the large plate glass office window. I guess we can go in now," Allen replied. My new husband seemed not too tired to carry me across the threshold of our honeymoon cottage. One full wall of glass offered a tremendous view of the white capped, diamond-tipped waves sparkling in the moonlight and crashing onto the shore of Laguna Beach, but Allen pulled the drapes. We could see the view in the morning. By then, at 4:00 a.m., we were dead tired from the excitement of a long day. I wondered how many hundreds of other couples find themselves exhausted on their wedding night? Weariness overcame us and we fell immediately into sound sleep.

It was years later before I recalled an old family superstition that shattered glass forewarns of death. It was a strange beginning.

*

A SHADOW APPEARS

Allen won't speak to me. He seems to have withdrawn into his own dark cave. For three days now he's said nothing, hardly acknowledging my presence. And this is our honeymoon! How can he be so silent and detached? What have I said to make him angry? I sit quietly beside him as we drive, wracking my brain, going over conversations of the past few days, but coming up with nothing that could explain this deep withdrawn silence. We hadn't had one cross word. Is he sorry he married me? Am I a disappointment to him? It is terribly upsetting.

We had been having a wonderful time. He was a gentle lover, demonstrating the devotion he had professed in letters these past months, and I had felt warm and protected in his arms at night, happy and carefree daytimes, as we drove across the U.S. It had been a good trip, even though it was the dead of winter and we had taken a chance, driving back to the midwest, that the weather would hold and roads would be clear. Allen had wisely chosen the southern route. Roads were only two lane then, but driving them was pleasant.

We'd had our first glimpse of the Grand Canyon. What a remarkable work of Nature! Later we went to the Carlsbad Caverns of New Mexico. We descended into the depths, many hundred feet, and struggled back up the long climb. What astounding beauty Nature forms in the bowels of the earth. My legs ached and Allen had to almost carry me at the end.

We laughed our way across the Texas Panhandle, listening to the local accents and particularly to the Texas twang of Lefty Frizell and his band coming over our auto's radio. This station was the only one on the air in Texas.

Allen seemed eager to tell me stories of his military life. Many were humorous, many poignant and sad. We talked and shared, exploring one another's minds and hearts, for each of us had much to learn about the other. I was a most avid listener, for my mind is curious by nature, and I am intensely interested in the many wonders of life.

Then suddenly yesterday and today Allen had become withdrawn and silent, a stranger by my side. I was puzzled and hurt.

"Is something the matter?" I gently inquired. "You are so quiet." His answer was noncommittal, even cool, telling me nothing. It was clear he wished no further questioning. Allen seemed aristocratically dignified, while placing an invisible, but very real, shield between us that defied penetration. Not wishing to irritate him further, I asked nothing more, and we rode in stiff silence through the wintery landscape which had been beautiful, but now seemed simply drab and cold.

During those days of long silent riding I had many hours to think. I put on a happy face, but how could I not wonder if I had been wise to marry this man I really didn't know at all. I thought again of the beautiful, masterly voice I had heard speaking clear, real instructions, "Marry this man. He needs you." The words had been explicit, unmistakable. I did admire and respect my husband immensely and had found a deep love for him stirring within me. But now, as the silence deepened, I wasn't so sure.

Suddenly I felt uprooted and alone. I wanted to ask Mama's advice, but I knew that wouldn't do me much good, as

I could almost hear her voice in my ear, "You've made your choice, now you will have to live with it." Mama was a practical woman and always had been a stern disciplinarian. But she had liked and approved of Allen from the very beginning. It was she who asked him to drive Evelyn and me to the airport. Mama had heard only the best things of him from her sister, Elsie, with whom he had taken a room for eighteen months. And Mama had been thrilled to be able to attend our wedding and had given us her warmest blessing.

The morning we were due to arrive at Allen's mother's home in Missouri, he playfully threw a pillow at me as I awakened, asking in a bright and jovial voice, "Hey Sleepyhead! What would you like for breakfast?"

I stared at him in disbelief! What happened? Here again was the man I had married, smiling into my eyes with love and tenderness, urging me to get up and see the shining new day. I was speechless.

"Why the look of amazement? Don't you believe in breakfast?"

I breathed a silent sigh of relief, still unable to speak, while wondering what had caused his three-day dark, ominous silence. But I was fearful to make reference to it lest I risk breaking his new, happy mood. If Allen wished to ignore the last few days, well then, so could I, I thought. I reminded myself he was soon going to war. Maybe he had dark and fearful thoughts I knew nothing of. Maybe he, too, had the premonition he would not return. This thought I had purposely put behind me in recent days, but now it loomed strange and frightening. I decided not to think of that — not now. It was my place to make his last weeks of leave happy ones. I was determined to set aside my qualms and questions, in favor of pleasant repartee and, I hoped, warm companionship and lovemaking.

My new mother-in-law was a delight. And she seemed delighted with me. Mother G. had been a belle from Tennessee, and she greeted us with the warm graciousness of a southern lady. She was rather short with a gently rounded figure, her head topped with a thick mound of silver grey hair. Her outstanding feature, though, was her sparkling brown eyes. They twinkled and danced, clearly expressing her good humor and happy heart, as she laughingly welcomed us. She was the warm and adoring grandmother so often pictured, who stands waiting at the door with flour on her apron, greeting eager little children who have trekked with their parents over miles of snowdrifts in horse-drawn sleigh to have Christmas at Grandma's. Her name was Christine. She had raised six children — four girls and two boys — my husband being third in line. They were all grown and gone now, but she talked a great deal about them as we sat rocking together on the porch swing. One could almost picture them still romping around her, rather than married with children of their own. I could see she really missed her family, while she regaled us with humorous tales of things they had said and done through the years. Some of the stories included Allen. As she helped me to become acquainted with my new family, I could also see she was reliving the joys of the past, for she was born to be a mother. She had graduated from the University of Tennessee with a degree in Home Economics, and there seemed to be no more attractive thing she could have or would now wish to have done with her life than to raise a large and happy family.

Allen was to be in Seattle to ship out within a few short weeks, so time was of the essence. In a day or two we journeyed on to visit other members of his family. They were all exuberant and welcomed me like a sister, which, since I was an only child, held great importance to me. Finally now I had four sisters! But on this trip I was to meet only two of them. Barbara, a beautiful dark-haired girl and the youngest of the six, was Allen's favorite. She bubbled over with enthusiasm and laughter upon seeing him.

Our stay with Barbara was unique. Two of her three children were twenty-month old twin boys, adorable as only children of that age can be. I saw firsthand both the wonders and the hard work of raising twins. My hat was off to my enthusiastic, bouncy sister-in-law with the ready smile, seemingly endless energy, and the love that shown on her face for her brother.

In the evening after dinner we had tea, and somehow the subject of tea-leaf-reading came up. Bobbie (her family nickname) asked me quite jokingly what I saw in her cup. I seldom remember anything that comes through in a tea-reading, since the thoughts do not come from my own mind, but are only 'passing through,' so to speak. But I remember what I saw in this one all too clearly, for what I saw caused a furor.

"You will have six children . . . just like your mother," I calmly stated.

Well! Barbara rose straight up off her seat, and denied the idea explosively. "No way! I've had it! Three is my limit! You've got to be crazy — or those tea leaves are crazy!" She fairly pounced on me. I didn't press it. I was afraid I had offended my new sister-in-law, but I'd only spoken the truth as I saw it. Within a few years' time, Bobbie and her husband had six beautiful children.

Soon we swung back across the country to Los Angeles to pick up Mama, who we had decided should accompany us north to Seattle, that I might have her companionship on my drive back to L.A., as the route crossed the Siskyou mountains in the dead of winter.

Driving across the states back to Southern California, the same dark, cold silence once more engulfed my husband. What had I said? What was wrong? Again I was hurt and bewildered. This silence was worse than if he had accused me of something specific, for then I might defend myself or apologize. Instead, I was shut out, almost as if I didn't exist, left outside of this invisible, impenetrable wall. The mood became worse if I ventured a question. I was left to wait it out. I wanted to understand, but it would be quite a long time before a light of understanding would shine through this darkness.

We picked Mama up in Los Angeles, and she was wonderful company on the last leg of our trip north. Mama was a walking jokebook, with a marvelous memory for funny stories that kept us in stitches most of the way to Seattle. She claimed she had memorized 200 jokes, "in order to train *my* memory." That was just like Mama.

We took the scenic route up coast Highway 1, and gained our first glimpse of the magnificent California Redwoods. In 1952 the coast was still rugged with virgin forest. The slow two-lane road along the ocean's edge twisted and turned through many miles of beautiful dense greenery, and later crossed and recrossed the lovely Smith River that seemed forever with us. Mama counted twenty-three crossings.

After we got to Seattle Mama had an adventure that was comical, but could have been tragic. In order to give her newly-married daughter and son-in-law time alone the last day before his sailing, Mama announced in her genteel way that she was going out for a walk. It was mid-afternoon and we thought nothing of it, while we enjoyed last-minute togetherness. But as the hours went by, she did not return to our motel room. It had begun to rain heavily, as is usual, we found, during Seattle winters. As time dragged on, Allen and I began to worry and berated ourselves mightily for allowing her to wander out in a strange city alone. We hadn't dreamed she'd be gone longer than forty-five minutes or so. Several hours passed. Just as we were getting desperate and were talking about calling the authorities for help — for it was by now quite dark and late — Mama appeared, wet and bedraggled (as she had no umbrella), with, as usual — a wild tale to tell.

It seems that not long after she left us, the heavy rain began and she took refuge in a church she found open nearby. She was surprised to hear the organist practicing as it was a Thursday afternoon, and she said she sat down to listen to the lovely organ strains. After a time, the music ceased. Mama continued to sit quietly meditating, enjoying the gentle calm atmosphere, waiting, hoping the rain would stop. When the downpour turned to a patter she walked to the door to leave. Horrors! Locked in! She tried both outside doors but they wouldn't open without keys. She realized now the church had only been open earlier because the organist was there.

Mama's startled thoughts encompassed her situation: My husband and I would not know where she was, and we, nor authorities, would ever think to look inside a locked

church. This was Thursday. Church service would not be
held until Sunday — good Heavens. Allen was supposed to
sail away in the morning. I could not leave Seattle without
her and would be frantic. Clearly she was in a terrible
pickle. She checked the church office door where there
might be a telephone. It was locked!

Her only recourse was what it had always been — prayer.
And her prayer was very fervent, she later related. She had
always taught me that God's Love was ever with us, and now
she must know it for herself, as this was a desperate situation. An hour went by. Mama thought of Allen's possibly
being jailed (she always gave a humorous twist to the worst
of situations). How could her son-in-law explain to authorities the unaccountable disappearance of his mother-in-law
on his honeymoon?

As the specter of the many strange and awful consequences paraded through her mind, she heard the heavy creak
of a door opening. She bounded up shouting, "Hello! — Anyone there?"

It was the organist. He had forgotten his music. He was
astonished to find someone in the church, as he had not
seen her there when he left, and he affirmed that *he never
before* had left his music. He confirmed Mama's fears. "The
church would not have seen another living soul until Sunday morning."

How amazing! He stared at her and wondered, too,
what she could have done for two days and three nights
while her family frantically searched the city.

Who now dare say prayer doesn't work? God knew
Mama was inside, and so, the organist left his music, in his
own words, "for the first time ever." We laughed and nearly
cried at her narrow escape.

Early the following morning we saw Allen off with
tears and prayers for safety, and I was so grateful for Mama's
comforting presence after he sailed away and we drove the
treacherous way back to Los Angeles over the Siskyou Mountains, often in dense fog. For many miles I had to hang my
head out the open car window to gauge where to drive. The
white line was all I could see, and I had to trust that it would

lead me home, just as I had to trust the guidance which had led me into this marriage. With neither could I see my destination nor even the landscape directly ahead. I must trust.

The two years passed swiftly. My job at the County Administrative Offices filled my days. Writing letters to my husband helped fill the evenings, while I prayed daily for his safety. His rich and wonderful letters came regularly in return. I continued whistling for occasional programs and attending the uplifting classes at the Agashan Temple. In addition, I had discovered a most inspiring study group, already mentioned, called The Astara Foundation,* begun the year before in Los Angeles by Drs. Earlyne and Robert Chaney. There I found a beautiful vibration of love and fellowship, coupled with a teaching that dove-tailed with, and yet added to, the Agashan studies.

Astara had a simple beginning, as most groups do, with a few attendees in the home of the Chaneys. As time went on, I knew I had found a spiritual home, and was quickly led to become a member. This small Church of All Religions, which taught the universal brotherhood of all men, quickly grew, and a simple white elegant temple was built on Mariposa Boulevard in the Wilshire District. I soon found that Astara published correspondence Degree Lessons, and I could continue studies whether I was near or far. And since I would be following in Allen's footsteps as an Army wife, mostly it would be far. This was ideal. Astara was to become a source of support, in spiritual strength through many future years.

Allen's letters from the Republic of South Korea in 1952-53 were so well-written and fascinating, reflecting the country and the charm of the South Koreans with whom he worked closely, that the son of my landlady, who was at that time an Assistant Editor of the Los Angeles Times, upon hearing some passages I shared with him, wished to publish Allen's letters regularly in the *Los Angeles Times*.

"All families with sons in Korea would want to read these," he said. "They are so descriptive, with such vivid word

*Astara, P.O. Box 5003, 792 W. Arrow Hwy, Upland, CA 91785-5003

pictures describing the people, the culture, and the war as well. Few men there could write such informative letters."

Allen's letters were far more than love letters, you see. And yet, in attempting to edit out the very personal portions, written for my eyes only, I gave up in despair. I also worried that Allen might not appreciate having his letters spread out in the *Los Angeles Times*, for all the world to see. This was no ordinary man, and he had a very private side. So, even a news editor agreed his letters were unique.

Sometimes he sent pictures to complement his descriptions: a picture of him bundled up like an Eskimo in fur-hooded parka in the 9 degrees-below zero winter temperature, or another as he received a commendation plaque from the South Korean Republic Commander for his leadership as a respected officer.

And then one day came the news. The war in Korea was over!

* MY SOLDIER COMES HOME

As the war came to an end and I came to the realization Allen would return, I was overjoyed. My prayers for him had been answered. Yet my gratitude and joy were mixed with other feelings. There was a small flutter of fear in my breast, the fear of the unknown. I had spent only four short weeks with him on our honeymoon, a time that had been both wonderful and strange. And now Allen had a new assignment and would be sweeping me up to go away with him. I would have to leave my beloved California.

Meeting my husband at the airport, I was both excited and nervous. He had seen two years of fighting. I didn't know what to expect. Allen appeared pale as he stepped off the plane, and thinner. But his arms opened wide and held me tightly for a long time. I could feel the slight sob catch in his chest as he felt the reality of being home. For he did love me, very much. His every letter had declared it.

Now he was back — safe and sound. For that, I was overjoyed. He had not lost his life after all, as I had feared from the prediction. He had had some strenuous months and one very narrow escape from death, when enemy fire hit and blew up the high Lookout Tower which he had visited and left only moments before. He was only a few yards down the hill when the concussion knocked him to the ground, stunning him. The shock and grief for the Lookout soldier within overshadowed his own good fortune, I could see, as he related the sad tale.

So much more he told, not only of the war and its deprivations and struggles, but of the Korean people, their beautiful singing voices, their stamina in the face of war, and of his respect and admiration for the South Korean officers he worked with. There were relief times on weekends toward the end of his tour when he especially enjoyed the company of the South Korean officers, with whom he went fishing, out to the countryside in the peace of natural surroundings. Allen's American co-workers preferred to go into town, and this was never his choice. In fact, he often was disappointed not to find one American officer who preferred quiet recreation, and thus he made good friends among the Koreans.

One South Korean officer especially enjoyed Allen's company and invited him to dinner one evening in his home. He found the gracious wife had worked all day preparing "special food for the American Officer." But to Allen's dismay, before the Korean meal, as a first course she proudly presented to him a huge plate of fresh doughnuts. She had found a recipe for this popular American dish, which she thought would truly please him.

Allen said he knew if he did not eat a good number of them it would be the greatest discourtesy to his host and hostess. However, unfortunately, after stuffing himself with several doughnuts (which had never been a food he ate even in America), he was hardly able to enjoy the fine local dishes she had prepared and served next.

That Korean Officer kept touch with our family and wrote to me for many years at the Christmas holidays. My husband was highly respected in that battalion. One Korean Colonel gave Allen a beautiful gift, a jewelbox hand-inlaid with mother-of-pearl, for me, his wife.

Allen had written from Korea that after a few days of

rest, upon his return he would gather me and my belongings up and we would set out for his next assignment, a small town in mid-Missouri, where he was to teach R.O.T.C. for the next three years.

My heart was in my throat at the thought of tearing up roots from California. I had come to love it; the balmy sunshiny days, the wonderful classes at Astara and the Agashan Temple. Worst of all was the idea of leaving Mama alone in The Big City, but knowing Mama's astute mind, I felt she would have no real problems. And, I would have to leave my secretarial position, which was then with the Los Angeles County Board of Supervisors.

My friend and former boss, Smith Griswold, had been away these two years also, serving in the war as Commander of the Hospital Ship *Repose*. This beautiful white ship, a city unto itself, came into port at San Diego at war's end, several weeks before my husband was to return. Smith, of course, was on it, and he telephoned me, inviting me to luncheon aboard and a tour of the vessel.

What a treat to see how meticulously clean and complete this huge ship was, a floating hospital city — four stories, with every possible need fulfilled for crew and the care of hundreds of wounded. But the real treat was being the only lady at a luncheon with fourteen handsome Naval Officers! I was so entranced that even if my life depended upon it I could not relate what we ate for lunch. They all grinned and were most courteous, though they took delight in ribbing their Commander with good humor about his blonde date. When he protested that I was his secretary, they responded, "Oh, yeah. Sure!"

That I had married in his absence was a shock to my good friend. Smith had expected me to continue as his Administrative Secretary upon his return to civilian life. He had now accepted the position of Director of the Air Pollution Control District for Los Angeles County, and in this capacity it was he who initiated the elimination of all outdoor rubbish-burning in the county and who later became the author of the law requiring all new American automobiles made in America to be equipped by 1963 with the first

air pollution control devices. Later Smith moved on to work
with the U.S Department of Health and Welfare in Washington D.C., as the American representative at Air Pollution
Control meetings world-wide, attending conferences in
Geneva, Buenos Aires, Singapore, London, and other world
centers. Had I chosen the other path and remained as Smith's
secretary, I may have accompanied him on some of those
global hops, as he had hoped, for we were a very good
working team.

When we come to a crossroads and choose a way, we
never know the future we miss in not choosing another. We
can only trust God's guidance within. Now many years later,
I know that I chose rightly, though at the time marrying Allen
seemed the least known and most daring path. It was like
holding my nose and diving in. But, like all of us, my soul had
a mission it had come to achieve in this life — this time —
which needed to be fulfilled, although it was not the easiest.

So much had happened to change my life and guide my
steps in California. I had a deep love for this beautiful state.
Now a new chapter of my life was opening. I had to turn my
face to my future with Allen, who in some ways still seemed
a stranger. Most of our courtship, and even marriage, had
thus far been via the written page, and in two years time, I
had been with him physically exactly six weeks.

The inner reluctance I had felt in joining my life to
Allen's was not without basis. In later years, when I looked
back on the magnitude of challenges I have faced and overcome, I saw my hesitance had been more than justified. But
in the overcoming I have found new knowledge, understanding, and, wonderfully, even joy. I hope that those who
read my story may find answers to ease and illumine their
own pain and struggle, may find the courage to meet life
with faith, and learn to trust that in all of their difficulties
there is a reason, an order, an ultimate beauty.

Life is difficult, but it need not be a battleground.
There are so many joys if one makes room for them. I soon
found I wouldn't lose friends, or past pleasures, if I kept
them in my heart and memory. Rather I was to gain many
new friends and greet experiences that would open entirely

new vistas of living. This was an important attitude I learned to carry always, as an Army wife moving onward every few years. You never lose anything or anyone you don't wish to lose. One must meet life with open arms and an open heart.

Once again we headed east. Settling in the picturesque midwest town of Fulton, Missouri, where Allen was assigned to teach at Westminster College for Men, we spent a delightful three years. We found Fulton to be a town of historical significance, with Westminster College having attained a special place in recent history.

Our new neighbors in the attractive brick apartment building we occupied were friendly and welcoming, and decidedly individualistic. Ola and Elrow Crane were a nice retired couple, Elrow having been Water Commissioner of nearby Columbia, seat of the University of Missouri. Ola and Elrow loved to square dance and soon introduced us to that delightful recreation. Ola's smiling face would pop in almost every forenoon with a southern "Yoo-hoo! How're ya'all doing this morning?" to make sure her new neighbor was not lacking for anything. Ola never knew anyone as a stranger.

Judge James Yates and his wife, Ada, were also retired, a bit more austere, believing themselves to be a solid vertebrae in the backbone of the town. But they were very good-hearted folks. Their truly colloquial attitude was captured in one of Ada Yates' remarks as she told me that her nephew was choosing to move to Wyoming. With great indignation she huffed, "I can't for the life of me see why James would want to move out west with all those Indians!" Believe it or not, she was serious, and this was 1955.

Another quaint and frail little couple down the hall were so dear in their concern for us as newcomers. He was eighty-two and she eighty-four years old, which alone was not so unusual. What was unusual was that one weekend a month they climbed up into their 1920's square black Model T-Ford and chug-a-lugged across the Missouri/Illinois state line to visit her parents, who were one hundred-three and one hundred-six years old!

In my first year of marriage I suffered from an intermittent and continuing condition, a urinary infection that causes incontinence and was becoming intolerable. Since this condition plagues others, I shall relate the easy cure I finally found, after much travail, in hopes it may be helpful. This cure has helped many women friends with whom I have shared it.

Before discovering this help, I went through some horrid experiences. This complaint had been with me earlier while I was yet single, and at times was extremely embarrassing because of the incontinence, with almost complete loss of bladder control. I was chained to the bathroom. Once, months earlier, while still at work in California, I was asked to take on the spot dictation while standing in an employer's office, when to my horror, I found myself wetting the carpet between my feet!

My experience with medical attention at that time caused even worse travail, as the doctor I went to for help injected a pint of medicine, a heavy dark brown fluid, into my bladder. Then he said, "Go on home, but you must hold it for at least an hour." He made no offer to allow me to remain lying down in his office for that hour.

I learned early how uncaring some doctors can be regarding what a patient suffers. If my bladder muscle was already so weak it could hold no more than a teaspoon at a time, as I had related to him, how in the world could it hold a full pint of this medicine for an hour? What a horrible consequence! I got only as far as the street. While I attempted to flag a taxi, a large puddle of that dark brown fluid splashed down with a gush making a dark widening circle on the pavement around my feet. Under the astonished stare of nearby pedestrians I fled, sloshing in my shoes, to the nearest gas station to remove and wash all my soaked underclothing. God only knows what those people thought.

That experience, and others I had undergone, went a long way toward turning me off to the expertise of the medical doctors. I turned instead to prayer and the intuitive feeling to heal myself of my condition through dietary means, avoiding acid-forming foods like coffee, tea, chocolate and sugars. This actually helped a great deal, but the infection was recurring. In 1953 no one ever spoke of diet or foods being a factor in bodily conditions. In fact, it took almost thirty years for this idea to be generally accepted, and the medical profession has been the last sector to concede.

Later, in my marriage, I found that intercourse seemed to re-activate the condition, for I was also somewhat weak, recovering from surgery for a tubal pregnancy. The bladder condition had become severe enough that tests were done at the University of Missouri's Urology Clinic. The doctors there recommended urinary surgery, to ream out the urethra tube leading from the bladder, saying " . . . there is a growth." This sounded so miserable that I told the doctor, I'd have to think about it," while begging for delay. Again I turned to prayer, asking Holy Spirit Presence to guide me.

That very week I was led (oddly enough) to speak of my health problem on the telephone to a woman who called, asking to speak to her husband who was in our home as a service person fixing a minor breakdown. He could not come to the phone immediately, so she and I conversed for a time. One would not ordinarily discuss their bladder infection with a complete stranger. But something she said prompted the subject. I'm sure my Angel was prodding me, for I found myself babbling out my worries.

What that lady told me made a complete change in my health from that day forward. And I have been able to help numerous other women in years since with this simple advice. I do not even know the name of this blessed person.

She said, "I have had this same condition. It became so severe that it extended to an enlargement of the kidneys, and the doctors decided to remove one. A month later the other kidney was laboring under the strain of the same problem. The cause, you see, had never been corrected. The medical doctors were then recommending removal of my one remaining kidney and proposed placing me on a dialysis machine the rest of my life. I was desperate, and asked in prayer for another way out. The very next day my attention was drawn once again to my neighbor, a cheery ninety-year old gentleman, who sang and whistled in his garden next door almost daily. Spry as a youngster, he was. So I boldly asked him his secret for good health, and told him about my worries. He laughed and said, 'It is simple. I just take a tablespoon of apple-cider vinegar and a scant tablespoon of raw honey in a tall glass of warm water every morning before breakfast and wait an hour before eating. I've never had a prostate or urinary problem. It cleans out the system and keeps everything going like clockwork.'"

The lady told me she then tried it, and within ten days of taking this remedy every morning, her symptoms went completely away. She added that it had been ten years ago now, she still had her kidney, and it was working just fine. She went on to relate that she asked her neighbor, "Why don't the doctors tell us something so simple?"

She said, "He twinkled a smile and replied, 'Ignorance. Ignorance and money.' "

I was elated and decided to gave it a whirl, and sure enough, in only five days I was feeling quite well. I canceled my appointment at the University Hospital and never went back. That was thirty-five years ago and I've never had a recurrence.

I still take the vinegar and honey remedy a few mornings each week as a preventative. The apple-cider vinegar should be natural, non-pasteurized, with no preservatives. It can be obtained from any health store. The praises of vinegar were touted in a book called *Folk Medicine: a Vermont Doctor's Guide to Health.** The honey is best if raw and unheated, only strained. This drink is actually very refreshing and nourishing, as well as healing.

You see, both honey and vinegar are germ killers. Honey also is a natural antibiotic. A keg of honey was found in King Tut's Tomb in Egypt years ago. It was ascertained to be over two thousand years old. Upon opening the cask, the archaeologists found the honey perfectly preserved, and perfectly good. Honey is its own preservative.

I have since read that in the 1970's the Sloan-Kettering Foundation did an experiment, placing a tiny drop of honey in a test tube of germs. Under microscope, the amazed scientists watched as all the germs died within moments.

Folk Medicine: A Vermont Doctor's Guide to Health, D.C. Jarvis, M.D., 1958, Fawcett Publishers, 201 E Fiftieth St., N.Y., N.Y. 10022

They found that honey dehydrates germs, and they die quickly. Besides being a germ killer, this mixture has a natural balancing action on the acid and alkalines of the body as it floods the system and the urinary tract first thing in the morning. I have given this simple remedy to a number of women suffering from yeast infections and bladder problems of various kinds, and invariably I have heard stories of near 100% success, with much gratitude. I am sure it would work equally well for men.

Our modern society's food preparations with many preservatives, and the wide use of sugars in almost everything we eat, has upset the body's ability to handle the quantities of toxins, resulting when there is an imbalance of acid-alkaline ratio. Organs and glands become acid-loaded and sooner or later breakdown wherever a genetic weakness may exist. Unfortunately, for seventy years and more the medical profession's solution to all problems has been drugs and surgery, as opposed to looking at causes and supplying the body's natural needs. Cutting out and disposing of an organ is not healing it, whether it be the uterus, prostate, kidney or breast.

When the body becomes too acidic, arthritis can sometimes become evident. I recalled Mama's home remedy she found to be a help. When the joints of her fingers bothered, she painted them with brown iodine at night before bedtime. This cleared up the trouble. By morning the stiffness and pain had disappeared and her hands were white again. In some areas of the country iodine is lacking in the water and diet, which affects the functioning of the thyroid gland. Interestingly, this malfunction can also extend to mild heart palpitations creating nervousness, in some instances. Applying iodine to the palms of my hands before bedtime has at times calmed this condition completely. The body absorbs the iodine and the palms are often white again within an hour. Obviously, if the condition continues, one should seek professional help. But this home remedy has served me many times.

The body is a miraculous, dynamic organism with the ability to heal itself, but it must be given the right nutritional tools, and not given cell-damaging chemicals in the form of additives and/or preservatives that never were natural to its existence in the first place. The knowledge that took shape in my mind in those early days was to be of major importance a number of years later — and actually the means of saving my life at the age of forty-four.

It was here in Fulton, Missouri our first son was born. Believing in natural-health methods I chose natural childbirth with preparatory exercises at a time when it was considered exotic, and heavy anesthesia was the norm. I had a very strong inner guidance, to not have even a local anesthetic. This decision saved our baby's life, for the labor was long and tiring. I had carried Jeremy eleven months. My doctor said if delivery had been delayed one more week, he could have written my case up in the American Journal of Medicine as a record in gestation! (Like a baby elephant!) It seemed the entire town of Fulton had held its breath waiting for our baby, as we had become well-known and liked by then.

One evening, before the birth when I had carried for about ten and one-half months, I was out for my solitary daily walk in the early twilight. A townsperson we knew passed in his auto. Slowing down, he jovially shouted out the window to me, "How are you folks tonight?"

My doctor had chosen to not do a Caeserian, but instead, gave shots to trigger birth. Even so, it was a week later before our little guy finally emerged, blue and not breathing, and was rushed into an incubator. I knew then if I had been anethesized, he would have been also, and could easily have not survived. So I am grateful I followed my strong inner guidance to stay awake for the work I had to do.

Allen was anxiously waiting as I was wheeled out of delivery (fathers were not allowed in the delivery room in those days). I smiled wanly up from the cart and said, "Hi, Daddy." The poor dear looked like he wanted to cry. Allen was a very grateful father, as he was by then thirty-eight years old, and earlier that year I had lost a pregnancy that was tubal, a very dangerous situation requiring surgery. In a tubal pregnancy the woman does not know she is pregnant until nearly too late, as menstruation does not cease. The tube can burst and peritonitis often results.

Besides losing this early pregnancy, I lost a second pregnancy later in my marriage while traveling. Ten years later I was told by a minister in a psychic reading in San Francisco, "Your grandparents in Spirit want you to know they are raising your two sons for you in the heaven-world." I was amazed! This minister knew nothing of me or my history.

"Is it true then," I asked, "that the souls of miscarriages are still considered family even though they are not physically carried to term or born into this world?"

"Yes, that is true," she responded. This has since been confirmed to me. I was given a message just two years ago, some thirty-seven years after these losses, through another remarkable trance medium, this time in Honolulu, concerning these same two miscarriages.

"You are being asked to pray for your two sons in spirit, as due to the lack of growth-inducing challenges that earth-life would have given, they are not maturing normally, but remain child-like."

This I think is very interesting, and throws a new light on lost pregnancies and also on abortions, a raging controversy in our time. Also, the fact I would be asked to pray indicates our prayers have a decided effect even on souls not in the body.

Our newborn son was a joy to his father and me, and to our many friends in Fulton, as they had all waited with me. I was deluged with thirty-eight plants and bouquets during the one week I remained in the hospital. I was well-known by then, having been a headliner whistling on a local talent show.

Jeremy was a fine healthy baby, except for one harsh reality: he suffered from colic, crying day and night the first three months of his life. I was so exhausted from lack of sleep, on the heels of a long labor, that I might have given him strychnine if someone had told me it would help! I had tried everything else — I thought. I had nursed, not nursed, given various formulas made up by doctor, and still Jeremy had stomach gas that caused milk projectiles to shoot in a streak halfway across the room. Poor little guy. I was frantic. Again, by grace, I was shown a remarkably effective and easy remedy. Someone suggested I should get a distillation of the herb fennel from the druggist and put a few drops in the baby's water bottle. I tried it that very day.

It was nothing short of a miracle — my anguished crying baby was taken away overnight, and a sweet smiling angel replaced him! We both slept a long night through for the first time in three and a half months. I heartily recommend fennel extract, a distillation of the herb, one teaspoon diluted in 6 oz. of water in the bottle once or twice a day, to aid digestion and alleviate gas. Or cooled tea made from steeped fennel seeds can be used if the extract is not available, and diluted in water. Being a very gentle herb, fennel is harmless and good for any baby's digestion, colic or not.

Baby Jeremy chose a famous mid-America town in which to be born, for it was here in Fulton, Missouri that Winston Churchill gave his world-famous Iron Curtain speech in 1946, right after World War II, warning that the Russians, although having fought with us against the Nazis, were not really our allies. It was soon proven he was right.

Churchill had wanted, on his visit to the United States that year after the war, to speak in mid-America. Since Harry Truman, who was President at that time, was from Missouri, and also had a young friend attending Westminster College, Fulton was chosen for the site of the speech. From this event Fulton gained a good deal of notoriety.

In the late 1950's, to honor Churchill's having spoken here, a Christopher Wren Church was disassembled brick by brick, brought over from London, and re-erected on the Westminster Campus. It is a beautiful addition in this small town to this day. Christopher Wren was a renowned English architect, having designed the great St. Paul's Cathedral in London, as well as many other famous structures in England, including fifty-two churches and museums. A large bronze statue of Winston Churchill was also erected in Fulton in honor of that day. Even as I write, on this day of May 6, 1992, CNN Television News is carrying coverage of Mikhail Gorbachev arriving to speak in — yes, Fulton, Missouri — with interesting remarks on Russia's stance forty-six years ago.

Former President Harry Truman visited Fulton and Westminster College while we were assigned there in 1953,

and I had the pleasure of shaking hands and exchanging pleas-
antries with him. This rather short, insignificant appearing
gentleman smiled as he peered pleasantly at me through his
round, steel-rimmed glasses. But he certainly was *not* insignificant as President during the latter days of World War II.

It is worth remembering that one can never tell a book
by its cover.

There is a true story told by a woman friend of the family
who sat next to Bess Truman while Harry was giving a speech
to a group of farmers. Our friend whispered to Bess, "Can't
you get Harry to use the word fertilizer instead of manure?"
Bess leaned back and whispered to her, "I don't think so. It
took me thirty years to get him to say 'manure!'"

Earlier, Fulton was the setting of a notorious tale behind closed doors that was brought out in the book, *Kings
Row*, which was made into a movie in 1942 starring Ann
Sheridan and Ronald Reagon (while he was still in Hollywood). The story was based on a scandalous tale involving a
southern family who were considered the backbone of the
County in Civil War days. The author was sued shortly after
his book came out by the elderly matriarch of Fulton, as she
recognized the town's setting, and the story as her own
family's dark history, replete with slavery and illicit sex. She
could not prove it was libelous, however, so lost the suit.
The national publicity from the whole uproar only served to
draw attention to the truth of the tale. Which goes to show,
one should keep one's mouth shut if the cat is already out of
the bag. Cats once loose, are hard to catch!

Fulton sits in the midst of Callaway County and Callaway
County prides itself on being the very last county to secede
from the Confederacy and to accept joining the Union after
the Civil War. Many residents there still feel a great deal of
southern pride in that area. So to land in Fulton for three
years was certainly not a boring experience for this Little
Big-Ears-from-the-Backwoods, with an avid curiosity about
human nature.

*
EVELYN COMES TO VISIT

Through these years I had kept touch by mail with my dear friend, Evelyn, who had, you will recall, gone to Italy with the U.S. State Dept. She met and dated a young Italian medical student there in Florence. Suddenly she was transferred to Montreal, so she planned to fly down to Missouri to see me. I was ecstatic! It was an enthusiastic and exciting reunion when we met in St. Louis.

Evelyn looked as beautiful as ever, even more chic, if that were possible, her short, dark auburn hair shining in the sun. I could hardly believe she had really come, it had been so long. She brought her warm friendship, plus a whole trunk full of fascinating Italian-made prsesents for me: two long slim umbrellas with jeweled handles, delicately gold-etched leather wallets and belts in Florentine motif, Italian silk scarves, a polished wooden music box shaped like a grand piano. Oh, it was a King's Treasure! We hugged, and stayed up late catching up on girl talk. She planned to stay ten days.

Suddenly, the very next day — a phone call. To my amazement, her young Italian doctor, now taking his medical residency in Buffalo, New York, stated he was flying down the following day. He arrived, and of course, most of her ten-day visit in my home was spent with him. After four years of dragging his heels in Italy where he saw her regularly, he now proposed to her in our small apartment in Missouri. How incongruous. Fate — Thou hast a bitter twist. There went my few days' visit with her alone, which I had *so* looked forward to having. Dear beautiful Evelyn was agog at finally receiving the proposal for which she had nearly given up waiting, and they lolly-gagged off on long walks and moonlight trysts.

Her swain was a tall and handsome young man of quiet, distinguished demeanor who spoke perfect English, and I thought it great to have the opportunity to meet my friend's future husband. But shucks . . . at the expense of my long-awaited chance to hear exciting and vivid details of her

European experiences, the people and parties at the Embassies. Well, life is always full of surprises and this was surely one of them. I understood later that because of his custom and honor, her young man had wished to finish all of his medical schooling and be established in his residency, with the future assured, before offering his proposal of marriage, and thus had delayed over-long in stating his intentions.

Soon they made marriage plans and took off in a pink cloud of love. I was glad for Evelyn's happiness. Evie and Giancarlo have been happily married all these years. Many years later, in 1978, I had the joy of spending several weeks vacation with them in Bologna, Italy where Giancarlo is a Professor/Doctor, Director of Neurology in Johns Hopkins University Hospital. Evelyn became Registrar at the University after leaving the State Deptment, as mentioned earlier.

Evelyn was a supreme hostess and there I had my long-awaited togetherness time, as well as her first-class guidance to Bologna's historical sights, delicious food, and classy shops with exquisitely beautiful wares. It is a memory I treasure.

It was on this same journey to Europe that I was privileged to visit England and the home of Brett and Missy Arnold, who drove us through southern England and King Arthur Country. How thrilling it was to see in reality the old family castle in the village of Beckington, England, still sturdily standing in worn medieval splendor since 1049.

*

HOLY PRESENCE ANSWERS A CALL FOR HELP

A memory that stands out like a beacon in my mind from those three years we lived in Fulton involves a young widow, Lois, who had the apartment next to ours. It turned out to be another beautiful proof of the Spirit Presence ever with us.

I had continued my enlightening studies with Astara through correspondence courses, and held my personal devotions in meditation daily. After some months Lois and I became acquainted. She often came over in the evenings while Allen was still at the office. Lois began asking questions of a religious nature, so I shared my philosophy of life. To say she was entranced with the ideas I presented would be a mild understatement. She sat in my apartment literally for hours on end, asking more and more questions, like a dry desert traveler who has found a cool well. Lois had an intense need for answers that the local fundamental churches simply had not supplied. (Shades of my past?)

Her earnest visits with our deep conversational dialogue had gone on for only two months, when out of the blue, Lois fell ill. Local doctors in the little hospital in Fulton could not agree upon her malady, so she was sent to St. Louis. From there the diagnosis came back: it was fast-acting leukemia, cancer of the blood and bone marrow. She was given less than six weeks to live, but in the 1950's doctors did not tell a patient this. Her sister and family were devastated and said they were not able to tell Lois either. They turned to me, as a friend with whom they knew she had shared many spiritual discussions, and asked me to break this news to her.

Lois was returned by ambulance to our local hospital to spend her last days. She was white as the sheet upon which she lay, the red blood cells having been slowly consumed by the rapid growth of white cell anemia. Her body was becoming stiff; soon she could move only her eyes and mouth. As I sat talking to her and gently explaining the doctor's verdict, her lovely eyes filled with tears. She thanked me profusely, because, she whispered, she had many legal concerns to clear up. She called instantly for her attorney. Lois told me also that she was not afraid to die because of what I had shared with her about the reality of the World Beyond the Veil, the wonder and beauty beyond any known here.

This world truly is very close, but because it exists on a higher vibratory level, it is invisible to our eyes. But this realm wasn't invisible to my great aunts who gave us early descriptions and sound proof in so many ways. Nor was it invisible to my own Mama who glimpsed it now and then, or to the dear souls who founded Astara, Drs. Earlyne and Robert Chaney, or to Master Yogananda and many other great teachers who have all told us over and over again of the freedom and light of the spirit, as opposed to the temporal nature of this third dimensional world we live in.

I had earlier told Lois this earth-plane is a schoolroom, a kind of laboratory in which we are to learn the real chemistry of our own nature, and just as we celebrate the graduation of students out of high school on their way to college, we should be even more joyous for our dear ones graduating to their higher level of learning. I held Lois' hand and told her again of the beauty and wonder of that Higher World she was entering, promising that she would not be alone in her crossing and telling her not to be afraid, that she had something new and wonderful to look forward to.

Lois had only a few days left. Alone at home I prayed deeply and earnestly to my Beloved Presence that Holy Spirit and my many loved ones in the Heaven World would be with Lois, that she would not be alone for a minute, that my promises to her, made in unshaken faith, would be fulfilled.

Lois could not move a muscle, or even speak or open her eyes the last afternoon when I held her hand and said a quiet "goodbye for now." She was as white and stiff as death itself. When I left, her sister Virginia stayed with her. Only a few hours later, Virginia came rushing to my home quite excited and amazed.

"I have to tell you," she could hardly catch her breath, "It was so astonishing! You know Lois has been white as a sheet, stiff as a board, not able to move for days. Only a few hours after you left, all of a sudden she sat bolt upright in bed! Her eyes flew open and raising her arms and outstretching them, she exclaimed, *'Viginia! Look! The whole room is filled with golden light!'* And instantly she fell backward and was gone. What do you think of that?" Virginia asked in amazement.

Well, I knew what to think of it, and I sent out a warm, silent "Thank you!" to all those who hear our prayers and respond to them, for only the combined auras of a number of loving Beings in the Light of Christ, could fill the whole room with golden light. That Lois was able to sit up and speak her ecstasy in that last moment was so very comforting to me. I was moved that Holy Spirit, knowing the changes Lois would soon face, had guided her to learn all she could before her illness struck, so she would face death without fear, being prepared with new understanding. Fear comes mainly through lack of understanding. Is it not so? That we fear the unknown?

It behooves us, while we are here on earth and there is yet time, to learn all we can of the trip we are all destined to make. We would not dream of going to a foreign country without learning a little of the customs, the coinage, the weather, what we might be expected to know of the country when we arrived.

Why then are so many of us so ill-prepared for the most important journey we will ever make? Yes, some of us go to church on Sunday and warm a pew or bench, and are seen as pious by other members, but do we choose a church where the minister actually knows through true understanding what he or she speaks of?

Unfortunately many mainstream religions in recent centuries have not met people's need for true understanding, the nature of the soul and its relationship to the Creator, understanding that would contribute to human spiritual evolution, to the ability to understand self and fellowman, that would promote tolerance and love in the treatment of all humankind, despite differences. Change, whether individual, social, or institutional, seems to be the most difficult of all aspects of life to achieve. People are creatures of habit. Generally change doesn't come until one has suffered enough to desire to change (finally figuring out in desperation that he or she must be doing something wrong). Thus there will always be suffering.

It is sad, as this is not the desire of the God who created us all, the Creator of Beauty, Love, Wisdom and the Power of the Universe. However, in this great love, the Lord of the Universe also gave us free will. Just look what we have done with it.

Well, Lois did her best to prepare, not consciously knowing why, nor did I have even an inkling at the time of our talks. I blessed her on her way in her adventure, and wished her Godspeed, content in knowing she was cared for.

While we were in Fulton we kept a close eye on Allen's mother who lived in nearby Columbia. Christine's life had been her family, and once her chicks had all grown and flown the coop, she seemed to begin to go backward in her mental condition, living more and more in the past. Finally, a few years later, we made arrangements for her to spend the next few years visiting from home to home with her grown children, for she could no longer keep her own house. She suffered arteriosclerosis of the brain.

I mention this by way of sharing my observations over the years regarding why some elderly folks develop hardening of the arteries (arteriosclerosis) of the brain and are mentally incompetent for any number of years, while other oldsters go merrily on being quite productive in society, or at least alert and sharp to a grand old age. Medical science has, of course, determined possible genetic causes, and recently has looked into the all-important role nutritional deficiencies may play in these deteriorations, including Alzheimers. But I have an additional observation to share, that thus far has not openly been spoken of as a factor.

In cases I have personally observed, it appears the mind's health depends a great deal upon whether that elder continues to have an on-going zest and enthusiasm for life, maintains an avid interest and participation in the current events of the day, and continues to render service in some immediate capacity to the community. For, invariably, I have seen that those who lose interest in new things, that is, in making new friends, or taking part in new activities, or in developing a new talent, but instead retreat down memory lane, living the majority of their waking hours reclining in a chair, rethinking and speaking of the past, it is these folks that are most often stricken with Arteriosclerosis of the brain and/or Alzheimers Disease.

The two are very similar. You see, what we don't use, we lose. If the brain is not given new ideas, new challenges to make it think and work, which brings blood to the vessels and cuts new channels for new memories, it will atrophy and die. Neurologists have found that we use only a very small percentage of our brain capacity in a lifetime, roughly 10%. What a shame to use even less and allow laziness and malaise to cut us off early in life, to thus become a burden on others.

The shining example of one who certainly was not letting this happen to her was Mama, who arrived from Los Angeles to visit us in Fulton in the Fall of 1955 to see her first grandchild, our new baby boy, Jeremy. What a happy reunion! Mama had survived remarkably well in Los Angeles where I had deserted her in a large and strange city to run off with my husband to Missouri. She animatedly told us of making new friends at the Authors' Club, the Philosophical Society, a local church, etc. Mama was sixty-eight years old by then, and as enthused about life as anyone ever could be.

One new friend she made in particular was a woman named Helen Olson, who lived at 433 Harvard Boulevard in the Wilshire District. There was an instant soul attraction between them, and after a short few weeks Helen asked Mother to move in to live in her spacious home. It seemed a nice idea and Marlena accepted. She was given her own wing of the house on the ground floor from which she could step out onto the sunny patio and backyard enclosed garden.

Helen and her husband, Roland, had four tall, lovely daughters, all of whom studied ballet, so the household was an especially active and vital one. Mama became a kind of live-in grandmother, who served as the unofficial secretary everyone checked in and out with, and through whom everyone kept tabs on the others. When Mama moved in, little did she anticipate the special kind of excitement that was in store for her.

✳

A YOGI IN THE HOUSE
MAHARISHI ARRIVES

Helen Olson, Mama's friend and house-mistress, was the Assistant Director of the Greek Theater in Los Angeles. In this position, she contacted, booked, met, and welcomed, many visiting personalities to Southern California, some even from foreign countries. Artists, dance troupes, actors, etc. from all over the world passed through her office. She often brought home unusual people to stay for a night or two, though many times their stay stretched into months. There were several quiet wings in her large home where Mama lived, and Helen had a flair for, and enjoyed talking to, interesting creative people. It was she who introduced Harry Belefonte to the United States, and into musical productions and films in L.A. and Hollywood. Mama said there was never a dull moment at 433 South Harvard.

One day Helen brought home an East Indian Yogi. His name was Maharishi Mahesh Yogi, and Helen worked diligently to introduce him to the western world, throwing open her home to his entire entourage from India, as she believed wholeheartedly in his teachings. Thus, for six months the first Transcendental Meditation meetings in America were held in the living room of the very home where Mama lived.

While in Los Angeles, Maharishi took residence upstairs in the largest wing of the house, together with a few devoted female devotees he had brought from India, who kept his personal silk robes and who cooked his special spicy vegetarian food in the kitchen. It was here that Mama could chat with the gentle and sweet East Indian ladies about their culture and the teachings, as the hallway to Mama's wing led past the kitchen and to the back garden. Every day that Maharishi was in residence spicy, delicious fragrances floated down the hall.

Maharishi was a quiet and gentle addition to the household, with his beautiful warm smile beaming on all he passed, as his orange silk robe swished down the curving staircase at the times he was visible.

Mama loved to ask questions and listen, during moments of his quiet relaxing with the household, and she found him very devoted and sincere, but she already had her own pretty solid philosophy of life (as I've described), and although she appreciated the concept of Transcendental Meditation — TM — and knew it would help many who were spiritually hungry and searching for a Path, she was not inwardly guided to join the Order or take a personal mantra for herself. She attended the early first lectures given in the large living room, to which fifty to seventy-five people attended evenings. Mama saw the value of the teaching, but had some reservations. For one, she told me she did not entirely approve of charging an individual $75.00 for a Mantra (meditation chant) as this seemed quite excessive in 1954. Many hungry souls who needed this help could not afford to pay she thought. (Of course, we know that where there is a will, there is a way. And if the seeker is sincere, some way is found to earn the amount.)

Later Mama told me she could not help but hear everyday scuttlebutt in the kitchen through those many months, but her integrity kept her from commenting upon it. Months later when Maharishi became well-known and TM was sweeping the country, she and Helen were offered $50,000.00 by reporters from *Ladies Home Journal* magazine to tell the inside story. Of course they refused. Mama could not be bought. Naturally, there were no tales to tell as such, but people's insatiable appetite for any and all details of such a famous figure's personal, at-home life tends to lure gossip-hungry reporters, especially in those early days of his notoriety.

Transcendental Meditation swept the country, here and in Europe. Helen wrote her own book, entitled *A Hermit in the House*,* describing in western terms Maharishi's philosophy and mission. The book sold quite well, and later Helen Olson moved to Zurich, Switzerland to lead the movement there, and to give initiation to new members who came from all over Europe. Helen's youngest daughter, Theresa, left a ballet career to join Helen as teacher and initiator. The Movement presently has its U.S. headquarters at their Maharishi International University in Iowa,** and is a living testament to humanity's hunger for peace.

All this wild activity with people coming and going kept Mama pretty well occupied in the Los Angeles scene. She was also compiling notes for her own book, *Awaken Your Awareness*,*** which was published in 1965 by DeVorss and Co.

Through those years she attended the Authors' Club, meeting and making friends with a number of interesting

A Hermit in the House, by Helena Olson, Forenede. Trykkerier Press, Oslo, Norway. 1967 (Out of print).
**Maharishi International University, Fairfield, Iowa 52556.
***Awaken Your Awareness*, by Marlena Beckington, 1963. DeVorss & Co. L.A. — Out of print.

individuals, including J.Allen Boone, who wrote the book *Kinship with All Life,** in which he describes his remarkable relationship with animals including movie dogs. Boone had trained the original Strongheart, the famous canine hero that preceded Lassie. He was well-loved in Hollywood and beyond.

Mama was a special lady. She was strong-minded about right and wrong (I can bear witness, having felt the willow switch as a little shaver who failed to mind). But on a broader scale her heart was open to people on many levels. She was a living testimony to unconditional love.

Unconditional love means totally accepting an individual as they are, where they are, and extending caring and concern to them, rather than saying, or feeling, "I will love you only if and when you shape up, and fit the mold I see as right." That is conditional love, and has no place in the life of a person who seeks to walk the path Jesus showed us.

Mama made friends with church ministers and corresponded with government officials and politicians who were running for office. Her files contained personal and in-depth answers even from Presidents. Sometimes they accepted her sage advice regarding the political scene. But Mama was especially available to souls who crossed her path who had no one else to turn to in times of emotional or psychological need. She would spend many hours listening to them, sharing their worries. They came as friends to find a haven in the storm and invariably returned again and again.

Such a one was Tom-Ann. If Tom-Ann had a last name, I never knew it, for Mama was discreet, but Mama did share with me, and no one else I believe, her interest and concern for this young man of about twenty-two, named Tom, who was very unhappy and threatening to commit suicide. After many in-depth conversations, Mama encouraged him to follow his heart, and he finally had a series of seven sexual operations in Mexico, with the blessing and help of his own mother. Earlier, before talking with Mama, he had been too frightened to tell his psychological agony to his mother.

Months later when he finally returned to visit, Mama

Kinship With All Life, 1954, Harper Bros., 49 E. 3rd St., New York.

said *she* was beautiful, complete with a lovely hairdo, make-up, a dress and high heel shoes. But most of all, Tom (now Ann) wore a brilliant smile expressing a genuine happiness within. The name was now Ann, but ever after, Mama referred to this individual as her friend, Tom-Ann, who remained happy and devoted. She went on to lead a quite normal enthusiastic life as a young woman. This story had a happy outcome.

The stigma that surrounds this kind of problem is still significant in our society, though we are gradually becoming more accepting. People are not only bodies and minds, but also souls. Most souls have reincarnated many times before, as both male and female, in order to experience the many facets of earth living. This fact is not understood or taught. In cases such as Tom-Ann, it is likely that the individual has been female many times over, perhaps over many centuries, in a longer series of lives than usual. When suddenly this soul incarnates in a male body attempting to balance its nature, the psyche cannot adjust to the new environment of being male, and thus experiences frustration and unhappiness that, if severe enough, manifests in depression or even suicide. A female-oriented soul feels trapped in a male body. This can, of course, happen vice-versa, as a female desiring to again be male. The trauma is much deeper than desire, and can break a life when not understood.

This same condition may exist in some who are homosexual or lesbian. They have difficulty making the shift, and it may take a few lifetimes, as it's all an experiential process eventually to reach a perfect state of male/female balance. "Male and female, maketh He them," states Gen. 1:27. The word and, if read esoterically, indicates we are, as human beings, endowed with both male and female qualities and characteristics.

So you see, we have both natures that must be developed within each of us: masculine energies such as strength, and courage to face danger, protecting the family unit, with the power to drive ahead through challenges, but also the feminine energies of the inclination to bring harmony to situations, creativity, sensitivity and the nurturing quality to embrace the weak and needy, with a respect for life in all its expressions. Some among us have these male/female qualities in better balance than others, through becoming developed and refined over many incarnations.

Thus, although discrimination in regards to our own thoughts and actions according to our understanding is necessary, we should not be judgmental of others, for we don't know the burdens they carry, nor their life's path. Jesus warned us of this. The American Indians also have a saying common to many tribes: "I will not judge a man until I have walked in his moccasins for six moons." Who among us qualifies?

During these years Mama kept copious notes of her thoughts and gleanings, and published her book in 1965. I typed and helped to put the manuscript into shape for the publisher. It is a gem, a string of avant garde thoughts on philosophy and personal experiences, pearls strung on threads of humor and wisdom. It is presently out of print, I am sorry to say.

I was thrilled to see Mama when she made the trip to Missouri, and she was thrilled with our baby, Jeremy, her first grandchild. Amazingly, three years later, at seventy-two, Mama would travel even further to see her second grandson, this time across the Atlantic to Europe on an ocean liner.

I was overjoyed when Allen came home one day to casually announce, "I have new orders. Guess where — we'll be living in Germany — at Nuremberg. I leave in August to find quarters for us, and you and Jeremy will follow later."

I hadn't dared hope of ever seeing Europe. During my childhood my dreams at night often took me to an old European castle or manor house, that seemed in those dreams very ghostly, with long, dark and mysterious stairways and corridors, past damp and dripping stone walls. Such dreams were often fraught with anxiety, and yet it all seemed so familiar and natural. And *so real*. Then I was thrilled at the thought of actually living there (but of course, not in a castle).

And so, at the end of our very pleasant three-year stay in Missouri, which had been eventful in many ways, we packed and sorted our belongings. Allen drove Jeremy and me to Los Angeles where we were to wait at 433 So. Harvard, Mama's interesting home, for three months while he flew

ahead to his post in Europe. We had a tent, and as it was late
summer, we camped out-of-doors enroute to the west coast.

One night after entering the amazing Rocky Mountains
from the east, we set up camp inside the high eastern
entrance of Yellowstone National Park. I shall never forget
that night, for I had a most unusual psychic experience. We
had found an enchanting, delightful spot alongside a clear,
cold rushing stream, an open place like a round room midst
an encirclement of tall trees, creating a cathedral-like setting, with an open dome to the sky above. Moonlight streamed
through. An ethereal magic captured us.

It was late and we were weary from the long day's
drive across the strange moonscape of the Badlands of South
Dakota and the high mountains of Montana, so we set up
our tent and turned in to sleep on our air mattresses. After a
time, I awakened, feeling extremely cold. I could not get
comfortable enough to sleep again. It may have been around
3:00 a.m. Suddenly, a brilliant light flashed. Like a flash bulb
going off. Startled, I opened my eyes. There was nothing,
only the soft cold darkness, and the sound of the running
stream outside our tent. I shut my eyes. Another flash!
These were like camera flashbulbs, flaring like rockets inside my forehead. I saw them only when my eyes were
closed. Then, I became aware of Indians around me. They
were spirits of those whose meeting place this cathedral
meadow had been, I seemed to be told. Multitudes of them.
The flashes of lights continued for many minutes as I lay
amazed at what I was sensing, the sacredness of this place
in the hearts of those who had lived and loved here, and
now were welcoming me to their hallowed grounds. Awareness of my cold aching body faded into the background as I
allowed myself to accept and appreciate what I was being
given. It was truly a light show, an inner radiance I have
never forgotten all these thirty-some years. Nothing like
that has ever happened again.

And so we arrived in Los Angeles, and my fourteen-
month-old son and I rested and enjoyed three months in the
house of travelers with Mama, Helen Olson and family,
while awaiting our call to Europe. During this time we had

early morning breakfast daily with the currently visiting artist-in-residence — the Director of London's Royal Ballet. He was a jovial and rotund gentleman, born in Latvia, but a resident of Switzerland for some time. He had made a trip to the west coast seeking new dance talent in America, and Helen's daughters were dancers. We became quite good friends, as he had two baby boys at home in Europe whom he missed, so enjoyed playing with and talking to Jeremy. Our friendship culminated two years later when we received complimentary box seat tickets for the opening performance of the London Royal Ballet Company in Zurich, Switzerland as his honored guests.

After the long drive to Los Angeles I had the misfortune to miscarry a pregnancy that was only a three-month gestation, and this was the second of the two sons I later was told are being raised in the heavenly realms by my grandparents. The packing, moving and auto trip from Illinois had apparently been too strenuous for my body. As mentioned earlier, I did not know at that time that even souls of the earliest of pregnancies seem to be considered family members, and remain so. They have to grow up and develop in the astral realm without the benefit of the character-building challenges that earth life brings, and for which reason souls come here in the first place. This illustrates why it truly is against God's law and Divine Plan to deliberately take another's life, or one's own, at any point in time. It deprives that one of the experiences he or she needs on this plane of life to develop the soul qualities necessary for evolution to higher levels of consciousness, which is our eventual destiny. Thus short-circuiting a life sets that life back in time, and that person must make another attempt at some later point to gain the wisdom and experience he would have gained earlier. This becomes a karmic debt for the perpetrator, for which the unchanging universal law will at a later time demand a balance. Dr. Ernest Wilson, while in his 80's, once stated humorously, with tongue-in-cheek, that he is grateful he was born before The Pill or abortions had become in vogue. "Otherwise," he said, "I am afraid I wouldn't have made it!"

Of course, there often are certain extenuating circumstances such as the medical condition of the mother, whose life may be in danger. Accidental miscarriages are not considered karmic debt. It is taught that sometimes the child, itself, will instigate the leaving while still a fetus, the soul having ascertained this setting is not to its best advantage. Paramhansa Yogananda said that a person who commits suicide will be miscarried, even repeatedly, until the soul yearns for, and realizes, the value of earth life.

By earth time, my two sons lost in pregnancy would now be thirty-eight and thirty-six years old. I am looking forward to the joy of becoming acquainted some day.

During this time in Los Angeles I had an amazing astrological reading in which the reader stated there were three major cities in my future: Nuremberg, Germany; Seattle, Washington; and London, England. The woman reading my astrological chart had not the slightest idea that I was *that very week* preparing to embark for Nuremberg, Germany to join my husband. It was to be a joyful three-years, a splendid highlight in my life, with intriguing stories of which I am eager to tell.

*

CHAPTER SIX

ANOTHER WORLD –
THE OLDE WORLD

How can one possibly describe Europe in 1956 before many tourists had come? It was living history. Everything we'd read in books, spread out before our eyes: medieval villages with narrow cobblestone streets, flower boxes at windows, overflowing with colorful blooms, picture-perfect pastoral scenes just like the postcards we had seen years before – nothing was changed. I was struck with a feeling that time had stood still in this part of the world, had waited just for us, that we might feast our eyes on scenes out of the past. Here it all was, waiting through the centuries, as it had always been. There was the feel of ancient tranquility, as cities were not yet so grossly overcrowded. Flocks of geese, and donkeys with sacks of grain on their backs were seen being guided along the narrow roadways.

After a long plane flight from America aboard an old propeller-driven military aircraft, we landed in Frankfurt where Allen was waiting to enthusiastically greet little Jeremy and me. Jeremy was now seventeen months old. Dashing away from me, he ran in and out between the legs of several men in uniform, crying, "Daddy! Daddy?" until one of the tall soldiers – his father – snatched him up into a big hug, then reaching for me in sweet embrace. Next came the adventure of traveling by German train to our new home in Nuremberg.

On weekends after becoming settled, we took joy-filled trips into the countryside, frequenting a particular Gasthouse in the area famous for its homemade strawberry wine. Or we might stop at noon when we came upon a sunny outdoor cafe with colored umbrellas, to munch on the famous brotchen, cheeses, tiny smoked bratwurst and other tantalizing and tummy-filling freshly-made foods.

It would take reams to adequately describe the many fascinations of Nuremberg. To be living in one of the oldest and most famous towns of Germany was for me a blessing untold, and every day was an exciting adventure. The immense churches with their gorgeous stained glass windows and magnificent artwork centuries old (often on the ceilings so I got a crick in my neck from upward-gazing), left me awestruck at the dedication involved in the creating. The masons of those days were inspired, dedicated men who were the foundation of the Masonic Lodge.

Koenigstrasse (King Street) is the main thoroughfare, with many narrow side streets wandering off in all directions, as though in early days a pail of worms had been thrown on the ground and whichever way they crawled became the plan for the narrow cobblestone streets. There was no such thing as a square block, and this was indeed a strange idea (or lack of idea) for Americans to deal with. You just had to point your nose in the general direction you wished to go, and keep heading that way at every turn. Eventually you would reach your destination. I was reminded of the thought-provoking poem "The Medieval Calf" which relates how the pathways people now travel were originally created by the meandering trails of the medieval calf. First the footpath, then the cart, the wagon, and finally the autos all continue on the same narrow winding course, the trail through the woods first trod by the calf. (This concept can also apply to the habitual mental roads most humans follow. Rather than exerting the effort to forge a new and straighter, clear-cut path through the wilderness of ideas to deal with life and its challenges, they defer instead to follow the established meandering path of the sociological medieval calf, the early-set cultural ideas they've never bothered to question.)

The shops of Nuremberg held delights of every description, wonderful handicrafts to suit every taste: hand-
carved wood, woven woolens, items of engraved silver and
gold, delicate embroideries and mouth-blown, hand-cut crystal.
Many were originals, not turned out by the thousands as in
our U.S. factories. In the mid 1950's prices in Europe were
reasonable and reachable. With Allen's modest military salary I could purchase, with great care, a few precious items
to use and cherish for many years. I had learned to speak a
little German so I might converse with shopkeepers. The
local populous was considerate and helpful, never laughing
at my stumbling attempts to be understood.

One very memorable activity was the German-Ameri-
can Club whose members were the American ladies of our
Battalion and the wives of the city officials of Erlangen.
Erlangen, a small town near Nuremberg where we first
lived, is a very lovely park-like university town which had
been given an award a few years previously as the most
beautifully refurbished town in West Germany. Flower-filled
parks and newly painted facades created a happy and colorful atmosphere. The local women were especially hospitable and warm; most spoke excellent English, and we soon
made lasting friendships.

Once a month the German wives escorted us American
ladies on tours to local factories such as the well-known
Shuko Toy Factory and the Hummel factory, where we
watched those delicate, lovely original figurines being made.
We visited one of the finest tapestry factories in West Germany, and admired the wares in a nearby crystal factory.

Also once a month we women, that is about fifteen
Americans and fifteen German ladies, got together for a
cooking class. One month the German ladies taught the
Americans secrets of their best traditional dishes, such as
Sauerbraten or Rouladen (sliced rolled beef with special
stuffings cooked in wine sauce), or Weinerschnitzel (veal
cutlets). The next month the Americans taught the German
ladies our stand-bys, such as Southern Fried Chicken, Texas
Chili, Boston-baked beans and other regional dishes. Then
at suppertime the thirty husbands would show up to enjoy

the fruits of our labors, which had been great fun to prepare. It was a memorable international relations experience, and over time we all became one social family.

There was an ambience in daily living thirty years ago
that allowed a graceful flow of ideas and a sharing of fellowship which has been fast disappearing in recent years as the
world and its peoples become more stressed. The Germans
have a word for this gentle, graceful outlook on life that
allows time to enjoy new things and new people, to share
leisurely and graciously the simple pleasures of life.
Gemutlischkeit describes in one word what in English takes
an entire paragraph to explain.

Nuremberg is one of the oldest great walled cities of
Europe. It was, in fact, founded as early as 1000 A.D., being
a stopover or resting place for the Roman Caesars traveling
from Rome to visit the Kings of France. This was in the days
before there was a Germany, when the area was all a part of
the Holy Roman Empire. A castle with moat was built on the
highest hill of this area as a fortress to house Caesar and his
entourage as they rested on their journey. As years passed,
serf huts sprang up around the base of the castle and lodg-
ings for merchants hoping to do business with the Caesar.
Gradually growing into a medieval town through the Middle
Ages, Nuremberg became one of the most important cultural centers of Europe.

Many famous buildings hundreds of years old stand within
its walled inner quarter. The first German gymnasium was
established in Nuremberg, and the first German paper mill
stood in this city. Peter Henle invented the Nuremberg Egg,
hailed as the first pocket watch. It was also a center of the
Protestant Reformation under Martin Luther. To be living in
the midst of such history was for me a dream come true.

The castle was impressive. The immense high stone
fortress was surrounded by a large cobblestone courtyard
which is empty now, except for the tourists in summer who
wander through. The deep and broad moat around the castle
was dry, and interestingly, its bottom had been planted in
small vegetable gardens worked by city dwellers who had
been fortunate enough to receive a plot. It was comparable

to our city pea-patch gardens. We were told that the soil in the moat was particularly rich, as the moat, when filled with water in days gone by, had been the handy receptacle for all the garbage and human 'night soil' flung out castle windows or off the walls through several centuries past.

At the base of the castle sat a simple but famous little hut. It was the true Hansel and Gretel Cottage that had inspired the well-known *Grimm's Fairy Tale*. Why it had been moved from its original location in the woods of Northern Germany near Cologne to this spot in Nuremberg was obscured in history. Somehow I was saddened, as it seemed out of character on display like this, away from its true home deep in the mysterious forest, the fairy tale setting that has fired the imaginations of so many children through the centuries. Nevertheless, Allen took my picture standing beside its small door near the base of the castle.

Nearby was another landmark attraction, the home of the German painter, Hans Drurer. His *Praying Hands* portrait is world famous, but is just one of his many works. The Drurer house itself was rustic, typical of that century. How fortunate that a few such museum pieces, the homes of a few city fathers, had been spared during the bombings of Germany in World War II, for such historical architecture cannot be replaced. Nuremberg took much bombing. The areas of new stone, built to match against the old, were distinctly visible. Even portions of the medieval wall itself, surrounding the inner city had been rebuilt but kept in the same architectural fashion. The clean, light stone stood out in bright contrast against the old, making a stark age comparison. The priceless goldleaf-covered Fountain Statue covered with hand-carved bigger-than-life figures, that stood in the center of the town square had, with great foresight, been dismantled and hidden underground in the early days of the war. Thus, it was miraculously saved when the town square inevitably was bombed.

Nuremberg was a prime target of the Allies as it was Hitler's favorite German city, and where he had already begun constructing the World Congress Building from solid granite blocks brought in from Denmark. There was to be a room in it for every country, including the United States. His plan was to make Nuremberg the capital of the world. This World Congress Building still stands, only two-thirds finished, on the edge of the Deutsendeich, a small park with a lake and swans on the water that was only two blocks walk from our housing quarters. After the war the Germans were nonplussed as to what to do with this building, for it would cost more to tear it down than to finish it. They thought perhaps to use it for a sports arena, but to my knowledge, nothing at all has ever been done with it. It still sits as a jagged monument to the wild dreams of a power-driven man who sought to be ruler of the entire western world.

Regarding those unique centuries-old houses that were turned into museums, I will never forget my astonishment at how short the people actually must have been in the 12th and 13th centuries. At five-foot six, I actually had to duck considerably to enter the front doorways! It was obvious folks then were little over four feet, perhaps four and one-half feet tall. The chairs within the houses were built very close to the floor, since obviously people's legs were much shorter. But these chairs also were very wide, to accommodate the many layers of clothing: gowns, velvet coats, petticoats, etc. Of course, none of the residences had heat other than the few fireplaces, so petticoats and underwear were worn layer upon layer against the cold. I have also read, and Mama told me from her knowledge of German family history tales, that much of this underclothing was *never taken off from fall until spring*, by rich and poor alike. I know for a fact that the olfactory nerve can be deadened against odor if subjected for any length of time to a strong scent. My father, a farmer, spent many hours in or near the barnyard and animals, and he claimed he "never smelled a thing," defensively calling Mama "a fibber" when she said his overalls needed changing. So I suppose those folks in medieval days had no problem either, if they all smelled alike. History books don't record such amusing and down-to-earth facts.

One vivid memory of the Altstadt (Old City) Museum stands out in my mind — the row of full suits of armor worn by knights of old. They were so small, can you believe, that they would have fit an average twelve-year old American boy. This again pointed out that medieval people were amazingly short. The movies depict these heroes as huge goliaths of men riding immense snorting war horses. I began to wonder if they were not more like dwarfs on ponies.

The implements of hand-to-hand combat were heavy, mean and ugly-looking. Despite their small stature, the people must have been very strong and fierce to wield them. Double-edged battle axes; and clubs — on the end of which were metal balls studded with razor-sharp nails; thin curved blades shaped to whip off a man's head in one stroke; swords of various lengths and description. These all lined the walls or were displayed under glass, creating vicious mental pictures best not harboured.

I stopped short. One item riveted my attention. I'd never dreamed of actually seeing it in this lifetime. I had read of the chastity belt in history books, a clumsy harness a man fastened around his wife's waist and pelvis to insure her faithfulness while he went off to war or on Crusades. It had sounded like a mean contraption, and it was. I could see that the heavy metal strip would surround the woman's waist to be locked on. An attached piece passed down and between the legs from front to back. In the crotch, firmly attached, was a small metal circlet, which was obviously meant to fit up against the vagina. The center of this metal circlet was cut to form fine sharp teeth turned inward like a small trap, as a multitude of fishhooks, so that anything that went in would be torn to shreds when pulled out. This I could see would be a most potent deterrent to any would-be lover, or possible rapist of a woman whose husband was away.

But tragically, a most horrible death awaited a young wife whose husband left her so shackled, but unknowingly pregnant. With the belt in place there was then no way to give birth. Some who were isolated had no means available to remove the contraption as the metal belt was bound on with a heavy metal lock and made not to be removed, the key taken or hidden. Sometimes the man never came home from the war or religious crusade, and the woman was left in this abject condition.

Women have suffered untold hardships and atrocities through the ages. Fortunately this pattern of inequality has been brought strongly to the forefront in this century, and strides have been made toward change. It has been pointed out that because women in general were not even given the privilege during the medieval years of having a physician to attend them when they were ill, their only recourse was to turn to the naturalists, or herbalists, who usually lived in huts in the forest where the various plants and herbs grew, and who brewed teas and herbal distillations from these plants. This is where the witches cauldron idea came from. It was no more than the medieval counterpart of our herb teapot today, only it was a large metal cooking pot hung over an open fire, as we see in pictures. We now know these natural brews often healed the ill person.

Men who had little knowledge, understanding or aware-ness of this kind of cure, called it a *witches brew*. Living a quiet life in the forest close to nature and the earth, these ones sometimes developed intuitive faculties as well, and could thus diagnose an illness by inner sight (just as my Great Aunt Kate did), so this of course added fuel to the fire. The early Christian Church built upon this ignorance with the attitude that looked on all forest and nature-oriented practices as pagan, evil, and of the devil. History shows many good people — usually women — were burned at the stake as witches because they were in league with the devil. Isn't it a shame what ignorance has perpetrated upon the more gifted through the ages, with resultant atrocities.

Nuremberg had many delightful customs. One of the most memorable was the annual *Christkindlsmarkt* — Christ Child's Market — at Christmas time. Year 'round the market in the town square, in the center of which stood that mag-nificent golden fountain, was always a pleasure to shop. With its colorful umbrella canopies, shading enticing farm-fresh fruits and vegetables, fresh breads and sausages, armloads of brilliant flowers for sale, it offered the eye and the fancy an abundance of goods from dozens of vendors. But at Christmas — Ahh! It became a fantasy-land for child and adult alike. For several weeks one could wander among the stalls, finding almost anything the heart desired, or just enjoying the beauty of the scene. In addition to choice wares from town shops, there were all the Christmas trimmings, including fresh greenery and wreaths, dried flowers and berries from the surrounding forests. The scene resembled old-fashioned paintings.

We needed to bundle up as the air was nippy. Our breath made smoke as we laughed and chatted together, while our feet scrunch-scrunched on the clean, snow-covered cobblestone streets. The nippy cold air induced hunger and there, crowded between the umbrella-covered stalls, wafting enticing scents onto the air, sat booths of vendors selling hot bratwurst sausages served between crunchy, tasty fresh brochen (hard rolls), sauerkraut and bratwurst, and hot-spiced apple cider. How could anyone resist? My! Those were memorable times that brought old-fashioned Christmas card pictures back to life, and one could fool himself into thinking he had somehow, by magic, stepped into just such an old lithograph.

Around December 18th, on an evening of the week before Christmas, the annual Children's Parade of the Lanterns was held. This event was publicized throughout Germany and surrounding countries, and visitors came to Nuremberg from far and near, gathering in large numbers along the streets of the parade route many hours before dark to get a desirable spot for the best view. The town was built on an incline, the impressive eleventh-century castle sitting at the very top of the hill. The streets curled and wound around, ever upward, finally ending at the base of the castle wall.

Many weeks before Christmas all the children of the town and surrounding area, ages twelve and under, worked industriously making colored rice-paper lantern-creatures in every shape and figure imaginable. There were replicas of fish, birds and various animals, bells, angels, dragons and butterflies. These paper lanterns were attached to a carrying pole and inside the figure would be placed a light, perhaps a small flashlight, which brought the colors of the creature to life. As darkness fell on the eve of the big event, traffic was closed off and the children gathered at the lowest part of town. All the street lights in the entire city were turned out, and for a few moments all was blackness, except for the moonlight glistening on the snow, etching the city's outline in a ghostly skyscape. The people waited breathlessly. Then the enchanted moment arrived – the lanterns went on. And an audible gasp went up from the thousands lining the streets above. Then the strange procession, every form of glowing bird, animal and fish in single-file, began to curl through the winding streets of the city tracing a long snake-like trail, multi-colored and brilliant, the paper creatures bobbing life-like at the top of their poles. An adult or two led the Column of Light, with others interspersed to guard against mishap. Under the cover of darkness, the four-hundred children were invisible; only the magnificent colored creatures could be seen in their Christmas Snake Dance through the inky black of night. Up and down the narrow curling streets they went, winding around and around until they finally emerged after an hour or so on the very crest of the hill in the castle courtyard. This area was then brilliantly lit, and a replica of the Passion Play was presented by the older children for the lucky onlookers who had earlier crowded into the castle courtyard.

This annual event was unique in its originality in all of Europe and imprinted a picture in the mind not soon forgotten. I imagine any child who walked this special Parade of Lanterns, and witnessed or acted in the Passion Play, would throughout life remember having played a part in a truly meaningful Christmas Story.

I felt a deep connection to Germany's medieval years, sensing a life in the time of the Crusades, the War of the Roses, and the pageantry and struggles of that era. During the latter period of Germany's domination by Hitler, I was a child and young teenager in America, but I still followed the news with avid and sad interest. Now in Germany, I could understand why an entire nation of young people could be indoctrinated into Hitler's leadership. German youth are taught early to respect authority. One never saw a German child stepping on the grass if a sign forbade it – not a single

ANOTHER WORLD — THE OLDE WORLD   261

blade — while the American child runs free and uninhibited. I saw German parents give one command to their child: "Sitzen!" And the child sits. Sometimes for an hour or more. An American child told to sit may stay put for two minutes before he is up and dashing about. And so, the German child grows up not only obeying the authoritative voice of the parent, but of any authority, including that of the government. As is true of so many leaders gone amuk, Hitler had brought his country up economically and socially, and restored the people's confidence in themselves and their country after the defeat of World War I. In the early years Germans looked on him as a savior. Even today, people of virtually every nation still excruciate over which leader to place their confidence in, for power corrupts and great power corrupts greatly. It is only a true man of God that can safely lead.

Due to the many military activities required even of wives in our battalion, it was the custom to have live-in help. Our little boy, Jeremy, was only two years old, so I found it especially necessary. Our maid, Angelika, was quite a special girl. She had been born in Czechoslovakia, but had fled with her mother and other siblings just before the invasion by the Russians in the 1940's. She was a very pretty girl of 25 years, and a very competent maid, who also, by the way, spoke five languages. This was somewhat of an embarrassment to me, having been taught in school that America was, in general, an advanced nation. I, an American, spoke only English (and a smattering of German). In the Midwest of the 1930's, foreign languages were not even offered in school. I did, however, study before going to Germany.

Angelika had quite a tale to tell of those frightening days, when her father had gone off to fight somewhere, leaving her mother responsible for the family's safety. They had to flee Czechoslovakia leaving all possessions, even clothing, behind, if they wished passage out of the country on a night train of boxcars. So, Angelika told me, her mother ingeniously dismantled her sewing machine and sewed all the necessary parts inside the clothing the children would wear on their bodies. Later, in Germany, with no money or job, she reassembled her machine and was able to piece

OVER AN ANGEL'S SHOULDER

together scraps of material she salvaged to sew make-shift clothes for her growing family. Angelika remembered the nightmare train ride out of Prague, with dozens of people jammed into the boxcar, standing up, until some fainted; there was no latrine and no food or water. The train ride lasted eighteen hours, and during daylight the sliding door had to remain shut. Some died of suffocation, or trauma, "and then," she said, "under cover of darkness in the otherwise peaceful countryside, the door was slid open enough to fling the dead bodies out alongside the tracks."

Angelika, her mother, brothers and sisters survived the journey, and then lived partially on green grass the first weeks after arrival. It had been ten years now, and they had obtained a foothold and a home in a small village near Nuremberg. Her mother raised geese and a vegetable garden, so I took the opportunity to buy fresh vegetables and some very nice goose down pillows from her. She was a woman much to be admired for her bravery, ingenuity, and will to save her family. Angelika took her salary home to her mother, for she received free room and board with us as a live-in. I did not feel guilty in having a maid; it was a help to all.

Most Americans, isolated from Europe by an ocean, as we have been since Pilgrim days, do not appreciate the sufferings Europeans have endured. War is a tragedy on this planet, but it appears we have not yet learned this lesson, even with the instant communication of television. They say, "Seeing is believing." I say, "Experiencing is believing." It is also said, "The nation that does not learn from history is doomed to repeat it." I fear the word "doomed" is all too accurate.

Nuremberg and the surrounding areas offered ceaselessly fascinating sights and destinations, so when Allen could be free of duty we seized the summer weekends for short vacations and delightedly drove around the countryside and even over the towering, beautiful Alps to Italy, Switzerland, or Austria. It was a bliss-filled period for me, as truly I sensed I'd come home. Viewing the scenes of old Europe, I felt a very real connection, a *deja vu*, and soon some amazing flash-backs and visions confirmed my intuition.

*
OUR NEW BABY BOY

During these summer months I had been pregnant and our second son was born, a beautiful little boy with big blue eyes, sweet, sweet smile and the best nature a baby ever had. We named him 'Jason.' Allen was a wonderful husband and father, so very good to me in all ways, never once speaking a cross word for any reason. After six weeks of military exercises in the field the men would return and we wives would be there at headquarters to greet them. Allen's delight on seeing me was so-o-o evident. With a shy grin he would say, "Gee, how did I rate having the prettiest wife of all to meet me?"

I came to admire Allen immensely and to be much in love, but at the same time I was very disturbed, as those strange silent spells were still with him from time to time and placed a very real pall over our joy. I never knew when his personality might change and, as a result, any plans we had would have to be scrapped. Allen's work in the military seemed at times to place a real strain on him, and I knew that as a sensitive and very artistic man who was highly intelligent, he struggled with the mold in which life had placed him, and the struggle often created much stress. He had not chosen the military as a profession, but rather had been drafted at an early age as a private in World War II, and had served in North Africa and Italy, as mentioned, rising to the rank of Captain by virtue of good leadership. In 1951 he was pulled back in for the Korean War. By then we had married, so Allen remained in service as a Reservist to support us. The officers Allen worked with now at times quietly indicated to me that his superior leadership abilities outweighed the frustration of his intermittent personality changes. They too had noticed and were concerned, wondering if I had an inkling.

I often prayed for understanding and an answer to his troubled days, which he would not, or could not, speak of. His quiet dignity was not conducive to discussion. When he felt fine and was happy I was reluctant to confront him about it, feeling, since I did not know the cause, that speaking of it might throw him back into another of those cold silences, and so I kept my peace. In all medical physicals he was given an A-1 bill of health. I continued to hold faith, knowing there had to be an answer, somehow, somewhere, for I had never before known anyone with such a strange alter ego, inexplicably triggered with no apparent cause. These strange dark spells in personality overshadowed the joy in our new son that should otherwise have been evident. Allen often remained distant, and I tended our sweet baby alone.

It would be another five years before a light would shine leading me to an answer to this strange puzzle. As fate — and heredity — would have it, variations of this problem were reflected in the lives of my children, one yet unborn. I pray that the answer I found may be of help to others who read this.

✳

MAMA SAILS THE ATLANTIC

"Guess what? Grammy Becky is coming!" Jeremy, now the very bright age of three, danced with joy as I made the announcement. I used the name he had renamed Mama. She chose to sail over the Atlantic by ship, being an adventurous soul, then to see Paris and the French countryside enroute, as she continued by train to Nuremberg. I thought it pretty brave of Mama to travel so far alone, all the way from Los Angeles, as she was now seventy-two years old, and had not been out of the U.S. before. But Mama was eager to see her new grandson, Jason, then seven months old, and also Germany which was her family heritage. She sailed on a British ship and the service, she reported, was excellent. Her only complaint was that when news was announced over the loudspeaker, she could not understand a word of it due to "that strange British accent."

Mama's parents were born in Germany. Grandfather came from Baden-Baden, the beautiful city of health-spa fame in southern Germany, and Grandmother from Westphalia in north

Germany. This spa in Baden-Baden is, even now in the 1990's, considered No. 1 in the world for beauty and health benefits.

In our travels we had the joy of visiting Baden-Baden and the Black Forest, a most beautiful part of Bavaria. The city itself is a mass of flowers, and the many parks, with lovely cream-colored buildings house the spas, which gush healthful healing mineral waters. We did not experience that delight however, to my sorrow, as taking the waters was a bit expensive. These places cater to the more well-to-do strata of society the world over. Seeing the Black Forest area, mountainous and thick with old growth forests, was a memory to hold in one's heart forever, for there is a pristine beauty, a feeling of mystery that lays over this land. One could almost sense fairies dancing in these woods, with elves and gnomes and other elementals about. I could now see how my grandfather, being born and raised here, nurtured by the ethereal atmosphere midst some of the richest natural beauty on the face of the earth (even moreso in the late 1800's), would have developed the sensitive psychic nature of which I spoke earlier.

We were all delighted to have Grammy Becky arrive safely, and she was thrilled seeing the land of her parents' birth for the first time. Some evenings we took her out into the jovial atmosphere of the Gasthaus, the rooms filled with song, the many voices raised in the German melodies Mama remembered from her girlhood, the decorated beer steins filled-to-overflowing, lifted in toasts to everything and everyone. What fun! The Bavarians did know how to enjoy life and the simple pleasures of fellowship. On weekends everyone went out walking. This was the national pastime, and a healthy one at that. Sadly, much has changed since the 1950's, even in these simple ways, as every passing year finds Germany and all other countries grappling with change faster than people, or governments, can adjust.

In those days a small railroad track ran behind our quarters, and once a day an antique-looking, picturesque Toonerville-type engine pulled a few old-fashioned railcars past. Jeremy, at three, found it enchanting to watch a "real live train" up close. He would wait religiously by the window and then seeing the train, would dance with excitement and shout, "See Grammy! The Funny Nu-Nu! The Funny Nu-Nu!" as the train whistle sounded so *Nuuu—Nuuuh!*

Allen's Battalion Commander, Colonel Molter, was a very well-liked and popular man, who ran a good competent outfit, and at the same time cared about his men and their families. He and his wife hosted all the officers from time to time at receptions and we became good friends. Suddenly he received orders from Army Headquarters; he was being given command of an American Battalion stationed at Dachou in Southern Bavaria. We all would miss him and his wife and were sorry to see them leave.

*

DACHOU — A VERY DARK SHADOW

Several months later an invitation arrived. Allen and I and several other officers and wives in the Nuremberg Battalion were being invited by our friends, Colonel and Mrs. Molter, to come down for the weekend, a buffet supper Saturday night, and to stay over Sunday in their new quarters at Dachou. Mama was still with us and insisted we should go, as she would enjoy being with the children. This, we thought, would be more than interesting, for we knew Dachou to be the scene of one of Hilter's concentration camps during the war, complete with the terrible crematoria ovens. We were eager to see our old Colonel and his wife, who admitted they missed all of us and the fellowship, but we had a morbid foreboding about visiting this place of ghastly reknown.

It had been only ten years since World War II ended, so there were yet no monuments or a park created to the sad memory of the many thousands whose lives were sacrificed there. That would come in later years. Now, as we arrived, it was as it had been. I saw the several smoke stacks sharp against the sky, indicating the ovens into which the Jewish people had been herded under the pretext of taking showers, and there were several rows of high mounds of earth, grass covered now, mingled with wild flowers that marked the mass graves. Strangely it was a peaceful scene, giving no clue, if one did not know of the atrocities committed there.

Our Colonel and wife gave us a rousing, warm welcome. The main house was their quarters where we also were to stay, and we were soon to see that it had been the headquarters for the notorious German S.S. Guards during the war. I immediately noted the outstanding pattern on the elegant parquet floor in the huge main dining room: The sculptured darker inlaid wood edge all around on four sides formed a running series of swastikas.

We were introduced to and soon became acquainted with some of the American officers and wives who were stationed there under the command of Colonel Molter. Some seemed oddly high strung, their conversation rapid and superficial, as though they were on a high, although these years were long before drugs were used.

After supper, which was excellent, a party with music and dancing came into full swing. The carpet was rolled back in one of the larger front rooms, revealing a smooth, elegantly polished floor. The atmosphere soon became electric and hilarious in the extreme, and I saw that a great deal of drinking was going on, much more so than at any other duty station I had been, including our own in Nuremberg which was sedate by comparison. Could it be that these people were trying to cover-up or cope with the bad vibes of this area that seemed to make everyone nervous? Some of the wives told me that everybody stationed here was very unsettled, unhappy, and had a difficult time waiting out the end of this duty-tour. This was a far cry from what we enjoyed in Nuremberg. I became more and more aware of the strange tension in the air, and although I do not drink, even so I found myself dancing wildly with as rare an abandon as the rest. I didn't even pay attention or care to see what Allen was doing. Fleetingly, I wondered what had gotten into me to act so. At 3:00 a.m. we guests began to trickle off to our assigned bedrooms, and the local folks on base there went home, or so we thought.

We had barely flung ourselves into bed when we were roused by a commotion in the hall — shouts of "Get someone quick! There's blood!" We grabbed our robes and dashed out into the corridor, to see three frightened people gaping at a broad trail of blood running out from under the bathroom door, which was locked tight. No one responded to our pounding. We stood there, astounded, not knowing what to expect. Our host came bounding up the stairs with a crowbar and broke the door open. On the floor lay a woman from the party, her wrists slashed with a knife, and there was blood all over the place. Someone grabbed for towels and bound her arms. The doctor had been called when the blood was first seen, and now the woman was rushed to the hospital.

I heard later that the suicide attempt had been prompted by a fit of despondency. It was not a new phenomenon we were told, as more than a few people stationed at this post in recent years had suffered psychiatric problems, people who had never had them before. This woman's husband had gone home earlier, too drunk to even miss her.

This is an indication that the extremely unhappy, unseen vibrations of traumatic, tragic past events remain to plague such a location, and to have very detrimental effects on anyone unlucky enough to land there, even many years later.

This strange experience has hung in my memory through the years, and I have often prayed for the area and others like it to help clear the subtle astral, to free the sad souls who died there, and those who may still be tied to this place through their part in the horrendous emotional traumas.

This same principle lies behind haunted houses. A soul who has either died a violent death or committed a crime in a house, is locked into the event by the tragic emotion and is unable to rise to higher realms. Its own anger, sorrow or guilt is so intense, this becomes all dominating to them. Usually such a one has never learned that there is a better existence awaiting him/her, if they will only give up strong negative emotions.

Another type of ghost may not be connected to a violent crime, but rather is powerfully attached to, or protective of, his money or his home. His unreasoning love and desire to keep these earthly possessions holds that one to them like a magnet. Thus, folks may move into a house recently purchased and find someone still living in it, a discarnate, which is nothing more than a soul who is refusing to or cannot leave the earth plane after he has died, for a variety of these reasons. This happens much more commonly than we might think and is told of in many true stories. Recently scientific investigators have proven the presence of ghosts by recording undeniable magnetic vibrations in one specific spot. These vibrations were picked up using three distinct technical methods, i.e. three separate types of electronic instruments, measuring magnetism. This was aired in Seattle May 29, 1992 on the program Sightings, with producer Henry Winkler.

Much good work has been done by real ghostbusters, in a ministry whose purpose is to help free misguided souls that they may become willing to let go and move on. Usually a medium who is able to see or hear the entity will work with a Light Worker. Two of the most famous in this field were Dr. and Mrs. Carl Wickland, whose work is described in the book *Thirty Years Among the Dead.** But there are many, many others as well. This ministry is a blessed sacrifice because these ghostly entities are lost souls, in a temporary sense. Temporary, because their condition can be changed, but they may go on for years, even centuries, before they find release. This no-man's land is a part of the purgatory spoken of by the Catholic Church. This is why prayer for the deceased is so important. Ghosts are simply unenlightened humans, who have now passed over, but still not aware of any world or existence other than the earth, and thus they continue to cling to it. They are to be pitied rather than feared.

It is of the greatest importance that we learn all we can while we are here in the body, by way of preparing ourselves for the best possible passing for our transition to the Heavenly Realms. Prayer for souls at the time of death as they are passing over is a great help, as it brings assistance from the Astral and Angel realms to aid that one in crossing.

Thirty Years Among the Dead, 1924, Amherst Press, Amherst, MI

I know these things to be true as I have had personal experience with it. Shall I tell you?

∗

A LOST SOUL IS FOUND

This vivid instance occurred seven years later in 1964 while we were living at the Persidio of San Francisco. I happened to be visiting in the home of a dear friend named Eddie who had been a fellow member of the Agashan Temple ten years before. He was the chap who, when younger, as I wrote, had skated in Sonja Heinie's famous Ice Capades. Later in life he enjoyed success as an artist. Eddie possessed an innate sensitivity and inner knowing. Another friend, Verna, who had also been a fellow Agashan, was visiting us in San Francisco from Los Angeles where she lived. Verna was a fine woman with rare spiritual wisdom and psychic ability, and with whom I had enjoyed a long-time friendship, almost as family. There seldom had been any need or the setting for me to read tea-leaves for a number of years, but this day we three were having a warm reunion after my return from Europe. So we had tea like old times and enjoyed reminiscing, as we had not seen one another for quite some time.

On the spur of the moment, Ed asked me to look into his cup to "see what I might see." As I become quiet and at peace, the cup serves as a focal point for a kind of tranquil concentration for me, and amazingly the shapes of the tea leaves create pictures and thoughts drop into my mind.

After a few moments I plainly saw the South Pacific Islands and one in particular. I asked, "Ed, who do you know that may have died on Iwo Jima?"

Ed answered, "My friend, John."

He had no more than spoken, when friend Verna nearly toppled off her chair. Ed caught her, and steadying her on the chair, we saw she had instantly dropped into a trance. Now Verna did not do this kind of thing voluntarily, nor seldom ever, but it had been known to come upon her *involuntarily* at rare intervals. This was one of them.

Her body seemed to be struggling to speak, and her voice changed: A young man's frightened tone came forth, "Eddie! Oh, Eddie! I've found you! Please help me! I'm lost. And the noise . . . shells shrieking . . . its terrible! Oh-ohhh! I can't stand it any longer!" He screamed and covered *his* ears (with Verna's hands).

Ed was astounded! He recognized him. "Johnny? Is that you, Johnny?

"Yes. It's me."

"I heard you were killed on Iwo Jima!"

"I'm not dead! I'm lost in the fog . . . I've been wandering around for so long . . . I finally saw a light and followed it . . . and now I've found you. Eddie, please help me. I can't stand the noise. The bombs are terrible . . . and the shells!" He appeared to be crying.

Ed and I looked at each other in astonishment, as this was our first personal experience with such a happening. Ed quickly told me he had gone through grade school and high school with John, and then John had been sent to the South Pacific in World War II and been killed on Iwo Jima *twenty years before.* Yet here he was, lost in the no-man's land of the living-dead, not realizing he had lost his body.

At this point I sprang into action and began a running conversation with John, who was using Verna's body but apparently not aware of it. I called to him by name, introducing myself as Ed's friend, and began to explain to him his situation. I told him he needed to understand that the war had been over for twenty years, there were no more bombs, that it was all only in his mind, and he must let go of that thought and look to the new world of Spirit, which awaited him. It took awhile for these ideas to sink in, as he had a difficult time understanding.

He kept saying, "Help me! Help me!"

I told him he was out of his body now and in a spirit body, where there was a new and wonderful life to experience if he could let go of the thought of war. I thanked him for coming to us, and told him over and over that he would be helped if he would listen closely and believe me. As he became more quiet, I said we would all pray together for an angel to come to rescue him, and he would then be taken to a beautiful land where there were no bombs or war or fog. I then proceeded to pray aloud most fervently to Holy Spirit for assistance in this dire circumstance, while Ed silently joined me.

Only a few moments elapsed before John broke in, saying, "Oh! I see a bright light! It's coming toward me. I'm frightened!"

"No, no," I comforted him. "Don't be frightened, John. That is the Angel who has come to care for you. Be quiet and wait."

Shortly, he breathed a tremulous sigh of relief and his tone became sweet. "Oh yes, it's so beautiful. It's beckoning me to come . . . Thank you. Thank you! I'll go now." There was a pause. Then faintly, "Goodbye, Eddie."

Verna, our lady friend's body, relaxed again in an unconscious slump as the spirit of John departed. We waited a few moments, both Ed and I still astonished at this unique happening. Suddenly Verna sat up straighter, opened her eyes and asked, "What happened? Did I faint?" (She had in the past suffered low-blood sugar and was known to faint at rare intervals, thus her assumption.) She knew nothing of what had transpired, her consciousness having been out-of-body while John was in, and she was as astonished as we when we related to her this amazing event.

The authenticity of all this was unquestionable due to the unique circumstances requiring we three individuals, each with a different capacity, working together to give this service, through God's grace, to a soul lost in the no-man's-land between worlds. (Neither Verna nor I had known of Ed's having a childhood friend named John, or of his wartime service.) I opened the door by psychically seeing Iwo Jima in the cup and asking Ed who he had known that had died there. When Ed said the name, John, it gave this tormented spirit entry to Verna who was a natural trance-medium, and being relaxed and receptive she was instantly taken out. Now I wish to stress that there must have been one or more Guardians here, mine, Ed's, Verna's, and our own High Selves even to allow this to happen, knowing full well that we all three worked in the Light, that this would be for a good purpose. Because there is no danger of negative or evil entities taking over during such a happening with those who work in Christ's Light. Such ones are always protected, and this is the importance of loving God and Christ and faithfully being in daily prayer meditation.

When we give ourselves to Christ in being open to His leading, all manner of special work may be given us, depending on our conscious knowledge, lack of fear, love of humanity, and willingness to serve. One may think, "That's just one soul. How important is it, when there may be thousands in that situation?" True. However, it is still of supreme importance to that one soul. Would it not be so to any one of us, were we trapped for twenty years in a fog-ridden, bomb-blasted, shell-shrieking place driving us crazy, with no idea of how to escape? Remember, Jesus caring for just one lost lamb? He uses any and all who are willing to do the much-needed work.

War creates havoc on the inner planes as well as the earth-plane. This is why it is imperative that Humankind evolve beyond the need to settle differences with violence, which creates many years of tragedy for so many.

It is a decided misconception humankind has in general that those who die to this earth are *automatically* elevated to a warm fuzzy existence of all-knowledge, perfect health, loving friends and beautiful surroundings. Nothing could be further from the truth. Believe me. It is true only when that soul has grown in consciousness here to believe in and accept such an existence, and yearn for it with good deeds, heart's desire, and love for God.

Yes, with the tremendous strides we have made in spiritual education in this century, more people are advancing in understanding, but even so, many drift along, too involved in earth-living to pay much heed to an inner awareness of who they really are — a Child of the Most High, who is on the all-important journey home. Again, this is why prayer for the newly departed is essential, and this is the true meaning of the Catholic Last Rites, that the one passing over may be properly received and taken to the level which their consciousness is attuned to.

Our famous President, Abraham Lincoln, was a very advanced soul with knowledge most were not aware he had. My mother admired Abraham Lincoln very much, and always stated he "was a special soul, chosen for a mission, and he understood spirit survival and communication." After he passed, Lincoln was so tormented by the thought of the many souls killed in the Civil War, for which he felt responsible, that he sought for years from the spirit side of life for an appropriate channel through whom he could speak. Due to certain laws of vibration not all spirit entities can function through all mediums. There has to be an inner compatibility, and acceptance.

Finally, he chose a woman in an Eastern state to be his vehicle, and she stated that when Lincoln entered she did not lose her consciousness completely, but was aware of her voice becoming masculine and very commanding, speaking out from a higher level of knowledge. The walls of her room seemed to open and dissolve as she saw, on the ethereal plane, souls beginning to gather by the hundreds as far as the eye could see, while Lincoln spoke through her. They appeared to be mostly soldiers.

"As he spoke," she wrote, "one would see a flash of light here and there in the crowd, and a soul would disappear, having received a new and enlightened understanding, a conscious awareness of himself, and be automatically lifted to a higher plane, released from his entrapment in an earthbound state."

These interesting, true reports were written in a book entitled *Abraham Lincoln Returns*,* by Harriet M. Shelton. This is a wonderful book full of fascinating information. Unfortunately, the book is now out of print, but can be found used. Heaven is described in glowing terms and would give hope to many.

It is natural to wonder why these souls are not simply rescued by spirit guardians, angels if you will, from higher

* *Abraham Lincoln Returns*, 1957, The Evans Pub.Co., 299 Madison Ave., N.Y.

realms. The answer is that the unfortunate earthbound entities are still too consciously tied to earth-awareness, thus
cannot see or hear the angel who comes any more than you
or I see them, and therefore cannot be reached. We all have
free will conferred by the Creator and are never forced to
go anywhere our consciousness does not take us. Discarnate
souls, however, can see us. (We know this, as ghosts resent
any human invading 'their' space.) They can hear a human
who teaches, whether in the earth body or in one's astral
form when one may leave the physical body at night. Indeed, Light Work can be done at night while one's body is
asleep; we may, if we so desire, work in the astral as necessary. Memory is seldom retained of such work, however,
only at times by a few advanced souls who have developed
memory of out-of-body experiences as they have spoken
and written of this.

I should explain that there are several levels to the astral
plane. We, as humans, enter the first level beyond the material
plane if we leave our bodies during sleep. This is the same
level most discarnates move into upon first passing over, and
is the vibratory level on which we may contact those who
linger there. Angels, on the other hand, exist at levels beyond
the first, but come down — lower their vibration — to work, if
called, to the lower levels, including earth.

Perhaps this may dispel some of the mystery and fear
surrounding ghosts. A ghost is only one of us who has had
the misfortune to care nothing for any reality beyond the
material, or who may have been shot onto the Other Side so
suddenly that the realization of death has not occurred
because he/she is still very much alive. Ghosts also may be
ones, perhaps, who have lived only for selfish and/or evil
purpose, have renounced all things Godly, and even proclaimed, "When you're dead, you're dead," as did my own
father for many years.

Years later my father, surprisingly, came to Mama through
a psychic in Los Angeles (who of course had no way to
personally know my mother's affairs). She accurately described my father, who spoke to her from spirit, and then
said to Mama, "Your husband seems distressed. He tells me

he wishes to give his deepest apologies to you. He is saying, 'I did not understand. And I want to thank you, and to say *how sorry I am*, because if it had not been for the things you said over the years, which I heard, even though I resisted, I would have been in very dire straits indeed on this side of life.'"

And so we see that whatever prayers we send out, whatever love we can give to those in need, whether here or there, are of greatest value in the Divine scheme of things, and it should be always in our awareness to be open to guidance, to help without imposing.

Back in Europe, an opportunity came up to take the vacation to Italy we had been longing for. Since Mama ("Grammy Becky") was visiting us, and would be there to stay with our two small sons, it seemed to be the perfect time. Angelika, the German maid would, of course, be there too, to do the necessary housework. Allen had thus far taken no time off, so this would be our first real vacation. Little did I know that Italy's terrain would bring astonishing flashbacks of past-life memory.

THROUGH VISION'S DOOR

If, by chance, I were to glance
        a 'backward glance' —
Through Vision's Door — into days of yore,
Spread before my startled eye,
Nostalgic scenes of days gone by
Would dance across my screen of Mind —
And there I'd find — Identity —
With those behind — in history books.

I'd find my life was woven tight
Into the fabric of the fight
Of men and nations down through an age —
And that today — is but a page
        Torn from my book —
Were I to give a 'backward look.'

And if — by chance — I were to glance
Through Vision's Door —
Across the threshold of time unborn —
And walk a 'ways with tomorrow morn,
My heart would soar! I'd cry no more

For there I'd find I was reborn!
Alive with life, and joy as well —
In a bright new world — where I will dwell
        Through Time Unborn.
Were I — by chance — to 'give a glance!'
Through Visions Door —

                    Bonnie Ann Gilchrist

*

A STEP INTO THE PAST — IN ITALY

There in the hot sun, high on a hill ahead of us, lay the glistening walls of historic Assisi, our immediate destination and future, and also, though I did not yet realize it, the setting of a hidden but vivid part of my past. We had driven over the magnificent Alps to Venice, where Allen had thrilled me with a romantic gondola ride on the famous Grand Canal, the gondolier serenading us in the dusky twilight evening. I was enchanted. This was a replica of the gondola picture Evelyn had sent me years before. But now I was in the gondola, gliding along as in a dreamy medieval portrait.

Pigeons, so tame, they sat on my head in the immense and romantic St. Marks Square, where the famous four bronze horses that had been brought from Constantinople in days gone by stood magnificently above the Doges Palace entrance. The huge bell in the tall tower tolled the hour. And there seemed no end to the enticing sidewalk cafes filled with Italian townsfolk, who appeared to have all the leisure time they wanted to enjoy animated conversation with friends. In Murano nearby, we watched Venetian Glass being blown, famous around the world for its beauty. I bought, and still treasure, a necklace of tiny blown glass canaries.

Then there had been exciting days and nights in Florence. I gazed with a feeling of *deja vu* at the scenes Evelyn had written about, had described to me in great detail years before. Now they seemed to be dream-pictures come true. Many days could be spent in gazing in rapt appreciation of the magnificent artwork in Florence alone. It was difficult to leave each unique city with its colorful history.

On the way to Florence, as we had driven through the countryside, Allen stopped at one special farmhouse. There were two white bullocks in the yard, hitched to a wagon as we might hitch horses. They were large and striking, very beautiful animals. The yard was neat, the house moderate in size and of stucco, built many years before. Several people poured out of the house, looking surprised and questioning, as our American auto pulled into the yard.

Suddenly the older of the group, a middle-aged woman, broke into shouts of laughter, throwing her arms into the air and running toward us crying, "IL AMERICANO CAPITANO! IL AMERICANO CAPITANO! They laughed and cried all at the same time, as the older of the children caught on. It was wonderful to see, as they hugged Allen enthusiastically. Nothing would do but we must stay awhile and have something to eat and drink, and we didn't object as it was a hot summer's day and a most pleasant respite. I saw why Allen had such fond memories of these warm and wonderful people. This was the farm home — and the family — where he had been quartered for some time during World War II, when the Americans, moving slowly forward, had liberated the Italian people from the Nazi invasion. The Nazis had strung mines in their wake as they retreated Italy, and it was one of these which had killed his driver, sparing Allen only by the grace of God.

The Italians had been stripped of food. Their garden produce, animals and poultry all were taken by the German Army, so the starving Italian people welcomed the Americans with great gusto, not only as their liberators, but because our forces brought food with them. Allen's company battery set up headquarters for a time in a farm house in Northern Italy at the foot of the Appenine Mountains. He told me that at the end of a work day when it was quiet, he would go down and milk the couple of cows for the farmer's daughter so that she would have time to visit with him for awhile and relate to him the experiences of the Italian people.

Now, as Allen and I drove over these very roads he had traveled with his troops, it was almost weird to hear him say, "Up ahead now is a curve in the road, and then the hill drops away and there will be a magnificent view," and to find it to be exactly so. It was a moving and nostalgic experience for him, as those war-torn days had been traumatic, yet touched with the pathos and memory of the warm and loving Italian people, appreciative of the men who had given them back their land and their freedom.

The road across the plain to Assisi which sat beyond, higher in the mountains, was straight and uneventful. I felt

impressed to converse and share with Allen many truths of
the spirit, which I had become so aware of through the
years, for my inner self felt joyous in once again being in
this sunny area. Allen was an active and busy professional
man, so there had seldom been time to talk on this level of
concepts that were so close to the heart. He listened intently, asked questions, and was in a relaxed and receptive
mood. There was a deep and tender closeness between us
and we were very happy.

Assisi came into view, high on a distant hill, shimmering white in the sunlight, its high stucco walls reflecting a
beauty that comes with age, and a character acquired through
centuries of sheltering lives and loves, witnessing many
births and deaths, standing against wars and standing in
peace. The closer we came the more a feeling of joy welled
up within me.

Upon arriving, I found a delight in wandering the narrow winding streets that was difficult to express in words,
a joyous feeling of having come home, and I said to Allen,
"I'd be very happy if we could just chuck the whole trip
and stay right here."

Here and there people stood in their doorways, warm
and laughing. One lady brought her beautiful baby daughter out onto the sunlit cobblestone street, holding her out
in her arms to show to me. The little girl's big black eyes
were striking as she gazed openly but solemnly at me without a trace of shyness.

We were enchanted with the architecture of the magnificent Church of St. Francis, which was built in the shape
of an immense cross at the highest point in town. Delicate
wrought-iron grillwork graced the doors leading into the
central courtyard, and also the clean sweep of arches. It is a
huge church, and quite unique in concept.

I wandered a distance away from the city streets with
an urge to visit the Shrine of St. Claire, who had led the
Monastic Order of Women followers of St. Francis, and I
felt as I knelt there in quiet meditation a strange and powerful inner longing — an inexplicable sort of homesickness.
Suddenly, as if in response to my longing, I was engulfed in

a wondrous, comforting love that swept over me in wave after wave, and I dissolved into tears of joy. It is difficult to describe, but I then knew I had once belonged here — I had come home, to a place I had known intimately in years past. It was a strange and unusual emotion. I seemed for awhile to be transported back in time, feeling the hood of a cloak around my head and stones under my knees. Later I looked to see — there were no stones, and I, of course, wore no cloak on a warm summer day. Coming back to now, my emotions were mixed with a tinge of regret that life moves ever onward. Our only comfort is a knowing in our heart, an inner promise that one day we will again be with those souls with whom we lived and loved.

If the past seems shadowy, mysterious, fascinating, so also is the future, for I had no way of knowing then that one day my daughter, yet unborn, would find herself equally attracted to Assisi and would choose to make her home there for a time. What mysteries lie in Heaven's store, awaiting us in Evermore.

Later that evening, in our room in the hotel in Assisi, something happened that sealed my knowing regarding the importance of both Assisi and Rome in my past. As we traveled, I had selected and purchased an item for each of my sisters-in-law to give to them as a memento (there were four of Allen's sisters). Earlier that day, in Florence, I had found a most delicate and beautiful, deeply glossed enamel thimble with colorful hand-etched floral design. It was for Ellen, who was a talented seamstress. She would appreciate something useful, as she loved beauty, but she was also practical. I watched the little white box containing the thimble tumble out onto the bed coverlet as I emptied my purse, intending to move these few items into my suitcase. *I plainly saw the thimble box lying on the coverlet.*

But as I turned back from my suitcase to reach for the little box with the thimble — it was gone! I searched the bed, the floor, my suitcase. In short, I searched everywhere, and there was no little box to be found. Allen came out of the shower where he had been all this time and joined me in the search, but he was no more successful than I. I knew I had seen it quite plainly only moments before, lying openly in the middle of the coverlet. We finally abandoned the hunt, left instructions for the maid if by some miracle it should turn up, and went out to enjoy more of the village.

Allen and I stayed in Assisi two more delightful days. Later, traveling on down the narrow winding road through the barren hills to Rome, lazily enjoying the passing scenery of the Italian countryside. I reflected on my ecstatic experience at the shrine of St. Claire and then on the puzzling disappearance of the small, but significant item. Could it be, I mused, that Spirit had somehow taken the thimble as a sign to me, to confirm my inner sense that this area had played a special place in my past? Even so, it seemed a strange kind of happening. "Well," I sighed almost aloud, "I mustn't let the loss dampen my enthusiasm. It's just such a puzzle."

Rome was immense. Seeing the dark heavy buildings smudged with soot and age, and awash in grey rain was not uplifting to my spirits. (Now, environmental scientists tell us that acid rain has inflicted more damage on these famous Roman landmarks in ten years, than the simple effects of time have in two millenniums. But restoration fortunately has begun.) Allen seemed to be doing fine, as he had good memories of Italy. We wished to see as much as possible in our few days.

The ancient Roman ruins of this city are unique in Europe. So we trudged about in the rain, then took refuge in the ghostly and amazing underground catacombs, where early Christians met and hid in the 1st Century A.D. There was a cool, quiet peace under there, a sense of calm from the outer world, despite the dusty evidences of old burial crypts midst the winding narrow passageways. Hadrian's Tomb, St. Peter's Cathedral, the Sistine Chapel in the Vatican, with its awe-inspiring ceiling of *The Creation*, painted by Michelangelo, all were amazing in their immensity and quiet dignity, monuments to an age we can only muse upon.

Near the end of our day we came to the huge Roman Coliseum. No sooner had we entered the arena than a strange and eerie depression settled over my being, a kind of whirling darkness so intense that I found myself falling to the ground before Allen could grasp me. I felt, rather than heard, shouts and screams, a far off roaring noise and an encompassing terror. Allen half-guided, half-carried me from the arena. I soon realized I had plugged in somehow, psychically re-entered the horrid events that had taken place here. Either I was remembering my own experience or those of others in the days of the gladiator fights, and the sacrifices of Christians to the lions. Allen held and comforted me while I forcibly brought myself back to the present, somewhat embarrassed and apologetic.

I knew I had no desire to remain in Rome. It had been, I felt, the scene of terrible personal trauma (but also of a great personal spiritual conquering, I was told several years later). Whatever the life, it had left its mark, lingering deep in my subconscious memory. I had no desire to pursue it.

Early the next morning we awakened at our hotel in Rome to find it was still raining. A dreary grey fog, vaguely visible, covered everything. We made plans to leave, to drive directly back to Nuremberg, and Allen went to take a shower. Taking off my nightgown, I thought of my little sons, as I often had on this trip, and longed for my baby boy, just nine months old. I was by now most eager to return home.

I carefully folded my nightgown and placed it in the case. Then, as I turned away to pull on my hose, a wave of sadness passed over me realizing that now, because of the weather, I'd had no opportunity to shop for souvenirs in Rome. And so I had nothing to take as a memento of Italy to dear Ellen, as the beautiful and delicately made enamel thimble was lost. In the midst of this thought I turned back to my case — and I blinked, not believing my eyes — for there, *directly in the center of the nightgown I had just folded and placed there, lay the little white box with thimble inside.* I was astounded!

What is the explanation? I can think of only one, as I know what I saw now, and I know what I didn't see. Beloved Presence, Holy Spirit, had in this way shown me what I already clearly felt through my intense experiences:

I had close ties in past lives to both Assisi in the days of St. Francis' ministry, and to Rome in days of the Christian persecutions. Spirit gave me this affirmation with the simple sign of tele-transporting my little thimble in its white box. If this was true, it was dematerialized in Assisi, held in limbo, and rematerialized in Rome four days later.

There is simply no other explanation, and to this day this memory serves as a wonderful example to me of the love and Presence of Spirit in our lives. As an aside, when we presented our gift to Ellen, she was delighted with the precious enamel thimble, handcrafted as only European artisans can do. In a sense, it had been to Heaven and back.

We arrived home late the next day, very happy to have had the trip, but also happy to be back with our little family. They were all safe and well, including Mama, who had gotten along famously with the children. Later when we were alone Mama quietly told me of an interesting happening that had taken place two nights previous while we were still in Rome. She said she had wanted to keep close watch on our nine-months old baby boy, Jason, so she had taken to sleeping in the nursery with him, in the extra bed there.

"That night," she said, "I had just retired at 9:00 p.m. but was still awake. As I lay quietly watching the baby sleeping in the dim glow of the night-light, I plainly saw you enter the room and glide over to the crib. As you gazed down at the baby for some minutes a soft glow of happiness seemed to emanate as you looked at him. Then, satisfied as to his welfare, you moved on out, not even glancing in my direction, — disappearing directly through the wall. I realized I had seen you plainly in an astral visitation, as this bedroom is on the second floor. You must have intensely desired to come to your baby." I told her that yes, I had that very night yearned to see him.

This was another example of Mama's intermittent clairvoyant sight, and also conveyed the interesting knowledge that my concern for my baby while I was in Rome had prompted an astral visitation to his bedside in Nuremberg, though I had no conscious recollection of it.

The days blended into months. Two of Mama's aunts arrived from America to visit us (who had themselves been born in the Westphalian area of Germany, and now were in their eighty's), so I drove them and Mama to visit their hometown in Northern Germany before Mama returned home to America. Our relatives there welcomed us warmly. However, I did have difficulty understanding a completely different dialect from the Bavarian and had to rely on interpretation. The family ran the only bakery in that small town, so were very busy with many people coming and going. We daily enjoyed delicious *brochen*, still warm from the oven, and at coffee time, *apfel*, peach, and plum *kuchen*, among other special baked goods, as well as wonderful meals. The Germans are some of the most hospitable people on earth, and I recalled Mama complaining that during her youth, "Grandma always wanted to feed everybody!"

There was a tragic accident a few months after our visit. We had become acquainted with a fine young man in his late twenties named Hans, the handsome son of Mama's German cousin, who more-or-less ran the family bakery. He rose very early mornings to make the wonderful fresh baked goods for the entire village. He was so courteous and nice to me, smiling warmly and attempting to visit (in German), whenever I entered the shop. Shortly after our return to Nuremberg, we heard his hand had become entangled in the sharp knives of one of the mixing machines very early one morning and severed at the wrist. This was a terrible tragedy for the family, as he was the main worker there and also had a wife and child. I heard that he went into deep depression for a time as well, for he could no longer work normally. I had great sadness for Hans, whom I had come to know and care about, and kept in touch by mail with the family for a number of years after.

True to form, while returning from her visit with us in Germany, Mama had another exciting adventure. It was a good thing I didn't know she came very close to being dunked in the Atlantic ocean until later when she told us of it. Having come over by ship, she returned by plane — a propeller driven one. Over the Atlantic, approaching the north American Continent, the pilot announced on the intercom, "We are experiencing an emergency situation. Due to unusually strong head winds, we are close to empty on fuel. I am going to try to coast into Goose Bay, Labrador. Do not panic, but please prepare for evacuation in case we don't make it."

Well! Mama was seventy-two years old. She also had earlier suffered a shoulder break that caused one arm to be semi-crippled. Nevertheless, in her indomitable way, she donned a life jacket and quietly went into prayer. She later told me, "In addition to feeling God's grace, I had no fear because Eleanor Roosevelt was sitting in the seat directly in front of me, and nothing ever happens to Eleanor. So I knew we would be all right. And we were. We just barely made it, and feeling the ground under my feet upon disembarking, I grabbed Eleanor's hand to shake it and thank her for being on my plane."* So Mama was safe, but with yet another adventure under her belt.

During this time, to my dismay, Allen continued to suffer those strange periods of silence when he seemed very depressed and remained aloof, so he did not go with us on our visit to Northern Germany. He was sometimes in the field with the troops for six weeks at a time. When he was home and felt well he was an attentive, and fun-loving husband and father. I continued to be silently concerned, for as I said, he would never discuss his changeable moods with me, and often they seemed severe and were disruptive to social plans and to our companionship.

I haven't spoken much about my own health in these nostalgic pages, but I must record that in addition to concern for Allen, I myself had not been well since the birth of our second beautiful little boy. Rather than obviously physical, the problem seemed to be emotional, as I sometimes felt on the edge of a nervous breakdown.

In later months, after Mama had left for home, I found

---

* Eleanor Roosevelt spent a number of years flying all over the world after her president husband's death, gleaning knowledge of other countries, which she used to write a syndicated column, "My Day." She also worked diligently for civil rights.

I could barely cope with stress of any kind, had to struggle to hold my emotional balance, and felt pushed towards hysterics just from the noise of a vacuum cleaner. I pressed on with family household duties of a mother and the social requirements of an officer's wife, but my natural up-beat sunny nature was missing, replaced by vague fears and unnamed nightmares that had no foundation. The doctor on Post could find nothing wrong.

Since I had recently given birth, I asked if that could have a bearing. "None whatsoever," he assured me, and offered only tranquilizers. Being one who seldom if ever took medication, I knew this was not the answer, and turned to prayer for peace from this inner turmoil, asking God's Loving Presence to bring relief. My lower back pain also flared up and the physical stress added to nervous exhaustion was becoming a very real burden. I thought inwardly, "If I could only get away." It had been over a year since our short trip to Italy.

It was eight years later that I finally discovered the physical cause of this temporary near-insanity. Definitely related to the birth, it was caused by the hormonal drop. How strange that the doctors failed to recognize this, when giving birth was obviously the most recent and significant change in my condition. I also found that some women commit suicide during this agonizing period, and I shall touch on this later in my story. Meanwhile, there was a heaven-sent surprise in store.

*

A GIFT FROM ANGEL GUIDES

My prayers for complete rest and change were answered — in a whirlwind fashion. One month before we were to return to the U.S., at the end of Allen's three-year tour of duty, we suddenly received word that our names had come up to have vacation time aboard the military ship that accommodated a few officers and their wives when cabins were available. The ship plied its way from New York to Barcelona, Spain; through the Mediterranean to

Italy; thence to Tripoli, North Africa; Athens, Greece; Istanbul and Izmir, Turkey; and back to Naples and Leghorn before returning to New York. At that time troops from the States were often carried abroad via ship rather than planes. As troops coming from the U.S. disembarked, staterooms became available. So military personnel stationed in the area were granted vacation privilege rather than leaving the staterooms empty for the entire circle trip around the Mediterranean. A good idea, really.

Hurray! Hurray! Three glorious weeks on the Mediterranean! I could hardly believe it — a most dramatic answer to my prayer. Although Allen had put our names on the list upon his arrival in Europe three years previously, our chances were considered virtually nil. We had not even dared hope as there was a long backlog; also these spaces were first given to those personnel assigned to what were considered hardship posts in the Mideast desert regions. But now they had actually called us. Even so, it was nip and tuck, as we had to put all our affairs in order immediately. If an officer was called, he had, of course, to be on post and able to secure leave, that is, not be out on field duty. The wife must have someone ready to stay with the children for three weeks.

Allen phoned me. "We must be packed and ready to board ship in Leghorn, Italy within twenty-four hours!"

The blessing continued. Holy Spirit had it all planned. We had just become acquainted with a young lieutenant and his wife, newly arrived from the United States, who were living off-Post in a German economy cold-water flat, awaiting quarters on-Post. Sandra had been a nurse before they were married. I had instantly liked her warm, charming, open personality. She seemed like an old friend, and Gustav was much respected at work. They had been married five years but thus far had no children, and appeared delighted at the idea of staying in our furnished, comfortable quarters on Post. Sandra and Gustav made perfect companions for our boys. I still had our efficient German maid, Angelika, as well.

What serendipity! I sang a song of praise in my heart to God and 'my Angel' while we quickly packed and took a

train across the Alps traveling through the night. We were
in Livorno (Leghorn) on Italy's west coast by the next
afternoon just in time to catch the ship.

There are no superlatives high or wide enough to
describe the Heavenly blessing this restful sea voyage was
to me. It was the summer of 1959. The weather was warm,
the Mediterranean was the bluest blue imaginable. It was a
huge sparkling sapphire in a ring of the gods. The ship
plied its way south to Naples and later on to Tripoli on the
north coast of Africa. The sunshine and sea air were balm to
my soul and health to my body after a dark and dreary
winter without sunlight.

I have since learned of the tremendous value of sunlight
in healing all manner of illness, including tuberculosis, as in
Mama's case while I was yet a child, and arthritis, as demon-
strated by the impressive work of Dr. John Ott in Orlando,
Florida. Dr. Ott is the talented photographer responsible
for the early, effectively beautiful time-lapse photography,
including the series of films *Nature's Wonders*, produced
by Disney Studios many years ago. He is now retired from
the Disney Studios and has his own photographic research
laboratory in Orlando, Florida. Several scientific papers have
now recently been published on the value of sunlight in
alleviating depression, especially in areas of the North where
darkness dominates many winter months.*

Drinking in the peace and calm, lulled by the gentle
roll of the ship as it balanced on the smooth blue sea, again
I contemplated and could only glimpse how much God
loves us; a loving Universe rushes to fill our real needs as air
rushes to fill a vacuum. Allen, too, was delighted to have
this rare opportunity to visit countries whose history he
had studied. He was a scholar and could relate to me from
memory stories of Roman conquerors and myths of Greek
Muses, gods and heroes. I was most fortunate to have in
him a personal history guide who briefed me before we
arrived in each ancient city, augmenting my understanding

Light, Medicine of the Future, by Jacob Liberman, O.D., Ph.D. 1991,
Bear & Company, P.O.Drawer 2860, Santa Fe, N.M. 87504-2860

and appreciation immensely. My husband's main joy in life had been reading. He loved the classics, history, and anthropology. I knew, he had earned the Phi Beta Kappa key he wore, the insignia of his fraternity in college. I also loved to read, but as you may have guessed, my attention seemed more drawn to esoteric philosophy and the mystical. At home we spent many an evening together, quite joyfully in silence — just reading.

Now our two loves, history and philosophy, seemed to meld, coming to life before our eyes in the places and ancient cultures we had only read and dreamed of.

The sun bathed us in its golden radiance; we were in another world. The ship was a haven, large and safe, although not opulent, being a military vessel. Our stateroom was small but comfortable, and meals were excellent. I felt euphoric freedom. It was simply heavenly. It seemed there was no past and no future, only today. But that would change.

✳

POMPEII — A PICTURE OF THE PAST

Our first stop came the very first day out, at Naples. We had a 24-hour lay-over here and though there was an array of choices, we were drawn to a tour of the ancient City of Pompeii, a few miles to the south. Pompeii had been built around 800 B.C. on a plateau of ancient lava, less than a mile from the foot of Mt. Vesuvius and near the Bay of Naples. The climate was warm and beautiful, conducive to the building of elegant homes in the country. Pompeii had paved streets, and a great wall with eight gates that surrounded the city.

For many years Allen and I had both felt a dark fascination with Pompeii. In the year A.D. 79 Mt. Vesuvius spewed lava and hot ash down in such a sudden torrent that over 2,000 people died a horrible death, suffocating, as the town was buried under twenty-two feet of volcanic ash. It vanished so completely that it was not discovered in excavations until 1,700 years had passed. We saw the Forum in the center of the city still standing, its tall pillars forming a rectangular shape, with the keystone arch still in place at the top. How strange to see the town bakery, also topped with a stone arch, containing twelve loaves of petrified bread, still intact in the oven.

It had been amazing to archaeologists to discover that the consistency and chemical content of the ash was such that as it drifted down like heavy rain, it settled around and engulfed buildings, house walls and statues in gardens, preserving them exactly as they were. Even the paintings in homes — beautiful full murals painted right on the walls — were preserved in their original rich colors. These paintings were so clear they have been reproduced on postcards and in history books through the years since discovery. It is of note that chemists could not ascertain the pigment used to create the particular red the Pompeiians used and have not been able to duplicate it. The unique beauty held me rapt, as the murals seemed to have been painted only yesterday.

The most gripping items on display in the small museum were the plaster-of-paris casts of humans, curled in a crouching fetal position, and even a crouching dog, still in the position in which they died, smothered in the ash. As archaeologists dug carefully with spoons and brushes, they would come upon what appeared to be an empty space in the otherwise solid ash. Very carefully they would pour plaster-of-paris into the hole and after allowing this plaster to harden, then the ash surrounding it could be scraped away. Lo-and-behold, the crouching form of a dying person was revealed, replicated exactly — in plaster, recording the tragedy. Chemicals in the ash had dissolved the entire body over the centuries, including the bones, while the ash itself had hardened to preserve the form in minute detail.

I found myself moving slowly through the unearthed streets of this ancient town which were laid out in blocks in surprisingly modern fashion. Moving as in a daze, feeling transported back in time, I *saw* certain houses *before* I turned the corner and beheld what was now only the standing walls. Many were of beautiful white building stones. In one, I *knew* before I arrived where I would find the garden. I could see in my mind the sunny courtyard with small white statue of a naked boy nymph spouting a fountain of clear running water. As I stepped over the threshold, it was as I had seen, but now the fountain stood dry in the hot sun of the deserted garden. How strange. This feeling of knowing this place so well, yet it was not a sad feeling, but more a nostalgia for days when I was carefree and happy, when life and love were simple and one lived as a child, delighted with life's beauty and wonder.

I stopped to sit on a stone that had tumbled from one of the walls. In a few moments of quiet meditation, pictures easily came to my mind's eye: the original beauty of these lovely white-walled homes in sunny Southern Italy, the dresses we wore, a country style with full skirt, low bosom, and wild colors bright as the red and yellow poppies in the field. And often we sang as we went about daily tasks, barefoot or wearing only strapped sandals.

What a shocking end to this beautiful carefree way of life — as the Mountain Goddess erupted in anger. I was glad some bit of this remembered beauty could see the sun again, even if it were only the silent white walls and the somber dead statue of the little boy, still standing in his garden, keeping guard near an empty urn that had once held masses of brilliant flowers.

Allen called to me. His voice seemed far away. As one awakening from a dream I found myself drawn back into the now. It was time to return to the ship and sail to the next port on the coast of North Africa. As I rose to leave, I felt refreshed and filled with an exhilarating new energy, as though I had been released from the ties of this segment of my past, even though it had not been a sad one. I reflected on the Soul — and its amazing journey through Time.

ODE TO POMPEII

Where is the glory of yesterday
    in the mouldy ruins of Pompeii?
My heart cries out for the day — when I lived
    as a queen along these avenues of clay.

How little we knew what the morrow
    would bring
As we sang in our carefree way
    Of the beauty of earth and the good of the sod
and enjoyed passions of the day

It is well that we knew not
    what the morrow would birth,
The terror, the loss and the pain
    On the day our mountain spewed fire to earth
and death came down like rain.

Where — oh where — is the glory now?
    Does it hang in the deathless air?
Unseen by eyes that look on the death
    With only a vacant stare?

How could they know those wonderful days
    of happiness under the sun
When Love and Life were deemed supreme
    and all the world seemed won.
The earth gives birth — and yet retains
    the power to take away.
When the mountain breast stirs
    The choice is Hers —
And the time? — No man can say.

                    Bonnie Ann Gilchrist

*

A GLIMPSE OF NORTH AFRICA —
AND THE MIDDLE EAST

From the deck of the ship we saw it sparkling white in the sun, like an Arabian oasis, its stucco walls sending rivulets of shimmering desert heat rising into the bright blue sky. The City of Tripoli on the shores of Libya had come into view. Our stay there of one day was far too short, but the tour through the city was a memorable one. What a different world it was in the 1950's for a girl from the Midwest, who had only seen Arab garb and camels in picture books. Now, in the 1990's, the world lives with a very much closer view. Amazing, the changes in forty years. It would be dangerous now for Americans to stroll through Tripol, a stronghold of Moammar Khadafy. At that time the U.S. still maintained Wheeler Air Force Base on the edge of Tripoli. It had served as a base from which American troops could cross the Mediterranean to fight in Italy during World War II.

I was entranced to see this exotic (to the western eye) culture at close range. At that time we were not allowed to converse with the people even if we had known the language; in fact, they seemed most shy and avoided even coming close when we were on foot. I also discovered by accident and to my embarrassment, that a camera was very much frowned upon, when a robed father jumped quickly in front of his little boy, and running, led him and their camel out of my range. I found later their religious belief is that a portion of the soul is taken into a picture and thus lost. So, no pictures, and I was sorry to have offended him in my American ignorance. Thus, I did not return home with any close-ups of the people. The differences were startling.

The outdoor market place at the center of town would turn a hygiene-conscious westerner's stomach. Swarms of large flies buzzed hungrily over open chunks of meat, and raw whole plucked chickens with heads still attached and beaks gaping open, hung by their feet on hooks from the ceiling of make-shift open stalls. A bloody camel's head sat grotesquely on a tabletop in the foreground, the eyes half-closed as though only dozing. It was for sale. There was dust everywhere as there was no paved roadway, just the sandy ground packed hard by the pounding of many human and animal feet over the years. Gusts of wind swirled eddies of hot dry silt from the road into the air and around the stalls, stinging the ankles as one walked through.

Later a tour bus took us around the perimeter of the town. There was only a scattering of moderately well-to-do homes, but slum shanties spread for miles and miles on the edge of this rambling city. Beautiful, dark-eyed, but shabbily dressed children eyed us openly, while standing quietly back from the road in polite deference. My heart was sad for them. We saw none of the forward inquisitive bounce and laughter that, in the main, are trademarks of western children. These peoples were too poor to be joyful, and of a sedate nature. Those more well-to-do were probably kept behind closed doors.

The dust and heat were oppressive, and I was painfully aware once again of the needs of people the world over, for the simple blessings of clean food, clean water, and safe homes, free of filth and pestilence. After only one day's visit, when the ship's incoming troops had been exchanged with those leaving Wheeler Air Force Base, we sailed on to Greece and to Turkey.

Suffice it to say that visiting the Acropolis and the glorious beauty of the Parthenon among other ancient sites in the legendary Greek culture, was the highlight of our lives. Climbing the steep steps, we felt the luxury of the marble under our fingertips. Allen, I believe, was now having his own feelings of time-warp. He resembled a little boy in a candy shop, viewing the masterpieces he had long dreamed of seeing. He excitedly recounted the legend behind each statue, as he knew the mythology well. We bought a couple beautiful replicas of Allen's favorite gods and goddess. We saw the American Archeological Society's large modern building there, as well, with a staff studying the ruins of ancient times. The shops of Athens had remained open to accommodate the visitors from our ship, and a delightful, beautiful woman tour guide was at our disposal.

Interestingly, she said she was Egyptian.

Our one day was altogether too short to do justice to the wonder of it all, but we found time for a fabulous Greek meal. I felt very adventurous ordering octopus wrapped in grape leaves. It was simply delicious! Any lobster lover would have liked this dish, for it was much the same, perhaps even more rich. For hors d'oeuvres we sampled marinated polyps. These resembled tiny baby octopi with many legs, and although the appearance might cause reluctance, this remains in my memory as the most delicious delicacy I have ever tasted anywhere.

Turkey was altogether different. I would have to write for days to fully describe Istanbul. We sailed through the Dardanelles, emerging upon a huge, bustling city spread over the banks of the Bosporus. Later, after disembarking, standing on the bank of the river that separates Turkey from Europe, we realized we were looking across to another continent. It was a strange sensation to consider the closeness, and yet the distance between the cultures of those countries.

The autos and clothing gave me the feeling of being back in the early 1940's in the U.S., because I discovered that, at that time, old American post-war autos were much in demand and were being shipped over to Turkey to be snapped up at good prices. The clothing styles too resembled the U.S. fifteen years previous. Turkey was just beginning to be westernized. It seemed incongruous. Being allowed only one day's layover from the ship, with time of the essence, we headed for the world's largest covered bazaar — ten acres under one roof in mid-town Istanbul.

It was astounding. Thousands of shops, pressed one against the other, some only three-feet wide, jammed with the most beautiful goods, and of greater variety than I imagined could be found in the entire world. Gold, silver, Turkish rugs, hand-hammered brass, objects d'art abounded. A six-by-nine gorgeous, richly patterned Turkish rug was being sold for $100.00, but I thought to myself, how in the world will I get it home? Later, I suspected I'd been foolish. For that price Allen and I should have carried it home over our shoulders. And we would have had to. I was not sure it would ever have arrived if I had asked to have it sent.

We visited the grandiose domed and turreted mosques, including the famous Blue Mosque and St. Sophia's. These are beyond imagination. The harem quarters in Topkopi Palace, which was residence to the last Sultan, but now stood empty, retains the beautiful appointments and jeweled artifacts of those fabulously opulent days, giving rise to vivid, indulgent images.

One more stop, as we sailed on to Izmir, completed the eastern edge of our wonderful tour. But the evening we left Istanbul, Allen suddenly reverted into his strange silence, so I knew that if I wanted to see Izmir upon our arrival, I would have to go alone, for he refused to leave the stateroom. I was dismayed and hesitated to leave him, but I also did not want to miss the only chance I ever hoped to have to view a part of Turkey that wasn't its largest city, so I trotted along with a few people on a short tour. I am *so glad* I did, for I saw a totally different life from the large city-bustle of Istanbul. Smaller cities and towns always give a closer and more correct view of a country and its people than the largest city.

Izmir's ancient name was Smyrna, which may be familiar to some from Bible stories. Lying on the hill above the Marmara Harbor, this beautiful city was a delight to the eye, and is my favorite memory of Turkey. The people with whom we came in casual contact on the street were friendly and seemed happy. They spoke simple English. Again, I marveled at America's isolation, for who among us can easily speak simple Turkish?

A smiling shoe-shine boy had set up shop right on the open sidewalk and offered to polish our shoes on the spot as we passed. He carried his equipment in a large wooden box of mahogany and elegant shiny brass filigree. The box had obviously been handed down from father to son, and was so ornate it looked like a priceless antique. I was sorry my shoes were not of the type to be polished, as the young man was the epitome of graciousness.

Our little group was on our way to see Roman ruins, which we were surprised to find in the center of Izmir. These were more of the many Roman ruins scattered over most of the Middle East. That Empire had been expansive.

The central mosque in Izmir was smaller than those in Istanbul, but was an artist's delight, easily the most beautiful in all of Turkey. Its lofty stained glass windows, depicting religious figures in exquisite detail and rich colors, were simply breathtaking. The mosque's many-colored dome could have come right out of Heaven.

Built on the side of a high hill overlooking a magnificent view of the harbor, Izmir was a blue and white vision emerging from the lights and shadows of a sapphire blue Sea, a sight never-to-be forgotten. Our little group tasted local delicacies in the food shops before reluctantly returning to our ship for the journey back to Italy and home. I can easily understand the peoples of these ancient cultures, with centuries of tradition, looking upon the Americans as brash up-starts, teenagers, one might say, in the life-span of human history. (Teenagers are renowned for thinking they know all there is to know.)

As we set sail to the West, across the iridescent sea, I felt we had been richly blessed. Many tourists have since traveled our route, and visited the countries that ring the Mediterranean, so these words seem not so special. But in the mid-1950's, such travel was unusual and modern life had not yet deeply penetrated these regions.

There were few tourists visible other than our small group from the ship, and everywhere we went the natives treated us with the utmost courtesy and respect as visitors in their land. We saw the richness of ancient cultures midst the lack of modern conveniences. The old way of life hung on with thin worn fingers though the modern world was pushing in to claim territory. I am grateful to have seen these countries as they were, for people were now grappling with a world having recently emerged from World War II, a war that had touched almost everyone. Change was coming quickly, yet they seemed unsure how many of the new ideas they could inculcate, or tolerate. On the surface they welcomed us with pleasure, yet I couldn't help sensing their reticence. I felt as I spoke with them that they stood in awe of the West, and with a wary concern for what the future held.

Our ship set sail on its return journey to Naples. We rested and enjoyed the warm Mediterranean sun. Thankfully, we could afford this trip. (It was offered free of charge — except for our meals — since the military ship was sailing anyway and the staterooms, as troops disembarked, would otherwise sit empty, as mentioned earlier.) We docked and had a few hours to see Naples quickly, enjoying a meal of true Italian pasta, and then on to Livorno and our train home.

I felt I'd been given a very special gift from Spirit, a new lease on life. Yet my puzzlement steadily grew. What could be the cause of Allen's silent spells? For now he was himself again, happily sharing new memories, wondering how his many color slides would turn out, and eager as I to see our small boys. We had been away only three weeks. It seemed years in the knowledge gained, centuries in the ancient memories retrieved. I had found a part of my soul's place in the life and reality of the historical past.

Back in the U.S. the following year, I was introduced to the wife of an Army General who had also just returned from Europe.

"Gilchrist . . . Gilchrist," she mused, "where have I heard that name? Ah yes! You are the ones! It was you folks who were the only family to receive the Mediterranean Cruise last year out of Occupied Germany. Was it enjoyable?"

"Enjoyable" would never cover it. The Beloved Presence had heard my plea, had renewed my health through sunshine and rest, and given me a gift beyond any I could have imagined. As I mused once again on these wondrous weeks, I felt beloved of God, and truly a Traveler through Time.

*

CHAPTER SEVEN

HOME TO THE U. S.

"I've received orders! We go home in a few weeks!"
Allen smiled as he stepped through the door. I caught
my breath. I'd known the time was drawing near, but I'd
put it out of my mind. My European experience had been so
rich and diverse, touching deep regions of my inner self,
that this announcement produced a certain sadness in me,
even though I dearly loved America and was very grateful it
was our home. Some other military wives had counted the
days 'til they could return, and seemed to feel they had
spent three years in purgatory here. It had not been so for
me. It had been a great blessing to savor the medieval flavor
that still clung to so many towns and villages, with history,
art, and music everywhere. The churches and cathedrals
were magnificent with their gorgeous stained glass windows and painstakingly carved architecture. I spent as many
hours as possible soaking up the atmosphere before the
time came to pack up, board ship, and sail for New York.

Saying goodbye to the many friends we had made, and
to my young German/Czechoslovakian maid, who was always cheerful and had been a great help to me, was difficult. Having a live-in housemaid had been a necessity as
there were many functions at which our presence was man-
datory and my little boys needed someone they were com-

fortable with, a kind of *member of the family*. The disadvantage was that all the maids of the military compound knew one another, and thus few secrets, family disagreements, or a rare infidelity could be kept quiet and behind closed doors. I had no worries, as Allen and I had never had a cross word in our many years together, probably because we were apart so much that our times together were precious. Gossip can be very harmful not only to the one whispered about, but ethically and spiritually to the one doing the gossiping as well. We don't fully realize that thoughts are things, and negative energy sent forth has a dynamic unseen power to destroy.* Angelika knew she had had a good household and she feared not finding another so compatible, but I knew her good record would smooth her way.

Coming back from my reflections, I asked Allen, "Where are we being sent? Where is your new station?"

"Seattle, Washington," he answered. "I am to be on the R.O.T.C. Staff at the University of Washington."

Amazement hit me as a memory surfaced. In that astrology reading in Los Angeles three years previous, before I had sailed for Europe, Maria Moody, a most enlightened lady had said to me, "There are three major cities in your future — Nuremberg, Germany; Seattle, Washington and London, England." At the time she had no way of knowing that Allen had already left for Nuremberg and I was at that very moment I spoke with her awaiting the call to join him. Her readings were right on. Here we were preparing to go to Seattle. At this writing, I have since spent thirty years in the Greater Seattle area. I am left wondering if the third city, London, is still in the mists of the future. Only Time will tell.

Remembering the value of preparing the way before traveling to a new destination, I began creative visualization, believing and knowing that just the right house would

---

*The harm that is done to young minds by violent television shows is incomprehensible. Only now as we observe the violence of the youth around the world and watch the population in our prisons soar are the results being clearly seen. And still people don't wake up, see the connection, and demand change! Instead we continue to pay out-of-pocket (and from the heart and with lives) for our ignorance.

be awaiting us, comfortable enough to raise a family, but with style and beauty surrounding it. As an extra I added mentally, "and quarters or a little guest house for Mama when she visits would be so nice." Smiling to myself I built the picture in my mind.

After a flurry of packing and a scenic train ride from Bavaria to Northern Germany and the Baltic Sea, we sailed away from the port of Bremerton, Germany. Crossing the ocean by military vessel took six days in 1959. However, the ship lay outside New York Harbor two more days awaiting entry. I vividly recall that the warm, muggy air, even two hundred miles out from shore, was so heavy in August that Baby Jason's diapers I hung to dry were still sopping wet twenty-four hours later. Jason was such a good little fellow, never causing a disturbance by crying — ever. And Jeremy enjoyed the excitement of a ship as only a four-year old can.

We did not dally in New York in that hot humid weather, eager to turn our faces westward to the adventure awaiting us on the opposite side of the continent. We had brought our auto aboard ship, also a large German tent as we planned to camp most nights. But in visiting family and friends across the U.S., many of whom we had not seen for three years or more, it turned out we didn't need the tent until we hit Utah.

An entirely new and different chapter of our lives began in Seattle. There was nothing military about our life there, except Allen's uniform, which he wore to the University as a teacher in the Reserve Officer Training Corps. Since Allen was a member of the faculty, we were included in many University functions.

"This is the house!" I exclaimed. After three weeks of fruitless search, we'd been led by the agent down a lovely, quiet dead-end lane, off the beaten track and thickly lined with tall evergreen trees. Golden sunlight rippled through the branches above us as we drove. And then I saw it. A house of Roman brick. We hadn't even gone inside before it was purchased in my mind. It looked like a rambler, set back from the road on a slight rise among tall graceful cedar trees. It was built of exactly the same dark red brick I had admired as a child when for years I had passed my aunt's home on my way to grade school in the village. "If I ever have a house, it shall look like that," I had mused in my mind those long years ago. Now here it was, waiting serenely for us, amidst the trees. Our agent interrupted my thoughts.

"This house has been on the market for many months, but hasn't sold even though the price is extremely low, as the previous owner filed bankruptcy. It is puzzling, for this house is the best buy in the entire north end this year."

The price *was* low, within what Allen had set as the limit we could afford. What's more, there was almost an acre of grounds as well. Granted, it would take a lot of work to clear the back area, which was covered with a thick tangle of wild blackberry bushes and second growth trees. But as it turned out, it was perfect therapy for Allen who spent five days each week in an office or classroom for the next three years. Being an outdoorsman, he truly enjoyed all the months of work clearing the grounds which he did *by hand*. This took all of his spare time, but clearing by hand allowed him to leave lovely large mountain ash, hawthorne and dogwood trees to bloom in their seasons.

Even after eight years of marriage, I found I did not yet know my husband, for here he was, exhibiting talent as a lumberjack. Climbing tall trees, using a winch single-handedly, he felled certain large dead trees, bringing them down to the *exact* spot he had designated. My admiration for his prowess grew by leaps and bounds! Swinging a machete, he attacked the overgrown wild blackberries, and as they came down, we saw to our amazement a little one-room cabin standing midst the tangle. We later discovered on old plat maps that this cabin had been one of the first structures on the north end of Lake Washington, so it was actually an historical building. Someone from Old Seattle had built a mountain retreat here in bygone days. At this point it looked pretty sad and we thought that would have to be torn down. But as we cautiously poked our heads through the ancient door, instead of the old moldy interior we had expected, we were met by the delightful scent of cedar wood. We found the entire interior beautifully paneled in matched knotty cedar boards; even the ceiling was solid cedar paneling. Thus Allen's next project was the restoration of our very own guest-cabin. Then it hit me: Here was the fulfillment of my visualized wish months before while still in Germany, expressed to the Beloved Presence, ". . . a little house for Grammy's use when she visits." What better proof of Divine Mother ever eager to fill our needs, if it is for the good of all.

Marveling once again at the ingenuity and gentle leading of the angel guides, I joyfully worked with the earth alongside Allen for many months, making a lovely home and grounds lined with rhododendrons, azaleas, camellias, forsythia and other flowering plants of many kinds, where before had stood only a wild jungle. Allen cleared a nice wide lawn space so the boys might play ball, croquet and other games.

Our Baby Jason had his second birthday the very day we moved into our new home and he was the sweetest, most loving child parents could ever wish for. He was always happy, affectionate and unselfish, adoring his bigger brother Jeremy, who was two years older. The word "No" did not seem to be in his vocabulary, even to age five when he began school. I recall with irony that I often thought in those days, "If all my babies could be like Jason I would have a dozen!" He truly was a joy. Well, famous last words, to say the least, as the curtain was yet drawn over what lay ahead.

I have learned that it is God's grace that we cannot know what lies in the mists of the future, or remember past lives either, for the weight of this knowledge would be too heavy. To safely handle the experiences of the day is enough. If we can learn to live joyfully each day, savoring the now and the love of dear ones and friends, we are building the foundation for happy tomorrows. If those tomorrows should bring travail, we can know, if we have the wisdom to see the broader expanse and the faith to trust in God's Love, that we are working through the effects of what we put in motion, somewhere in our own long-forgotten past. These experiences come to clear our slate, and to instruct us.

*

EXPERIENCES WITH
THE MIRACLES OF HEALING

Allen's health continued to fluctuate, with those depressed dark moods of changed personality coming more frequently. In addition he was becoming thin and tired, and his face assumed a grey pallor. Doctors could find nothing wrong, despite repeated physical tests. Finally he was hospitalized in a military hospital with the horrid diagnosis: psychosomatic. This is a way for doctors who do not know what is wrong to cover their own ignorance by placing the blame on the patient: "It's all in your head." This would be a harsh and very detrimental verdict on Allen's records.

In desperation, while Allen was in the hospital, intuitively feeling there was a need to get a new perspective away from the environment of illness, I took the boys and drove south to California. While discussing this strange condition with my brother-in-law, a light went on in my mind.

I immediately wired Allen. "Go to a dentist . Get deep ex-rays of your teeth and jaws."

He did, and there it was — deeply implanted — a huge funicular cyst, slowly poisoning him.

The dentist told him, "One might say you have been taking, as it were, a teaspoon of poison every day for three years. Soon your heart might have failed."

"This explains the bad taste in my mouth and ringing in my ears I've been complaining of for weeks," Allen exclaimed. The medical doctors had not considered these symptoms important enough to notice, saying, "It's all mental."

Naturally Allen did not recover overnight. Though the cyst had been removed, his system still needed cleansing from the poisoning, which had permeated the bloodstream and organs. Disillusioned with medical aid, we sought help elsewhere. We found a delightful old gentleman, a Naturopathic doctor who was sympathetic and understanding. He put Allen on a blood-cleansing nutritional diet of fresh raw vegetable juices and healing medicinal herbal teas.

"It is obvious the two and a half years of working hard

out-of-doors in your yard has saved your life. You perspired out much of the poison that otherwise would have engulfed your heart."

And so, with deep gratitude I once again silently thanked the angels of guidance and mercy, who brought us to this home where heavy duty yard-clearing was required, work that would have daunted a lesser man than my valiant husband. In the end it was quite possibly the means of saving his life for a few more years, years that were important to our children's future.

Meanwhile, I had made friends with a like-minded neighbor woman. Together we began a prayer group that was to be a spiritual step forward for everyone involved. My friend Virginia has since written several noteworthy books on astrology and spiritual teachings under the pen name Gini, and sometimes, Oreana, helping many people through her insightful interpretations of their charts, with guidance to esoteric studies.*

In those years however, our days were mainly taken with raising our families, so we met only once a week. The group grew to seven members, then ten, and eventually became several groups of ten as more and more women were attracted by what was experienced in the group. I cannot stress enough the value of group meditation and intercessory prayer for those in need. Each of the women in our group was helped with the personal problems that naturally arise for everyone living on this earth plane. In some ways we were a do-it-yourself psychotherapy group, gratified to see our group prayer affecting actual changes and healing in our own lives, as well as in the lives of others whose names we lifted. We always asked that the Christ Spirit be the Leader and direct our gathering. No one person led per se, but rather, we took turns moderating the sessions. In this way all of us grew in understanding through the ensuing years. Family relationships were healed, old scars and grievances were forgiven, physical problems were

*Her latest titled: *The One Remains*, by Oreana, 1992 Gray Wolf Publishing, 2900 Canyon Rd. #91. Ellensburg, WA 98926

often healed quickly. It was during this period that I was led to know Allen should have his jaws x-rayed by a dentist when the doctors had not thought of it.

One miracle that took place in those months was the healing of a gangrenous leg of the elderly mother of one of our members. Her name was Mabel and she was a diabetic. As often happens in diabetics, the circulation to one leg had become so bad that gangrene had set in. The toes were almost black and her doctor was recommending amputation of that leg, as that is the usual practice in such a case. Her daughter, a fellow prayer group member, asked if we would all come to her home and pray together.

Mabel was in her wheelchair with her right leg propped up. The lower leg was cold with no feeling, the flesh rock hard and stiff, with toes an ominous discolored darkish purple. There was no feeling left in it, she said. She was happy we had come, as she was a devout lady who had lived a serviceful life.

In our laying on of hands we visualized her legs engulfed in White Light, seeing them well and strong, while asking Christ Jesus to be there with His Grace. After perhaps fifteen to twenty minutes, to our joy we saw the darkened toes begin to turn faintly pink, and to feel the leg becoming warm under our hands. Mabel, with tears in her eyes, whispered, "I can feel my toes! I can feel my toes! Thank God!"

It always amazes me that even though we pray with faith in the power of the healing energy of Christ, still we are surprised when we see the wonderful results. Mabel's healing was dramatic and very rewarding because Mabel was able to keep her leg until she passed away four years later. Her doctor was surprised. "He thinks it is the medicine he is giving me," she told us. " I never could tell him what happened — he would not have believed it." But Mabel knew. She had taken the medicine for many weeks before with no change whatsoever, until that day we called on the power of Christ, and saw a change within minutes. "When two or more are gathered in my name, there am I among you," (Matthew:18:20).

Through those many months, I looked forward to my own hour of meditation at 10:00 p.m., when the day's work was finished and my family was in bed. Allen also retired early, weary from his day's mental or physical labors. I have been forever grateful for his lovingly allowing me the freedom to pursue spiritual studies in these ways, though I sought to never neglect my duties as wife and mother. After the boys were tucked into bed, he and I often read quietly together through the winter evenings, enjoying the glow of dancing flames in the large fireplace. He preferred scholarly articles, but only once remarked, "Dear, why don't you read something useful rather than that nebulous stuff?" It was a statement, not a question, but he did not press it. He was always, to the very end, a courteous gentleman (I tell this in passing only as a comparison to the change I shall relate that took place after his Near-Death Experience five years later.)

One night close to midnight, while I was meditating, the telephone rang. It was one of our prayer partners named Ruth calling on the telephone prayer-chain we had formed. She was frantic, crying and pleading: "I just received a call from my brother in Sacramento. His wife, Mercedes, is dying in childbirth! It is their fourth child and he will be left with four small children. He is devastated! The doctors cannot stop her hemorrhaging and have told him they are helpless. Please pray for her as there is no other hope."

From the phone I returned to the meditation room and went immediately into prayer for Mercedes. Seeking the deep quiet space within, feelings of love rose within me for this other mother. I almost felt myself in her place — what it would be to have to leave four little children. That I had never met her did not matter. I asked with intense fervor and love for the Christ Spirit's healing light to bring life-giving energy to Mercedes, whose children and husband needed her badly. I spoke to God as a Friend by my side.

"Beloved, you cannot desire these little ones to be without their mother. We ask in all love, and desire that her life be spared, if it is for the highest good of all. If my prayer can be answered, please give me a sign that I may comfort Ruth who is so worried."

I have not spoken much of it before, but all through these years I had suffered recurring backaches, the hangover results from breaking my coccyx as a child and the resultant curvature of the spine. Now, within a few seconds my spine began to tingle. Waves of energy passed up and down in thrilling ripples. I was near ecstasy with the joy of it! These pulsing warm energy-rivulets did not cease, but continued many minutes and I felt a wonderful peace flow over me.

With great happiness I phoned Ruth.

"Mercedes will live — it is all right." Two hours later at 2:00 a.m. my phone rang again. I had retired, but could hardly sleep. It was Ruth. The good news was confirmed.

"My brother called. He said a miracle had happened! At midnight Mercedes suddenly came back from death's door. The bleeding miraculously stopped and she will be all right. The doctors cannot explain what happened, he said, as they had given her up."

Well, we knew what happened, the Angel Guides and I. I knelt in thanksgiving that our prayers were heard. The crowning touch for me was that my spine continued to tingle with energy, at intervals for the next three weeks, and I was healed of all backache for the next twenty-five years, after suffering from the age of seven. God's Love is boundless. In the Bible it states: "Pray one for another, that *ye* may be healed," (James 5:16).

Another night a vision was granted to me while in prayer for the dying husband of one of our prayer members whose name was Benita. She had watched her husband slowly waste away, his kidneys failing. I suddenly sensed a spirit couple standing to my left, and slightly behind — an older man and wife. The lady held out her hand that I might see in her palm a beautiful brooch set with precious stones, and her words seemed to enter my mind.

"We are the parents. We will watch over Frank. Tell her not to worry, it is all right." And they disappeared.

I drove over to see Benita the next morning, saying that her parents had brought a message. I related it, describing the brooch, its shape and colors, adding "I have no idea why that was shown to me as it seemed to have no bearing."

Benita looked at me intensely with tears in her eyes. "Oh, yes it does! Those were not my parents. Those were Frank's parents. My mother-in-law gave that brooch to me upon my engagement to her son years ago. You have described it perfectly. That was her way of identifying herself and the message." She hugged me in relief that though he might soon pass, Frank would be safe on the Other Side of Life, met by loved ones.

These are only a few instances, of personal highlights that came to bring solace during those many months when we made group prayer a strict weekly ritual with which nothing could interfere. The group grew, and then split off to form new prayer fellowships, so eventually there were several in the area. I wish to relate an interesting follow-up.

The next year after we had moved again, this time to the Presidio of San Francisco, I attended a metaphysical church in San Francisco one Sunday morning. The minister gave an excellent sermon, and at the end of the service, with eyes closed she read for a few people of her choice in the congregation as she picked up on certain needs. To my surprise, (since I was new to this church), after two or three messages had been given, she clearly identified me.

Speaking directly to me, she stated very enthusiastically and rather dramatically, "When I touch this lady's vibration I want to stand ten feet tall!" She drew herself up as she spoke, visibly seeming inches taller. "There is, surrounding and within you, a beautiful aura of light that is not yours alone — but of a group. There are several who are One, that is, doing or having done a spiritual work and who are still connected in this way. The value from this group work still continues to ripple out and leaves a trail of good for all . . . Blessings be yours." So if one needed confirmation of the value of prayer, that was it, coming through a new minister, in a different city.

It was during this period of heightened awareness, while working with the prayer group, that I was blessed with the appearance of the Master Kuthumi. One evening during meditation, I saw the face and head of a radiant Being, slightly above and to my left. He was looking at me, though not actually smiling, his large, soft brown eyes very gentle and loving. He wore a white turban with a gorgeous jewel set in its center above the forehead. The Master's dark hair hung in ringlets to his shoulders.

This clear vision lasted but a minute and I did not receive a mental message, but there was a distinct feeling of approval and blessing. For me, it was a blessing just to see him, for I had always had a special feeling of love for Kuthumi. It was he, together with the Masters Rama and the Egyptian Healer-Pharoah Zoser, who had worked from the astral side with Drs. Earlyne and Robert Chaney to found Astara forty years ago, the Church of All Religions, which I had joined at that time. Master Kuthumi's last lifetime was Tibetan, but he is a Universal Being, one of the Great White Brotherhood. We are told that these Masters keep watch over their disciples, guiding and teaching them as much as the disciples are able to accept, through repeated incarnations on earth.

✳

A RETURN TO CALIFORNIA

Again we move, this time to the beautiful Presidio of San Francisco. What a blessing this move is. The Presidio is one of the loveliest military posts in the United States, with its red tiled roofs atop clean white stucco buildings built in Spanish style in the late 1800's. The Presidio sits upon a hill with an even rise, giving a perfectly magnificent view of San Francisco Bay and the Golden Gate Bridge, with portrait scenes of the city below.

San Francisco's history is colorful and adventurous. Its Bay was the most important west coast port during World War II. The Presidio, built on the original site of the Spanish Mission founded by Father Junipera Serra as he traveled up from Mexico, has been a military garrison under the flags of three nations: Spain, Mexico, and the United States. The original structure of the Post Officers Club dates from 1776 and was built over the original walls of the early mission. A sliding panel allows one to see the old mission wall beneath. This building was the very beginning of the City of San

Francisco, which grew up around and below the Mission. During the great San Francisco earthquake in 1906 the Presidio, as a military garrison, was a haven for all the city's people, who were fed and given tents before rebuilding began. It was exciting to be stationed at a place of such historical significance.

We were given quarters on the Fort Winfield Scott section of the Post, in a house built in 1880 along a clean tree-lined street. This huge white stucco, red-tiled roof duplex, was built with cement walls three feet thick between the two living areas so one never heard a sound from the opposite side. The house was four stories. The rooms of our new home were enormous. The front hall alone seemed like a room, with an open staircase curving gracefully up to the second floor. We found our bedroom to be 30' x 30', so one half became a comfortable upstairs sitting room. The guest bedroom was 30' x 20'.

In all, I had twenty-two tall windows to curtain. Off the spacious kitchen was a butler's pantry, from which a steep back staircase led upstairs, used by the maid as was the fashion when these houses were built. The attic on the fourth floor was light and expansive so it became Jeremy's bedroom, with a large play area attached. He was excited to have "a whole floor all my very own!" Now eight years old, he coveted the privacy, though the first few weeks it was amusing to see him screw up his courage each night before climbing the narrow stairs to the dark attic to go to bed.

It was great to have the space because through the next three years we discovered we were welcoming quite a number of out-of-state guests, relatives and friends passing through San Francisco enroute to Hawaii to vacation, or military people on their way to Asia. Some dear ones came and stayed with us as long as a month at a time, including Mama and Great Aunt Alvina, one of Mama's aunts who had come to Germany while we were there. She was 94 years young, still traveling and going strong.

Our little German-born Jason now five years old, had been a nearly perfect child, loving and gentle, charming everyone with his terrific sense of humor and happy smile.

We loved him dearly. He was especially bright and observant and liked to tell me with great enthusiasm about everything he had seen and heard.

When he began kindergarten, however, we noticed a
change. He became jumpy and nervous, and seemed unable
to settle down or to be calm as before. Soon his teacher was
calling me in for consultations.

"Jason cannot sit still and concentrate long enough to
finish a project. He runs about in class annoying other
children. He is never mean, just continually restless."

We tried teaching him at home and found he easily
picked up his lessons and seemed unusually bright. In fact,
he appeared to me to be an exceptional child. So it was
difficult to understand the problems at school.

Soon however, Jason began acting jumpy and too silly
at home, too. Other children began teasing him and making
him the butt of their jokes. We did all we could to alleviate
this, but nothing would change the basic pattern which was
emerging, a troubled little boy who somehow did not fit the
norm or fit in with others. The more he was teased by other
boys, the worse it became. Children can be cruel.

Meanwhile Allen was gone three weeks out of every
four, as an officer of the Sixth Army's Inspector General's
Office. He traveled to all the eight western states inspecting
everything from National Guard Headquarters to Language
and Radar Installations. I came to respect and admire his
wide range of knowledge and versatility even more, as he
memorized hundreds of pages of rules and regulations, needing
to be precise and correct when citing a particular regulation in his formal critique after inspection of any particular
unit. Thus he was home only one week a month. He spent
those few precious hours with our sons, fashioning home-
made bows and arrows and teaching them archery, working
with them in Scouting, or going on beach-combing expedi-
tions. Warm summer weekends we all escaped on delightful
family camping trips to the beaches or down the coast.

Allen did not seem entirely well. He was pale in complexion and more often now retreated within himself into
those silent depressed spells. His annual physical had shown

no problem. I was becoming more concerned and one day sought out the minister of a church I had attended, thinking to receive some guidance. She was an excellent clairvoyant and the advice she gave me was in-depth, and penetrating far into our future, though it did not answer the causes of Allen's problem, per se. One very esoteric message stands out in my memory. I did not understand it until several years later.

"Your grandparents, Augusta and Christopher are here. They greet you with much love. They are bringing a very special gift to you, a very beautiful gift! I cannot adequately describe the wonder of it, for it glows with an effervescent radiance. Your grandmother extends it to you and it seems to be in three parts. She is telling me that this gift is not from them, but from God. They have only been given the great honor of presenting it, for it is A Gift of Life!"*

And then they were gone, leaving me with the memory of an unusual and precious puzzle.

Allen's increasing depressions and absences were especially hard on Jason, who continued to exhibit erratic behavior and could have used a father's time and attention. Jeremy was very well adjusted, smart at his studies and he got along well with others. Naturally, Jeremy also did not appreciate his younger brother's often acting too silly.

The school psychologist didn't have much to say. "He will grow out of it. Just a matter of adjustment." Physically Jason seemed perfectly well. A visiting dentist who had come to school to give a lesson on tooth hygiene and brushing chose Jason to stand in front of the class to show off his perfectly formed and well-cared for teeth. He did have a beautiful smile. He also possessed a sweet, melodious singing voice. He immediately learned and carried any tune he was taught, singing precisely on key and exhibiting a natural ear for rhythm. I tried to believe the psychologist, hoping Jason would outgrow his restlessness, as it was badly affecting his studies and grades in early grammar school.

*These are not names one can pick out of a hat. Only one other medium had ever stated my maternal grandparents' names and that was Dr. Robert Chaney of Astara.

Meanwhile, in answer to my prayers, when the boys were eight and ten years old we were blessed with a baby girl. Believe it or not, she was due on my fortieth birthday. One might say, "She squeaked in under the wire." *This time* during the early months of pregnancy I experienced no early morning nausea because, after the first and only signs of sickness, I was given Vitamin B-6 shots once every ten days for the next six weeks. This doctor was certainly better informed. The B-6 alleviated the problem completely. I have since advised women in the early weeks of pregnancy to take Vitamin B-6 in some form, and in this way always avoid nausea. I wish I had known this with my firstborn!

I might also add that in later years I found this same antidote of B-Vitamins, particularly B-6, to be a great help during menopause, in alleviating the symptoms of hot flashes that annoy so many women. There seems to be a need for an increase in this vitamin during changes in the hormonal metabolism.

I knew our baby would be a girl. For five years I had thanked God in advance for a girl. Also a very 'sensitive' lady friend had told me a number of times while visiting us in earlier months (before I conceived) that she *saw* a little girl skipping along by my side, waiting to come through, she said.

Our baby girl arrived the last of May in 1965. I was isolated from the other expectant women at Letterman Hospital because of my age, along with one other forty-year old expectant mother. It seems the chance of the child being born with a problem increases with a woman's age. Our little girl was perfect in every way. The other woman also gave birth to a girl, but unfortunately the baby did have an abnormality: her right arm ended at the elbow. The mother, the wife of a full Colonel, insisted she had never taken a drug of any kind, nor did she drink or smoke. I felt very sad for them.

Our boys were thrilled to have a little sister, and Allen especially was overjoyed to finally have his little girl as he was now forty-eight years old. Jeannine was a blonde with blue eyes and sported a curly 'top-knot' of hair. Young Jason, who adored her from the start, nicknamed her "Doll."

Jason's loving, gentle and devoted nature shone when he was with her. He spent many hours through the next few years reading to her and happily playing small games. I could always count on him to faithfully babysit if I had to be gone for a short while. Jeremy was studious and often had school and Scout projects to work on, or went off with his older friends, which was natural.

When our baby was only three weeks old, Allen came home with news that he was being sent to the Far East, as America was now at war in Viet Nam. So the Presidio tour ended, and we were to move once again. We chose to return to our home near Seattle. That is, the children and I did, for Allen was being sent over as an "American Advisor to the Republic of South Korea." In 1961 he had been promoted in rank to Lieutenant Colonel. Now he was to train a South Korean Regiment and take them to Viet Nam. We did not know how long he would be gone. Once again I faced wartime and my husband's absence.

Three weeks later we were in Seattle, lock-stock-and-barrel, including cat, dog and baby. We hugged Daddy goodbye, not knowing when — or if — we would see him again. I found myself alone in our house on the wooded lane, with two young sons and our six-weeks old baby girl.

*

ILLNESS — AND AN ANSWER

This period following our move back to Seattle, necessitated by Allen's departure for Korea, became a time of deep distress. I was left alone to cope, and I found myself again suffering the symptoms I had experienced in Germany after the birth of Jason. But this time the illness was more severe, and I crept dangerously close to a nervous breakdown. While I kept up the home and yard, repaired neglect left by the renters in our absence, nursed and cared for the baby and the two boys, I was also writing to Allen and attempting to keep a stiff upper lip for his sake. The boys were a help, but they were still young and sometimes when they argued or fought in play, this simple stress would cause me to become hysterical. Crying uncontrollably more than once, I would break down, frightening the children. To make matters worse, I totally lost control of my right arm. With no muscle strength, it hung helplessly at my side. It was tricky indeed to cook meals, and feed and diaper a new baby with one hand. There were no relatives in the area that I could call on, and the boys were in school.

I made repeated visits to several doctors, but these consultations produced no noticeable help. I was even x-rayed by a doctor who wanted to see if I had a spare rib pressing against my arm nerves. Doesn't that sound silly? At the age of forty, wouldn't any problems a spare rib might produce have shown up long before? Another doctor actually offered me muscle relaxants, which I did not dare accept or take, as my muscles were already so weak I didn't have the strength to lift the baby or a kitchen pan. Just imagine what that prescription would have done to me.

Each time I told a doctor that I had only weeks before given birth at the age of forty, and suggested this might have something to do with it, I was brushed off with the wave of a hand or a shake of the head. "That's another area. It has nothing to do with this." By this time I had seen five doctors to no avail and feeling worse than ever. Once again I gave up on the medical profession. And I sorely missed my husband.

Early one morning just before waking I had a strange and vivid dream. (Our subconscious sometimes tries to reach our conscious mind with pictures as a warning.) This particular dream is an example of why we should pay attention to our vivid dreams, the ones that leave a strong impression and remain in the memory.

In this dream I was sitting petting a coal black cat in my lap. The cat jumped from my lap, and then walked into my sons' bedroom. At that point I became aware of a packet strapped under its neck which was opening, releasing a swarm of small black spiders which crawled out into the room. I was so horrified at the thought of their biting the boys that I awakened with my skin tingling and hair prickling on my head. Before coming too far awake, I mentally and immediately asked in my mind:

"Father-Mother God. What — oh what — does that mean?"

I lapsed back into semi-sleep and a new dream seemed to bring the interpretation. It came vividly clear. The black cat represented a bad habit or something I was holding; it was the illness I was nursing (stroking the black cat in my lap). The cat had jumped down, entering the boys' room. The spider in a packet around its throat, were the harsh, negative, nerve-racked words coming from the throat of a sometimes hysterical mother, which were potentially damaging to the boys — biting them like unseen spiders. I came sharply awake, horrified at having allowed my illness to reach such a point, and grateful for being shown the danger this was causing.

When we are emotionally ill, or going through times of need, we sometimes forget to turn in prayer to God and Holy Spirit for help until we reach a point of desperation, whereas we should ask at the outset to prepare the way. I was guilty of this at times as a result of being too overloaded with material daily duties. Like many, I had forgotten the help that is available, which silently waits to be called.

Needless to say, with the urgency of the picture my subconscious had shown me, I went into deep prayer for answers, giving thanks and gratitude *in advance* for God's ever-present help. In the turmoil since arriving back in Seattle, I had not called or seen my friend Virginia, who had been my prayer-partner in our group three years previous. One tends not to burden others with one's problems. I should have known better, as this is a mistake. We should always call on prayer partners for their prayers in our behalf, as they too are blessed in the praying.

The very day after I prayed, Virginia appeared, saying, "I had an urge to call and see you." Shocked to hear my tale of woe, she insisted, "You must see *my* doctor, as I had a similar problem a few years ago and he helped me." Weary of doctors and still dubious, I yet knew God usually answers through other people, so I consented to go *just one more time.*

Well! That dear man did not even give me a test.

"You've already had too many tests. I've listened to you for only five minutes and it's clear what is wrong. I've treated many women with similar post-birth problems. Some have been suicidal and we caught them just in time, and were able to achieve a dramatic and complete turn-around in their health. What you need is estrogen. Has any previous doctor you've seen suggested this?"

"No one," I answered.

"When you relate that you felt better during pregnancy than at any other time, that clinches it, because the placenta, present during gestation, produces extra estrogen, helping the expectant mother to feel great. Then when the placenta is expelled at birth, the woman experiences a sudden drop, causing these extreme symptoms. In some women such as yourself, the body does not pick up on estrogen production on its own after giving birth for some reason, and the hormone system then suffers the loss. From what you describe you apparently have been somewhat short of it all of your life."

He gave me a prescription, I took it, and I was a changed person overnight. What an immeasurable and immense relief! Even my useless right arm was soon functioning normally again. All this came after I gave up running around seeking answers from many doctors and gave the need to God. I have found He almost always answers us through other people. Just the right person will appear on the scene — with just the right answer. One year later my body had righted itself. I found it no longer needed the extra assistance, and I have not taken any estrogen to this day twenty-six years later.

The role of hormones has become more commonly understood in these intervening twenty-six years, so now few women would be shuttled about as I was without proper diagnosis. I am, nevertheless, quick to give the medical profession its credit where credit is due, especially in the case of very astute doctors who have done a tremendous amount of good. We are all aware of this. However, I relate all this because I recall a particular happening.

Years earlier I had a cousin whose young twenty-six year old wife completely lost her mind after the birth of their second son for no reason the doctors could ever ascertain, and she was confined to a mental institution for the rest of her life. At that time no one could understand it, as she had been a perfectly normal, delightful young woman before the birth and during pregnancy. She and my cousin had had an ideal, happy marriage. But immediately after the birth, Audrey changed completely. She had a nervous breakdown (just as I was headed toward), suffered hysteria (as I did), and even chased her husband, Melvin, one day with a butcher knife. At this point she was committed. With Audrey, as with me, the doctors could find nothing physically wrong. Her change from normal to mental was so sudden and so like mine that I am thoroughly convinced that all poor Audrey lacked was estrogen. The hormone system becomes so unbalanced it affects the entire nervous system, the glands, and the brain's neurons. How many people through the years, I wonder, were called crazy and put away simply for lack of proper diagnosis of their physical condition, when what they needed was only some form of body-nutritional help. How tragic.

To my joy, my immediate change to good health coincided with my birthday week. I felt that the renewed health I was experiencing was a gift in answer to my prayer. Angels were in attendance, it seemed, wishing to cheer me, for during my birthday week, I received thirty-five birthday cards from friends all over the United States, the most ever. But what was amazing was that *every single card was roses* – pink, yellow, red, lavender, even blue and green – but all roses! It was then I recalled that two weeks before, talking with a neighbor as we looked at flowers, I had mentioned to her, "I love all flowers, as they are so very precious, carrying God's love to us, but I love the rose most, since besides its beauty it has such a heavenly fragrance." I now saw that my Angel had heard and took the trouble to whisper in the ear of every friend and relative, to let me know the Loving Presence is always with us. It was too astounding and wonderful to be coincidence.

We all can have an angel, but we must always be aware. If we ask for angel help, it will be given, but it is well to watch and fully expect. In this instance the flood of roses on the cards was a surprise gift as I had no inkling my words were heard. I was being told I was loved all through my illness. We are all loved, but we must be open to the signs with a grateful heart. Jesus said, "Pray, believing ye have, giving thanks, and it shall be given." This is a literal statement from our Lord.

One can ask for a Health Angel who will strive to give help as I had, or a Mechanical Angel to help keep one's auto running safely (I have received numerous amazing assists in that area). Truly, the Angels appreciate recognition and will strive to please, as to serve is their joy. But do watch for the Gift, for it may not come in the form you expect, or through the one you are looking to. Never close the door on an unexpected opportunity or ignore an idea when it comes to you out of the blue. Many times the rational mind which has been conditioned to demand proof, reasons us right out of the good the Universe, through our angels, seeks to bestow. "Having faith as a little child" means to remain open-minded and open-hearted. That's when what we call miracles can happen. And — always give thanks.

Since that time I am happy to find others who have discovered this truth and written excellent books on angels.

Angels not only serve the Lord, but they have been asked to serve humankind and it has been told many times that these pure Beings truly delight in answering our sincere calls for assistance. Angels are transducers of energy and can control and direct instant energy to whatever happens to be their personal area of assignment and responsibility, be it plant life, animal, or humankind. If one has sincerely asked for angel guidance and protection, an angel often will step in at moments of danger and one can find oneself miraculously saved from what could have been a disastrous situation. I often think what a challenge our modern day lives, with fast-moving automobiles, must present for angels, and what credit they are due.

I often speak directly to my Mechanical Angel with love and thanksgiving, who has charge of my auto whenever I am on the road. This protection has been true now for many years, from simple flat tires or other breakdown (which, when they rarely happen, have been amazingly in *very* convenient places) to more alarming experiences. During the years I was driving the long distance at least twice a year from Seattle to Los Angeles to visit Mama, often alone or with one or two of my small children, there were a number of instances that will forever stand out in my memory.

One day before I was to leave for Los Angeles, I was to have my auto checked, as was my custom. I normally kept it in good condition, but that morning while on errands the car developed a loud CLUNK every time I turned the wheel to round a corner. It was alarming! I decided not to wait for my appointment but to head for the garage, which was at the military base four miles away over heavily traveled roads. It was a scarey drive, as at every turn the CLUNK became louder, and there were many turns. I am sure I prayed to my Angel to help me arrive safely. Driving into the base, I wheeled the auto down to the area of the garage — CLUNK — pulled in — CLUNK — backed into a space — CLUNK — and parked — CLUNK! After describing the problem to the mechanic, I left to shop while he checked it out.

One hour later I returned to an amazed mechanic. "In the past you have told me you have an angel on the roof of your car. Today you must have had two of them! I couldn't even drive it into the garage! I drove it one foot forward and the idler arm between the front wheels broke completely in half. If you had been on the road when it broke, you could have easily tipped over."

I never cease giving thanks and love to my Angels. You may have an angel. You need only ask, and give thanks daily.

✳
HEART ATTACK

Allen had been home only five weeks, having survived the Viet Nam War, when it struck. Our season of joy had been brief, and now a terrible fright clutched at the hearts of our little family. It was hardest on the boys, now ages nine and eleven, as they had waited two years for their Daddy's return. We had been so grateful, for the loss of life in Viet Nam had been terrible, but Allen had been spared. And now this! After several weeks stay in the hospital, he recovered moderately and, being an optimistic soul who always had looked to the best in himself, he went back to work and also to working out-of-doors in our large yard.

I had earlier planted rows of Cascade seedless blackberries, raspberries, and boysenberry bushes that bore delicious fruit as large as a man's thumb. Thanks to Allen's devoted care, we had luscious pies and fresh breakfast berries for many summers to come. He seemed fairly well now physically, but Mama cautioned him not to overdo. When Allen persisted in tending our big yard, she exclaimed on the phone from Los Angeles in exasperation, "Well go ahead and work outdoors! At least you will die healthy." Mama dearly loved her son-in-law and they got along like peaches 'n cream. We changed his diet and he stopped smoking cigarettes (we now know this alone is a killer). But the stress of action in three wars had taken its toll on him, and food in the field was not the best. Allen had survived two very close misses, as previously mentioned, the first time in World War II when his driver had been killed as their jeep rolled over a land mine seconds after Allen had climbed out to scout ahead, saying they must be very cautious. He was knocked to the ground but not hurt. Grieving for his driver was the worst, he said. The second time happened in Korea when a hilltop *crow's nest* was blown sky-high by enemy fire only a few moments after he had climbed down, having spent an hour with the lookout on duty to go over computations. Allen told us he was only thirty feet down the mountain when the lookout position was hit. Again, he was knocked to the ground from the concussion, but escaped unhurt. These were dramatic instances, but day-to-day battle is draining. There is only so much stress the body can take without showing damage. Mental breakdowns among Veterans is well-known.

Mama came to visit us again, as she had years before when we first moved here. The beautifully paneled Little House which we'd fixed up and furnished seemed to be there just for her. She adored having the quiet privacy in the woods, just a short walk away from our house when she wished to retire from the normal ruckus children create. I was delighted, for with this sanctuary, she was able to stay with us awhile. Mama said she liked to listen to the soft swish of the cedar pines that surrounded the cabin as the night breezes stole through the limbs, and she told me she often sat out-of-doors in the stillness, listening to night sounds of the forest and communing with nature. Our woodsy place was very different from Los Angeles and more like our long-ago well-remembered home on the farm in Illinois.

During these next several years I continued my metaphysical studies, and after seven years of evening classes, received my Doctorate in Divinity and Metaphysics. My teacher, Dr. Anna Maye Dahl, was a unique woman with an exceptionally fine mind. She had a memory like a steel trap that could close in on any point in a flash. Dr. Dahl was a respected scholar and speaker, a leader in the metaphysical community, serving many years as Moderator at annual meetings of the International New Thought Alliance. In 1946 she had applied for the Academy of Universal Truth to receive Washington State accreditation as a legal College of Spiritual Studies. Dr. Anna Maye was often referred to as Seattle's Spiritual Godmother. She made her transition to the Higher Realms in 1986, having taught and graduated many students as ministers and teachers. I was privileged to be among them, though I chose, due to family obligations, not to be in the forefront of organizational work at the Academy. My talents tended more toward working one-on-one with individuals, and in the art of natural healing in which I later became actively involved.

Allen felt well enough to go on family outings. He and the boys went fishing and boating on Lake Washington, happily trolling for salmon in the fall. He worked with the Boy Scout troops the boys belonged to, and they camped in the mountains, a special privilege of this area. Allen spent precious times with Jennine, now two and one-half, whose babyhood he had nearly missed. She was a favorite.

Then we discovered a very special Family Summer Camp, which brought new friends and unusual experiences into all of our lives, especially mine.

*
C. F. O. –
AND A DRAMATIC FLASH-BACK

"That music! Where is it coming from?" A beautiful *classical melody drifts on the gentle evening air, mesmerizing me. The tones of the piano rise and fall, capturing my soul as I follow the sound to the large empty meeting hall, empty save for the slight figure of a boy perched at the piano in the front. I can see only his slender back, but the music is like a magnet. I am hypnotized as the notes weave through my mind and pull me forward by my heartstrings. In a kind of dream I sit down to listen. I absorb the waves of sound that flow through me, and I am transported.*

Now, a strange other world feeling engulfs me. Suddenly, I am crying, deep shaking sobs from the depths of my being, but my conscious mind is a thing standing apart, watching in amazement as the Soul is touched. The feeling is pure joy — joy to hear this music! My inner being exults as long as the music lasts, and something inside is crying out, "He's playing again! Thank God — he's playing again!"

How strange. I could not see the face of the young man. I had not left my seat. I was alone in the room. He was not aware of my presence. It was as though I were two people, one watching surprised, the other crying with joy at finding this music, and this musician again, as someone known and loved.

The music stops. He turns and sees me. He is only a boy, but a most handsome one, with gentle wavy brown hair and serious clear eyes that probe into mine very intently. As we look at one another, Time seems to stop, and we are struck immobile. We are alone in the hall, but for a long moment we are alone in the Universe.

Finally I found my voice. "Your music has deeply moved me. I pray you will never give up your aims, for this music has touched my very soul. Do you mind that I had listened?"

"No, not at all. I like an audience, as I intend to become a concert pianist. I hope to attend Julliard."

Adrian was still a student, so although his playing was

good, it was not its greatness that had moved me. Truly, it
was my inner being that could not help rejoicing that he
was playing again. There was a deeply personal connection
and significance in all of this that I could not understand
(but would be revealed to me later). Adrian reached for my
hand and seemed instantly comfortable with me, a strange
woman — who really was not. We were both experiencing
instant soul recognition. Needless to say, we spent as much
time together as possible in the remaining days of Camp.
We were eager to catch up on lost time, enjoying one
another's company immensely, and at week's end we could
barely stand to say goodbye. Adrian and I kept in close
touch through the following years, though he and his family
lived in another state.

The Camp we were attending was Camps Farthest Out,*
or C.F.O., as everyone calls it. C.F.O. is a wonderfully struc-
tured spiritual life family camp program, founded in 1938
by Glenn Clark, a deeply devoted, Christ-filled man who
was the author of several excellent books on the deeper
meaning of the spiritual life.** The founding idea to "go
farther out with Christ" has spread with the camps throughout the United States, and camps are now offered annually
in beautiful natural settings in almost every state and part of
Canada. One could call C.F.O. an ecumenical movement,
crossing denominations, for those who wish to rise above
the confines of one church and join hands with all who
desire fellowship in Christ. C.F.O. camps are attended by
folks who come from all religious affiliations, or perhaps
none at all — it does not matter. No one asks what church
you attend or even what profession you may be in. We
knew one fine gentleman friend through six years of summer camp fellowship, for example, before discovering he
was a judge in his home town in Eastern Washington.

It was a wonderful week of spiritual renewal that sum-

*Camps Farthest Out Association, 1569 Grand Ave., St.Paul, MN 55105
**God's Reach, by Glenn Clark, 1951 Macalester Park Pub.,St.Paul, MN
Also: A Man's Reach, What Would Jesus Do?, The Way the Truth
and the Life, I Will Lift Up Mine Eyes, The Soul's Sincere Desire,
How to Find Health Through Prayer

mer, guided by excellent leaders for all age groups. Many healings were witnessed and lifetime friendships made among people who shared a common bond — their love for Christ Jesus. The healings were moving experiences, not only for those healed, but for family and new friends who saw torn relationships made new as forgiveness was received, as Christ-love poured in through the power of group prayer and powerful leadership.

Some dramatic physical healings, as well, brought deeper faith to many. We saw for example, one young man toss his crutches into the air and walk, free of the multiple sclerosis he had suffered for years. For some, healing comes as a matter of right timing in their soul's journey. Others may have to wait awhile, until they learn necessary lessons. Only the God within knows this time table. During these days of Camp, many lives were changed and burdens were released that had been carried for years.

I prayed that my dear Allen might be among those healed, for his heart condition was worsening. He tired easily and was becoming quite thin and pale. In those days (it was 1967) heart bi-pass surgery had not been perfected and was not commonly practiced or recommended. Allen was, however, taking medication. But healing of the body was not to be, although Allen participated in his quiet way and partook of the beauty of the setting and richness of the Spirit that moved through the group.

Our boys, now ages ten and twelve, found Camp life a delight, with the youth gathered 'round bonfires at nightfall, under excellent leadership, sharing with each other in heart-to-heart ways young people cannot always achieve with their parents. Our eldest son, Jeremy, especially, was touched through the ministering of Reverend Cliff Custer. Since that time, Jeremy's entire life has been motivated with a deep love for God and the desire to work with the Divine Plan in whatever way is open to him. Rev. Cliff Custer has since founded Christophos Institute* in Southern Oregon, where he and his wife lead a Christ-filled ministry and have

*Christophos Institute, 14324 E.Evans Creek Rd, Rogue River, OR 97437

been a moving force in bringing, through deep and dynamic emotional healing, Christ's love into the lives of hundreds of individuals across the U.S.

The spirit-filled music of Dr. Charles King* was a highlight of those wonderful days. His marvelous voice and personal example showed hundreds of seekers the joy of worshiping our Lord through music, then and now. He, too, was a guiding light for Jeremy and became a good friend and kind of God-father figure through these ensuing years.

Another of our fine speakers in those years was Ruth Carter Stapleton, Past-President Jimmy Carter's sister, whose life was devoted to Jesus and who founded a healing ministry in Texas.

The Camp setting in each state is chosen for its natural beauty and serenity, far from the maddening crowd. In Washington State it was held that year, as in many other years, at Holden Village, an historic mining camp turned church camp, perched high above beautiful Lake Chelan and accessible only by boat. Steep cliffs rose above either shore as we sailed up long narrow Lake Chelan nearly 50 miles, disembarking at Lucerne.

We then boarded buses which carried us 1,000 feet higher, winding slowly upward along a steep, wooded mountain road and into a high pristine valley. Arriving, we stood in the midst of sun-splashed, snow-capped peaks, stark against the blue sky, feeling dazzled and deliciously dizzy at being half-way to heaven at the top of the world. Needless to say it was a rare escape, void of newspapers, telephones and television. The spirit is refreshed and made new in the clear, wonderful air and quietude, and by the unique inspirational program of creative music, creative writing and art, shared prayer times, and the love-bonds, new and renewed.

For my young friend and I it was both new and renewed, for we shared a soul-recognition, the special thrill of finding a soul we love once again, in a new lifetime, in a new land, through the blessing of reincarnation, which God has given us. No loved one is ever lost to us you see, for we

*Charles King Musical Church, 16330 N.E. 4th, Bellevue, WA 98008

will meet again, somewhere, someday, on this plane or on another. The true love bond between souls, even in deep friendship, cannot be broken. The Law of Attraction is automatic. It draws us together again and again, across the millennia, and though it is a great mystery, it is infallible.

For all strong emotion sets in motion the Law of Attraction, and hate is only love's 'other side of the coin.' Hate, as an intense emotion, will attract it's object to us just as surely as love will, and at some point we will be faced once again with the person or the situation we despise, being given an opportunity to resolve and master our own emotional creation. We are wise to consider this universal law before we let our emotions run away with us in our relationships in life.

Neither Adrian nor I knew where or when our bond was forged, or what it would mean to meet again. That eventful week when time stood still, Adrian was fourteen and I was forty-two. It was 1967. The years passed. Our friendship deepened, as did my love for this handsome youth and his musical talent, and for his gracious and loving family.

In answer to my intense inner ponderings, two visions came to me that brought back deep and traumatic memories, helping fit the pieces of the puzzle into the pattern of our soul's experiences. These visions were a revelation which told me why I had been so overcome to hear Adrian playing hauntingly beautiful music *once again*. The explanation I will save for later. Meanwhile another major event came crashing down on us.

*

A NEAR-DEATH EXPERIENCE

I often enjoyed sharing nuggets of faith and wisdom with Allen, who always listened patiently, but was sometimes dubious, as intellectuals tend to be. Allen believed in God, and we often prayed together, but that we all have a Divine Destiny, with angel comfort and help through the Christ Light ever at hand, close as breathing, or that reincarnation was a fact, he wasn't sure.

The moment of truth arrived exactly one year plus one day after Allen's first heart attack. The second attack was very severe.

"Help! Help me!" His strangled voice from the bathroom shower one evening sent cold chills cascading over me. I rushed in. He lay on the tub floor gasping, with water still pouring over him. There was no '911' to call in those days and doctors' offices closed at night. I managed to dry and cover him, and after a short time when he felt he could stand, helped him don pajamas and a warm robe. Then, half-lifting and half-supporting him, we got to the car and made the trip to Madigan Military Hospital at Tacoma where he had previously been a patient. We arrived just in time — with me praying all the way. Upon arrival he had another heart attack, and barely survived as doctors worked to save him.

Actually, Allen did *die*. He was gone over five minutes, I was told, before miraculously being brought back to life. When the crisis passed, I was sent home (the children were alone) and I was not allowed to see him that night.

When I returned early the next morning, Allen's doctors met me, reporting they were astonished after the extreme severity of his heart attack that at 5:00 a.m. my husband had sat up in bed and announced he was well now and wanted to go home!

"The doctors refuse to believe me!" Allen complained in exasperation as I entered. "They label me delirious." Greeting me with outstretched arms, a smile on his face and tears in his eyes, immense love poured from him as he enthusiastically exclaimed that he had "something wonderful to tell me." Was this my calm, usually cool and collected husband? Had they taken him away and given me a new one? Yes, in a way that was true, for as his story unfolded I saw indeed, he seemed to be made new.

He told me he had been taken to see a glimpse of Heaven, and it was so marvelous he had not wanted to come back. His soul had actually left his body (during those five minutes when he *died*) and didn't want to return to it. But now he was sitting up, vivacious and enthused, not at all like one who has just had a severe heart attack. I perched on a chair and held his hand while he unfolded his amazing experience

"I suddenly moved upward and outward very fast, and I found myself on a kind of raft, that floated on what I can only describe as living water, for it sparkled and shone and was alive, bubbling and kind of singing! The atmosphere was very bright, emanating a clear beautiful Light that touched everything with magic. Faster and faster I traveled, then suddenly was in a place with scenery and I saw trees and birds and flowers similar to earth, but far more wonderful, as these flowers radiated life, in effervescent glorious colors everywhere! There were birds like here, but their colors were far more brilliant and unusual like one might see in a prehistoric jungle and — amazingly — I saw and felt the beauty of their songs coming forth in streams of color, blending with the Light which was so radiant. I don't know how else to say it, for everything was just so beautiful."

He stopped and lapsed back into dreamy inner contemplation. I waited, and soon he spoke again.

"The wondrous thing though was the tranquility and bliss, for I felt a happiness impossible to describe, as though I were a part of these scenes, and totally surrounded by love . . . that I finally was home with my heart's longing fulfilled. As I sped forward I heard singing up ahead, voices rich in melodious harmony, like nothing on earth, and instinctively I seemed to know it was my welcoming committee, and I rejoiced! But in the midst of my joy there came a sharp tug to my whole Being and I blacked out.

"The next thing I knew I was back in my body, and I was never so disappointed in all of my life. Then I recalled, perhaps two minutes later, that you and the children were here and needed me."

Allen stopped speaking, with tears in his eyes, looking at me so lovingly while holding my hand. "I guess it's not yet my time to go."

I realized then that the doctors had been giving shock treatment to the heart to bring it back to beating, causing the soul to be actually yanked back into the body by the silver cord of life which connects the two.

I had not in those days of the late 1960's heard the term Near-Death-Experience, although I knew this was possible, as Great Aunt Minnie, who had been the remarkable clairvoyant I spoke of earlier, had had such an experience and told our family of "going to heaven" just three weeks before her actual passing. She was waved back by loved ones, she said, who impressed her with the thought, "It is not yet time." She came back knowing the exact day she would die. She prepared for this event by giving away every item she owned to the very person she wished to have it. On the last day the house was empty except for the bed she lay in, the table and lamp beside it, and a chair for a visitor. This was ideal I thought.

So I was personally thrilled that such a wondrous thing had happened to Allen, for it changed his entire outlook on life. He insisted I call a couple we knew to ask them to come to the hospital. The man was a co-worker with whose views he had disagreed and whom he had somehow strongly disliked. Now he wanted desperately to ask the man's forgiveness and make amends. We did that. They came and were touched by his humility. Also, every single morning beginning on the first day at 5:00 a.m., he sat up in bed, and said, "God spoke to me." He was inspired to write deeply expressive poetry and short stories, all the while claiming he was healed.

Allen's psychic sense had opened so he 'knew' which nurses weren't feeling well and which ones had troubles at home. He discussed this with them, and they were pleased and surprised by his knowledge and concern. He wrote a letter to the hospital superintendent demanding a lounge for the nurses that they might rest on their breaks, as at that time there was no lounge. He had ascertained this without anyone's telling him. The many prayers for him at C.F.O. Camp four months earlier had been answered after all, but in God's own way. I was overjoyed and gave thanks to Holy Spirit.

The doctors, however, were very upset over all of this as they'd never had a heart patient act so sprightly and gregarious only hours after an attack. So they proceeded to pump him full of tranquilizers. Terribly dismayed, I could do nothing, for if I had taken him out of the hospital against doctors' wishes, the military rules were such that we would then have been responsible for all costs, and we could not afford it. I helplessly watched as eight days later the tranquilizers had done their dirty work, and he came down from his spiritually elevated state to a rather numbed, docile, almost depressed condition again. This, then, pleased the doctors, and they allowed him to be released. Allen was given a medical discharge from Service. Once again, we had run afoul of the medical profession's answer to illness, although they had saved his life with shock to the heart.

For me, the memory of Allen's moments of joy will never be erased. Now, in recent more enlightened years, three books have been published by prominent medical doctors, documenting similar cases of Near-Death Experiences. The first was published in 1975, called *Life After Life*,* by Raymond Moody, Jr., M.D. This was a landmark book, being a 'first' on this subject. The second book, *Closer To The Light*,** was recently published by Melvin Morse, M.D., who practices at Children's Orthopedic Hospital in Seattle.

Dr. Morse, impressed with Dr. Moody's work, chose to document one step further, and published his findings on the many experiences reported by children, many of whom had been his own patients. This book is a wonderful follow-up, as children could hardly make up such stories, all with similar reports of seeing the wonderful Light and feeling the peaceful, even blissful, state that accompanies passing in so-called death, with all pain and discomfort gone.

Dr. Morse tells of a small boy of four, who upon hearing his parents' talking of "going to see a play about Jesus" at Christmas time, suddenly asked them, "Will He look like the Jesus I saw when I died?" The parents were dumbfounded, as this was the first time the child had ever mentioned the subject of death, nor had they ever told him that he had *died* for a short time, when he was very ill at the age

*Life After Life, by Raymond Moody, M.D.,1975, Bantam/Mockingbird Books, Covington, GA
***Closer To The Light*, by Melvin Morse, M.D. 1990, Random House New York, N.Y.

of nine months. Previously he had been too young to speak of this, nor could he have learned of it from them as they had never discussed it.

Dr. Raymond Moody's first book was published rather belatedly, as for many years those who'd had such experiences, his patients among them, were reluctant to speak of this even to their doctors, afraid — understandably — of being called crazy or being accused of hallucinating. However, in the last ten-to-fifteen years an explosion of interest in this subject has occurred, so the reality and confirmation of the Truth is now openly discussed and more widely recognized.

So much so that Dr. Melvin Morris has compiled exciting new information in an additional book entitled, *Transformed By The Light*.* This book is a follow-up to his previous work on near-death studies. In *Transformed By The Light* he examines how people are changed by the Near-Death Experience. Dr. Morse states that this experience defies description, for the Light has a powerful effect on people's lives. They often will go on to in-depth work in their community; also they have no more fear of death. Their lives are always changed for the better. Dr. Melvin Morse is a Seattle area pediatrician who has conducted studies at the University of Washington on this phenomenon. In an interview on KING-Radio in October of 1992 Dr. Morse offered some of the results of his work.

"The Near-Death Experience has been called an hallucination by those who do not understand it. A person in a Near-Death Experience knows who they are, where they are, and they are in no way unclear about what they see. It is not in any way similar to an hallucination. To call it that, trivializes this joyous and marvelous spiritual happening. People are transformed by the Near-Death Experience."

One of the ongoing results of the Near-Death Experience is an expanded or heightened intelligence in many cases. Dr. Morse told of a man who had been a mediocre student of chemistry before having a Near-Death Experi-

Transformed By the Light, 1992, Random House Subsidiaries.

ence in which he said he saw a lot. Now this man has over one hundred chemical patents! He claims all of his present knowledge was simply the working out of the initial basic knowledge he was given during the N.D.E. Another subject was a physicist who had a Near-Death Experience, after which he found he understood sub-atomic particles, long before they were discovered in the laboratory.

When Dr. Morse is asked, "Is it real?" he states, "Yes, it is. In fact, the findings of our research team at the University of Washington corroborate reports published in the American Medical Pediatrics Journal. The Near-Death Experience is as real as math, as real as languages. It is just not understandable by people who do not understand the brain. We have circuit boards of mysticism in our brain. There are many dimensions to time which exist outside of our third-dimension reality. When our mind steps outside this dimension, we are then in this timeless zone. Our psychological abilities are located in the right temporal lobe of the brain. Telepathy also is utilized by this right lobe. The N.D.E. activates this telepathic area of our brain that we normally under-use.

"Dr. Raymond Moody is recognized as the father of the Near-Death Experience study. Dr. Moody is helping people to learn to activate the portions of their brain the N.D.E. stimulates. Joan Rivers, nationally known T.V. talk-show hostess, recently went to Dr. Moody's lab, and was placed in a hypnogogic state, or a state of reverie. She went out of her physical body, traveled across the state, and visited her sister in her home. The sister happened to be in the shower. Immediately after this session, the staff telephoned the sister, who stated, 'Yes, I just got out of the shower.'"

Dr. Morse continued, "The lesson in all of this is interconnectedness. Those who attempt suicide come back and say they were told, 'Don't do that again! When you do that you hurt everybody.'

"Doctors have evolved a technical ritual around death and dying.

"They have become the Medicine of Death. But death is more than a technical, medical ritual. We have lost our old societal rituals. We must learn to give dignity to the dying experience by creating a spiritual climate where we can talk about the Light and the family can understand this wonderful experience. If the patient sees the Light, he must be able to speak of it. We must have more communication on this subject.

"Paying attention to this area of life is also economically sound," continued Dr. Morse. "Listening to these experiences could save our health care system 10%-15%, because we needlessly keep people on resuscitation machines when it is not really necessary. We must empower the dying patient to take his life into his own hands."

In a September 24, 1992 interview on the Oprah Winfrey Television program, Dr. Morris stated: "We are on a new link now, in the way neuroscience is meeting the psychic." He also pointed out that all of his subjects agree on one point: Because of their Near-Death Experience they now know LOVE to be the most important thing in all of life.

The International Association for Near-Death-Studies,* under director Kimberley Clark Sharpe, offers once a month meetings in Seattle to those who have had experiences or may wish to attend out of interest. The International Office of I.A.N.D.S is in Hartford, Connecticut.**

It gratifies me to see the new awareness expanding people's minds, as humankind slowly releases frightening ideas about death implanted over the centuries by unenlightened clergy who portrayed a fearsome God eager to wreak hellfire and damnation upon his created subjects.

Slowly but surely the truth is seen that God is Pure Love in Self-Expression, having created everything in the light of this love. This, then, is the central core of our being, our true nature. It cannot be otherwise. Anything in our lives that does not express this essential Love is born of

*I.A.N.D.S., Seattle Chapter, P.O.Box 84333, Seattle, WA 98124
**International Association for Near-Death Studies, 638 Prospect Ave, Hartford, CT, 06105
Note: In 1991 the prestigious University of Virginia Medical School, among several others, funded a study of Near-Death Experiences, under Dr. Ian Stevenson, who was recently interviewed in an in-depth radio broadcast on KING out of Seattle.

misunderstanding, of ignorance.

Those who pass over and come back tell of this pure love and bliss that is unlike anything felt on earth while we are entrapped in a physical body. Isn't it worth listening to them and adjusting our attitude to understand that our life is just a part of a much greater, wondrous Life? So-called death is really a doorway to a new and expanded life, not an ending, but a new beginning! Death is never to be feared or mourned if a person has done their best with the lot they were given in life. They can instead look forward to an exciting new chapter in their inter-galactic existence. Mama humorously and wisely remarked, "When life here gets so crazy one can't stand it any longer, God provides a trap door."

When mankind understands the universal immutable Law of Cause and Effect, and lives and expresses it through love for all fellow beings, with kindness to animals as well, and the earth itself, only then may the Golden Age in all its glory be brought to the planet. For all are created equal in God's love, through the Creative Force that wishes to express more of Itself.

Many younger souls on earth have not yet gained the experience or the wisdom needed to awaken to the power of the Spirit within, and therefore relate to and operate on only the physical plane. One must have understanding and compassion for these individuals. It has been said that behind every saint walks a sinner, and ahead of every sinner walks a saint. We are all on the Road to Becoming, and it is a wondrous road that has no end.

Humankind in general has, by personal greed and selfishness, held itself back from achieving the potentials that are possible to it. We are all cells in the Body of God, so what happens to one affects the many. Subtly but surely, in the course of time, the effects of all our actions or thoughts are seen. Whatsoever we think or do is tossed out into the sea of our surroundings, and eventually, after touching many around us, washes up on the shores of our circumstances, carried by the relentless, unerring tides of universal justice. One cannot escape one's own creations; they are boomerangs. But foolishly, we often blame God or bad luck for our misfortunes.

The law of cause and effect is a law of electromagnetic energy operating on a subtler plane within our own being which is not yet generally understood. This law involves vibration and attraction, which unfailingly designs the outcome, with the purpose that the individual may realize in broad daylight, so to speak, the results of past actions, whether done in the dark or in the light. The law is, actually, quite scientific and logical.

Kindness is Love in Action. *True prayer is Love in Action on unseen levels. Every single living thing is a channel through whom love can flow to others.*

Recently, at San Francisco General Hospital, Dr. Randolph Byrd in Clinical Medicine directed a study of four hundred heart attack patients. All were treated identically, except that the names of two hundred (half) were farmed out for prayer. None of the four hundred knew they were involved in this study. The results were even more astonishing than the researchers expected.

The two hundred who were prayed for appeared to have been given a miracle drug. *Not a single one of these two hundred died*; all recovered, and far more rapidly than expected. The other two hundred had to remain on various machines or medications, and some died. It was said by the researchers that had this been a new drug that was discovered, it would have been hailed as a miracle and people would line up down the block to receive it. One on the team of surgeons, a Dr. William Noland, who had been the greater skeptic, was greatly impressed. He was heard to speak of this study in detail on a recent radio broadcast in Seattle in 1993.

Numerous books have been written describing the power of prayer to heal, many based on controlled research. An article entitled "The Power of Prayer — Old Approach — New Wonders" is a comprehensive excerpt from *Recovering the Soul, A Scientific and Spiritual Search,* and *Prayer, The Mind's Roll in Healing,* both compiled by Larry Dossey, M.D. (Bantam Books, 1989). These are a sampling.

Love is the quantity and the very necessary quality. When

the Law of Love is understood and rightly used, and the Mother Planet likewise treated with love and respect, the New Heaven and New Earth of biblical prophecy will become a reality. With humankind's tremendous potential for achievement unleashed on all levels, through the removal of past and current negative energy blocks, think what vistas this knowledge and life force could open to our wondering eyes.

We are yet babes in using the power available on inner creative levels. A few down through the ages have made this breakthrough, contacted the Universal Omniscience, and proceeded to express a multitude of talents to help uplift humanity.* Most are familiar also with the phenomenal works of the scientist Nicola Tesla, for example.

This potential is realizable to all who truly seek with perseverance and with love for God. For doesn't the drop of ocean water contain the essence of the ocean? If the drop is *in* the ocean, it moves in tandem and with the power of the ocean. Thus Jesus' statement: "I of myself can do nothing. It is the Father within that doeth the works." Jesus tried to get this idea across in His teachings.

> A greater law I give you: Love one another as I have loved you, (John:13:34).
> I have said ye are gods, and all of you are children of the Most High, (Psalms 82:6).
> These things I do, greater things than these shall ye do, (John: 14:12).

However, the organized church (in the 1st Century A.D.) seemed to pick up the ball and run with it in a different direction (witness the Dark Ages, the Spanish Inquisition, the Salem witch hunts — all directed by the church). Someone has facetiously remarked, "There is nothing wrong with true Christianity. It just hasn't been tried yet."

Churchianity is not necessarily *Christianity*. There is

The Man Who Tapped the Secrets of the Universe, by Glenn Clark, 1946-1969. Macalester Park Pub.Co., St.Paul, MN; and *Breakthrough to Creativity*, by Shafica Karagulla, M.D., M.R.C.P.Ed., DeVorss & Co., Inc., Los Angeles, CA 90041 to name only two.

a difference. Many churches do a tremendous good work, and the needs to which they minister are monumental. Many individuals have lived sainted lives, sung and unsung. All of this is in the spirit of love. It is the basic underlying untrue dogma we speak of, for it has taken centuries for men to begin to understand that God is Pure Love and Life Itself. Anything of a lesser nature has been created by humankind.

We find it humorous that those who proclaim "God is dead" are denying their own existence. Genesis 1:26-27 clearly states, "And God said, Let us make man in our image, after our likeness." Does that not mean man is a creator also, if he is in God's image? It is time we individually realize this, its effect and promise in our lives, and live accordingly.

So my dear husband had a glimpse of the glory that awaits, and it was as though he had been made new in spirit, even though his body, we found over the long term, was not healed of the plague of heart disease or of the intermittent depressions. However, his gentle love, with new knowledge and faith, shone upon our little family during the next two years, as his soul was healed. He had received something far more meaningful than a physical healing.

He and Jennine, then two years of age, became the best of pals. He taught her simple ways to learn mathematics with ingenious card games and books, and she would have two years to know and love her father. Also, he planned and finished the lower level of our home during those two years, paneling, plumbing and creating a lovely, livable recreation room, with added bedroom and downstairs bath, even though building had never been his profession. I never ceased to be impressed with Allen's talented hands and creative mind. The boys often worked with their father in the tool room, making boats, bows and arrows, repairing household items, and learning to use hand and electric tools.

A number of years earlier, when Jason was two and one-half, he intently watched Allen working at the carpentry bench. The little guy had heard me exclaiming now and then in moments of curiosity or exasperation, "What on earth are you doing?" Now as he watched his father, he asked with wide-eyed interest, "Daddy, what are you doing on earth?"

Allen, surprised and amused, said, "Son, sometimes I wonder myself."

"LIFE EVERLASTING"

Where are the tulips that bloomed after slumber?
Do you think they have passed through Death's door?
Where is the fruit our apple tree bore —
As she gracefully embraced the summer?

Where is the glory of the rhododendron bush
As she wore her prettiest gown?
With luxuriant blooms of crimson, purple and gold
Encircling her form like a crown.

You say, "This beauty is a fleeting thing,
It was meant to be this way —
So, we do not weep or in sorrow wail
When the flower or fruit has had its day.

And so, I would that you should see
Your soul — as the hidden bulb would be,
Absorbing the growth of a long summer's day
Into its depths and stored away — yet
Destined to burst forth in more glorious array
In the golden light — of another New Day!

Bonnie Ann Gilchrist

✳

WE FIND AN ANSWER

Depression. It is depressing — and hard on any family. To our dismay, Allen's withdrawn spells seemed still to plague him from time to time, despite all the wonders that had occurred and the healing in spirit he had experienced. It was a sadness to me to which I never ceased seeking the reason, as I believe that at the heart of every problem there is an answer. All the doctors could do was to prescribe tranquilizers, and it was obvious that this only glossed over the cause and definitely made things worse.

I reasoned that the depression must in some way have a physical origin, since Allen had had such a beautiful spiritual healing, so I was very careful to keep him on a healthy heart diet, and yet now and then he still would retreat into that dark area of his mind that allowed no one to enter.

One day quite unexpectedly Beloved Presence guided my footsteps. I entered a health store intent on buying a certain item. Instead, I immediately felt my head being turned left to the book section, and my feet followed quite involuntarily. As I walked forward, right at eye level, the yellow letters of a black book jumped out at me.

*How To Live With Schizophrenia.** Picking it off the shelf, I opened it, and found myself riveted. The words I read on the pages which had fallen open described Allen's case exactly! Mesmerized, I sat down on a nearby chair and read for over an hour, for here was my answer. Purchasing the book, I excitedly brought it home for Allen to read, for by now he was feeling amiable again and readily took my suggestion.

You cannot know the relief these doctors findings brought to him as he read that his illness truly had a physical cause and could be treated with large dosages of Vitamin B, particularly B-3, or Niacin.

"And all this time I thought I was crazy!" Allen's candid exclamation was warmth to my heart, after long years of his silent suffering and refusal to discuss his feelings.

According to Drs. Hoffer and Osmond, who have treated a wide variety of cases successfully over many years, what

*How to Live With Schizophrenia, Hoffer & Osmond, Second Printing 1974 Citadel Press, Secaucus, N.J.

is called schizophrenia does not always express itself in the form commonly associated with the word, e.g. hearing voices, split personality, or strange behavior that is easily recognized. They state:

> This illness can oft times be a mild form, which evidences as periodic depressions, dark moods which tend to make the sufferer isolate himself from the rest of society, having dark and foreboding thoughts that create a most unhappy state of mind. This is extremely hard to detect and diagnose because of its periodic appearance *caused by bio-chemical imbalances in the body which are co-related to the sensory nerves of the brain.*

The doctors go on to relate that particular foods, or lack of others, as well as emotional stress, can cause these bio-chemical imbalances which in turn trigger the symptoms. Thus, the term schizophrenia is a misnomer, for this imbalance can cover a wide variance in symptoms. The particular reaction which Allen suffered has recently been named by the medical profession *Bi-Polar Personality Disorder*. Canada has promoted schizophrenia research while the United States has hindered it, and therefore in the 1960's Canada was way ahead in medical research and discovery in this field.

Understand that thirty years ago nutritional therapy through vitamin and mineral supplements was in its infancy. Few spoke of it, and the medical profession in the U.S. poo-pooed it, calling any such solution quackery. The American Medical Association actually harassed, persecuted, and even black-balled their own members who tried to initiate and incorporate its use. These were very sad years for a number of very fine forward-thinking doctors who, simply for their far-sightedness and desire to add to the understanding of the human body's basic nutritional needs, suffered unheard of criticism and slander, had their offices ransacked and legal action brought against them by their own American Medical Association, in an effort to bar them from their profession. Many of these doctors were forced to leave the U.S. if they wished to continue practice. Drugs and surgery alone were the accepted methods of treatment, and sadly, in many areas, still are. One could mention the enormous financial interests of the pharmaceutical industry, in league, of course, with the A.M.A. and F.D.A., who stand to lose a lot of business through natural nutritional approaches.

It seems only rational, does it not, that the body builds on the food it receives, and if some basic element is missing in the body's fuel or is not assimilated, or even lacking in sufficient amount from birth through genetics, this would cause a change in glandular and nerve function? Now, after thirty some years, this fact is finally being looked at and confirmed by open-minded medical people in laboratory studies, corroborating what Drs. Hoffer and Osmond had shown in the 1960's. People with long-standing illnesses, even Alzheimer patients in some instances are now being helped to lead more normal lives in their later years.

Recent (1990's) articles in *Biological Psychiatry and Nutrition Reports International*, report that psychiatrists have found a significant relationship between depression and Vitamin B-6 (pyridoxine) deficiency. The use of B-6 is now being promoted as an alternative therapy for schizophrenia, based on recent success with this nutrient. So the work of Drs. Hoffer and Osmond is proven out twenty years later. As an added note: recently it has been shown in Naturopathic studies that one tablet each of Vitamin B-3, that is Niacin, and of Chromium Picolinate taken together in combination once daily will significantly reduce cholesterol in the body and bloodstream. This is a very helpful breakthrough, as high cholesterol is known to be a precursor of atherosclerosis and heart attacks, being currently much discussed.

Allen began the natural vitamin therapy that was recommended and within days felt an immediate and dramatic improvement in his outlook and personality. Also the buzzing in his ears disappeared and he said he was no longer cold. But above all, the spells of depression which he had suffered his entire lifetime disappeared during the ensuing month. This was cause for great joy, after eighteen years of concern.

"I always wondered why," Allen said to me, "of all the six children in our family at home, I was the only one who developed rickets as a child, when we all ate the same food."

In their book, Drs. Hoffer and Osmond explain: "Anyone with this particular biochemical imbalance usually also lacks a sufficient amount of Vitamin C, as the body does not retain it from the food, and this can often lead to rickets." For Allen, this observation was the clincher. One of his married sisters had years earlier confided to me when I sadly spoke of his depressions, "Oh, yes. He was always like that. When we walked to school as kids together, sometimes he wouldn't speak to me for three weeks. The family just thought, 'That's Allen.'"

In those days children's needs were not high on the list of priorities, and most parents didn't have the time to spend seeking answers which, as we see, were not available anyway. How sad that so many, like Allen, have had to go through life with these biochemical imbalances and other hidden illnesses (such as my mother's undiscovered blue-baby heart) causing aberrations of behavior that affect their entire life's relationships and work in negative ways, never finding answers, understanding, or help. As mood-related studies are more commonly conducted to test B-vitamins and other nutrients including minerals, more medical and psychiatric researchers are realizing that nutrients play vital roles in mental health, *and that there is a direct relationship between nutrition and personality swings, including violence.*

One of the reasons I write this book is in the hope that more children and adults may be understood, enlightened and helped to live more normal lives, free from stigmas that are the product of ignorance. The terribly frightening thing in this decade is that the Federal Drug Administration (F.D.A.) is working to make the nutritional supplements of ordinary food vitamins illegal, or required to be by prescription only (thereby costing a great deal more: a $5.00 bottle of vitamins would cost around $45.00), as the powers that be seem to want our entire society to rely solely on drugs and chemicals. It would seem that by now we would have plainly seen the fallacy of this approach. But fallacious or not, drugs are profitable. Naturopathic doctors' offices are being broken into at gun-point and their records and products confiscated, without warrant or warning. We wonder what is happening in our free America.

Allen felt so much better; he was no longer tired, or as cold or pale in the face, and the incessant ringing in his ears stopped.

Enormously gratified by our discovery, which lifted a great mental burden from both of us, he smiled and said to me one day,

"Hon, I feel so well now. Why don't you make the arrangements for a house exchange? You always have wanted to go to Hawaii."

Oh Joy! Joy! I thanked the Guardian Angel who had shown me the help we had long prayed for. But as fate would have it, such a trip together was never to be, for one day, only a few weeks later, two sudden, and shocking events occurred.

*

A WARNING – CANCER

Cancer! It had become a word that struck fear into the hearts of the strongest. Slowly, agonizingly, by 1969 I had lost fourteen friends and relatives to this modern-day scourge. All had received the best the medical world had to offer, and generally, it had only prolonged the agony. In the 1940's Allen's father had to be given quantities of morphine to withstand the never-ending pain, and finally, dying at home after many long months of suffering, he begged Allen to give him a dosage that would release him from what he no longer had the strength to bear.

Now, these weeks while Allen was feeling better, we had gone to hear a well-known herbologist, Dr. John Christopher from Provo, Utah, who was visiting and speaking in our city. Dr. Christopher gave a wonderful talk on the benefits he had achieved with herbal treatments. He also made a significant statement that alluded to the receptivity to new approaches, or lack of it, by suffering humanity. He said, "There are no incurable diseases. Only incurable patients."

Also attending this meeting was an Iridologist who, after the lecture, offered to look into Allen's eyes with his special magnifying instrument and give a diagnosis of the body's condition. Iridology is a fairly new but reliable way to see problem areas in the body by studying the eyes under magnification. Few people are aware that all the physical conditions in any organ of the body, including old injuries and bone breaks, show up in the eyes, and can be read by the experienced practitioner of iridology.

Interestingly, the Iridologists's observations regarding Allen's physical condition coincided with the medical doctor's diagnosis exactly, so I knew this man was well-qualified and a good iridologist. As he finished discussing Allen, he turned to me and asked, "How about you? Would you like an examination also?"

Shadowy thoughts raced through my mind. I had been overly tired for many months, and the tiredness had in recent weeks turned to a dragging fatigue. I had ignored it, even though upon awakening mornings I felt I had slept with a heavy stone on my chest. I had consistently refused to acknowledge my own body's needs, giving my husband's three-year heart illness more urgent precedence. His illness, and the unique difficulties of our troubled youngest son, as well as the care of our other two children, all had placed significant strain on me and I was prone to accredit my tiredness to this strain and to overwork. I had neglected my regular meditations in recent months, and occasionally had given in to the poor me's. For long months there had seemed very little hope of Allen improving (until just recently) despite all my efforts. All this flashed through my mind, though I had not spoken a word aloud.

The iridologist asked again, "How about it? Shall we take a look while I'm here?"

"Sure," I finally found my tongue. "Good idea."

I sat down in the chair and he brought the magnification instrument close, looking intently first into one eye and then into the other.

"Mmmm. I see what looks like an old break and a calcification healed over it in the lower 5th lumbar of the spine and the coccyx area . . . And, you have had your appendix removed."

"That's right," I responded.

"And . . . amazing!" he murmured as if to himself. "You are the first person I've seen without any drug ring in the eyes whatsoever!" He paused, then continued, "Drugs always show up, you know, and you have none."

I confirmed that I had never taken any drugs, not even for the births of my three children, who had been delivered in natural childbirth without the use of any medication.

I was impressed. This man saw everything! He really knows what he's doing, I thought to myself.

He continued to look intently, and then longer. Becoming more quiet, he turned to his wife. Handing her the magnifier, he said, "Would you look?"

She took the glass, and leaning close, studied my eyes very carefully. Then slowly lowering it, she looked at her husband and he at her. Then in an undertone, "Shall we tell her?"

"Tell me? Tell me what?!" My voice rose to a squeak.

Quietly and seriously he looked at me. "You have developed lymphoma. I'm sorry to say this, but it's quite evident and cannot be mistaken. I feel obliged to tell you. It is through the lymph glands, although not too far advanced." In those days just to be told one had cancer — almost any form of it — was a death sentence. For a moment my heart stood still, but in the next instant I knew that somehow, some way, I would be all right — that the mighty God Presence would show the way. I also fully believed in my heart of hearts that I was to live a long life, for I still had work to do. That year I was only forty-four years of age.

Allen was very disturbed. He had been so involved in his own illness, it had not occurred to him that I might have any problem, as I had always been there to hold the family together while he was gone to war and through his many weeks in the hospital. I did all I could to comfort him and quell his fears, but I knew he was not at peace.

This did not, however, seem to be the time for me to jump headlong into treatment, considering the other illnesses in our family, and I told myself I wasn't really all that bad, making light of the matter. He could be mistaken, I thought. No need to make a big to-do over one simple eye exam. But Allen had enough stress without the added worry over me, so I promised I'd have it checked further.

When trouble strikes, one must turn to the God within. It seems these challenges come into our lives to cause us to do just that, to remind us vividly that we cannot stand alone without the undergirding of faith. So, as I always had done, I went into prayer for guidance. When we take steps toward the Light and God's love, Divine Grace comes to meet us. In meditation I proclaimed Divine Order in my life and affairs, to direct my health and that of my family. A gentle peace, akin to bliss, settled over my being as I gave my concern to the Higher Power that is available to all.

How necessary this was at this time, for an amazing thing happened. Only a few mornings later I found myself surrounded by an unearthly peace, a kind of insulated bubble. Invisible but very real, is the only way I can describe it. It was strange, for I could see and hear my sons' sibling scuffles and arguments, but could not feel any emotional vibration or reaction whatsoever. It truly was as though they were on a screen somewhere outside of my space and I was only watching. What I could feel was this very real and utterly peaceful bubble of bliss radiating around me, in which I was at the center! For the next three days this profound peace continued, and in silent amazement I wondered somewhat in awe, Have I been given the peace that passeth understanding?

I later came to understand this peace was a Gift from Spirit and the Angels that was prearranged, for it carried me calmly through the shock and trauma that was to come the afternoon of the third day.

*
DEATH – A GRADUATION

"I killed Dad! I killed Dad!"

Young Jason, only eleven years old, came crying and screaming through the door, followed by his older brother Jeremy, whose face was white with shock. Our youngest son's face contorted with grief and tears as the boys poured out the happenings of the past hour.

It was 5:00 p.m., the afternoon of a school day in early Fall. An hour and one-half earlier at 3:30 p.m. Allen and I had been concerned when young Jason had not returned home from school. Phoning, we found to our dismay that the Junior High had actually closed that morning at 9:30 a.m. due to electrical power failure and all the children had been sent home. A woman had lost control of her auto, crashing into the power pole directly in front of the school. Little do we ever fully know the many consequences of our actions to the lives of others, like ripples in a pond that touch the far shore when a stone is thrown.

We were continuing to experience deep concern for Jason's emotional stability, having sought for several years the finest mental health counselors, and had even gone regularly to family counseling. The really disturbing part was that Jason, even at age eleven, had taken to hanging out at school with older boys who were strongly suspected of using drugs. The principal of this Junior High School had actually told me in conference that at least 78% of the students (in 1968) were on drugs! And he didn't know what to do about it.

So our fears were very real and we counseled our son over and over, but as every parent knows, peer pressure, and being accepted by the guys, often takes far greater precedence with the young than any words voiced by parents. Jason knew how we felt, but had grabbed the opportunity to run around free all day with those older boys. Allen, with sudden apprehension became very upset and, being already in an ill state, was more sensitive to such a problem. He took Jeremy with him in the auto to search for

Jason and track him down. Jeremy later told me the sequence of events.

As they drove past an open and rather rundown house belonging to one of Jason's friends, they spotted the boys inside. But when Jason saw Jeremy approaching, he sneaked out the back door hoping not to be seen. Jeremy ran around to the back of the house and chased Jason down a steep canyon and up the other side, where he caught him and dragged him by the arm, back down the canyon and up again, to the car on the road. Jeremy was angry with Jason for causing us distress.

It must have been that deep concern and emotional anger at his son's disobedience which caused Allen to lose good judgment regarding his own heart condition. Angry words passed as my husband shoved his wayward young son into the front seat beside him, then starting the motor he backed the car out of the driveway to head for home. The moment the car began to roll on the road, his body could no longer take the strain of both emotional stress and physical exertion.

Heart Attack! Falling to the right with his head in his little boy's lap, Allen gasped his dying breath under Jason's frightened face.

Now in motion without control, the auto careened downhill, off the roadway and toward another canyon drop! It was God's grace that Jeremy, age fourteen, was along. With desperate effort, Jeremy lunged over the top of the back seat where he had been sitting, across his father's body, and head down, pushed both hands on the brake pedal, stopping the car just in time before it rolled on down into the canyon with all three, helpless inside.

When a neighbor who happened to observe this scene through her kitchen window, rushed out to where the auto came to rest, she later told me she found, "Your older boy praying in tongues!" This was amazing, as we did not attend a church where this was practiced, although Jeremy had been immersed in the Spirit at C.F.O. Camp two years previously when he was 12. It has never been a phenomenon for him since. Quickly the neighbor called the Fire

Department believing they might resuscitate my husband. The firemen put the boys into their truck-van to wait while they worked over the body.

And here is another unusual thing. Jeremy reported to me that in those first few moments as they waited there, his father came into the van and smiling at him said, "It's alright Son. I'm fine," but then dissolved before his eyes! So apparently for a few moments Allen himself did not realize he had *died* — and in the emotional trauma of that moment was able to materialize enough that Jeremy, in a super-sensitive state from the shock, was able to see him in the astral body looking well and quite happy. This incident was a tremendous proof to our older son, at a very young age, of the reality of life after the passing of the body, and a great comfort and memory for him. In subsequent years he has gone on to be a shining light to others, quietly teaching spiritual truths.

Sadly our little guy, the sweet and gentle Jason, was not so fortunate. He was already disturbed by a world he could not seem to handle well, or fit into, and now his screams — "I killed Dad! I killed Dad!" rang in my ears. It was like a red flag before my eyes.

The amazing bubble of grace, in which I still felt contained, carried me through this strange and shocking experience. Calmly I wiped my crying son's tears and tried gently to dispel the grievous guilt in which he felt engulfed. Realizing the danger to his psyche, I quietly told him over and over, "No-no-no, Dear. *You did not kill Daddy*. You did what any small boy would do who runs from a possible spanking. Daddy's heart could have stopped over any exertion. It is just too bad that it happened this way. It is *not* your fault."

The next hours and days were, of course, filled with activity, as neighbors, wonderfully concerned teachers, and relatives from afar came to console. And there were the memorial preparations. So time for continued consolation of my youngest son was minimal. Also our little daughter Jennine, still just four, was confused and frightened by these strange happenings. Through days to come she deeply missed him and in later years the scars of this loss became even more evident as unspoken sorrow returned to haunt her. Children need their fathers.

I must relate that an unusual telephone call came early the first morning after Allen's sudden passing. Answering the phone, I heard the worried voice of my dear life-long friend, Verna, from Los Angeles. It was she, you may recall, who had suddenly left her body in our unusual meeting in the Bay area a few year's previous to make way for the young shell-shocked soldier killed in Iwo Jima to speak to us. I heard her anxious voice.

"What has happened at your house? I met Allen on the Inner Planes last night and he seemed agitated. He kept saying over and over: 'Tell them it wasn't Jason's fault! I love my Son!' It was so frightening I had to call!"

When I told her what had happened, the impact of Allen's message was all the more poignant, and of course, confirmed what I knew.

Recalling Allen's amazing and beautiful Near-Death-Experience two years before, I remembered how he had not wished to return from the wonder and peaceful bliss of the Other Side of Life once he had glimpsed it. I knew that his soul was now released from entrapment in a body that had been a burden to him for three years. He was a man who had before been strong and capable of any work he chose to do, and his illness had been a great frustration. Now he was free. I could have nothing but joy for him!

I saw that in an unusual manner my prayers for his well-being had been answered in God's own way. Also amazingly, *I felt his joy.* As I laughingly greeted friends at the funeral service, I think I was looked upon askance. They could not know this joy within me that seemed to bubble up, engulfing me, and over which I had little control. For you see, I know it was his joy at being released into a more beautiful existence which was reflecting through me.

Yes, of course, I grieved in my own way. I later allowed myself that bit of selfishness, but I also knew it is not well to grieve for long, as our strong emotion holds the dear one in an unhappy state. They long to comfort and say, "Here I am! I'm fine! Don't cry!" But usually we cannot hear.

One unique experience at this time gave me a glimpse into the purpose of the Wailing Wall in Jerusalem, where folks there go to mourn their dead, and I now know why it is called the Wailing Wall.

The day I brought my husband's ashes home, preparatory to final disposition, I entered the house carrying the small interment box against my solar plexus. Suddenly, with no thought from my mind or feeling of emotional grief in that moment, my body began to wail the loss of its mate. It was a very objective experience in that I, as a thinking person, seemed to be standing aside, listening to the wails coming from the deepest part of my throat and inner being. It was not crying, it was not moaning, but loud wailing. That is the only description that fits. I was alone in the house and I was quite astounded. It did not last long, but I felt a distinct difference afterward, a release of tension I had unconsciously been carrying until that moment, when a new peace and a kind of refreshing acceptance flowed through me. Now I know the real value of the Wailing Wall.

Through later weeks, when the blessed bubble was no longer with me, and in the months and years ahead while faced with the physical and emotional work of raising three children alone, I missed Allen very, very much. But my sorrow was but for myself, and that too is softened with time. Wonderfully, I often felt his love close to me, a kind of warmth wrapped around me, a special sweetness, and I was comforted, for now he was again healthy and strong in spirit and could express his love much more freely than while encased in an ill body.

I also knew the timing of his passing was divinely planned so I did not question it. Hadn't I received the prediction many years before. (*"He needs you, for he will die."* I didn't know then it would be eighteen years later.) And he had needed me, for many women would not have understood or loved him through those long years of strange and dark depressions. And hadn't Spirit lovingly surrounded me, even before the happening with that amazing insulated bubble of grace and peace to soften the shock?

Strangely, Allen had been in three wars on three continents, over three decades, had three children, suffered three heart attacks, and died three blocks from home with three dollars and three pennies in his pocket. His three heart attacks had been in three consecutive years — on October 18th, October 19th, and October 20th, the date he passed, after having been ill exactly three years.

Now drifting back in memory, I recall there were three out-of-the-ordinary occurrences at the time of our wedding. During the ceremony we had parked the auto on the street outside. Strangely, a neighbor across the street backed her car so far out of her driveway clear across the street, smashing in the door on the driver's — Allen's — side of our auto. Due to lack of time we had to drive on our honeymoon all the way to the midwest with a smashed-in door. Secondly, that first night, as related, the plate-glass window of the office to our motel had to be shattered to reach the keys to our cottage. Later the next day, while stopping at the home of our friend who had been the hostess of our wedding supper, the center diamond fell out of my diamond wedding band. It was later found on the kitchen floor, so not lost, but I mused, "How strange . . ." and tried not to think of omens.

My husband had earlier told me that every man in his family named Allen had died at or before the age of fifty, including his Great Grandfather, General Charles Allen Gilchrist, for whom he was named, and in whose honor a statue stands in Tennessee for bravery during the Civil War.

What is even more strange, *Allen was fifty when he 'died' in the Near-Death-Experience, fulfilling this prediction.* But he was returned to us. We had been given a gift of life, a two years' reprieve, so to speak, as now he left us at age fifty-two for the Higher Realms he had justly earned.

There could never be a more devoted or loyal husband and father than Lieutenant Colonel Charles Allen Gilchrist. Drafted into the Army as a Private at an early age, he left a legacy of courage, faith, hard work and leadership in North Africa, Italy, Germany, South Korea and Viet Nam, as well as here at home in America, helping to keep our country free. He never faltered in his leadership, despite illness, isolation from his family, which his work often demanded, and the stress of combat action through three wars fought by America. Charles Allen remained gentle in all of his relationships, in love letters and spoken words to me, and in purposely making delightful and instructive playtime with his children. His life reflected his high ideals, both at home and abroad, in his teaching years, and in daily actions towards all whom he touched.

The South Korean officers, who were his co-workers both in the Korean War and in his Advisory position during the Viet Nam War, admired him so much that twenty years later, when they knew he had passed on, still wrote each year at Christmas to inquire after the health of the children and me. Colonel Gilchrist gave total dedication to family and the country he loved — the United States of America.

*

CHAPTER EIGHT

PRISON

It is God's grace that keeps us from foreknowledge of the heart-wrenching traumas we are to suffer, until we actually must suffer them. Through the years that followed, I carried on with raising the family. Our young daughter, Jennine, was only four when Allen passed and she missed her father terribly. Our oldest son, Jeremy, had been for some time discontent in public schools being, as he was, highly motivated spiritually and finding the social life and most of his studies shallow and dissatisfying. His spirit soared when, through a friend from C.F.O. he discovered the Ananda School at the Ananda Community in California, where the teachings of Paramhansa Yogananda were followed. At seventeen Jeremy left our home to attend and graduate from this ashram school in the oak-and-pine-forested foothills of the northern California Sierra. The beautiful Master Yogananda was touching our lives once again in a most profound way!

Meanwhile, after a long series of seemingly inescapable events, Jason, who had been the sweet and very gentle one, was sentenced and incarcerated in California State Prison at the age of sixteen. Prison! Despite endless and near-heroic efforts on my part. Despite countless hours with school and health counselors. Despite many thousands of dollars to mental health therapists and psychologists beginning when Jason was seven, and then larger sums to private schools from ages eleven through thirteen. Despite all this, Jason's destiny took him steadily down hill.

Jason had been beautiful, with large blue eyes ringed with black lashes that were innocent and clear in their gaze. He had straight teeth which flashed in a ready smile, a tall, lithe body, and expressive, artistic hands. Jason's manner had always been gentle and loving with me and with smaller children, whom he adored. A year after his father passed, when Jason was twelve, he asked me if we could adopt a baby boy.

"Why do you want our family to have a baby boy?" I asked back.

"So I can be a big brother to him and take care of him the way I didn't have anyone take care of me."

So many times older boys had beaten Jason because he was erratic or acted silly. There was no one around to protect him, including Jeremy who was more irritated than the rest. Very early Allen and I had suspected medical problems, possibly in the head or sinuses as Jason could never breathe clearly through his nose and had very flat cheekbones. But doctors' cursory evaluations found nothing definitive to treat. Not knowing what else to say, their advice was, "Let's hope he outgrows it." As Jason hit puberty, he shot up very quickly, but he did not outgrow it. In fact, exactly the reverse took place. He became much worse.

He was often nervous and restless and created disruptions by being a comedian, hoping to gain the acceptance of his peers. This had begun as early as kindergarten. He always had a great sense of humor, seeing the laughable side of things, but his humor seemed to alienate rather than ingratiate, and Jason found himself rejected by many, even his teachers. I was dismayed when he came home very sad from school one day while in the 3rd or 4th grade and told me his teacher had said to him, "You can't be Jeremy's brother. You don't act nice like him at all!" Playmates began calling him "M.R." (Mentally Retarded). Children can be very insensitive, and some adults too. Jason was unusually smart, but suffered from a short attention span. In the quiet of our home Jason was usually stable, loving and helpful, and finished his studies easily when not put under stress. When he was eleven years old his Scout Master told me with surprise that, "When the boys have a project to accomplish, Jason is the quickest of all. He has his work finished before the others even figure out how to do it!"

It was the disruptive 1960's and soon Jason fell in with older boys who were drug users at school. The biggest tragedy of all was that we did not recognize he was using drugs since he had always acted somewhat erratic. And, after all, he was only eleven years old!

In 1968, we didn't even suspect drugs. It was only shortly after we began to be suspicious that the events occurred which led to Allen's death. Jason could not handle the stress of school and, although I continued taking him to various mental health specialists including the University of Washington's Child Psychologist, nothing changed his pattern of behavior. "He is an unhappy little boy," they said. This was no help at all (and I was still charged a hefty fee).

Jason had lost his father in a terribly traumatic way, and despite my efforts to alleviate his feelings of responsibility and give him as much love and attention as I could, this event was undoubtedly deeply impressed in his psyche. His restless behavior and school problems, however, had begun many years previous.

I called the Big Brothers Organization which I heard paired young men with lads like Jason who needed a male friend in the absence of their father. They turned me down, saying, "he is a month past the age of acceptance into our program." This was a disappointment, but typical of the disappointment I encountered along every avenue of help I pursued. All doctors could suggest was the drug Ritalin, to calm him down. No one looked to a possible imbalance in his body chemistry, as I tried to suggest. They assured me that this wasn't possible. He felt calmer on the Ritalin, but I believe it helped him down the road to taking stronger drugs to feel better.

Soon Jason began running away from school. He was not running from anything in particular, except himself, and the confinement and stress school represented. This was my sweet and gentle little boy who wouldn't hurt even a fly, but who couldn't seem to handle the normal responsibilities of life. The insensitivity of some adults was unbelievable. On the day he first ran away from school, when he was found, an adult had been overheard saying in his presence, "Oh! This is the boy who killed his father!" The person reporting this to me added, "I looked at Jason and his face was so twisted, I thought he was going to cry."

Even the school principal did not understand and felt Jason simply lacked discipline. But the more restrictions that were placed on him at school, the worse he became.

Deciding he should be out of this setting and since he was receiving no visible help from mental health counselors to whom we had been referred by the school, I placed him when he was twelve years old in the privately run Marymount Academy near Tacoma. He liked being there very much and did well, as it was well-structured, and there was love and concern for each child. One day while playing saxophone with the band, Jason fainted dead away on the parade ground. Much later I found he suffered petit mal, a mild form of Grand Mal — or epilepsy, which he had apparently inherited from his father. We did not know this at that time, however, nor had it been detected by any doctor among the myriad who had seen him.

Unhappily, after only one year at Marymount, Jason was expelled for smoking cigarettes in the yard. Their rules were very strict and he wasn't given a second chance. It was then that I felt abject dismay and defeat, for we had interviewed for, and exhausted, all educational possibilities available at that time, except the Ryther Children's home in Seattle. Since Jason was not considered mentally handicapped, nor physically handicapped, there was no school of any kind for borderline emotionally disturbed children. Since the Ryther Children's Home was an institution for troubled children, it was a last resort.

Teachers in neither public nor private schools could understand Jason's needs, nor were they equipped to do so. Thirty years ago the condition we now call hyperactivity had not been identified by psychologists and educators, much less its causes, the emotional turmoil it creates, or its proper treatment. The term *Hyperkinesis* was unknown, and medical doctors would not awaken to the implications of this problem until it was too late to help many thousands. My heart aches for the mothers and fathers who have lost their children to this syndrome through the lack of simple treatments unknown even fifteen years ago. I am one of those mothers, and I recall only too vividly the many nights my pillow was sodden with anguished tears and God's Angels alone heard my sad heart's prayers.

Social psychologists have since observed that, "If not treated, serious hyperactivity in children will result in adults who become either alcoholics or criminals."* We have seen the results in our society in the last twenty years, at a tremendous cost to taxpayers.

Our prisons in every state are teeming. With proper medical evaluation, how many lives and dollars might have been saved?

I too was ignorant of causes thirty years ago and knew that if love alone could heal, my Jason would have been perfect. But his body and brain needed something more and I didn't know what. I had pursued every available professional channel to no avail.

The Ryther Children's Home was a disaster, the beginning of the end. At the age of twelve Jason was not kept at the Home in Seattle as I had expected. I was told that due to his size (he was very tall and lanky) and due to his record of running they told me, he would be taken to their School/Clinic on Cypress Island in Puget Sound, which was isolated away from the city and the availability of drugs.

"There are tennis courts, a swimming pool and good teachers," they said. But I was not allowed to visit nor even to inspect the premises beforehand. The administrators said they felt separation from old associations, including par-

* *Improving Your Child's Behavior*, Lendon Smith, M.D., 1977, and *The Children's Doctor*, Lendon Smith, M.D., 1969 Pocket Books, 1230 Ave.of the Americas, N.Y. 10020.

ents, was necessary. I should have smelled a rat right then, but naively, I trusted that professionals know best. Jason's time at the island school was traumatic. It is difficult to relate everything that happened.

"The place wasn't what they said, Mama. They lied to us. There was no swimming pool or tennis courts, and it wasn't nice at all. The first day I arrived they set me to digging a big ditch six feet long and four feet deep, without telling me why. And when I had it done and was dead tired, they ordered, 'Now fill it up again!'"

Jason was thirteen years old and had not transgressed other than to run from stress at school, and probably marijuana smoking with other boys. Now, he had been placed under even greater stress! This was, I suppose, an attempt on the part of Ryther School officials to establish discipline and to break his spirit right at the beginning. The upshot of it was that it did just the opposite, making him a very angry young man. He also was a very bright one (later showing an I.Q. of 145), and became the only boy ever to escape from that 'school' on Cypress Island!

After a few more very harsh and traumatic days, determined to get out and back home to me, quietly, in the dead of night when all were asleep, Jason formed a plan. Silently he donned his boots and heavy coat, leaving all his clothes and the personal items I had provided for him behind. Under cover of darkness, he hiked across the isolated thickly forested island, pushing his way through the dense undergrowth to the opposite side. Lying down on the beach he waited until dawn, and in the early morning mist Jason flagged down a family in a passing fishing boat, telling them that he had beached his canoe to rest for the night and it had floated away while he slept. They took him to the mainland where he attempted to hitchhike home. Unfortunately, he was picked up enroute by police and taken to the County Jail, as the Cypress Island Ryther school had turned in a "runaway call." At that time in Washington State *being* a runaway was a criminal offense.

All my efforts just to obtain schooling for my son were ending in disaster. Now he was in jail, barely the age of thirteen, and through no fault of his own other than attempting to escape harsh treatment, at a time when his only real problem was he could not handle stress.

What had I done? I'd sought schooling in a safe environment away from the city, having been told this was a "fine place with excellent facilities." I felt the misrepresentation was criminal.

"It was not the kind of place they told us at all, Mom. It was a jail with guards, and a lot of the guys there were sixteen and seventeen years old from Chicago and Detroit who had been in real trouble. They lied to us and they wouldn't let me call you. I had to leave!" Jason was terribly distraught as I visited him in lockup.

The City Jail is a terrible place for a thirteen-year old to be confined. In the first few days, Jason's back was raked with the sharpened tines of an angel-food cake knife while he was naked in the shower, for no reason other than that he was white. Jason carried those scars the rest of his life. This was his introduction to confinement and to the dark side of race relations. Until then he had had no prejudice, as I had raised my children thus.

From that day on, life was a waking nightmare. Jason's assigned social worker was a bulldog, who had no understanding whatsoever of his real needs, a self-important functionary who went by the book of those ignorant days. She had no desire to understand nor appreciate my views.

"How dare you try to keep a boy at home who obviously needs 24-hour care? What kind of mother are you anyway? Can't you see he needs to be in the hands of the State where he will receive proper discipline in a contained setting? Why have you waited so long?" On and on she harangued at me for days, absolutely refusing to sign a release from jail for him so I might take him home in my custody. The badgering went on until I was in tears and totally worn down, and I began to believe she might be right, for I was now up against a stone wall with no public or private school available to meet his emotional needs, and also I now was running low on savings. All of my attempts at expensive, available private help had been fruitless.

The bulldog continued to call me names and shoved a paper under my nose to sign which stated Jason was incorrigible, that I was not able to handle him, and that I was releasing all legal claim to my beloved son. I was told over and over that his problems were all my fault, that if he were away from home he would be all right. I had no husband to turn to or to back me up, and I had no relatives in the Northwest — not even an uncle or a brother.

Trying to control my grief, and with eyes blinded by tears I signed the paper I was given.

It was the biggest mistake I ever made, or so it seemed for many years. Under State control Jason rolled steadily down a seemingly unswervable road to full prison life. He was incarcerated for the next fourteen years.

Many youths, once locked into the correctional systems typical of most states in our country find themselves caught in a maze from which it becomes increasingly difficult to extricate themselves. Becoming progressively more alienated and anti-social, their self esteem eroded, there is little chance for them to come back whole in mind or body — if they come back at all.

After a short court hearing where the bulldog's recommendations were rubber stamped, Jason was taken away to a Youth Forestry Camp in southwestern Washington State. I came home and cried bitter tears. For up to that point, he had done nothing really illegal. His crime had been to try to escape pressure placed on him by adults. Adults who lacked understanding and education regarding what body imbalances can do to sensitive children, altering their ability to handle particular situations and environments. These physiological imbalances, I found too late, were the real underlying problem.

Hyperkinesis (hyperactivity) is caused by biochemical imbalances in the body which result from faulty nutrition or allergic reactions to certain foods and chemicals. The condition affects fully one-third of American young people. When left untreated hyperkinesis manifests in a range of behavioral symptoms including short-attention span and the inability to concentrate on studies. These learning disabilities

create poor self-image, which often results in school drop-
out and the downhill slide into drugs, thievery and ultimately prison. It cannot be ventured that hyperkinesis is the
cause of most drug taking, but it is one major underlying
factor and a factor common enough that it should be addressed with a very conscious strategy of prevention.

Of course I continued to ask "Why? Why!", but the
answers, for our family, came too late.

Through intensive research on my own I found in ensuing years that certain forward thinking medical doctors and
many other parents were beginning to seek answers to this
exploding phenomenon of hyperactivity in children. However, to my dismay, the State would not allow Jason to be
tested further, nor would they allow vitamins and minerals
to be sent in, even with a doctor's special prescription.

Meanwhile, new medical research was showing that
good results in control of this ailment could be achieved
through specific tests ascertaining what toxic metals might
be present, and what nutritional minerals lacking. One of
the new successful treatments was high dosages of Multi-B
Vitamins, particularly Niacin and/or Niacinimide, and ad-
herence to a diet totally free of all foods containing chemical preservatives and/or pesticide sprays. The elimination
of refined sugars was also shown to be necessary. Amazingly, this was close to the same treatment that was helping
some forms of schizophrenia and manic/depressives. Immediately I thought of my husband and his depressions — was it
possible our son had inherited a syndrome, a shade of this
illness, only manifested in a different way?

In subsequent years, brilliant doctors from all over the
United States and Canada began writing and presenting the
results of their research, as there were far too many disturbed young people showing up in their offices. Finally
some prominent psychiatrists turned their profession completely around and became allergists, for they found, as I
had with Jason, that standard psychiatric and mental health
treatment was achieving nothing whatsoever with most of
these patients. On the other hand, when they changed the
patient's diet, eliminating all sugars, foods containing caf-

feine, such as chocolate and colas, all prepared foods containing synthetic chemicals such as artificial preservatives,
flavorings and colorings that are foreign to the body, and
put the patient on a purely natural food diet, many of the
patients' symptoms cleared up entirely.

At a large symposium in Seattle one doctor spoke of his
testing the theory. He had been treating one disturbed child
with the conventional psychiatric approach for over two
years with no noticeable improvement. After many months
of seeing material on allergies come across his desk, during
which time he usually dumped it into the wastebasket, he
one day, in desperation, decided, "Oh, why not give it a try?
What's to lose?" He put this one really difficult child on the
natural diet. The child's mother reported a phenomenal
change, which was also evident on his next visit.

"I thought," the doctor stated, "perhaps it was a fluke,
so I experimented. When I allowed the child's mother to
return him to his usual foods for two weeks, that is, to cold
cereals, hotdogs, candy and the like, he became a wildcat
again, tearing up my office upon entering and even snatch-
ing the glasses right off my face. I was astounded at the
difference! When I put him back on the restricted pure
natural foods plan once again, the child became a normal,
intelligent manageable youngster — a pussycat. It was so
amazing, I gave up psychiatry on the spot!"

The speaker was Dr. William Philpott, one of the most
respected allergists in the U.S. today.

Jason's problem was more complicated, but this approach was the first bright light on my horizon. Once in
awhile when he was allowed out of State Camp for a day
with me, I saw that the B-Vitamins I gave Jason made an
immediate change within hours. He became calmer and
more attentive, genuinely interested in our conversation
and activities. But there was no hope for treatment then, as
I could not get doctors in the system to even understand my
viewpoint or requests for tests. In fact, in his records a
court-appointed social worker had already labeled me "psychotic" because of my views that he may have a medical
need, and continued to advise that the boy be taken away

from me. Imagine the ignorance only twenty years ago. If I had not known of God's love, and certainly of His love for my son, who began as one of the most beautiful sweet little boys anyone could ever find, I would have been totally devastated. As it was, I realized we were being shown a great need that had to be put in the spot light, and I began working to do what I could to help educate others who had hyperactive and allergic children, that they might avoid the fate Jason was suffering.

I could not change the past, but I might somehow assist in altering the future. I became a volunteer member of the Well Mind Association* in Seattle, which is affiliated with the American Schizophrenia Association, and for several years served as Board Secretary. This group, through the consistent efforts of many parents such as myself, has done more than any other action group in the Northwest to bring public attention to the major role biochemical illnesses play in childhood learning, emotional, and behavioral problems, which carry over into adulthood, and to point out the lack of proper diagnosis, which is helping to fill our mental health hospitals and prisons to overflowing. Through the founding efforts and guidance of a remarkable woman named Elizabeth Gentala, and others devoted to this work, who hold monthly meetings, open to the public, bring brilliant researchers and medical doctors as speakers from all over the country, and especially to the Annual Fall Symposium sponsored by The Well Mind Association.

The wealth of new information on this subject suddenly became a flood in the late-1970's, available to any who sought it. But the problem remained how to stop the flow of young people into our mental hospitals and prisons, many of whom need medical attention on this level. Slowly, over the next five to ten years, we saw young medical doctors incorporating alternative therapies into their practices, using new-found tests in their diagnoses. More patients are now being served by these natural methods, as many people, especially children, react to the side-effects

* The Well Mind Assn., 4649 Sunnyside No., Seattle, WA 98103

OVER AN ANGEL'S SHOULDER

related to prescription drugs.

The tragedy we are trying to address is multi-fold. Not only is the cost to American taxpayers staggering, and becoming worse daily through the explosion of prison and hospital population nation-wide, but our society is losing the intelligence potential of thousands of young men and women who need innovative help early to assist them in achieving that potential, as opposed to confinement which serves no real purpose other than to take them off the streets, often truly destroying their lives in the process.

In the twenty years since the time I was dealing with Jason's difficulties, we have gained a more sophisticated understanding of these needs. Many doctors have written excellent books on this subject.* It is gratifying to see therapy centers and special schools springing up like mushrooms all over the United States to deal with hyperkinesis, allergies, and emotional instabilities. One such center in the Seattle area is called New Beginnings.** But unfortunately, the pattern already has been set for many young people who cannot be helped in this way and must remain confined.

Jason was an example of those who are not originally criminal, but due to professional ignorance of their medical needs, suffer increasing loss of self esteem, social acceptance and adjustment, and fall into criminality, adding one by one to the swelling statistic of failure. Jason possessed one of the most alert minds I have ever encountered, with a memory for detail that was phenomenal. He was musical, artistic, and articulate, as well as sympathetic to those even less fortunate than he. In addition, he acquired a rich philosophy and faith in life despite everything that had happened to him.

Hyperkinesis in children now, thirty years later, has become widely recognized as a major problem in American families and has proven to have accelerated in tandem with the advent of sugared foods and chemical additives that manufacturers have surreptitiously placed in our prepared

* A list may be obtained from The Well-Mind Association, as only a few are mentioned here.
** "New Beginnings": 1-800-DO-BEGIN

foods since 1940. This was the beginning of Jason's school problems as a boy, for I had no inkling he was being poisoned by his regular meals, that he was suffering brain allergies from the chemical additives in foods as common as popular prepared juice drinks or chocolate milk. No one ever heard of such a thing at that time. He had no real trouble at home in the early years. It was after beginning school with attendant sweet snacks, plus the stress excitement, that his behavior changed.

Finally, in only the last few years, as hyperkinesis has become widespread and widely recognized, and after cancer in its multiple forms has run increasingly rampant, a significant and vocal portion of the public is awakening and demanding truly natural foods that have not been adulterated by the manufacturers and pushed by advertisers.

Thirteen years ago, Alexander Schauss, Director of the American Institute of Biosocial Research* in Tacoma, Washington, wrote in his landmark book, *Diet, Crime and Delinquency:***

> In 1978, over 12,000,000 arrests were made of children under the age of eighteen for non-traffic crimes. *Over one million children* were placed in detention centers for some period of time in 1979. Estimates of the cost of maintaining the criminal justice system range from *30 to 50 billion dollars per year.* [This was written in 1980!]
>
> Environmental exposure to the toxic metal lead has mushroomed to over 500 times that experienced by 16th century man. In 1971 the United States had the dubious distinction of becoming the first people on earth to consume processed foods for more than 50 percent of their diet. *Over 4,000 additives* can now be found in the American food supply, none of which have ever been tested thoroughly for their effects on our central

* Am. Inst. of Biosocial Res., P.O. Box 1174, Tacoma, WA 98401
** *Diet, Crime, & Delinquency*, 1980, Parker House, Berkley, CA 94784
Also: *Eating for A's*, Life Sciences Press, Box 1174, Tacoma, WA 98481

nervous system. We have become a nation of coffee and soda pop drinkers, fast food consumers and refined carbohydrates junkies, without regard to their disastrous consequences, particularly on our children.

He went on to say that a young man could be put through Harvard (at that time) for what it costs to keep him in prison just one year. This was figured by averaging the maintenance costs of our huge prisons plus personnel salaries across the U.S. It is more monumental than most people have any idea, and growing rapidly.

Ten years ago when representatives, including myself, of the Well Mind Association appeared before Washington State legislators to ask for a new law that would provide for early testing, we were told that it would require a public vote, since new taxes would be involved. Balderdash! Research for *Diet, Crime and Delinquency* had shown the cost just to keep people in prison was $64,000.00 per year per man, in 1980! The figures now are even higher and amount to tens of billions of dollars. A preventative program would surely save money!

"A stitch in time saves nine," is the old saying, and it still applies. The problem lies in the unfortunate fact that America was not paying attention and did not apply a preventative approach. And sadly, to this day, in the 1990's, not enough clinics can be found that offer an enlightened approach to early prevention. But Praise God! There are some who do, as recently Eastern State Hospital in Washington State, as one example, has elected to begin a biochemical testing program for new patients.

The cost of total biochemical medical diagnosis, education and proper application of therapy, if need be, for youngsters in trouble would be only a fraction of the present day cost of keeping them locked up in hospitals and prisons for years, with no rehabilitation or hope of change. As I write, American prisons hold 1.8 million individuals (nearly 1 per 100 citizens).

At the October, 1991, Well Mind Association's Fall

Symposium, Dr. William J. Walsh of the Health Research Institute, Carl Pfeiffer Treatment Center* in Illinois, presented the results of his research in an Illinois State prison where he gained permission to administer biochemical tests. He found that all the men he tested who were incarcerated for violent crimes had very high percentages of toxic metals such as lead and mercury in their bodies, and very low percentages of the minerals necessary for good health such as calcium and copper. The tests were conducted on several hundred men. The control group of inmates tested who had no record of violence showed a significantly lower level of toxic metals. Small attention, however, is given even now to the results of this and similar studies. It is difficult to change perceptions. Bureaucrats, by and large, resist change. And prisons have become big business in America.

When Jason was first confined to Youth Forestry Camp, his younger sister Jennine and I drove to visit him across the entire state every other weekend for the eighteen months of his sentence there. He was always sweet, smiling and delighted to see us. The boys had some studies and also had work now and then fighting fires in the woods by clearing fire breaks. During the latter part of that year a friend of mine, knowing of Jason's situation, suggested a particular doctor to me who had an office in Portland.

"Dr. Stober is the only specialist in chiropractic skull adjustments," she said. "He is achieving amazing changes in many children, even those retarded or who have not been able to walk or talk." I thought of Jason's difficulty breathing through his nose. On a rare weekend when he was allowed a pass to go with me, we drove to Portland to see Dr. Stober. After examination, the Doctor looked at me very seriously.

"I don't see how this lad has been able to function at all — his sinuses are so totally crushed in with the nerves pinched. He desperately needs help." The doctor shook his head in wonderment. Then he proceeded with the treatment. Jason "Yelped!" It was painful, but only for an instant. Dr. Stober told me Jason definitely needed a series of treat-

*Carl Pfeiffer Treatment Ctr, 2100 Manchester Rd, Suite 1610, Wheaton, IL

ments, as changes in the bone structure could be made only a little at a time. But of course, as always, I was stymied, not being able to extricate him from the camp to bring him to the doctor except on very rare occasions. Knowing a help and not being able to take advantage of it is very frustrating.

Nearing the end of his eighteen months' confinement in the Youth Camp, Jason ran away, and for no apparent reason the counselors could see. The result was an additional two-year sentence just for running, although he had committed no other crime. This time he was sent to a different facility. Suffice it to say, that from then on it was a fast downhill road. During the formative years of twelve to sixteen Jason's only companions were other very troubled youngsters in confinement, many of them from the inner city (and my Jason was a fast learner). Again I heard those famous last words of the social worker, ringing in my ears, who had proclaimed that Jason needed 24-hour care in a guided and guarded setting. Ah yes, guarded from all that would have helped him to normalcy, from the new-found, and now denied, medical treatment for his illness and from the daily love of his family, and guided into criminality.

Jason continued the pattern of escaping and running away, as stress, for obvious reasons, was far worse in State institutions than it had been in any outside school. Details are unnecessary here, except to say that Jason progressed from Youth Camp, where his only friends were other delinquents, to becoming entangled in larger and larger institutions. No rehabilitation was given that produced any changes, although he did receive *some* basic schooling. I ended up visiting him in prisons in Washington, Arizona, New Mexico, Texas and California, as he always managed to run away. In New Mexico I was told, "Jason is unusual among the youth here as he has an I.Q. of 145. The norm here is 85, with no other child over 90." The official related this in astonishment. So they, too, were puzzled by his situation. They said he definitely did not belong in prison, but could offer no alternative because of his running record. He was fifteen by then.

Consulting with case workers in all of these states, I attempted to get proper medical assistance for him, but it was hopeless. I was met by a stone wall. Some case workers were sympathetic, but totally helpless in a system with no method for evaluation to separate youngsters with hidden medical needs from others who were truly criminal. Twenty years later, our prison system is still in the Dark Ages.

Meanwhile, Jason's values and ideas, through association, were being seriously and dangerously altered. His troubles increased. Finally, at 16, he was arrested for robbery and assault committed while running and on drugs. Due to his long confinement record and because he was tall for his age, he was tried as an adult and confined to a maximum security prison in California. At sixteen he was the youngest in a prison containing over 5,000 adult men. A rooster cannot survive in a cage of foxes. Jason had to become a fox to survive. Survival is the key word here. My agony over my son and the fate I felt I had allowed by signing that paper knew no bounds. My pillow remained soaked with bitter tears for many months, as I prayed for his safety.

The trauma was heavy for all of us, as I know his brother and sister suffered as well. They had lost their father, and now their brother was in deep, deep trouble. Jason always wrote loving, cheerful and intelligent letters, despite everything. His sweet nature never seemed to fade where his family was concerned. In the early years he wrote, "I don't think you should even come again soon, Mom, because it hits me hard how much I miss you and Doll, and our house, and I feel worse after you've left." He sometimes described the often deplorable conditions. Crowding, even in the mid 1970's, was bad.

"Four men are put into cells made for two, and some guys who come in have to sleep on the floor of the dayroom and in the walkways. They have no place to toilet and are beaten if they attempt to use someone else's."

I gathered later what he did not let me know at the time, of course, that as a young handsome sixteen-year old, he suffered the horror of any number of rapes before a powerful, respected man claimed him, giving him protection from the others. This was the only recourse. Any time he got into a fight to protect himself or another young boy (he always had compassion for the underdog, being one himself), he was slapped with two or more years of time just for fighting. Racial tensions those years were even worse than they are today. Even if one didn't want to belong to a faction, the color of your skin denoted it automatically. One time, after about six years, Jason wrote, "It seems I'm doing a life sentence in two-year stints."

The years went on. He wrote beautiful long letters descriptive of emerging talents and ideas which had no outlet. The prisons were so crowded there were only 350 job opportunities in an institution of over 5,000 men. He was an avid reader and clearly understood the spiritual teachings I sent to him. Also, he took as many courses as was possible through correspondence in college studies. Jason's art drawings, sent in letters, had delicate detail etched in thin pen, an art form reminiscent of Celtic times, and the intricate tracings which decorated the first books. He had never had an art lesson. His ability came naturally, apparently from soul memory.

Jason never gave up hope of release, and attempted to introduce reforms that would give more work and study opportunity to inmates. But by becoming embroiled in prison politics he was labeled a boat-rocker and a trouble-maker by the administration.

He usually tried to keep the harshness of prison life from me, but when long periods passed without a letter, I always knew something had happened. We here on the outside have had little idea of the atrocities and conditions that prevail inside prisons, until recently when news stories have focused attention upon them. I asked Jason one time while visiting him if there was any hope of the prison doctors taking an interest in deeper medical biochemical testing. He laughed sardonically.

"Mom, I don't even go when I'm ill with simple things, for all these doctors seem to know is to give you an aspirin — if you're lucky. But they *do* know surgery. They are damn good at that! I've seen them open a guy up and operate right where he fell on the tier after a stabbing."

Drugs were at that time nearly as available inside prison

as out. When Jason was in his early twenty's and had been
moved from San Quentin to Folsom Prison, I did not receive
his usual regular letters. The men were moved around due
to space problems and Jason generally lost his property. I
had come to know something was wrong when he did not
write, for he considerately tried to keep bad news from me,
later saying, "I didn't want you to worry, Mom."

One thing was clear — psychically I was tied to him. I
always knew when something was wrong and I was in
prayer daily for his safety (one can never call the prison to
ask for information — not at all). Soon a mutual friend from
the area telephoned me. She had been on a visit to see
Jason, but had been allowed to talk only through a glass
partition. Her voice was agitated.

"I saw Jason today. Has he written you?"

"No," I replied, "and I'm worried."

"He looks pretty dreadful," she continued. "He's been
badly beaten by the guards. He didn't want me to tell you,
but I feel I must."

"What happened?" My heart was a lump in my chest,
pounding heavily.

"The guards accused him of passing drugs, but he said
he was innocent and knew nothing about what happened.
They didn't believe him. He told me he had been just quietly
minding his own business, reading one evening, when two
guards came into his cell, made him strip, then handcuffed
him and beat him senseless!"

I was horrified and could hardly respond, as anger rose
inside. I felt ill.

I flew down to see for myself that he was still alive, and
I, too, was allowed to talk only through a glass partition
even though I was his mother. Jason told me that after being
stripped, he had been forced to kneel while two guards
thrust his head into his cell's toilet bowl in an effort to make
him confess. He could not, as he said he knew nothing of
what they accused him. Then he was beaten unconscious
and left naked on the floor. He awakened in a pool of blood
which appeared to be coming from the penis, so his kidneys
were injured. He said he felt dizzy and nauseous and could

not see very well. His head throbbed, and his body ached so badly he could hardly move to rise. He had been unconscious forty-five minutes to an hour.

I was aghast. He looked awful, with swollen face and purplish/blue bruises even two weeks later. As a result of this beating, Jason lost complete hearing in his left ear and 70% vision loss in his left eye. This, for no reason he could ever ascertain, other than someone had possibly falsely accused him. He told me it also happened to others from time to time, as certain guards chose to wield their power and indiscriminately beat men.

This began a dreadful string of events. While still inside he decided to bring a lawsuit against those particular guards due to the loss of his hearing and sight, and his professed innocence for the alleged misconduct. However, to get the papers out to an attorney was not so easy. Four times his mail was intercepted, a totally illegal action, as inmates have constitutional right to mail privileges. The case never reached the courts because his papers were always apprehended. He was, after that, on their black list, and several times was thrown into *the hole*, as solitary confinement is called, with no yard or meal privileges, on trumped up charges or for the slightest transgression.

He looked so wan and pale through those days when I drove down to visit, at ages twenty-three to twenty-five when a young man should be in his prime.

One winter, while in the hole for two solitary months on a lower basement level of the building, he wrote, "There is no heat and the window pane is broken out, so I sleep with all my clothes on, day and night because of the cold." In summers, on upper tiers of those large cement buildings, the heat was suffocating, often rising to 108 degrees with no ventilation or air conditioning of any kind.

One July day after my visit to Jason, I stood outside in the burning sun with grief in my heart, watching the heat rise in rivulets from the roof of the huge cement building, and wondered how anyone survived the stifling atmosphere and the crush of sweating humanity within. Men in such conditions with nothing to do can go mad. Is it any wonder there are riots?

The reader may wonder why I, from the outside, did not press charges or make attempts at rectification by writing a letter to the warden. Jason always begged me not to — *under any circumstances.*

"Mom, if you do, they find ways to punish the guy in here, and I will have hell-to-pay! Even worse than I do now. I've seen it happen."

Even so, he continued to read and educate himself. He looked forward to visits from his brother, Jeremy, who visited as often as possible. Jeremy found himself astonished in later years at Jason's knowledge of world affairs, politics and philosophy. Jason also found solace in drawing, as mentioned, and rediscovered a latent talent in art that was meticulous and beautiful.

No, he most certainly was not an angel. But Jason was special and gifted in his own unique way. Life educates people by circumstance, and often a certain hard shell has to develop in order to survive. Jason's generous nature remained intact. He always requested extra treats in his once-a-year box (allowed only at Christmas) "for guys here who don't have anybody to send them anything, Mom." He usually ended up giving away over half of his box, though it wasn't that much, the poundage being limited.

In later years when Jason finally achieved a few weeks release, his first act, with the meager amount of his own money, was to purchase toys for the small children whose fathers were his friends inside. He would then deliver them in person with words of comfort. I know this because he asked me to drive him to the department store and then to their homes. He never lost his love and empathy for children, while often expressing a yearning for some of his own.

Rape, beatings and stabbings were commonplace inside, and many fight fire with fire, becoming tougher than the next guy in order to stay alive. It is the very few who know Christ who are able to wrap themselves in faith and the Light of God's Love, to walk untouched through the madness year after year. Even then it is extremely difficult, for the environment fosters not love, but hatred. One letter during those days I found especially interesting.

"This month I have had a lesson in patience. I have 'held mud' when I felt at times like tearing things apart and yelling my lungs out. I haven't, though, and the pressure I feel allows me to test my inner strength under stress. Instead of getting bummed out, I have analyzed my stress capacity which will prove valuable in the future. I doubt if many people know their strengths, weaknesses, pressure points, etc., as well as I do mine now. In any confrontation situation, business, pleasure, or whatever, I'll hold the edge. I've tried to train my mind to be aware of things most people miss. I listen to conversations on the tier and analyze motives, actions and reactions, sometimes before the speaking parties even do.

"For the past 72 hours I have spoken to no one except the doctor. Even to the cops I only nod or shake my head. Various people have tried to involve me in conversation and I just kick back, relax and stay quiet. I have beaten two of my faults: 1) To put in my two-cents for no reason other than recognition, and 2) To listen without hearing. I used to have to jump up and say something if two people were arguing over a point that I knew the answer to. Now I just listen and laugh to myself if two people argue and both are wrong.

"This whole exercise is to heighten my level of awareness and to hold an ace in the hole instead of showing it unnecessarily. For a socializing person like me, it is quite an exercise."

It pleased me that Jason worked consistently at self-improvement in a variety of ways and was able to share his thoughts in this manner. Most sons, I doubt, would be so open with their mother in such a situation. He was, in addition, an articulate letter-writer. He was, in this way, his father's son.

The high and growing cost of simply holding men in prison with very little education and/or vocational training is not generally realized by an inattentive public. One report from the Department of Corrections of the State of Washington in the Spring of 1991 revealed that it costs our country $16 Billion a year. The cost has doubled in the past two years, but crime continues to increase at an alarming rate. The statistics are changing so rapidly with the exploding prison population, they are obsolete soon after compiled. Suffice it to say that a point-of-no-return is approaching and most inmates who have had no chance to learn a means of self-support, simply having been locked up and left to vegetate, will be out on the streets to wreak havoc out of sheer anger and frustration.

In May of 1992, as I write these words, Chase Riveland, Washington State's Chief Corrections Officer went to Washington D.C. for an exchange of ideas about crime and punishment. A news article in the Seattle Times, May 18, 1992, reported his disappointment.

> "Instead of exchanging ideas, what [Riveland] got was a U.S. Justice Department monologue, a sermon on how to lock up more people. If the prison population trend of the late '80s and early '90s were to continue for the next fifty years, everyone in Washington State would be in prison. In this state alone an average of $4,000 a year is spent for each student in the K-12 education system, while it spends an average of *$26,000* a year *on each inmate* in the state's correction system. Enrollment is capped on the state's colleges and universities while prison population expands unchecked. Chief Riveland calls these facts, 'A confusing message about our priorities. It is not a matter of being soft on crime or hard on crime. You've got to be smart on crime, and being smart on crime means rethinking sentencing reform, creating more community-based, closely supervised alternatives to incarceration, especially for first-time drug offenders." As Riveland said in a letter to U.S. Attorney William Barr after the recent Justice Department conference, "The incarceration of millions of Americans should be treated with alarm and concern, not with self-righteous smugness."

How can we afford to not pay attention to this? For I

know that what is true of Washington State is representative of other states across the United States.

I want to shout from the housetops that spending our money to incarcerate thousands of young people in environments so unhealthy they only become real criminals instead of spending the same money to educate them and draw forth their potentials — is criminal in itself. The cycle of arrests, rearrests, punishment and more punishment is unending and fruitless. The cost is measured in billions of dollars, in thousands of lost lives, and in untold wasted potential.

Television can and should be a powerful teaching tool not only for children but also for adults. To achieve this while also entertaining the adult is a specialized art. Through recent years I have appreciated the show *In The Heat of the Night* because the star and producer, Carrol O'Connor, has helped create episodes that encompass moral issues such has racism, bigotry, human rights, and judgment of ones fellow man. But in dealing with these issues, deep caring, heart-touching drama is displayed in stories that highlight our failures, or now-and-then achievements in following the teachings of our Lord. This is often done with subtle humor and down-home wisdom sprinkled throughout, while depicting life in a typical small southern town. O'Connor's character, the local Chief of Police, once, stated, "I hate prisons. I would rather look at the horizon and see a cyclone coming."

I give undying praises to the small groups of ordinary citizens who have, here and there, started live-in country camps for troubled inner-city youngsters. There they are taught self reliance and responsibility in caring for animals and gardens, serving freshly grown vegetables from the fields they themselves help to tend, while building strong bodies and bright minds in the process. We need many more of these.

In Henry County, Georgia, one such camp called Snap Back is being run for boys ages 12 to 15 — those with an attitude problem, or disobedient teens who constantly talk back. Parents help fund the camp through fund-raisers such as country barbecues. It is reported to be very successful, and the kids enjoy it.

In San Francisco a Rehabilitation Center for men on

parole from San Quentin and other prisons, called the Delancey Street Foundation* was founded and is directed by one brave woman, Mimi Silbert, and is highly successful. Not a single Delancey Street graduate has re-entered prison. Delancey Street helps men reconstruct their own lives.

They learn trades, work at forming new businesses, and work together as teams, giving support to one another. (This latter, I believe, is a lot of the secret.) There have been a few marvelous, innovative changes since the 1970's when I found nothing. Delancey Street Foundation is so successful, other states are looking to it as a model. This gives much hope!

Ours could be called the Age of Chemicals, as the public has been sold down the river by the chemical companies who produce chemical fertilizers for crops, chemical sprays for insects (which have nearly decimated numerous species of birds, including some of the grandest like the bald eagle and the peregrine falcon), chemical preservatives for foods and even chemical drugs given by mouth and injected as therapy to heal bodies already polluted with chemicals! Is it any wonder we have a population plagued by the highest rate of cancer in its many forms of any country in the world, as well as many other major illnesses? In 1991 it was projected by the American Cancer Association that one out of four individuals in the U.S. will die of cancer. This, after forty years of research. Can this be called normal? Little was spoken of connecting the breakdown of organs and body systems to toxic materials ingested in food, water and air. Fortunately, a few alarms are now being sounded.

The populace is slowly awakening and demanding chemical-free foods, but irreparable damage has already been done to thousands of our children who are now young adults, and it is yet continuing. We are seeing an unprecedented number of violent acts of men beating their wives or their children, even women inflicting damage on children out of stress and anger. What is the cause of this wave of anger and violence in adults, even in their own homes? Life is supposed to be easier with all the modern conveniences available.

*Delancey St., Fn., Dept. P, 600 Embaracadero St., San Francisco, CA 94107

It is well-known there are many contributing factors to the stresses felt in our society: The breakdown of family life with one-parent families or both working, the lack of a sense of community that sustained our ancestors, and the resultant alienation most people feel. Growing materialism and economic pressures play a large part as well. However, when the body and brain are clear and strong, stress can be dealt with and alleviated. Could one cause of stress run-rampant be an imbalance in the body's chemistry, causing brain aberrations?

In *The Decade of the Brain*, Dr. Allan Bromley, Ph.D., Science Advisor to President George Bush, and Director of Science and Technology Policy writes, "It has always seemed astonishing to me that we know vastly more about the first microsecond of the existence of our universe, or about the constituents of any atom, or about the interior of the sun, than we do about the three pounds of tissue inside our own heads. Brain research is truly one of the great frontier areas of Science."

Could it be that the brain is naturally the first organ, because it is the most sensitive, to react to foreign chemicals in the body's bloodstream and glandular fluids, and then triggers a total body reaction? An excellent book, *Brain Allergies*,* by Dr. William H. Philpott and Dwight K. Kalita also lays out a very strong case that this is true.

After I became more educated in this area, I clearly saw from the symptoms Jason had earlier shown that he suffered brain allergies to particular foods that did not trouble our other two youngsters. Another doctor, Lendon Smith, M.D., noted speaker and author, stated, "Hyperkinesis usually strikes boys in a family, often the middle child, and usually the blonde, blue-eyed children."

Jason fit that description precisely. He was of a sensitive, artistic nature, so the body was sensitive as well, and the doctors who began research in this field stated that this first strikes the most vulnerable organ — the brain. When this happens the impressions such a child receives from the outside world *are* different than those seen by normal people,

Brain Allergies, 1980 Keats Publishing, 27 Pine St., New Canaan, CT 06840

and often frightening, causing the child to react in an abnormal way.

In their work with prisoners, Alex Schauss and his associates found that psychiatric counseling *has no real effect whatsoever when the body and brain are biochemically deranged, for the person is not emotionally capable of truly hearing what is being said.* The counselee is actually antagonistic towards the counseling process for he is seeing the world differently. Only after physical biochemical treatment has brought the brain back to a normal condition does the individual become receptive.

The allergic reactions were only one dimension of Jason's multiple difficulties. He also suffered malformed sinus cavities (apparently they were crushed in at birth), which resulted in a constriction of the cranium and resultant pinched nerves. Couple his physiological problems with his grief at feeling he had caused his father's death, and we had a very explosive situation. Through the years in prisons, Jason changed from a near angelic, intelligent, gentle child to a very strong, wary and somewhat hard-shelled young man who had to battle for survival amidst violent circumstances. A generally unaware and unsympathetic public rarely entertains any idea of young men in prison other than to label them bad people, criminals, or convicts.

Later, when Jason was allowed on the yard, he spent time with weight lifting, as many do, so his body would not become weak in confinement. In the last years Jason put himself on a dietary regimen, refusing all sugared foods and flavored drinks, as well as caffeine, and he wrote to me, "I feel much better, Mom, more calm and level-headed." He had a beautiful build finally, lean and strong, and stood six feet, four inches tall. Jason had received our guidance of God's love, ever-present, and did spend many solitary hours in meditation, which helped him retain his inner spirit, and the gentleness often shone through.

In years since Jason's incarceration, Transcendental Meditation programs have been introduced into many prisons across the United States, with very rewarding results. (The reader may recall in an earlier chapter I spoke of Maharishi Mahesh

Yogi coming in the 1950's to Los Angeles, bringing the practice of Trancendental Meditation to the West, and being first hosted in the home where my mother lived.) Since those days T.M., as it is popularly called, has been taken up by millions all over the United States and Europe.

Recently Larry King, the well-known talk-show host, interviewed a Dr. Charles Alexander, Professor of Psychology at the fully accredited Maharishi International University.* With Dr. Alexander was Pat Correm, who had been a prisoner in California for twenty-five years. Mr. Correm states that after discovering T.M. his life changed completely, as T.M. is one of the most simple techniques as an antidote to stress. When stress is released, one's value system and very lifestyle changes. Mr. Correm later became active in contacting prison group leaders in San Quentin from the Mexican Mafia, Black Panthers, Black Gorillas, Black Nationalists, Arian Brotherhood, American Nazi Party and Hell's Angels, forming study groups in T.M. with these leaders and their followers before he himself was released. He is now in college studying law.

"Of all the 'Lifers' who took T.M. in California prisons," Mr. Correm states, "not one has ever returned, despite the fact the Jailhouse Door is called a revolving door!" He relates that meditation made tremendous changes in the prison atmosphere, as men's lives became more stable.

Often, due to traumas in a child's environment, a person's emotional development becomes frozen at age nine or twelve, remaining juvenile no matter how old the body grows. Practicing meditation seems to unfreeze this block in development, and a person then continues to mature emotionally. When an individual can release inner stress and pain, healing begins. Transcendental Meditation thus has a powerful effect in reducing addictions. Such programs are needed in all prisons and their presence would be invaluable. But meditation, and the desire to change, are of course, very personal matters. An individual must desire change.

Meditation is also the foundation of the teachings of Paramhansa Yogananda who sought to help people find ex-

*Maharishi Intern'l. University, Fairfield, Iowa 52556, Ph: (202) 723-9111.

panded awareness and inner peace. At the time of this writing, Yogananda's techniques are being taught at the California Medical Facility at Vacaville in a meditation/study group there. Reports are that the benefits are observable and very gratifying. Yogananda always stressed the scientific nature and universality of the practices of yoga and meditation, rather than their exotic nature. His first book, *The Science of Religion* points out the common thread in all mankind, wherever they may be or what relgion they follow, in their relationship to their Creator, and how these practices may help them to grow toward a deeper understanding of their own nature.

Jason did not have such opportunity, but helped himself considerably as he matured and was able to look at his own condition objectively. He always admitted to his failures openly. Tears fill my eyes as I remember how, through everything, he remained loving, gentle and sweet to me, his mother, whom he honored to the end by never once using harsh language in all those difficult years, or a single word of condemnation, reprisal, or blame towards others for his troubles. He took that upon himself. To me the beauty buried within him was always visible, and my sorrow at the loss of his artistic creative mind and sensitive, caring nature was overwhelming. My personal faith had reached its ultimate test, but through all the tears and turmoil I saw a loving soul putting himself into a position of gaining strength through challenge and pain, continuing to hold his own in the face of situations most of us out here can hardly imagine. Many thousands of others are in these same horrendous conditions.

In looking back, it is possible also for me to see that nothing could change the course of Jason's destiny because he himself charted it before coming into this life. Something in his soul needed a prison experience, as was shown to me a few years later in a remarkable reading, which you may find interesting as I relate it later on in my story, for nothing I nor anyone else did seemed to be able to change his course. It was like standing in front of a steam roller and shouting "HALT!" It simply ran right over you. I had through those years held consistently to the comforting belief that his experience was preparing him to be a force in society in

later years to help alleviate these same obvious and horrendous problems suffered by other young people, because
one who has been there is the most powerful mover. He
often said to me, "When I get out I'd like to take courses in
social work, Mom, and then be able to help kids like me."

But this was not to be. Later, I was given a vision, a
piece of the puzzle, which helped me to understand.

*

DREAMS AND VISIONS

There is a difference between dreams and visions, and
one who has visions finds no trouble differentiating between them. Dreams are common to everyone. Researchers
have long studied dreams and find that, for the most part,
they are a way for the mind to relieve itself of stress that has
occurred during waking hours. The imagination, or subconscious mind, is never idle, even while one is asleep. However, dreams are almost always wispy and smoke-like, disappearing within moments after awakening. Like everyone,
I have experienced hundreds of dreams which I would not
have been able to relate to you in detail even moments after
I woke from them.

Even so, in times of need or changes in our life, we
should pay attention to our dreams, because they can be a
very useful tool in helping us gain answers to important questions. Questions such as, "What is the best decision in this
matter?" or, "What do I need to do to be healed?" or simply,
"What is the cause of this condition?" Even for help in relationships, answers can come in our dreams. However, it is important to *ask* for an answer from our Inner Guardian upon going
to sleep, *and pay attention immediately upon awakening*
before they dissapate, to the outstanding symbols that can be
remembered. They may not make sense at first, and like anything, it may take practice, but can be very rewarding when
sincere cooperation is desired with the Inner Self. *You* are the
best interpreter of your own dreams, because pictures mean
different things to different people.

I will give a short but interesting example. One time in

therapy, I was working with a woman who seemed not to improve in her unique psychic condition regardless of my efforts over many months. One evening, in reverie, while almost asleep, I asked, "What can I do for Peggy?" Soon in the darkness of my mind I saw a white emvelope, addressed as a letter, float past the left side of my head. I had to turn that idea around for awhile, in having seen a *letter go by*. Soon it rang clear. *"Let her go by."* I was to let go and let God take care of her. Now isn't that cute? Our Inner Guide is very imaginative.

Visions, on the other hand, remain sharply in our memory for years, even for our lifetime, as they are of a different quality altogether. Mine come in bright color, every detail sharp and clear and, I find, relate specifically to a circumstance or relationship of importance in my emotional life or urgent physical health at that time. The soul working through the subconscious mind might bring a past experience up from deep memory banks in answer to the consistent longing to know, "Why?"

Sometimes visions can be the soul warning us of an impending event, and can be startling and hair-raising. If we heed the warning and lift the concern to God in sincere and devout prayer, the circumstances can be altered, changing what otherwise could have been a tragic event that was not in the divine plan. This is so because spiritual laws supersede the psychic realm. Visions of guidance and visions of warning are different, but both serve very real purposes.

I have observed, however, that if an event is in divine plan it cannot be altered. It is programmed in, so to speak, by that soul's Higher Self before it is born into earth life, that a certain lesson may be learned through experience. We cannot know another soul's Plan for this life, and we need to keep in mind that we must give this situation to God for the highest good of all. It has been said, "God does not always come when called, but He always comes on time." This does not mean our time – but His. We, naturally, in compassion and empathy, must do all we can to relieve suffering. In this we are the comforter in many ways, but since we cannot know what another's Soul Plan is, nor its outcome, we must not overly grieve or blame God. For our sight is very short. We are looking at the karmic picture through the keyhole of this life only, and, as you can readily see, that is only a very small slice of the overall soul-pattern. If the help or the healing hand is meant to relieve or heal, it will. Nothing is ever lost by a loving thought or touch, sent out in the Light of the Master. And many times, though we cannot change the course of events for a loved one, we may lighten the burden, or change his or her attitude about it. If there is no obvious benefit or change, be not dismayed, for many times this love sent in prayer goes to work on an unseen level, not apparent to our human eyes.

And so it was for my son, who seemed on a crash course with his destiny. And I, too, wondered why all my valiant efforts seemed not to have altered it. Then, a vision came to me.

One evening at home, deep in meditation, a clear scene rose before my inner eyes, like a movie inside my forehead. It was a huge wooden Viking Ship. The bow rose high in the water to form a large sculptured hawks-head with beak open wide. Many oars extended through the sides, moving in rhythm, as it was fast propelled through the sea.

Suddenly I am given clear sight through to the inside, where men are chained, straining against the oars. Their upper bodies glisten as they strive to keep the steady rhythm of the drumbeat. The orders rise to a shout, "Faster! Faster!" The order is clear, though I do not 'hear' the words.

My attention becomes riveted to one man in particular, sitting in mid-section on the right side, a very handsome young man in his prime, perhaps mid-twenties, with strong muscular shoulders shining with sweat, his sinewy arms keeping the rhythm steady with the drumbeat. BOOM! BOOM! BOOM! A wave of shock and intense sadness passes over me as I recognize my son! — the same soul I now know in this world, though here he seems a bit older. He is beautiful, in face and form. As I watch from somewhere above, I hear the shouts and the drumbeat increase to a frantic crescendo and I realize the ship is in battle with another — to the death! Even as I watch, horrified, I see the great warship rammed by another at its center, right where my son sits chained, with no way to escape. The water rushes in and somehow I 'see' or 'know' that he does not die from drowning, *but that the crash of the great ships crushes in his face and head . . . and he dies instantly.*

The scene faded, and understanding of the full meaning swept over me in hot waves. I was given a 'vivid realization' that as his mother in the days of the Vikings, I had stood by, allowing him to be sold into slavery in order to obtain money for food for the other children of the family. He was a strong elder child, loving and giving then as now, and had understood the reason and accepted his fate, not knowing how harsh it would become. Even so, the tragic stress of those many months at the oars had taken its toll on his emotions and left a deep scar of rebellion and a desire to escape from authority, with intense inner fear stamped in his psyche. And I, having given him away then had to suffer having him taken from me now against my will, and to watch, helpless, the resulting karmic out-workings of the effects.

You will recall that even in birth this time, he brought in as a carry-over the flattened cheekbone area of his face, causing sinuses to be blocked and nerve flow impaired, physically creating a condition for erratic nervous reaction to the slightest stress, that would lay the foundation for his downfall.

And so I was shown in my vision, in answer to prayer, one clear cause-and-effect example, even several lifetimes later, of how we unknowingly create our own future.

*

MAMA RECEIVES HER DIPLOMA

In these years of quiet sadness, while Jason was confined and Jeremy had graduated from college with a degree in Literature and had gone back to California to teach school, Mama (Grammy Becky) suddenly left us for her Higher Home.

She was a miracle in her own way, for although her eyesight had failed in the last years, she independently wished to live alone and keep her own apartment in Los Angeles' Wilshire District. She had helped to comfort me through

Jason's tragic experiences and had written faithfully to him, for she never ceased being interested in life's happenings. Mama always retained the courage to be herself and not be influenced by what others might think.

I recall the year she put up with the intense racket involved in the construction of a multi-storied office building, the immense Amundsen Building, directly across the street from her apartment. The noise of cement mixers and cranes and the shouts and curses of workmen continued daily for a full year. To Mama's tremendous relief it was finally finished, and she saw that at the street level was a brand-new elegant restaurant. She vowed to be one of the first to patronize it, treating herself and Jeremy, who was then 15 years old and visiting her, to the best dinner in the house.

As the Maitre'd seated them at a table of linen, crystal and silver, she saw the restaurant was so new there was only a sprinkling of patrons, with actually more waiters than customers. But those waiters were very elegantly outfitted in short red bolero jackets and black tuxedo pants, with the usual immaculate white towel over the arm, obviously prepared to fulfill their slightest wish. After ordering, Mama and Jeremy sat with only their water glasses filled.

Jeremy later related that every time he took one swallow from his water, the waiter standing behind him jumped to fill it again. Soon, Mama piped up, "Stop! Stop! Are you trying to drown him?"

Well, despite all the waiters and only a few customers, they waited for their dinner, and waited — and waited some more. After a time, Mama became exasperated. Jumping up, she waved her handkerchief in the air and called to the waiter standing by the kitchen door, "Yoo-Hoo! What happened? Did the cook die?" Young Jeremy said he wanted to slink under the table, but that Grandma was always so comical, he had to laugh instead.

At the age of eighty-nine Mama's voice on the telephone was that of a forty-year old, her spirit yet filled with humor and her handwriting firm and clear. She had written three books, two unpublished.

One night while writing a long letter to me, she apparently felt tired, lay down on her bed and left. Just like that. She remained totally clear in mind and body to the last moment. Flying down by the first plane available, I found the nine-page, unsigned letter open on her desk with pen beside it, for she had not planned to leave. I was blessed with her last loving thoughts. Her faith had been so positive that she refused to ever carry hospital insurance. She always said, "God has promised me I will never go to a hospital or be in a nursing home." Such faith was rewarded. She was not ill, even one day (I am not advocating this for others. Only relating my mother's strong spirit). I was her only chick and she often called me her angel.

We were very close and I missed her immensely. We had shared so many wonderful things in life, as it was she who first pointed the way to my expanded concepts and encouraged my freedom of thought. It was she who taught me that we are not to be bound by mass consciousness, but must truly know ourselves as Children of God and beloved of the Lord. It was she who tried to teach us there is no death, only continuing life, to be lived ever more fully.

Once she shared with me her revelation as to why she had been born into this lifetime as a farmer's wife, restricted by hard work, poor health, and an uncaring husband who lacked understanding.

"God has shown me a vision of a life wherein I was a wealthy aristocrat in Austria, perhaps a duchess. But I was selfish and self-centered, not caring for the common man or for the needs of the poor. Now, it appears my soul chose to learn firsthand of such trials; first on the farm with my family, and then on the farm with your father, in those harsh physical circumstances. And you, my child, my Angel, followed me into incarnation to be a comfort through it all. Love is a saving grace."

> Do not stand at my grave and weep.
> I am not there, I do not sleep.
> I am a thousand winds that blow;
> I am the diamond glints on snow.
> I am the sunlight on ripened grain,
> I am the gentle autumn rain.

When you awaken in the morning's hush,
I am the soft star with dawn's first blush.

So do not stand at my grave and cry.
I am not there; I did not die.

—Author Unknown

One day as I cleared her things, an involuntary tear rolled down my cheek, and I heard her chuckle as she reminded me of a poem I had sung and whistled. She was telling me she is free now to be her real Self, that wonderful spirit filled with life and humor, no longer restrained by the fetters of earth, but free and light as the butterfly.

THE BUTTERFLY

A butterfly rested upon a flower,
Gay was he and light as a flake,
And there he met a caterpillar
Sobbing as though his heart would break;
It hurt the happy butterfly
To see a caterpillar cry.

Said he, "Whatever is the matter?
And may I help in any way?"
"I've lost my brother," wept the other,
"He's been unwell for many a day;
Now I discover, sad to tell,
He's only a dead and empty shell."

"Unhappy grub, be done with weeping,
Your sickly brother is not dead;
His body's stronger and no longer
Crawls like a worm, but flies instead!
He dances through the sunny hours
And drinks sweet nectar from the flowers."

"Away, away deceitful villain,
Go to the winds where you belong,
I won't be grieving at your leaving
So take away your lying tongue.
Am I a foolish slug or snail,
To swallow such a fairy tale?"

"I'll prove my words, you unbeliever,
So listen well, and look at me,
I am none other than your brother,
Alive and well and fancy free!
Soon you'll be with me in the skies
Among the flirting butterflies."

"Ah!" cried the mournful caterpillar,
"Tis clear I must be seeing things,
You're only a specter sipping nectar,
Flicking your ornamental wings,
And talking nonsense by the yard.
I will not hear another word."

The butterfly gave up the struggle.
"I have," he said, "no more to say."
He spread his splendid wings, and ascended
Into the air and flew away.
And while he fluttered far and wide,
The caterpillar sat and cried.

                                        — Anonymous

                    *

RELEASE FROM PRISON — AND EARTH

Jason was finally released on parole at the age of twenty-seven. He had spent fourteen years in confinement. It was now the late Fall of 1983. California insisted Jason be paroled within the state. They would not consider any out-of-state placement. Nevertheless, he made a major effort to come home to Washington for Christmas week, as he had a premonition that all was not well. He said to me at the time, "My parole officer doesn't like me, Mom. I have a weird feeling about him. He even told me I didn't have to report in next time, when I know the rules are that I'm required to report every week."

We had a warm and wonderful family reunion for a few days. Jeanine was so happy to see him, she clung to him like a burr. It was well that the mysterious curtain of tomorrow remained draped over our eyes, that we did not know these would be our last hours together, or suspect the horrible shock and grief that lay ahead.

Five days after Jason left us to return to California, the telephone rang. It was a mutual friend in California who had heard a shocking report over a local news broadcast. Jason had been shot to death by the police.

There was something strange and mysterious about the entire happening. We were *never notified* by the authorities, and have not been to this day. I know Jason lived in fear. He had told me only a few days before he was killed, "The guards in the prison want me out of the way." I had a very strong suspicion, almost a psychic intuition, that certain authorities at the prison were in cahoots with the parole officer and the police on the outside, although this is a harsh thing to say. Most people believe they can have faith in the force hired to protect them. However, I was finding otherwise, and recent months have exposed the raw brutality of some on the police force as sting operations have come vividly into the spotlight. What Jason tried to tell me began to make sense. Even today the mystery is still unfolding, and his words proving out.

In 1991, seven years after his passing, the Sheriff's deputies appeared at the door in a community in California where he had lived the few short weeks he was out, asking for him by name. The person who answered the door did not know he had passed over seven years previously, so only said, "We do not know of him." But how does it happen the current police force themselves do not know? Was his death hushed up due to covert actions?

After my friend's heart-rending phone call, I caught the first plane available at our fogged-in airport and joined Jeremy and Jennine, who had flown down from Denver (as she was attending the Air Force Academy at the time) to identify Jason's body which had been taken to a local mortuary. I noted the head was covered from the eyebrows up, bound in a white cloth wrapping, and more cloth wrappings were around the torso's midsection. I make mention of this for a special reason, as it bears on the story later.

Yes, it was my son, but the cold, still, pale form did not resemble the warm and loving soul I knew. Jason was gone. Yet that moment, that last strange sight of the form he wore, will remain stamped in my memory, never to leave me.

The press reported that there had been a robbery and that the police had chased the suspect, who had a gun and was dangerous.

Jason knew he was being hunted and foolishly acquired a gun hoping to protect himself, though he knew it was unlawful for him or any parolee to carry one. As before, when fear possessed him, Jason always ran and in every way became irrational and reacted badly. He was desperately afraid of being returned to prison and told Jeremy quite seriously that he would rather die than go back. There was no report that Jason fired any shots when the police stopped his car and he got out to face them. No policeman was harmed. No less than five men were after him, and their simultaneous gunfire felled him outright, at a deserted gas station. Also, there was never any proof shown, or further mention made, that he was connected to the reported robbery.

Whatever had happened, my delving into it, seeking reasons, causes or blame, would not bring him back to life, nor change the events. My shock was intense — only a mother or father can know the grief, and I had no husband with whom to share it, or so it seemed. Actually, Allen *had* shared it — amazingly — and I'll come to that shortly.

Jeremy made arrangements for a quiet memorial service to be held in the community where he lived, led by a kind and gentle minister who had known Jason, and his sister Jennine and I were surrounded by loving friends there where the knowledge of God's ever-present help brought comfort to my heart. But the greatest comfort of all was soon to come.

There is a beautiful saving grace in knowing there is no *death*, only a shedding of the heavy body as one might shrug off an outworn or too heavy overcoat, or as the lovely emerging butterfly sheds the outgrown cocoon, leaving it behind on earth that it may be free to fly into the sunlight. For death truly is only the passing from one dimension to another. Somehow I could sense Jason's very real relief at being released from a lifetime of distress. And for me there was a kind of comfort, too — that at last it was over.

Jennine returned to Colorado to school. Jeremy chose to fly home with me to the Northwest as a comfort to both of us for a few days. Soon I received a very strong impression that we should have a sitting with, Sandra, a lady who had recently been recommended to me as an excellent psychic. Since we had never met her, she would have no knowledge of our family whatsoever so whatever she said would not be biased. It was now only five days after Jason had been killed. We called and made the arrangement. If we needed proof of spirit's presence, we surely got it — most emphatically!

Sandra arrived on a sunny afternoon. Jeremy and I sat together with her in a quiet room of our home. She simply closed her eyes and spoke a sincere and fervent prayer, surrounding us with Christ's Light and asking for guidance from Holy Spirit. Sandra did not know I had any son other than the one seated before her, as Jeremy and I had not divulged the purpose of the sitting to her. Moreover, our tragedy had occurred in another state and was not known here in Washington. After a few quiet moments she immediately stated, "There is a young man here, very close and very eager to come through. He seems to be giving me the impression he is part of your family. Do you have a son in spirit?"

Before I could even answer, she laughed with amusement and said, "This is funny!" Imitating him with gestures and a gleeful expression, she continued. "He is sort of dancing up and down and saying, 'I'm free! I'm free! They can't hurt me now!' He comes through *very strong* and is almost trying to speak through me! It seems he has just passed over and he wants you to know he is fine and is with his father." (True!) Then she added, "He has a very nice voice, rich and mellow." (True also. Jason's voice was deep and smooth.)

Suddenly Sandra became agitated and said she was being shown a street scene. "It looks like a gas station . . . with several policemen about. I see them in uniform, but there is also a plainclothesman there . . . (pause) . . . who somehow has a key role in this scene." Remember that Sandra knew nothing previously of our family and no one here in Washington knew of the shooting. Now she became excited and even excessively agitated, gasping out, "There is gunfire!" With a quick frantic motion she clutches herself stating, "The young man is taking my body to show where he was shot twice in the stomach and once in the head." At this I recalled the wrappings around his body's midsection and around the head in the mortuary. It all fit like a glove.

Then she began to choke. "Blood is coming from the mouth . . ." as she clutched her throat, and gasped for breath. "He drops to the ground . . ." Sandra then relaxed and became quiet, as though listening, and soon spoke again, quieter now.

"He is telling me he was at first very angry at what they had done to him, but soon realized he was finally free. And he is telling me he was immediately met by his father and also by a Master."

In a sitting seven years later, through a quite different medium in Honolulu, Hawaii, Jason again reported this meeting, but this time clearly stated it was the East Indian Master Paramhansa Yogananda. This was thrilling to us because, of course, the Ananda Community which Jeremy had joined ten years earlier, and where he now was living and working, was founded on the beautiful teachings of this master, as I have written. Also recall that I had met Yogananda while visiting his church on Sunset Boulevard years before in 1946. That the master would be watching over and taking a personal interest so as to be present at Jason's transition was a tremendous comfort to us, as was knowing that Allen, his father, was there to meet him as well.

Our lady continued, "He wants you to know he is fine and very happy to be free." There was more, of a personal nature. Jason was spending time with his father, resting.

And so, once again, came unmistakable proof that there is no death, only the shedding of the physical body, and the assurance that whether death happens naturally in an easy passing, or unnaturally in violence, the spirit is not harmed.

A few months passed before Jason again appeared at a sitting to tell me he had been busy, as he put it, "studying universal teachings and how to make recompense for the mistakes I made while on earth." He also said he was often with me evenings in our home and that "he liked to ride with me in the car, as it was a comfort to us both." I could attest to this for I had several times while driving distinctly felt his presence, a quiet feeling of love surrounding me.

One time in particular, only two weeks after his passing, as I was traveling along thinking of his harsh prison life, having so little of the joy a boy should have had in a normal home life, the involuntary tears trickled down my cheeks. To my amazement, I suddenly heard his voice in my mind.

"Aw Ma, quit snivelin'. I'm just fine."

This struck me so funny I burst out laughing, for that is exactly the way he would have reacted to tears. Could I communicate with him? I wondered. So emptying my mind as much as possible, I thought one clear question: "What's it like over there, dear?"

Mentally listening, I received only one distinct word, "Different."

From my lifetime of study and research, I realize this to be true, for on that plane we learn to function in the lighter body of a higher dimension where Mind creates through visualization whatever we need, be it traveling about, etheric clothing, or a house. For yes, one has a home of one's own there on the Inner Planes, just as here, which however, must be built and furnished with mind-power. Likewise, in a denser slower degree this is also true on this physical plane, for anything, before it is built, is first visualized in the human mind. This is why the development of the creative imagination is so important in order to strengthen this, our

God-given faculty, the ability to create with mind-power.

One of the main detriments in a child's over-watching television is that the picture is always built for him or her, so the child's creative imagination is undermined. Thus the practice of visualization, which is naturally achieved through reading books, is side-stepped. Creative visualization is very important in soul development.

Many great minds, some known, and others quietly unknown, have used this faculty in dramatic ways. Inventive individuals in all fields use this creative ability consistently. In some cases a picture may appear in the mind, not nebulously, sketchily, as most of us grasp an idea, but clearly, even in finished detail, as in a photograph or motion picture. Examples of this are outlined in a book written by Shafica Karagulla, M.D., called *Breakthrough to Creativity.**

The stories of the works of Nicola Tesla, the great inventor and genius, is a case in point. Tesla worked for years with Thomas Edison and was the creator of many of the inventions for which Edison was later given credit. Tesla, way ahead of his time, wrote,"I cannot divulge my most amazing discovery. The world is not ready for it."

How true his statement was, for scholars now believe Tesla had discovered atomic energy. Power without wisdom, he knew, is very dangerous.

I write Jason's story for him, for he is not here to tell it as we had hoped he would be. He is not here to work toward changing a prison system that is a pox on the face of our nation. Our system has become hopelessly inadequate, the scene of physical and emotional violence which serves neither the improvement or reform of inmates nor the long term interests of our country.

The unseen, insidious, villains of nutritionally deficient, chemically adulterated foods, poison-sprayed fruits and vegetables, and polluted air and water, are now making their effects known in an immense wave of biochemically imbalanced, brain-disfunctional citizens of all ages. Suffering from inexplicable irritations, anxieties, and restlessness, these

* *Breakthrough to Creativity*, 1967, DeVorss & Co. Los Angeles 90041

individuals cannot gain the emotional control and stability necessary to lift themselves above their trouble or even to improve their environments. Consequently, they succumb to the ravages of drugs and alcohol, striking out in myriad ways against a society they see as the enemy. Evidence: the alarming increase in split families, wife beatings, child abuse, rape, violence in schools, assault and murder in many forms on every hand.

Recent news items across the nation report that in a number of U.S. cities children's bookbags must be searched as they now carry weapons to school — clubs, knives and guns. Teachers have been attacked, many are becoming afraid to teach. This is abnormal and frightening to the entire citizenry. Everyone sees these results. I write nothing new. If we are to save ourselves and our children's futures, we must act on new knowledge.

Obviously, we do not say that chemically laden food is the sole cause of crime. Of course not. We all know better. However, there are root causes that help lay the groundwork for abnormal behavior and drug abuse. There is a domino effect we should look at. Going back to basics: Children in particular are more sensitive to changing body chemistry and cannot accept the amount of foreign substances that their elders may handle. On-going stress is the result on all levels, but particularly in the brain, as this is the most sensitive organ in the body, as previously noted. While brain-stressed, an individual reacts abnormally, even violently, to situations that otherwise would not have caused a stir. Relationships deteriorate and reach breaking points. Adults divorce. Children adopt anti-social behavior, leave home to wander the streets and join gangs. Some even turn and kill their parents without serious provocation.

It is well known that many children are born deficient of nutritionally deficient parents and/or drug addicted of drug addicted parents.

"The sins of the parents shall be visited upon the children." states the Bible.

In the days when these words were transcribed from the Aramaic, sin, scholars say, did not carry modern connotations, but could be understood to mean shortcomings. A deficient body is a shortcoming. If parents are physiologically, biochemically imbalanced, the child in the womb is likewise biochemically imbalanced. Thus, the sin or shortcoming, is visited upon him. Generationally passed infirmities in the forms of inherited susceptibility to particular diseases is a reality doctors are well aware of. A more immediate and dramatic face of inherited illness we see now in the drug addicted and AIDS infected babies being born by the thousands.

A less dramatic, and thus less obvious example of generationally passed infirmity is the inheritance by children of the nutritional deficiencies and biochemical abnormalities of their parents. The rash of chemical preservatives and poisonous sprays Americans of all ages have routinely ingested for the past forty to fifty years, as they unsuspectingly sat down at their daily meals, they are now passing on to their children. Only recently have people begun to watch the ingredients in the prepared foods they buy, but the damage has already been done to thousands upon thousands of our second generation youth who are exhibiting psychotic reactions in gang violence and vandalism. Substance abuse and the money needed for it is the heavy cause. That lure often traps a deficient child already suffering stress and anxiety, who is unable to study sufficiently to learn in school. The child then eagerly tries anything to relieve his or her dis-ease and emotional unhappiness.

Truly healthy, well-balanced young people, who are happy both in mind and body, are not attracted to drug taking. Researchers have found in repeated studies that when healthy children are asked about drugs they will answer, "I don't have the need."

Our family paid dearly for our, and society's, lack of understanding of these principles thirty years ago. Neither Allen nor I were entirely well when Jason was conceived. Allen, of course, was suffering from the periodic and often extensive depression, which had been evident even in his childhood, and which, we later found, is called Bi-Polar Personality Disorder. His condition later improved dramatically with heavy natural vitamin and mineral intake. I was experiencing nervous exhaustion, and realized too late that while pregnant with Jason, I had been extremely deficient in B-Vitamins as well as in some basic minerals. We always had so-called well-balanced meals, but everyone's body chemistry is distinctly individual and the vitamin/mineral needs for some can be much greater than for others. The U.S.D.A.'s minimum daily allowance (M.D.A.) often falls far short of filling the basic needs of many people in these days of depleted and chemically-laden soils on which the food is raised.

Thirty years ago, while I was pregnant with Jason, I was not aware of these facts, but came to understand many things only after it was too late to help my son, and I had to watch as he was wrestled from me and confined at an early age by a state government that allowed neither testing for deficiencies, nor nutritional supplements to be admitted to institutions. We must be observant of our children, especially if they are hyperactive and have problems in school.

Jason and I, after his fourteen years of imprisonment from ages thirteen to twenty-seven, submit that confinement is not the answer for many young first offenders whose needs are not being met. They become much worse in prison. I am grateful now in 1991-92 that there is a gradually growing recognition of the needs of borderline children, with schools and clinics available in many states.

Young forward-thinking doctors have formed the American Orthomolecular Medical Society.* One of the earliest presidents of the group was the brilliant orthomolecular psychiatrist, Michael Lesser, M.D., author of *Nutrition and Vitamin Therapy*, which became a best-seller. Lesser, and doctors like him, have incorporated into their practices specific tests to determine the biochemistry of a patient's body that they may pinpoint missing nutrients, or determine if there are high levels of heavy metals absorbed from the environment.

Some well-known allergy physicians are finally being heard. One, Dr. Doris Rapp, who in the summer of 1991 was

*American Orthomolecular Medical Society, Mary Haggerty, Exec.Dir., 900 No. Federal Way, Suite 330, Boca Raton, Florida 33432.

featured on the television show *Medicine Today*, is the author of *The Impossible Child*.* She spoke at *The Well Mind Assn's Annual Symposium* in *1978* and gave startling proof (*even then*) of the efficacy of these tests and the proven results of the effects on the psyche of certain chemical-laden foods. In Dr. Rapp's new book, *Is This Your Child?*** she describes the medical breakthroughs that have come as a result of further research in this explosive area. Dr. Rapp, with her last mentioned book were, on Feb. 2, 1993, featured on the Phil Donahue television program before an enthusiastic and interested studio audience. It has taken a slumbering public from 1978 (and before), until 1993 to recognize this biochemical connection, while the unfortunate young people haunt the streets, disrupt the schools, and fill our prisons.

The aforementioned Dr. William J. Philpott gave up his psychiatric profession of many years to become a medical allergist after witnessing successful results in only a few weeks in cases where psychiatry had made no improvement whatsoever after as long as six years' treatment! His talk, heard in Seattle twelve years ago, was electrifying, but he was forced to move to another state to practice due to prejudice and lack of sympathy here from the medical community, despite his *proven* methods.

Two books which deals with this subject directly are *Help for the Hyperactive Child**** by William Crook, M.D. and *Why Your Child Is Hyperactive* by Ben F. Feingold, M.D., Chief of Allergy at Kaiser Permanente Medical Center in San Francisco. One would think such help would have been greeted with bugles and drumbeats. Instead, years pass, while the mainstream medical association and criminal justice systems deal in effects, pouring young people off

Impossible Child,1986 Life Sciences Press, Box 1174,Tacoma,WA 98041
**Is This Your Child?*, Doris Rapp, M.D., Wm. Morrow, Pub., 1358 Ave.of the Americas, New York, N. Y. 10019
***Help for the Hyperactive Child*, William Crook, M.D., 1991, Professional Bks./Future Health, Box 3246, Jackson, TN 38301
†*Why Your Child is Hyperactive*, Ben F. Feingold, M.D.Contact: The Feingold Assn. of the U.S., Box 6550, Alexandria, VA 22306, (703) 768-3287

into prisons and mental hospitals rather than looking toward causes and *prevention*. Why must *thousands* suffer and be locked up before these dedicated avant garde healers are given serious attention, and a connection made between the health of our children and the open violence in our society?

Just today, as I write, it has been found and reported that the serial arsonist who caused millions of dollars in damage to property and the peace of mind of thousands of people in the Greater Seattle area recently, before being apprehended, has had problems since very young, in fact, *he was a hyperactive child.*

In addition, the violence seen daily on television teaches them that violence is the normal way to react to problems. How long will such damaging insanity be tolerated? Quoting Jennifer James, a well-known national columnist who recently wrote in the Seattle Times, "We need new ways of thinking and acting. Why? To overcome madness. Madness is doing the same thing over and over again and expecting different results!"

Unfortunately, money has become god in this consumer age where advertising and marketing brainwash the public. Truth is obscured so products will sell and profits roll in, *regardless of the cost* to human health and well-being. Our children are our future, and our nation is the loser, for our nation is destroying its own future.

Once a youth is caught in the correctional system, coming out unscathed is all but impossible. The latest report as I write is that costs exceed *$14 Billion* a year to keep prisons running in America.

Now, health care for our citizens is on the front burner. Recently C. Everett Koop, a former U.S. Surgeon General, appeared on an in-depth television interview on this subject. His remarks confirm what I have written.

> Health Care Reform is not a matter of passing new legislation, but can only be accomplished by the way both doctors and patients think about such care. 160 million people are happy with their

health care program because their insurance is covering it. But for the people to depend totally on insurance to pay for everything, fosters individual greed, in that they then do not care about the cost. They have the opinion that because insurance pays, it's okay. But this is not true, as it is being paid for by all of us.

This also engenders rapid advances in high technology with attendant costs. But every dollar of cost is someone else's dollar of income.

He then gave statistics such as, hospitals are costing $114 Billion, drugs $35 Billion, etc. Dr. Koop continues:

"Doctors perform at least 30% more High-Tech tests than are needed in fear of malpractice, which also raises insurance costs. High-Tech has brought us to the brink of bankruptcy. If we could understand the outcome of all that we do, we could save 25%-30%. Low-Tech treatment can be very useful and includes proper prevention."

He then gave some explicit and surprising examples, such as proper shoes for diabetics. Dr. Koop emphasized:

"Prevention *should be our top priority. It is the ethic that is the most important of all because it is cheap, effective, but not glamorous. There are 741 lobbyists who want to see things stay the way they are because it benefits the few, but not the many. The barrier is selfishness. We must do all we can to return the ethics in medicine that made it the great profession that it is.*

"My graduates will appreciate Low-Tech as well as High-Tech, as so much can be helped with Low-Tech, which is much less costly."

Dr. Koop then discussed individual care of one's self, saying: "Individuals can make the first step by focusing on their own health and becoming informed."

It is now gratifying to hear that Senator Edward Kennedy has presented a bill in Congress that would limit the amount of pesticides that could be used on fruits and vegetables. It is long overdue. Senator Kennedy states, *"Studies have shown the Environmental Protection Agency miscalculated the risks while setting the allowable exposure limits, and this needs to be changed!"*

Across our nation facilities overflow as young Americans behind bars reaches a new high. Justice officials in several states are seeking alternatives to incarceration for juveniles, and are paying particular attention to Massachusetts where a statewide program appears to be a success. Despite the fact that Massachusetts spends far less per delinquent than most states, they have one of the best records in deterring juvenile crime in the nation. Rather than automatic lock-up, 80 percent of juveniles committed to the Department of Youth Services are given intensive supervision in community-based programs or at home. The remaining 20 percent who are deemed a threat are held in small facilities where education, skills and behavioral development are emphasized, with a teacher-to-student ratio of one to four.

Ned Laughlin, director of Massachusetts Dept. of Youth Services states: "We've cut costs, we've cut repeat offenders and we don't have a juvenile crime wave." Only 23 percent of all juveniles committed are incarcerated as repeat offenders, compared with 63 percent for California's Youth Authority, as an example. *At the center of the Massachusetts program is the belief that most delinquent children do not require custody, but development.* And I would like to see health checks that include attention to nutrition, with food that is grown on soils free of pesticides. This common sense approach could do a great deal to alleviate a dangerous trend in our nation, if other states would follow the example Massachusetts has set.

There are now more schools available for children who need extra help and understanding in our country, but one that has drawn my recent attention is the Santa Fe Mountain

Development Center in New Mexico,* a school for learning disabled children. One avant garde teacher, Richard Kimball, Ph.D., stated in a television interview on January 11, 1993, that there are millions of learning disabled children in the United States who are not being educated properly, or even given the basic schooling required by law. As a result, they are often lost in classes for the retarded or emotionally disabled, which can be tragic for their self-esteem and personal development.

Dr. Kimball is presently seeing great success in the Santa Fe Mountain Development Center with a program that combines strenuous mountain climbing exercises with regular scholastic classes. By exerting the effort it takes to make it to the top of a mountain through strength and skill, the students also climb an inner mountain, reaching a higher level in their own self-esteem, and their performance in academic classes. This teacher advises parents to understand their rights under the law for the schooling of their children, and to work with their local school to seek individualized education for their child's need.

It is my daily prayer, and the purpose of this writing, that our son has not suffered and died in vain, that his story may help awaken the sleeping giant of public awareness before it is too late. Time is running out. We are only a few strokes short of midnight.

*Santa Fe Mountain Center, Rte. 4, Box 34-C, Santa Fe, NM 87501

THE FENCE — OR THE AMBULANCE?

"T'was a dangerous cliff," as they freely confessed,
    Though to walk near its crest was so pleasant;
But over its terrible edge there had slipped
    A duke and many a peasant.
So the people said something would have to be done,
    But their projects did not at all tally:
Some said, "Put a fence 'round the edge of the cliff,"
    Some, "An ambulance down in the valley."

But the cry for the ambulance carried the day,
    For it spread to the neighboring city;
A fence may be useful or not, it is true,
    But each heart became brimful of pity
For those who had slipped o'er that dangerous cliff,
    And the dwellers in highway and alley
Gave pounds or gave pence, not to put up a fence,
    But for an ambulance down in the valley.

"For the cliff is fine if you're careful," they said,
    "And if folks even slip or are dropping,
It isn't the slipping that hurts them so much
    As the shock down below — when they're stopping."
So day after day when these mishaps occurred,
    Quick forth would the rescuers sally
To pick up the victims who fell off the cliff
    With their ambulance down in the valley.

Then an old man remarked, "It's a marvel to me
    That people give far more attention
To repairing results than to stopping the cause
    When they'd much better aim at prevention.
Let us stop at its source all this mischief," cried he
    "Come, neighbors and friends, let us rally;
If the cliff we will fence, we might almost dispense
    With the ambulance down in the valley."

"Oh, he's a fanatic," the others rejoined,
    "Dispense with the ambulance? Never!
He'd dispense with all charities, too, if he could;
    No, no! We'll support them forever.
Aren't we picking up folks just as fast as they fall?
    And shall this man dictate to us? Shall he?
Why should people of sense stop to put up a fence
    While their ambulance works in the valley?"

Thus this story so old, has beautifully told
    How our people, with the best of intentions,
Have wasted their years and lavished their tears
    On treatment, with naught for prevention.
But a sensible few, who are practical too,
    Will not bear with such nonsense much longer;
They believe that prevention is better than cure,
    And their party will soon be the stronger.

Encourage them, then, with your purse, voice and pen,
        And (while other philanthropists dally)
They will scorn all pretense, and put up a stout fence
    On the cliff that hangs over the valley.

                              by Joseph Malines

✳

CHAPTER NINE

SLAYING THE DRAGON — A CANCER CURE

I awakened in a cold sweat — with the nightmare fresh in my mind. My body ached with a heavy oppression. I felt an inexplicable sense of fear, a strange foreboding of doom. Once again, as for many nights now, I felt as if I had slept with a load of bricks on my chest. Cold and clammy, I rose to change my damp nightclothes. The specter of the dream still haunted my mind, creeping with a shudder down my spine. I allowed myself to recall being sucked into swampy dark water filled with crabs, their claws clinging to me like blood suckers. The terror of it had awakened me and I now was grateful that it was only a dream.

Calming myself, I looked around my familiar room with relief, wondering what such a horrifying dream could mean. The realization soon came that in the turmoil of Allen's recent passing, I had pushed aside the pronouncement of the Iridologist to me a few months ago: cancer of the lymph. Now I knew. The ever-alert inner Guardian was sending red-light warning signals in vivid pictures, I couldn't ignore it. The ugly crabs and the cold sweat were very real. I would call a doctor in the morning for an exam.

Results of the preliminary tests were positive: malignancy of the lymph system. Lymphoma, the doctor called it. He urged me to have surgery immediately to remove the glands he'd identified under my arms. At the same time he informed me that lymphoma can spread quickly to the lymph glands throughout the body system and that not all of these glands can be removed. Radiation, a recently developed treatment, would be required. It was not encouraging.

Only too clearly now, I saw I had gone off the track. By not being true to my own being, by allowing stress and deep concern for my family over many months to override every other concern, I had neglected my own principles of health and wholeness. This is always dangerous and fruitless, as worry over others only doubles the negative. I was now paying the price for not having practiced the truths I knew. It is by stumbling into the brambles that we realize we have wandered off the path. Vividly, I was once again shown the value of paying attention to our dreams, for the message the Inner Guardian is trying to convey could be life-changing, even life-saving.

I pled with my doctor for time to consider, as I was more than loath to take the dubious, and likely futile attempt at recovery down the medical route which had led my many unsuspecting friends and relatives, who had placed their faith in medicine, to often agonizing, slow deaths. I had learned through repeated observations that cancer cells, once released into the blood by surgery, often spread like wildfire to other parts of the body. Cancer, by its very name, has claw-like extensions as the crab, and it is therefore difficult to remove all its pieces with the knife. I had watched patients, after short and deceiving periods of remission, suddenly and rapidly deteriorate, as the cancer flared up more virulent than ever in other areas of the body. And then there was little hope, and little help.

The use of radiation and chemotherapy were beginning to come into prevalent use, but these often caused greater pain and suffering than the cancer. After prolonged agony, patients usually died anyway. I knew this so well because I had watched sadly the disintegration and loss of no less than fourteen relatives and close friends through those methods during the 1950's and 1960's.

Clearly, I saw that I faced a very serious situation. The

verdict of my own near-certain death came only months after my husband had passed away. I had to get well or my three children would be orphans. Jeannine was only four years old and had just gone through the trauma of losing her beloved Daddy. Jason was in the midst of his increasingly difficult problems, having recently been confined for running away, to which I was wrestling to find solutions. There was not the slightest doubt in my mind that God's loving Presence, so real in my life, would show me the way. I also knew that the human body, with its many miraculous systems, is far more intelligent and resourceful than any of us fully realize. I knew my body could heal itself. But I had to find and give it the help it needed. For it was I, after all, who through overwork and emotional stress, had allowed this illness an entrance.

Every emotion affects the immune system. The glandular system, the guardian angel of the body, is highly affected by the emotions, and in turn influences them. When subjected to chronic stress, the glandular system tightens with tension. If stress is prolonged, this can slow or shut down some of its very important functions. In observing loved ones with cancer, I had discovered an emotional condition common to all of them: Longstanding, chronic anger or resentment turned inward. These individuals were always too nice to speak out against a spouse, or some family member or old situation which was still hurting them. In my case, I saw it was frustration over the prolonged illnesses of Allen and Jason, over which I seemed to have no control to help or change. Some of this was now released, having been taken out of my hands, but the damage had been done in the body.

One night soon after, while I was in prayer and meditation seeking guidance in my need, there flashed into my mind a conversation I'd had a few months previous with a spiritually motivated woman named Margaret Watson. She was the wife of the late "Tick" Watson, a courageous polio-stricken minister-at-large. Margaret and I had been discussing health aids. She had related the tale of a man she knew in Arizona who had a cancerous tumor growing on the left side of his face. She said it had grown large and alarming.

She had seen it hanging on his cheek, the size of a large lemon. The man had refused all surgery and instead had tried another approach. He was well-versed in herbs and their uses, so had collected the sun-dried medicinal herb Chaparral off the hot Arizona desert floor, made tea of this herb and drank several cups of it daily for a number of weeks. Slowly the tumor became smaller, finally disappearing altogether. My friend, Margaret, was very impressed with this, as she had seen this change with her own eyes.

Margaret also related that she had found the juices of raw root vegetables, particularly carrot which contains Vitamin A in the form of Betacarotene, to be marvelous body cleansers and helpful in healing a variety of illnesses. This conversation took place in 1969, long before such things were generally ever heard of.

This memory flashed through my mind like a light beam, and I resolved what I would do. I faced no ordinary adversary. I needed to fight for my life and I could not use halfway measures. I had always known there was life energy in totally raw, fresh vegetables and fruits, the life force called prana in the East. My own father stayed so healthy eating raw vegetables and horseradish, he never saw a doctor until he was seventy-seven years of age. He never went to a dentist nor lost a tooth in his entire life, eating mainly the freshly grown products from our own family garden, especially raw celery and cabbage which he loved. Mama, you may recall, with no other choice in her circumstances, had recovered from tuberculosis with the same natural methods, plus sunshine and intermittent planned rest.

I had learned through my studies that the body cells renew themselves constantly, and that the mind, when applied, can assist in drawing in the proper energy to build new healthy cells. We need to visualize our body's renewal daily, while feeling new life flowing through our body cells, knowing we truly are in charge as the master of our life and the captain of our soul.

I bought a juicer, and for the next two and one-half months made and drank daily two quarts of fresh raw root vegetable juices of carrot and celery, with sometimes radish and parsley juice added. I used mainly organically grown vegetables. Also, because beets are more difficult to juice and not always available, I purchased Biota Brand beet juice bottled in Europe which for bottled juice was surprisingly fresh and rich. Diluting the beet juice with fresh spring water, I alternated drinking this mixture with the carrot and celery juice. In addition, remembering Margaret's story of the man with the tumor, I learned to drink six to eight glasses of Chaparral tea daily (fresh quarts made each day can be kept in the refrigerator). I found the chaparral herb to be an ancient medicinal remedy of certain American Indian groups, and it has since the time I used it become more well-known for its healing qualities.

One has to be really dedicated, for this wonderful cleansing herb (the Chaparral) tastes and smells like creosote — you know, that smelly tar that is used to black-top roads? It does smell like that, and is, in fact, called the creosote bush. But when it's a matter of life and death, who cares about smell or taste? You hold your nose and gulp it down.

One can alternate chaparral with two other blood cleansing herbal teas: red clover and dandelion root, or mix the three together. These latter make much more palatable teas, but the chaparral is by far the most potent and efficient cleanser of toxins in the body and blood. It seems to kill cancer cells, so one should *not* use a substitute if the goal is to get well. In between, pure water with lemon can be taken.

During this cleansing time I ate no solid food whatsoever. I also drank no coffee, no tea, milk or any canned juices or sodas. My entire intake consisted of raw, fresh vegetable juice, the teas, and water (fresh purified spring water is preferred). This strict diet is stressed, for the idea is to give the cancer cells nothing to grow on. The cancer must be starved out, while the immune system is strengthened, and healthy cells renewed with the concentrated minerals and life force in fresh raw vegetables. Potatoes are a root vegetable, but too starchy (the starch feeds the cancer cells). The potassium, however, which potatoes are famous for, will keep one from becoming low in this important mineral. Therefore, I sliced a raw potato, soaked the slices in fresh water overnight, and then in the morning drank just the water, using the potato slices in other ways for the family. This I did twice a week.

During the cleansing period, *keeping the colon and intestinal tract clean daily is imperative.* This can spell the difference between life and death, for when the body begins throwing off the toxins in large quantities into the blood stream, then into the liver and kidneys, and thence into the intestines, autointoxication can set in if the intestinal tract is clogged, and death may ensue. Then the medical establishment will say, "See, that quack natural method killed him or her!" So one needs good daily warm-water enemas for the first few weeks, and/or a professional colon cleanse at a naturopathic clinic. Strange as it may sound, alternative health therapists have recommended diluted warm coffee enemas as being the most cleansing.

I did not speak to anyone of my battle with the devil cancer, other than one very good woman friend, for I did not wish the negative thinking and objections of others to place obstacles in my path. I knew my approach was highly unorthodox at that time, and the few occasions any such nutritional approach was mentioned, it was called quackery. Many doctors went so far as to state that what one ate had no bearing whatsoever on one's health. Just imagine such arrogance. And such ignorance. This was only twenty-five to thirty years ago.

It has been my great joy in the past few years to find a rapidly changing attitude toward this subject, as nutrition and health have come explosively to the forefront in mainstream thinking, especially among the younger generation, who now stress diet in conjunction with aerobics. Something had to change, for too many people were dying, and many began to wonder why. A growing body of the populace has begun to lose faith in the efficacy of foreign chemicals, surgery, medicines and radiation to heal, as in the face of these treatments, too many patients die.

The rate of heart disease and cancer has risen in tandem with the use of powerful preservatives and chemicals in our foods and on our soils beginning in the early 1940's.

Even ten years ago, research scientist Alexander Schauss, in his book, *Diet, Crime and Delinquency* (already named in Chapter 8), told that progressive Norway had, by 1975, outlawed *all* chemical preservatives in its foods; Sweden allowed only seven; Germany — seventy; while America uses over 4,000! Is it any wonder recent statistics state that one in every four citizens will die of cancer?

The frighteningly high incidence of breast cancer in women is of great concern in current times. This year 175,000 American women will battle breast cancer. Statistics show that at the current rate of incidence, one in four American women now living will eventually die of breast cancer. That is 46,000! Yet, in most reports we hear, doctors seem nonplussed. I find it astounding that more is not said in favor of a nutritional approach to prevention of this deadly disease. As far back as 1980 it was found that noncancerous lumpy breast tissue is often relieved by the addition of vitamin E to the diet, as reported in *The Journal of The American Medical Association* (Sept. 5, 1980), in a study conducted by Robert S. London, M.D., director of reproductive endocrinology at Baltimore's Sinai Hospital and faculty member of The Johns Hopkins University School of Medicine. Dr. London prescribed vitamin E over a period of several years to a group of 20 patients. At least two-thirds of the women responded to the treatment, their lumps disappearing, along with the discomfort. He states:

> "Women with at least some types of fibrocystic breast disease are thought to be at a twofold to eightfold greater risk of developing breast cancer. Even those whose lumps remain benign often experience extreme discomfort. Breasts ache and become quite tender."

On the basis of current (1980) findings, Dr. London recommends that physicians try prescribing vitamin E for their patients with cystic breast disease. "It worked in a high percentage of patients and no side effects were noted," he said.

It is encouraging that the National Insitutes of Health

also is now finally conducting a study under the supervision of Dr. Carrie P. Hunter of the Office of Research on Women's Health, working with 48,000 postmenopausal women, ages 50 to 79. The women will be assigned to groups receiving different diets and on-going counseling. Cardiovascular disease, mainly heart disease and stroke, is the leading killer of women in this country. It kills nearly 500,000 women a year.*

The body cannot easily digest preserved food containing alien chemicals, so chemical residues remain in the tissues, sometimes combining to form new toxins, while the overworked organs slowly break down, particularly at any point where there may be a genetic weakness. It is amazing to me that more is not spoken of in this regard.

Also, as we know, many people breathe chemicals in their work place or live near a chemical plant and breathe them at home. This tragedy is now more commonly recognized. The findings of international research on anti-oxidants published in 1992, show the importance of vitamins C, E, and Betacarotene (which is the precursor of vitamin A) as preventatives to major diseases.**

Mama used to say, "Bugs are smarter than people. You never catch one bug in a bag of white processed flour. They won't eat the stuff!" Mama was very wise and way ahead of her time sixty years ago in figuring out such things. She also told me, "Processed white sugar can be poison to the system when eaten too often." We have since found this also to be true.

Habit is very strong and hard to break. Advertising agencies for large companies sold the populace a bill of goods, tantalizing tastebuds with sugared, packaged and processed foods of all lovely descriptions. Companies flourish and grow wealthy, while the people who consume such 'food' die like flies. No, this connection is not easily recognizable, or provable, as the culprits (thousands of additives) are legion and it is all but impossible to pick out this additive or that one, and say "this particular substance causes this particular condition."

How many people stopped to think only a few years

---

* Citizens for Health, P.O.Box 368, Tacoma, WA 98401
** Seattle Times, March, 1993.

ago what is clearly recognized now, that the life-giving live enzymes in foods are killed by cooking, freezing, and processing, leaving dead food which is much more difficult to digest and does not encourage the building of new, live cells? Some colorings and flavorings also, I suspect, would endanger or kill live enzymes on contact.

The Food and Drug Administration (F.D.A.) recommends we take certain amounts (the Regular Daily Allowance, or R.D.A.) of vitamins and minerals. However, that is only part of the story. Vitamins and minerals are essential nutrients, but the body's ability to utilize them depends on enzymes, which are never mentioned.

Our body can be compared to an automobile which is built to run on certain fuels. The proteins, starches and oils are to the body as the gas and oil is to the auto. Vitamins and minerals are the fuel additives normally within the food, which help the body run smoother. But will the car start with only gas and oil, even though filled to the brim? No. It must have the electric spark from the battery. Live enzymes in raw foods provide this electric spark of life energy that help vitamins, minerals and other food substances to be properly utilized by the body processes.

It strikes me as an interesting phenomenon that people will take better care of their auto than of their wonderful body. They wouldn't dream of putting milk in the gas tank and then wonder why the car doesn't run. But, unthinkingly, they will ingest strange chemicals in food, alcohol, and drugs of all descriptions, and then wonder why they are ill, while researchers still search for germs and viruses.

The body was created to run on fresh food from the ground and off the trees of Mother Earth, provided by a loving abundant universe. Evolutionarily speaking, you can say the body is the product of hundreds of thousands of years of adaptation to its environment — the earth — and the food sources provided by the land. This dependency and connectedness of the body to the land is an obvious reality which, strangely, few stop to realize. Different groups living in different regions adapt to the food sources of their region over hundreds of generations. Eskimo bodies are highly adapted to eating raw meat, for instance. But other native groups, who have traditionally eaten primarily grain and vegetable diets, when put into a culture like ours with a diet high in fat, become obese, as their bodies are adapted to conserve any fat or surplus calories they ingest. Most individuals can adjust to some extent to diets of different regions or lifestyles when they move to other locales.

But nothing in our biological history of endless millennia has prepared our bodies to accept and process intelligently the totally foreign substances, synthetic pesticides, colorings, flavorings, preservatives, conditioners, etc. now introduced for the first time into the human diet in the last 50 years. Our bodies are literally in shock.

This miraculous body attempts to adjust and tolerate material that has been devitalized, through canning, cooking, freezing, packaging and storing, and chemically tampered with and adulterated by laboratory scientists and now recently radiated, until there truly is little if any life force left. After a time the body's magnificent storehouse of live enzymes runs low (it was found the body is generally able to manufacture enzymes to approximately the age of thirty). Then if enzymes are not replaced, the immune system and cleansing organs slowly break down as the system strives to work with a flow of foreign debris, largely devoid of adequate life-giving sustenance.

The effects of our artificial diets have become frighteningly obvious throughout society. Why are so many thousands suffering from immune deficiency, and all manner of named diseases?

Back to the battle. All of the above became ever more clear to me as the days passed and I continued to follow the intuitive regimen I had set. Shockingly, the dear friend in whom I had confided, found she also had cancer, a tumor in the colon. So she came to live in my little guest cabin, and we did the raw-fresh-juice-and-medicinal-herb-tea diet together. She was with me six weeks. We took the opportunity to give each other castor oil massages, as caster oil was a highly recommended remedy for many ailments by the seer, Edgar Cayce. This was a blessing for both of us, a time of renewal and mutual support, as we also included prayer and healing visualizations. An individual's mind set is also a very important element of the healing process.

"Be ye transformed by the renewing of your mind." (Romans 12:2)

My weight slowly dropped from 133 pounds down to 109. I continued, even so, to care for my children and to tend all necessary household duties of a one-parent family. I took time to rest often.

Early, in the first two to three weeks of the diet, I experienced days of strange illnesses as toxins began circulating through my bloodstream, preparing to eliminate by pouring out through normal excretions. *It is not uncommon to experience headaches, dizzy spells with blurred vision, bad breath, even nausea and gas pains, during such a cleansing, as the body excretes its poisons.* It is important to remember this when one embarks on a cleansing diet, and not be dismayed or give up. As I stayed on my program, continuing to rest often, these problems cleared, and after about three weeks I began to feel light as a feather.

Two and one-half months after I began the daily juice diet, there passed in my stool a strange bright green lump, as large as a goose egg. This was unusual, because for weeks there had been only the small excretion from juices. This lump was green as grass and had a bad odor. Since my health was my main objective, curiosity overcame me. I found the lump to be smooth as clay. Obviously it was old congested bile from the liver or gall bladder. I deduced that if the liver bile duct had been clogged, the backup would then clog the lymph glands, as the lymph are the purifiers and cleansers. (I had heard one doctor call the lymph system "the body's guardian angel"). As the system becomes clogged and toxins build up, radical cells then can take over, as radical cells grow in a toxic environment.

I had passed the clog!

From that moment I knew I was well. I felt differently, a kind of quiet elation and inner squeaky-clean feeling, with more energy emerging daily through my entire being. My intelligent wonderful body had won the battle! All it needed was a fighting chance.

It has been twenty-three years since that day, and there has been no recurrence of a symptom or slightest need for concern. I have seldom had even a simple cold. There has remained, however, an intense interest in helping others as needs arose.

I have, since that time, found many others who have taken similar paths back to health, some of whom have written books and given lectures to tell their stories. Health stores across the country are filled with such books which can be easily located. A very few will be named below.*

One cure came from fresh grapes, and that meant only grapes, with no other food added, as grapes contain abscisic acid. Cancer cells cannot tolerate this, but healthy cells can. Sloan-Kettering Foundation did a study, discovering and confirming this interesting fact. Wheat grass juice, squeezed from fresh wheat sprouts, also contains abscisic acid. Wheat grass juice has been used extensively as a health drink in healing serious illnesses by Ann Wigmore, Director of the Hippocrates Health Institute in Boston, Massachusets, as well as by others.

One's state of mind is of utmost importance. *Deciding to be well*, to look at and release the stress in life, can spell the difference. Joy, love, and laughter lift the immune system, as there is a need to pick up the threads of a love for life. Dr. Bernie Siegel wrote a wonderful book on this subject: *Love, Medicine, and Miracles,*** relating case histories from his prac-

---

The Gerson Therapy and *Ten Cured Incurables* — The Gerson Institute, P.O. Box 430, Bonita Calif. 92002

Killing Cancer — 1980, The Jason Winters Story, M & R Publishing Co., 732 South Fourth St., Las Vegas, Nev. 89101

How I Conquered Cancer Naturally by Edie Mae with Chris Loeffler Harvest House Publishers, 17895 Sky Park Circle, Irvine, CA 92714

The Grape Cure, by Johanna Brandt, The Gibson Auer Co., 721 Sheridan Ave., Cody, WY

** *Love, Medicine, & Miracles*, by Bernie Siegel, M.D., 1986 Harper-Collins Publishers, 10 E. 53rd St., N.Y. 10022

tice, of patients who had miraculous recoveries when their mind was focused on health and life. This is, in fact, what I did, by treating the whole body.

My diet regimen was very simple, did not cost more than a normal food budget (less in fact) and belied the need for millions of dollars in research monies. I was fortunate indeed to be guided to find out early in the illness so it was cleared more quickly. An early detection is most helpful for a natural cure such as this to work.

More advanced severe cases can also be healed although it may take longer, requiring faith and real perseverance, and a truly sincere desire to recover. Guidance by a naturopathic physician would be helpful, even necessary.

To my joy my lady friend, Val, also recovered. After the cleansing period, to be really safe, she had her tumor removed. Interestingly, by then it was found to be only shrunken white dead tissue, quite different from the red angry tissue first found during biopsy. The cleansing had worked for her as well.

For those interested in this approach, The Association of Cancer Victors and Friends is a good place to seek information. There are now chapters in every state in the U.S. One can find literature and many who will help with support.

It has been widely publicized that the American Cancer Society's decades of research and billions of dollars asked in contributions to find an answer to cancer is the biggest rip-off of the American public since Watergate. Granted, some good has been done, but I actually heard the Northwest Director of the American Cancer Society state emphatically on the radio about four years ago, in answer to the moderator's query regarding a cure. "Oh, we aren't interested in a cure — only in research!"

I could hardly believe my ears! The moderator sounded shocked, too. It was no surprise to me to hear on the news about three months later that this particular director had been arraigned for misappropriation of Cancer Society funds. But oddly, there was never another word about it or a follow-up.

Many in medicine are looking for better ways to health.

One fine group is The World Research Foundation* with headquarters in Sherman Oaks, California. They have held symposiums in recent years entitled "New Directions for Medicine — Focusing on Solutions." It has always been my opinion that we should have a system such as was practiced in China for centuries. The personal physician was paid as long as the patient was kept healthy. When illness struck, payment stopped. That would change the focus of medicine in a hurry.

After my healing I gradually went back to a normal diet of solid food, but I continued to eat mainly fresh vegetables and fruits, both raw and cooked, with some grains and nuts. I then added a variety of vitamin and mineral supplements to help build my system. During the cleansing, as described, one should *not* take vitamin or mineral supplements, for this, too, would feed the cancer. Use these to build the system, after the cleansing. I did not return to the medical doctor for a check, as there was no need. I knew I was well and also felt I would not be believed, but would be told there had been an error, that I probably had not had cancer in the first place. This has happened to others who went through natural therapy. Now to add some seafood seemed to be good for my body. Each person must listen to his/her own body's reaction and find the nutritional program that brings good energy and a happy emotional nature. Allergies are common, and are not easily recognized as the underlying cause when tempers flair and irritations to the actions of others are unwarranted. Some people cannot tolerate wheat or eggs, or soy, or milk, and as stated in a previous chapter, the brain is the first affected. The body system may also be more sensitive after an extended cleansing.

It is well also to read the ingredients on any prepared food one may wish to purchase. The slogan should be "Buyer beware!" Even foods as common as milk can become an allergen through processing, as the homogenization changes

*World Research, 15300 Ventura Blvd., Suite 405, Sherman Oaks, CA 91403. Regional Center: P. O. Box 2818, Sedona, AZ 86336. European Hdqtrs: 1 Kriegerstrasse 17, D-7000, Stutgart 1, Germany.

the molecular structure. (Homogenization makes the calcium in milk less available, and also not as easily digestible.) Other foods may fall into this category, with young people, children especially, being susceptible. The phrase, "he went bananas," could be altered to read "he went peanut butter," or "he went soybeans," depending on the person's allergy and behavioral response. A person may think he/she is allergic to bananas, but it can be the chemical insecticide sprays liberally used on the cargo, which comes, of course, out of foreign countries. These chemicals can penetrate the skin, leaving residue in the banana flesh. This condition is even more dangerous in fruits and vegetables that are eaten skin and all. One help is to soak the fresh fruit and vegetables for ten minutes in a sink full of water, to which two tablespoons of Clorox have been added. Then rinse thoroughly with clear water before refrigerating. This dispels most of any poisonous spray that has been left on the surface. Another safeguard, and a better one, is to purchase only organically raised fruits and vegetables, even though this may be a bit more expensive.

In 1962, upon its publication, I read the book, *Silent Spring*,* written by Rachel Carson. Even at that time in my life, I was horrified at the prospect she drew, warning of the dangers in America's wide use of chemical pesticides, to which few people were paying attention.

After receiving reports from U.S. citizens of the dreadful occurrences of death and illnesses in areas that had received pesticide spray, particularly DDT, Mrs. Carson's conscience would not let her rest until she had thoroughly researched the situation. Four and one-half years later, after reading thousands of technical reports, consulting with hundreds of American and European scientists, investigating a catalog of illnesses, including cancer, and the death of her own mother, she wrote her revealing book.

In a special report to the *Baltimore Sun* on October 11, 1992, H. Patricia Hynes wrote an anniversary commentary to Rachel Carson's *Silent Spring*, and I wish to quote a few excerpts:

Silent Spring, 1962, Houghton-Mifflin, 1 Beacon St.,Boston, MA 02108

Upon the publication of *Silent Spring*, there was a firestorm of protest from the agri-chemical industry. Mrs. Carson was vilified in many monied quarters. However, President John F. Kennedy's Science Advisory Committee corroborated her findings, and the *New York Times* proposed that Rachel Carson receive the Nobel Prize for her work. DDT was eventually suspended in the U.S. in the early 1970's as a consequence of *Silent Spring*.

Thirty years after its publication, *Silent Spring* is regarded as the cornerstone of the modern environmental movement. Yet, while the book has been heard and debated, it has not been heeded. At its most rigorous, the focus of pesticide regulation has been on the individual chemical, not on the model of industrial agriculture.

Thirty years later nearly five times as many pesticides are manufactured for use in U.S. agriculture, forests, and homes, and for export than were in 1962. More than 440 insect species are now resistant to certain insecticides. In 1945, 7 percent of crops were destroyed by insects; in 1990, 13 percent. Out of 129,249 employees in the U.S. Department of Agriculture, *only two are assigned to the development of organic agriculture.*

Nearly 50 million pounds of DDT have been manufactured each year and exported to foreign countries after the chemical was suspended in the U.S. *It is then imported back on fruits and vegetables in what has been labeled a circle of poison.* [my emphasis] *Silent Spring* merits, on its 30th anniversary, a fresh reading to recast its singular contribution and to take up its unfinished business — an ecology centered agriculture. Until then, we have not even achieved a cease-fire in our war on nature.

Feeling so well in those ensuing months, I embarked on an isometric exercise regimen, coupled with certain yoga postures to strengthen and tone my muscles. These exercises can be performed on one's living room or recreation room floor. The expense of a health club is not necessary. When done in rhythm to favorite music, the exercises become a most pleasurable daily practice.

Periodically, the sexual energy rose, tingling through my body as those organs, too, experienced rejuvenation, this being a whole body healing. I found it beneficial to lift this force consciously up through the spinal column, while joyfully visualizing new cell growth renewing my body's youth and vigor. My appearance continued changing to that of a much younger woman with sparkle and bounce; in other words, I was literally given a new life to live. (I recalled the same result for my father in his involuntary fast years ago.)

Interestingly, because my body again became lithe and energetic and a new sparkle brightened my eyes, a few friends teasingly asked, "Who's the new man?" Well, yes, I *was* in love — with life and the beloved God Presence that had shown me the way back from what could have been Death's Door, but was instead, a blessing in disguise.

It was then I remembered the spiritual reading I had received in San Francisco five years previous, when the minister had clearly seen my grandparents in spirit offering to me a Gift of Life in Three Parts, a gift that was sparkling with life-energy and which they said was from God. With awe and humble gratitude, I now realized these to be,

First: the birth of my baby, Jeannine, the year after the reading. As I was forty, she squeaked in under the wire;

Second: Allen's being brought back from his Near-Death-Experience two years later — to receive two more years of life with us;

Third: my healing from cancer — my gift into new life.

One morning, while giving thanks for these gifts and God's answers, this poem came through, as a prayer from me, rather than a message from Him, as I meditated on love.

LOVE

L ord
O f
V ast
E ternity -

L ift
O ut
V anished
E nemies

L ingering
O n
V arious
E extremities,

L ike
O ld
V eils
E ntangling me.

L et
O versoul's
V ibrant
E nergy

L ight my
O ngoing
V ision -
E ternally

That I may through
L ove — more truly be — the
O ne perfect individuality, tho
V eiled in earth — You did
E nvision me.

Bonnie Ann Gilchrist

*
THE JOY OF MUSIC

I am humming a tune — and words start to flow through my mind. I run to the piano, and a new song gives birth to itself. The melody is the story behind the words, and it brings flickers of remembrance — a lifetime I only partially glimpse as in the mists of a dream.

The song comes now during this extraordinary period of grace in my life, this upswing in health that is not only of body but is a renewal of my spirit. My inner vision is intensified and expanded through a new exultation that is bringing vistas I've never before glimpsed. I find a new thrill in composing songs and poetry, perhaps more for myself than for anyone else. It seems that in giving birth to something brand new in the world, we become a channel for the Life that continually wishes to express more of Itself. And in being that channel — we are blessed.

Also there comes to me again the positive realization that I feel the reality of the continuum of my Being, through the many days of many lives. Shadows of memories reach through the Veil of Forgetfulness to help me into a conscious knowledge of wholeness, of completion. Even though we know this lifetime to be full of many happenings, sorrows and joys, loves and losses, successes and mistakes, all of this together is truly only one piece of our whole Self, each life- time is like one small piece of a whole and perfect picture puzzle. The reality of our True Being will one day be as the very colorful and finished panorama, no longer a puzzle, but the completed story of a soul — Ourself. And looking back we wouldn't have missed any of the parts for all the tea in China.

And so, my rejuvenation brought more than bodily health. It brought the gift of the creative spirit that sang joyfully from within, and with it a certain new light to my days and peace to my nights, the new life we so often yearn for, but so seldom achieve. In that sense, the dreaded Cancer was a friend, for in the light of God's Love *it helped me to find the path to the creative source within, that Source from which flows the Life*

Force, that can then be directed and activated by mind. We truly must KNOW that in His Love — all things — Yes! ALL THINGS — can be turned to good!

> At what point in time do our tears turn to joy?
> When the light of new knowledge — old concepts
>   destroy.
> We find a new freedom — a freedom to be
> Open and loving — a total "Care — Free!"

One day while listening to especially inspiring music during meditation a unique vision swept me up and away . . . and I tried to capture its beauty.

THE ORCHESTRA!

Quietly I sit with Thee — to meditate,
        my soul set free. And then:
Clear blue sky — white bird I see,
I Am The Bird! Sailing free . . .
Earth and sky somehow are One —
        Blended by the gold of setting sun.

Wings that glint — turn and glide . . .
It feels so good to swoop and dive,
Then rise again, effortlessly,
        On the wings of melody.

Whence comes the song that seems to be
So beautifully a part of me?

(Continued)

Far below . . . what is that I see?
Rainbow bright! — streams of Light!
Like a rising, falling, waterfall . . .
Down I glide . . . I must go see
What can this beauty be?
An Orchestra! Alive and free — Like me!

The instruments . . . oh glory be . . .
      Each one a personality,
Dancing, playing, glad to be
      Expressing life, joyously !

Marimba rings — bell-like tones,
Flutes sing clear, like crystal stones
      In pinks and greens. . . .
Deep blue — moan the Saxophones.

Violins slim, with bows poised high
      Toss their notes into the sky . . .
Gay colors, like confetti fly . . .
      Trailing streamers,
While Woodwinds sigh . . .

Big fat Cello — jolly fellow!
His "boom-boom" voice so mellow
Forming shades of purple, mauve and wine,
Fat round notes that shine,
      Marching out in timely line.

The Clarinet! — a slim Jack-Sprat . . .
Oh that I could make notes like that.
How the colors rise and fall —
      A rainbow-painted waterfall . . . Of Light!
Dancing shimmering sparks so bright
Like fireflies — sparkling in the night.
I float upon the melody . . .

(Continued)

I let it lift and carry me
Into a realm of ecstasy
Where Light and Color and Sound and Joy
Mingle and blend — old forms destroy.

Then who can know — who can see . . .
Which is the Orchestra —
And which is Me?

Bonnie Ann Gilchrist

＊

VISIONS OF ADRIAN

During this year of heightened awareness, periods of brilliant visions came to me as my soul answered my conscious mind's persistent question. "Why this strange and impelling attraction I feel for this young pianist who is yet a lad?"

As the years passed I seldom saw my young pianist friend, Adrian, as he lived in another state, but we kept close touch. He now was twenty years old and became engaged to be married to a girl of nineteen. Instantly I felt an inner animosity toward her, for I believed that I knew she would not be good for him. I strongly felt she would lead him down a path away from his music; this, despite the fact that I had not yet met her.

My feelings were so overwhelming that I said to myself, "This is crazy! These young people have a right to their lives! What business is it of yours anyway?" Even talking to myself like a Dutch Uncle did not seem to help. I continued to be troubled with a feeling of foreboding, that Adrian was being blinded by this girl and his career threatened, for I had taken a genuine interest in his very promising musical career. Ernestly I prayed that my unasked for and unwanted feelings be extricated so I could give my blessing to my friend on his marriage.

My subconscious Guardian again came to my rescue, bringing an explanation to my misplaced possessive love. One evening while I drifted in the state between waking and sleeping, I suddenly found myself in a century or more past, in Europe, though I did not try to distinguish the country. It may have been Austria:

I clearly experienced myself to be a large, rather plain woman of middle age. In a fit of intense anger, I saw *myself slamming the piano lid down over the hands of my son, screaming, "Go then! Marry her! And don't ever come back!" I seemed to* know clearly, *as a poor widowed mother of this one son, that I had sweated and slaved long years as a cleaning woman and seamstress to provide not only the necessities, but also the expensive music lessons needed for my boy, who was nothing short of a genius at the keyboard. He was well on his way — until he fell in love. And now he planned to run away with the girl, deserting his promising career,* totally mindless of the sacrifices I had made to provide for it and our dreams for his future.

I also knew, with shock, that the piano lid, in the strength with which my anger had slammed it down, broke his hands — and his career was settled. He could not ever play again, even if he had wanted to. My grief was long and intense. For he then left with her, leaving me totally alone, with the shame of what I had done staying with me to my life's end.

All this flashed through my mind with great clarity in only moments, and then I came back to the present, still feeling the very real hot flush of shame washing over my body. In putting the pieces of memory where they belonged, I was able to see why my soul had cried in deepest joy that amazing day six years before, when I first heard his beautiful music in the hall at summer camp. Involuntary tears had streamed down my face, tears I could not quench.

"He is playing again! Thank God he is playing again!" I gave thanks for God's grace that gives us a second chance, a chance to make amends, when understanding comes to us.

The girl whom Adrian now planned to marry was perhaps, or perhaps not, the same soul as the girl in the former incarnation, who had taken his mind and his heart from his music. But I saw that Adrian's current marriage plans had triggered in me the old fear, still lurking darkly in the dungeon of my subconscious, which I now was able to face and dispel, through understanding.

Adrian did marry, repeating the pattern again in this life, but the marriage did not last. They were divorced, and Adrian returned, this time, to his music. We all make our own choices – and rectifications if need be – sometimes two or three times over. No other person, even parents, can make our choices for us, or take them from us.

Soon after, another vision concerning Adrian came in brilliant color. I have learned that visions always come to me in color, unlike the wispy, smokey grey images of normal dreams which usually disappear instantly upon waking; one can barely recall such dreams moments later. Visions of traumatic past-life experiences, on the other hand, stay imprinted in the mind for many years (as I have shown).

I am in a state of reverie, and I suddenly find myself, a girl of 20, in a lovely home in Southern France. I am sharply aware of my gown which rustles as I walk. It is rich, of a sumptuous elegant satin, a soft shimmering golden green, like the feathers of a hummingbird. Wide, stiff skirt panels stand out on either side at my waist, as is the style. The cut of the dress is low, exposing a great deal of my bosom, and the sleeves are loosely puffed. (All this I know in a flash.) The rich setting feels quite natural. It is my home.

I am walking around an inner courtyard. In the center of the courtyard directly in front of me is a graceful kidney-shaped, garden pool. The tile is colorful and its edge raised. This pool is shallow, not for swimming. I see delicate, pink lilies floating on the glassy surface of the water. Small statues adorn the parameter of the pool. Despite the lovely setting, I am deeply distressed, pacing in consternation. I wring my lace handkerchief in my hands as I look across the pool towards my mother, standing on its opposite side. We are discussing my brother, Robert (pronounced in my mind, 'Ro-bair'), whose absence has us both terribly worried. My father has died earlier leaving Robert as head of the household. But Robert had gone off on horseback some three months before to attend to business, saying he would return in a fortnight. Now he is more than two months overdue. He should have returned two months ago!

I feel my fear growing. What could have happened? Where can he be? I cry to my mother. Suddenly, I see Robert appear before me in spirit form — dressed in his riding habit and reaching out his hands and crying, "Sister! I cannot come back! My horse stumbled and I was thrown into a stream, hitting my head on a rock and drowned." Then he fades from sight.

In amazement I step quickly backward, and then I am falling — a great distance. I re-enter my current body with a shocking jolt and awake abruptly. My scalp prickles as every hair on my head seems to stand on end. Instantly I know the soul, Robert, my brother, is now this young pianist, Adrian, to whom I have such an unusual attachment.

An interesting point in the story is that several months later, in quiet conversation, Adrian happened to mention that he had a great fear of drowning. So he wondered if he had drowned at some previous time. I had not before, told him of my vision, but I did then. He exclaimed to me with excitement, "I feel that is true!"

And thus I saw I had been both mother and sister to him, and perhaps more in other lifetimes. But these two visions served to satisfy my longing to know, "Why this intense and loving attraction?"

Physical age has no bearing when souls meet who are of the same Cosmic Family and have gone around the Universe together, for who knows how many lifetimes. In such instances, sex is not the motivating factor. There are marriages of young men to older women and vice-versa, that until lately, many people have looked askance on. They simply do not understand. Such a soul relationship is naturally, not always the condition in such marriages, but if there is a deep, lasting (often instant) attraction, and/or a feeling of *deja vu*, past incarnation ties can well be the reason. These individuals likely have been together before and have something to work through — always for the good

— as it is for the growth and consciousness of the soul that these relationships are needed. Thus, they are reunited, if only for a short time. And, even though such alliances may appear to produce disagreeable results or events, or even lead to what is humanly called a tragic outcome, still the relationship is for soul growth.

These ideas are fairly common, even well-known, these days. Many therapists and healers have written books on their findings, full of case histories. However, until a person has some sort of personal experience in this area, he cannot really know for himself the truth of these words. Thus, I know — I do not just believe.

Everything in life, our relationships, challenges, successes and failures are for our soul growth. We absorb the lessons — sometimes through pain, but also through joy — provided for us by a loving God and a Universal Plan. No matter how challenging, our experiences are all ultimately a privilege and a blessing.

How harsh it is to have any other belief. One lifetime cannot possibly give a soul all the wisdom it needs to return to the Godhead. If that one lifetime is flubbed (i.e. used for personal gain and power over others, even murder), what horror that one faces on his deathbed! We see this on the faces of some people who die with great terror in their last moments, not knowing a God of pure love, who gives a second, third, fourth chance, indeed infinite opportunities for us to grow in grace and wisdom. We can shorten this long and sometimes bumpy span of earth experience by awakening to Reality.

Christ, ever with us and ever available, has the power to wash clean a soul of its transgressions and give new life to us, but only if our effort and repentance have proven it is time. Only the Spirit within us can know this — no outside person can know. This spiritual cleansing does happen, and this is what gives true meaning to the powerful prayer meetings held by devout and sincere leaders around the world.

Some masters, those who have conquered all earthly ties, are able with godly insight to see a soul's karma, and to know if it is time to give guidance and help in this cleansing.

OVER AN ANGEL'S SHOULDER

The many who seek a guru go to such souls attempting to be free of the sticky ties of this earth. We are all like swooning bees, tantalized by the subtle sweet scent of false pleasures offered by this three dimensional world. But now we find ourselves stuck to the flypaper of earthly desires. The harder we struggle to make it by earth standards, the tighter we are held.

The fairytales in many instances embody true metaphysical teachings. One shining example is the tale of Pinnochio, who was enticed by the Candyman on his way to school, telling him of a "land where all was a party with good things to eat and drink, lots of fun, with no work." We all know what happened to Pinnochio on his journey to "becoming a Real Boy," including finding himself in prison, with changed facial features.

The answer lies in letting go — letting go of intense earthly ambition for money, power, fame and notoriety, gluttonous desires for food and drink, beyond what is needed for bodily health, and even letting go of the need for love from others, particularly lustful sexual appetites. When we turn to and live in God's Love, our true needs are filled with abundance, in His right time and in a sacred way.

Rather than being consumed with needs and desires, we must, instead, give and serve the true needs of others. God is in *all* creatures, man and animal. When we give with wisdom, we are careful to give in such a way that does not deprive another of his or her need to stand alone, to grow in strength of body and soul. In right giving, *our* real needs are in right time met, fulfilling all that we have first released. Then we are surprised with the overflowing of gifts from the Universal Storehouse. The bread on the water returns — a hundred-fold!

A VISION OF HAWAII PAST

Hawaii! For many years this single word has conjured up visions of soft balmy breezes whispering through waving palm trees, paradise beaches and carefree happiness, for every one who heard it spoken. And I was no exception. All my life I had yearned to go to the Hawaiian Islands. But my wish never came true, even in travels with my Army Officer husband. Now, in celebration of my new-found exuberant health and joy in life, my dream was fulfilled with some lovely trips to the Islands.

As I write, I look out over the beautiful blue-blue water of the Pacific Ocean, rippled faintly with shades of pink and lavender from the hidden coral reefs which surround these Islands. Whitecaps dance on gentle rhythmic waves, and colored sails of small boats float lazily past on this clear spring day. The green expanse of the park at Ft. DeRussey on Oahu spreads out below my balcony, with dozens of white doves floating like lazy paper airplanes among the palm and banyan trees. This is a small piece of Paradise in an otherwise hectic world. I am blessed to enjoy these vacation days.

It is a dream come true, for even as a small child I thrilled inside, not knowing why, when I saw pictures of the South Seas in magazines. I cut out the palm trees and hung them on the wall in our old farmhouse in Illinois. It was not until many years later, widowed at the age of forty-four, that my first opportunity came to visit the soft, warm tropics I had yearned for all of my life.

One day a vision visited me that helped to explain this joyful feeling of being home once again. Lying on the sand in a meditative state, I became immersed in the soft breezes, blue water and waving palms. It was evening, and I was not asleep — only totally relaxed.

As my mind opens, I feel and see myself to be a strong brown-skinned young man standing in the prow of a war canoe. There are others seated behind me, paddling swiftly, mightily. I am very excited; I feel power rushing in my veins — for we are approaching an enemy. The water and sky are a bright blue, the canoe long, large and sturdy. All this I see in a flash, as I stand in the prow of my canoe at the forefront of a number of other canoes, for I am a leader. I am the son of the Chief of our tribe.

Suddenly, a sharp blow to my chest! A spear! Intense shock, blackness all around.

And then, I am back in the here and now, under the blue sky, this centuries-old scene etched vividly in my mind after who knows how many years and lifetimes. The vision had been of short duration, but I knew I had experienced a traumatic moment of a past life when I was abruptly removed from the world I loved, as a healthy young man in the prime of life. This would help explain my yearning to return.

I know I have lived several incarnations in these beautiful South Seas Islands, but this particular lifetime carried a deep trauma at its conclusion. Such moments create an indelible mark on the memory, which are held in the *astral seed atom* that is carried within the soul from lifetime to lifetime. Memories of such lives are more apt to be brought forth out of the mists of the past to the conscious mind when we seek answers, when we ask ourselves "Why?" I had for years wondered "Why do I love the Islands I have never seen? Why do I yearn to go there with a desire that is far deeper than the simple urge to travel ever could be? Why do I feel I want to live there and leave all this behind?" In response, my subconscious had answered me from its' storehouse of memory in the only way it can — with pictures in the mind, so vivid one feels the emotional (not physical) pain and the excitement. The hair stands on end, the flesh prickles, and the vision never fades. This is all quite different from common dreams which, as stated, within moments of waking, dissolve completely.

Thus, to satisfy my yearning, I have returned to one Hawaiian Island or another whenever possible, and I am blessed each time. For I am sure that the water is the same blue, the sand holds the same golden warm crunch beneath the feet, and that the air caresses one's cheeks with the same balmy fluid strokes and lovingly ruffles the hair, whatever island in the South Pacific one may visit, from Tahiti to Pango Pango, and whether in 1590, 1790 or 1990.

Many people, feeling the attraction, have discovered these island paradises on earth. Sad to say, the quiet serenity, and even the clear skies, are changing with the encroachment of modern civilization. A balance must somehow be found so that many may enjoy, but not despoil these glorious places.

Thankfully, an awareness is finally beginning to grow that there is pain on the planet. The increasing severity of storms and extremes of weather and climate shifts, the huge number of species extinctions, the desecration of huge areas of land and some ocean regions, and perhaps even the warming global temperatures and holes in the ozone layer, are all painful symptoms which indicate disease in the earth system, disease caused by human destruction, pollution, and general desecration of the global environment.

Extreme discomfort, a form of pain, was the alarm-system my body used to alert my conscious mind (in charge of the body) to the presence of radical cancer cells – a danger on the threshold – and the need to take *i*mmediate remedial measures.

"As above – so below." Our nurturing mother-planet is now in pain, as well, and the pain has the same purpose: it is an alert. Pain is a signal the physical body gives. Storms, floods, droughts, and species die-offs are a pain alarm the planet is giving. Extremely severe hurricanes and floods are becoming far more frequent and intensely damaging, worldwide.

By eliminating foreign toxic foods and stressful thoughts from my body, cleansing with nature's own fresh foods, and consciously eliminating stress, I allowed my body to heal itself. All the expressions of life, the human body and the earth as a whole, are directed by intelligent Life Energy, which is self-perpetuating, self-harmonizing, and self-healing if not subjected to ignorant interference. Healing of the planet can take place using this same principle as the healing of an individual body, by allowing the intrinsic wholeness, health and beauty, and the order of its natural system, to restore itself by the specific elimination of toxic pollution.

As with my fight against cancer, half-way measures will not attain the goal. What is needed is an all-out dedication from an enlightened and concerned populous. My stake in my effort to heal my body was my life on this earth. Is not our stake in Mother Earth's health the same?

※

CHAPTER TEN

THE WONDER OF
CREATIVE HEALING

I stand in amazement at the body's ability to heal its
dis-ease when given a minimum of help. The year is 1974
and I've been introduced to a wondrous therapy which has
proven itself in my own body.

I met Don Arnold at the Washington C.F.O. camp on
Lake Chelan in 1972. We had kept up a lively correspondence since that time, exchanging ideas on the topic of our
growing mutual interest — healing. Don soon became involved in a year-long course of study in Southern California
at the Creative Healing Headquarters in Lake Elsinore. I was
intrigued with this unique therapy he was learning, and so I
invited him to come to Seattle upon his graduation from the
course, as he was now prepared to practice this amazing
therapy and was looking for a location to begin. The term
Creative Healing is comprehensive, referring to a spectrum
of techniques, but its premise and purpose is *to create a
condition within the body that will allow it to heal itself.*

During these recent years of Jason's confinement, I
had set out on an intensive search for answers (and causes),
looking for means of healing by natural methods, that is,
without the use of drugs or surgery. I took classes whenever
possible, gaining considerable knowledge through a variety
of excellent courses which prepared me to practice thera-

peutic massage, to understand and treat the body's magnetic energy field, and to work with body meridians in polarity therapy. I also undertook additional study in the use of herbs and certain foods as medicines, in this way incorporating the holistic approach, (having proven the efficacy of this in successfully healing myself of the dreaded cancer). Also, there was the continued advantage of attending lectures sponsored by The Well Mind Association, which featured eminent doctors from the entire North American continent presenting their latest findings in health science research. I also continued studying the powerful influence of the mind on the body's health or dis-ease.

This subject of health, in its many dimensions, has recently exploded into mass consciousness. I was in the forefront of this avant garde movement twenty-three years ago, and often, when speaking of these ideas, was called a "health nut" and scornfully ridiculed by the three-squares-a-day-meat-and-potato people. How strange it is that new ideas or new approaches that challenge old habits are so difficult for the majority to accept. Many people will fight to the last ditch to defend their ingrained habits, even though they may have been given a death sentence by their doctor. A few outstanding adventurous souls chose through these years to open the windows and doors of their minds to new ideas, refusing to accept such sentencing. As a result, many individuals reversed their desperate situations, and not only returned to complete health, but went on to become best-selling authors and teachers, thus assisting others who needed help and would listen. Such writers include Jason Winters, Ann Wigmore of the Hippocrates Health Institute, Edie Maye, Max Gerson, Gaylord Hauser, and Dr. Paavo Airola. There are literally scores of others, including numerous physicians practicing alternative medicine, whose books are now available in all health stores and most standard bookstores.

With these undergirdings of personal experience and formal study, giving me a broad base of understanding from which to draw, the concept taught by Creative Healing fit like a glove. It seemed to be the next logical step.

Creative Healers have one common desire — to help

alleviate human suffering. But one of the rules we were asked to always adhere to was never to solicit in any way. Those in need of help must *ask* of their own accord. For when a person asks to be shown a new approach to health, it indicates that his or her mind is open and ready for healing.

My friend Don arrived and settled in our small suburb nearby. It was a joy to see him and to share our mutual interest. As Don described the background of the amazing man who had brought the Creative Healing approach to America from his birthplace in Wylam on Tyhne, England, I became more and more intrigued.

Joseph B. Stephenson was born in 1874, a seventh child, and a man centuries ahead of his time, as some few are. Stephenson had the marvelous ability to see clairvoyantly into a body to observe where blood arteries and veins flowed, and where nerve channels extended, connecting nerve centers to specific organs. Mr. Stephenson was a sensitive, a healer/medium of the finest order. With his special sight, Joseph Stephenson could locate energy blocks that caused organs to malfunction, and he was guided to know exactly what to do to release the blockages, using *specific* massage techniques and mental imaging. His story is fascinating. I will only touch on it briefly.

As a young boy in England, Stephenson healed his uncle of a kidney ailment through his particular vision and hands-on massage. He later came to the United States, settling in Pennsylvania with a family named Hunt. The young son in that family, John Hunt, was especially intrigued, and closely observed Joseph Stephenson in his work. Mr. Stephenson continued to practice in Pennsylvania for several years. Later he felt a calling to go to Long Beach, California, where he had a very successful practice until his death in his mid-80's. During those years he also lectured at Long Beach College, attempting to enlighten the medical students.

In 1929, during the early years of Stephenson's work in Pennsylvania, the medical establishment, as often happens, had him arrested for practicing medicine without a license. Stephenson's frustrations poured out on paper in the late night hours. As recorded in *The Stephenson Story*, he wrote,

"It is against the law to heal the sick, to make a cripple walk, to restore a dying child to its mother if I use my hands and a little olive oil. Common sense tells us that medicine cannot reach all the ailments that cause physical suffering. Everyone who comes to me comes as a last hope, they have tried everything. So if healing the sick is against the law, I am guilty and proud of it. Let the law take its course. I will not ask for mercy."

The battle had not been his alone. Over a hundred people signed a petition in 1934 to Gifford Pinchot, then Governor of Pennsylvania, which read:

WE THE UNDERSIGNED DO HEREBY PROTEST AGAINST THE LAW THAT INTERFERES WITH THE HEALING OF THE SICK BY MR. JOSEPH STEPHENSON.

Many personal letters begged that something be done to allow Stephenson to continue his work. Even so, for six months a sign on his door told the public that he was under oath not to heal.

At the time of his arrest, he healed the Sergeant who brought him in of a long-standing ailment. Later, in the courtroom during the proceedings on his case, Joseph Stephenson spoke up to the presiding judge.

"Excuse me, Your Honor, but if you will do [such and such] you can then remove that steel plate from your hip."

The astonished judge, wearing a heavy black robe and seated behind his enormous bench with only his upper body visible, dismissed the case on the spot (for he did have a steel plate in his hip), and Joseph Stephenson went back to his therapy.

He became well-known for his work in that area of Pennsylvania. For many years ensuing the police department there called upon him for assistance at particular times to help accident victims, as he was able from a distance to stem blood flow in an individual for perhaps an hour, until the injured person could be transported to a hospital. This was in the days before aid vehicles with sophisticated medical equipment were on the road.

Meanwhile, John Hunt came of age and enlisted in the U.S. Navy at the outbreak of W.W.II. While in the service

John frequently contacted his wise friend, Mr. Stephenson, just to keep in touch. At the conclusion of his Navy tour, John moved to Long Beach, California, where he fulfilled his desire to become fully tutored in Creative Healing by Mr. Stephenson, who had in the interim moved to that area and who wanted John to further the work and teach others. Young John Hunt worked beside Stephenson, studying and mastering his massage technique, as well as acquiring knowledge of the inner body systems that Joseph Stephenson saw and taught him.

John eventually teamed up with Hildreth Coulter, his star pupil, and together they founded the Creative Healing Headquarters in Southern California, which has served to teach hundreds of eager therapists, as well as several hundred doctors and nurses, through the past thirty years. They have, as well, healed many of the ill, nation-wide, for whom doctors had found no cure.

My friend Don was enthused and eager to work, as he had seen some remarkable case results during the year he studied at the headquarters. But he needed new territory in which to begin, and so upon my invitation, he came to the Northwest. I liked and respected this handsome quiet man who belonged to the Masonic Order, and who had similar idealistic goals as myself. In the days that followed his arrival we enjoyed exhilarating philosophical conversations and humorous exchanges of viewpoints. I was impressed with Don's gentle manner, his sweet spirit and caring for the ills of men, and his deep love for God. He seemed closer to having a lack of personal ego than anyone I had ever known, wanting only to be of service to suffering humanity. Don raised three children in his marriage, but had experienced tragedy when his only little girl was struck by an auto at the age of six, causing her to develop severe epilepsy. To his dismay, he then saw the damage the indiscriminate use of drugs had done to her persona and psyche during the years of her later commitment to a sanitarium, halting her personality growth. He then believed, as I did, that there were better treatments for many illnesses. We only need to find them. I agreed to help in any way I could to further the work of Creative Healing by providing a place to serve.

Oddly enough, despite earlier healing and wondrous changes, I had in recent months developed an intermittent pain in the right side of my abdomen. It was sharp, but came and went at odd times. Eager to display his new knowledge, Don offered the Creative Healing Abdominal Treatment to me, a most gentle massage, that requires light but steady strokes in a specific pattern, using only olive oil as a lubricant. Mr. Stephenson taught different massage patterns for each and every condition or area of the body that is affected.

I found this massage to be the most relaxing I had ever experienced. Generally, the client falls asleep during a Creative Healing treatment. In the ongoing months of our work together, we found this happening invariably, but the clients would then awaken and feel as refreshed as from a full night's sleep. I was no exception, as my body relaxed, responding to this gentle, yet powerful, imperceptible energy.

Forty-five minutes to an hour after Don began treatment, I awakened, totally rested, wondering what he had done, for I felt quite well. However, that evening an odd, very thick, dark brown, smooth-as-clay-like substance began to issue from my vagina, requiring a sanitary pad. This emission continued slowly for three days and nights during which time I felt wonderfully well, with no return of my pain.

In the ensuing weeks a steady flow of patient-clientele found our little clinic by word of mouth, because Creative Healing, as practiced on a small scale by Don, and taught to me, was most successful. People who had given up on the medical (or the medical had given up on them) or who had run out of money, found our door as they had no other hope. We saw some desperate cases and made no monetary charge. It was very safe, being a most gentle treatment, with no body adjustments as in chiropractic practice.

After practicing for some months we found that, while treating, our hands became 'charged' in an otherwise inexplicable way with healing energy, that remarkable life-giving force that flows from God through all of life and can be directed by mind. The patient would often comment on the delightful feeling he or she experienced, saying, "Your hands are so warm and wonderful."

In my ministerial capacity, we always began with an interview, offering any needed counseling before accepting anyone as a client, for we had found it was most necessary for each person to understand and accept personal responsibility for his or her own condition and state of health before any real and lasting healing can occur:

"What is your diet — drinking, smoking, etc? What stress are you experiencing, aside from health worries (i.e., Who is upsetting you)? Do you have work-related tension? Are you carrying old resentments, or guilt, or anger?" All these areas and more we gently probed. Often long-buried feelings were brought to light, pointing out their important bearing on physical health. We made it clear that we, as Creative Healers, were only facilitators.

"We may point the way and help you and your body to heal through the God-power within. Together we must work to create the conditions for healing. We do not wave a magic wand. Just as medical doctors' magic pills can't change conditions that will bring a lasting healing, but only bring a temporary relief through masking the pain, or repressing the symptoms. The true seeker of health needs to find and root out the cause behind the illness, or dis-ease, before our combined efforts can be lasting. In this way we are partners on the crusade back to wellness."

Many desperate folks, who saw and were willing to change old, damaging habit patterns, to release emotional hang-ups, making ready the path for Creative Healing energies to heal, were helped to new life and went on their merry way. Space here does not allow to describe more than a couple of the recoveries we saw, some had been long-standing for many years before they found Creative Healing.

One such case was a young woman named Sally who had heard of us and came in a kind of last hope. She had been under doctors' treatments for seven years for an open, draining abscess on her lower spine. Long ago it had become impossible for her to sit down. When she went out in the auto with her husband, she had to lie down in the backseat. She was in her mid-30's and life was quite miserable, she said. She was required to go in to her medical doctor's office regularly to have the abscess drained, and usually, after scraping and cleaning, a small drain pipe was placed in the open wound under the bandage. We had never seen a case like this, but Don, with his experienced hands, found that her lower spine at the coccyx was off-center by one-quarter inch. He worked during several bi-weekly massage sessions to correct this. My part was to discuss her diet. We eliminated all foods such as meats, coffee, citrus fruits, sugar etc. that create an acidic reaction. This drainage fluid was very acidic and caused a hot and burning feeling in Sally's spinal area. We also suggested healing herbal teas in her diet, and as many fresh green and yellow vegetables as she wished. Sally was one of the most co-operative, willing and eager patients we had.

Within three weeks the draining ceased, and in six weeks the wound was almost completely healed. Sally was ecstatic! She could sit again, and go to movies, concerts and games with her husband. She remained on her diet, as she had observed other benefits such as weight loss and more energy, as well. She enthusiastically told a number of ill friends about our work, some of whom then came to us.

Sometimes the treatments were very simple, in helping a shoulder joint to slip more correctly into place, when the client came complaining they could not raise their arm above elbow height, for instance, or others had a constant, nagging ache in the arm. They were always amazed at the almost instant results.

Some of the most gratifying times were experienced when imminent heart attacks were avoided by using the specific heart-treatment Stephenson had taught. One such time I recall was the following year of 1975 when Don and I attended another C.F.O. camp meeting in Washington State. A beautiful black lady was there, whom we happened to engage in conversation. She told us she was a missionary, and that she planned to leave for a mission in Africa soon, but she was very worried, as she had a heart condition which caused her to have shortness of breath, and she had already experienced one heart attack. She had put off surgery, being afraid of the outcome. Don offered to give her the Creative Healing heart treatment to see if it would help. (This is very gentle, and can never hurt.) She was most willing, being a person who preferred natural methods. That evening we found a suitable, comfortable private room. The heart treatment as taught by Stephenson and applied by Don, with my presence in prayer-support, was totally successful. We heard a distinct gurgle as the clogged passage was cleared. Our lady, whose name I do not recall, took a very deep, expansive breath for the first time in many months, and with tears in her eyes, exclaimed, "A weight has been removed from my chest! I can breathe again!" We heard from her in a follow-up letter weeks later. She was on her way to Africa and felt just fine.

Some healings that I helped to facilitate during those years were not always at home in our little clinic. While I was on a trip through California, the heart treatment was successfully applied to my niece's husband, Bob Castner. I had stopped for a visit and found my niece very worried about him. Bob had been visiting the local hospital, where very high blood pressure was diagnosed. Also, he suffered apnea, a breathing difficulty while sleeping. Bob is a favorite of mine, a fine young man interested in spiritual growth. Toward the end of the treatment, Bob gave a gasp and exclaimed, "That felt like a lightening bolt going through my chest!" He felt much better the following morning, and in keeping his hospital appointment the next day, was told the attendants were surprised that his blood pressure was now normal. Suffice it to say I considered the heart treatment another fine success.

In stopping on a trip to visit a lady friend named Estelle, I was shocked to find her to be pale and wan, looking quite ill. She confided that her menstrual had not ceased in the usual five days, but continued to flow, with continued loss of blood for over eight weeks. No medical efforts to stop it thus far had been successful. Her face was a frightening dead-white. I immediately offered an abdominal Creative Healing treatment that evening, during which time she fell sound asleep. In the morning Estelle greeted us with the joyful news that the bleeding had stopped. For the first time in over six weeks she felt strength returning, and her face was returning to a normal pink color. We were very gratified, and this alone was our reward.

We could not work with others, however, who were not willing or able to change ingrained destructive habits, or negative conditions in their life, or who had minds set in cement (as Mama used to say). A few were simply too ill to reverse the process, or perhaps, as we found, had the will to die buried in their subconscious and sometimes even admitted that. These could not be helped, and one can then only bless them and let go and let God.

During these early months, in the course of discussions with women clients, I sometimes had revelations about my own health history. One lady in particular told me of having had surgery for cysts on her ovaries. My ears perked up as I recalled the pain I had experienced in my right abdomen and the dark brown thick emission that had flowed after receiving the abdominal Creative Healing treatment under Don's experienced hands.

She continued, "My doctor showed them to me after removal . . . three large, brown clay-like lumps the size of hen eggs," she said.

"Dark brown?" I queried.

"Yes, they are even called chocolate cysts and can form after surgery near scar tissue."

I was amazed and thrilled, for I remembered again that I had, years before at age thirty, suffered a tubal pregnancy and had surgery on my right side, removing the tube!* Apparently there had been enough trauma to the area to create the formation of cysts that had grown slowly through the next fifteen years, and large enough to create the pain I had begun to feel when Don arrived. Again, I realized, God's grace had brought Don and Creative Healing to my door; a simple one-hour treatment of properly directed healing energy had dissolved the cyst or cysts I did not even know I had, which then flowed out naturally, saving me the trauma, expense and pain of surgery.

*Chapter 5

How wonderful is Divine Guidance that brings answers and help to us, often before we ourselves are aware of the need. And how I praised the new knowledge of Creative Healing, which has proven itself time and again with hundreds and hundreds of grateful people who found new health in visiting the headquarters at the Lake Elsinore ranch.

Later I, too, went to California for further study, where I met dedicated therapists of both sexes from many states. These healers have since fanned out throughout the U.S., and even other countries around the world, working quietly to meet and alleviate life's illness and pain.

The two most dedicated to continuing this work in our century have been John Hunt and Hildreth Coulter, who have given their lives to this path, solely to do God's work, through their hands, in the world. They have taught hundreds of doctors and nurses, whose patients, they report, recover in one-third the normal time. John and Hildreth were honored on a trip to South India by the Holy Man, Satya Sai Baba, by his giving them his own private apartment to use during their stay at his ashram. He knew, and gave recognition to, the value of these dedicated ones.

Recently in May of 1990 the saintly woman, Hildreth Coulter, made her graduation to the Higher Realms at the age of 97, active and alert almost to the last. John Hunt has also retired, finding plenty to do on the ranch. At the time of this writing, Creative Healing, and its education program world-wide, is being carried on by the Joseph B. Stephenson Foundation,* located in Santa Rosa, California, under the direction of its current, very dedicated directors, Patricia and John Bradley.

It is so easy to see all the tragedies and troubles in the world, but there is also so much beauty, and truly angelic beings among us. We are indeed fortunate and blessed when they touch our lives.

After a few years of work in our clinic, Don was called to California for personal reasons. Rather than shouldering the whole work myself, and aware that I needed to give

*The Joseph B. Stephenson Fn., P.O. Box 8446, Santa Rosa, CA 95407.

more time to Jeannine as I was, of course, her only parent, and to travel at times to visit Jason, I decided to cease working with Creative Healing.

I have always intuitively known the nature of the power that can be channeled through the human hands as an instrument of healing. It is a higher vibration or unseen higher counterpart of the electricity in nature which we know and understand. It is now commonly known that the human body emanates a subtle electro-magnetic energy (which is this higher electrical force) and that these emanations can be directed by the mind. This subtle electricity is Life Energy. It has two basic qualities: It is self-governing and it is basically harmonious.

Water contained in any vessel, no matter what position the vessel is tilted, will automatically maintain a level parallel to the sea. Air rushes to fill a vacuum, through the smallest of holes. Mercury, broken into small particles, takes the form of small spheres and is instantly attracted to itself again if the spheres touch. Governed by physical laws, these elements consistently seek balance and unity. In the same way, governed by its intrinsic nature, the life force always seeks balance and unity. This self-governing quality is especially invaluable in healing and does away entirely with the necessity of the facilitator's knowing the nature and location of an ailment in a person who has asked for assistance. All one needs to do in magnetic treatment is to direct the Life Energy to the patient, and the Force, being self-governing, will rush to fill the spot where it is needed.

Primal Energy, being the foundation for all there is, by its very nature is perfectly harmonious. It is mind, when misdirected, that covers the life energy particles with a negative film. But whenever it comes from Infinite Source it flows free, harmonious, healing, and constructive. *This magnetic current carries such a sense of harmony that it harmonizes even the operator through whom it flows.* I knew wonderful health during the years I worked with Creative Healing.

In a very simple example, the effect of this electro-magnetic energy which emanates from a true healer's hands can be likened to the old-fashioned method of priming the pump that had gone dry. Years ago on the farm, by simply pouring a pitcher of water down the pipe while pumping fast to bring the new water up, we were able to restore the flow, as the water poured in from above contacted the water from below and brought it up. Likewise, the sparks of energy from the hands and mind of the facilitator touches the life energy within the patient's own body that has somehow gone dormant or been blocked in certain areas of bodily systems. The inflowing energy stimulates and activates the patient's own internal life force and brings it back to functioning. We have seen these results.

The book, *The Gift of Healing* (Harper and Row, 1976), is a remarkable narrative of the healing successes of Ambrose and Olga Worrall, who for many years worked through their church in Baltimore, Maryland. Ambrose Worrall refers to para-electricity, corroborating my long held sense of this energy.

"I believe that most so-called miracles are not miracles in any accepted sense, but only the working out of . . . immutable laws on a higher level of consciousness than we know. Laying-on-of-hands," he says, "can bring healing by altering the body's atomic thermal patterns. The undefined energy which passes from the healer to the patient, can be called para-electricity."

It is interesting to contemplate that the magnetic-electrical-creative energy generated in our bodies, the creative force that builds new cells, is the same force that works in healing and can be directed by mind from one body to another. It is also the same force we feel when we are in love which culminates in mating, and if left to nature, creates a new human. This electrical force is Life/ Love, and helps to explain why people, from babies to older folks and all in between, respond to waves of true love and become in the presence of love healthier and happier beings.

It is well known that a total lack of love can quickly lead to stress and dis-ease in humans, and even in the higher mammals. This is the very real reason why all true spiritual teachings emphasize love as the answer, and state that God is Love. Love is *the creative life force, the subtle energy, from which all things are made.*

This reasoning formed the basis for the original requirement that priests be celibate, for priests were originally considered healers of body and soul, as well as spiritual mediators. This creative force in the human can be directed by mind, as stated, either through the hands or through thought waves to affect physical healing in others. It can be used to create beauty through the utilitarian works of art, philosophy, or physical invention. But it can also be dissipated through the sexual organs in personal physical gratification. If used for the latter, the electrical force then is lost (if not used with intent to create a new life form, or to sanctify deep, true love between two people). This force is then not available, or at least not to the same extent, for higher altruistic purposes such as sending forth in healing. If the physical and meta-physical reasons for celibacy are not understood (or better, experienced), and if the individual is not strongly inclined toward altruistic and selfless work, then the yoke of celibacy chafes heavily on his shoulders and the person is likely to bolt from the commitment or live in hypocrisy.

When truly understood, this electrical life force can be generated by mind to not only heal but even to create new healthy cells in one's own body. Such a flow of energy, in combination with good health habits and positive happy thoughts, can create an enthusiastic love for life that will slow down and remarkably alter the aging process.

Perhaps it is clear now how true understanding can alter our lives in remarkable ways, not only to help us care for others, but to bring dynamic health and energy to ourselves. It behooves us to be aware how we daily use this wonderful gift of Life Energy from the Creator, which we, too, use to create.

IMMORTALITY

The days of your years are more
    than you knew —
For Life is alive! — and even in "death"
    still seeks to renew Itself,
As tree leaves and flower bulbs -
    each season do.

So awaken! — dear friend,
    and know that you too,
Have Life in continuum —
    tho centuries accrue
Across many borders, You —
    will always be You!

Your lifetimes are as seasons,
    in new worlds — it's true,
But never, no never, must you ever construe
    Death as the end. Oh No!
For I say what is true.
Look to Nature; you will see -
    Her reflection — in You!

For Life moves in cycles —
    the long winter days
Recall Nature's promise — in glory to raise
Blossoms — bursting forth
    in the Spring,
When new life and joy through all
    Nature rings!
Thus Nature's cycles — will your life renew —
As in the grace of God's Love — You are
Forever — Made New!

Bonnie Ann Gilchrist

*
THE HEALING POWER OF
WELLSPRINGS THERAPY

Another special blessing came during the years of the mid-1970's while my talented friend, Don, and I were using my small clinic for Creative Healing. This experience further confirmed my understanding of the effects sometimes felt in a current life of causes begun in the distant past. There arose an opportunity for me to become part of a group of twelve people who would participate in a therapy training session called Wellsprings. The teacher and facilitator was a remarkable woman named Kaye Ortmond, who operated a healing sanitarium and retreat center at Ben Lomond, California. She was offering a full week of teaching the Wellsprings method to those in the Seattle area who were interested and who had professional massage experience.

Kay hailed from England. She had received, years before through intuition, knowledge of a totally original spiritual and emotional healing therapy which combined the use of classical music with massage. She was not, however, to use ordinary music or ordinary massage. The music chosen, through intuitive guidance, was to be the finest classics of the masters, played at high volume, while massaging the patient in particular patterns, with mindful intent to release from the body cells the negative energy patterns that unconsciously held old emotions — even from past lives — that were yet creating pain and/or emotional trauma to the body and person in this present life.

Music has power not fully understood by most people, even today. Especially powerful are the classics of the great masters, for most of these works, it is acknowledged, are inspired. Body cells are in reality units of pure energy. Kaye was given the inspiration to couple the sound-wave vibrations of special music with deep massage, with intent to release pent-up or held-in traumas in the form of energy patterns held within the body cells. The patient, of course, comes to the therapy in complete agreement and desire to achieve this purpose as well, as many are at their wits end due either to their physical pain, continued emotional turmoil, or both.

Her work has been amazingly successful, both in California and in workshops across the country, to which Kaye traveled for many years reaching people who could not come to California. We were very blessed to have her arrive in our city, in this instance in February of 1977, to teach this innovative technique.

Twelve interested therapists together rented a large home in a quiet part of Seattle. We were to stay there one full week, not leaving the entire time. Kaye as the facilitator/teacher was the thirteenth person. I was fortunate to be among the twelve.

The ensuing work and learning/healing experiences were nothing short of astonishing. There was not one among us who did not come away deeply enriched, and many had healing experiences as well, some quite dramatic. We were divided evenly, six and six, so we took turns on the massage tables, first being the patient/receiver and then the masseure/facilitator. We were a mix of men and women and all of us had experience in massage. We were there in a prayerful spirit with high-minded intent. This is essential. The results at times were electrifying and moving. Sometimes the trauma was a life-long maladjustment with a family member, such as one woman revealed. I'll tell of that in a moment.

Kaye saw to it that the day's program was varied and balanced. In addition to each morning's music/massage session, we also had meditation/prayer time listening to uplifting specially chosen music that took one into the deepest regions of the inner self. This was a valuable foundation for the work. Afternoons included art and dance as therapy, where people learned to relax and let go of stress and the outer world's pace, and was a meaningful sharing time. This was in preparation for receiving, or giving, an evening massage, the second session of that day. (Those who gave a massage in the morning received one in the evening). Meals were planned to be both healthful and socially delightful.

Kaye had been shown in her intuitive spirit which classics to play for each part of the body massage. That is, the melody for massaging the legs would be quite different in tone and rhythm from one played for work on the chest and upper body, with another piece for the abdomen, etc. While six worked on six, Kaye moved about, instructing here and encouraging there. When an individual receiving the massage began to show signs of agitation with the rising to the surface of some old trauma, Kaye would be immediately there, probing with appropriate gentle questions to encourage the release.

Some of the stories that came out were both gratifying and sad. Gratifying for the release and relief from the old trouble-causing memory, and sad to hear what some souls had lived through in the past. Invariably, these were past-life experiences. The person found himself *in the scene*, feeling the emotion, often crying or groaning or frightened, but *not* reliving the physical pain, only the emotional turmoil — momentarily. *Since the individual himself brought up the memory from a relaxed reverie-state but was still quite conscious, he/she knew the experience to be authentic, not something concocted by a psychic or reported to them by a hypnotherapist, for example, that they were expected to accept on faith.*

As a traumatic experience rose out of the subconscious, up into the conscious mind, the individual would be encouraged to experience it only as something to be looked at, to be seen as only a memory. As the fallacy of holding onto the trauma in this life was realized, they would sigh in relief, consciously letting it be gone — out of the deep memory-bank, not to cause pain any longer. Kaye helped bring this about, while the music and massage continued, to help that person see and discern reality from unreality.

One woman described an anguished scene of being tied to the yardarm of an old-time pirate ship and having her tongue cut out for lying. She said later she had always wondered why she had a speech difficulty when required to express an opinion in public or when confronted with a sudden question. She was relieved to know, and now could let it go, saying she felt a weight lifted from her.

Though such delving into past lives may seem exotic and unnecessary, even unbelievable, recent research is showing a factual basis for this work and the phenomena of remembering. An awakening is beginning. The television show *In Search Of . . .* hosted by Leonard Nimoy of *Star Trek* fame, recently investigated reincarnation. Highlighting a number of scientists in research projects working with patients in regression, the program focused particularly on the eminent theologian and scholar, Dr. Alan Young. Dr. Young documented cases of remembered past-lives, the individuals under regression giving data that was irrefutable. One subject spoke an ancient Egyptian language, wrote hieroglyphics, and while in regression related the meaning of the glyphs (which was later found to be authentic). It was clear that in his present life the man had no knowledge of the Egyptian language whatsoever. Dr. Young stated, "Those who have experienced this no longer fear death, for they confirm that there truly is life after life."

In our Wellsprings sessions, one evening a particularly poignant clearing began. As the music swelled in volume, filling the room with vibrant sound, one of the ladies under massage began sobbing like her heart would break. Then she screamed, "Mama! Mama!" Kaye comforted her. "Where are you?" Plaintively came the answer in a little girl voice. "I'm in a box in the ground! She put me in a box and threw dirt on it! It's dark . . Mama!" She screamed again.

Kaye quieted her with soothing words, suggesting that she would be all right and then asked her, "Where are you? What country is this?" There was a pause, "China," came the answer.

"How old are you?" asked Kaye.

"I don't know. I'm a girl baby."

Gently Kaye took her through release of it (as she died there), pointing out it was long past. Then, after the woman had quieted, Kaye instructed, "Now, you can go back in time to see why your mother would bury you like that. Take yourself back to another time, to find the cause." There was a long pause while music and gentle massage continued. Soon Joyce again showed agitation, her face twitching.

"Now where are you?", Kaye asked.

"In Italy." She spoke roughly in a strong matronly voice,

blurting out with anger, "I've had her walled in . . . behind the bricks . . . she did an evil thing! She is with child and this is forbidden! She and the child will die together for her transgression." She paused, and with a slight choke, " I harden my heart against her screaming . . . I cared about her very much."

"Why would you have done this?" Kaye asked.

"Because I am the Mother Superior of this Convent and it is my duty . . ."

Kaye spoke again, "Now bring yourself forward to see if these events have a connection."

Suddenly the woman's face showed great surprise. "She is the same one. This girl I care for and must punish, was my mother in China!"

She continued to sob for awhile and then, as massage continued, she gave a sigh and slept.

Later, fully awake and recalling it all, Joyce saw the pattern of cause and effect. She also realized that this same soul was in this life once again her mother. The antagonism between them, though less violent, still lingers. They are being given another chance to clear the karma. Joyce felt much better after this release. She said she could finally love her mother without restraint, now that she understood, and now that the old emotions which she found she had been holding in the body cells, even into this life, were cleared.

Often it is necessary only to look consciously at old emotions and strongly decide "I don't need that anymore." It takes energy to retain (even unconsciously) troublesome memory patterns, energy we should use instead for positive purposes. It is an amazing and wonderful mystery, that the cells of the body have intelligence and memory of their own and can hold onto experiences, including traumatic ones, sometimes lifetime after lifetime, through the pattern carried over in the seed atom of the soul, until they are given a clear signal to release such memories from the One they take orders from — the True Being of You.

One of my personal clearings was not nearly so dramatic, but certainly was helpful to me. All my life I had suffered poor circulation in my lower extremities, causing cold legs and feet. One evening, receiving the Wellsprings

massage on my legs which often ached, I drifted in a comfortable half-reverie, deeply feeling the music. Suddenly I
clearly saw, as in a movie, a large old-fashioned many-masted
sailing vessel in the distance, silent against the sky. It was
trapped, locked in a vast expanse of solid ice in the northern seas of the Arctic. At first, afar off, it appeared as a small
painting against the sky, and then as I seemed to move
closer, it became larger in my vision. I then realized it was a
dead ship. There was no movement of life upon it. Immediately, the scene shifted. I found myself slowly trudging
across the vast, snowy tundra of this far northern landscape. Two male companions were laboriously moving beside me, and I, too, was male. I felt the bundled weight of a
heavy coat with parka rimmed in fur; my face was cold and
frost covered my beard. But my attention was on my feet. As
I tried to lift heavy, snow-covered boots, my feet were like
lead weights and I felt the pain in a detached sort of way.
White ice and snow, unending, stretched in every direction,
and I was aware that we had come from the ship, locked in
ice. Our only hope had been to somehow walk out to civilization; but for me, hope was gone. I was tired unto death
and could no longer lift or move my heavy frozen feet. My
legs were numb and I heard myself telling my companions
to go on without me. I drifted off in unconsciousness, and I
knew that I died there. And the scene faded.

There was no crying out or exchange with Kaye. This
simply was like a very clear movie that I was watching behind
the screen of my forehead, and as I looked at it, the strange
dull pain I had felt in my legs disappeared under the deep
massaging fingers of the one working on me. It seems that just
becoming aware of the original cause, and consciously lifting
the locked-in memory from the body cells up into the mind
was the healing factor. From that day forth my legs and feet
have been normally warm, with renewed circulation.

Another most vivid vision came two days later as my
lower back was being massaged. Throughout my life I'd
experienced pain in my lower back as a result of the childhood break I'd sustained in the fall from the haymow on the
farm. As the deep massage continued, in rhythm with a mov-

ing passage of music, I became very relaxed and felt myself drifting through a kind of swirling mist. Without warning I found myself hurled into a vivid and dramatic scene that must have taken place several centuries past. I saw brilliantly a wild chariot race, somewhat like the scenes of *Ben Hur.*

I am one of the drivers, a young and handsome man about twenty-two years of age, with sun-bronzed skin over strong rippling muscles. What's more, I am the son of a high ranking family and I am expected *to win. My horses are beautiful and fast and we will bring in the prize. I urge my straining horses on, feeling the exhilaration of the race and exulting in my sure victory. The prize, I know, will not only bring me great honor, but will bring me the hand of the young queen, as well. I am the favorite. I carry the young queen's colors and have her vow of love, and her promise I will be her consort upon my success.*

I come to a short corner and — My God! the chariot lurches and careens over on its side. As it flips, my left foot is caught and I am dragged on my back. I hang tightly to the reins attempting to avoid other chariots bearing down on me as the horses scream and charge wildly ahead. I feel a rush of panic and intense shame.

The scene fades, and shifts to another awareness. I become conscious that I have lost all, except my life — which is now worthless. I am a cripple, the lower half of my body paralyzed from the damage to my spine, for the rest of my years. Death would have been better. My family is dishonored — all hope is gone. Shame and guilt wash over me in hot waves as I recall my earlier pride, my cockiness over a sure victory. No longer can I even pretend to be a man, much less have the life I thought was assured.

All this flashes across my inner vision and I know it's veracity beyond the shadow of a doubt, for such a vision is irrefutable when one experiences it oneself. There is no mistaking it, as the emotions are strong and specific.

The scenes melt into the mists from whence they came, and I gradually find myself back hearing the music, feeling the massage. An amazing new realization fills me of the hidden ancient cause for the present effect, the lower back condition of the body I now inhabit. I contemplate why this should be shown to me now. Obviously I called it up myself, from the depths of the Inner Self, with the help of the music and the massage.

In this instance, however, the seeing alone did not result in instant healing, although this is a clear example of how extreme trauma can follow one lifetime after lifetime. Since the etheric body serves as a blueprint to the physical, circumstances are laid to create a carryover of the condition. Healing, therefore, takes place only over a period of time as the cleansing of the etheric pattern, through recognition and release, becomes slowly manifest in the physical.

Wellsprings therapy helps us understand that we alone carry our traumatic memories as harmful deadweight, restricting the life flow, just as trash and deadwood pile up to create a muddy dam in a stream. It is we alone who can decide to release the blockages that will clear a way for new energy and new life to flow through the body and psyche, just as a fresh stream of sparkling clear spring water brings new life to the hills and meadows of Mother Earth.

Truly, we are more closely aligned to the patterns of the earth than we realize, for our bodies are created from its elements. Therefore, we, too, embody the unseen finer vibrational magnetic energies of the planet from which we receive our lifeforce.

Many people, healthy and well-balanced, happy with their lives as they are, have no need for these helps. I write not for them, but for the many troubled people, and there seem more each year as hospitals, institutions and prisons fill to overflowing, who would be assisted to happier lives and healthier bodies with the help of alternative approaches to emotional healing. Psychoanalysis has its place, and serves a specific area of need, but too often such treatment is drawn out over many years, while the deepest buried *causes* of the distress are never found and released.

Sometimes very serious personality and health aberrations which often ruin lives can be traced to simple biochemical allergic reactions within the physical, and can be cleared up in a matter of weeks without delving into deeper analysis. This has been proven at clinics here in Seattle, as well as other cities throughout the nation.

A cousin of mine, Wesley, was a man of forty-two who lived in another state. After many years of unhappiness and depression and six years or more of expensive psychotherapy, which produced no visible improvement, he came to the point of considering suicide. Upon my insistence, Wesley flew out by plane to my home on the west coast. Biochemical testing revealed that he suffered severe hypoglycemia. His psychoanalyst in six years had not looked at this area of health, nor had normal regular medical check-ups disclosed it. Advanced hypoglycemia can cause severe mental aberrations.

Upon being given immediate heavy vitamin/mineral injections over a period of five days and then a complete change of diet, Wesley became a different person, finally able to handle his life for the first time in many years. He did suffer some setbacks until he realized he was severely allergic to coffee and sugar. He now knows his own responsibility in staying well, and today is a happier, healthy man with the inclination and time for a new love in his life. This, of course, also added to his being a healthier individual, as true love does wonders for the body's glandular system.

Dr. Brian Weiss, a Psycho-Pharmacologist and Medical Psychologist, stated in a radio interview in Seattle on October 1, 1992, that his studies have shown that caffeine (in coffee, colas, etc.) can actually cause panic attacks in some people.

A European report from the World Research Foundation* Newsletter 1st and 2nd Quarter, 1992, states that the tool of blood diagnosis called Aurasscopy has proven to be a very successful holistic method for physical diagnosis. The following quote illustrates the holographic principle that, the whole can be found in every one of its parts.

> "A drop of blood can represent the status of
> health, which has been developed during 30 years

* See Page 423 for address.

of research work, into a simple but highly effective technique.

> "Several drops of blood are taken from the tip of the little finger of the patient's left hand and spread evenly on a microscope slide according to standardized method. The dried blood smears are stained and then examined at a magnification of 1250 under a binocular microscope to obtain a diagnosis. Examined in this manner, the blood smears provide an illustration of a person's overall physical condition. The blood stains reveal diseased organs, such as the pancreas, and diseased or injured bodily parts, such as the femur or eyes."

Furthermore, it can be determined how a disease is linked to different bodily parts or functions. Biochemical deficiencies or abnormalities are also seen.

> "As is shown by photographs taken through the microscope, the imaging forces at work create a natural, anatomically faithful reproduction, one with great color variation, of the bodily part or organ in question. The size and color intensity of the images for interpretation are directly proportional to the severity or degree of advancement of the disease or disturbance. Aurascopy is an especially valuable diagnostic tool in those cases where clear-cut assignment of symptoms to causes is not possible, or where the patient is suffering from vague complaints that cannot be explained by other diagnostic methods."

I find this thrilling, for this diagnostic tool would provide an invaluable (and quite simple) test for biochemical disturbances, and apparently has been in use in Europe for some time.

In recent years Alternative Health Clinics are springing up all over America, with doctors who are astute enough to include a variety of comprehensive and in-depth therapies in their treatment, rather than the cover-up of the problem using a drug approach to simply deaden the pain. One such excellent treatment center that teaches many drugless healing methods is the Heartwood Institute* at Garborville, California.

Pain is the body's only warning system, and it is the wise man who pays attention, whether the pain be physical or emotional. We are seeing far too much of the latter recently in people striking out against others, both within the family and against society.

Hypnosis therapy often achieves results similar to the Wellspring sessions, and may be preferable in many instances, but we found the Wellsprings sessions superior in the sense that the individual being treated is conscious and aware of the visionary break-throughs, and feels and remembers them personally. In traditional hypnosis one is asleep, and awakens with little or no memory of what transpired, and must hear what he or she said from the therapist or played back from a tape.

In our week of revelation and learning at the Wellsprings retreat, not all of us experienced such dramatic results, although there were several breakthroughs. A person's experience depends, of course, on his personal needs and what lies buried. (Some may not have a deep need, while with other individuals more time and more sessions may be required.)

Incorporating the Wellsprings massage therapy into my work I was able to affect in some individuals deeper healing than might have been otherwise possible. We worked out an amazing past-life trauma in one instance for Jim, an older gentleman who was also a friend of our family. During the session, on an inner emotional level Jim appeared to be reliving being hung by the neck until dead. Jim did not express his feelings to me during or after the session, nor did he mention the era or the reason for the event. He did not seem to remember these, as during the session Jim appeared to be in a trance state. However, the nature of his experience was obvious to me, as his body became grossly

*Heartwood Institute, 320 Harmony Lane, Garberville, CA 95440.

contorted, his legs jerked, and his head twisted to one side with very taut neck muscles. I called on all my faith and prayer to the Christ Light in this instance, while continuing to work with gentle massage, for it was a rather frightening session and lasted quite a few minutes. Although there was nothing visible to cause this contortion (I had used only gentle motions), the rope around the neck could not have been more real. You may find this hard to believe, as even I did while watching it, but it is true, and the session did bring forth very good results, releasing old long-held negative trauma in his body cells, which, of course, was the purpose of the work.

Jim came through with flying colors, and was not at all disturbed by the experience afterward, and no longer suffered the stiff neck and shoulders he had lived with and complained of most of his life. His personality also changed amazingly, from a rather grumpy, negative outlook on life, in which he often found fault with any and all circumstances, to one of warm joviality with a beautiful sense of humor. Jim became really quite easy-going. He began then to love himself enough to change his diet to incorporate healthy nutrition, including glasses of fresh raw carrot juice and his own home-baked bread, which was very tasty. Our friend Jim was fun to be with and had so few health problems after that, he lived well into eighty-plus years of age and didn't look a day over sixty-five. I do not wish to say this therapy alone caused Jim's total well-being, but I know it did contribute to a release of the entrapped negative energy, so healing could happen and life could be happier.

There is so much yet to learn about the wonderful Being that makes up the One whom you think you are. Thomas Edison once said, "We do not know one/one-millionth about anything!"

We can already see how right he was by simply looking at the marvelous advancements that have been made in electrical inventions and technology in the few short years since the wonder of the light bulb, harnessing electricity in his time. With the advent of the computer and the laser, great advances have become possible in all areas of society, from science and the medical, to military and outer space. We know some factories now have robots working twenty-four hours around the clock. These wonders are now all known, used and accepted as a part of everyday life.

Could it be we also are just on the cutting edge of new discoveries about our Inner World? Could it be that the wonders possible by this Inner Self may be as remarkable, or even greater, than the achievements in the outer world of technology? The Master Teachers through the ages have tried to tell us this is so. Even Jesus stated quite bluntly, "Know ye not that ye are gods? These things I do, even greater things shall ye do," (John: 14:12). Jesus also repeated Psalms 82:6, which states, "I have said ye are gods and all of you are children of the Most High."

I believe that one day in the future, the 100 years we are now living will be considered the second Dark Ages. Nations yet war between themselves, millions starve on a planet of abundance; medical science cuts and burns, thinking to eradicate illness; and personal greed among those who govern is more outrageously destructive than ever before in history.

There is much we yet need to learn about ourselves, about our relationship to each other and to the rest of the planet. A few brilliant men have spoken out. A little later, let us look at what they have to say.

＊

CHAPTER ELEVEN

GUESS WHO CAME TO MY HOUSE — AND SURPRISING ADVENTURES

"I know you!", we silently say to one another as our eyes meet with curiosity and surprise. I also feel a certain shyness, for I know we haven't met, at least not in this lifetime. A dark-haired man with a lanky frame stands before me. Around six-feet, six inches tall, his warm brown eyes twinkle with hidden mischievous humor as though he knows an unspoken secret. His well-trimmed beard is dark and full, with just a sprinkle of grey; it compliments his handsome strong-featured face. He wears a tweed hat with brim turned down all around, making him look as if he just strode in off the Scottish Moorlands.

He greets me, here at the lower outdoor level of my home, with a few words and a most pleasant smile, eyeing me openly but mannerly, and I see the personal interest evident in the sparkle in his eyes. Somehow I know this man, but I don't know how I know him. He, with other early comers, strolls about, surveying the items I have strewn over the tables under the trees. I am contemplating the sale of my home and a garage sale is just the thing to clear the clutter.

As this man and his companion continue looking around, a name suddenly pops into my mind, so clearly it seems spoken aloud. "Klaus! Klaus!" I approach him.

"Excuse me. Did I hear you say your name was Klaus?" His head snaps up like a startled animal as he stares at me with undisguised surprise.

"No . . . my name is Frank. My father's name was Klaus . . . but how did you know that?"

His voice is deep and rich, with a foreign accent — German, I think. Now I *know* I have never met him, and embarrassed, I lamely mumble, "I don't know. I just wondered . . ." My voice trails off. He is still looking at me with a puzzled expression.

Frank introduces his companion, a realty agent, and before they leave they ask to look further around my property on which stand many large trees and extensive plantings. Our small guest cottage crouches in the woods too, Mama's hideaway (and later our Healing Clinic).

"Of course . . . take your time."

That night, alone in my room and not quite asleep, I heard the same voice once again, but this time the impression came to my mind more clearly. *"Klaus . . . Klaus! Help my son!"* Three times the voice came and I knew it was the same Klaus of earlier in the day. *"Help my son! Help my son!"* The voice held an urgency. Klaus who? What kind of help? I was baffled and finally, giving up, I dropped off to sleep.

Amazingly, I found the tall, bearded gentleman on my doorstep the very next day. Frank asked if he could talk with me. It seemed he was urgently in need of living quarters. "I fell in love with your little cedar-paneled guest cabin under the trees, while I was looking around your property yesterday."

"Ah Ha!" I thought to myself. "*This* is the help I'm being asked to give: He needs a place to live." I was expecting to sell my large home with an acre of grounds and cabin, as with my family gone it had become too much for one person to care for. Nevertheless, I agreed to the rental arrangement but made it clear the arrangement would likely be temporary. Frank was simply delighted, and soon moved in.

In the days that followed, Frank revealed that he, too,

had experienced an instant, unexplainable recognition of me. He felt very much "at home" on my property, especially with the gentle healing vibration that still permeated his new residence.

One day Frank held a book out to me. "Since you asked about my father, I brought this to show to you. It's in German, but it tells the well-known story of my father, Count Klaus von Stauffenberg."* He opened the book to pictures of his family: his father, his mother, and his brothers, one still living in Germany, and active in government and business.

I looked at the pictures, and as my eyes fell on an early picture of Klaus, — an even greater jolt of recognition hit me. Klaus did not resemble Frank, but was strikingly handsome in a different way. A shiver passed over my body, and involuntary tears filled my eyes. What did this all mean? . . . and where did I fit in, that this man, long dead, should come and speak to me in my mind with such urgency?

Klaus' strange, tragic story is, indeed, well-known history. A PBS television documentary of the late 1980's describes Count Klaus von Stauffenberg's brave efforts to save his beloved Germany, as he had masterminded the only almost-successful plot to assassinate Hitler in the latter days of World War II. Klaus Schenk von Stauffenberg and at least eight other high-ranking commanding officers realized full well that Hitler was mentally unbalanced and that the war against the Allies could not be won. Seeing that Hitler's wild rampaging orders would be the downfall and total ruin of their beloved fatherland, these officers sought to bring an end to the madness, with no further useless loss of lives.

Frank sadly told me some of the story, adding personal details. These were intelligent men. Klaus von Stauffenberg's family was of a line of intellectual aristocrats, who were active in German politics for many years prior to Hitler's rise to power. Frank's great grandfather, in fact, knew King Ludwig II personally, and it was he who persuaded King Ludwig to allow Bavaria to be annexed to the German Reich, rather than

* Klaus Graf von Stauffenberg, 15 November 1907–20 July 1944

requiring Bavaria to remain a separate principality, as King Ludwig proposed. Frank's grandfather was a Master Mason, a man of great influence, spiritually and in government.

The story of the almost-successful assassination attempt is riveting. Two books in English tell it in detail: *Code Name Valkyrie, Count von Stauffenberg and the Plot to Kill Hitler*,* and *Stauffenberg, Architect of the Famous July 20th Conspiracy to Assassinate Hitler*.** I quote from the fly-leaves.

"The German aristocrat who was the leader in the plot to overthrow the Nazi government and assassinate Hitler was Claus Phillip Maria Graf (Count) von Stauffenberg. The book *Stauffenberg* is the first full-length biography in English and an invaluable record of the only active resistance during the Nazi regime — the secret conspiracy that resulted in an attempt on Hitler's life in 1944.

"Stauffenberg was a member of the old German aristocracy in whom the principles of duty toward God, man, and country were embodied. He had been seriously wounded in Africa, losing a hand and an eye, after having served his country in the Rhineland, Czechoslavakia, Austria, Poland, Russia, and finally North Africa. Now, while convalescing from near fatal wounds, slowly the conviction grows in Klaus von Stauffenberg that loyalty to mankind and to Germany takes precedence over his oath of allegiance to his superiors and to the man who is the author of all the horror and destruction that is engulfing the world — Adolf Hitler.

"After Col. von Stauffenberg's release from the hospital, he joined the staff of General Olbricht, also a secret anti-Nazi. This modern-day true story contains the details of a high-grade thriller, as suspense builds, event upon event, with the conspira-

*Code Name Valkyric by James Forman, 1973. S. G. Phillpis, Inc., Pub., 305 West 86th Street, NY 10024.
**Stauffenberg . . ., by Dr. Joachim Krumarz, 1967, The MacMillan Co., 866 Third Avenue, New York, 10022.

tors meeting in secret, making plans for the assassination of Hitler, setting up a nationwide command
structure, specific orders for army units and communication with officers in outlying areas. Klaus
von Stauffenberg became the driving force and co-
ordinator of the plot to eliminate Hitler and the
Nazi regime, preparatory to setting up a new government dedicated to peace and reconciliation."

Despite Klaus von Stauffenberg's wounds and his handi-
cap of having only one hand with two fingers remaining, he
decided to make the final effort himself, as other officers
involved were reluctant. Klaus prepared the deadly bomb
personally, and timed and set the detonation. Carrying it in
a briefcase to a staff meeting, he placed the bomb under the
conference desk at Hitler's feet.

The course of history might have been changed, but Fate
decreed differently. Hitler rose from his seat and left the spot
only seconds before the explosion, — the plan was aborted.

Frank told me the grisly ending. Hitler ordered the
execution of all the involved top military intellects of Germany, who were faithful to their homeland, but anti-Nazi.
Hitler's retaliation was diabolical. These officers, which included several generals, were hung on meat hooks, through
the shoulder blades, to die. Due to his high station in life,
Klaus was accorded the courtesy of a firing squad. Moments
before the shots rang out, Count von Stauffenberg was heard
to shout, "Long live my beloved Germany!" He was thirty-
seven years old. Hitler still lived. History books tell the rest.

The striking dark man, now living in my guest house, was
the youngest son of Count Klaus Schenk Graf von Stauffenberg.
Frank never saw his father; he was yet in his mother's womb
when his father was executed. One can presume that his
mother's shock and intense grief around these events and her
husband's death impacted the unborn child.

Countess Nina von Stauffenberg, in great fear for the
lives of her sons, hid them elsewhere, as Hitler vowed vengeance on the entire family. Nina von Stauffenberg was sent to
confinement, Frank was born shortly thereafter. Soon came

Allied liberation and she fled to Austria as she had friends there, including the Hapsburg family, who had been the reigning monarchs of Austria before Hitler's rise to power.

Little Frank was placed in a Catholic Monastery School. His traumatic boyhood experiences there left his psyche terribly scarred, with deep-seated angers and resentments against the Church, and even against his mother, who, for many long years, he felt had abandoned him.

Frank and I talked often over the following months, especially in the evenings when he came to use my kitchen. He found me an interested listener, for I well remembered the years of World War II. He told me of terrible beatings at the hands of the monk school teachers and other sad stories of an emotionally lost little boy. As his life slowly unfolded I saw that he carried yet, as a man of forty years, the scars both physical and emotional of those beatings, and the misunderstanding of teacher-monks and even of family members.

As Frank spoke, expressing what he was not able to do as a child, I saw clearly that this little boy had been learning disabled, as we have recently come to understand it. Frank had not been able to comprehend the written word in books. This could have been due to dyslexia or an attention-span deficit. But the monks in their ignorance regarded this inability as stubborn refusal to study, and beatings were their standard punishment. It never occurred to them, of course, that there could be a physical disability involved. Little Frank's grades were consistently F, but because he was the son of Countess von Stauffenberg, the school could not expel him. He had no possible escape. As Frank spoke with intense emotion of his boyhood I could see there were, even yet, significant symptoms of hyperkinesis and much deep-seated fear and anger, which created emotional instability and mental blockages.

To my amazement, I saw in Frank mental and emotional symptoms similar to those my Jason had suffered in the days when I also was ignorant of causes. But my son, at least, had received family love and kindness, if not any help from schools. Frank had received neither.

As a boy, Frank suffered a terrible lack of love from

anyone at all, especially from his mother, who he felt, for reasons he could not fathom, had abandoned him to a harsh fate for a little boy. He told me the loneliness was so profound, he often sat in a crevice within the cold grey stones of the monastery and cried, feeling his heart would break in two, while he felt the walls closing in to smother him. Frank's sensitive nature was further assaulted as he witnessed atrocities against other boys which caused him intense grief and horror. One little boy actually had an ear torn off, he said, it was jerked so hard by a teacher. And there were beatings until blood flowed, including his own. I was stunned to hear these tales.

Strangely, his mother only rarely brought him home for short visits where, he said, "I did not even have a room of my own, but had to sleep on the couch." I suspect she did not know what to do with this odd child who seemingly could not learn. For, if I had no professional help whatsoever twenty-five years ago for a child with these strange behaviors, there certainly was no understanding in Europe thirty-five years ago.

Frank said his only joy was that sometimes in summer he would get to visit his grandfather, who took him on long walks in the beautiful Austrian mountain meadows and forests. His grandfather, whom he adored, taught him a wonderful knowledge: the medicinal lore of many herbs. Frank learned where various plants grew, learned how to recognize them, and to make healing potions from their leaves and roots. His grandfather also told him the stories of old Germany and its formation as a country. These visits were few, and very precious.

As Frank became more comfortable with me, his angers against the Church, and against anyone that represented authority over him, began to boil more and more to the surface. Then he vehemently vowed vengeance against that authority, particularly religious, and I saw, as we allowed the depth of his feelings to come out, that Frank could become violent. He was physically very tall and strong, and it was obvious he had the potential to erupt explosively when with others whom he perceived as trodding on his toes, possibly with disastrous results. When I pointed this out, Frank admitted that he had come precariously close to such violence a few times, but that he had been saved by the skin of his teeth (perhaps by the grace of God), and possibly from a prison sentence. In addition, he suffered severe migraine headaches from this on-going stress, which made his job, too, an added, almost unbearable strain.

In the days that followed, we found that allergies to certain foods were a problem for Frank. He had an allergy even to wine. In Germany wine is a national drink, given to children with meals. This sensitivity may also have contributed to his early hyperkinesis.

As the weeks progressed, although time for discussion was limited to a few evening hours and some weekends, I began to see the urgency of the instruction I had received from spirit in the voice of Klaus to *"Help my son! Help my son!"* There was a far deeper need and purpose here than I had at first discerned, and the order was a full one.

Rather than simply giving Frank a place to live, I was to work quietly and prayerfully, one-on-one, with a very troubled man. The need, as I perceived it, was to help him become the watcher of his own emotions. This receptive watching was necessary if Frank were to understand himself, as understanding was the only thing that would break his pattern of automatic subconscious reaction to situations he perceived as threatening, but which were, in reality, not leveled at him at all.

No matter what situation we find ourselves in, in a particular period or lifetime, surrounded by certain individuals or situations which present challenges or trials to us in certain specific ways, perhaps drawing forth our deepest, darkest sides, we should be aware that all karmic situations have but one underlying purpose. That purpose is to teach us to observe our reactions, and learn to deal with them constructively. Through consistent observation — being the watcher — coupled with meditation and prayer for God's grace, we can come to balance our emotions, releasing the old negative patterns, and consciously drawing, instead, higher energies and aspirations to bear on our life's challenges. In this way we act, or remain calmly passive, rather than re-acting out of old subconscious habit patterns. Then slowly, through right use of will and desire, with understanding, we can change and dissolve old hurts and angers.

If we carry old negative energies of hate, anger, resentment, and so on, within our being for our entire lifetime, just who is hurt? Mainly ourselves, of course, but also our loved ones. The past is past and was meant only as a learning tool. The past has no reality, except as a memory, an energy pattern within our minds and emotions. The individual, himself or herself, is the only one who can release this negative energy and replace it with positive, by accepting the purpose of past events and griefs as learning experiences for the soul. We need to throw out the ballast of old trash, that our balloon of consciousness may rise to higher levels.

In this light, forgiveness is the key. Forgiveness is an attribute of unconditional love. No clearance of negative energy patterns can ever be achieved without forgiveness. Jesus the Christ admonished, "Let him who is without sin throw the first stone." We can never know or judge why others act in certain ways until we have "walked in their moccasins for six moons," as Native Americans have wisely taught. Since obviously that is not possible, we must not ever judge.

Nevertheless, we can learn to forgive in order to cleanse our own being of harmful emotions that otherwise restrict our joy in life, dampen our relationships, threaten our physical health, obstruct our love for our Creator, and even retard the rate of our soul's evolution. Our energies, positive or negative, tend to be passed on down the line to others we meet and with whom we associate, in that way affecting many, like the ripples of water in a pond that reach the far edge after a stone has been tossed. In this way too we are all connected in hidden ways, along energy lines of life force.

Changes in long-held emotional responses and patterns do not usually happen overnight, except in some miraculous healing instances. Actually, the slower, conscious work on oneself is more beneficial, for a person can observe his or her own progress and take personal claim in achieving freedom. In Frank's case, the healing process took place over two years' time through quiet talks and facing some heavy emotional upheavals.

The wonderful part was that Frank was open and ready to investigate and entertain these healing ideas, as we emphasized Jesus' teachings to which he was truly devoted, even while he reiterated that it was the Church — which he hated with a passion — that had crucified Him. Frank eagerly read certain passages in books we referred to, and began to see his life in a new light. (After leaving school, Frank had taught himself in his own way to read, and had, in fact, learned several languages by living in a variety of countries.)

Frank's life story was simply amazing to me. He had become world-traveled so we had some fascinating conversations. I remarked once, "You should write a book," and I offered to help. His answer, "No one would believe it."

Out of school, he had run away to Sweden at age eighteen, never having made peace with his mother or family. He married and fathered a child, divorced, then migrated alone to Canada and then to the United States. Frank became accomplished in many fields of endeavor as he learned by doing, not from books. As an American citizen during the Viet Nam War, Frank told me he worked for the U.S. Government teaching languages in the Pentagon (he spoke six fluently). Later, he worked as a deep-sea diving instructor who took groups into many oceans of the world. At one time he lived in Venezuela, raised bananas (he gave me the huge machete knife he had used there), and took pleasure in learning the healing uses of South American herbal plants to augment his knowledge of nature's medicine. Later, as a travel guide to the handicapped, he escorted groups of paraplegic tourists up the Great Wall of China, carrying some himself on his broad back. I mention only a few of his adventures — but everywhere he traveled, Frank carried with him his old unresolved angers, through and including a couple more marriages and divorces. Thus he became a rolling stone, who could never feel happy, never become settled.

I found Frank to be *very* bright and creative, but also a

OVER AN ANGEL'S SHOULDER

natural artist, perceptive in the ways of Nature. But none of his talents had been recognized or encouraged when he was a child, no support given to help him achieve his inner potential. This same lack exists for many young people today who object to learning by rote from books. These often are creative souls bringing in new ideas for a new century.

When one wife in particular, whom Frank loved very much and to whom he gave much (they worked together deep-sea diving), left abruptly after five years of marriage, he became distraught and set sail alone in his yacht across the Pacific for Tahiti, "hoping," he said, "I would drown enroute." Three agonizing months on the water in Pacific storms only served to teach a harsh lesson: to never again attempt crossing the ocean alone, for he came very close to losing his life.

"It was then I found I really did wish to live after all."

Our conversations were stimulating and enlightening for both of us as Frank discussed his experiences and took a hard look at his life and the continuing emotional problems created by an inability to let go of past trauma. It was a joy to see the eagerness with which he desired to change his responses and attitudes, and to accept the wonder of God's love and help, *always available if we will only turn and ask*. Frank had previously blocked God out, for in his youth, through the years when a child builds an inner creed and foundation, he had seen those who professed God, and who supposedly were his representatives, to be actually very cruel. He saw and experienced no love there. We were able, in deep work together, to separate God — and the reality of Divine Love — from those sad figures of the Church of that time with their misapplied dogmatic teachings. Frank was then able to reach a more emotionally mature understanding and thus, eventually, an ability to forgive. As stated, his healing did not happen overnight.

One morning, months later, on a bright and beautiful Saturday, 10:30 came and went and Frank had not yet come down to breakfast. I, wondering if he were ill, walked up to the guest house along the tree-shaded path. I knocked; he bade me enter. Frank was still in bed, although awake, appearing dazed and somewhat confused and perplexed. He sat up and said abruptly, "I have just had an amazing experience which seems like a dream — and yet it was *very real*! I've just returned from somewhere . . ." His voice trailed off as he stared into space, reflecting. Then he continued.

"A beautiful, small, dark man in an orange robe came here to me. He had a large head of dark hair like a halo around his face, and he took me to a place I've never seen. We sat on the floor, he sat cross-legged in front of me. We were in a small room, no furniture, but with a stand, kind of a statue beside an open window behind us. I noticed the breeze was blowing the yellow curtains. We talked, but I can't seem to remember what about . . ." Frank paused, his brow furrowed as if in contemplation.

"I remember only that at the end of our talk, he blessed me and then I blessed him — and suddenly I am back here — and you are here. This is weird. What time is it?"

I told him it was mid-morning and I was concerned he might be ill. Frank said he felt fine, and I left. Puzzling, and with a jolt of wonderment and surprise over his description of the small man in an orange robe, I went to my library and pulled out the book, *Sai Baba, The Holy Man and the Psychiatrist,** by Samuel H. Sandweiss, M.D. When Frank came down from his quarters, dressed and ready for a late breakfast, I showed him the picture of Satya Sai Baba on the cover, and another inside the book. His response was electric.

Immediately jumping up from his chair, he almost shouted, "That's him! That's him! That's the one I saw who took me with him! Where did you get that book? Who is he?" Wide-eyed with excitement, he eagerly asked if he could take the book to read.

"Of course," I responded. He proceeded in the next few days to pore through it cover to cover. This book he absorbed like a sponge absorbs water, becoming more enthralled with every page. Frank asked many questions which I tried to answer from my past studies. Then suddenly, one

---

Sai Baba, The Holy Man and the Psychiatrist, 1975, Birth Day Pub. Co., Box 7722, San Diego, CA

day soon after, Frank announced, he would quit his job and leave for India. He believed he was being called by the Indian Master Sai Baba to come to the Ashram in Southern India at Puttaparthi, near Bangalore. He wasted no time in acquiring a ticket and taking flight.

As God's Plan would have it, this event gave a big boost to confirm the teachings I had offered, for Frank's visit to the Ashram at Puttaparthi gave him a great leap forward in his outlook on spiritual realities, and was like a door opening to a new world. This was a dynamic stepping stone in his life.

Frank returned after six weeks time, glowing and full of vitality. He excitedly informed me that upon his arrival at Sai Baba's Ashram, he had been given the very room he saw in his astral flight with the holy man, complete in every detail. There was the bare room, except for a bed, and there was the statue under the open window, with yellow curtain blowing in the warm breeze. This confirmation, which he was able to make for himself, was invaluable to Frank in cementing his knowing the Truth I had sought to convey, of God's love and the wonders of higher realities.

Thousands of seekers from all over the world visit Satya Sai Baba's Ashram daily from Germany, Italy, South America, the United States, Mexico, etc., to receive this holy man's blessing. There, the very first morning after his arrival, at the darshan gathering in the compound where all visitors receive Baba's blessings, Frank later told me of his acquiring a front row position, where he seated himself cross-legged on the ground, on the side of the compound reserved for men. As Sai Baba softly glided past, he lightly touched only a few individuals. However, when Sai Baba saw Frank he stopped. Looking at Frank intently, he said, "So there you are. What took you so long?"

This personal recognition, among a crowd of hundreds, put Frank on Cloud Nine. It also made him the star of the week with the men who were his roommates. Thereafter, he laughingly told me, everyone tried to sit near him in hopes of being acknowledged by the Holy Teacher.

Even so, he did not receive the personal audience in private quarters that he had hoped for, as there were others present, with very real needs, from all over the world. I believe Frank's private audience had already taken place, weeks before, in the personal visit he received from Sai Baba, right here in my little healing cabin in the trees, when Frank was transported in his astral body to India.

This was the beginning of Frank's real transformation, and I gave thanks in my meditations for the amazing assist to my efforts. He was full to overflowing with stories of his experiences in India, and the beauty of the Spirit he had felt at the Ashram. He often urged that I must go there too, to experience this unique setting and its blessing. In addition, he was primed up with an idea to import certain hand-crafted goods from India for wholesale in America.

"You should see. There are bea-u-u-tiful things there and they are very inexpensive. You would really be great at choosing things to bring back here," he enthused.

Then he asked if I would join him in such a venture. This was a startling thought. I had never been to the Far East, much less India, and it would be a great adventure for me. We would not travel in a tour group then, but as buyers of merchandise.

"We could visit Sai Baba's Ashram. You must see how beautiful is the spirit there, with thousands of people from all over the world eager for his teachings that are food for the soul. There is a peaceful vibration everywhere that is a special blessing, and you already know him through your books and studies." His enthusiasm overflowed and caught me in its wave.

I was truly tempted, as I had not taken time, due to the responsibilities of raising my family and Jason's troubles, for a major trip for many years. After a few days contemplation, I agreed to go on an investigative buying trip, provided we would include a stay at the ashram and perhaps visit Brindaban, the Spiritual Retreat with University for higher learning, founded and guided by Satya Sai Baba. This University is highly regarded throughout India. Through Sai Baba's guidance, its graduates have been trained in practical skills, as well as in the professions, to help lift the level of living in India. They fan out throughout the countryside, teaching better methods of agriculture, nutrition, sanitation and other basics of hygiene, as well as spiritual ideals and disciplines. This University, a vision of Sai Baba's, was a first in this broad effort, and is much needed there.

I have, since this time, heard that Sai Baba has also directed to be built a new and modern hospital in connection with this university that will encompass many forms of natural as well as medical healing modalities. The wonder of it is that it will be free to all who cannot pay. This is in line with this wonderful Teacher's living example of love in action for all of God's humanity. And even more recently, the exciting word is that Creative Healing will be among the natural therapies offered there through the person of a fine facilitator from America, by specific invitation of Satya Sai Baba.

*

OFF TO INDIA

My decision to accept the challenge of this trip was a major one as it opened quite another exciting and entirely new chapter in my Book of Life. We arranged for the long flight to Bombay. My stay at Satya Sai Baba's Ashram was all Frank had said it would be and more, even though I was only one among hundreds of women from all over the world. I was the only American lady housed in a dormitory with thirty-six German women. I was grateful to have a cursory knowledge of German. It was gratifying to see the thousands, of many nationalities, eager for God's love and spoken wisdom through a living master, as they sought a path to higher understanding. Sai Baba's teachings parallel those of Jesus in many ways, carrying the message that Pure Love is the answer to the ills of the world.

The Ashram was an oasis of cleanliness and good food, all was permeated with a wonderful uplifting atmosphere, and the joy that everyone felt at being close to Sai Baba and his teachings. In the center of the ashram stood a lovely white and gold temple, with a large, clean, paved compound where Sai Baba daily walked among and blessed the devotees who gathered there. The surroundings were beautifully landscaped with flowers, trees and fountain.

There is controversy in some circles over the miracles Sai Baba performs, bringing healing ash, and objects of beauty which he bestows as gifts, out of thin air, so to speak, just as there was controversy in Jesus' day as to who and what He was. One need only speak with those who have received lasting healings from a myriad of ailments, psychological and mental as well as physical, to believe in this Master Teacher's truth and worth. I had ample opportunity for this, as well as the healing testimony of personal friends, John Hunt and Hildreth Coulter, the teachers of Creative Healing, who had earlier visited him and received a private audience. The materialized objects, Sai Baba always states, are only to help the faithless to believe, for he laments, "Why do you ask for baubles when I can give you Life?"

Many times Sai Baba has shown mastery over the material world. Dr. Sandweiss, who personally witnessed startling instances of this mastery, describes his observations in the aforementioned book, *The Holy Man and the Psychiatrist*. Also, Sai Baba seems on call when a need arises among his devotees anywhere in the world.

Very recently in the Fall of 1991, Larry King interviewed the movie star and authoress, Shirley MacLaine. She related a story involving Sai Baba that had happened not long before, while she was present. While she was in India with Richard and Janet Bach, who were filming Sai Baba at his ashram, Richard ran out of film. Unfortunately it was at a point where a materialization was to be filmed. Sai Baba excused himself and went in to meditate, while Richard Bach took a break and wondered what to do. Coming back shortly thereafter, Richard was astounded to find a fresh bag of film by his camera, and filming proceeded.

Shirley Maclaine told Larry King and the radio listening audience that soon, upon returning to Los Angeles, she sought out the owner of the film store printed on the mysterious bag which had appeared by Richard's camera in India, and asked him if someone had purchased that certain number of rolls that particular day.

"Yes," the owner replied. "It was so strange that I remember it well. This odd little man came in wearing an orange robe and he had a shock of black hair. I thought he was someone on location from a film company. He paid me, and when I turned back to give him the receipt, he was gone!"

Many devotees have reported receiving visits from Sai Baba in America in times of need, even while he was also at home in India. He is a master of bi-location, and remains in telepathic touch with his devotees. One personal instance I recall was just a few years ago when a hot-burning brush fire swept over the hills of Southern California and threatened the aforementioned Creative Healing Ranch at Lake Elsinore. John and Hildreth called to Sai Baba for protection. The fire stopped directly across the road, and swept around them, leaving the ranch safe.

As well as first visiting Frank in my little guest house, I also know Sai Baba answered my call in a strange way, by coming right into my home. Earlier, while we were yet planning the trip to India, we debated the wisdom of including a certain woman in our new business. She had approached Frank, offering to invest money, and asking to be included as a business partner with us. Financially, it was an important decision for me to make, so we invited her and an adviser of hers to come to my home one afternoon to discuss this. I was dubious, as I did not know her well, and so I prayed earnestly to Sai Baba to guide us in a decision that would be for the good of all concerned.

An odd thing happened. The woman and her friend arrived and I decided to serve the refreshments first. I cut my homemade pie and made a large pot of black coffee from fresh beans which Frank, himself, had just ground at that moment. Frank always insisted on fresh-ground coffee. So he not only saw, but helped pour the finished perked coffee with its dark color and rich aroma into the silver serving pitcher. I carried the pitcher into the dining room where I had other food on the table. Then, when I began to pour coffee for our guests, imagine my astonishment when from the silver pitcher came forth pale, almost clear water! In over thirty years of serving coffee from this serving set, this has never happened before nor since.

There was only one answer to this phenomenon. In an amazing way, Sai Baba had announced his invisible presence, coming to answer my call. As Jesus turned water into wine at the wedding, Sai Baba turned coffee into water at my business meeting. There was absolutely no mistaking it, for both Frank and I saw the strong coffee made from freshly ground beans as we transferred it into the serving pitcher. We felt Sai Baba's presence and message in this, and we quietly agreed, the lady was not meant to be a business partner with us. The strength of the work would be weakened; the metaphor was clear.

As events unfolded, it became evident that our decision was a very good thing.

The trip to India in its entirety was for me an experience of a lifetime. In our search for specific samples and items of merchandise, we traveled the length and breadth of the country. From teeming Bombay where our plane landed and where we did some business with a dealer of fine gemstones, we took a train to Jaipur in the north, as Jaipur is famous for its gemstones and we planned to deal in them. Frank had as fine a knowledge of precious gems as any true gemologist. He could hold a stone in the palm of his hand and know the carat weight and value instinctively. Also talented as an artist of exquisite jewelry, he hoped to use these precious gems in new and distinctive ways.

Jaipur is called the Pink City, as the great majority of its buildings are built of pink sandstone, really very pretty. This city is surrounded by rugged hills and is truly a slice of the real India, its market streets thick with shops of all conceivable wares, swarms of people, vehicles, and small animals loose to run in the town square.

After a number of days in Jaipur (a few of which we spent being violently ill), but did visit the Palace of the Winds, we bused down to New Delhi, and then on to Bangalore in the south, where we arranged to spend the week at Sai Baba's Ashram at Puttaparthi, a small village four hours drive beyond Bangalore that is also Sai Baba's birthplace. Here in the south of India, we had the nicest weather. It reminded me somewhat of Hawaii, with palm trees waving in a warm breeze and wide clean streets. My visit to the Ashram was a most memorable experience.

I was shocked by the unbelievable pollution and dense population in the larger cities, though I had seen vivid pictures in movies and on television for many years. In reality, living conditions for the large majority are becoming rapidly worse as the population explodes. There are hardly words to describe the deplorable situation in which many live. I can only say that as buyers of merchandise we walked among and spoke with people in the labyrinth of streets and tucked-away shops, and saw an inside view of India, different than that usually seen by tourists who travel by tour bus, visit temples, and stay only in five-star hotels. Garbage in the streets of the larger cities is common, which is eaten by various animals roaming loose. We saw no evidence of city garbage pickup — if there was such — or street repair of any kind. The government sadly neglects such services. Everywhere are beggars, some crippled from birth, and the homeless are counted by the thousands. At night the streets are lined with the sleeping indigent. Calcutta, for instance, India's largest city, contains over 15 million people. About one-quarter of them, or 3.5 million people, live on the streets or in one-room slum lean-to's built of cardboard, wooden crates, and sheets of scrap metal. We saw such structures stretching for many miles on the outskirts of the cities.

In the midst of this outward impoverishment, the shining smiles and sweet faces look up at one with innocent candor that bespeaks of souls long accustomed to physical hardships, but who do not allow outer conditions to affect their happiness. The spiritual calm displayed by the people is a testament to the efficacy of the time-honored teachings of Hinduism and Buddhism which permeate this land with the notion of the supremacy of the spirit over the material.

The many temples throughout India, built over the centuries by various moguls, are famous for their beauty. The Taj Mahal in Agra is one of the Seven Wonders of the World, built of carved white marble. It was ordered built by Shah Jahan, in memory of his beloved wife, Mumtaz Mahal, who died in childbirth with his fourteenth child in 1630.

The Taj Mahal took 22 years to complete by 20,000 workers at the expense of the poor, history shows. (Is this not often true?) The Taj Mahal is actually a mausoleum, containing the bodies of both the Shah and his wife. I was disappointed that we did not have the time on this trip to visit Agra.

One of the leading tourist attractions in New Delhi is the simple grave of India's beloved leader, Mahatma Gandhi. A flickering eternal flame near Gandhi's gravesite casts eerie shadows upon a cemetery where grass is being mowed by oxen pulling giant blades behind them, a kind of lawn mower on the hoof. I have read that another memorial to another martyred Gandhi will be built in New Delhi, a spectacular $600 million modern cultural Taj Majal to Indira Gandhi. This memorial, a National Center for the Arts, is heralded as the largest publicly sponsored project ever in India. The museum will combine elements of Hindi, Moghul, and classical architectural styles to reflect India's multi-cultural heritage. So everything is not poverty in this country, as there is a beautiful respect and appreciation, as well as talent, for the arts, and businesses are flourishing, especially in the last few years. But the lower classes have it very difficult.

The Indian masses are generally sweet and rather childlike in some ways, not sophisticated as are westerners. I was amused one day to approach the main Post Office in central Bombay where I was to meet Frank, to find a throng of people, some 50 people raptly watching in quiet fascination someone who stood by the door to the building. To my amazement it was Frank. Being a tall westerner, he stood head and shoulders above the general Indian populous. While waiting for me, he had brought out his simple magic trick of causing a series of brightly colored silk handkerchiefs to disappear for a few children waiting for their parents. But in only a matter of minutes the throng of adults grew so large that it was almost impossible to push through to enter the Post Office. Some were attempting to give him gifts for his efforts.

I managed to get through and found him laughing happily, simply delighted that he had such a rapt audience. Frank was in his glory being the center of attention. I always thought he would have been a great actor on stage. But we had to break it up as this was a public thoroughfare being jammed.

You cannot imagine the crush of being a sardine in a can until you attempt to jam onto India's commuter trains. The rush hour is a stampede. There are women's cars and men's cars in this country where the sexes have for centuries been separated in public. This is a good thing, for bodies can hardly be distinguished one from the other, as they stand tightly wedged until not one more can fit in. Just to find and jump onto the right car is tricky, for very little time is allotted at the stop. Once on, you can only hope not to have need to scratch an itch, for if you can move at all, you are likely to scratch your neighbor. I was told that if a woman got on one of the men's cars by mistake, the men were very apt to take liberties in this tight situation.

I learned the veracity of this first hand, for one day, in fear of losing Frank altogether in the crowd, and not knowing fully at what station we were to get off, I jumped onto the men's car with him. I was the only woman in a sea of men. His long arms surrounded me in the crush in a kind of protective circle bear-hug, for all bodies were jammed tightly into the compartment. After a short time I was startled to feel a hand (I could not tell from where) caressing my upper thigh. I managed to inch my own hand down and gave the bold stranger a deep, sharp scratch with my fingernail. That instantly ended the problem.

Later, when I told Frank of this incident, he roared in his deep voice, "Why didn't you tell me. I would have killed him!"

"Yes," I said. "That's what I was afraid of. You would have created an uproar. For who could tell from which direction it came? I settled it myself, very quietly."

I now found it easy to understand the pictures I'd seen of trains in India with people riding outdoors on the top, or clinging to the sides. The reason was obvious. There was no way for these people to cram themselves inside.

We found the businessmen, however, to be very clean and bright, and sharply astute in dealing with money. As we stepped from crowded, dirty streets, awash with a surging sea of humanity, autos, bicycles, jitney taxis, and animals, with fruit and vegetables laid out for sale on the streets' edge on squares of burlap gunnysacks, and into neat shops laden with lovely wares to be greeted by smiling business-men in spotless white shirts, we were always amazed at the contradiction. I wondered how they did it.

It was here in New Delhi that we found the large, multi-level shop of Raj Mathur and his family, who exported many of the beautifully hand crafted items that filled the shop to overflowing. We were especially impressed with delicately hand-carved stone jars containing exquisitely scented natural solid perfumes. As time unfolded its hidden mysteries, we found this meeting to be a propituous one.

The handcrafted beauty of Indian arts is well-known. Time there has not the same connotation as in the western world. Artisans often take years to perfect their work with loving and painstaking care, and it shows. We found far more wares we would like to have imported than was fea-sible. As it was, we could only carry home samples of very special items and make contacts for future imports.

Toward the end of our stay we were caught in Bombay in the July monsoons and found ourselves wading ankle deep in tepid, swirling, refuse-laden water running in tor-rents in the streets. On my bare feet I wore old sandals that I immediately threw away, as the pollution in the water was obvious. Woe be to one who has an open sore on his leg or even a scratched mosquito bite. Frank had such a sore, unfortunately developing blood poisoning that needed strong treatment, and which hospitalized him upon our arrival back in the U.S.

We traveled by plane, train, bus and taxi, and experi-enced the length and breadth, the swarm of humanity, the animals, and the variety of scenery that is India. We saw many herds of handsome black and white goats, patient elephants at work pulling full carts, and large cud-chewing, humped camels with loads on their backs. Dozens of agile, long-tailed monkeys swung from trees whose branches hung over outdoor country restaurants, waiting to be given — or to steal — someone's food.

While traveling through the countryside, I was intrigued to see at the edge of a village, twelve stately Indian women, wearing bright red, yellow, and green saris to the ankles, working together to lay the foundation of a large apartment building. Some were carrying wooden boxes of wet cement on their heads to others who then poured the cement into the wooden forms. There was not a man in sight.

My adventurous daughter, Jennine, then twenty-two, had nine months earlier strapped a pack on her back, withdrew her savings, purchased a one-way ticket around the world, and set off alone. She mainly would be in the Southern Hemisphere, so she left during our Fall season in October. With open-ended flight dates in major cities in a variety of countries, Jeannine traveled in Tahiti, New Caledonia, New Zealand and Australia, Indonesia, Singapore, Thailand and India on the first legs of her trip. She spent five months in India, traveling the length and breadth of the country, while also visiting very special holy shrines, before Frank and I arrived.

To my joyful amazement, we actually connected; she found us in a hotel in Bombay. What a warm and heartfelt reunion. We hugged and cried and hugged again. For I had felt myself a pretty brave Mom to stand back nine months before, allowing her to experience her dream to go on this trip entirely alone. Through many earlier months I had not known what country she may be in at any given time. However, I had raised her to have faith in God's constant protection, and she believed in that protection wholeheartedly. So, when she announced her amazing trip plan, I had to put my money where my mouth was.

And now, here we were in India. Standing back, I held her at arm's length. "Let me look at you!" Jeannine was very thin. Her blonde hair was short-cropped and sun-bleached, her face and long bare arms an Indian tan, her clothes hung loose on her tall easy frame. Upon my concerned questioning she admitted she had been on antibiotics for dysentery, a common ailment in eastern and now even western countries, but was fine otherwise. She told me she had been hospitalized for several hours a few weeks before, when she fainted from exposure in the 115° F. temperature. Otherwise, Jeannine assured me, this had been a magnificent once-in-a-lifetime experience, as she had been touched by the lives of many people in several countries. Such heart-to-heart contacts can never be known through reading books.

A woman she stayed with in Tahiti, for instance, had suggested she visit her sister in New Caledonia. On arriving, Jeannine found herself on a farm run by this French-speaking woman and her twelve children. Jeannine stayed to work with them three weeks; it was a high point of her trip. Only the mother spoke a little English. The entire family arose at 4:00 a.m. daily, each having an assigned task, and all sang and were happy all day. She enjoyed working in the fields with them, but they were sad to see her leave. The mother warmly pleaded, "Go home. Be with your mother in the United States for a year. Then, come back and stay with us."

Traveling on, Jeannine hiked in Nepal and even spent a week in a cave with an Indian guru. She said she found joy in visiting several well-known ashrams of Indian Masters, particularly the home and family lineage of Paramahansa Yogananda. She spoke of traveling to Varanasi, also called Benares, to the Ganges, the holy river where millions of East Indians make pilgrimage annually to bathe and thereby, as they believe, receive salvation. The river is polluted by any standard. Brown and heavy, flowing a thousand miles through countless villages and plains, accumulating sewage along the way, it is, in fact, among the world's dirtiest rivers. Jeannine reported seeing garbage floating continually past, and even the dead bodies of animals. But the river is held sacred, and the belief in its spiritual qualities to purify each soul who bathes in it attracts millions to its banks. Many people who can, come several times a year. Others feel lucky to make the trek once in their lifetime. And no one becomes ill from bathing in the water but are, it is said, often healed.

Jeannine remained to accompany us on our train trip to Jaipur. It was God's grace she had arrived just at this time, for it was now that both Frank and I became very, very ill. The germ we had picked up was more serious than the usual intestinal complaint, and Jeannine was there with us to find a doctor and to nurse us for several days until we were again able to travel.

Later, when Jeannine and I were both home in the U.S., I asked her, "Of everything you saw and did and felt during your year away, what do you consider the highlight of your trip?" Her answer was meditative, thoughtful, and touching.

"Without a doubt, it was the days I spent with Mother Theresa's nuns, working beside them in the Children's Hospital in Calcutta. It is a soul-service they are doing. The children are so sweet and beautiful, and many are in such very sad condition. It was a privilege to be a part of their work for even a short time. One sister even arranged a meeting for me with Mother Theresa. It was an amazing time, an incredible memory. But you know Mom, I didn't feel it was my life's calling. And then too, I'm not Catholic."

Jeannine's closest call happened, of all things, in an ice cave in New Zealand while she was exploring. A several-ton block of ice suddenly came loose from the ceiling and crashed down onto the floor of the cave only a few feet from where she was standing. "That would have been a strange way to die," she pondered, "killed by a block of ice in a cave in New Zealand!" I have a gorgeous picture, taken by a traveling acquaintance, of Jeannine poised on the edge of a crevice, halfway up a steep shining glacier while on a hike in that area. It is a shot worthy to be in National Geographic Magazine.

From India my daughter journeyed on to Italy, staying for a number of months at Assisi, the birthplace of St. Francis, where Yogananda's followers have established a European Center and Retreat. Run by the Ananda Brotherhood (based in Nevada City, California) the Assisi Retreat is housed in a lovely old villa on a hilltop, and commands a magnificent view across the central Italian countryside. Subsequent to her visit, Jeannine became a disciple, studying the teachings of the master, Paramahansa Yogananda, as her brother, Jeremy, had before her.

I think how life's circles go around and come around, as I recall my visits to Yogananda's eautiful temple on Sunset Boulevard in Los Angeles when I was but a young woman in 1946, feeling the attraction of love. And I remember my visit to Assisi with Allen, when I received the moving recall of my past life connection to this area, to St. Francis, and remembering too my small thimble apport.

Ananda Centers have since sprung up in many U.S. cities, as well as in Nigeria, and now seekers come from all over Europe to the Ananda Assisi Retreat Center. Yogananda's dream to teach the truth of God's love and the wisdom of Self-Realization through deep meditation has exploded in many directions in the western world. There are as of this writing altogether 171 Ananda ministers working in the field and at the home community.

The day that Jennine left India, traveling from New Delhi on to Rome, Frank and I headed back to Bombay, and then home to the U.S., via Manila in the Philippines and Bangkok, Thailand.

*

PSYCHIC HEALING EXPERIENCES

What an amazing happening! My story would not be complete without describing our stopover in the Philippines that included a bus trip to Baguio City, outside of Manila. After riding through the countryside for a number of miles, I was intrigued to find our crowded bus climbing up into an indescribably beautiful, thickly forested mountain valley. Baguio City, a quiet little town, sits perched high up on the mountain. Disembarking and wandering through the streets, we found the shopkeepers to be open and friendly. It was easy to arrange a visit to a Philippine Healer, which was the reason we had come here.

For many years I had known of the Philippine healers who, using neither instruments nor anesthesia, perform surgery with their hands on patients who feel no pain, and who report many healings.

Since 1968 I have owned the book, full of graphic colored pictures, *Wonder Healers of the Philippines,** by Harold Sherman, who discovered the healers during his stint in the Philippines during World War II. As I had long

*Wonder Healers of the Phillipines, 1964, DeVorss & Co., LA, CA.

been intrigued by this type of healing, and since our travels had brought us so close, the opportunity to see this amazing work for myself seemed too good to pass up. Back pain still plagued me from time to time as well, a kind of residue from my fall as a child on the farm. Frank, also, had some scar tissue from old accidents which bothered him (his right thumb had been cut off by the miscalculated slice of a machete and sewn back on in Venezuela), so he, too, was eager to see how this was done.

After a quiet walk around the beautiful, quaint town square of Baguio City, where we enjoyed some refreshment in one of the local cafes, we made inquiries and were taken by taxi to the modest home of a recommended and respected healer and his wife, who lived in the residential area above the town. We were greeted by a nice young man in a simple home that was very clean and attractive. I noted an abundance of colorful flowers and tropical plants gracing the downhill steps and entrance. Paul introduced himself and his tiny, charming wife. We exchanged casual pleasant conversation, Paul inquiring courteously about our trip, and asking the reason for our visit to him. He spoke of his spiritual faith and guidance in this work. Then we discussed a donation for his time that would be suitable.

Paul ushered Frank and me into the treatment room. It was sparkling clean and stark, containing only a chair, a small table holding a bowl of water and cotton balls, and the treatment table itself, which was covered with a clean white sheet. There was no cabinet or any other equipment.

Paul began with a sincere and reverent prayer to Christ. (The healers are devout Christian). I was then shown to a small anteroom and asked to undress only enough to expose my lower back and stomach. When I emerged Paul directed me to lie down on the table. The entire preliminaries were straight-forward and simple. Paul's short-sleeved shirt exposed bare arms. His hands touched my abdomen, seeming to seek direction where work was needed. I can here report that as I watched carefully, tilting my head forward, I saw with my own eyes the healer's fingers enter my abdomen and remove scar tissue, during which time I felt no pain whatsoever. There was no blood save a bit of watery pink fluid that was easily wiped up with a dab of cotton. The scar tissue was residue from the surgery of my long ago double hernia. Paul showed me this scar tissue before he dropped it into the bowl of water with his left hand. As the fingers of Paul's right hand drew out of the small pocket of my abdomen where they had been working, the flesh snapped shut instantly, leaving visible only a thin, clean, faintly pink line that resembled what otherwise one would assume had been a small cut, now in its last healing stage. After a few hours even that disappeared. It was astonishing and beautiful to see the wonders that are possible in this world by those who truly believe in the help of Holy Spirit.

Paul now asked me to turn over so he could work on my back. I felt only the pressure of his fingers, removing scar tissue around the spine. Afterward that area did feel less stiff, though not entirely healed. Orthopoedic surgeons had diagnosed me as having disintegrated disks, and that apparently was not changed. It appears to me that the healer can *take out* unwanted tissue, but apparently did not, or could not at that moment, *replace* tissue that is missing. I rose from the table, perfectly well, without discomfort of any kind.

Frank had problems with the back of his neck, so asked for help in that area. I was allowed to watch from very close range the same marvelous entry and withdrawal of Paul's fingers from the flesh, releasing a tension for Frank which he had suffered in his neck for years. Paul also worked on Frank's lower back, as his fingers sensitively sought out troubled areas, and included work on his hand. Frank said it felt only like a massage, not uncomfortable in the least.

This was a unique experience that I had never imagined I would have. Years before, in reading about this psychic surgery, I had in meditation asked Holy Spirit, *"How can this be? Please tell me the law by which a man's hand can enter the body of another without cutting, pain, or blood."* I was sincerely and deeply eager, as a disciple and student of the mysteries of life, to understand. Soon the answer came into my mind and a picture was shown to me. This is what I received.

"The phenomena involves magnetism and polarity. During such healing work, the fingers of the healer emit a polarity opposite to the polarity of the cells of the body being worked on. All cells are held together by the Law of Attraction. When an opposite polarity is introduced, the body cells are repulsed and spring apart naturally without severing, and they stay separated as long as the negative or opposite polarity remains intrusive. As the repulsion polarity of the fingers is withdrawn, the healthy cells of the body snap back together again in perfect formation under the same Law of Attraction, with no harm done. Diseased or dead tissue emits a different energy, felt by the healer, and can be withdrawn."

This made sense to me and I was happily satisfied. In years past, as today, many poor or destitute people lived in the Philippines. God, in His goodness, made a way for them to receive help without expensive medicines and modern surgery, which was not often available. Patients gratefully brought a chicken or some vegetables from their garden to the healer in payment.

Before you scoff at what I write, please remember, there is nothing impossible under the sun. In seeking wisdom from the Universe we must not go to the ocean with a thimble. If we wish to grow and evolve, we need to keep an open mind and an open heart as our receptacles. Dr. George Washington Carver did, and he revolutionized the economy of the South with what he received from the Universal Fountain of Wisdom: a myriad of uses for the lowly peanut.

Frank and I returned home enlightened but weary, and glad beyond measure to be American citizens, although we had been very grateful before, of course. The next two and one-half years I was deeply involved in my new corporation, Trans-World Trade, Ltd., importing from India and successfully distributing sixty-two fine handcrafted items. I traveled to, and participated in gift shows throughout the U.S., from Seattle to Chicago, Dallas to Los Angeles, San Francisco and points between.

At the outset I had great difficulty dealing with East Indian banks. To say this was a challenge is an understatement; it was a nightmare. All export buy and sell monies must pass through the Indian banks. No direct exchange, as we have in the U.S., is allowed. The Indian government is fraught with corruption and the banks held our monies for many months to gain the interest on them, thereby not releasing payment to our merchant contacts so goods could be sent.

After a time of business struggle, Frank and I helped sponsor and bring to America a fine East Indian gentleman from New Delhi who eventually became my business partner. His name is Raj Kumar Mathur, and he now is distributing in the U.S. the products of the four factories he owns near New Delhi, which his brothers in India continue to run. Our business, which I sold to and now under R.Expo, U.S.A.,* keeps 4,000 East Indian families working, and contributes to the trade between our two countries.

It was a privilege, later, to sponsor Raj's beautiful wife and three lovely small daughters as they settled in America. They all were becoming ill in India's unbelievably polluted air. Raj is truly well-deserving. His brave efforts and struggles to succeed at holding the family business together after the death of his parents is quite a story. When Raj first arrived in the U.S., he stayed in my home, out of which we operated the business for six months until his wife and family could join him, and new business space be obtained.

Frank continued to study the spiritual truths with great enthusiasm, and over the months gave voice to fewer angry or other negative thoughts about his past, and having been touched by the spirit of a living master, seemed much happier and mellow toward life. Though there are always higher hills of spiritual growth to climb, Frank's achievement of a plateau of emotional control after many turbulent years is to be applauded. As Raj took on more of the business with me, Frank felt free to go on to other work, as he always seems to be a pioneer.

A year later, Frank told me he had telephoned his mother in Austria on Mother's Day. This was his first contact with her in many years. Before this call she had not

*R.Expo-U.S.A., 1112 S. 344th St., #309, Federal Way, WA 98003

known where he was.

Then Frank told me, "I want you to know I am leaving for Europe in ten days. Mother was absolutely delighted to hear from me and has invited me to come home for her eighty-fifth birthday celebration. Some two hundred guests are expected, including some of our old friends from the Hapsburg family (ex-monarchs of Austria, ousted by Hitler's invasion). Recalling what you have taught me, I wish to make peace and a reconciliation with Mother before she passes from this earth. If I do not, I will always bear the burden of my neglect to make the attempt."

How wonderful it was to hear these words. I had prayed through many months that this deeply fractured and hurtful mother/son relationship could be healed by forgiveness, compassion and understanding, with peace returning to the hearts of all, including the one in spirit who had several years before whispered so urgently and passionately in my ear, "Klaus . . . Klaus . . . Help my son!"

I had not then imagined the depth and breadth of Klaus' urgent plea from the Inner Planes, as a father, tormented to see the dark unhappiness of hurt and anger buried in the breast and mind of his youngest son. Klaus had been denied the privilege of raising this boy because of his fateful execution in mid-life by Hitler's firing squad. And it was fortunate I'd had no inkling of what his request would mean for me, nor how it would affect my life through several years of steady, patient, sometimes emotionally painful effort, quietly teaching Frank of God's love for him and for all His creation, despite appearances and man's inhumanity to man.

In addition to working with him personally, knowing Frank also precipitated the whole India scene in my life, the import business, Trans-World Trade Ltd., our help in bringing an East Indian family to America, the amazing events in the Philippines, and the visit to Thailand. God works in wondrous ways, to bring forth the Plan for our lives.

Frank was an extrovert, the very opposite of a shrinking violet. He enjoyed joking and creating outlandish humor, even with strangers. In addition, being six-foot, six inches tall, he was often very much in evidence. Sometimes someone would ask me discreetly, "Where in the world did you find him?"

I could truthfully answer, "At a garage sale."

This was not a love affair. Frank was twenty years my junior. Oh, no! God's Plan intended something far more meaningful to inner healing, soul growth, and wisdom for all involved than that would have been.

I do know, however, that in the past our lives have crossed in a meaningful way. Whether as family members or otherwise I cannot say, but we understood and felt we knew one another from the moment we met, and that, undoubtedly, was why Klaus came to me for help, help that was badly needed. I also could recognize and understand Frank's symptoms and resultant problems as a learning disabled child, you see, because of my experiences with my own son, our beloved Jason. Holy Spirit, I am sure, planned it all.

Frank invited me to come to Austria with him to meet his mother and family, and to attend her birthday celebration. I refused, however, feeling this to be a special time for him to renew and heal relationships, better done on his own, without my back-up.

In a month's time my larger-than-life friend returned from his visit to Austria, pleased and proud of his gentle behavior during the time with his mother, because, as he related, he had for the first time in his life of emotional turmoil felt relaxed, happy and at peace in her presence. Frank had let go of old, long-held resentments.

"Mother laughed and we enjoyed many hours together," Frank related. "Although at eight-five she suffers some arthritis and pain now. It was a wonderful birthday celebration for her with two hundred guests." He told me his mother still resides in, and manages, the very large family home.

It seems mother and son have achieved forgiveness and a certain peace of mind at long last, and surprise of surprises, his mother requested that Frank return to Austria to live. "I've decided to go," he announced.

My assigned task from Spirit, to help Frank change the course of his beleaguered life, to take control of his Ship of State on the stormy Sea of Life, has apparently so far succeeded with God's grace and ever-present help. Only time can tell.

It proves once again that, "God will not do for man, what man must do for himself. But what man cannot do for himself, God will do."

*

CHAPTER TWELVE

A STRANGE VISION — AND A HEAVENLY VISITOR APPEARS

For a person of Gemini nature, born under the sign of The Twins, many events in life seem to happen in doubles, at least it always was so for me. Mama used to say, "As a little girl you couldn't just swing, you had to be eating a peanut butter sandwich at the same time, and often you dropped it, and the chickens got it." While astride my horse watching cows, I read books. In my teens when I came down with measles, mumps also appeared to give me chipmunk cheeks the very same week. A year later on top of fiery red scarlet fever, with skin so sensitive that a light sheet was painful, chicken-pox chose to break out, spreading ninety-six of the ugly pustules over my face alone. Soon they covered my entire body, making matters doubly worse. Later, while playing the piano, I doubled the fun by whistling in accompaniment with the tunes.

So now, I should not have been surprised that in the midst of my active and demanding schedule (which included the trip to India, and setting up business), the recurrent lower back pain was coupled with a strange stiffness through the pelvis, a feeling of being strapped that made walking difficult.

Since my business distributing the fine handcrafted work of the East Indian people (including many natural floral perfumes packaged in beautifully carved stoneware that resembled marble) was helping to keep over three or four hundred families in India employed (which has since increased to over one thousand), it presented not only an adventure, but an altruistic venture and the gratification of giving something of benefit to both countries. Thus, I felt a desire to continue the business, even while carrying pain and discomfort.

The plan was to help Raj get a foothold in the U.S. I had great admiration for this very fine, gentle East Indian who had experienced great struggle in life, losing his mother while he was only eighteen. She had been the guiding force in a small family perfume business. His father was a semi-invalid. Raj had, through tremendous perseverance, since age eighteen, not only obtained his education in commerce while supporting his brothers and sister, but also built up, and now owned, the factories that produced most of the products we imported. He and his family were often ill due to the horrendous pollution in India, so Raj had a strong desire to come to America and to bring his wife and three daughters as well. We found a mutual benefit in our arrangement.

However, this was a terribly inconvenient time for physical impairment to bring me such discomfort, and I wondered how I could alleviate it. The pain seemed especially strange considering the healing work that had been done in the Philippines.

Earlier, when I sought relief through traditional methods, the orthopedic surgeons and a variety of therapists I consulted could not agree on treatment. Some stated they had never seen such an abnormal skeletal structure and expressed surprise that I walked. A variety of surgical methods were offered as a trial, with no guarantee of the outcome. I refused them for obvious reasons; being a guinea pig was not an attractive prospect. One doctor diagnosed disintegrated disks in the lower spine causing pressure on the main nerves to the legs.

Others said there was a separated pelvis, still another, "Perhaps new hips will do it." But all agreed, ex-rays showed no signs of arthritis in the spine or hips. At least that was encouraging.

The best relief came from chiropractic adjustments, but this was always short-lived. I visited twelve chiropractors over those few years. I must say, I gave my best effort to so-called normal routes to recovery. I even attended physical therapy at the hospital twice weekly for a year. Amazingly, even this effected no change.

I also flew to California to receive the Creative Healing technique from the masters of this therapy themselves. To everyone's surprise, this also effected no change, even though Creative Healing had shown a tremendous success record in healing all manner of illnesses, in the practices of a large number of graduate therapists, including my own, as related earlier.

And so, I ceased looking to outside help and continued gentle exercises at home to forestall total crippling. I also gave myself morning and evening rubs, massaging the affected areas with castor oil, as recommended by the renowned healer Edgar Cayce, and alternately with olive oil as recommended by Joseph Stephenson of Creative Healing. It is this home ritual, which included healing prayer and giving love and praise to my body, that I credit with keeping me on my feet and out of a wheelchair, so that I was able to make the trip to India and work the import business.

I never ceased asking of the Beloved Presence, "What does this mean? What is happening?" For I have tried through my life to live on the high side of ethics and love, to live up to my soul's purpose in life. Now, when it seemed there should be freedom after years of responsibilities, including the travails with Jason's life, I found myself semi-crippled, carrying this strange condition which seemed to have no purpose. I sought answers.

I tell all this for a special reason, for answers came in a surprising way. A beautiful description of the deeper reason behind much human suffering is given in the book *Cosmic Healing, a Comparative Study of Channeled Teachings on Healing* (DeVorss & Co. 1988) by Alan Young. The following paragraph carries a wonderful truth that is applicable in many lives:

"Knowledge is born of suffering until man attains to

the consciousness of God. When we reach the conscious awareness of the only one Real and existing Power expressed in ourselves, we will realize that suffering has been the means of the unfoldment of the awareness, and then suffering ceases. The darkness that surrounds us unfolds the Christ in us. When a seed is planted in the darkness of the earth, the life in the seed unites with the life in the earth, waiting to reproduce it; it grows out of the darkness to express itself in the image and likeness of the seed sown. So does the Spirit of God; *the Christ is the seed that is within us and grows out of the darkness that surrounds us.* The beauty of the Christ manifests in us as the image and likeness of God. We must not be discouraged if immediate results are not forthcoming, for work is being done in accordance with our thought. This law is infallible."

During the time of being overshadowed by, and carrying, this strange condition of the pelvis, I actually felt bound by an invisible harness even while lying in bed half awake and half asleep. Daily movement was often stiff and awkward, causing me much wonderment. At certain times I could hardly walk. Remember, there had been no diagnosis of arthritis. Oddly, the severity of this condition also seemed to come and go. I often prayed asking "Why?" One evening in meditation a vision came, suddenly, dramatically, as have so many events in my life.

While in the reverie state I saw or, more specifically, felt and was shocked to find the binding of a chastity belt, as used in medieval days, tight around my pelvis. This I experienced and saw on the etheric level, as though a pattern from the past was casting a very real shadow into the present, manifesting its effects on my physical. I recalled then the vivid image of the old chastity belt I'd seen in the Altstadt Museum in Nuremberg, which I described in Chapter Six. At the time I was repulsed by the ugly contraption, made of chain metal and heavy straps, to be locked onto a woman's torso. An ugly, small metal trap at the crotch was fashioned as a circlet of sharp metal hooks turned inward, shaped to tear anything that dared to pass the forbidden gate.

The knowledge swept over me in those moments of

vision that this was one evidence of the cruelty to women down through those years when the men went on Crusades and to war, often never to return, leaving the woman, many hundreds of them I'm sure, locked in this contraption to suffer the miserable consequences. The agony endured for one left pregnant can only be imagined, for there was no means to break free of this torturous contraption which was fashioned to not be broken. Women were a man's possession, a sort of chattel, like his land and his horses, and the cruelty of the thing was not considered.

In this moment of realization it became clear that I was to lift these atrocities to God for forgiveness. An electrifying thought then hit me. "Could the chastity belt also have been my fate in ages past? And if so, why is it evidencing now?"

It is said that "The mills of the gods grind slowly, but they grind exceedingly fine." It seems that patience is a prime requisite if one wishes to receive deeper answers from the Universe. So I was patient. I drifted off to sleep, and the answer to the mystery was not revealed to me until many months had passed.

✳

A HEAVENLY VISITOR APPEARS

One day a young friend of our family who thought of me as his second Mom, phoned. Paul was a student teacher, and was now, he said, in the process of moving to a new residence. "May I stay with you a few weeks until I can get settled?" he asked hesitantly.

"Of course! I'd be happy to have you," I replied. We had plenty of room since Jeremy and Jennine were away from home. Paul is a delightful chap with a light and bright nature, who has been a really warm and loving friend of our whole family.

A week later my young guest announced, "I'm meeting a friend of mine from Honolulu at the airport tomorrow. Arthur is passing through on his way to Los Angeles on business. I've invited him to lay over in Seattle enroute as I'd like to take him sight-seeing on the Islands this weekend (in Puget Sound). Would it be alright if Arthur stayed here two nights with us? We would be away through the days . . ." I smiled, "Certainly! He is most welcome. And the guest room is empty. It will be no problem at all." I had become accustomed to having young people overnight through the years.

An hour before Paul drove to the airport to meet his friend, he casually remarked, "Oh, by the way, Arthur is a trance medium. You ought to have a sitting with him." Well, that was a surprise. But I declined, pointing out I had work to do and was quite tired (I was at that time devoting sixteen hours a day to my India import business, getting out orders, keeping books, etc.).

I might mention here that we, Raj, the business partner who had come to America, and I, were required by the U.S. Immigration Department to sell over $100,000 in gross wholesale products the first year, if Raj were to be allowed to continue his end of the business in America. This was a very harsh regulation for my small import company. Expenses of importing by air freight were high, so net profit was far lower, and there was also my start-up loan to pay off. Thus I generally took no time off whatsoever, so I was weary to the verge of illness.

Paul's friend from Honolulu arrived. He was a charming and disarmingly open young man, with whom I felt an instant rapport. We laughingly agreed we both felt as though we had known one another for long years, though it was, of course, our first meeting. Arthur was a delight. A fine looking man, in his mid-thirties, with a warm and infectious sense of humor, it was obvious he truly enjoyed people, giving his full attention to whomever he was with. I thought, here is a chap who fully lives life! At the same time he seemed humble and devout, devoid of pretense. In short, I found our guest to be an all-around joy to be with.

Arthur is a spiritually gifted young man. It would be many months before I learned of the wide reputation he has gained through his integrity and accuracy in his special work, for which he is called to all of the Hawaiian Islands, as well as to the west coast of the U.S. He also has since been invited to New Zealand, where six hundred people attended his lecture on the north island. I knew none of this on the day I met him, however. After a few hours of relaxation, refreshment, and making plans with Paul, Arthur insisted on giving a reading to me, gratis.

"I really wish to, in thanks for your warm hospitality," he stated with a beautiful smile. How could I refuse? I decided to take a break from work and accept.

This reading turned out to be a most precious gift from God, a highlight in my life, the most beautiful, helpful, emotionally moving, remarkably soul-serving, and healing experience I had received for many years. Not since the wonder of the expanded consciousness experience in my teen years, while in meditation in my bedroom that night long ago in Illinois, had such a spiritually uplifting event come to me. I was told in this reading that this meeting had been planned. It was Holy Spirit's response to my intense, prayerful need for answers.

We retired to a quiet room in my home, and at Arthur's suggestion I set up a tape recorder to record the message. Arthur began the sitting with a deeply sincere and reverent prayer to God that we be surrounded by the Christ Light, and guarded that only the highest good should come forth for us this day. This, by the way, is standard procedure and a necessity in all legitimate, or legal, trance sittings, for if those involved are not workers with and children of the Christ Light, trance should be avoided for reasons of psychic safety. For in this, as in all things on all planes, there are laws that govern actions. When properly conducted, with a guardian at the gate of inner levels, it is totally safe and can be beneficial beyond all belief. Since some may not understand what this entails, I will digress to give a very sketchy overview as I have understood it.

There are some certain individuals who have developed, through long hours of meditation and devotion to God, or in some cases have been born with, because of similar disciplines in past lifetimes, the ability to temporarily take their consciousness out of their body at will, giving the body over as a service for a short time to a Being, a discarnate we shall say, from the Unseen Higher side of life. The Being can then step in and speak in a natural way to the loved one here in the physical, using the body's vocal chords. In one sense this is miraculous, for one can hear the voice, in reality, of another who has long since passed over. It is, indeed, a very special thrill when this happens.

Now here I must stress that this is not done haphazardly, by any stretch of the imagination. There are higher laws of magnetism and vibration with which we are not generally familiar governing this work. In any legitimate trance sitting the medium, or sensitive person, is guided and guarded very carefully by an unseen guardian called a gatekeeper, and generally only one or two specially appointed Beings whose vibration blends with that of the medium are allowed to come through. Usually only one Higher Being comes through, having found a physical medium with whom he or she can work. This work, when legitimate, is always done as a help and benefit to those here in the physical world who need comfort and advice.

There is, as in everything in this world of duality, the flip side, whereby illegal entry to human consciousness can be gained by lower astral entities, through one in the physical body inadvertently opening their psychic centers with the use of drugs, alcohol, or intense uncontrolled emotions. Herein lies a very real and frightening danger, which has, in fact, become a far greater cause of all forms of possession and resultant crime than people realize. Unenlightened earthbound entities are ever seeking such opportunities to again experience vicariously the sensual pleasures of earth life. They are often trapped in limbo, so to speak, unable at their level of consciousness to advance to higher realms, and now without a physical body as a vehicle. So when the psychic centers are artificially forced open with drugs, the unaware human leaves himself wide-open, without protection from such lower astral intruders. He may then become a victim by being temporarily displaced and his body used to commit all manner of crimes by the intruder! Later the astral entity withdraws, leaving the rightful owner, the human, (who sometimes claims no remembrance of the act as he was out of it) to face the dire consequences. Thus the accused one here may say, "Something came over me, I don't know why I did it," or, "The Devil made me do it," as they realize they were not in control.

Nothing like this can happen in a legitimate trance sitting. Higher Forces *never* come without prayerful invitation, and then only for a good and uplifting purpose, under the protection of the Christ Light with a known gatekeeper present. In this way, all involved are workers for Truth and Love. There is nothing to fear in this latter setting, and much information to gain.

Bear in mind that this medium and I had just met. Arthur knew nothing of me or of my family, nor had our mutual friend Paul apprised him, as Paul also had no knowledge of my personal life. In fact, most of the amazing information that came through concerned my soul's past lifetimes. Some of the information that was given no other person but myself could have known, and much of it applied only to me in ways no one other than Spirit could have been aware of.

The sitting began with Arthur's beautiful opening prayer, and then, before going into trance, he offered a number of clairvoyant messages that he received directly. He spoke of the colors and extension of my aura and what this showed to him of the many and varied experiences of life. He then gave me valuable information on what he perceived regarding my life's future time-frame, all of which was very helpful.

Soon, to my amazement, Arthur spoke of a man in spirit who had come to greet me. He described perfectly his coloring and build, even to the suit he was wearing and the particular ring on his finger which he had always worn as identification. I recognized the description as Smith Griswold, my friend, and handsome ex-boss from my days in the office in Los Angeles forty-five years ago. I have not before written that Smith had succumbed to a rare brain tumor, passing on over twenty years before in a hospital near where he had been working in Washington, D.C. Now he had come to me at the first opportunity.

Arthur continued, "This gentleman wishes to tell you that he, from spirit, saw and was concerned about what you were involved in, that is, your spiritual studies. He says he had not understood them . . . He is telling me he began to investigate and . . . (here Arthur paused listening, and then chuckled) . . . He says, 'And you know what happened!' He is telling me that he, through you, has found the Path, and has been very active over here in such studies." I expressed surprise and delight to hear from Smith, and asked how he was getting along.

Arthur listened for awhile, and then continued. "He is asking me to tell you that he has recently been occupied with translating a rare book of spiritual text from Chinese into English so others may take advantage of the truths contained therein." (Apparently books are still used for study by some souls on the Inner Planes.) Arthur paused, and appeared to be listening again. "And he also wants you to know he loved you more than you knew."

I am sitting enthralled. For you remember, as a young girl before my marriage, this man had been my ideal, a dream walking. And now to have him return to speak to me, and to bring a distinctly personal message was something I had never even imagined.

Later, on September 4, 1992, on the television program *Unsolved Mysteries*, hosted by the well-known television actor, Robert Stack, a woman named Coral Pogue of Sussex, England, was interviewed. She is a psychic artist who, for a number of years, has drawn sketches of individual souls from inner vision as she sees them appear. Over 100,000 deceased relatives and friends of the people who come for sittings have been seen and drawn by her. Ms. Pogue claims the subjects are alive and come to her in person for the sittings. Her clients invariably identify the spirit entity. But Arthur was speaking again.

"I feel now I am to go into trance. There is someone who works through me and he desires to come in."

Arthur appeared to fall immediately asleep, his head dropping slightly forward. After a few moments, the head came up, the throat cleared, there was a short period of adjustment. Then an entirely different voice spoke in a most beautifully precise, and unmistakably classic, English accent.

Here I shall interject that the reading which followed was such a remarkable and profound experience, pertaining so explicitly and helpfully to what I was going through, that months later I thought to myself, "I must ask his permission to divulge his name and to speak of him in the book I am writing." For this speaker from Spirit was, and is, a special personage whose name everyone will recognize, but whose identity I did not know until the very end of my message from him, at which time I asked him for his name.

Two years later, when visiting Honolulu where Arthur lives, I asked for and received a second sitting. To my great surprise (after Arthur had gone into trance and this same individual again had entered the body), before I had an opportunity to greet him and certainly no time to ask a question, this delightful Entity's first words in that precise English accent were, "Yes, my dear.You have my permission to write of me in your book. In fact, you may wish to give the entire transcript."

He had read my thoughts! This should not have surprised me, but it did surprise me that he gave permission to write in its entirety the enlightening and personal message he had given in my home that amazing day over a year earlier when Arthur arrived out-of-the-blue, the unexpected guest of my houseguest, and brought me heaven. So now, I shall share those exact words of my Heavenly Visitor.

In that delightful English accent, his first words came clearly. "There, I think we've about got it. The connection's a bit weak, but we've got something like contacts here. It's a bit difficult to adjust to another location, as the lad presently wishes to live in the Islands, you know.

"Let me begin by introducing myself. It is only proper. I function as a Spokesman for a particular Council and we are working, more or less, through the medium's vocal chords at the current time. The purpose for the coming is to give a delineation upon certain things that have been, things that yet are to be, the main events in your own life, as seen. This is not the first time we have contacted, not in this life, but in another."

He then told of a time when I was a member of a brown-skinned people who settled in this same approximate area. "These came to be known in time as the Nez Perce Indian tribe. We do not find this to be of recent time, but taking it back two or three centuries or so. You were married to two men, obviously not simultaneously, but the first being killed, ironically enough, by a very large brown bear. I say ironically, because he, himself, was called Brown Bear. We all thought it very interesting, eh?

"The second husband, I believe, is the same gentleman you were married to in this current embodiment, the one you've got now. And . . . hold a minute . . . the two of you were interested at that time in the bartering of some land which another tribe from farther down south were trying, in a sense, to get from your people. And though you were willing to concede some of it, you wanted certain fishing rights, you know, things like that. And the two of you became, as it were, negotiators for the whole tribe. For this purpose, and others too numerous to go into here, we say to you thus the good karma returns in your being able to establish the home you have here at this time. Also, when the time arrives when you may choose to let go of the home, which no doubt will be prompted by . . . hold a minute . . . by your man, I believe it's Allen, who is here in the Spirit World, he would let you know through a solid feeling — now is the time.

"Your man, Allen, is quite about the task. In other words, as you know good and well, he's not quite left you, but has been in and out. He has, in fact, contacted you in the dream state, and has from time to time inspired your writing on occasion. We might literally say has been right by your side. At such a time when his impulse is upon you, he would let you know when it is time for the sale of the house, he being able to see from here when the economic climate is right."

"That's good," I interjected, "I need the help!"

"Yes, there's no question about it. You shall have it. He is now, you might say, greater than he was. Although his own interest in the world of spirit was not equal to yours, still he now, of course, knows it to be the open waterway to eternal truth.

"And I know I don't surprise you when I tell you that you have the typical band of Red Indians who come and go and watch the property. From time to time you might even have sensed the presence of them."

(Here there was discussion regarding spirit doctors who were working together on my metabolism so that surgery to correct the back condition would not be necessary. And recommendations were given for a helpful remedy for the viral condition tiring me, which I still carried from an infection sustained in India.)

Then he continued. "The entire work of India and the function of what you are doing now has to do with an old . . . how shall I call it . . . not a debt, not a debt . . . no, rather an inward sense of obligation to aid somehow in the plight of India, if even symbolically. And it is done by aiding in the distribution of those things which have been made there that the world will continue to note the beauty of the Indian artifact.

"Then it was meant to be that I do this work?"

"Only for the nonce . . . only for now, as we are approaching the crisis. You have been doing it at personal expense, and as this thing is part of the ancient tradition of India, having to do with surrender . . . surrender and the emotional aspect. That you are thus functioning as a bhakti yogi,* and that your karmic involvement in this also dates back to the 12th Century or so. You had been in the lineage of the one known as Akbar, the great Mogul Emperor.**

"I was in his lineage?" I asked.

"Knew him . . . and you pledged to work for the soul of India in times to come. For as he was leaving that life . . . you were not related, but were his handmaiden, very young and lovely, and he took great comfort in having you about. It was a platonic thing . . . At that time he told you that in his

*One who surrenders to his 'soul's plan' for most spiritual growth.

**Akbar was the Emperor who built the beautiful and famous 'Hanging Gardens of Kashmir'. I had always wondered why involuntary tears sprung to my eyes upon seeing the beautiful films of that country.

eyes of the future he saw India disintegrating. And you said to him, 'As long as I've got breath and life I shall do all I can to keep India holy in the eyes of the world.' So he thus said that, and later, when incarnate as the great Master El Morya Khan, did also bring blessings upon your head."

"Thank you so much for expressing this! I have often wondered why."

"Yes. Very ancient, and yet, the pact was such that it only held until . . . well the End Times, as some have called it. And as you know, water doth boil at 212° F. or so, and generally not before that, so also the changes that are meant to change the face of this earth began at the point when the earth has reached the vibrational pitch predetermined by the great Minds that sustain the Universal Flow, and upon your earth calendars, as you shall call it, would be the year 1990 and the whole decade soon to come. And that though your own — you might call it karma if you will — shall allow you to remain in the physical body . . . oh years and years from now . . . that you might elect at any point after that — to leave, and it would not be catastrophic."

"In other words I would have fulfilled my obligations and karma after 1990 or 1992?"

"Yes. 1992 precisely. And after that you may find yourself thinking in terms of quitting the body, though those thoughts already steal through you now."

At this I am utterly astounded! For I had thought that, but no one knew it — or so I assumed! I answered, "It is simply because I am so very weary, with this condition upon me plus the long hours of work."

"Yes, and yet the work shall cease, as we speak of the business side of things."

"I try to make joy of it, but it has been my health that held me down."

"Yes, but in the times to come, called again the decade of the '90's, you shall find yourself again more able to place thoughts upon paper, fulfilling the dharma of the hierarchical energy of Gemini, which is the Mercury shining mind."

"I want to do that so much! And I want to say the things from spirit that need to come through —"

"Oh yes. And you'll find that the book, as we see it, has a strong probability of getting out and published . . . shall have reminiscences of your life, of the many you've known and seen, of even the phenomena you've witnessed . . . of the various things you have noted, even to the point of apports. You also shall mention the whole Oriental element and how it all blended into the life of this one woman (me) who also has her roots in Europe, going into England and Germany. And all of it shall get annotated. You'll need a little help with it — and it shall come.

"And the son who yet remains on the earth plane . . . he is guided by his brother in Spirit. Though he scarcely knows it, but shall come to know it more fervently. And the one who passed (Jason) was greeted by the Holy Man Yogananda, who received him in Spirit, as well as others."

"Oh!" I exclaim, "Was he? How wonderful!"

"Yes, it has been some years now — forty or more since he passed."

"Yes. How happy I am that my son was met by him. Jason was a beautiful boy. He just had, well, problems."

"Right. And yet his passing taught many lessons you see, and they yet continue. And in your writing phase, various from our world shall take turns standing at your side and you will have them coming, almost dictating, giving the information through. In the times of the German life before this one, you were the sister of the one who writes under the name of Montgomery — Ruth Montgomery."

"I was?" I ask, somewhat in awe.

"Yes, sister then. And she is soon to join us in the world of Spirit."

"Oh . . . That's the first I've heard that."

"Yes, the two of you had quite a passion for writing, though in this life its been her lot to do so and yours only sporadically."

"I seem to have been held back all through this life by the material aspect of physical living, and I've had a large question in my mind of why was I detained so long."

"Well . . . well. We know that in the Universal flow of things the soul ever seeks balance, and you know, it occurs . . . as we look into the records of Akasha . . . what we find is . . . this particular soul, you whom we are addressing, has very often had lives of strong, beautiful spiritual influences on the earth plane. So you see, it was a time, in a sense, to handle the nuts and bolts of the whole matter, and I believe that's what you are doing."

I laugh, somewhat sardonically. "Yes, and its not been easy."

"No, not easy. Not easy ever, for the soul that is born of spirit remains of the spirit, and you've been constantly aware also that the earth plane is not your home. Not your home at all. Nor the home of anyone really, for we are all spirit-beings and our true home shall ever be in the spirit . . .

"That also the blessings of the Lord Kuthumi have streamed forth into the world, many a time, dating from the time when you served by his side in the life as Francis, the Mystic of Assisi, long ago."

"Yes! I was there then, was I not? I knew this!"

"Yes, of course. And even sometimes your fondness for animals has been echoes of those old times. You were a musician then, among other things, and played something like a harp. And sang upon it."

"I knew that, too. I came into this life knowing I played the harp. I always yearned for one, but we were too poor."

"Yes. Interesting. Your soul-memory, you see, was somewhat intact. Also, you had once learned the harp in Greece from the one who was in this life . . . well, she is no longer with you, but is now with us . . . known as Lotus Ballard and was the female counterpart of Godfre Ray King."

"Of the I AM Foundation?" *

"Yes. You had learned this string instrument long ago. It was Grecian. Also . . . hold a minute . . .we've got some more here . . . We've got also to let you know of one man who is of the Indian persuasion, who has known of your work, and he simply gives the name Red Cloud. He was a Chieftain, and says he has watched your work. In times

*The Magic Presence, Unveiled Mysteries, & I AM Discourses, Saint Germain Press, 1934, 1935 (Out of Print)

past, he said, you have often graced the Indian race with your presence."

"I'm not surprised," I murmur.

"It's come again and again. And, oh my god! Look here. I should think this would be in the 1940's as you would count time . . . You were spending a lot of time astrally out of the body. And amongst your various functions, one of these was to form part of the great spiritual battery surrounding those terrible things that were known as the Trials of Nuremberg, that you were one of those who acted, you might say, as a truth agent. It was quite an expanse of the spirit. Many were there and caused the truth to be known that all the world see it and understand it clearly."

"Oh, I see. Working from the astral side?"

"Yes. Part of the invisible helpers. And also, before this current embodiment, you were very active in the spirit world helping with the movement known as Theosophy, and did function as an aide for both the clairvoyants Besant and Leadbeater."

"Leadbeater . . . Yes! I feel very close to him. I'm not surprised at all to know that. Thank you so very much."

"And hold a minute . . . I temporarily shall let go of the vehicle that another might speak. I will return."

At this point the head of Arthur's body slumps a bit, there is a pause, then, straightening, a most deep and magnificent voice, rich and strong, bursts forth.

"I speak only in few words, my daughter. I am Golden Eagle of the Lokota."

"Greetings. Bless you."

"To make your heart now rest at ease . . . to tell you that the property that you love and value shall not fall into foul hands, but shall easily slide, when the time is right and the moons have been fulfilled, into the hands of those who shall know how to keep the place holy. The grounds shall remain undefiled. This thing is assured, and you will find yourself after that time living in different locales. You may also descend to the Northern area of California, there not far from children, yet happy and content in your own way. You can also go and cross the Great Water and be where you have lived also when in Tahitian body. The message is simple. I leave it with you, as one who has known you and loved you in life. Life goes on, and I remain for you . . . a Scout . . . A Shiloka."

"Oh, thank you so much for coming . . . Tahitian body? . . . Yes, I know," I murmur.

There now is a pause while Arthur's body is again relinquished. Then it straightens once again as the English speaking gentleman returns.

"I am attempting to get the medium's vocal chords in a way that I shall again be able to use them . . ." comes the precise English accent.

(It must be an effort, I think.)

"Yes, and moreso as the old boy has been traveling a bit."

"I appreciate your work and your efforts in coming through to me."

"You have given much, my dear, and so we come through quite happily. By the bye, when you do the writing which shall yet come in the future, you will find also there is one here who prefers to work with you, who in life was known as Anna Lee Skarin, an author, and the one, Cerminara — Gina Cerminara. The two are friends, and you might say have collaborated on a lot of the books now being released in the so-called metaphysical movement through authors that might not be so well-known. And those but acting as amanuenses for these particular ladies. Hold a minute . . . yet more . . . There's something else here we've got to bring through to you . . . Interesting. Have you found anything in the yard of this property whilst diggings have been done?"

"Yes! You're right! I was told this . . . some ten years ago, in a reading in San Francisco, but I did not try to dig it up. Yes. In fact, a psychic there spoke of an Indian Treasure buried under my BIG tree . . . in the yard of my home up here in the Northwest."

"Yes — old burial grounds and things. Indian property apparently. Yes, and 'tis about here."

"That's why I'm reluctant to have the property bull-dozed, afraid of desecration. Now Golden Eagle told me it would not be defiled."

"Apparently not. It shall no doubt be bought intact. At least, that's the plan as we've got it here. And . . . oh! We've got one here who wants to let you know that the soul who once inhabited the body of Edgar Cayce has now ascended to quite a high plane, but that this one yet, from time to time, does come to those many and sundry who have called out to him, whether in their pain or simply their curiosity. And that you have been such a one and he has found ways of reaching you through the threads of Light which go forth into the bodies and into every aspect of the continent." (Proof of what I saw years ago.)

"That's great!"

"These things are so. Now we want to answer any questions you may have, as we have quite a bevy here who seem to feel they can give the answers as quickly as you can ask them."

"How marvelous!" I say, laughing. "I thank all of them, such as Edgar Cayce, who have helped my physical condition that I could continue to work when feeling disabled. I really thank whoever has helped me — always. I want to conquer this condition that my back and pelvis may be healed that I may walk straight and do the things I need to do."

My amazing visitor then proceeded to give me some stretching exercises, recommending the asana known as the cobra, also deep pranic breathing, which I am familiar with, sending the breath into that lower back and pelvic area and releasing.

"Now, we'll not make any bones of it my dear, we want to tell you the straight and narrow, as they say. We want you to know that a portion of your own deeper Self has in a sense chosen, shall we call it this temporary malady, in that it's been her particular determination — yours in that sense, by undergoing the pain of it, to balance a certain portion . . . not of personal karma . . . but of *planetary karma*. Even as the Master Jesus did take unto His body a great torment, ultimately physical transition itself, in the so-called balancing of planetary karma that was not His own. In other words, He gave so unselfishly that the balancing action was incredible. He, of all entities, had no right to suffer and yet did so voluntarily.

"The elders of the race, of which we count you as one, do from time to time do such a thing. We tell you this, knowing it might alleviate to a degree. So, a deep portion of Self, in a sense, my friend, my dear friend, rather willingly lives life on a cross. It is an ultimate sacrifice, not consummated in three hours, but over the years."

"I appreciate so much your telling me this, for it does make sense to me . . . considering the vision I had."

"Very good. And this is why we bring it, that once one understands psychologically what goeth on . . . in that you see, you of all people, so quite aware of the reality of the spirit world and of the reality of your own spirit self, thus then you might say, put that knowledge on the line. To put it . . . well, I don't like to use vulgar colloquialisms, but as some have said . . . 'To put one's money where one's mouth is.' So what you have done is said, 'Not only do I know the reality of Spirit contact in the world and myself, but I prove it by . . . little by little, not focusing in the physical body, but on those things which keep me going onward . . .' So in a sense, its a self-elected condition. But we stress it, *it's not a matter of personal karma as much as the voluntary giving of self, to the point of pain and discomfort for a few short span of years, for the purpose of balancing planetary karma*. It is, as it were, a gift that you give in parting, for from this time hence, no further need to return to the physical body shall be necessary as we see it."

"Oh, my . . . " I manage to murmur, as I am totally swept away emotionally by this revelation.

"Though you may elect to — yes, you may elect to return, one more time, to demonstrate your full mastery."

"Thank you! That is so very meaningful to me, because I have asked, 'Why, when I know so much, should I be experiencing this?'"

"This is why, my dear. It is precisely because you know so much. That you, in a sense again, do it out of love. For you see, there are so many under-developed ones, that they know not of giving selflessly, much less to the point of their own discomfort. So the balance has got to be held; and it is held by an elder such as yourself, who yet occupies a frame, and yet has been through so much proof of spirit world reality, that you can hold it safely."

"Very, very enlightening."

"So this thing we have been instructed to bring to you. And now that I sense the medium's vitality grows low, I cannot stay much longer. I must let you know . . . the thing we want you to know . . . is that 'twas on our own, you might say, preparation for this particular sitting, that enroute here we were intercepted by a vast and Holy Light. And suddenly, much to our grateful gaze, did appear the incredibly lovely face and Presence of the Master Jesus, Who did want us to let you know, that as *He also had spoken to you when last in His body, and had comforted you then and physically knew you, that He had told you that you would elect to suffer a lot as He had elected to suffer. But that ultimately your goals would be the same. And if you will tarry, He will come as He ever has, for He has kept his promise in receiving you at the termination of every embodiment since that time . . . and in this one it shall be no less glorious. That your destinies have been intertwined long before you came to this planet."*

"Yes. I felt I knew that. Thank you so much . . . He has always been my Lord . . ." The tears are flowing now, as I am overwhelmed.

"His blessing — as always — is with you, and we are but privileged to bring it. And thus my dear, though we should like to tarry, we may not, and yet we feel we have addressed the most essential. Know that in the fortnight to come there shall come yet other answers to you . . . some spontaneously, some in the sleep state. And ultimately all things answered and all things known."

"This has been a marvelous, marvelous help to me. I shall no longer be sad about anything."

"God bless you, my dear."

"And please, may I send love to my son, Jason, and my husband, Allen, and to my mother."

"Yes, they all stand in attendance, although they humbly, took a backseat, so to speak, that we could bring you the information that all deemed to be the most useful. The reality of what has been said and done here will continue to grow . . . and grow . . . and grow . . . in the fertile soil of your own spiritual Self. God Bless you, my dear."

"Sir, before you leave, please give me your name." His answer was immediate and clear.

"I have been on earth — Sir Arthur Conan Doyle."

"God Bless you . . . and thank you so much!"

Of course. The accent, the style and beauty of verbal expression, the wisdom and truths I had been privileged to hear. I was thankful and honored to the depths of my being, and stated so. I felt I could never again be sad, and could now carry my body's burden with thanksgiving and in trust, until the timing of its release by the Higher Self within. With that, he was gone, my new friend, and yet one from ages past, who had shown me the honor of appearing in my own home. Through no previous planning on my part, Spirit had planned and brought the finest gift one could receive — food for the soul.

I sat profoundly humbled by this amazing transmission, and it would be many days before I would fully assimilate it into my consciousness. I know Holy Spirit came in this manner, in the person of Sir Arthur Conan Doyle, to bring hope and peace of mind at a time when I was near collapse, bone-weary from work, and depressed with the strange state of my health. This was a most in-depth Akashic Record reading, and it was truly an answer and a healing for my soul's cry of "Why?"

When we understand, we can then more easily deal with whatever comes, but it must make sense. If we know the purpose, we can see any challenge through and survive. Our Lord had fulfilled His promise to send a Comforter, a carrier of the message, in honoring me with the presence of one so renowned as the famous English author everyone recognizes as the creator of Sherlock Holmes. His mystery/ adventure stories and novels continue to be published for an admiring audience to this day, and are still shown weekly as television plays in the visually romantic and authentic settings of 19th Century England. I shall quote from the fly-leaf of the book, *The Complete Sherlock Holmes:**

"In Memoriam: Doctor, novelist, dramatist, historian, athlete, war correspondent and spiritualist — Sir Arthur Conan Doyle was a vigorous and ardent lover of life. But it is chiefly as the creator of Sherlock Holmes that more than two generations of readers hang upon his name."

Sir Arthur's travels to Australia and New Zealand in the later years of his lifetime to further the cause of Truth are compiled in an interesting autobiography, *The Wanderings of a Spiritualist,*** first published in 1921. And he spoke of his White Papers the following year during a sitting I had in Honolulu when he honored me once again with his presence. He also wrote another autobiography, *Memories and Adventures.**** Sir Arthur is so utterly charming, with such a distinctive voice, that it seems nothing short of a miracle that we can hear the words of one so beloved still, even though he is presently in spirit realms. I am grateful to have his voice and messages on tape, which I may replay and enjoy whenever I choose.

It was during those late Fall days of mentally assimilating what I had received, that I heard in successive early morning hours, the trilling, thrilling song of a wren in the tree branches right outside my bedroom window. The tiny bird sang a most delightful song, a long and melodious aria, rich and sweet. Then it always flew to the trees over the Little Guest House and sang up there for many minutes. I was so entranced that I took my tape recorder outdoors and recorded it's song, that I might replay it on mid-winter days. It was very special and unusual, so late in the season when no other birds were about.

Five months later I flew to Honolulu on vacation, where Arthur lives. †Of course, a top priority was to visit with him,

---

The Complete Sherlock Holmes, 1906-1927, Bantam Doubleday Dell Pub. Group Inc., 666 Fifth Ave., N.Y., N.Y. 10103.
**Wanderings of a Spiritualist,* Ronin Publishing, 1988, Box 1035, Berkeley, CA 94701
***Memories and Adventures,* Little Brown & Co., 1924, Waltham, Mass.
†It is interesting that they are both named Arthur.

and also to make an appointment for a second sitting. I wanted to contact my mother and Allen in spirit, and possibly Jason, as they had not come through at the earlier meeting in my home. I relate some of this second reading as it may be of general interest.

Early in the sitting — to my joy — I am thrilled to hear young Arthur, the medium, see and speak to me of Jason's spirit-presence. Remember, my new friend Arthur knows nothing of Jason, having only come to my home the previous Fall, at which time I did *not* discuss the loss of my youngest son. With another beautiful opening prayer, Arthur closed his eyes and after a few quiet moments, he speaks clairvoyantly, not in trance.

"There is here a very angelic looking being . . . a man. He doesn't look to be very old. I'd put him in his late teens or early twenties . . . and fair of hair. He stands close to you. Well, you know . . . he loves you like a son! His name . . . I can't quite get it . . ."

But then, after a couple attempts, Arthur does proceed to receive Jason's true name. I now confirm to Arthur that, yes, I have a son in spirit who passed at age twenty-seven.

"He is telling me his life was troubled — emotional, mental problems and all of that . . . some drugs . . ." This confirms it is Jason.

"He's angelic now?" I ask, in thrilled wonderment.

"Oh yes! Very much so. He is a very beautiful Being. He says, 'It's fun to ride around with you — to be with you wherever you go.' He is here in Hawaii with you now."

You may recall I had felt him in the auto with me only days after he passed, as I wrote in Chapter Eight of receiving his message — "Ma, quit snivelin'! I'm just fine." — at a moment when tears were flowing involuntarily.

"He says to tell you he can give you a bit of information he had not given before . . . Did he ever come before?" Arthur asks, rather puzzled, as he, naturally, had not known I had a son in spirit.

"Yes, he has come," I respond. "But not through you. He had come to us through another clairvoyant in Seattle shortly after he passed."

I recall only too vividly the sitting in my home when Jason told us how he was shot by the police and died on the spot, of his father and a Master meeting him, and of his joy at finally being free.

"He seems to be saying he needed one lifetime to play out his foolishness, or troublesome side, and he needed parents who would love him enough that they would not reject him for it. That's why he chose this time . . . And you apparently agreed to go through that with him before you both incarnated this time . . . He indicates an amethyst, and is saying he had something to do with your receiving it. Do you have an amethyst?"

"Yes! A beautiful ring that was brought from India, I had not chosen it. It was given to me. I have often felt Jason's influence when some special gift comes my way. So, *he* chose that ring. How surprising, and lovely! "What is he doing with his time now?" I ask.

"He says he is helping with the children whom his brother teaches on the earth-plane, and also to tell you his own real work has not begun yet, as he is working through certain phases preparatory for it. He is also studying to learn the best ways to make restitution for mistakes made while on earth. He is smiling and says, 'When you get into your own writing and . . . he uses the word 'ministering,' then his work may begin."

Arthur listens awhile and then goes on. *"He is saying that he looks at the years he spent on earth as though it were someone else's life."*

"Like a dream?" I interpose.

"Yes, he says . . . it was like a bad dream. And for all that you gave and tried, certain dark elements of his own psyche had to be out-pictured so he could deal with them face to face, so he could correct them or die trying, and that's what happened. But the fact he was willing to give up the incarnation to totally work his way through all of that . . . he says . . . now he is done with it."

"I'm so glad it's past." I sigh, recalling the horror of his long years in prison and my anguish leading up to it, and through it.

"Yes. That's really one of the main things he wanted you to know, and he says he felt Hawaii was a good place to tell you."

"I love him so much. Even as a baby I felt we had been together before. And I want to ask his forgiveness for the mistakes I made in handling his life. It was a stumbling kind of thing on my part, as I was on such unfamiliar ground, and these were such difficult things to deal with."

"He indicates the plan included mutual mistakes — mutual — that you would bounce off one another so that the both of you worked out deep, deep areas of the psyche you had not known before until the deep love catalyzed it, and much was learned on both sides. No one else could have done it. And so it has been totally cleared and you are now both free. He says it took a strong love bond or it never could have happened. There would have been rejection on one side or the other, avoidance or something. But there was not, and that's why you both went through it with flying colors in the grand picture. And that was all agreed upon before.

"He says he marvels now at the incredible drama of life . . . that life is far more than any of us realize while we are in it." Then laughing, with wry humor, Arthur adds for himself, *"Yes, we can certainly agree intellectually, although we cannot see it as he does, but believe me, I know too. It can be very heavy!"*

"His was particularly so," I comment. "You have no idea. It is amazing as young as he was the amount of strange experiences he had."

"He also is telling me there were things that occurred that you never knew about."

"Yes, I know. Jason always protected me from the harshness . . ."

"He says he will remain here in Hawaii with you for the remainder of your vacation, and even attend the Magic Show with you tonight. He smiles . . . and says he already has his seat picked out. Now he states he will turn the microphone over to someone else."

I am so touched by this visit. It is wonderful to again have confirmation that loved ones can be closer to us than we know, that we can continue to feel the love for them and from them as it flows back and forth between their world and ours. I want especially to pass on these simple, yet beautiful, from-the-heart messages as the final act of the harsh drama of Jason's troubled life, which included fourteen years in prison. This young lad apparently came into this life with a soul plan, set up in such a way that he would experience these happenings as power-boosts to soul-growth, not only for himself, but for me. One cannot go through experiences that bring such emotional trauma without changes in attitudes, patience, acquired knowledge about oneself, compassion for others, and above all, unconditional love. Now, to hear that he appeared to Arthur as an Angelic Being was a special joy, for this confirmed my earliest impression of this beautiful little boy. And I found it deeply meaningful that Jason should say, "The drama of life is far greater than any of us realize, while we are in it."

Now Arthur's head slumped forward for a few moments, and I saw he was entering the trance state. Soon came the beautifully strong and rich, full-toned Indian voice.

"The name is Golden Eagle. And I have chosen now to land, as eagles do from time to time. However high we fly, we must always find the branch and take our rest, for flight, though it encompasses our life, is yet something that is temporary. Eagles come to know something of the winds, of course, and thermals that take them high into the heavens, but always they must return to the earth. So it is with yourself. Your soul is as an eagle, a great white eagle, and this was a name you yourself used in a male incarnation long ago when you were of my people, the Lakota. For there it was that you knew the one known as White Buffalo, who now watches over you as a father." (It had earlier been given me that White Buffalo was my Gatekeeper who keeps all harm from my presence, particularly in any psychic work.)

"Many times we were together then — all of us — and we did pass the pipe and smoked, and in the smoke saw *vision. We knew all things to be sacred. Wakan was our word. Now I control this man's body and I also give praise to Wakantanka, the Great White Spirit. There is then in your future a great awakening of past memory. The ways and means to accomplish it shall come to you, even in this very hour you will be shown how to unlock doors of memory. For this reason we have come. Mine is to announce and to bring a blessing, and so we bring it.*

"*Long ago, I of the tribe was known as Shiloka, meaning guide — scout. I went out in the early morning, and while others hunted and some gathered, some sewed and some trained the young, I was the eyes of the tribe. Shiloka — the Scout, though my name, Golden Eagle held, and as an eagle I watched. I knew the comings and the goings of the bears and the deer, and if the summer would be long or the winter unusually harsh. All these things I would awaken in you and the rest of the tribe, and before long you were all as skillful as I. For I awakened it in you, even as I am in this hour awakening your memory of the Lakota.*

"*White Eagle was your name then. And though white eagles were not seen, your name was given to your father who had seen a white eagle in a dream the night before you were born and so he knew your name. And a boy child came forth and he said, 'This one — White Eagle.' The elders said (and here he mimicked the ancient, cracked voice of an Elder), 'Eh. Good name. But there is no white eagle. They are all golden, or black and white as the bald.' He said, 'No matter. My son is named this, for Wakantanka has shown it to me.'*"

"That's beautiful," I murmur.

"*The word is delivered. My message is given. As you know, we do not waste words. I now happily go, but the Englishman has words for you.*" The body slumps as though asleep.

Then, as the body straightened, once again came the one with that beautifully enunciated English accent — Sir Arthur Conan Doyle.

"*There, I think we've about got it. How are you, my dear?*"

"Oh greetings, Sir Arthur. Look! I've been reading your book," and I hold out a copy of *The Wanderings of a Spiritualist.*

"And enjoying it, I presume? And yet, you know my dear, that which lies ahead of us all I find far more fascinating than what has been. In those days my ideas were quite colored by the British and Toryan society of which I was a member. Now, of course, I see those things as tight-fitting and altogether inhibitive." (There is further exchange of ideas.) Then Sir Arthur asks if I have personal questions. I have thus far received no word of my family, so I ask how my mother is faring on the Inner Planes.

"The Lady Lena has been right here for some time. She is very well and happy to be speaking with us. She has regained much of her youth she wants you to know. She tells me you are wearing her ring."

I am pleasantly surprised Mama noticed this, as I had taken her gold wedding band from her hand after her passing for memory's sake, and I now use it as a ring guard. Again a simple, yet solid proof of authenticity of the visitation of loved ones. No one else would know.

"The Lady Lena is pursuing her personal interests, working to prepare those who are soon to take leave of the body."

"Helping as they pass over?" I ask.

"Rather before they pass, my dear, at night in the astral, so they will be more at peace without fear. Also, she has located a group in the New England area with whom she is working, as the medium there is actually an old friend from way back, and she says she actually has been able to take over and speak right through from time to time."

"Oh for goodness sake."

"Yes, she smiles, and says she is up to her old tricks! She visits you often, and feels you are more like a sister than she the mother. She is asking if you have heard a songbird about lately?"

"Why Yes . . . I have! A most beautiful wren."

"She is saying it was she who sent the bird to you — as a sort of gift, to let you know of her love and presence."

"How amazing! I thank her, for it was most thrilling." (Here is yet another proof of the reality of loved ones near.)

"The Lady Lena is saying she also goes to Italy to see

the granddaughter, and has been with her on her travels."

"To see Jennine! And went with her on the world trip? Oh, that's good to know."

"Yes . . . and to Italy to visit her."

Now I ask if Arthur has a message for my son, Jeremy.

"Yes. Let him know that we have noted that he has often spent time at night in the Inner Dimensions, and he has made contact with the one known in your world as Maria Montessori and has spoken with her, philosophized with her, you could say." (Jeremy, as mentioned, is working in Natural Science as a teacher-at-large, and the Montessori Schools are known throughout America for progressive teaching.)

"She has shared with him and told him, 'Sir! You are every bit as gifted as I. It is only that someone had to do the work that was so desperately needed and so I did it.' She said to him, 'You shall do similar, and sell not yourself short.' She has encouraged him thusly."

"That's excellent," I add, "for he does need to place greater value on his own gifts and abilities."

"One other thing, let him know also that of late, and I speak within the last, oh it would be within six months in your time, that he, for a time there, was visiting the soul who had been known as Mahatma Gandhi in your world and discussing with him politics. Not in the earthly sense, but in the sense of spiritual livingness. And that your son's own, you might call them political views, have been touched by the one known as Gandhi, with whom he has an old and ancient tie."

"Oh Good. I shall tell him this. Does my husband Allen have any message?"

"The man, Allen, you refer to, has been here since the beginning of the sitting and simply says that he could not believe that he could enjoy you so much whilst you being here and he being there. But he says that he has, and continues to, and has of course accompanied you here to this lovely place. He says that, with your aid and in your light, so to speak, he has actually had memory of a past episode which you and he shared together. For you see, being in our world, my dear, does not automatically guarantee past-life

recall. It is something that must be striven for."

"One takes with them to the Other Side exactly what they have attained here," I add.

"Oh yes. *And he says though, that in your light and wake, he has been able to recall a time, and it occurred right on these Islands, when you both were in brown skins."*

"Oh, I can believe that! He knows my love of always wanting to come back to the Islands."

"Yes. And he has aided you in whatever way he could. He is happy that he has been able to leave that as a legacy. And . . . oh, bye the bye, he also says he has tried to get playful with you when . . . it looks like you were attempting to compose music or some such. You like to compose, my dear? Yes, alright . . . He says so. He says that . . . And oh look! He wants you to know that he has sat recently and had a very brilliant chat with the man who was known as Walter Disney in your world, and he says you had some tie with this man."

(I thought when I heard this that it was because I had made some whistling tapes for Disney Studios years ago when in Hollywood.)

"He tells you that Mr. Disney now works with one of the great masters, you might almost say right beneath him, and they are planning out a wonderful . . . shall we call it . . . project . . . to be initiated at the end of the next century, at which point Mr. Disney shall again take incarnation."

"Oh really? How wonderful! In the Golden Age?"

"Yes. Bit . . . by bit . . . by bit."

I then ask, "In the future might I be able to do something again with my music, the whistling in particular? I dislike letting it go entirely. But other projects have demanded attention."

"Well, that is yet to be seen. But here is something that may interest you. Several centuries ago in a life in India, you lived on the edge of a deep forest. You had two sons who enjoyed playing in those woods, but they could be dangerous with animals and such. You were psychic in that you could sense when danger was present, and you would then whistle *for them to return without frightening*

them. You had trained them so. And it was your father then who had taught you to whistle, the man and soul you know now as Walt Disney."

"Really? My father? Well! That *is* interesting!" This casts a whole new light on my late husband Allen's words about "sitting and speaking with the man Walter Disney, *with whom you have some tie.*" My goodness, so I was his daughter at that time!

"And now the time has come to depart, for we must not tire the medium, and I trust these words have been of benefit to you."

"Oh Yes! God love you for coming to me. You are a beautiful soul and I am so very blessed to have you grace my presence."

"We feel the same, in all truth. In that we feel so often we know the great love and admiration with which so many of you hold us, but I tell you my dear, in all honesty and no false modesty, that we — from the World of Spirit — find that our role is . . . well, a lot easier than yours, and our hats are off to you! So God Bless You, and may the roses of God's love blossom ever in your gardens . . . and sweet joy."

Arthur's body slumped slightly as though in sleep, and then for the second time, Sir Arthur Conan Doyle was gone, back to the vastness from whence he came, my friend . . . and Heavenly Visitor.

Once again, I contemplate on the wonder — that the very distinct voice, perfectly expressed with no flaws whatsoever, of one long gone from this earth-plane, could be heard once again, seated quietly as a visitor conversing in my own room in a perfectly natural way. Yes, most would say this truly is not possible. And yet, when one studies certain laws of the Universe the phenomenon becomes understandable and quite possible. Actually this work is not uncommon. In recent times a number of psychics have become well-known as they channel Higher Beings, who come as teachers in this age of new knowledge. This is a time in Earth's history that is propitious, when mankind needs guidance. Information on this subject is readily available in many metaphysical book stores. I feel these particular visitations to be significant, however, as Sir Arthur Conan Doyle is a personage almost everyone knows and has respected for many years, the voice and usage of words unmistakable. He is so utterly charming, speaking with his distinctive British accent. I feel especially blessed that he gave me permission to write out these messages for others to share.

Young Arthur awoke, back in his body, quite well and none the worse, though he appeared to be coming out of a deep sleep so he took a few moments to be totally here, just as anyone would upon awakening. He knew nothing of what had transpired during the trance portion, nor did he ask. Young Arthur saw my deep emotion and reverent thanks, and said he was glad I'd had a good sitting. Then added, "Yes, Sir Arthur has been working with me for a time, but he doesn't always come in, only on occasion." I was grateful *my* sittings were such occasions, to say the very least. Contemplating once again that both are named Arthur, I recalled being told earlier by Sir Arthur these two souls have a connection, as friends in past lives.

What sets Sir Arthur apart from other teachers who are channeled through and whom one can hear at special group meetings is that the master teachers from Spirit usually give wisdom teachings of a general nature for all those in attendance, impressing the message through mental telepathy to the channeler, who then uses his/her own voice. This is very good and much needed. I have heard many such lectures. However, these particular sittings were so distinctly outstanding and helpful to me, being personal akashic record readings of my soul's path, tying in especially with this life. Also my esteemed visitor and friend, someone so very well-known in modern times as opposed to often obscure, mystical beings who seem far removed from us, is that he, himself, was there, using his own voice, as was the Master Agasha, in the 1940's teachings in Los Angeles.

Sir Arthur humbly remarked on his surprise that his works, such as the Sherlock Holmes series, continue to be

of great interest to others. He, himself, was far more interested, he said, in his search for truth in spiritual matters,
commenting on his successful lecture tours to Australia and
New Zealand while on earth, as described in his autobiography, *Wanderings Of A Spiritualist.*

Now I also have a new friend in young Arthur as well,
and am delighted to see him when I visit Honolulu. His unique
and excellent work is in great demand in the Islands, the west
coast of the U.S., and recently in New Zealand, as mentioned.

*

I RECEIVE A VISION CONFIRMATION

There is a postscript to this part of my story that ties in
with the physical condition I have described, in addition to
the amazing information Sir Arthur related regarding it. Two
years after my first sitting with Arthur, while attending a
40th Anniversary Celebration at Astara, the wisdom school
and Church of All Religions in Southern California, I experienced a serendipitous happening. Of the many attendees, a
very special lady was assigned, through God's grace, as my
roommate for the three-day celebration. And guess what? She
was an excellent masseuse, born in Germany, who also was
gifted psychically to *see* the need in a body as she massaged it
with her strong and sensitive hands. Her name is Waltraud,
and she was a fount of information and wisdom.

Through this weekend celebration, Waltraud took time
to give short massages as a personal service to other ladies
attending. But I was blessed to have two lengthy massage
treatment sessions while alone in our room after hours. It
was during one of these that an amazing thing occurred.
While massaging my lower back, Waltraud began to describe seeing something.

"What is this? Your etheric body is bound — it seems
with metal links! And it lies over the body. You are mis-
shapen." She went on to describe in detail that unmistakable mental picture I had been struck with. I then confirmed that I had had a vision of the chastity belt.

"Ah yes. It was dreadful! More dreadful than anyone knew."

With her knowledge of European history from her birthplace of Germany, she poured forth details, some of which I had previously known and written earlier in this book, but with more horrid embellishments than even I had envisioned.

Waltraud said, "The men went away you see, to war or the Crusades, not realizing the hideous condition they perpetrated upon the woman, for due to daily urination, the menstrual cycle and the like, the metal became rusty and often infection set in, leading to poisoning and a slow agonizing death. In addition, if the woman were pregnant that horror can hardly be conceived, for even the poor babe within would die deformed as birth was impossible. Often then, due to the trauma experienced to the psyche of the babe, that soul could be born into its future life as a cripple or a hunchback." And then Waltraud went on to say something I had never thought of. *"This was often the hidden cause for such poor creatures as were seen in the Middle Ages."*

And so she gently led me through an emotionally cleansing visualization ritual, to clear the old memory pattern by throwing off the unseen shackles and instead, mentally bringing forth a healthy, beautiful baby.

I relate this for a purpose, for during this visualization and quiet massage, amazingly, there appeared within the vistas of my inner mind's eye, a myriad of women rising from the mists of time. Some wore old-fashioned dresses to the ground, others in garb I did not recognize, all with outstretched hands, weeping and crying out, "For me, too . . . Help me! Pray for me too!"

It was then I knew the nature of the message Sir Arthur had earlier given me. A part of the physical out-picturing I now carried were portions of the mass *planetary karmic residue of uncleansed pain,* of women even yet emotionally suffering from the ignorant treatment inflicted upon them through the ages. These dark clouds cling in the etheric energies of earth for many, many years. Acting as a proxy, I took them all into my heart and wept for them. Waltraud and I prayed together that this darkness be lifted, cleansed and forgiven, and I have continued in this prayer to this day, asking for purification. "Forgive them Father, for they know not what they do."

In this light, it is the tragedy of mankind that in our unevolved state, our actions and their on-going effects in the unseen vibrations of earth are not understood, and so humans in ignorance continue to perpetrate atrocities on one another, and even on entire races. They do not realize that in the process they are destroying themselves and the beauty of the planet, as it becomes slowly enveloped in darkness — not the darkness of a soft sweet night, but the darkness of evil, disease and death.

The second evening I spent with Waltraud, during her sensitive healing massage to my lower back, she again brought forth a second psychic insight.

"I am feeling something strange . . . A kind of metal plate has been ground into your lower spine . . . and I see horses . . . Did you have a fall from a horse? . . . as this is very severe, you were dragged . . ."

I am astonished! For here is another confirmation of my vision of the chariot race that had such a disastrous ending, with my being dragged and crippled. I then told Waltraud it had not been in this current life, but I had seen something of this in a vision of my past.

Waltraud exclaimed, "Yes! That would do it, for in those days the charioteers wore a metal plate strapped across the lower back, often with the crest emblazoned upon it, and set with precious jewels if the family was wealthy or of aristocracy. This was ostensibly to protect the spine. But in your case I see it was actually the undoing, for the sharp jewels and metal edges, as you were dragged on the ground, cut into the nerves of the lower back, causing the paralysis you describe."

If this sounds preposterous, please be assured it is true as described. Waltraud continued to give details of the European history she knew so well, having been born and raised there. This was a most remarkable confirmation once again of my own vision, brought to me in a unique way, and unsolicited, since this amazing healer/masseuse was assigned as my roommate in a by-chance(?) arrangement.

It usually takes time for healing to evidence in the

physical body after successful mental visualization has imprinted a vibrational change in the etheric body which surrounds and interpenetrates the physical. The etheric body is a pattern and a blueprint so to speak, like the paper pattern for a dress, and is influenced by thought vibrations of the individual. Intense emotional trauma in a past life can carry over and recreate a pattern impressed even in the current body, and so the work of bringing forth the new picture into the physical realm is needed. This will slowly take shape as the new visualized pattern from the etheric is transferred to the cells of the physical body. During this time the individual should continue to hold the desired result in the mind, accompanied by sincere prayer for healing. In recent years, it is becoming more well-known and accepted that our mental out-picturing has a definite effect on the physical. Sometimes in powerful healing prayer work the change will be almost instantaneous, as is seen in large spiritual mass meetings.

Obviously, in my case, there is much happening that was decided on a higher level of Self, and I live in knowing that it is all for the highest good, whatever each day brings. I shall be forever grateful to Holy Spirit that sends beloved messengers, both seen and unseen, bringing answers to my fervent prayers to know the reasons behind the events, the cause that brought the effect. With understanding comes mental freedom.

This idea was summed up very neatly in the words of the famous clairvoyant, Arthur Ford,* in his autobiography, *Nothing So Strange*.**

"In every phase of spiritual endeavor there are laws at work, and the adept, quite as much as the student, must keep lining himself up with them. Physical fitness, moral responsibility, mental equilibrium, emotional harmony, spiritual expectancy, a

*Arthur Ford worked with Sir Arthur Conan Doyle at points in their careers.
***Nothing so Strange*, by Arthur Ford, 1958, Harper Bros.,49 E.33rd St., N.Y. 10016"

dedicated will. All these are the supportive concommitants of expanded awareness."

And, I would like to add, of a closer walk with Christ and God's Love, that can then bring good out of all things.

How we act in the world is crucial. There can be a big difference between embracing religion and living the spiritual life. When spirituality is internalized, one is no longer tied to a specific religion, and intuition increases.

There also is a difference between being psychic and being spiritual. Many people are confused on this subject. A person can, for any number of reasons, be developed psychically without being spiritually enlightened, or without even being on a spiritual-growth path. Thus, there are those who have psychic powers but use them for selfish, even evil purposes, thereby unfortunately giving a bad name to this work, which has created for too long a deterrent in the United States to legitimate scientific research in this area of extra-sensory perception — our wonderful potential.

The former Soviet Union had, in fact, forged much further ahead in this research than the U.S. As early as 1978 American Dr. A. J. Lewis, a prominent psychologist of San Diego, California, visited the Soviet Union and Eastern Europe. He conferred with researchers in these areas which are considered by most American scientists to be "too far out" for study. Dr. Lewis found that the European scientists were using highly technical instruments to study psychic phenomena and had come up with break-throughs so dramatic that he felt their American colleagues would be bound to sit up and take notice. But it has taken twenty more years for significant work to surface in America.

The most basic theory being tested in the Soviet Union was that all live cells send out waves of energy like radio waves, and that these transmit messages, a kind of Morse Code of cells. This energy field sent out by the cells would explain the auras that have been depicted by artists around saints, but which also exists normally around all live creatures. The Russian scientists found that these energy fields showed a change if a person were in an early stage of an illness, even though doctors might not be able to find anything wrong.

This transmission of electro-magnetic energy could explain Extra-Sensory Perception, the picking up of signals by one person sent out by another.

In his talk at Western Washington State College in Bellingham at the time of his visit in the 1970's, Dr. Lewis told of the experimental methods being used in Eastern Europe to test these ideas of cell communication. For example: energy fields, or auras, were being recorded by high frequency Kirlian photography. The brilliant energy could be clearly seen on the photograph. (In the 1990's, this is now a well-proven fact.) This theory of energy waves, Dr. Lewis said, could explain why plants appear to register emotion when tested with a polygraph. When one plant is badly torn, *another registers a reaction similar to fainting.* * Dr. Lewis concluded that messages are being sent by plant cells via energy. There also was what he called the ghost leaf effect. When one-half of a plant leaf was cut off, a Kirlian picture taken afterward showed the distinct sparkling electrical energy still in place where the missing portion had been. The energy-pattern still outlined the whole leaf! This remained so for quite some time. This could explain amputee patients who later state they can still feel their toes, even when said toes are missing.

Dr. Lewis also said that Czechoslovakian researchers were using the idea of energy fields in medical diagnosis. "They pick up the energy about five feet from a person with a machine called a bio-energy accumulator, feed the information into a computer and then can tell how that person is going to respond to medical treatment. To determine if cells communicate, a mass of cells is separated and half of the cells are invaded with a virus. The other half goes through defense mechanisms, indicating that somehow the infected cells have transmitted a message."

*This, in fact, has been proven by other researchers, such as Clive Baxter in the 1960's when he hooked six philadendrons up to lie detectors. When one plant was crushed by one man among six who walked through, the others "went wild" on the graph when the "murderer" returned to the room, while ignoring the other five.

Dr. Lewis believes the source of a person's energy waves may be the brain and that there actually is an energy circulation system in the body separate from the known nervous system. He cited experiments with desert ticks, which apparently pick up energy waves to locate their victims. He said the ticks head for the nearest human subject without error, unless the human's head is enclosed by a metal shield. Then the ticks aim for a person farther away, but with his head uncovered.

The presence of this energy circulation system is now well-known by many therapists who use non-invasive methods, and easily relates to the healing work done with acupuncture, which deals with balancing the energy. American medical personnel had, until recently, been willing to credit acupuncture with anesthetic powers, but not with actual healing powers, because the idea of an energy circulation system remained in the area of the unknown and unrecognized.

However, this has, I am thankful to say, recently been changing. In the United States, the National Institutes of Health has created the new Office of Alternative Medicine, which is seeking proposals from researchers who wish to explore the merits of therapies outside mainstream healing.

Some parapsychology laboratories in the United States are now working with experiments and reporting some very advanced and startling findings, as per a television documentary aired on station TNT out of Atlanta, Georgia, on January 1, 1993. This program reported the experience of a California businessman named Calvin Westerbeck who had been diagnosed through Kirlian photography as having an inoperable tumor of the pituitary gland. Therefore, medical science could give no hope. So the gentleman went to the Philippines and through the psychic healers there the tumor was successfully removed. One laboratory presently working in research in this area is The American Society for Psychical Research.*

Russian scientists and doctors, also police, have been using this telepathic ability developed in some people to

*The American Society for Psychical Research, #5 W. 73rd St., N.Y.,NY

both help find murder victims for law enforcement, and as healers on staff in hospitals. In an interview on a television program aired on April 16, 1993, Dr. Galperrin, who heads the Center for Clairvoyance and Physic Research in Moscow, reported their success in these areas as 80%. This is recognized as a legitimate and useful tool in Russia.

We humans are *whole beings*, composed of interrelated and interconnecting systems, so wonderfully created that our finite minds cannot conceive of the Infinite Intelligence that made them. When one part is damaged, or changed to a higher or lower vibration through thought or action, all the other parts are affected. We have been given the means to think, understand, and use our powers of discrimination to create new circumstances, even new cells of our body, to better serve the upward thrust of our soul growth.

This sixth sense called the extra-sensory, which is inherent in all individuals, but often is left dormant, was intended to be a useful power to these ends. Used rightly, it would be of tremendous advantage to mankind. One can readily see that many of earth's confusions would disappear. No longer would we be duped by swindlers or those with only selfish interests which cause all manner of turmoil and there would be no need to muddle through expensive court suits that create months of backlogs which line the pockets of a plethora of lawyers, to name only simple examples, for the intentions, or guilt, of all would be readily seen, through the clear sight of our psychic vision.

Plato said: "Temperance, moderation, balance, self-control, and order within are the remedies."

Buddha said: "All thy sufferings are of thy own making, no one compels."

In the *Maitryana Upanishad* it is written: "Thoughts cause the round of new birth and new death . . . what a man thinks — that he is, is the secret," (Chap. VII:34).

Jesus said: "As a man believeth in his heart . . . so it shall be done unto him . . ." and "Know the truth, and it will set you free."

The author, Howard Thurman wrote: "The spiritual life resembles a fertile egg whose embryo is surrounded by the exact sustenance needed for its development. The egg grows by feeding on its environment, achieving the strength needed finally to peck through the shell. So, likewise, the spiritual germ, the spark of the soul within each human being, is surrounded by the exact food needed for its development. This food consists of the essence of all the circumstances, the difficulties, the opportunities, the relationships, both personal and in work, in which each person at every moment of time is environed. But often rather than working with, and overcoming, the human tends to resist, even to fight against this given sustenance. He or she fails to recognize it as the perfect nutriment for his or her spiritual growth."

In her book *Fifty Years A Medium*,* Englishwoman Estelle Roberts, who was talented in many clairvoyant abilities, and the most famous medium of her time, writes:

> "The teachings of Jesus, Buddha, and all of the world's religious leaders are meaningless if the concept of everlasting life is not upheld. Without it, the only philosophy open to us is 'Eat, drink and be merry, for tomorrow we die.' This philosophy leaves one wallowing in self-gratification, which can only lead to eventual despair.
>
> *"In contrast, the Truth of the soul's eternal nature floods the mind with light and warmth. It opens up an endless vista of glorious life, a perpetual expansion of the consciousness, each advance bringing enhanced love and happiness as we travel along the road to Perfection.* We no longer mourn for the dear ones who have left us, for we know they live and that we shall meet them again. We no longer fear death and disease for ourselves, for we know these are but temporary conditions and that we shall re-awaken to a new life in a perfect body."

Fifty Years A Medium, Story of Estelle Roberts, Avon Books, 959 Eighth Ave., New York 10019. Last pub. in 1972 Barrie & Jenkins Ltd., London 1969

For me, personally, this truth was proven many years ago. The frosting on the cake was the unmistakable reality of visits in spirit by my son Jason, with his easily recognized messages of love and personal references, as well as messages from my husband, Allen, and my mother, Marlena. In addition, to have been honored by the personage of Sir Arthur Conan Doyle with hours of personal revelations and encouragement, was a blessing beyond measure. I wish only to pass along these joyful truths, truths that are life-changing when fully accepted and "real-I-zed" within oneself.

Estelle Roberts guide called himself Red Cloud, a pseudonym. He was a great teacher who chose to return to earth to give courage to hundreds who had lost loved ones in World War II and before.

Red Cloud states, "Stand upon the hilltop and watch the setting sun, and in your heart be calm. Watch the blending of the colors as they fall behind the hills and in that quiet stillness God will be. Stand among the yellow of the buttercups in the open fields when the dew lies upon the grass. Watch the bird rise with a flutter of wings, its throat trembling in the beauty of its note. It is there God will be found. In the laughter of a child when it runs to its mother's side, there too, God will be found. May I always find within your world the beauty of God and the wisdom of His kingdom expressed in the one simple word: Love."

"... For now we see through a glass darkly, but then face to face; now I know in part; but then shall I know even as also I am known. And now abideth faith, hope, love, these three; but the greatest of these is love," (I Cor. 13:12-13).

※

CHAPTER THIRTEEN

THE MIND MIRACULOUS

These words emblazoned across a brochure throughout the Greater Seattle area in October of 1977, caught the attention of over 3,000 people who attended the Mind Miraculous Symposium in the Seattle Opera House in November. This Symposium presented a range of speakers known as pioneers at the forefront of their fields, fields as diverse as communication, physics, and philosophy.

One speaker that day was Dr. Fritjof Capra, then Director of the Physics Department at the University of California, Berkeley. Dr. Capra electrified the audience as he presented on huge screen startling photographs of the interactions of the new sub-atomic particles. Capra was the first eminent scientist to announce publicly through his writings that Science was now compelled to concur with teachers of ancient eastern religions, that matter, physical matter we think of as solid, simply does not exist. "There is," he said, "no *thing* at the heart of *anything*."

To illustrate this verity Dr. Capra showed films of a variety of sub-atomic particles of materials including stone, wood, metal, and flesh. What we saw on the screen were points of bright light, energy whirling in distinct patterns, constantly moving. When another atomic particle was shot into the midst of these patterns under the camera's eye, a sudden flurry of energy points changed direction and formed new geometric patterns. Dr. Capra's book, *The Tao of Physics*,* published a few years later, describes his work.

"Everything in the known physical world," stated Dr. Capra, "including our bodies and the planet we call home, must be made up of pure energy, atomic substance held together by a force unknown. It is assumed this force is an Intelligence within the energy itself that creates the pattern it will become as a result of the rate of its vibration or speed and the number of positive electrons and neutrons in its structure."

At that I am taken back in my memory to 1947 when I attended classes at the Agashan Temple in Los Angeles. We'd been told exactly that by the ancient Egyptian Master Teacher, Agasha, as he channeled through the sensitive, Reverend Richard Zenor. So now Science had caught up, proving conclusively what the spiritual teachers have taught for centuries, that there is no reality (as we think of it) to the body, that matter is, instead, a cluster of pure energy particles held together by mind power. This is indeed mind-boggling to many, and still difficult to recognize when one can feel and touch what one believes to be our solid reality.

So what is this mind, this Intelligence that molds atomic particles into eyelashes in one place and fingernails in another, and can also build a planet? Could this mind be God — in Action? Or Supreme Intelligence, Allah, Great Spirit, the ultimate Reality known by many names in many beliefs? I believe so. Rather, I know so.

Some people have been amused by others who declare, "God is dead!" For it probably is their church and its ministry to which this phrase should apply. I always appreciated Mama's remark when approached by self-appointed soul-savers who demanded of her, "Have you found God?"

Looking at them in feigned surprise, she would reply, "Why, I didn't know He was lost!"

The French writer Voltaire, like most of the greats in our literature, spoke of his faith very clearly. "If a clock, by

The Tao of Physics, 1983, Random House, Dist. 400 Hahn Rd., Westminster, MD.

its very being proves the existence of a Clockmaker, and the Universe does not prove the existence of a Supreme Intelligence, then I consent to be called a fool."

Recently another outstanding doctor/scientist has appeared on the lecture circuit with a message similar to Dr. Capra's. That man is Dr. Deepok Chopra, an eminent Aruveydic physician, man of Science, and author of several books, among them *Quontom Healing: Exploring the Frontiers of Mind/Body Medicine,** *Unconditional Life and Perfect Health,*** and his most recent, *Ageless Body - Timeless Mind.**** Dr. Chapra held over 3,000 people in rapt attention in the Seattle Arena in May of 1991 as he spoke on who and what we really are, setting forth proven principles in lucid understandable terms. He discussed the energy pattern of thoughts, the memories we harbor and how these daily affect and shape our lives. Since this information dovetails perfectly with the remarkable therapy sessions in 1975 in the Wellsprings work, which I related in Chapter Ten, regarding the release of old memories as negative energy held in the cells of the body, I'll quote Dr. Deepok Chopra in a portion of his talk given in Seattle in that Spring of 1991. Dr. Chopra affirms the same scientific conclusions elucidated by Dr. Capra, and then he carries the understanding a step further. Dr. Chopra states:

> "Our bodies are literally the music of nature. We are part of a symphony that has been there forever. Behind the mask of mortality is that quantum mechanical body, and that quantum mechanical body or subtle Causal body is something you *always* had. You've always had that.[Here he quotes the ancient Indian scriptures, the Vedas.]
>
> "Fire cannot burn it, water cannot wet it, wind cannot dry it, weapons cannot cleave it. It was

*Quantum Healing, 1989-1990, Bantam-Doubleday
**Unconditional Life and Perfect Health, Bantam-Doubleday, 2451 So. Wolf Rd., Des Plaines, IL 60018.
***Ageless Body-Timeless Mind, 1993, Harmony Books/Div. of Crown Pub., 201 East 50th St., New York 10022

never born and it never dies!"

"Is there any basis for that? Today we are seeing in fact that there is basis. If you could see the body again as a physicist would see it, all you would see is atoms, and if you could see the atoms as they really are, not through the artifact of sensory experience, you'd see these atoms are particles that are moving at lightening speeds around huge empty spaces. These particles are not material objects at all; they are fluctuations of energy and information in a huge void of energy and information. If you could see a body not through this sensory artifact, you'd see a huge empty void with a few dots and spots and a few random electrical discharges here and there. 99.999999 percent of your body is empty space, and the .00001 percent of it that appears as matter is also empty space. So, it's all empty space! So we question, What is this empty space? Is it nothing or is it full of non-material intelligence? In fact, it is a fullness of non-material intelligence.

"Intelligence can sound mystical, and as a scientist I like to keep away from mystical terms, so we can say this intelligence is information that, in fact, influences its own expression. With that definition it is very obvious that this empty space is not an emptiness of nothing, but the Womb of Creation. And Nature goes back to exactly that same place to fashion a galaxy and a rain forest, as it goes to fashion a thought. It's the same place, and it's inside us! It's our Inner Space, which gives rise with amazing fertility to all things that are so crucial to us: right, wrong, God, Heaven, sin, salvation, damnation, grace. All this comes from the same place.

"A scientist by the name of Herbert Spector did an experiment about twenty years ago, working at the National Institute of Health as Head of Molecular Biology. In laboratory experiments using small mammals he found they interpreted the memory of certain smells to decide how they should react at given times. Once again, the crucial difference between survival and death was the interpretation of certain smells. Is this relevant to us? Yes, it is, for like those mice we have conditioned ourselves to respond to memories in a certain way. We link stimuli to certain memories and every time we are exposed to those stimuli we reinterpret the universe and ourselves according to those memories. We become the victim of the stale repetition of outworn memories! It is estimated the average human has 60,000 thoughts a day. This is not surprising. What is disconcerting is that 90% of the thoughts you have today are the same ones you had yesterday!

"So, through the same mechanics we become bundles of conditioned reflexes and responses, constantly being triggered by people and circumstance into the same predictable biochemical responses, and ultimately into the same behavioral responses, and ultimately into the same patterns of disease, aging and death. *We accept our sensory experiences to be real.* So in that sense we can say the reason we grow old, age and die is because we see others growing old, aging and dying. We are locked in to mass consciousness. What we see — we become, because we behold that to be true. We do not see the world with fresh eyes. [Here Dr. Chopra quoted an Indian Saint,]

"I wish to use my memories. I do not want my memories to use me."

Could Jesus words, "As ye believe, so it shall be done unto you," be applied here as well?

There is a great deal of food for thought in these words uttered by an outstanding thinker of our time, who sees behind the veil of appearances. A man of science and spirituality, Dr. Chopra combines the best of both worlds, so to speak, and by the concepts which he so clearly describes, he shines a brighter and more practical light of understanding on the heretofore hidden nature of that Life Force that energizes all things, including human beings. And as humans, we are controllers and motivators of this Life Force within us, and have the ability to shape and reshape through our thoughts, our mind power, not only the circumstances surrounding ourselves, but our own bodies and beings as well. What of these thoughts? Allow me to continue to quote Dr. Chopra:

> "Findings in medical research show clearly that mind has escaped the confines of the brain — it is *not* confined to the brain — *it is everywhere in our body*. And so, as if that wasn't enough, it seems that now it is breaking the confines of the body — out there. Our mind is not even imprisoned in our body. It is completely non-local, it's everywhere in space and time; in fact, our mind is part of a non-local field of information that we can only call The Cosmic Mind. The German philosopher Nietche said, 'We live on the presumption that we think, when its entirely possible that we are being thought.'
>
> The Yogi of all Yogis, Shiva Himself says, 'If you want to recreate the world, then look at it with fresh eyes . . . Look at it without the camouflage of memories.'"

Dr. Chopra continued, saying we do not "see with new eyes" because we are not in touch with the One who is seeing. We are rather just a bunch of conditioned reflexes, the outcome of our thoughts and feelings. But the One who is having these thoughts and feelings is not the thought, but the *consciousness* behind the thought. It is the Source of thought."

Dr. Chopra then told the story of one of his patients who had, in his work, inadvertently picked up a wire not knowing it was a live electrical wire, and he was electrocuted with 12,000 volts passing through his body, stopping his heart instantly. He fell fifteen feet to the ground, and Dr. Chopra related:

"As luck would have it, he landed in such a way with enough impact, and in the right position and location of his chest, that the jolt caused the heart to begin beating again. It was as though God called him and then changed his mind!"

Dr. Chopra said he later asked Bob what happened, and this young man answered, "I went into the gap."

When Chopra then asked him what was there in the gap, he answered, "It was sheer unbounded joy! It was absolute total bliss."

Upon further questioning, Bob said, "No, there were no thoughts there; No, I didn't have a mind; No, I didn't even have a body."

"What was there?" Dr. Chopra asked.

"I was just aware. I was aware that I was aware! But it was pure wakefulness. I was grounded totally and completely in the experience of my own immortality."

In his book, Dr. Chopra goes on.

> "So much so that he does not now know the meaning of fear. In fact, was he not only lucky to have this experience, but like a true scientist, he started experimenting in this field of pure aware-ness. He would go into the gap, as he called it, now that he knew how to slip into it, and from there would put his attention on his leg which had com-pletely burnt. There was no muscle, nothing. The femur was exposed to the atmosphere. There was just bones and nerves and some vessels. And over the course of two years, by diving into the gap and projecting his awareness from there, he has actu-ally regrown a new lower extremity, because he has found that place from where everything is cre-ated. It is his own Self!
>
> "And where is this Self? Is it in the brain? Is it in the body? Where is it? Because this is really the only important experience.

"The Vedic teachings of India say that, "All your problems exist because you never paid attention to your Self, only to your experiences."

"And you are not your experiences. You are the One who is having the experiences. Enlightenment is not another experience — it is the discovery of the timeless factor in every experience. And who or what is that Timeless Factor that scientists have been looking for, for a long time? It is you!"

How exciting it is to me to now hear individuals of fine intelligence, respected in the accepted fields of Science and Medicine, speaking out in confirmation of the underlying truths of life that I have known and that have been my undergirding through *all the days of my years.*

In contemplating my late husband's Near-Death-Experience, I see how similar it was to Dr. Chopra's patient who went into the gap where there was only total awareness and absolute bliss and unbounded joy, where one is grounded completely in the experience of one's own immortality. This is the very definition that Allen had tried to give me of his memorable soul experience while the body lay dead on the hospital table. And I recall Allen glowing as he believed himself healed upon his return to this world, but eight days of tranquilizers given him brought his elevated consciousness down to a state more acceptable by his doctors.

This blissful state was also central in the experiences as told by many individuals in the books *Life After Life, Reflections on Life After Life,* and *The Light Beyond,* by Dr. Raymond Moody, and of the children who *died* whose stories were told in *Closer to the Light,* by Dr. Melvin Morse, as earlier mentioned and noted in Chapter Seven. These are not isolated experiences, but happen time and again, and are only now being given attention and credence. Undoubtedly there are many more stories that are not told, for fear of ridicule.

THE PEARL

The Way of Life is a long, long path
One cannot recall when he first began
the trek —
That many years did span.
For conscious mind — in the mind of Man
Does not reveal the wondrous Plan.

The conscious mind does questions ask -
Whence?, Where?, and Why?
It begs to know —
Silence reigns — there is a mask
Life wears — and does not show

For therein lies the answer,
and each must seek
To delve the deep and inner Self
Where quietly hidden from mortal eyes
the Treasure lies..

The Pearl of Great Price —
the name is known,
While in the search — o'er the earth
one doth roam.

One day we find — to our surprise
in that quiet place within the Mind
The Pearl we sought
need not be bought!

We are beguiled — as we are shown
that all the while
T'was right at home.
Surely —
God must smile.

Bonnie Ann Gilchrist

And so I ask, when will we advance to a Celebration of Life for those near and dear who graduate to Higher Realms, to the beautiful bliss and joy they richly deserve, rather than weeping at funerals?

Understandably, we honor and miss our loved ones who pass over, but truly we weep for ourselves, left behind. Or we weep for those who were cut short early in their life through accident or violence. Losing such dear ones is far more difficult, but I think of my son, troubled beyond the help of any professionals of those days, dying in violence and trauma, who yet came back to comfort me. He related how joyful and happy he is now, filled with bliss to be in the Higher World, and he continues to study, to learn and grow in soul-depth, free from earth's turmoils and troubles.

The level we attain on the higher planes of life is dictated by how courageously and steadfastly we meet the turmoils and troubles we encounter during our lifetime on Earth. Our well-being there depends also on whether we grow out of the need for such challenges, which work as the building blocks of soul strength in character and ability to love. Do not be deceived! The final journey comes sooner than we ever expect, for the years pass swiftly, and the days become like many-colored autumn leaves soon scattered by the winds of time.

It is the wise man who, knowing he is to embark on a journey, seeks to learn something of the country he will encounter, the customs and the language, and what he can expect upon arriving. The Mind, our creative imagination, plays a very necessary part in the higher dimensions, we are told. We create our own surroundings, wearing apparel, travel, and even build our homes with mind-power. Therefore, the more clear the mind, and the more free it is of destructive or negative thought-forms carried over from earth, the more powerful will be our use of mental energy.

Through the past one hundred years authentic teachers have written voluminously. Books and lessons are readily available which offer interesting and educational study on many levels of spiritual growth. *Astara, A Church Of All Religions** is one of the best such establishments, presenting classes and correspondence studies on all aspects of the mysteries of our Being. The teachings of Paramahansa Yogananda, as earlier mentioned, are available through *Ananda Church Of God-Realization,*** or through Self-Realization Fellowship. If we listen to inner guidance in our search, through genuine desire for the highest path of learning and soul growth, we will be led to the right material or teacher at any given time in our life. It is all there for the asking.

It is also well to come to the realization, as laid forth, that all of humankind is connected through atomic magnetic vibrations, that the harm one does to another harms all.

Likewise, the good, light-filled, loving thoughts and actions that we send out into the ethers lifts all, and in that way also lifts our beleaguered planet that has suffered much because of human selfishness, cruelty and greed. Only if a person has been filled with the dark passions of jealousy, hate, or avarice need so-called death be feared, for these emotions become dark thought-forms that cause the soul to be bound to them, tied as surely as with chains. On the other hand, if one loves God and has lived as Jesus The Christ and His Brother Masters taught, the transition is truly a birth into an expansive new life

For just as the wonder of awakening to conscious life in this physical world with its sounds and smells and colorful scenes of earth is a miracle to the babe who comes from the dark of the mother's womb, how *very much more magnificent is our awakening to the beauty and glory of the Higher*

*Astara, 792 W. Arrow Hwy., P.O. Box 5003, Upland, CA 91785.
**Ananda, a Church . . . ., 14618 Tyler Foote Rd., Nevada City, CA 95959

World as we emerge from this womb-cocoon of Earth life into the Reality of Spirit. And our new body there is as gloriously light and beautiful as the magnificently hued butterfly, emerging from the earthbound cocoon shell, transformed from the lowly caterpillar, and free at last to fly.

Now, while we stand facing into the cave of this third dimension, with our backs to the Light, we are filled with fear by the shadow we see on the wall of the cave. Little do we know, the shadow is only the shadow of our own reflection. All we need do is turn, face the Light, and the shadow disappears.

Facing the Light means living in Love, love for God and love for all His/Her creation. Facing the light means acknowledging and accepting beauty in all its forms. Facing the light means nourishing the good in others and rejecting purely selfish aims in oneself, refusing to be engulfed by negative rampant forces. Thus, in following Christ's admonition to "Love one another as I have loved you," (John 13:34 and 15:12), we can bring heaven to earth for ourselves and for those around us.

Humankind has become densely entangled in the drama of material involution. Now we must accelerate our *evolution* into Oneness and the glory for which we were created, for it is in this union with True Beingness that we will find the answers we seek, the Peace we desire, and the Love for which we yearn.

Were it not for the Enlightened Ones, the true spiritual teachers, the children of Light and Truth among us through these centuries, our plight would be close to hopeless. It is said there is now a foggy, murky aura around our Earth severely blocking the clear flow of pure cosmic Life Energy, relayed by our sun from the Great Central Sun, which every living organism needs to survive. The pollution in and around beloved Mother Earth's atmosphere is not only on the physical *seen* level, a collection from years of chemical fumes and radiation from atomic bombs, etc., *but also on the unseen level, the emanations of centuries of extremely cruel and selfish thoughts and actions of humankind against all life forms including itself, and against the planet as well.* The majority of humankind has for centuries acted like selfish children, quarreling over earth's toys and their space on the Sandpile, acting as though the Sandpile belonged to them. And the selfishness is escalating.

The hour is late. It is crucial that we grow up to a greater realization of our true spiritual nature and heritage, and into an understanding of a spiritual relationship with our Mother Earth. Only a few of the more enlightened are sounding warnings — of the disasters that await us, as results of our dismal custodianship of our home in space — the beautiful gift God gave us.

THE ILLUSION

What does it matter — the heave and the ho,
The sweat and the blood, the toil and the woe?
What does it matter, this tremendous ordeal,
This battling for place, this winning Life's deal?

They want to excel; they want to be kings,
As driven by hungers, they fight for the things
Displayed on the tables of Life's Barter Hall
Where everyone comes and tends his own stall.

Each seeks a position — some want to be seen
Out front and center, to display
　　their wits keen.
Others cower in corners, afraid of the light;
They work in the shadows and do trading
　　by night.

They cheat and they haggle
    to build up their pile
Of earth's paltry baubles, to travel in style.
But where are they going,
    as they jockey for space?
Afraid they will lose the material race!?

If only they'd pause in their mindless pace
To wonder a moment — Will I find grace?
When I take that long journey
Leaving Earth's Market Place.

                  Bonnie Ann Gilchrist

The acts and consequences of war are so horrendous as to be inconceivable. It seems that we never learn from history that no good can ever come from hate and violence. So many millions of innocents suffer, not only maimed and murdered children, but animals, trees, the land itself. People have, it seems, become almost immune to horror, unless it affects them directly. Most are unaware that causes, — for good or bad — return unavoidably as effects, for these are their own creation. This is the explanation of Jesus' words: "Whosoever soweth the wind shall reap the whirlwind."

It behooves every soul who cares for his own future, and for that of the planet and of future generations, to spend a certain time daily directing Life Energy through creative visualization in a meditative state toward healing the planet, just as Dr. Chopra's patient (an average individual) was able to grow a new leg with mind power. As our thoughts and our actions have caused the damage, (each of us is part of mass consciousness), our thoughts and our actions can also assist Nature in alleviating it. Do you think this is much too idealistic? We don't have any idea how powerful positive thoughts are, and the good they do.

Matter is the condensation of the radiant energy of Light. That Light is Life, and that same Light is Cosmic Mind, and these are what many call God. This same Light and Cosmic Mind condense and take form as us. Just as the instruments we call radios bring free radio waves into sound waves that can be heard, so we are the God-created human instruments that *bring etheric energy into form through the dual concentrations of Mind and Feeling*. The masculine mental energy of mind and the feminine energy of emotion work in tandem to create form. We all have this masculine energy *and* feminine energy within our Being. Male and female created He them, (Gen: 1:27).

Prayer in daily meditation directed first toward centering oneself in God's Infinite Love, and then bathing Mother Earth in Love and Light are desperately needed now. Meditation becomes more than a habit, but rather a way of life, like breathing. Leaving the world and going to the Father is not a final act of quitting the body, but an hourly act of the mind. The secret of the higher power is the uniting of the outer expression with the power that works from within.

Many children of Light already know this, but I hope all who read these words will join the work. You are a miraculously created individuality! It is you (not your human ego self, but your High Self) who controls your destiny and can bless your surroundings. These are the gifts you were given by God: Free Will and the Creative Imagination. With these gifts come responsibility. Imagination gives you the ability to rise above all appearances. *But you must want the vision more than the pain and misgivings of the illusion.* It is not work that hurts us, but rather the strain and conflict we experience when we believe that everything depends on our lower personality self, when we are unaware of our connection to the powers of the universe, the powers of the Higher Self.

Just as the small trickle that begins as a rivulet in the mountains becomes a mighty river by the time it enters the vast ocean, so *we need not be perfect or whole before we make a start.* We are as the small rivulet. If we take this moment and begin, we start the flow. As in any creative activity, we grow into wholeness as we work toward our dream.

Take your imagination and your enthusiasm (which is

creative energy in action), hitch them to the farthest star of your dreams and forget about the weather of circumstances. What the Mind can conceive – it can achieve! And always remember: *The highest desire placed in the heart of Man is, in itself, the promise of fulfillment from the heart of God.*

The evolution of humankind is a series of immortal stepping stone experiences to ever higher plateaus, and the vistas – once glimpsed – are breathtaking and life-changing. Think on this for a moment:

> The babe placed in your mother's arms had the man or woman within it that you are now. Just so, the man or woman you are now – has the god within it – you are to become!

Stand tall! Accept your heritage. That Man be created in Our Image . . . after Our Likeness, (Gen:1:26). Turn your face to the Sun (Son) and the Light. Then no more will you be frightened by the shadows on the wall of the cave of your mind.

It has been an inspiration to me to contemplate this: When one man harnessed electricity that illumined the light bulb and brought light into the darkness of the world, he discovered it for all of us. Everyone benefits, no one has to invent the lightbulb over and over again. Just so, when Jesus the Christ (one Man) broke through the illusion of mortality, showing us immortality, he broke through the wall of mass consciousness for all of us. Thus His true declaration, "Be of good cheer . . . for if I be lifted up from the earth I will draw all men unto me," (John 12:32).

Most of us need not understand the intricate law behind the electronic wizardry that can bring a single television picture into every room simultaneously in order to have it be there for us to enjoy. So we need not understand His inclusive statement to have it be true for us, but only accept it with grateful hearts. It is also not necessary to have a Near-Death-Experience to be given a glimpse into the wonder of the immortal world. Many individuals have had just one precious moment that engulfs their being, and their lives ever after take on new meaning. Emerson wrote of this in his essay on Love:*

> "But be our experience in particular what it
> may, no man ever forgot the visitation of that power
> to his heart and brain, which created all things
> anew; which was the dawn in him of music, poetry
> and art; which made the face of nature radiant with
> purple light."

A good friend of mine had such a singular glorious few
moments many years ago on an Oregon beach early one morning ". . . when all the world suddenly turned a soft shade of
purple before his enraptured gaze, and he felt himself in a
holy space, One with all Life." This lasted many minutes before slowly fading. Since those unforgettable moments, he has
given his life to quietly exemplifying God's love.

My own experience at the age of seventeen in entering
an expanded consciousness state, of being embraced by that
wondrous holy love, continued to shine through and influence my entire life, bringing me an awareness of unseen help
acting as a life jacket in stormy waters and shining as a Bethlehem
Star during my dark nights of the soul.

A highly respected Northwest writer, lecturer, and columnist, Dr. Jennifer James, recently wrote in affirmation:

> "When we are quiet, sometimes our intui-
> tive intelligence is able to open a path to con-
> sciousness, to the heart of life. Sometimes the
> gods will tap you on the shoulder just to remind
> you of the way.
>
> "I remember the first time I felt the under-
> standing. I was ten, walking along the railroad
> tracks into the future and knew the whole world
> in an instant. Another powerful opening was at
> age seventeen, on the dorm lawn at college, read-
> ing a book about evolution and suddenly realiz-
> ing how closely all life is linked. All of the wis-

*The Complete Essays of R. Waldo Emerson, 1950, Blacks Readers Serv.

dom traditions, including Christianity, describe such moments and encourage us to seek them. Satori, enlightenment, nirvana, ecstasy, ascension, all are described as the loss of self in the feeling of Oneness; the end of separation. Some people are never touched by it, their lives keep consciousness at bay. They can stay in their own backyards and miss nothing. Others hear the call and they are never the same again. They must follow their hearts. Whatever you may think, whatever others may think, you are not just you, you are a part of the world. You hold a silent promise for the future."

And here I wish to add the words of Geoffrey Hodson, a man of uniquely clear sight who wrote in his book, *Kingdom of the Gods*:*

"A digression is necessary in order to present the point of view from which I write concerning the life and consciousness of Nature. Under certain conditions of heightened awareness, the universal indwelling, Divine Life becomes visible, although translation of such vision into brain consciousness and words presents many difficulties. When this state is attained, the Divine Life in Nature is seen as an all-pervading, glowing, golden Life-force, omnipresent as an ensouling principle in every atom of every world. Physical forms then disappear. One is within and part of an all-pervading ocean of golden glowing Life, which consists of myriads of points of light, interconnected by lines of force, the whole being part of an apparently infinite, living web of exceedingly fine mesh which pervades all beings, all things, all worlds. Each of the points is found to be a source of Life, almost a sun, within which Life-Force wells up as

Kingdom of The Gods, by Geoffrey Hodson, 1953

from an inexhaustible fount. From these centers, the golden power flows along the great web, vitalizing all substance. There is no dead matter. All beings and all things are seen to be filled with the indwelling Life or Fire of God."

We have so much to learn about even the physical side of the unseen world, much less the mental and spiritual, that we have only scratched the surface of knowledge. And can you believe that the Director of the Bureau of Patents of Washington, D.C. resigned in 1887 because he stated, "Everything has been invented. There is nowhere else to go."

Today I read an article of an interview with a delightful, very active lady, ninety years young, who shared her busy schedule and formula for living. Her name is Beatrice Cole. She lives in Manhattan and has been the subject for interviews on television and featured in the news. Mrs. Cole states, "I greet each day as a gift that I unwrap with anticipation."

How wonderful! Imagine feeling an ever new joy at ninety! She stated she achieved contentment by having a happy heart through a lifetime, with full appreciation of everything and everyone in her world. At the end of the article she said exactly what I believe.

"There is still one adventure ahead of me that is the greatest experience of all, the only perfect happenstance in life, with no strings attached, no loose ends. Absolute perfection. That is death. I think of it as the perfect ending to a long and happy life."

This is the way the loving Creator intended for us to live, and to die. Death is an inappropriate word for the greatest adventure in time-travel we will ever experience, arranged by the greatest Travel Agent of all time!

It is good to know of kindred souls who share the ever-new, miraculous beauty of our world, both seen and unseen. May we also continue to work in the seen and the unseen to restore the beauty that was given us. Trees are gentle, beautiful silent friends benefiting us in so many ways, not the least of which is the constant supply of oxygen they provide, which is the breath of our existence, and which they emit as they help to absorb the massive amounts of carbon monoxide produced by our automobiles and industries. Trees literally give us the breath of life.

It is imperative we come to understand our oneness with all of life, the unity that appears as diversity. A glob of the metal mercury can be splintered into innumerable individual particles and yet can as quickly rejoin into a single unit. So our natures only appear as diversity, many individual human particles functioning on this dimension of duality.

We, too, will one day know unity, just as the many droplets of water eventually join with the ocean, powerful and full of grandeur. We are created only a little lower than the angels, and like the angels, we will not lose consciousness of Self in the Ocean of God, but are destined to retain full knowledge of our individuality as wondrous Beings.

As parts of the amazing human experiment, being created in the image of God and given free will, we were given also the stewardship of the earth, (Gen:1:26). Now in the last decade of this century the end of this Age is upon us as prophesied. This is not a theory; it is a fact.

We are told the earth is approaching a great change in the process of her evolutionary cycle which will mean a raising of vibration that is to take the planet into a finer dimension of energy and consciousness. This shift may necessitate a radical cleansing. Scientists of many universities now agree that major earthquakes in the near future are inevitable. They cannot pinpoint dates, of course, and in this they agree with the prophets, who are actually more specific. The planet is giving warning with hundreds of minor tremors monthly.

The cleansing is foretold to come as a preliminary to earth's evolution into the new era. This is a blessed time in history which we are privileged to experience. We should be aware of our ability to be as beacons of light through the perhaps very difficult days ahead.

How we meet the change will be up to us, for as individuals, we must decide now to attune ourselves with these finer vibrations, these new emanations of Light and Love, and to express them toward one another and toward

God. If we do not attune ourselves, we are warned we will find ourselves leaving this planet for we may not be able to tolerate the new vibrational level.

This shift in Mother Earth's vibration has been foretold by many prophets of various centuries and traditions including biblical prophets, and it behooves us to listen to their message. The curtain is coming down at the end of the act in the play of this age. Beginning with Revelation in the Bible,* continuing with,

> "Howbeit when he, the Spirit of Truth is come, he will guide you into all truth; for he shall not speak of himself, but whatsoever he shall hear, that shall he speak: and he will shew you things to come." (John: 16:13)

> "So shall it be at the end of the world: The angels shall come forth, and sever the wicked from among the just . . . and shall cast them into the furnace of fire; there shall be wailing and gnashing of teeth," (Matthew 13:49-50).

Nostradamus' writings in 1555,** and then in channelings through readings of *The Sleeping Prophet*, Edgar Cayce,*** the message is always the same. This same message is echoed in the prophecies of the Navajo people, the Hopi tribes, writings of Paramahansa Yogananda,† in the writings of author Ruth Montgomery†† and others, too numerous to mention. One recent book, *Mary's Message to the World*,††† I highly recommend as a must-read

*Holy Bible, King James Version.

**Nostradamus, *The Man Who Saw Through Time*, 1984, Greenwich House, Crown Publishing, N.Y.

***The Sleeping Prophet, Story of Edgar Cayce*, by Jess Stearn, 1967 Bantam Books, 666 Fifth Ave., N.Y. 10103

† *The Road Ahead*, by Paramahansa Yogananda, edited by Kriyananda Crystal Clarity, Pub., 14618 Tyler Foote Rd., Nevada City, CA.

†† *Threshold to Tomorrow*, by Ruth Montgomery, 1982, Ballantine Books and Random House, New York.

††† *Mary's Message to the World*, by Annie Kirkwood, 1991, Blue Dolphin Publishing, P.O. Box 1909, Nevada City, CA 95959.

book. This volume appears to be a sequel to the famous messages from Mary communicated through the visions described in *Words from Heaven, Messages of Our Lady from Medjugorje.** Her recent book clearly reiterates the old prophecies, and carries her loving advice for meeting the future. We are given a choice, as we always have been, but this time it is a final call.

Christ Jesus cautioned many times: "He who has ears to hear, let him hear," (Matthew:13:30). And there's the old proverb: "He who does not have hold of the rudder will have to be taught by the rocks." I quote here a few lines from Mary's Message to the World:

> "Evolution is always towards growth. The process of change is in this world, and in each individual. The evolutionary processes are already bearing fruit in the world. For the past hundred or so years, the psychic processes have become more active in man. Some call it a gut feeling or intuition. Many call it a mother's sixth sense.
> "What is evident is the refining of the sixth sense in mankind. No longer will man live by his five senses: now a sixth sense has been added, although this sixth sense has been in you from the beginning of time. Recently it has been activated to an extent that it is now becoming commonplace. It is an inherent sense, much as your sight or hearing. It is the use of the emotional body to see into the unseen, to feel the directions of the Almighty. Evolution is not a one-time process, but one which is now slowly changing man into the new species."

Mary's message covers a magnitude of information and has a

**Words from Heaven, Messages of Our Lady from Medjugorje*, 1990, St. James Publishing, P.O. Box 380244, Birmingham, Alabama 35238-0244.

very real urgency:

> "Our mission is to warn and alert the common man of the coming catastrophic events. The planet Earth is in dire danger and all its inhabitants are also in this peril. The wars, chemical use on the soil and in the minds of men is destroying your planet.
>
> "My words are for all people, all nations and all religions. This is a global warning and not simply a national or a religious matter. The events which are already happening are happening to the whole world. Every person will be affected by the coming events. The prediction of events are of such a magnitude as to be unbelievable. Not one solitary person on earth will remain unaffected by the coming changes. "It is not for God's or my benefit that you should seek God. It is for your benefit alone. Who you are saved from will be yourself! God is all Love. You and every being in the universe are surrounded in his Great Love. The love of which I speak is so wonderful and so unwavering you cannot imagine how great it is."

She urges all men to pray, to pray daily, for yourselves, your loved ones, the planet; that true prayer is asking God to set your life in perfect alignment with His will that you may feel the protection and receive guidance in the days ahead. Mary states:

> "The predictions will happen as I have stated, over the next few years. After this, there will be little doubt left in anyone's heart . . . My message is to instill hope, love, and care for each other and this beautiful world."

Gordon Michael Scallion, modern day prophet, and author of *The Earth Changes Report*,* and recently featured on

The Earth Changes Report, Matrix Institute, Gordon Michael Scallion, P. O. Box 336, Chesterfield, NH 03443 or 1-800-MATRIX-3.

the prime-time television program *Ancient Prophesies,* states:

> "Changes are natural, but they have been ac-
> celerated to move or shift more than otherwise
> due to the misuse of spiritual and natural laws.
> Thus, spiritual laws may also be used to bring
> about safety during this era. An individual is not to
> focus on the world changes but to focus on self,
> not in a selfish or personal way, but the changing
> or upliftment in awareness of yourself and the
> community you live in. Begin the 'earth changes'
> where you live. Respect must be given to all forms
> of life on our planet. There is already a great
> awakening, and community is beginning to come
> back among people.
>
> *"Prophecies given are not to create fear, but
> to help the awakening of humankind to their
> free will in creating harmony on the earth* [my
> emphasis]. Tribulation is the time period of judg-
> ment, not of judgment by someone out there,
> such as Saint Peter at the Gate, but the judgment
> of each soul by his own inner Self. During this
> time called Tribulation, each soul has an opportu-
> nity to choose. During this time period all souls,
> bar none, on this planet are being awakened. How
> they respond to this awakening — this is indi-
> vidual. We must give thanks each day for being on
> the earth at this crucial and life-changing time, for
> indeed — these are blessed times."

Native Americans cared for the land that gave them
their sustenance, and gave thanks to and honored the Great
Spirit (God) for that privilege. Robert Moss, who is a student
of American Indian traditions and has written *Fire Along
the Sky*, states:

> "After many years of urging Native Americans
> to take up our ways, we may have at last realized
> that it's time to take up theirs. This is not merely a

venture into the exotic. As the year 2000 approaches, we are threatened by an environmental catastrophe and afflicted by a spiritual malaise. By providing a different way of looking at the world and what it means to be human, American Indian culture could be our salvation.

"Many Indian nations have prophecies about the end of the world that resonate chillingly today. Tom Porter, a Bear Clan chief and spiritual leader of the Mohawks, related one: 'First the elms will die. Then the maples. Then the fish will go belly-up in poison waters. The strawberries will no longer bear fruit, and then our world will be close to dying.'

"There is no exact translation for the word "religion" in Indian languages, because in their traditions there is no clear divide between the sacred and the secular. Religious values are enacted in everyday life. While American Indian traditions offer many such warnings, they also offer us guidance on ways to restore our balance with the earth that sustains us."

In his talks with elders, clan mothers, and spiritual leaders of many of the more than 500 tribal groups, Moss has found they all share underlying values and beliefs that could help our society. In a nutshell, some of these are:

* Everything is spiritual.
* We are all related.
* We must seek personal truth.

Robert Moss goes on to say that the late Jaime de Angulo, an anthropologist who lived with the Pit River Indians of Northern California, observed, "The life of these Indians is nothing but a continuous religious experience. To them, the essence of religion is the spirit of wonder, the recognition of power as a mysterious concentrated form of nonmaterial energy, of something loose in the world and contained in a more or less condensed degree by every object."

The recognition that everything is alive and everything is connected is at the heart of Native American spirituality." Black Elk, the leader of the Lakota tribe, has said: *"Peace comes within the souls of men when they realize their relationship, their oneness, with the universe and all its powers, and that the center is really everywhere. It is within each of us."*

This is the very truth that was given me many years ago, in the expanded consciousness experience as a young girl in Illinois, when I sought the spirit within. And is this not the very essence of what we heard Dr. Deepok Chopra sharing with us? We must come to realize this oneness fully if we are to relate peacefully to one another and to all creatures and to the earth.

Native Americans continue to struggle to remember the old ways. Robert Moss speaks of a Mohawk prophecy, as told by Tom Porter:

"In the beginning, our Creator gave all the races of mankind the same songs and the same drums to keep in touch with Him, to keep faith. But people kept forgetting. In the fullness of time, the spiritual traditions of all Indian peoples — for they are the same — will be united again in a great gathering of their leaders. And they will gain power to remake the world."

For those interested in Indian prophecy, there is a recently published book that is comprehensive and enlightening. *Black Dawn, Bright Day: Indian Prophecies for the Millennium that Reveal the Fate of the Earth*.* Noted authoress Elisabeth Kubler-Ross M.D. has written a commentary: "One of the most important visionaries of our time teaches people why and how they must heal themselves and the earth now. I recommend this book wholeheartedly."

We must allow our hearts to open to the spirit within, and pray that we may be filled with love, for God and for one another. Love is the perfect fuel for all time and all travel through the momentous days ahead.

Black Dawn, Bright Day, 1992, by Sun Bear with Wabun Wind
Simon & Schuster, Rockefeller Ctr., New York 10020

A recent popular song melodiously carries a profound truth:

"On a clear day — rise and look around you,
And you'll see who you are.
On that clear day — how it will astound you,
The Being you are — outshines every star."

Let us toss out the ballast of ignorance and fear, and the restrictive consciousness of small horizons, that we may rise up and over the mountaintop, into a vision of that clear day when we shall see forever and evermore.

✳

EPILOGUE

Our lives are truly the never-ending story. For Life itself has no ending, on whatever plane we may choose to experience, and thus this tale also has no ending, but is only a pause on the breath of time. Perhaps one day I will write a sequel, for Life has a way of springing surprises, and although those may be challenging, or even shocking at the time, they often later make good stories.

General MacArthur once said:

"Old soldiers never die . . . they just fade away."

Allen used to say:

"Old fishermen never die . . . they just smell that way!"

And I have heard

"Old gardeners never die . . . they simply go to seed."

So I shall add:

"For old storytellers, you must not grieve,
As they never, ever, truly leave,
For though our vision may be blurred,
Their many voices can still be heard
In the wild and tangled tales they weave."

One might assume this writer's life has encompassed many difficult years of separations from loved ones, injuries and illness, even violence, but there have also been joys.

Very dear loving and giving neighbors and friends, both near and far, have been a joy in my life, as they must have been in yours. God always sends comforters, we are told, and it is so. In this way we are all One, for though the circumstances may be different, we find that almost everyone faces their Dweller on the Threshold in earth life.

This earth is a school, a kind of laboratory for experiments in living, where we are to learn what works and what does not. All, the dross — the lead of our lives — in time, will be burned away, and leave only the nuggets of gold — the wisdom gleaned by the soul through these lifetimes. The message I hope to convey is that each event in my life and yours, in its span, carries a hidden blessing; each is the piece of a puzzle, when seen in the full picture contains a meaningful and enlightening wisdom. This discovery brings understanding and absolute knowledge of Divine Order in all our lives. And in this understanding we achieve peace of mind.

We tend to forget that this world of duality has a very real purpose, for no one would ever truly know joy if he or she had never known sorrow. Would we ever fully appreciate the bounding exhilaration of health if we had never known pain? Golden sunny days are warm and wonderful on the body and spirit after many drenching dark days of rain. Conversely, nothing is so welcome as fresh, sweet, cleansing rainfall on a thirsty land that has suffered long weeks of parching drought. Similarly, there is a hidden blessing in knowing and overcoming trials, the pains and struggles of earth challenges. These are our teachers, bringing us knowledge we would never have gained otherwise. These are the building blocks of soul strength, strength of character, the ability to love and to have understanding and compassion for others.

In our struggle against adversity, we find eye-opening Self-discovery, the awakening of indwelling wisdom and the discrimination we truly need. Through challenges met bravely and with love, we return to the Godhead from whence we came. *It is not what happens to us that counts, but rather our reaction to what happens that leaves the mark.*

If, on life's path we should stumble or fall, it is important to bear in mind that it does not matter that we have fallen; what is important is that we rise and meet the obstacle, that we learn a lesson from it and advance in spite of it (or more often, because of it). So bless your difficulty, thereby sending out a positive thought about it. Never, never hold a strong negative resentment or an anger vibration toward any person or any condition that will then be the cause of this same obstacle appearing again to you in a different form. For be assured that it will — *until you have learned the lesson that it has come to bring.* Be the watcher of yourself and your life. Discover the big picture. It may amaze you. Sweeter and richer is the reward in the strength of overcoming, in obtaining the panoramic view from the mountaintop after the climb.

The Universe ever seeks balance, and as Sir Arthur summed it up to me: "After many lifetimes of high spiritual achievement, this was the time for you to deal with the nuts and bolts, so to speak."

And so, in this lifetime there came one big challenge after another, tying up the loose ends of lives past, fitting the left-over pieces of the puzzle into their place in the over-all picture. But along the way, I was gifted, through God's ever-present love, with surprising and enlightening blessings. The promised Comforter was there.

And so it is for you. In doing your best to meet life's challenges, while asking for strength from Holy Spirit, you will find that every rainstorm brings a rainbow, and every seed planted bears abundant fruit after its own kind. Be assured that nothing is ever lost, but comes around in its' cycle, in its own universal timing. Let us look to the harvest we would wish to reap.

Dear One, turn your face to the Sun (the Son), let Love be your guide . . . and for you Heaven's Door will one day open wide.

THE DAYS OF MY YEARS

They ask my age. What can I say?
I am young as tomorrow — old as yesterday.
Only those will understand
    who have passed my way.

For Time — around eternal events in its span —
    Is only a framework employed by Man.
The fruit of the loom hangs heavy on the vine
In the warp and the woof of the webbing of Time.
Every soul is a Weaver; who works each day through
To weave their own picture, every detail
    — real and true.

Memories, like ships on a journey embark,
Sailing forth from mind's mists,
Displaying their marks — on this tapestry
    woven in light shades and dark,
Some oh-so-delicate, others heavy and stark.
Here bright with joy, there wet with tears
As the mind — like a light,
    flicks over the years.

Sensing the length and breadth of the Plan
Wonder and awe then o'ertake the man.
Who awakens as tho from a long winter's slumber
To view with surprise, with a new-found wonder . . .
The Pattern, a puzzle, a strange tangle of tales,
In seeing "Life's Story" unfold — in vivid details.

(Continued)

When one tries to unravel it
   with eyes on the yarn,
Frustration and fury — and often — alarm!
"How can this be? I do not understand!"
The Weaver cries out to the Maker of Plans.
The silence is vast and answers come not,
One is left with the woe — and the oft-tangled plot.

Then, who can tell? — soon or late,
Flits a thought through Time, on gossamer wings
to light in the mind . . .
And the answer it brings
   is that we stand too close,
We can ne'er see the picture —
We are as one blind!

For the Pattern — this Tapestry
   must be viewed from afar,
As tho the Door to Eternity were left standing ajar.
'Tis the story of one soul's journey
   through this Time and this Space
While collecting the treasures of Wisdom and Grace.

The pictures entwine, with threads running through,
   one scene to the next — the colors blend true.
Each scene the forerunner of scenes yet to come,
As each weaves their own story
(and beats their own drum!)
The Tapestry's beauty — its dark shades and light
   depend on the Weaver . . .
The choice must be right.

(Continued)

Every Soul chooses what he or she will
As they weave many days — thru Ages — until
One day, in one instant, when Light — like a jewel —
    suspended in Time,
Shines thru the dark reaches of the mind . . . and —
Falling on this Tapestry created by their own hand,
With clear eyes they will gaze
    on the Pattern and Plan.

Voila! The beauty! The wonder and joy!
Each knows that not for a treasure
    would they now destroy — one detail —
Not a single thread or hue, for
All has its place — in the pattern, on cue.
And the Tapestry — tho centuries old,
    Is as New!

For Time has no meaning to the Maker of Plans,
Love and grace are His gifts through each Age,
    to each woman, each man.
With gaze transfixed - - Ah! What will it be?
Through pure sight, You then are destined to see,
    in beauty, and in rare clarity,
Your Soul's own unique —
    IDENTITY!

Oh yes — my age? What can I say —
Only those would understand
Who have passed my way . . .

                    Bonnie Ann Gilchrist

REFERENCES

BOOKS

Abraham Lincoln Returns, 274

Agasha, Master of Wisdom, and Agashan Discourses, 174

Ageless Body — Timeless Mind, 546

Autobiography of a Yogi, 171

Awaken Your Awareness, 244

Bible (The), 564

Black Dawn, Bright Day, 569

Brain Allergies, 382

Breakthrough to Creativity, 399

Children's Doctor (The), 361

Christian Agnostic (The), 61

Closer to the Light, 333,551

Code Name Valkyrie, 471

Complete Essays of Ralph Waldo Emerson (The), 560

Complete Sherlock Holmes (The), 523

Cosmic Healing, A Comparative Study of Channeled Teachings on Healing, 503

Decade of the Brain (The), 382

Diet, Crime & Delinquency, 369

Earth Changes Report (The), 566

Eating for 'A's', 369

Fifty Years A Medium, Story of Estelle Roberts, 542

Fire Along the Sky, 567

Folk Medicine: A Vermont Doctor's Guide, 230

Gerson Therapy (The), 421

Gift of Healing, 452

God's Reach & other Glenn Clark books, 326

Grape Cure (The), 421
Help For the Hyperactive Child, 403
Hermit in the House (A), 244
How I Conquered Cancer Naturally, 421
How to Live With Schizophrenia, 342
Impossible Child, 403
Improving Your Child's Behavior, 361
Is This Your Child?, 403
Kings Row, 235
Killing Cancer, 421
Kingdom of the Gods, 561
Kinship With All Life, 245
Life After Life, 333, 551
Life & Teachings of the Masters of the Far East (The), 190
Light Beyond (The), 551
Light, Medicine of the Future, 289
Love, Medicine, and Miracles, 421
Magic of Findhorn (The), 188
Magic Presence (The), 516
Man Who Tapped the Secrets of the Universe (The), 339
Mary's Message to the World, 564
Memories and Adventures, 523
Nostradamus, The Man Who Saw Through Time, 564
Nothing So Strange, Arthur Ford Autobiography, 537
One Remains (The), 306
Prayer, The Mind's Roll in Healing, 338
Quantum Healing, 546
Recovering the Soul, A scientific and Spiritual Search, 338
Reflections on Life After Life, 551
Road Ahead (The), 564
Sai Baba, The Holy Man and The Psychiatrist, 479, 483
Silent Spring, 424
Sleeping Prophet, Story of Edgar Cayce (The), 564
Stauffenberg, 471
Strange Story of Ahrinzaman (The), 59
Tao of Physics (The), 179, 545
Ten Incurables, 421
Thirty Years Among the Dead, 269
Threshold to Tomorrow, 564

Transformed By The Light, 334
Unconditional Life and Perfect Health, 546
Wanderings of a Spiritualist, Sir Arthur Conan Doyle, 523, 528
Why Your Child Is Hyperactive, 403
Wonder Healers of the Philippines, 493
Words From Heaven, Messages of Our Lady from Medjugorje, 565

POEMS
Butterfly (The), 392
Days of My Years (The), 574
Days of My Years — Journey Through Time, 11
Energy, 181
Fence — or the Ambulance? (The), 408
The Illusion, 556
Immortality, 454
Life Everlasting, 341
Love, 427
Ode to Pompeii, 293
Orchestra (The), 429
Pearl (The), 552
Through Vision's Door, 277

ADDRESS REFERENCES
American Institute of Biosocial Research, 369
American Orthomolecular Medical Society, 402
American Society for Psychical Research, 540
Ananda Brotherhood, 188
Ananda Church of God Realization, 554
Astara, Church of All Religions, 189, 222, 554
Camps Farthest Out, Assn., 326
Carl Pfeiffer Treatment Center, 371
Charles King Musical Church, 328
Christ Church Unity, 150
Christophos Institute, 327
Citizens for Health, 417
Delancey Street Foundation, 381
Earth Changes Report (The), 566
Guideposts Magazine, 35
Heartwood Institute, 465

International Assocation For Near-Death-Studies, 336
Joseph B. Stephenson Foundation, 450
Maharishi International University, 244, 384
Matrix Institute, 566
R. Expo-U.S.A., 497
Santa Fe Mountain Center, 407
Well Mind Association (The), 367
World Research Foundation (The), 423

BIBLE REFERENCES
Chapter 1 — John 14:17, 61
Chapter 3 — Gen. 1:31, 141
Chapter 4 — Gen: 1:27, 177
                    St.Luke 8:8, 178
Chapter 5 — Gen. 1:27, 246
Chapter 7 — Matthew 18:20, 308
                    James 5:16, 309
                    John 13:34 , John 14:12 & Psalms 82:6, 339
                    Genesis 1:26-27, 340
Chapter 9 — Romans 12:2, 420
Chapter 10 — John 14:12 & Psalms 12:6, 467
Chapter 13 — John 13:34 & John 15:12, 555
                    Genesis 1:27, 558
                    Genesis 1:26, 559, 563
                    John 12:32, 564
                    John 16:13 & Matthew 13:49-50, 564
                    Matthew 13:30, 565